LEARNING
Microsoft®
OFFICE XP
Deluxe Edition

Suzanne Weixel
Jennifer Fulton
Faithe Wempen
Sue Plumley

275 Madison Avenue, New York, NY 10016

Acknowledgements

Thanks to everyone at DDC Publishing, especially Jennifer Frew and Jim Reidel. I'd also like to thank Nancy Stevenson for her technical editing.

Suzanne Weixel

To my Mom, who inspires me everyday with her love, courage, and uncanny ability to nurture nature. Happy 80th birthday, Mom!

Jennifer Fulton

Thanks to the DDC staff for all their hard work.

Faithe Wempen

I'd like to thank Jennifer Frew for her encouragement and support. She makes it a pleasure to write for DDC Publishing.

Sue Plumley

Managing Editor	**English Editor**	**Technical Editors**	**Design and Layout**
Jennifer Frew	Ginny Wray	James Reidel	Shu Chen
		Nancy Stevenson	Elsa Johannesson
		Paul Wray	Elviro Padro

Educational Reviewer	**Cover Design**
Anna Solomon	Amy Capuano

ISBN: 0-13-036523-8

10 9 8 7 6 5 4 3   07 06

Contents

EXCEL 2002

Introduction

Microsoft Office XP is Microsoft's suite of application software. The Standard version includes Word, Excel, Outlook, and PowerPoint. The Professional version includes the above applications plus Access. This book covers Word (the word processing tool), Excel (the spreadsheet tool), PowerPoint (the presentation tool), and Access (the database tool). Because Microsoft Office is an integrated suite, the components can all be used separately or together to create professional-looking documents and to manage data.

How We've Organized the Book

Learning Microsoft Office XP is made up of seven sections:

- **Basics**
  This short chapter introduces essential Office skills—including starting Microsoft Office, using the mouse and keyboard, screen elements, and an overview of the applications. If you are completely new to the Office suite, you should start with this lesson. All of the lessons on CD can be printed out or viewed on-screen. See page ix for details on how to access the files.

- **Word 2002**
  With Word you can create letters, memos, Web pages, newsletters, and more.

- **Excel 2002**
  Excel, Microsoft's spreadsheet component, is used to organize and calculate data, track financial data, and create charts and graphs.

- **Access 2002**
  Access is Microsoft's powerful database tool. Using Access you will learn to store, retrieve, and report on information.

- **PowerPoint 2002**
  Create dynamic on-screen presentations with PowerPoint, the presentation graphics tool.

- **Challenge Lesson**
  This chapter combines critical thinking, application integration, and Internet skills. In the Challenge Lesson, you will retrieve data from the Internet, send Web documents via e-mail, download clip art and add it to a PowerPoint presentation, create a Web page, and more. In each exercise, only basic step directions are given—you need to rely on your own skills to complete the exercise.

Each chapter in **Learning Microsoft Office XP** is made up of several lessons. Lessons are comprised of short exercises designed for using Office XP in real-life business settings. Every application exercise (except for the Critical Thinking Exercises and the Challenge Exercises) is made up of seven key elements:

- **On the Job**. Each exercise starts with a brief description of how you would use the features of that exercise in the workplace.

- **Exercise Scenario**. The Office tools are then put into context by setting a scenario. For example, you may be a designer putting together a promotional sales flyer using Word or you may be responsible for tracking inventory for a gourmet-food store.

- **Terms**. Key terms are included and defined at the start of each exercise, so you can quickly refer back to them. The terms are then highlighted in the text.

- **Notes**. Concise notes for learning the computer concepts.

- **Procedures**. Hands-on mouse and keyboard procedures teach all necessary skills.

- **Application Exercise**. Step-by-step instructions put your skills to work.

- **On Your Own**. Each exercise concludes with a critical thinking activity that you can work through on your own. You may have to create a personal budget spreadsheet in Excel or a personal Web page in Word. You are challenged to come up with data and then additionally challenged to use the data in a document. The *On Your Own* sections can be used as additional reinforcement, for practice, or to test skill proficiency.

- In addition, each lesson ends with a **Critical Thinking Exercise**. As with the *On Your Owns*, you need to rely on your own skills to complete the task.

Working with Data and Solution Files

As you work through the exercises in this book, you'll be creating, opening, and saving files. You should keep the following instructions in mind:

- For many of the exercises you can use the data files provided on the CD-ROM that comes with this book. The data files are used so that you can focus on the skills being introduced—not on keyboarding lengthy documents. The files are organized by application in the **Datafiles** folders on the CD-ROM.

  ✓ See **What's on the CD** for more information on the data files.

- When the application exercise includes a file name and a CD icon ⊙ , you can open the file provided on CD.

- The Directory of Files at the beginning of each section lists the exercise file (from the CD-ROM) you can open to complete each exercise.

- If the exercise includes a CD icon ⊙ and a keyboard icon ⌨, you can choose to work off of either the data file or a file that you created in an earlier exercise.

- Unless the book instructs otherwise, use the default settings for text size, margin size, and so on when creating a file. If someone has changed the default software settings for the computer you're using, your exercise files may not look the same as those shown in this book. In addition, the appearance of your files may look different if the system is set to a screen resolution other than 800 x 600.

- All the exercises instruct you to save the files created or to save the exercise files under a new name. You should verify the name of the hard disk or network folder to which files should be saved.

- Instructors can purchase solution files to compare student work with the desired results.

What's on the CD ⊙

We've included on the CD:

- **Data files** for many of the exercises. This way you don't have to type lengthy documents from scratch.

- **Internet simulation** so that you can go to real Web sites to get information—without an Internet connection or modem. Following the steps in the book, you will experience going "online" to locate facts, data, and clip art. You will then use the information in Office documents.

- **Glossary of business and financial terms** used in the workplace, the financial arena, and *Learning Microsoft Office XP*. Key business terms help you understand the work scenarios and the data that is used to complete the exercises.

- **Touch 'N' Type Keyboarding course** was designed for those who would like to learn to type in the shortest possible time. The keyboarding skill-building drills are also ideal for those who wish to practice and improve their keyboarding. The exercises can be printed out, copied, and distributed. The files have been prepared in Adobe Acrobat format. You first need to install Adobe Acrobat (provided on the CD) before you can open the files.

- **Typing Tests with Automatic Scoring**. Use these to test typing speed and accuracy.

- **Computer Literacy Basics**. These exercises include information on computer care, computer basics, and a brief history of computers. Once Adobe Acrobat is installed, these exercises can be printed out and distributed.

To Access the Files Included with This Book ⊚

1. Insert the *Learning Microsoft Office XP* CD in the CD-ROM drive. A menu of options should automatically appear. If it does not, perform the following steps:

   a. Click Start>Run.

   b. Type D:\CDmain.exe (where D: is the letter of your CD-ROM drive).

2. Move the mouse pointer over a menu item to display information on how to install or access the files.

3. Click a menu item to activate it.

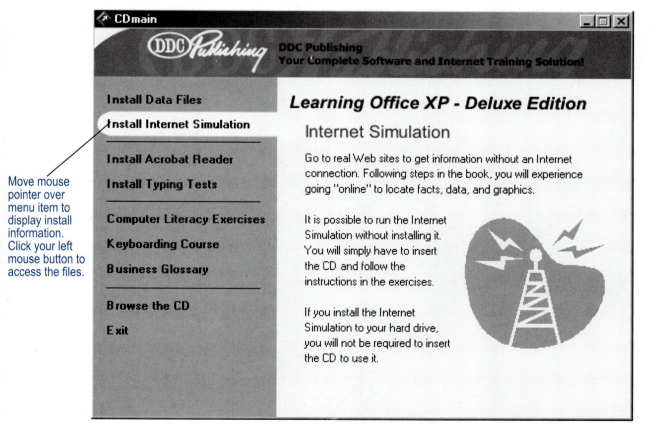

Move mouse pointer over menu item to display install information. Click your left mouse button to access the files.

Getting Started with Office XP

Lesson 1

Exercises 1-4

Exercise 1

Skills Covered:

◆ **About Microsoft Office XP** ◆ **Use the Mouse**
◆ **Use the Keyboard** ◆ **Start and Exit Microsoft Office Programs**
◆ **Common Screen Elements**

On the Job

Microsoft® Office XP Professional contains a suite of programs that may be used independently or together to create simple documents, such as letters, faxes, and memos, as well as complex documents, such as reports, tables, books, and interactive Web sites. Many jobs in today's workplace require knowledge of this best-selling software suite.

You've just been hired as the assistant to the president of Regency General, Inc., a Web startup company specializing in business-to-business Internet services for customer database management and purchasing. She has asked you to become familiar with Microsoft Office XP, since the company uses it throughout its business operations. In this exercise, you'll practice using the mouse and the keyboard to start and exit Office XP programs, and you will review the screen elements common to the different programs.

Terms

Software suite A group of software programs sold as a single unit. Usually the programs have common features that make it easy to integrate and share data.

Mouse A device that allows you to select items on-screen by pointing at them with the mouse pointer.

Mouse pointer A marker on your computer screen that shows you where the next mouse action will occur. The mouse pointer changes shapes depending on the current action.

Toolbar A row of buttons used to select features and commands.

Insertion Point A blinking cursor that indicates on-screen where text or data will be inserted in a document.

Scroll wheel A wheel on some mouse devices (called a wheeled mouse) used to navigate through a document on-screen.

I-beam A mouse pointer shape resembling the uppercase letter I.

Mouse pad A smooth, cushioned surface on which you slide a mouse.

Current file The file currently open and active. Actions and commands will affect the current file.

Menu A list of commands located at the top of the program window.

Window The area on-screen where a program or document is displayed.

Elements Menus, icons, and other items that are part of an on-screen interface.

Scroll To page through a document in order to view some part of its contents that is not currently displayed.

Notes

About Microsoft Office XP

- There are four editions of the Microsoft Office XP **software suite**:
  - The Standard edition includes Word (a word processing program), Excel (a spreadsheet program), PowerPoint (a presentation graphics program), and Outlook (a personal information manager and e-mail program).
  - The Professional edition includes the same programs as the Standard edition plus Access, (a database application), Publisher (a desktop publishing program), and the Small Business Tools (programs for managing a small business).
  - The other two editions are Small Business, which does not include Access or PowerPoint, and Premium, which includes all the programs already mentioned as well as FrontPage (a Web site development program), and PhotoDraw (a graphics program.)
- This book covers the most commonly used programs in the Office XP suite: Word, Excel, Access, and PowerPoint. Outlook is covered only as a tool for sending and receiving e-mail.

Use the Mouse

- Use your **mouse** to point to and select commands and features of Office XP programs.
- When you move the mouse on your desk, the **mouse pointer** moves on-screen. For example, when you move the mouse to the left, the mouse pointer moves to the left.
- When you click a mouse on a **toolbar** button, the program executes a command. For example, when you click on the Print toolbar button, the program prints the current document. Clicking a mouse button can also be used to move the **insertion point**.
- A mouse may have one, two, or three buttons. Unless otherwise noted, references in this book are to the use of the left mouse button.
- Your mouse might have a **scroll wheel**. Use the scroll wheel to move through the file open on your screen.

- The mouse pointer changes shape depending on the program in use, the object being pointed to, and the action being performed. Common mouse pointer shapes include an arrow (for selecting a button or menu), an **I-beam** (for inserting text), and a hand with a pointing finger (to indicate a "hyperlink" in a Web page).
- You should use a mouse on a **mouse pad** that is designed specifically to make it easy to slide the mouse.
  - ✓ *You can move the mouse without moving the mouse pointer by picking it up. This is useful if you move the mouse too close to the edge of the mouse pad or desk.*
- Newer mice include the Intellieye-type mouse, which uses light instead of a ball and pad, and wireless mice.

Use the Keyboard

- Use your keyboard to type characters, including letters, numbers, and symbols. The keyboard can also be used to access program commands and features.
- In addition to the regular text and number keys, computer keyboards have special keys used for shortcuts or for executing special commands.
  - Function keys (F1–F12) often appear in a row above the numbers at the top of the keyboard. They can be used as shortcut keys to perform certain tasks.
  - Modifier keys (Shift, Alt, Ctrl) are used in combination with other keys or mouse actions to select certain commands or perform actions. In this book, key combinations are shown as: the modifier key followed by a plus sign followed by the other key or mouse action. For example, Ctrl+S is the key combination for saving the **current file**.
  - The Numeric keys are made up of the 10-key keypad to the right of the main group of keyboard keys on an enhanced keyboard.
    - ✓ *Laptop and notebook computers integrate the numeric keys into the regular keyboard.*
  - When the Num Lock (number lock) feature is on, the keypad can be used to enter numbers. When the feature is off, the keys can be used as directional keys.

- The Escape key (Esc) is used to cancel a command.
- Use the Enter key to execute a command or to start a new paragraph when typing text.
- Directional keys are used to move the insertion point.
- Editing keys (Insert, Delete, and Backspace) are used to insert or delete text.

Start and Exit Microsoft Office Programs

- To use an Office XP program you must first start it so it is running on your computer.
- Use Windows to start an Office program.
  - You can use the Windows Programs menu to select a program name.
  - You can use the New Office Document command on the Windows Start **menu**.
  - You can use the Microsoft Office Shortcut bar if it is installed on your computer.
- When you are done using an Office program, close it to exit.

Start an Office program using Windows

New Office Document command

Start button   Programs menu

The Office Shortcut Bar

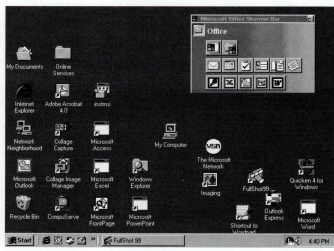

Common Screen Elements

- When a program is running, it is displayed in a **window** on your screen.
- The program windows for each of the Office applications contain many common **elements**.
  - ✓ You will find more information about the individual program windows in the other sections of this book.
- The following figure identifies the common elements you will find in the Office program windows.
  - ✓ There are many ways to customize the appearance of your programs. If your programs do not look exactly the same as the ones shown in this book, they may have been customized. You learn more about customizing each program in other exercises.

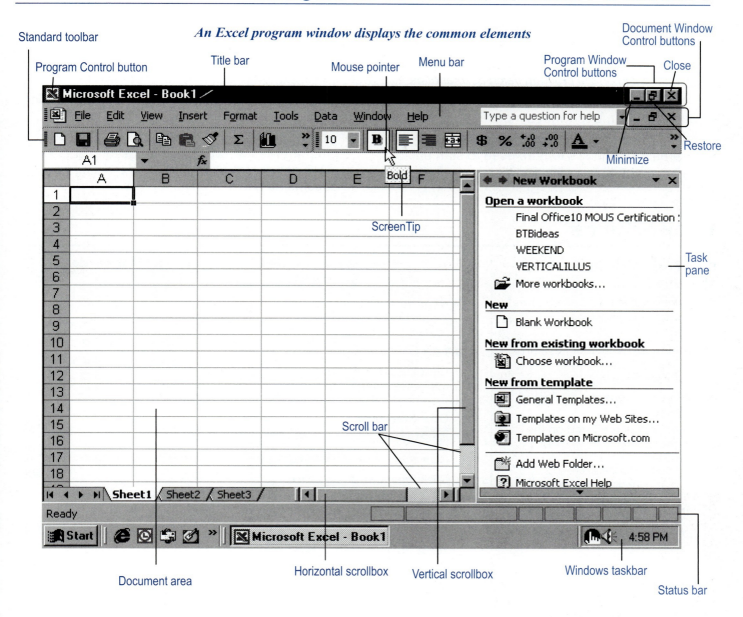

An Excel program window displays the common elements

- **Program Control button.** Used to display a drop-down menu of commands used for controlling the program window.

- **Title bar.** Displays the name of the program (Word, Excel, etc.) and the name of the current file.

- **Program Window Control buttons.** Used to control the size and position of the program window.

- **Document Window Control buttons.** Used to control the size and position of the document window.

- **Program Close button.** Used to close the program.

- **Document close button.** Used to close the document.

- **Menu bar** displays the names of the main menus. Select a menu name to drop down a list of commands or options.

- **Standard toolbar.** Displays buttons for accessing common features and commands such as saving, opening, and printing a file.

- **Formatting toolbar.** Displays buttons for accessing common formatting features and commands, such as centering text.

    ✓ *The toolbar buttons may vary depending on the program being used.*

- Mouse pointer. Marks the location of the mouse on the screen.
  - ✓ *The appearance of the mouse pointer changes depending on the program being used and the current action.*
- Scroll box/bar. Used with a mouse to shift the on-screen display up and down or left and right.
- Taskbar. A Windows feature used to start and switch among programs and files.
- Status bar. Displays information about the current document.
- Document area. The workspace into which you enter text, graphics, and other data.
- ScreenTip. Displays the name of the element on which the mouse pointer is resting.
- Task Pane. An area on the right side of the program window, which can be used to access some common features, such as creating new documents and searching for files.

Procedures

Conventions Used in This Book

Throughout this book, procedures for completing a task are documented as follows:

- **Keyboard shortcut** keys (if available) are included next to the task heading.
- Mouse actions are numbered on the left
- Keystrokes are listed on the right.

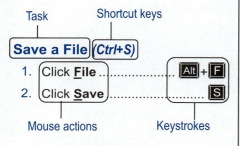

Display the Office Shortcut Bar

1. Click **Start** button
    .... Ctrl + Esc
2. Click **Programs**.................. P
3. Click **Microsoft Office Tools**.
4. Click **Microsoft Office Shortcut Bar**.
5. Click **Yes** .... Y
   to set the Shortcut bar to display whenever you start your computer.
   OR
   Click **No** .... N
   to manually display the shortcut bar when you want it.

- ✓ *If the Office Shortcut bar is not installed on your computer, Office will prompt you to insert the required Setup disk. Ask your instructor for more information.*

Start an Office Program

- Click the program button on the Office Shortcut bar.
OR
1. Click **Start** button
    .... Ctrl + Esc
2. Click **Programs**
3. Click the name of the Office program.
OR
1. Click **Start** button
   Start .... Ctrl + Esc
2. Click New Office Document button.
3. Click General page tab.
4. Click one of the following:
   - **Blank Document** icon

     Blank Document to start Word.
   - **Blank Workbook** icon

     Blank Workbook to start Excel.
   - **Blank Presentation** icon

     Blank Presentation to start PowerPoint.

- **Blank Database** icon

  Blank Database to start Access.

Exit an Office Program

- Click **Program Close** button
  X at the right end of the program's title bar.
OR
1. Click **File**..................... Alt + F
2. Click **Exit** X
3. Click **Yes**............................ Y
   to save open documents.
   OR
   Click **No** .... N
   to exit without saving.

Use the Mouse

Move the mouse pointer:

Right	Move mouse to right.
Left	Move mouse to left.
Up	Move mouse away from you.
Down	Move mouse toward you.

Mouse actions:

Point to	Move mouse pointer to touch specified element.
Click	Point to element then press and release left mouse button.
Right-click	Point to element then press and release right mouse button.
Double-click	Point to element then press and release left mouse button twice in rapid succession.

Drag   Point to element, hold down left mouse button, then move mouse pointer to new location.

✓ *Element, or icon representing element, moves with mouse pointer.*

Drop   Drag element to new location, then release mouse button.

IntelliMouse actions:

Scroll   Rotate center wheel backward to scroll down, or forward to scroll up.

Pan   Press center wheel and drag up or down.

AutoScroll   Click center wheel to scroll down; move pointer up to scroll up.

Zoom   Hold down Ctrl and rotate center wheel.

Use the Keyboard

• Press specified key on the keyboard.

For key combinations:

1. Press and hold modifier key(s)................ Ctrl , Alt , Shift

2. Press combination key.

✓ *Remember, key combinations are written with a plus sign between each key. For example, Ctrl+Esc means press and hold Ctrl and then press Esc.*

Exercise Directions

1. Start your computer if it is not already on.

2. Move the mouse pointer around the Windows desktop.

3. Point to the Start button.

    ✓ *A ScreenTip is displayed.*

4. Point to the Recycle Bin icon.

5. Click the My Computer icon.

    ✓ *The icon is selected.*

6. Right-click the Recycle Bin icon.

    ✓ *A menu is displayed.*

7. Press Esc to cancel the menu.

8. Start Microsoft Word 2002.

9. Point to each button on the Standard and Formatting toolbars to see the ScreenTips.

10. Move the mouse pointer over the document window. It changes to an I-beam as shown in Illustration A.

11. Minimize the Word program window.

    ✓ *Click the Minimize button ▬ in the top-right corner of the screen.*

    ✓ *Notice that a button representing the program is displayed on the Windows taskbar.*

12. Click the taskbar button to restore the window.

13. Exit Word.

    ✓ *Click No if a box is displayed asking if you want to save the changes.*

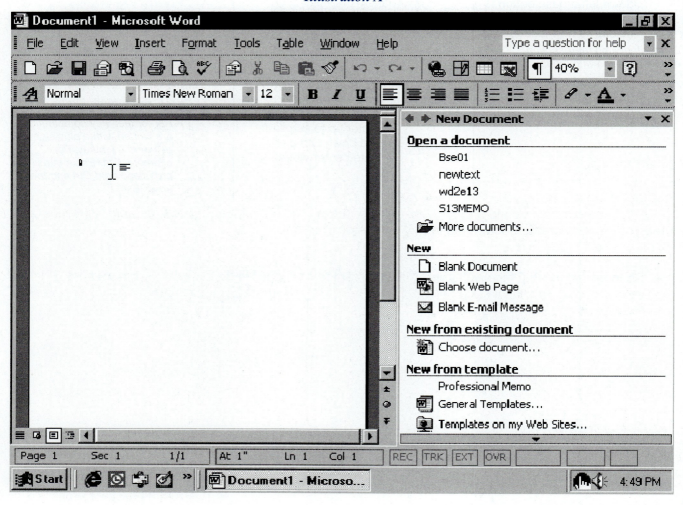

On Your Own

1. Practice using different methods to start and exit the Office programs.

2. In each program window, use the mouse to display ScreenTips to identify different elements.

3. Practice maximizing, minimizing and restoring the program windows.

4. See if you can identify which menu commands are the same in each program and which menu commands are different in each program.

   ✓ *When you are done, be sure to exit all programs.*

Exercise 2

Skills Covered:

◆ **Execute Commands** ◆ **Use Menus** ◆ **Use Toolbars**
◆ **Use Dialog Box Options** ◆ **Use Shortcut Menus** ◆ **Use Task Panes**

On the Job

To accomplish a task in an Office XP program, you must execute a command. You select the commands using menus, toolbars, and dialog boxes. Once you learn to use these tools, you will be able to access the features you need to create documents in any Office XP program.

To get up to speed using Office XP programs, you want to spend more time exploring the menus, toolbars, and dialog boxes. In this exercise, you will practice using toolbars, selecting menu commands, and choosing options in dialog boxes.

Terms

Command Input that tells the computer which task to execute.

Menu A list of commands.

Toolbar A row of buttons used to execute commands. Each button displays an icon (picture) representing its command.

Dialog box A window in which you select options that affect the way the program executes a command.

Icon A picture used to identify an element on-screen, such as a toolbar button.

Toggle A type of command that can be switched off or on.

Ellipsis A symbol comprised of three periods that indicate more will follow (…).

Submenu A menu that is displayed when you select a command on another menu.

Hotkey The underlined letter in a command name.

ScreenTip A balloon containing information that is displayed when you rest your mouse pointer on certain screen elements.

Shortcut menu A menu displayed at the location where the selected command will occur. Also called a context menu.

Task Pane An area on the right side of an Office XP program window in which you can access commands and options for certain program features.

Notes

Execute Commands

- To accomplish a task in a Microsoft Office XP program, you execute **commands**. For example, Save is the command for saving a document.

- Commands are accessible in three ways:
  - **Menus**
  - **Toolbars**
  - **Dialog boxes**
- You use the mouse and/or the keyboard to select and execute commands.

Use Menus

- Office XP groups commands into menus, which are listed on the menu bar.

- When you select—or open—a menu, a list of commands you use most often drops down into the window.

- You can expand the menu to see all commands in that group.

- Commands that are not available appear dimmed on the expanded menu.

- Command names are listed on the left side of a drop-down menu.

- If a toolbar button is available for a menu command, the button **icon** is displayed to the left of the command name.

- Some commands are **toggles** that can be either active or inactive. A check mark or bullet to the left of a toggle command means the command is already active.

- Shortcut keys and other symbols are listed on the right side of the menu.
  - An **ellipsis** (…) indicates that the command opens a dialog box.
  - An arrowhead indicates that the command opens a **submenu**.

- Each menu and command has an underlined letter called a **hotkey**. Hotkeys are used to select menu commands with the keyboard.

The Tools menu in Word

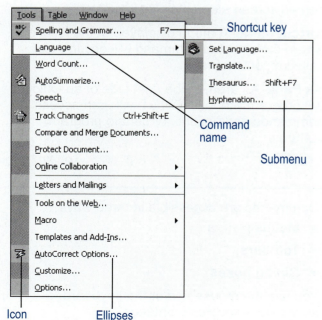

Use Toolbars

- Office XP programs come with many different toolbars, which provide quick access to common commands.

- By default, only the Standard and the Formatting toolbars are displayed.

- You can display or hide toolbars as needed.

- When you point to a toolbar button with the mouse, the button is highlighted, and a **ScreenTip** displays the name of the button.

- Some buttons are toggles; they appear highlighted when active, or "on."

- Buttons representing commands that are not currently available are dimmed.

- Using the toolbar handle, you can drag a toolbar to any side of the program window, or float it over the document window area.

- All toolbars have a Toolbar Options button you can use to select options for displaying buttons.
  - ✓ *If there are buttons available that do not fit on the toolbar, the Toolbar Options button will have a right-pointing double-arrow on it. Click it to select other buttons.*

The Standard toolbar

Toggled button

Handle   Dimmed buttons   Toolbar Options button

Use Dialog Box Options

- Microsoft Office XP programs display a dialog box when you must provide additional information before executing a command. For example, in the Print dialog box, you can specify which pages to print.

- You enter information in a dialog box using a variety of elements. Use the numbers to locate the corresponding element in the figures on the following page.

The Font dialog box in Word

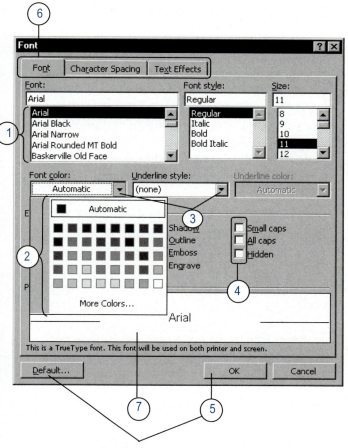

The Print dialog box in Word

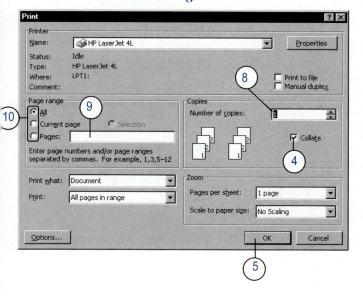

Palette (2)

- A display, such as colors or shapes, from which you can select an option.

  ✓ *Some commands and some toolbar buttons also open palettes.*

Drop-down list box (3)

- A combination of text box and list box; type your selection in the box or click the drop-down arrow to display the list.

Check box (4)

- A square that you click to select or deselect an option. A check mark in the box indicates that the option is selected.

Command button (5)

- A button used to execute a command. An ellipsis on a command button means that clicking the button opens another dialog box.

Tabs (6)

- Markers across the top of the dialog box that, when clicked, display additional pages of options within the dialog box.

Preview area (7)

- An area where you can preview the results of your selections before executing the commands.

Increment box (8)

- A space where you type a value, such as inches or numbers. Increment arrows beside the box are used to increase or decrease the value with a mouse.

Text box (9)

- A space where you type variable information, such as a file name.

Option buttons (10)

- A series of circles, only one of which can be selected at a time. Click the circle you want to select one item or one control in the series.

Use Shortcut Menus

- **Shortcut menus** are useful for quickly accessing commands pertaining to the current task using a mouse.

- Shortcut menus are sometimes referred to as context menus.

List box (1)

- A list of items from which selections can be made. If more items are available than can fit in the space, a scrollbar is displayed.

- Commands on shortcut menus vary depending on the action being performed.

Use Task Panes

- Microsoft Office XP programs have a **Task Pane** that you can use as an alternative method for accessing certain program features.
- For example, all programs include a **New Task Pane** that you can use to create new files, or open existing files.
- Other features that can be accessed from the Task Pane include the Office Clipboard, the Media Gallery, and the Search feature.
- Some programs have unique features that can be accessed from the Task Pane as well, such as Mail Merge in Word and Custom Animation in PowerPoint.
  - ✓ *You learn how to accomplish tasks using the Task Pane in the exercise in which that feature is covered. For example, in Word Exercise 10 you learn to use the Clipboard Task Pane to move text in a Word document.*
- Task Panes have some features in common with dialog boxes. For example, some have text boxes in which you type text as well as drop-down list boxes, check boxes, and options buttons.
- You can leave the Task Pane open while you work, or you can open it only when you need it.

Procedures

Open a Menu Bar Menu with the Mouse

- Click the **menu name**.

Open a Menu Bar Menu with the Keyboard

1. Press and hold .... Alt
2. Press **hotkey** in menu name.

Expand a Menu

- Click **expand arrows** at menu bottom

  .

  OR

- Click menu name and wait a few seconds.

Select a Menu Command

1. Click **menu name** .. Alt +hotkey
2. Click the desired **command** ....hotkey

   OR

   a. Press **up** and **down arrows** to highlight command....

   b. Press **Enter**................. Enter

   ✓ *If a submenu is displayed, select the command from the submenu.*

Close a Menu without Making a Selection

- Click the menu name again.

  ✓ *If the menu expands instead of closing, click it again.*

  OR

- Click in the document window.

  OR

- Press **Esc**.

Select a Command from a Toolbar

1. Point to a **toolbar button**.
2. **Click**.

   ✓ *If the button you want is not displayed, click the Toolbar Options button* *to display additional buttons, and then click the button you want.*

Display/Hide Toolbars

1. Click **View** .... Alt + V
2. Click **Toolbars** .... T

   OR

   Right-click any **toolbar**.

   ✓ *A check mark beside the toolbar name indicates toolbar is already displayed.*

3. Click **desired toolbar** to display or hide.

Move a Toolbar

1. Move the mouse pointer so it touches toolbar handle.

   ✓ *The mouse pointer changes from an arrow to a cross with 4 arrows*

2. Drag the toolbar to a new location.

Use a Dialog Box

1. Select a **command** followed by an ellipsis (…).
2. Make **selections or type text entries** in dialog box.
3. Click **OK** command button .... Enter

   ✓ *Sometimes command button displays Close, Add, Insert, or Yes in place of OK.*

   OR

   Click **Cancel** to close dialog box without making changes .... Esc

Dialog Box Options

Move from one option to the next:

- Click desired **option**.

  OR

- Press **Tab** key .... Tab

  OR

- Press .... +hotkey

Select from a list box:

- Click desired **item** ... [↑↓], [Enter]

Select from a drop-down list box:

1. Click **drop-down arrow** .... [Alt]+hotkey
2. Click desired **item** ... [↑↓], [Enter]

Select/deselect check box:

- Click **check box** ..... [Alt]+hotkey

    ✓ A check mark indicates box is selected. Repeat action to remove check mark and deselect box.

Display tabbed pages:

- Click desired **tab** .... [Alt]+hotkey

    ✓ If no hotkey is displayed, press Ctrl+Tab.

Use a text box:

1. Click in **text box** ..... [Alt]+hotkey
2. Type **data**.

Use an increment box:

1. Click in **increment box** ...... [Alt]+hotkey
2. Type **value**.

OR

- Click **increment arrows** to change value.

Select option button:

- Click **option button** .... [Alt]+hotkey

    ✓ A black dot indicates option is selected. Select alternative option button to change setting.

Select palette option:

1. Click **palette** drop-down arrow .... [Alt]+hotkey

    ✓ Some palettes are always open. If the palette is open, skip to step 2.

2. Click desired **option** .... [↕], [Enter]

Shortcut Menus

1. Right-click **element** on screen.
2. Click **command** .... hotkey

    ✓ If no hotkeys are available, use arrow keys to select command, then press Enter.

Open the Task Pane

1. Click **View** .... [Alt]+[V]
2. Click **Tas_k Pane** .... [K]

    ✓ A check mark indicates the Task Pane is currently displayed.

Select a Different Task Pane

1. Click the **Other Task Panes** drop-down arrow on the Task Pane title bar [▼].
2. Click desired **Task Pane**.

    ✓ Click the **Back** arrow on the Task Pane title bar to display the previously open Task Pane; click the **Next** arrow to display the next Task Pane.

Scroll the Task Pane Display

- Click **Scroll arrow**

    at bottom of Task Pane, if displayed, to scroll up.

OR

- Click **Scroll arrow**

    at top of Task Pane, if displayed, to scroll down.

Hide the Task Pane

1. Click **View** .... [Alt]+[V]
2. Click **Tas_k Pane** .... [K]

OR

- Click **Close** button [X] on Task Pane title bar.

Exercise Directions

1. Start Word.

2. Open the File menu using the mouse.
   - Click the word *File* on the menu bar.

3. Let the menu expand to show all commands.

4. Note the commands on the File menu.

5. Close the menu.
   - Click the word *File* on the menu bar, or press **Esc**.

6. Open the View menu using the mouse.
   - Click the word *View* on the menu bar.

7. Select the Toolbars commands.
   - Click the word *Toolbars*, or press the **T** key.

8. Look at the submenu of available toolbars.
   - ✓ *Notice the check marks next to the toolbars that are currently displayed.*

9. Close the menu.
   - Click the word *View* on the menu bar, or press **Esc** twice.

10. Open the Format menu with the keyboard.
    - Press and hold **Alt**, and then press the **O** key.

11. Select the Font command.
    - Press the **F** key, or click the command name.

12. Select *Bold* in the Font style list box.

13. Select the Superscript check box.

14. Select the Text Effects tab to show another page of options.

15. Select the Font tab.

16. Open the Font Color palette.
    - Click the drop-down arrow, or press **Alt**+**C**.

17. Select the color red.

18. Open the Underline style drop-down list.
    - Click the drop-down arrow, or press **Alt**+**U**.

19. Cancel the dialog box without making any of the selected changes.
    - Click the **Cancel** command button, or press **Esc** twice.

20. Display the Task Pane if it is not already displayed.

21. Change to the Search Task Pane.

22. Change to the Clipboard Task Pane.

23. Change to the New Documents Task Pane.

24. Close the Task Pane.

25. Click the Bold button on the Formatting toolbar.
    - If the Bold button is not displayed, click the More buttons button to expand the toolbar, and then click the Bold button.
    - ✓ *Bold is a toggle; it remains on (highlighted) until you turn it off.*

26. Click the Bold button again.

27. Right-click anywhere in the document window.

28. Select the Paragraph command.
    - Click the command.

29. Note that the Paragraph dialog box includes increment boxes, drop-down lists, and a preview area, as shown in Illustration A.

30. Cancel the dialog box without making any changes.
    - Click the **Cancel** command button or press **Esc**.

31. Exit Word.
    - ✓ *If Word prompts you to save changes, select No.*

Illustration A

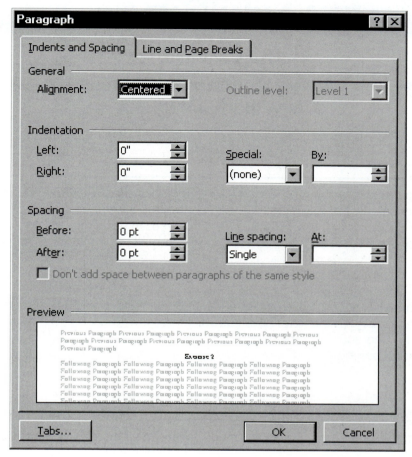

On Your Own

1. Start Excel and explore the menus.

2. Look to see which commands are on each menu.

3. Notice which ones open dialog boxes, which open submenus, and which have corresponding toolbar buttons.

4. Select a command that opens a dialog box. For example, try opening the Options dialog box from the Tools menu.

5. If the dialog box has multiple pages, check out each page. Note the different options available on each page.

6. Use the Toolbar Options button on the Standard toolbar to see what other buttons are available.

7. Try moving the toolbars to other locations on the screen.

8. Move them back.

9. Exit Excel without saving any changes.

10. Repeat these steps using PowerPoint.

Exercise 3

On the Job

Controlling the way Office XP programs and documents are displayed on your computer is a vital part of using the programs successfully. For example, you can control the size and position of the program window on-screen, and you can control the size a document is displayed. In addition, you can open more than one window on-screen at the same time, so that you can work with multiple documents and even multiple programs at once.

As you spend more time working with Office XP programs, you'll find that there are many tools that help you do your job more efficiently. In this exercise, you will learn how to maximize, minimize, and restore windows on your screen, and you will experiment with the zoom level. You'll also practice scrolling through a document, and opening more than one window at the same time.

Terms

Default A standard setting or mode of operation.

Maximize Enlarge a window so it fills the entire screen.

Minimize Hide a window so it appears only as a button on the Windows taskbar.

Restore Return a window to its previous size and position on the screen.

Zoom in Increase the size of the document as it is displayed on-screen. This does not affect the actual size of the printed document.

Zoom out Decrease the size of the document as it is displayed on-screen. This does not affect the actual size of the printed document.

Scroll Shift the displayed area of the document up, down, left, or right.

Active window The window in which you are currently working.

Tile Arrange windows so they do not overlap.

Cascade Arrange windows so they overlap, with the active window in front. Only the title bars of the nonactive windows are visible.

Notes

Use Window Controls

■ When you start an Office XP program, it opens in a program window using **default** settings.

■ You can control the size and position of the program window.

• You can **maximize** the window to fill the screen.

• You can **minimize** the window to a taskbar button.

• You can **restore** the window to its previous size and position.

■ There are three ways to control a program window:

- With the Control buttons located on the right end of the title bar.

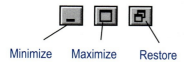

Minimize　　Maximize　　Restore

- With the Program Control icon drop-down menu.

Program Control drop-down menu

- With the taskbar button context menu.

Taskbar button context menu

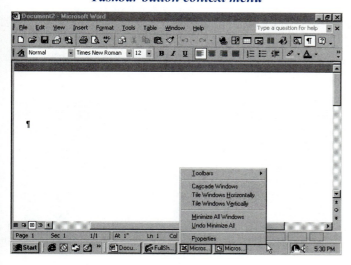

Zoom

■ In Word, Excel, and PowerPoint, you can adjust the **zoom** magnification setting to increase or decrease the size a program uses to display a file on-screen.

■ Set the zoom using the Zoom drop-down list box on the Standard toolbar, or the Zoom dialog box.
   - ✓ *The options in the Zoom dialog box will be different depending on the program you are using.*

Zoom dialog box in PowerPoint

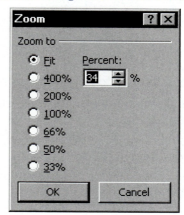

■ **Zooming in** makes the file contents appear larger on screen. This is useful for getting a close look at graphics, text, or data.
   - ✓ *When you zoom in, only a small portion of the file will be visible on-screen at a time.*

■ **Zooming out** makes the document contents appear smaller on-screen. This is useful for getting an overall look at a document, slide, or worksheet.

■ You can set the zoom magnification as a percentage of a document's actual size. For example, if you set the zoom to 50%, the program displays the document half as large as the actual, printed document would appear. If you set the zoom to 200%, the program displays the document twice as large as the actual printed file would appear.

■ In Word, you can also select from four preset sizes:
   - Page width. Word automatically sizes the document so that the width of the page matches the width of the screen. You see the left and right margins of the page.
   - Text width. Word automatically sizes the document so that the width of the text on the page matches the width of the screen. The left and right margins may be hidden.
   - Whole page. Word automatically sizes the document so that one page is visible on the screen.

- Many pages. Word automatically sizes the document so that the number of pages you select can all be seen on-screen.
  - ✓ *Some options may not be available, depending on the current view. Options that are not available will appear dimmed.*

Scroll

- When there is more data in a window or dialog box than can be displayed on-screen at one time, you must **scroll** to see the hidden parts.
- Scrolling is like flipping the pages of a book. You can scroll up, down, left, or right.
- You can scroll using the directional keys on the keyboard, or using scroll boxes.
  - ✓ *Some mouse devices have scroll wheels that are used to scroll.*

Tools for scrolling in a document

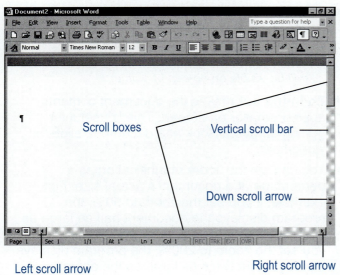

- ✓ *The size of the scroll boxes change to represent the percentage of the file visible on the screen. For example, in a very long document, the scroll boxes will be small, indicating that a small percentage of the document is visible. In a short document, the scroll boxes will be large, indicating that a large percentage of the document is visible.*

Use Multiple Windows

- You can open multiple program windows at the same time.
- Each open window is represented by a button on the Windows taskbar.

- Only one window can be active—or current—at a time.
- The **active window** is displayed on top of other open windows. Its title bar is darker than the title bars of other open windows, and its taskbar button appears pressed in.
- You can switch among open windows to make a different window active.
- You can **tile** windows if you want to see all of them at the same time. Tiled windows do not overlap.
  - ✓ *You can tile windows horizontally or vertically.*

Windows tiled horizontally

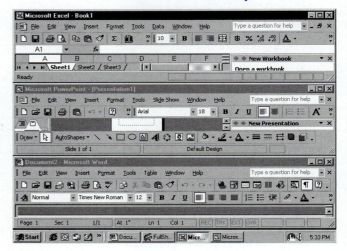

- You can **cascade** windows if you want to see the active window in its entirety, with the title bars of all open windows displayed behind it.

Cascaded windows

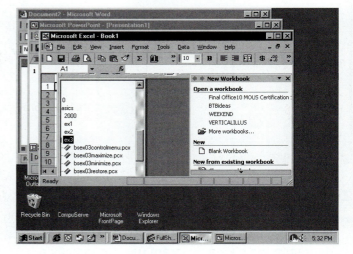

- You can open multiple document windows in Word, PowerPoint, and Excel.

Procedures

Control Windows

Minimize a window:

- Click the **Minimize** button ⬜.

OR

1. Click the **Program Control** icon.
2. Click **Minimize** .... ⬜N

OR

1. Right-click the taskbar button.
2. Click **Minimize** .... ⬜N

Restore a window:

- Click the **Restore** button ⬜.

OR

1. Click the **Program Control** icon.
2. Click **Restore** .... ⬜R

OR

1. Right-click the taskbar button.
2. Click **Restore** .... ⬜R

Maximize a window:

- Click the **Maximize** button ⬜.

OR

1. Click the **Program Control** icon.
2. Click **Maximize** .... ⬜X

OR

1. Right-click the taskbar button.
2. Click **Maximize** .... ⬜X

Adjust Zoom

Use zoom drop-down list:

1. Click **Zoom** button drop-down arrow ⬜ on Standard toolbar.
2. Click desired **percentage**.
   OR
   Click preset option.

OR

1. Click in **Zoom** button ⬜88%⬜ drop-down list box on Standard toolbar.
2. Type desired percentage.
3. Press **Enter** .... ⬜Enter

Use Zoom dialog box:

1. Click **View** .... ⬜Alt⬜+⬜V
2. Click **Zoom** .... ⬜Z
3. Click desired zoom option.
   OR
   a. Click **Percent increment box** ...... ⬜Alt⬜+⬜E
   b. Type **percentage**.
4. Click **OK** .... ⬜Enter

Scroll

Scroll down:

- Click **Down scroll arrow** .... ⬜↓

OR

- Click in **Vertical scroll bar** below Scroll box.

OR

- Drag **Scroll box** down.

OR

- Press **Page Down** .... ⬜Page Down

OR

- Spin scroll wheel on mouse toward your palm.

Scroll up:

- Click **Up scroll arrow** .... ⬜↑

OR

- Click in **Vertical scroll bar** above Scroll box.

OR

- Drag **Scroll box** up.

OR

- Press **Page Up** .... ⬜Page Up

OR

- Spin scroll wheel on mouse away from your palm.

Scroll left:

- Click **Left scroll arrow** .... ⬜←

OR

- Click in **Horizontal scroll bar** to left of Scroll box.

OR

- Drag **Scroll box** left.

Scroll right:

- Click **Right Scroll Arrow** .... ⬜→

OR

- Click in **Horizontal scroll bar** to right of Scroll box.

OR

- Drag **Scroll box** right.

Start Multiple Programs

1. Start first program.
   ✓ *Refer to Exercise 1 for information on starting Microsoft Office XP programs.*
2. Start additional program(s).

Arrange Program Windows

1. Right-click on blank area of Windows taskbar.
2. Select desired option:
   - **Cascade Windows** .... ⬜S
   - **Tile Windows Horizontally** .... ⬜H
   - **Tile Windows Vertically** .... ⬜E
   - **Minimize All Windows** .. ⬜M
   ✓ *Maximize active window to display active window only.*

Arrange Word document windows:

1. Click **Window** .... ⬜Alt⬜+⬜W
2. Click **Arrange All** .... ⬜A

Arrange Excel workbook windows:

1. Click **Window** .... ⬜Alt⬜+⬜W
2. Click **Arrange** .... ⬜A
3. Select desired option:
   - **Tiled**
   - **Horizontal**
   - **Vertical**
   - **Cascade**
4. Click **OK** .... ⬜Enter

Arrange PowerPoint presentation windows:

1. Click **Window**............. `Alt`+`W`
2. Click **Arrange All**................ `A`
   to tile windows vertically.
   OR
   Click **Cascade** .... `C`
   to cascade windows.

Switch Between Open Windows

- Click taskbar button of desired window.

OR

- Click in desired window.

OR

1. Press and hold `Alt`............. `Alt`
2. Press **Tab** .... `Tab`
   to cycle through open windows.
3. Release **Tab** when desired window is selected.

Exercise Directions

1. Start Word
2. Minimize the Word window.
3. Maximize the Word window.
4. Restore the Word window.
5. Start Excel.
6. Cascade the open windows on-screen.
   - ✓ *Right-click on a blank area of the Windows taskbar and select Cascade Windows.*
7. Tile the windows horizontally.
8. Tile the windows vertically.
9. Make the Word window active.
10. Maximize the Word window.
11. Click in the document window and type your name.
    - ✓ *Do not worry about making errors while you type. This is just a practice exercise, and you will not save the document. You learn more about typing in a Word window in Word Exercise 1.*
12. Press **Enter**.
13. Type the first line of your address.
14. Press **Enter**.
15. Type the next line of your address.
16. Press **Enter**.
17. If necessary, type the next line of your address.
18. Set the Zoom to 25%.
19. Set the Zoom to 500%. It should look similar to the document shown in Illustration A.
20. Scroll down to the bottom of the document.
21. Scroll up to the top of the document.
22. Scroll to the right margin.
23. Scroll to the left margin.
24. Set the Zoom to Page Width.
25. Make Excel active.
26. Maximize the Excel window.
27. Exit Excel.
28. Exit Word.
    - ✓ *When Word prompts you to save the changes, select No.*

Illustration A

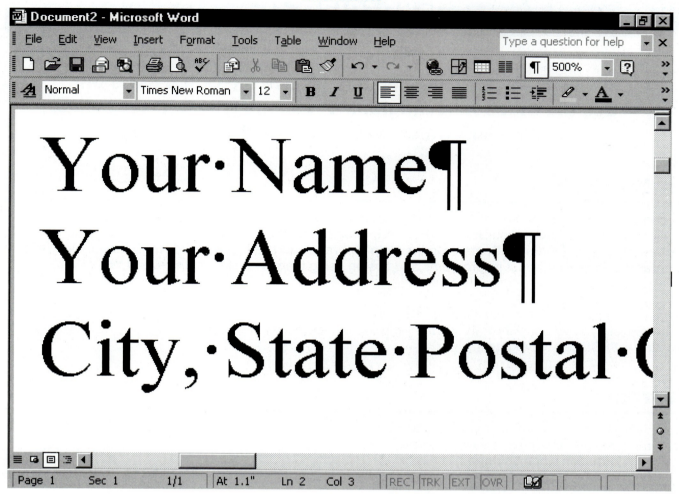

On Your Own

1. Start more than one Office XP program.
2. Practice maximizing, minimizing, and restoring the windows, using all three available methods.
3. Practice arranging the windows on-screen.
4. Type some text in the Word document window.
   - ✓ *Click the mouse pointer anywhere in the document window and start typing. You learn more about typing in a Word document in Word Exercise 1.*
5. Try different zoom magnifications to see how the display is affected.
6. Set the zoom very high so you have to scroll down to see the end of the document.
7. Exit all programs without saving any documents.

Exercise 4

Skills Covered:

◆ **Use the Ask a Question Box** ◆ **Use the Office Assistant**
◆ **Use the Office Help Program** ◆ **Use the What's This? Pointer**
◆ **Microsoft Office on the Web** ◆ **Recover a File**

On the Job

You can get help regarding any of Office XP's features while you work using a variety of methods. Type questions in the Ask a Question Box to start a Help program quickly and display specific information. Alternatively, use the Index or Contents in the Help program to locate the information you need. Microsoft also makes information about its programs and tips on using them available on the World Wide Web.

As a new employee at Regency General, it's important to learn how to solve problems on your own. In this exercise, you will learn how to use the Help system to answer the questions you may have while working with Office XP programs.

Terms

Office Assistant A feature of Microsoft Office Help program, designed to make it easy to locate helpful information when you need it.

Hyperlinks or links Text or graphics in a document set up to provide a direct connection with an Internet destination location or document. When you click a hyperlink, the destination is displayed.

Internet A worldwide network of computers.

World Wide Web A system for finding information on the Internet through the use of linked documents.

Notes

Use the Ask a Question Box

- There is an *Ask a Question Box* on the menu bar of each Office XP program.

- Type a question in the box and press Enter to display a list of related Help topics.

Ask a Question Box

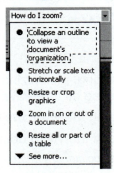

- Click the topic to start the Help program and display the associated Help page.

Use the Office Assistant

- The **Office Assistant** is an animated character that functions much like the Ask a Question box.

- You type a question or topic in the Office Assistant help bubble, then select from a list of available help pages. The Office Assistant starts the Help program and displays the selected information.

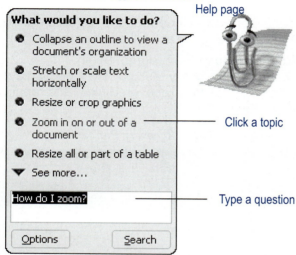

The Office Assistant

- Although the Office Assistant is not installed by default, you can install it by running the Office XP Setup program.

- You can also set the Office Assistant to display tips or suggestions about current features while you work. For example, if you start typing a letter in Word, the Office Assistant will ask if you need help.

- If a light bulb appears above the Office Assistant, it means a tip is available. Click the light bulb to display the tip.

- By default, the Office Assistant is represented by an animated paper clip, called *Clipit*. You can select a different animated figure.

- You can disable the Office Assistant if you want to be able to access the Help program directly.

Use the Office Help Program

- All Office programs come with a Help program.

- The Help programs provide thorough information about how to use Office XP features.

- The Help program opens in its own program window, which is split into two panes.

- Pages of information are displayed in the right pane.

- The left pane contains three tabs (Contents, Answer Wizard, and Index) designed to make it easy for you to locate the help information you need.

- The Contents tab is like a table of contents in a book.
  - Each topic in the table of contents appears with a small book icon.
  - Open the book to display its subtopics.
  - Close the book to hide its subtopics.
  - Click a subtopic to display the help page.

Select a Topic on the Contents tab

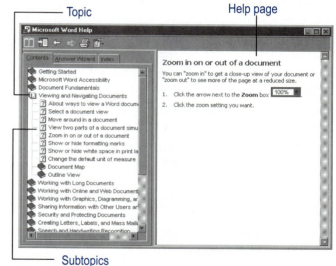

Type a specific question on the Answer Wizard tab

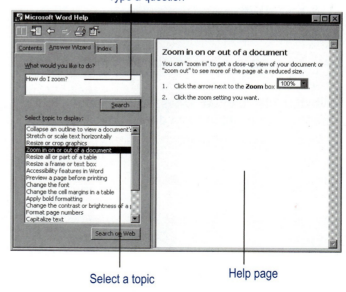

Locate a topic based on a keyword on the Index tab

Type keyword

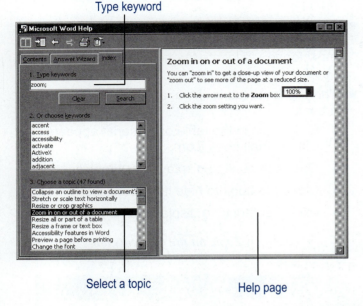

Select a topic

Help page

- Help pages use **hyperlinks** to make it easy to move from one topic to another.

- When the mouse pointer touches a hyperlink, it changes to a hand with a pointing finger.

- You can hide the left pane of the Help window to make more room on-screen once you find the information you need.

- You can tile the Help window with the program window so you can work in your file and read the Help information at the same time.

Use the What's This? Pointer

- Click a screen element or command with the What's This? pointer to display help information in a ScreenTip.

What's This? pointer

- What's This? can be accessed from the Help menu or from within most dialog boxes.

Microsoft Office on the Web

- If you have access to the **Internet**, you can connect to Microsoft on the **World Wide Web** and get up-to-date information and support for all the programs in Office XP.

Recover a File

- In the event of a system failure, Word, Excel, and PowerPoint will attempt to save your most recent changes.

- If any damage was done to the file data during the crash, the program will attempt to repair it.

- When you open the program again, the Document Recovery task pane will be displayed, listing original files, recovered files, and repaired files (if any).

The Document Recovery Pane in Word

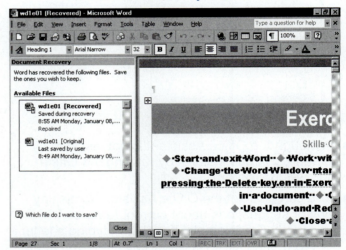

- You can review the files to see the changes and repairs.

- You have the option of saving one or all of the listed files.

Procedures

Display Office Assistant *(F1)*

- Click **Microsoft** *program name* **Help** button on Standard toolbar.

OR

1. Click **H**elp .... `Alt`+`H`
2. Click **Show the O**ffice **Assistant**............................. `O`

   ✓ If the Office Assistant Help bubble is not displayed, click the Office Assistant.

   ✓ If the Office Assistant is covering information you want to see on-screen, drag it out of the way.

Hide Office Assistant

1. Right-click **Office Assistant**.
2. Click **H**ide .... `H`

OR

1. Click **H**elp .... `Alt`+`H`
2. Click **Hide the O**ffice **Assistant**............................. `O`

Use Office Assistant

1. Display **Office Assistant** and Help bubble `[?]` .... `F1`
2. Type question in text box.

   ✓ Replace existing text if necessary.

3. Click **S**earch .... `Enter`
4. Click **See More** to see next page of topics............ `Tab` or `↓`, `Enter`
5. Click **See previous** to see previous page of topics.................. `↓`, `Enter`
6. Click desired topic... `↓`, `Enter`

Change Office Assistant Animation

1. Right-click **Office Assistant**.
2. Click **C**hoose Assistant ...... `Alt`+`C`
3. Click **N**ext .... `Alt`+`N`
4. Repeat step 4 until desired animation is displayed.

5. Click **OK** .... `Tab`, `Enter`

   ✓ If selected animation has not been installed, install it, or select a different animation.

Change Office Assistant Options

1. Right-click **Office Assistant**.
2. Click **O**ptions .... `Alt`+`O`
3. Select or deselect options as desired.
4. Click **OK** .... `Enter`

Turn Off Office Assistant

1. Right-click **Office Assistant**.
2. Click **O**ptions .... `Alt`+`O`
3. Click the **U**se the Office Assistant check box... `Alt`+`U` to deselect it.
4. Click **OK** .... `Enter`

Start Help Program *(F1)*

1. Turn off Office Assistant.

   ✓ See above for required steps.

2. Click **Microsoft** *program name* **Help** button `[?]` on Standard toolbar.

   OR

   a. Click **H**elp .... `Alt`+`H`
   b. Click **Microsoft** *program name* **H**elp ..... `H`

Control Left Help Pane

- Click **Show** button to display hidden left pane.

- Click **Hide** button to hide left pane.

- Click **AutoTile** button to tile program windows.

- Click **Scroll** arrows `◄` `►` to display hidden tabs, if necessary.

Use Help Contents

1. Start **Help program**.
2. Click **C**ontents tab...... `Alt`+`C`

3. Double-click **book** to display subtopics ..... `↓`, `Enter`

   OR

   Click **plus (+) sign** beside topic.
4. Click desired **subtopic**.................. `↓`, `Enter`
5. Click **hyperlink** to see related topic.

Use Answer Wizard

1. Start **Help program**.
2. Click **A**nswer Wizard tab. .... `Alt`+`A`
3. Type a question or a **keyword** .... `Alt`+`W`, *text*
4. Click **S**earch................ `Alt`+`S`
5. Click desired topic .... `Alt`+`T`, `↓`, `Enter`
6. Click **hyperlink** to see related topic.

Use Index

1. Start **Help program**.
2. Click **I**ndex tab. .... `Alt`+`I`
3. Type **keyword** in Step 1 box. .. `Alt`+`T`, *keyword*

   OR

   Click **keyword** in Step 2 box....... `Alt`+`K`, `↓`

   ✓ To select new keywords, first clear the Step 1 box.

4. Click **S**earch................ `Alt`+`S`
5. Click desired topic in Step 3 box....... `Alt`+`H`, `↓`
6. Click **hyperlink** to see related topic.

Close Help Program

- Click Help window's **Close** button `X` .... `Alt`+`F4`

Use Ask a Question Box

1. Click in **Ask a Question** box.
2. Type question.
3. Press **Enter** .... `Enter`

4. Click **See More** to see next page of topics............ Tab or ⬇, Enter

5. Click **See previous** to see previous page of topics.................. ⬇, Enter

6. Click **desired topic**.......... ⬇, Enter

Use What's This? *(Shift+F1)*

1. Click **Help**.................... Alt + H
2. Click **What's This?** .... T
3. Click any **screen element** or command.
4. Click **outside ScreenTip** to cancel What's This? .... Esc

Microsoft Office on the Web

1. Click **Help**.................... Alt + H
2. Click **Office on the Web** ..... W
3. Follow steps to **connect** to Internet.
4. Click **hyperlinks** to display related topics.
5. Follow steps to **disconnect** from Internet.

   ✓ *To connect to the Internet you must have a computer with a modem or other Internet connection and an account with an Internet Service Provider. For more information, see Word, Exercise 23.*

Recover a File

✓ *If your program was able to recover or repair a file, it will display the Document Recovery pane automatically when you restart your programs.*

1. Click desired file in Document Recovery pane.

   ✓ *You can review each file to see which one you want to keep.*

2. Save desired file.
3. Steps for saving files are covered later in this book.

   ✓ *If you save a repaired file, the program will prompt you to review the repairs before continuing.*

Exercise Directions

1. Start Excel.
2. Display the Office Assistant (if it is not already displayed).
3. Search for help topics about changing the Zoom magnification.
   a. Type **Zoom** in the Office Assistant Help bubble.
   b. Click **Search**.
4. Read the available topics.
5. Click *See more*.
6. Select the topic: *Zoom the display*.
7. Hide the Office Assistant.

   ✓ *If necessary, click the Help button on the Windows Taskbar to make the Help program active again.*

8. Read the Help topic.
9. Display the Contents tab in the left pane of the Help program.
10. Open the topic: *Managing and Printing Files*.

    ✓ *You may have to display the list of topics by clicking the book icon.*

11. Display the Index tab.
12. Search for topics about ScreenTips.
    a. Type **ScreenTip** in the step 1 text box.
    b. Click **Search**.

13. Select the topic: *About getting help while you work*.
14. Click the *Office Assistant* link on the Help page. The Help program should look similar to Illustration A.
15. Read the Help page.

    ✓ *Scroll down in the window to see the rest of the information.*

16. Close the Help program.
    • Click the **Close** button in the upper-right corner or press Alt + F4.
17. Turn on the What's This? pointer.
18. Click the **Bold** button on the Formatting toolbar.
19. Read the ScreenTip.
20. Turn off the What's This? pointer.
    • Click anywhere outside the ScreenTip or press **Esc**.
21. Use the Ask a Question box to locate information about displaying toolbars.
22. Close the Help program.
23. Exit Excel.

Illustration A

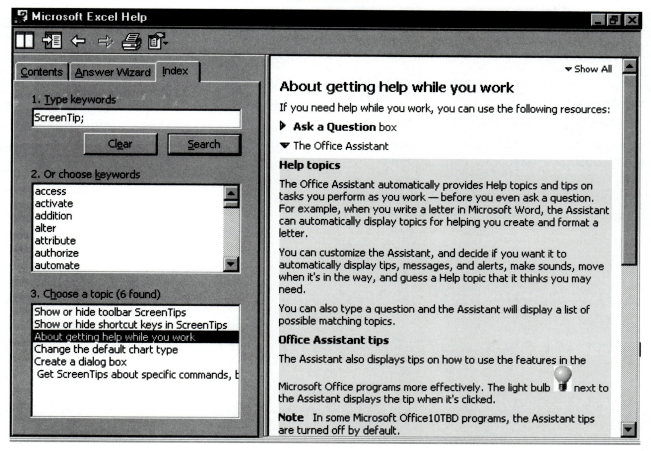

On Your Own

1. Start Word and display the Office Assistant.

2. Open the Office Assistant dialog box to see what other animations are available for use as the Office Assistant.

3. If you find one you like, select it.

4. Open the Office Assistant dialog box again to see the options available for controlling the Office Assistant.

5. Close the dialog box without making any changes.

6. Use the Office Assistant to search for help topics related to Menus.

7. Open any topic that sounds interesting.

8. Explore the topics on the Help Contents page.

9. Open any topic that sounds interesting.

10. Continue to explore the help topics as long as you want. When you are done, close the Help program and exit Word. Do not save the document.

Word 2002

Lesson 1

Getting Started with Word 2002
Exercises 1-8

Lesson 2

Basic Editing Skills
Exercises 9-14

Lesson 3

Formatting Basics
Exercises 15-21

Lesson 4

Using the Internet and E-mail; Creating Web Pages
Exercises 22-26

Lesson 5

Creating Tables
Exercises 27-31

Lesson 6

Creating Documents with Merge
Exercises 32-35

Lesson 7

Creating and Editing Longer Documents
Exercises 36-41

Lesson 8

Enhancing Documents and Automating Tasks
Exercises 42-49

Directory of Data Files on CD

Exercise #	File Name	Page #
1	N/A	N/A
2	N/A	N/A
3	N/A	N/A
4	N/A	N/A
5	N/A	N/A
6	N/A	N/A
7	N/A	N/A
8	N/A	N/A
9	09PRESS	77
10	10POLICY	80
11	11POLICY	83
12	12CONTEST	90
13	13CONTEST, 13MEMO	93
14	14CAVIAR, 14FLYER	96
15	15ANNOUNCE	100
16	16GRAND	103
17	17FIREDRILL	107
18	18PROGRAMS	113
19	19COURSE	118
20	20BUSINESS	123
21	21TRAIN	125
22	22LIST, 22RULES	130
23	INTERNET SIMULATION	136
24	24COURSE	141
25	25TRAIN, 25COURSE, INTERNET SIMULATION	146

Exercise #	File Name	Page #
26	26SPECIALS, INTERNET SIMULATION	150
27	N/A	N/A
28	N/A	N/A
29	29COOKING	166
30	30BASKET	170
31	31DEMOS	173
32	N/A	N/A
33	33SOURCE	188
34	34CALDATA	194
35	N/A	N/A
36	N/A	N/A
37	37HEART	210
38	38HEART	219
39	39CHD	226
40	40INHOUSE	235
41	41B2B	237
42	42GAZETTE	243
43	43PATIENT	249
44	44OPEN	258
45	45PATIENT	265
46	N/A	N/A
47	47WINNERS, 47MISSION	275
48	48BUSINESS	280
49	49ADINFO	283

Exercise 1

Skills Covered:

◆ **Start Word** ◆ **The Word Window** ◆ **Change the Word Window**
◆ **Type in a Document** ◆ **Correct Errors** ◆ **Use Undo and Redo**
◆ **Save a New Document** ◆ **Close a Document** ◆ **Exit Word**

On the Job

Word is the word processing application included in the Microsoft Office XP suite. You use Word to create text-based documents such as letters, memos, reports, flyers, and newsletters. The first step in mastering Word is learning how to start the program and create a document.

You are the office manager at the medical practice California Cardiology, Inc. A new doctor has recently joined the staff, and you must type up a brief biography that will be made available in the office and sent to prospective patients. In this exercise, you will start Word, create and save a document, and then exit Word.

Terms

Default A standard setting or mode of operation.

View The way a document is displayed on screen.

Elements Menus, icons, and other items that are part of an on-screen interface.

Word wrap A feature that causes text to move automatically from the end of one line to the beginning of the next line.

Paragraph mark (¶) A **nonprinting** character inserted in a document to indicate where a paragraph ends.

Nonprinting characters Characters such as paragraph marks and tab symbols that are not printed in a document but that can be displayed on the screen.

Undo The command for reversing a previous action.

Redo The command for reversing the Undo command.

Notes

Start Word

- To use Word 2002 you must first start it so it is running on your computer.

- You use Windows to start Word.

- When Word is running, it is displayed in a window on your screen.

- You can start Word using the Start menu, a desktop icon, or the Office Shortcut bar.

  ✓ *Different methods of starting Office XP programs are covered in "Getting Started with Office XP," Exercise 1.*

The Word Window

- Word opens a new, blank document using standard, or **default**, settings. Default settings control features of a new document, such as the margins, the line spacing, the character font, and the font size.

- Word starts with a new blank document open in Print Layout **view** and displays **elements** for accessing tools and menus to create, edit, format, and distribute a document.

- The following illustration identifies the default elements of the Word window. The numbers following each element correspond to the numbers next to the descriptions that follow.

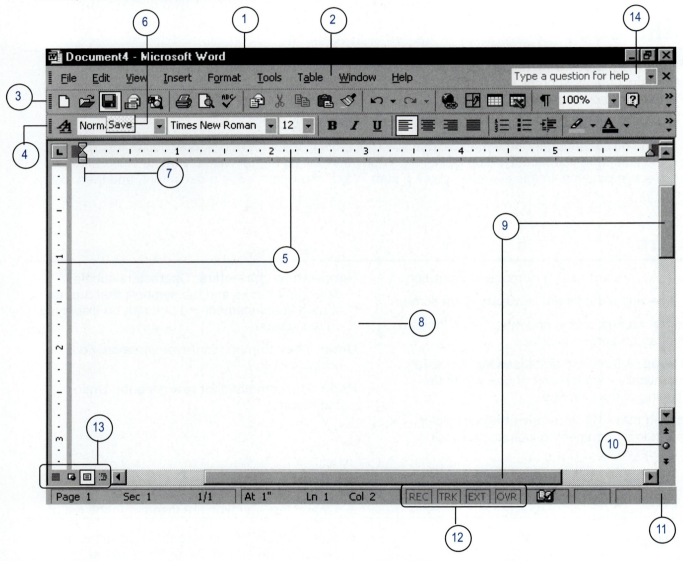

Title bar (1)

- Displays the program and document name.

Menu bar (2)

- Displays the names of the main menus. Select a menu name for a list of commands.

Standard toolbar (3)

- Displays buttons for accessing common features and commands, such as saving, opening, and printing a file.

  ✓ *Toolbar buttons change according to your most recent selections. To see additional buttons, click the Toolbar Options button* ⁇.

Formatting toolbar (4)

- Displays buttons for accessing common formatting features and commands, such as bold, italic, and centering text.

Rulers (5)

- The horizontal ruler measures the width of the document page; it displays information such as margins, tab stops, and indents.
- The vertical ruler measures the height of the document page.

  ✓ *The vertical ruler is displayed only in Print Layout view and Print Preview.*

ScreenTip (6)

- Displays the name of the element on which the mouse pointer is resting.

Insertion point (7)

- A blinking vertical line that displays to the right of the space where characters are inserted in a document.

Document window (8)

- The area where you type document text or insert graphics, tables, or other content.

Scroll boxes (9)

- Used with a mouse to shift the on-screen display up and down or left and right.

Select Browse Object button (10)

- Used to shift the on-screen display according to a selected object, such as by page, by picture, or by heading.

Status bar (11)

- Displays information, such as the currently displayed page, currently displayed section, how many pages are in the document, where the insertion point is located, and which mode buttons are active.

Mode buttons (12)

- Used to change the way Word operates to make creating and editing documents easier.

  ✓ *Active mode buttons appear bold.*

View buttons (13)

- Used to change to one of four available document views. These options are also available on the View menu.

Ask a Question box (14)

- Used to access the Help program. Type a question to display a list of topics for which help is available.

  ✓ *For more about using the Help program, refer to Exercise 4 of "Getting Started with Office XP."*

Change the Word Window

- You can change the default settings to control which Word elements are displayed.
  - You can show or hide toolbars.
  - You can show or hide rulers.
  - You can show or hide Task Panes.
  - You can change views.

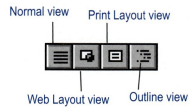

Normal view   Print Layout view

Web Layout view   Outline view

  - Normal view is used for most typing, editing, and formatting.
  - Print Layout view displays a document on-screen the way it will look when it is printed.
  - Web Layout view wraps text to fit the window, the way it would on a Web page document.
  - Outline view is used to create and edit outlines.

Type in a Document

- By default, the insertion point is positioned at the beginning (left end) of the first line of a new document.
- You simply begin typing to insert new text.
- Characters you type are inserted to the left of the insertion point.
- **Word wrap** automatically wraps the text at the end of a line to the beginning of the next line.
- When you press the Enter key, Word inserts a **paragraph mark** and starts a new paragraph.
- After you type enough text to fill a page, Word automatically starts a new page.

Correct Errors

- You can delete characters to the left of the insertion point by pressing the Backspace key.
- You can delete characters to the right of the insertion point by pressing the Delete key.
- You can cancel commands before you execute them by pressing the Escape key or clicking a Cancel button if available.

Use Undo and Redo

- Use the **Undo** command to reverse a single action made in error, such as deleting the wrong word.
- The Undo command also lets you change your mind about an entire series of actions used to edit or format a document.
- Use the **Redo** command to reinstate any actions that you reversed with the Undo command.
- If the Undo command and the Undo button are dimmed and entirely gray, there are no actions that can be undone.
- If the Redo button is dimmed, there are no actions that can be redone. However, sometimes when there are no actions to redo, the Repeat command is available from the Edit menu in place of Redo. Use Repeat to repeat the most recent action.

Save a New Document

- As mentioned, Word starts with a new blank document named *Document1* open on-screen.
  - ✓ *Subsequent new documents are named consecutively:* Document2, Document3, *etc. You learn more about creating additional new documents in Exercise 2.*
- If you want to have a file available for future use, you must save it on a removable disk or on an internal fixed disk.

- When you save a new document, you must give it a name and select the location where you want it stored.
- Word automatically adds a period and a three-character file extension to the end of the file name to identify the file type. By default, the file extension is *.doc*, which identifies a document file.
- To specify a disk for storing the document, you select the disk drive letter. Floppy disk drives are usually drives A: and B:. A hard drive is usually drive C:.
- You can store documents in a folder on your hard drive called *My Documents*, or you can select a different folder. You can also create a new folder when you save a document.

Close a Document

- A document remains open on-screen until you close it.
- Close a document when you are finished working with it.
- If you try to close a document without saving it, Word prompts you to save it.
- You can close a document without saving it if you do not want to keep it for future use or if you are not happy with changes you have made since you last saved the document.

Exit Word

- When you are done using Word, you exit the Word application.
- If you try to exit Word without saving your documents, Word prompts you to do so.
- If you exit Word without closing your saved documents, Word closes them automatically.

Procedures

Start Word

1. Click **Start** [Start] ... [Ctrl]+[Esc]
2. Click **Programs** .... [P]
3. Click **Microsoft Word** on Programs menu.

OR

1. Click **Start** [Start] ... [Ctrl]+[Esc]
2. Click **New Office Document** [New Office Document]
3. From the General Tab, double-click **Blank Document** [Blank Document] .

Change the Word Window

To show or hide toolbars:

1. Click **View** .... [Alt]+[V]
2. Click **Toolbars** .... [T]
   - ✓ *Check mark next to toolbar name indicates that toolbar is already displayed.*
3. Click the toolbar name.

To show or hide ruler:

1. Click **View** .... Alt + V
   - ✓ Check mark next to ruler indicates ruler is displayed.
2. Click **Ruler** .... R

To change view:

1. Click **View** .... Alt + V
2. Click **Normal** .... N
   OR
   Click **Web Layout** .... W
   OR
   Click **Print Layout** .... P
   OR
   Click **Outline** .... O
   OR
- Click a View button.

Correct Errors

- Press **Backspace** Backspace to delete character to *left* of insertion point.
- Press **Delete** Del to delete character to *right* of insertion point.
- Press **Escape** Esc to cancel command or close dialog box.
- Click **Cancel** Cancel .

Undo the Previous Action
(Ctrl+Z)

- Click **Undo** button .
  OR
1. Click **Edit** .... Alt + E
2. Click **Undo** .... U

Undo a Series of Actions
(Ctrl+Z)

- Click **Undo** button repeatedly.
  OR
1. Click **Undo** drop-down arrow .

- ✓ The most recent action is listed at the top of the Undo drop-down list.
2. Click last action in the series to undo all previous actions.

Redo the Previous Action
(Ctrl+Y)

- Click **Redo** button .
  OR
1. Click **Edit** .... Alt + E
2. Click **Redo** .... R

Redo a Series of Actions
(Ctrl+Y)

- Click **Redo** button repeatedly.
  OR
1. Click **Redo** drop-down arrow .
2. Click the last action in the series to redo all previous actions.

Repeat the Previous Action
(Ctrl+Y or F4)

1. Click **Edit** .... Alt + E
2. Click **Repeat** .... R

Save a New Document
(Ctrl+S)

1. Click **Save** button .
   OR
   a. Click **File** .... Alt + F
   b. Click **Save** .... S
2. Click **Save in** drop-down arrow .... Alt + I
3. Select **drive** and **folder**.
4. Select **File name** text box .... Alt + N
5. Type **file name**.
6. Click **Save** .... Alt + S

To create a new folder for storing files:

1. Click **Save** button .
   OR
   a. Click **File** .... Alt + F
   b. Click **Save** .... S
2. Click **Create New Folder** button .
3. Type **new folder name**.
4. Click **OK** .... Enter
   - ✓ The new folder automatically becomes the open folder.

Close a Document *(Ctrl+W)*

- Click **Document Close Window** button .
  OR
1. Click **File** .... Alt + F
2. Click **Close** C
3. Click **Yes** to save document .... Y
   OR
   Click **No** to close without saving .... N

Exit Word

- Click **Application Close** button .
  OR
- Double-click the **Application Control** icon .
  OR
1. Click **File** .... Alt + F
2. Click **Exit** X
3. Click **Yes** to save open documents .... Y
   OR
   Click **No** to close without saving .... N

Exercise Directions

✓ *Note that the Word documents in the illustrations use the default 12-point Times New Roman font, unless otherwise noted. Fonts are covered in Exercise 7.*

1. Start Word.

2. Type the first paragraph shown in Illustration A.

   ✓ *Remember that you do not have to press **Enter** at the end of each line. Word wrap automatically moves the text to the next line as necessary.*

3. At the end of the paragraph, press **Enter** twice to start a new paragraph and insert a blank line between the paragraphs.

4. Undo the previous action.

   ✓ *When you execute the Undo command, Word reverses the action of pressing Enter twice. Sometimes Word combines actions for the purpose of Undo and Redo. In this case, it considers pressing Enter twice one action (called Typing on the Undo drop-down menu).*

5. Redo the previous action.

   ✓ *Word redoes the action of pressing Enter twice.*

6. Type the second paragraph shown in Illustration A.

7. If you make a typing error, press Backspace to delete it, and then type the correct text.

   ✓ *Word marks spelling errors with a red wavy underline, and grammatical errors with a green wavy underline. If you see these lines in the document, proofread for errors.*

8. Change to Web Layout view.

9. Change to Print Layout view.

10. Change to Normal view.

11. Open the File menu.

12. Close the File menu.

13. Hide the ruler.

14. Show the ruler.

15. Hide the Formatting toolbar.

16. Show the Formatting toolbar.

17. Save the document with the name **DOCTOR**.

    ✓ *Your instructor will tell you where to save the documents you create for use with this book.*

18. Close the document, saving all changes if prompted.

19. Exit Word.

Illustration A

California Cardiology, Inc. is pleased to announce that Dr. Cynthia Ramirez has joined our practice. Dr. Ramirez received a BS degree from Stanford University in 1991 and an MD from the University of California at Los Angeles College of Medicine in 1995. She completed a residency at UCLA Medical Center and is board certified in cardiology.

We are certain that Dr. Ramirez will be a valuable addition to our practice. Her skills and experience make her highly qualified, and we are sure you will find her "bedside manner" to be professional and compassionate. Dr. Ramirez is currently accepting new patients. Please contact our office for more information or to make an appointment.

On Your Own

1. Create a new document in Word.

2. Save the file as **OWD01**.

3. Type a brief biography about yourself, using at least two paragraphs.

4. Correct errors as necessary.

5. Practice changing from one view to another.

6. Display and hide different toolbars.

7. Close the document, saving all changes, and exit Word when you are finished.

Exercise 2

Skills Covered:

◆ **Create a New Document** ◆ **Work with Show/Hide Marks**
◆ **Move the Insertion Point in a Document** ◆ **Use Click and Type**
◆ **Save Changes** ◆ **Preview an Open Document**
◆ **Print an Open Document**

On the Job

Mastering insertion point movements in Word is necessary to enter and edit text anywhere in a document. You save changes to keep a document up-to-date as you work. When you want to have a hard copy version of a document, you must print it. Preview a document before you print it to make sure there are no errors and that it looks good on the page.

California Cardiology has decided to issue a press release announcing the hiring of a new physician. In this exercise, you will create a new document and type the press release. You will practice moving the insertion point around the document and you will align text with the click and type feature. When you have completed the press release, you will save the changes, preview the document, and then print it.

Terms

Insertion point The flashing vertical line that indicates where the next action will occur in a document on-screen.

Horizontal alignment The position of text on a line in relation to the left and right margins.

Hard copy A document printed on paper.

Notes

Create a New Document

- As you learned in Exercise 1, when you start Word it opens and displays a new blank document called *Document1*.

- You can create additional new documents without closing and restarting Word.

- Each new document is named using consecutive numbers, so the second document is *Document2,* the third is *Document3,* and so on until you exit Word or save a file with a new name.

- In Word, you can create a new document using the New dialog box, the New Document Task Pane, or the New Blank Document button on the Standard toolbar.
    - ✓ *You can also create a new Word document using Office, as described in "Getting Started with Office XP," Exercise 1.*

Work with Show/Hide Marks

- When you type in Word you insert nonprinting characters like spaces, tabs, and paragraph marks along with printing characters like letters and numbers.

- Displaying nonprinting characters on-screen is helpful because you see where each paragraph ends and if there are extra spaces or unwanted tab characters.

- On-screen, the most common nonprinting characters are displayed as follows:
  - Space: dot (•)
  - Paragraph: paragraph symbol (¶)
  - Tab: right arrow (→)
  - ✓ *Other nonprinting characters include optional hyphens, and line breaks.*

Move the Insertion Point in a Document

- The **insertion point** indicates where text will be inserted or deleted.

- You can move the insertion point anywhere in the existing text with keystrokes or mouse clicks.

- Using scroll bars to shift the document view does not move the insertion point.

Use Click and Type

- In Print Layout view, you can use the Click and Type feature to position the insertion point anywhere in a blank document to begin typing.
  - ✓ *Click and Type can only be used in Print Layout view.*

- When Click and Type is active, the mouse pointer changes to indicate the **horizontal alignment** of the new text.
  - ✓ *You learn more about horizontal alignment in Exercise 4.*

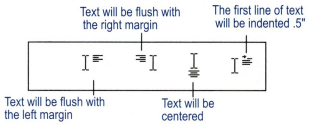

Text will be flush with the right margin

The first line of text will be indented .5"

Text will be flush with the left margin

Text will be centered

Save Changes

- To keep revisions permanently, you must save the document.

- Saving frequently ensures that no work will be lost if there is a power outage or you experience computer problems.
  - ✓ *The Document Recovery feature also helps insure that you won't lose your work in case of a failure. Refer to Exercise 4 of "Getting Started with Office XP" for more information.*

- Saving replaces the previously saved version of the document with any changes.

Preview an Open Document

- Use Print Preview to display a document as it will look when printed.

Print

- Printing creates a **hard copy** version of a document.

- Your computer must be connected to a printer in order to print.

Procedures

Create a New Document
(Ctrl+N)

1. Start Word.
2. Click **New Blank Document** button 🗋 on the Standard toolbar.

OR

1. Start Word.
2. Click **View** .... `Alt`+`V`
3. Click **Tas̲k Pane** .... `K`

   ✓ *If New Document Task Pane is not displayed, select it from the Other Task Panes drop-down list.*

4. Click **Blank Document** button 🗋.

Show or Hide Marks

- Click **Show/Hide ¶ button** ¶.

OR

1. Click **Tools** .... `Alt`+`T`
2. Click **Options** .... `O`
3. Click **View** tab .... `Ctrl`+`Tab`
4. Select **All** checkbox .... `Alt`+`A` in Formatting marks section.
5. Click **OK** .... `Enter`

Insertion Point Movements

To move with the mouse:

- Click mouse pointer in text where you want to position insertion point.

To move with the keyboard:

- One character left .... `←`
- One character right.............. `→`
- One line up .... `↑`
- One line down .... `↓`
- Previous word............. `Ctrl`+`←`
- Next word .... `Ctrl`+`→`
- Up one paragraph .... `Ctrl`+`↑`
- Down one paragraph... `Ctrl`+`↓`
- Beginning of document................ `Ctrl`+`Home`
- End of document .... `Ctrl`+`End`
- Beginning of line .... `Home`
- End of line .... `End`

Use Click and Type

1. Change to Print Layout view.
2. Click at location where you want to position insertion point.

To enable Click and Type:

1. Click **Tools** .... `Alt`+`T`
2. Click **Options** .... `O`
3. Click **Edit** tab .... `Ctrl`+`Tab`
4. Select **Enable c̲lick and type** check box .... `Alt`+`C`
5. Click **OK** .... `Enter`

Save Changes *(Ctrl+S)*

1. Click **Save** button 💾.

   OR

   a. Click **F̲ile**................. `Alt`+`F`
   b. Click **S̲ave** .... `S`

2. Select the disk and folder where you want to save the file.
3. Enter a file name.
4. Click **S̲ave** button

   `Save` ....`Alt`+`S`

Preview a Document

1. Click **Print Preview** button 🔍.

   OR

   a. Click **F̲ile**................. `Alt`+`F`
   b. Click **Print Prev̲iew** .... `V`

2. Press **Page Down** to see next page.
3. Press **Page Up** to see previous page.
4. Click **Close** `Close`.

Print *(Ctrl+P)*

- Click **Print** button 🖨.

OR

1. Click **F̲ile**..................... `Alt`+`F`
2. Click **Print**........................... `P`
3. Click **OK**........................... `Enter`

Exercise Directions

1. Start Word, if necessary.

2. Create a new document and save it as **PRESS**.

3. Click the Print Layout View button to change to Print Layout view if necessary.

   ✓ Select View, Print Layout.

4. Display all nonprinting characters.

5. Use Click and Type to center the insertion point on the first line of the document.

6. Type the text shown on the first line of Illustration A.

7. Use Click and Type to move the insertion point so it is flush left on the third line of the document. You will be able to see if you have positioned the insertion point on the third line by looking at the paragraph marks on-screen. There should be one paragraph mark at the end of the first line, a second paragraph mark on the second (blank) line, and a third paragraph mark to the left of the insertion point on the third line.

   ✓ If you press Enter twice to start a new paragraph and leave a blank line as you did in Exercise 1, the insertion point will still be centered. That's because Word carries formatting such as horizontal alignment forward from one paragraph to the next. You must use Click and Type to change the alignment to flush left.

8. Type the rest of the document shown in Illustration A.

   ✓ Depending on the default settings on your computer, Word may automatically format the Web address in the last paragraph as a hyperlink by changing the color to blue and applying an underline. If you click the hyperlink, your computer may try to log onto the Internet to locate the site. You can remove the hyperlink by right-clicking on it, then clicking Remove Hyperlink on the context menu.

9. Move the insertion point back to the fist sentence in the press release and delete the comma and the abbreviation **M.D.** following the name **Dr. Cynthia Ramirez**.

   ✓ You should delete the abbreviation because you have already used the title Dr.

10. Move the insertion point between the words **a** and **staff** in the second sentence of the second paragraph.

11. Type an **n** to change the word **a** to an.

12. Type a space, then type the word **exceptional**.

13. If necessary type a space between the new word **exceptional** and the existing word **staff**.

14. Save the changes you have made to the document.

15. Display the document in Print Preview.

16. Close Print Preview.

17. Print the document.

18. Close the document, saving all changes.

Cynthia Ramirez, M.D. Joins California Cardiology, Inc.

Los Angeles, CA -- California Cardiology, Inc. is pleased to announce that Dr. Cynthia Ramirez, M.D. has joined our practice. Dr. Ramirez received a BS degree from Stanford University in 1991 and an MD from the University of California at Los Angeles College of Medicine in 1995. She completed a residency at UCLA Medical Center and is board certified in cardiology.

California Cardiology provides high-quality cardiac care to patients in the metro Los Angeles area. With the addition of Dr. Ramirez, we now have six full-time physicians supported by a staff of nurses and physician's assistants. Our offices are thoroughly up-to-date with the most current technologies, and we have admitting privileges at most major hospitals in L.A.

n
exceptional

For more information about Dr. Ramirez or about California Cardiology, please call 310-555-2922, or visit us on the Web at www.ddcpub.com/calcardiology. We accept most major insurance policies.

On Your Own

1. Create a new document.
2. Save the file as **OWD02**.
3. Draft a press release announcing that you are taking a course to learn how to use Microsoft Office XP.
4. Using Click and Type, center a headline at the top of the document.
5. Using Click and Type, move the pointer back to the flush left or first line indent position to type the rest of the press release. Include information such as your instructor's name, the textbook you are using, and when the course will be completed.
6. Save the changes, then preview the document to see how it will look when printed.
7. Print the document.
6. Close the document when you are finished, saving all changes.

Exercise 3

Skills Covered:

◆ **Correct Spelling as You Type** ◆ **Correct Grammar as You Type**
◆ **Check Spelling** ◆ **Check Grammar** ◆ **Use the Thesaurus**

On the Job

A professional document should be free of spelling and grammatical errors. Word can check the spelling and grammar in a document and recommend corrections.

The marketing director has asked you to create a mission statement explaining the goals for Northwest Gear, Inc., a manufacturer of clothing for teens and young adults. In this exercise, you will type the statement, and then improve it by correcting the spelling and grammar.

Terms

Smart tag A feature of Word 2002 designed to let you perform actions within Word that you would normally have to open another application to accomplish. For example, you can add a person's name and address to an Outlook contact list using a smart tag in Word.

Thesaurus A listing of words with synonyms and antonyms.

Synonyms Words with the same meaning.

Antonyms Words with opposite meanings.

Notes

Correct Spelling as You Type

- By default, Word checks spelling as you type and marks misspelled words with a red, wavy underline.

> This·is·an·example·of·a·missspelled·word.¶

- Any word not in the Word dictionary is marked as misspelled, including proper names, words with unique spellings, and many technical terms. Word will also mark double occurrences of words.

- You can ignore the wavy lines and keep typing, correct the spelling, or add the marked word to the dictionary.

- If the wavy underlines distract you from your work, you can turn off the Check spelling as you type feature.

  - ✓ *Word uses a few other underlines to mark text on-screen. For example, blue wavy underlines indicate inconsistent formatting and purple dotted lines indicate **smart tags**. You learn about checking for inconsistent formatting in Exercise 19.*

Correct Grammar as You Type

- Word can also check grammar as you type, identifying errors such as punctuation, matching case or tense, sentence fragments, and run-on sentences.

- Word marks grammatical errors with a green, wavy underline.

> This·is·an·example·of·a·grammatical·errors.¶

- Word picks out grammatical errors based on one of five built-in style guides.

- The default grammar style is called Standard. You can select casual, formal, technical, or you can develop a custom style.

- As with the spelling checker, you can ignore the green wavy lines and keep typing, or correct the error.

- If the wavy underlines distract you from your work, you can turn off the Check grammar as you type feature.

Check Spelling

- You can check the spelling in an entire document or in part of a document.

- To check the spelling in part of a document, you must first select the section you want checked.

- The spelling checker identifies any word not in the Word dictionary as misspelled, including proper names, words with unique spellings, and technical terms.

- When Word identifies a misspelled word, you can correct the spelling, ignore the spelling, or add the word to the dictionary.

Correct spelling with Spelling Checker

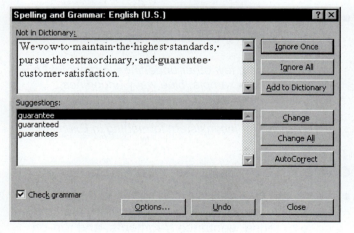

Check Grammar

- By default, Word checks the grammar in a document at the same time that it checks the spelling.

- When Word identifies a grammatical mistake, you can accept the suggestion or ignore it.

Correct grammar with Grammar Checker

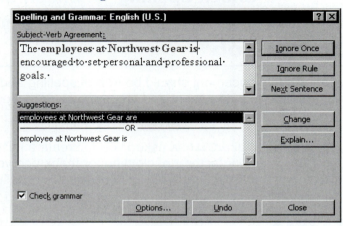

Use the Thesaurus

- Use the **thesaurus** to locate **synonyms**, definitions, and **antonyms** for words typed in a document.

- A thesaurus can improve your writing by helping you eliminate repetitive use of common words and to choose more descriptive words.

Choose synonyms with the Thesaurus

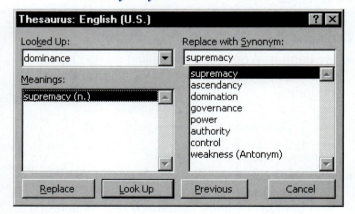

Procedures

Correct Spelling as You Type

1. Right-click red, wavy underline.
2. Click correctly spelled word on context menu.

   OR

   - Click **Ignore All** .... `I`
   - Click **Add** to add word to dictionary .... `A`

To turn off Automatic Spelling Checker:

1. Click **Tools**.................... `Alt`+`T`
2. Click **Options**...................... `O`
3. Click the **Spelling & Grammar** tab .... `Ctrl`+`Tab`
4. Deselect **Check spelling as you type** check box ..... `Alt`+`P`
5. Click **OK**........................... `Enter`

Correct Grammar as You Type

1. Right-click grammatical error marked with green, wavy underline.
2. Click **correct grammar** option on context menu.

   OR

   Click **Ignore Once** to hide the underline .... `I`

To turn Off Automatic Grammar Checker:

1. Click **Tools**.................... `Alt`+`T`
2. Click **Options**...................... `O`
3. Click the **Spelling & Grammar** tab .... `Ctrl`+`Tab`
4. Deselect **Check grammar** as you type check box ...... `Alt`+`G`
5. Click **OK**........................... `Enter`

Select Grammar Style

1. Click **Tools**.................... `Alt`+`T`
2. Click **Options**...................... `O`
3. Click the **Spelling & Grammar** tab .... `Ctrl`+`Tab`
4. Click **Writing style** drop-down arrow .... `Alt`+`W`

---

5. Click desired **style** .. , `Enter`
6. Click **OK** .... `Enter`

Check Spelling *(F7)*

1. Position insertion point where you want to start checking.

   ✓ *Word checks document from the insertion point forward.*

   OR

   Select text you want to check.
2. Click **Spelling and Grammar** button.

   OR

   a. Click **Tools**............. `Alt`+`T`
   b. Click **Spelling & Grammar** .... `S`
3. Choose from the following options:

   - Click correctly spelled word in **Suggestions** list....................... `Alt`+`N`
   - Click **Change** .... `Alt`+`C`
   - Click **Change All** to change the word everywhere in document .... `Alt`+`L`
   - Change the misspelled word manually in the Not in Dictionary text box.
   - Click **Ignore Once** to continue without changing word .... `Alt`+`I`
   - Click **Ignore All** to continue without changing word and without highlighting it anywhere else in document.... `Alt`+`G`
   - Click **Add to Dictionary** to add word to dictionary............... `Alt`+`A`
4. Repeat step 3 options for every misspelled word.
5. Click **OK** when Word completes check. .... `Enter`

✓ *Word may prompt you to check the formatting in your document. Click Yes to check the formatting, or No to close the prompt without checking the formatting. For more information on checking formatting, refer to Exercise 19.*

Check Grammar *(F7)*

1. Position insertion point where you want to start checking.

   OR

   Select text you want to check.
2. Click **Spelling and Grammar** button.

   OR

   a. Click **Tools**............. `Alt`+`T`
   b. Click **Spelling & Grammar** .... `S`
3. Choose from the following options:

   - Click the correct grammar in **Suggestions** list..... `Alt`+`N`
   - Edit the error manually in the Not in Dictionary box.
   - Click **Change** .... `Alt`+`C`
   - Click **Ignore Once** to continue without changing text......................... `Alt`+`I`
   - Click **Ignore Rule** to continue without changing text and without highlighting error if it occurs anywhere else in document .... `Alt`+`G`
   - Click **Next Sentence** to skip highlighted error and continue checking document............... `Alt`+`X`
   - Click **Explain**.......... `Alt`+`E` to display information about grammatical error.
4. Repeat step 3 options for every grammatical error.
5. Click **OK** when Word completes check............. `Enter`

Use Thesaurus (Shift+F7)

1. Click on the word you want to look up.
   - ✓ *The insertion point should be positioned within the word.*
2. Click **T**ools .... `Alt`+`T`
3. Click **L**anguage .... `L`
4. Click **T**hesaurus .... `T`

5. Choose from the following options:
   - Click **L**ook up to display synonyms for word highlighted in Replace with Synonym list. .... `Alt`+`L`
   - Click a word in the **Meanings list** to display synonyms for the word .... `Alt`+`M`, `⬓↓`
   - Click **Antonyms** to display a list of antonyms for selected word.
     - ✓ *The Antonyms option is not available for all words in the Thesaurus.*

6. Click the **replacement word** you want in the **Replace with Synonym** list. ..... `Alt`+`S`, `⬓↓`
7. Click **R**eplace. .... `Alt`+`R`

Locate a synonym as you type

1. Right-click on the word you want to look up.
2. Click **S**ynonyms on context menu .... `Y`
3. Click desired **synonym** on submenu .... `⬓↓`, `Enter`

   OR

   Click **T**hesaurus .... `T`
   to open the Thesaurus dialog box.

Exercise Directions

1. Start Word, if necessary.
2. Create a new document.
3. Save the file as **MISSION**.
4. Display paragraph marks.
5. Begin at the top of the screen and type the paragraphs shown in Illustration A, including all the circled errors.
6. As you type, correct the spelling of the word **committed**.
7. As you type, correct the grammar in the first sentence of the second paragraph.
8. Check the spelling and grammar starting at the beginning of the document.
   a. Correct the spelling of the word **clientele**.
   b. Ignore all occurrences of the proper name **Khourie**.
   c. Correct the spelling of the word **guarantee**.
   d. Change the double comma in the middle of the second sentence in the second paragraph to a single comma.
   e. Capitalize the word **we** at the beginning of the last sentence.

9. Use the Thesaurus to replace the word **excellence** in the last sentence.
10. Display the document in Print Preview.
11. Print the document.
12. Close the document, saving all changes.

Illustration A

Northwest Gear, Inc. is comitted to excellence. In order to meet the needs of our clientelle, we encourage and support creativity at every level of our organization from our president, Mr. Khourie, to Bob on the loading dock. We vow to maintain the highest standards, pursue the extraordinary, and guarentee customer satisfaction.

The employees at Northwest Gear is encouraged to set personal and professional goals. Following the leadership of Mr. Khourie, we respect all employees as individuals and believe that fostering a strong community within the workplace strengthens our position in the marketplace. we are confident that our commitment to excellence will make us leaders in our industry.

On Your Own

1. Create a new document.
2. Save the document as **OWD03**.
3. Type your own mission statement for this class in the blank document. Include information such as the goals you'd like to achieve and the things you'd like to learn.
4. Check and correct the spelling and grammar.
5. Use the Thesaurus to improve the wording of your document.
6. Print the document.
7. Save your changes, close the document, and exit Word when you are finished.

Exercise 4

◆ **Use AutoCorrect** ◆ **Select Text In a Document**
◆ **Replace Selected Text** ◆ **Align Text Horizontally**
◆ **Align a Document Vertically**

On the Job

As you type a document, Word's AutoCorrect feature automatically corrects common spelling errors before you even know you've made them. You must select text in a document in order to edit it or format it. For example, changing the horizontal and vertical alignment can improve the appearance of a document, and make it easier to read.

You work in the personnel department at Perry, Hawkins, Martinez, and Klein, a large law firm based in Washington, D.C. In this exercise, your supervisor has asked you to type a memo to employees about the new Casual Friday policy.

Terms

AutoCorrect A Word feature that automatically corrects common spelling errors as you type.

Caps Lock Keyboard key used to **toggle** uppercase letters with lowercase letters.

Toggle A command that turns a particular mode on and off. Also, to switch back and forth between two modes.

Select Mark text for editing.

Contiguous Next to or adjacent.

Noncontiguous Not next to or adjacent.

Highlight To apply a colored background to the text to call attention to it.

Horizontal alignment The position of text in relation to the left and right page margins.

Flush Lined up evenly along an edge.

Vertical alignment The position of text in relation to the top and bottom page margins.

Selection bar A narrow strip along the left margin of a page that automates selection of text. When the mouse pointer is in the selection area, the cursor changes to an arrow pointing up and to the right.

Notes

Use AutoCorrect

AutoCorrect dialog box

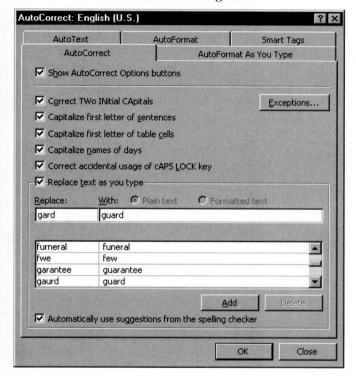

- **AutoCorrect** automatically replaces spelling errors with the correct text as soon as you press the spacebar after typing a word.

- Word comes with a built-in list of AutoCorrect entries including common typos like *adn* for *and* and *teh* for *the*.

- AutoCorrect can also replace regular characters with symbols, such as the letters *T* and *M* with the trademark symbol, ™.

- AutoCorrect also corrects capitalization errors as follows:
  - TWo INitial CApital letters are replaced with one initial capital letter.
  - The first word in a sentence is automatically capitalized.
  - The days of the week are automatically capitalized.
  - Accidental use of the cAPS LOCK feature is corrected if the **Caps Lock** key is set to ON.

- You can add words to the AutoCorrect list. For example, if you commonly misspell someone's name, you can add it to the list.

- You can also set Word to use the spelling checker dictionary to determine if a word is misspelled and to correct it automatically.

- If AutoCorrect changes text that was not incorrect, you can use Undo or the AutoCorrect Options button to reverse the change.

- If you find AutoCorrect distracting, you can disable it.

Select Text in a Document

- You must **select** text already entered in a document in order to edit it or format it.

- You can select any amount of **contiguous** or **noncontiguous** text.
  - ✓ *You can also select nontext characters, such as symbols, nonprinting characters, such as paragraph marks, and graphics, such as pictures.*

- Selected text appears **highlighted** on screen as white characters on a black background.

Selected text in a document

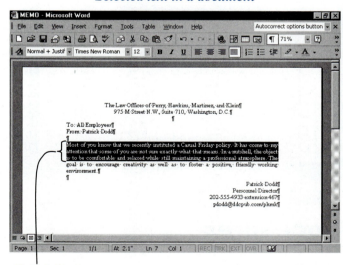

Selected text

Replace Selected Text

- You can replace selected text simply by typing new text.

- You can delete selected text by pressing the Delete key or the Backspace key.

Align Text Horizontally

- **Horizontal alignment** is used to adjust the position of paragraphs in relation to the left and right margins of a page.

  - ✓ *You have already used Click and Type to align text horizontally in a document.*

- There are four horizontal alignments:
  - *Left.* Text is **flush** with left margin. The text along the right side of the page is uneven (or ragged). Left is the default horizontal alignment.
  - *Right.* Text is flush with right margin. The text along the left side of the page is uneven (or ragged).
  - *Center.* Text is centered between margins.
  - *Justify.* Text is spaced so it runs evenly along both the left and right margins.

- You can use different alignments in a document.

Text aligned in a document

Align a Document Vertically

- **Vertical alignment** is used to adjust the position of all text on a page in relation to the top and bottom margins.

- There are four vertical alignments:
  - *Top:* Text begins below the top margin. Top is the default vertical alignment.
  - *Center:* Text is centered between the top and bottom margins.
  - *Justified:* Paragraphs are spaced to fill the page between the top and bottom margins.
  - *Bottom:* The last line of text begins just above the bottom margin.

- Centering vertically can improve the appearance of some one-page documents, such as flyers, or invitations.

- Vertical justification improves the appearance of documents that contain nearly full pages of text.

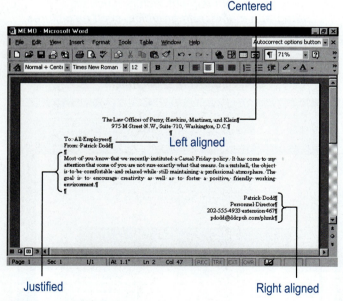

Centered

Left aligned

Justified   Right aligned

Procedures

Use AutoCorrect

Add words to the AutoCorrect list:

1. Click **Tools** .... `Alt`+`T`
2. Click **AutoCorrect Options** .... `A`
3. Click in **Replace** text box........................ `Alt`+`R`

4. Type misspelled word to add.
5. Click in **With** text box .. `Alt`+`W`
6. Type correct word.
7. Click **Add** button
   `   Add   ` .... `Alt`+`A`
8. Click **OK** .... `Enter`

Set AutoCorrect to correct words found in spelling checker dictionary:

1. Click **Tools** .... `Alt`+`T`
2. Click **AutoCorrect Options** .... `A`

3. Select **Automatically use suggestions from the spelling checker** check box................ `Alt`+`G`

Disable AutoCorrect:

1. Click **Tools**.................. `Alt`+`T`
2. Click **AutoCorrect Options** .... `A`
3. Deselect **Replace text as you type** check box. .... `Alt`+`T`

   ✓ *Clicking should remove check mark; if not, click check box again.*

Use AutoCorrect Options button:

1. Click word that was automatically corrected.

   ✓ *A small blue box is displayed below the word.*

2. Rest mouse pointer on **blue box** ═.

   ✓ *The AutoCorrect Options button is displayed.*

3. Click **AutoCorrect Options** button 🖋 ▾.
4. Select one of the following:
   - **Change back** .... `H` to reverse the change.
   - **Stop Automatically Correcting**...................... `A` to remove the word from the AutoCorrect list.
   - **Control AutoCorrect Options** .... `C` to open the AutoCorrect dialog box.

Select Using the Keyboard

1. Position insertion point to left of first character to select.
2. Use following key combinations:
   - One character right....................... `Shift`+`→`
   - One character left .. `Shift`+`←`
   - One line up .... `Shift`+`↑`
   - One line down........ `Shift`+`↓`
   - To end of line .... `Shift`+`End`
   - To beginning of line .... `Shift`+`Home`

   - To end of document ..... `Shift`+`Ctrl`+`End`
   - To beginning of document... `Shift`+`Ctrl`+`Home`
   - Entire document ..... `Ctrl`+`A`

Select Using the Mouse

1. Position insertion point to the left of first character to select.
2. Hold down left mouse button.
3. Drag to where you want to stop selecting.
4. Release mouse button.

Mouse Selection Shortcuts

One word:
- Double-click word.

One sentence:
1. Press and hold **Ctrl** .... `Ctrl`
2. Click in sentence.

One line:
- Click in **selection bar** to the left of the line.

   ✓ *In the selection bar, the mouse pointer changes to an arrow pointing up and to the right* ⬈.

One paragraph:
- Double-click in selection bar to the left of the paragraph you want to select.

Document:
- Triple-click in selection bar.

Select noncontiguous blocks

1. Select first block.
2. Press and hold **Ctrl** .... `Ctrl`
3. Select additional block(s).

Cancel a Selection

- Click anywhere in document.

OR

- Press any arrow key.......... ⬇

Replace Selected Text

1. Select text to replace.
2. Type new text.

   OR

   Press **Delete** .... `Del` to delete selected text.

Align Horizontally

1. Position insertion point in paragraph to align.

   OR

   Select paragraphs to align.

   OR

   Position insertion point where you intend to type text.

2. Click alignment button:
   - **Center** ☰ .... `Ctrl`+`E`
   - **Right** ☰ .... `Ctrl`+`R`
   - **Justify** ☰ .... `Ctrl`+`J`
   - **Left** ☰ .... `Ctrl`+`L`

Align Vertically

1. Click **File**..................... `Alt`+`F`
2. Click **Page Setup** .... `U`
3. Click **Layout** tab .... `Alt`+`L`
4. Click **Vertical alignment**.................... `Alt`+`V` drop-down arrow.
5. Select **Vertical alignment** option:..................... ⬇ , `Enter`
   - **Top**
   - **Center**
   - **Justified**
   - **Bottom**
6. Click **OK** .... `Enter`

Exercise Directions

1. Start Word, if necessary.

2. Create a new document and save it as **CASUAL**.

3. Display nonprinting characters, if necessary.

4. Open the AutoCorrect dialog box.

   a. Add the misspelled name **Martinex** to the AutoCorrect list; replace it with the correctly spelled **Martinez**.

   b. Add the misspelled word **personell** to the AutoCorrect list; replace it with the correctly spelled **personnel**.

   c. Add the misspelled word **casaul** to the AutoCorrect list; replace it with the correctly spelled **casual**.

   d. Be sure the *Replace text as you type* checkbox is selected, then close the dialog box.

5. Type the document shown in Illustration A.

   - Type the actual date in place of the text *Today's date*.

   - Type the circled errors exactly as shown in the illustration.

      ✓ *Notice that Word automatically corrects the errors.*

   - Press Enter twice to start new paragraphs and leave blank lines as marked on the illustration.

6. Save the document.

7. Horizontally align the text in the document as marked on the illustration.

   a. Select the lines marked for centering.

   b. Center the selected text.

   c. Select the three paragraphs marked for justification.

   d. Justify the selected paragraphs.

   e. Select the lines marked for right alignment.

   f. Right align the selected text.

8. Select the text **Personnel Director** on the *From:* line near the top of the document and replace it with the name **Patrick Dodd**.

9. Check the spelling and grammar in the document. Ignore all proper names.

10. Display the document in Print Preview.

11. Center the document vertically on the page.

12. Display the document in Print Preview again.

13. Justify the document vertically.

14. Display the document in Print Preview again.

15. Print the document.

16. Close the document, saving all changes.

On Your Own

1. Create a new document in Word.

2. Save the file as **OWD04**.

3. Add your last name to the AutoCorrect list.

4. Add other words that you commonly misspell.

5. Type a memo to your teachers asking them to be sure to spell your name correctly. Include the misspelled version as well as the correct spelling. When AutoCorrect changes the misspelled version, use the AutoCorrect Options button to reverse the change.

6. Change the horizontal alignment of some of the text in the memo.

7. Change the vertical alignment of the document.

8. Print the document.

9. Close the document, saving all changes.

Illustration A

The Law Offices of Perry, Hawkins, [Martinex], and Klein   } *Center*
975 M Street N.W., Suite 710, Washington, D.C.

↓ *Enter 4x*

MEMO

↓ *Enter 3x*

To: All Employees
From: [Personell] Director
Date: Today's date
Subject: [Casaul] Fridays

↓ *Enter 3x*

Most of you know that we recently instituted a Casual Friday policy. It has come to
my attention that some of you are not sure exactly what that means. In a nutshell, [teh]
object is to be comfortable and relaxed while still maintaining a professional
atmosphere. [THe] goal is to encourage creativity as well as to foster a positive, friendly
working environment.

↓ *Enter 2x*

As for what constitutes appropriate attire for Casual Fridays, please use common
sense. For example, do not dress for the beach. [ALso], if you have a meeting with a
client who is not expecting Casual [friday], you should not dress for Casual Friday.

↓ *Enter 2x*

} *Justify*

Here are a few guidelines:

↓ *Enter 2x*

Khakis instead of dress slacks or skirts
[SWeaters] instead of suit coats   } *Center*
Sneakers instead of [hgih] heels

↓ *Enter 2x*

If you have any questions, feel free to contact me. I think that in a few weeks we will   } *Justify*
all be completely comfortable with the Casual Friday atmosphere.

↓ *Enter 3x*

Patrick Dodd
[Personell] Director
202-555-4933 extension 467   } *Right align*
pdodd@ddcpub.com/phmk

Exercise 5

Skills Covered:
◆ **Format a Business Letter**
◆ **Insert the Date and Time in a Document** ◆ **Use Uppercase Mode**
◆ **Change Case in a Document**

On the Job

Write business letters as a representative of your employer to communicate with other businesses, such as clients or suppliers, or to communicate with individuals, such as prospective employees. For example, you might write a business letter to request a job quote from a supplier, or to inquire about a loan from a bank.

You are the assistant to Mr. Benjamin Boghosian, the owner of Coastline Gourmet Importers, a chain of specialty food retail stores. He has asked you to type a letter to a vendor about obtaining some Russian caviar. In this exercise, you will compose a full-block business letter regarding the caviar.

Terms

Full block A style of letter in which all lines start flush with the left margin—that is, without a first-line indent.

Modified block A style of letter in which some lines start at the center of the page.

Salutation The line at the start of a letter including the greeting and the recipient's name, such as *Dear Mr. Doe.*

Computer's clock The clock/calendar built into your computer's main processor to keep track of the current date and time.

Case The specific use of upper- or lowercase letters.

Notes

Format a Business Letter

- There are different letter styles of business letters.
  - In a **full-block** business letter, all lines start flush with the left margin.
  - In a **modified-block** business letter, certain lines start at the center of the page.
    - ✓ *Modified-block business letters will be covered in Exercise 6.*
- The parts of a business letter are the same regardless of the style.

- Vertical spacing is achieved by inserting blank lines between letter parts.
- Refer to the illustration on page 57 to identify the parts of a business letter.
  - Return address (may be omitted if the letter is printed on letterhead stationery)
  - Date
  - Inside address (to whom and where the letter is going)
  - **Salutation**
  - Body

- Signature line
- Title line (the job title of the letter writer)
- Reference initials (the initials of the person who wrote the letter, followed by a slash, followed by the initials of the person who typed the letter)
    - ✓ *Whenever you see "yo" as part of the reference initials in an exercise, type your own initials.*
- Special notations (included only when appropriate):
    - ◆ Mail service notation indicates a special delivery method. It is typed in all capital letters, two lines below the date. Typical mail service notations include *CERTIFIED MAIL, REGISTERED MAIL,* or *BY HAND.*
    - ◆ Subject notation identifies or summarizes the letter topic. The word *Subject* may be typed in all capital letters or with just an initial capital. It is placed two lines below the salutation.
        - ✓ *The word* Re *(meaning* with regard to*) is sometimes used in place of the word* Subject.
    - ◆ Enclosure or attachment notation indicates whether there are other items in the envelope. It is typed two lines below the reference initials in any of the following styles: *ENC., Enc., Encl., Enclosure, Attachment.*
        - ✓ *If there are multiple items, the number may be typed in parentheses following the notation.*
    - ◆ Copy notation indicates if any other people are receiving copies of the same letter. It is typed two lines below either the enclosure notation, or reference initials, whichever is last. It may be typed as Copy to:, cc:, or pc: (photocopy) with the name(s) of the recipient(s) listed after the colon.

Insert the Date and Time in a Document

- Use the Date and Time feature to insert the current date and/or time automatically in a document.

- The inserted date and time are based on your **computer's clock**. A variety of date and time formats are available.

The Date and Time dialog box

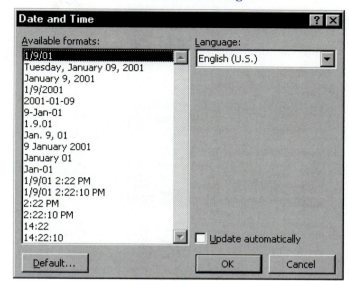

- You can set Word to update the date or time automatically whenever you save or print the document.

Use Uppercase Mode

- Use Uppercase Mode to type all capital letters without pressing the Shift key.
- Uppercase Mode affects only letter characters.
- When Uppercase Mode is on, the Caps Lock indicator on your keyboard is lit.

Change Case in a Document

- You can automatically change the **case** of text in a document.
- There are five case options:
    - Sentence case: First character in sentence is uppercase.
    - lowercase: All characters are lowercase.
    - UPPERCASE: All characters are uppercase.
    - Title Case: First character in each word is uppercase.
    - tOGGLE cASE: Case is reversed for all selected text.

Procedures

Format a Full-Block Business Letter

1. Start 2" from the top of the page .... `Enter` **4x**

   ✓ *Press Enter four times to leave 2" of space.*

   ✓ *If you are using stationery with a printed letterhead, you may have to adjust the spacing.*

2. Insert the date.

3. Leave one blank line and type the mail service notation .... `Enter` **2x**

4. Leave three blank lines and type the inside address .... `Enter` **4x**

5. Leave a blank line and type the salutation .... `Enter` **2x**

6. Leave one blank line and type the subject notation ..... `Enter` **2x**

7. Leave a blank line and type the letter body ...... `Enter` **2x**

8. Leave a blank line and type the closing .... `Enter` **2x**

9. Leave three blank lines and type the signature line .... `Enter` **4x**

10. Press **Enter** .... `Enter`

11. Type the title line .... `Enter`

    ✓ *If you are not using letterhead stationery, type the return address information below the title line.*

12. Leave a blank line and type the reference initials. .. `Enter` **2x**

13. Leave a blank line and type the enclosure notation .... `Enter` **2x**

14. Leave a blank line and type the copy notation .... `Enter` **2x**

Insert the Date and/or Time

1. Position the insertion point.

2. Click **Insert** .... `Alt`+`I`

3. Click **Date and Time** .... `T`

4. Click the desired format.

   ✓ *Select Update automatically check box if you want date and/or time to update when you save or print document.*

5. Click **OK** .... `Enter`

Uppercase Mode

1. Press **Caps Lock** .... `Caps Lock`

2. Type text.

To turn off Uppercase Mode:

- Press **Caps Lock** .... `Caps Lock`

Change Case

1. Select text.

   OR

   Position insertion point where new text will begin.

2. Click **Format** .... `Alt`+`O`

3. Click **Change Case** .... `E`

4. Click the case you want:

   - **Sentence case** .... `S`
   - **lowercase** .... `L`
   - **UPPERCASE** .... `U`
   - **Title Case** .... `T`
   - **tOGGLE cASE** .... `G`

5. Click **OK** .... `Enter`

   ✓ *You can also select text and then press **Shift+F3** to toggle through sentence case, lowercase, and uppercase. Release the keys when the desired case is in effect.*

Exercise Directions

1. Start Word, if necessary.

2. Create a new document and save it as **CAVIAR**.

3. Type the letter shown in Illustration A.

   - Press the Enter key between parts of the letter as indicated.

   - Insert the current date using the MONTH DAY, YEAR format found third from the top in the Date and Time dialog box.

   - Set the date so that it does not update automatically.

   - Use Uppercase mode to type the mail notation.

     ✓ *Word may display ScreenTips as you type certain parts of the letter (for example, CERTIFIED MAIL). Simply ignore them and continue typing.*

4. Change the text on the Subject line to title case.

5. Change all occurrences of the text **Coastline Gourmet Importers** and **Coastline Gourmet** to uppercase.

   ✓ *Do not change the text as it appears in the Web address.*

6. Check the spelling and grammar in the document.

   - Ignore all proper names.

7. Display the document in Print Preview.

   ✓ *If the document does not fit on one page, you may have inserted too many blank lines. Make sure you have nonprinting characters displayed so you can see the paragraph marks, count the marks, and delete any extras.*

8. Close the document, saving all changes.

Illustration A

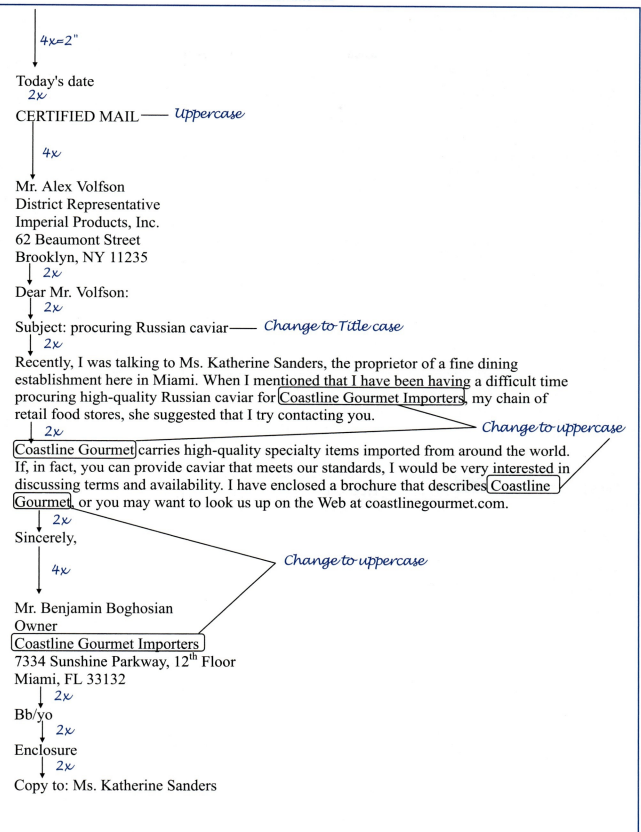

4x=2"

Today's date

2x

CERTIFIED MAIL —— *Uppercase*

4x

Mr. Alex Volfson
District Representative
Imperial Products, Inc.
62 Beaumont Street
Brooklyn, NY 11235

2x

Dear Mr. Volfson:

2x

Subject: procuring Russian caviar —— *Change to Title case*

2x

Recently, I was talking to Ms. Katherine Sanders, the proprietor of a fine dining establishment here in Miami. When I mentioned that I have been having a difficult time procuring high-quality Russian caviar for Coastline Gourmet Importers, my chain of retail food stores, she suggested that I try contacting you.

2x

Change to uppercase

Coastline Gourmet carries high-quality specialty items imported from around the world. If, in fact, you can provide caviar that meets our standards, I would be very interested in discussing terms and availability. I have enclosed a brochure that describes Coastline Gourmet, or you may want to look us up on the Web at coastlinegourmet.com.

2x

Sincerely,

4x

Change to uppercase

Mr. Benjamin Boghosian
Owner
Coastline Gourmet Importers
7334 Sunshine Parkway, 12th Floor
Miami, FL 33132

2x

Bb/yo

2x

Enclosure

2x

Copy to: Ms. Katherine Sanders

On Your Own

1. Create a new document in Word.

2. Save the document as **OWD05**.

3. Representing your school or organization, draft a full-block business letter to a local newspaper asking them to include information about upcoming events in a calendar listing. School events might include athletic contests such as a homecoming football game, club activities, field trips, band and choir concerts, or vacation days.

4. In the letter, indicate that you have attached the necessary information and that you are sending a copy to your instructor.

5. Test different case options for different parts of the letter.

6. Save your changes, close the document, and exit Word when you are finished.

Skills Covered:

◆ **Set Tabs** ◆ **Format a Modified-Block Business Letter**
◆ **Shrink to Fit** ◆ **Full Screen View**

On the Job

You use tabs to align text in a document, such as the date in a modified-block business letter. If a letter is just a bit too long to fit on a single page, use *Shrink to Fit* to automatically reduce the printed length of a document so it fits on one page.

The marketing director at Northwest Gear, Inc., a clothing manufacturer, has asked you to type a letter inviting a buyer from a chain of clothing stores to preview the new fall line. In this exercise, you compose a modified-block business letter using tabs, Shrink to Fit, and Full Screen view.

Terms

Tab A location (or measurement) you use to align text.

Font A set of characters with a specific size and style.

Notes

Tab stops on the horizontal ruler

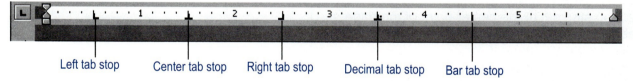

Left tab stop   Center tab stop   Right tab stop   Decimal tab stop   Bar tab stop

Set Tabs

- **Tabs** are used to indent a single line of text.
- Each time you press the Tab key, the insertion point advances to the next set tab stop.
- There are five types of tab stops:
  - Left: Text starts flush left with the tab stop.
  - Right: Text ends flush right with the tab stop.
  - Center: Text is centered on the tab stop.
  - Decimal: Decimal points are aligned with the tab stop.
  - Bar: A horizontal bar is displayed at the tab stop position. Text starts 1/10" to the right of the bar.

- By default, left tab stops are set every ½" on the horizontal ruler.
- You can set any type of tab stop at any point along the ruler.
- You can use the Tabs dialog box to set precise tab stops.
- You can set tabs before you type new text, for the current existing paragraph, or for selected multiple paragraphs.
- Once you set tabs, the formatting will be carried forward each time you press the Enter key to start a new paragraph.

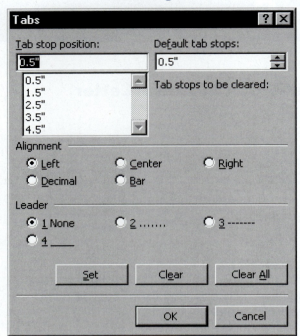

Tabs dialog box

Format a Modified-Block Business Letter

- A modified-block style letter is set up with all lines starting flush with the left margin except the date, closing, signature, and title lines, which begin at the center point of the page.

  ✓ *The parts of a modified-block style letter are the same as those of a full-block style letter. The special notations are used when appropriate.*

- A left tab stop set at the center point of the page enables you to position the insertion point quickly where you need it.

  ✓ *Using a center tab stop or centered alignment centers the text; you must use a left tab stop in order to position the text to start at the center point of the page.*

Shrink to Fit

- Shrink to Fit automatically reduces the **font** size and spacing in a document just enough to fit the document on one less page.
- Use Shrink to Fit if the last page of a document contains only a small amo
- unt of text.
- The Shrink to Fit feature is available only in Print Preview mode.

Full Screen View

- In any view, including Print Preview, use Full Screen view to display a document without the title bar, toolbars, ruler, scroll bars, status bar, or taskbar.
- Full Screen view lets you see more of your document on-screen at one time.

Full Screen view

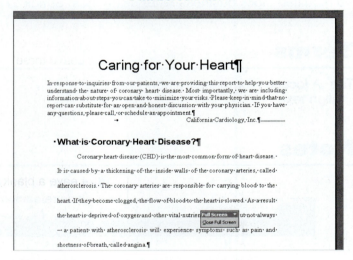

Procedures

Set Tabs

To set a left tab stop:

1. Position insertion point in paragraph to format.
   OR
   Select paragraphs to format.
2. Click ruler where you want to set tab stop.

To set a different type of tab stop:

1. Position insertion point in paragraph to format.
   OR
   Select paragraphs to format.
2. Click the **Tab** box .

   ✓ *Each time you click, the tab icon changes. Stop when tab stop you want is displayed.*

3. Click ruler where you want to insert new tab stop.

To set a precise tab stop:

1. Position insertion point in paragraph to format.
   OR
   Select paragraphs to format.
2. Click **Format**................Alt+O
3. Click **Tabs**..........................T

4. Select type of tab:
   - **Left** .... Alt+L
   - **Center** .... Alt+C
   - **Right** .... Alt+R
   - **Decimal** .... Alt+D
   - **Bar** .... Alt+B
5. Click in the **Tab stop position** .... Alt+T
6. Type precise position.
7. Click **OK** .... Enter

To clear a tab stop:

1. Position insertion point in paragraph to forma.
   OR
   Select paragraphs to format.
2. Drag tab stop marker off ruler.

OR

1. Click **Format** .... Alt+O
2. Click **Tabs** .... T
3. Click **Clear All** .... Alt+A
   OR
   a. Select tab stop(s) to clear.
   b. Click **Clear** .... Alt+E
4. Click **OK** .... Enter

Format a Modified-Block Business Letter

1. Start 2" from top of page .... Enter **4x**
   - ✓ *Press Enter four times to leave 2" of space.*
   - ✓ *If you are using stationery with a printed letterhead, you may have to adjust the spacing.*
2. Set left tab stop at 3".
3. Press **Tab** .... Tab
4. Insert date.
5. Leave three blank lines and type inside address ..... Enter **4x**
6. Leave a blank line and type the salutation .... Enter **2x**
7. Leave a blank line and type the letter body ...... Enter **2x**
8. Leave a blank line .... Enter **2x**
9. Press **Tab** .... Tab
10. Type the closing.
11. Leave three blank lines .... Enter **4x**
12. Press **Tab** .... Tab
13. Type signature line.
14. Move to next line and press **Tab** .... Enter , Tab
15. Type title line.
16. Leave a blank line and type reference initials .. Enter **2x**

Shrink to Fit

1. Click **Print Preview** button 🔍.
   OR
   a. Click **File** .... Alt+F
   b. Click **Print Preview** V
2. Click **Shrink to Fit** button.
3. Click **Close** button Close.

Full Screen View

1. Click **View** .... Alt+V
2. Click **Full Screen** .... U

To display screen elements again:

- Press **Esc** .... Esc

OR

- Click **Close Full Screen** button Close Full Screen.

Exercise Directions

1. Start Word, if necessary.
2. Create a new document and save it as **BUYER**.
3. Type the letter shown in Illustration A.
   - ✓ *When you type the letter as shown in the illustration, it will not fit on a single page.*
   - Set a left tab stop at 3" on the ruler.
   - Position the date, closing, signature, and title at the tab stop.
   - Press the Enter key between parts of the letter as indicated.
   - Insert the current date using the MONTH DAY, YEAR format found third from the top in the Date and Time dialog box.
   - Set the date so that it does not update automatically.
4. Check the spelling and grammar and make changes as suggested.
   - Ignore all proper names.
5. Display the document in Print Preview.
6. Shrink the document to fit on a single page.
7. Display the document in Full Screen view.
8. Display the screen elements again.
9. Print the document.
10. Close the document, saving all changes.

4x

Left tab stop set at 3"

Month, Date, Year   *Insert today's date*

4x

Ms. Rebecca Ling
Buyer
Mergatroyd & Wren
325 Fifth Avenue
New York, NY 10016

2x

Dear Ms. Ling:

2x

Did you see who was wearing a full Northwest Gear ensemble in the August issue of Teen People magazine? If you did, then you know that our clothes are currently the hottest trend among 12 to 20 year olds. And yet, Mergatroyd & Wren, one of the most popular clothing and accessory stores for teens, has yet to carry a single Northwest Gear item!

2x

My mission, Ms. Ling, is to remedy that situation. I am sure that you agree that we should take advantage of the phenomenal overlap between your customer base and ours. Together, you and I can certainly find a way to get Northwest Gear clothing on to the sales floor at every Mergatroyd & Wren store in North America. I know your customers would be thrilled by the new inventory, and you'd be thrilled by the positive impact on your bottom line.

2x

With that in mind, I am personally inviting you to come to Seattle (at our expense, of course) to take a sneak peak behind the scenes at Northwest Gear. Come for one day, two days, or for a week. You can tour our center of operations, meet our designers, and preview our new fall fashions. A dinner reception with our president, Mr. Khourie, will cap your visit.

2x

In case you missed the Teen People article, I have enclosed it with this letter. I eagerly await your reply.

2x

Tab   Sincerely,

4x

Tab   Nathan J. Pritchard
Marketing Director

2x

Njp/yo

2x

Enclosure

On Your Own

1. Create a new document in Word.

2. Save the file as **OWD06**.

3. As a representative of a school organization, draft a modified-block business letter to a company that sells music CDs by mail telling the company that your organization did not receive the complete order in the last shipment.

4. List the music CDs that you ordered and indicate which titles were missing in the shipment.

5. Preview the document. Make sure it fits on one page.

6. Display the document in Full Screen view.

7. Change back to display all screen elements.

8. Print one copy of the document.

9. Close the document, saving all changes.

Exercise 7

Skills Covered:

◆ **Format a Personal Business Letter** ◆ **Select Fonts**
◆ **Change Font Size** ◆ **Apply Font Styles** ◆ **Apply Underlines**
◆ **Create Envelopes** ◆ **Create Labels**

On the Job

Write personal business letters to find a job or communicate with businesses such as your bank or your insurance company. For example, you might write a personal business letter to your insurance company to ask about a claim that needs to be paid. The letter serves as a formal record of your inquiry. To send it, you need to print an accompanying envelope or label. Use fonts, font sizes, underlines, and font styles, to dress up the appearance of a document. Fonts are a basic means of applying formatting to text and characters. They can set a mood, command attention, and convey a message.

You are interested in obtaining a position as a graphic designer for Northwest Gear, Inc. In this exercise, you will create and format a personal business letter asking about job opportunities. You will also create an envelope to accompany the document. Finally, you will create return address labels and save them in a separate document.

Terms

Return address The author's address, typically appearing at the very top of the letter as well as in the upper-left corner of an envelope.

Letterhead Paper with a company's name and address already printed on it.

Font A complete set of characters in a specific face, style, and size.

Font face The character design of a font set.

Serif A font that has curved or extended edges.

Sans serif A font that has straight edges.

Script A font that looks like handwriting.

Font size The height of an uppercase letter in a font set.

Font style The slant and weight of characters in a font set.

Delivery address The recipient's address printed on the outside of an envelope.

Notes

Format a Personal Business Letter

- A business letter written on behalf of an individual instead of on behalf of another business is considered a personal business letter.

- A personal business letter includes the same elements as a business letter, minus the title line and reference initials, and plus a **return address**.
  - ✓ *If the paper has a **letterhead**, omit the return address.*

- A personal business letter can be full block or modified block.
  - In full block, type the return address following the signature.
  - In modified block, type the return address above the date.
    - ✓ *For more information on the parts of a business letter, refer to Exercise 5.*

Select Fonts

- Each **font** set includes upper- and lowercase letters, numbers, and punctuation marks.
- There are three basic categories of **font faces**:
  - **Serif** fonts are easy to read and are often used for document text.

A Serif Font

  - **Sans serif** fonts are often used for headings.

A Sans Serif Font

  - **Script** face fonts are often used to simulate handwriting on invitations or announcements.

A Script Font

- The default Word font is Times New Roman, a serif font.
- The current font name is displayed in the Font box on the Formatting toolbar.

Font box shows the font name

- Both Office and Windows come with built-in fonts; you can install additional fonts.
- Fonts can be changed before or after you enter text in a document.
- You can set the tone of a document by putting thought into the fonts you select.
  - ✓ *More than two or three font faces makes a document look disjointed and unprofessional.*

Change Font Size

- **Font size** is measured in points. There are 72 points in an inch.
- The default Word font size is 12 points.

- The current font size is displayed in the Font Size box on the Formatting toolbar.

Font Size box shows the font size

Apply Font Styles

- The most common **font styles** are **bold** and *italic*.
- When no style is applied to a font, it is called regular.
  - ✓ *Font styles can be combined for different effects, such as bold italic.*

Apply Underlines

- There are 17 types of underlines available in Word, which include:
  - <u>Single</u> (underlines all characters, including nonprinting characters such as spaces and tabs)
  - <u>Words only</u>
  - <u>Double</u>
  - <u>Dotted</u>
  - <u>Thick</u>
  - <u>Dash</u>
  - <u>Dot dash</u>
  - <u>Dot dot dash</u>
  - <u>Wave</u>

The Font dialog box lets you select a font, font size, font style, and underline at the same time

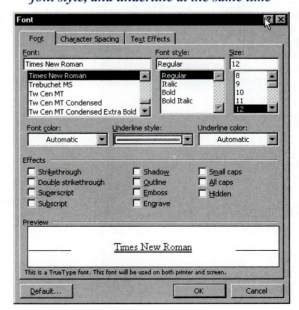

Create Envelopes

- Word has a feature that automatically sets up an envelope for printing.
- If a letter document is open on-screen, Word picks up the inside address for the envelope's **delivery address**.
- You can print the envelope immediately or add it to the beginning of the open document and save it to print later.

Create Labels

- Use the Label feature to create mailing labels, file folder labels, or diskette labels.

- The Label feature automatically sets up a document to print on predefined label types.
- You select the manufacturer and label type loaded in the printer.
- By default, Word creates a full page of labels using the inside address from the current document.
- You can change the default to create labels using the return address or to create a single label.

Procedures

Select Font

1. Select text.

   OR

   Position insertion point where new text will be typed.

2. Click **Font** drop-down arrow

   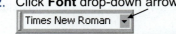

3. Click font name .... ⬇, Enter

   ✓ The font list is alphabetical; however, recently used fonts are listed at the top of the list.

   The Font list

   Recently used fonts

   Alphabetical list starts here

   OR

1. Select text.

   OR

   Position insertion point where new text will be typed.

2. Click **Format** .... Alt+O
3. Click **Font**.......................... F
4. Click font name in **Font** list .... ⬇
5. Click **OK** .... Enter

Change Font Size

1. Select text.

   OR

   Position insertion point where new text will be typed.

2. Click **Font Size** drop-down arrow .
3. Click font size .... ⬇, Enter

   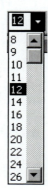

   ✓ You can also type desired font size directly into Font Size box, then press Enter. You can even type half sizes, such as 10.5, 12.5, and so on.

   OR

1. Select text.

   OR

Position insertion point where new text will be typed.

2. Click **Format**............... Alt+O
3. Click **Font** .... F
4. Click font size in **Size list** .... Alt+S, ⬇
5. Click **OK**.......................... Enter

Apply Font Styles

1. Select text.

   OR

   Position insertion point where new text will be typed.

2. Click font style button:

   - **Bold** B .... Ctrl+B
   - **Italic** I .... Ctrl+I

   ✓ To remove font styles repeat steps 1 and 2.

   OR

1. Select text.

   OR

   Position insertion point where new text will be typed.

2. Click **Format**............... Alt+O
3. Click **Font** .... F
4. Click font style in **Font style** list .... Alt+Y, ⬇

   ✓ To remove font styles click Regular.

5. Click **OK**.......................... Enter

Apply Underlines (*Ctrl+U*)

1. Select text.
   OR
   Position insertion point where new text will be typed.
2. Click **Underline** button [U] ....[Alt]+[U]
   ✓ *Repeat steps to remove underline.*

OR

1. Select text.
   OR
   Position insertion point where new text will be typed.
2. Click **Format** ....[Alt]+[O]
3. Click **Font** ....[F]
4. Click **Underline style** drop-down arrow ....[Alt]+[U]
5. Click desired underline type.
   ✓ *Click (None) to remove underline.*
6. Click **OK** ....[Enter]

Create an Envelope

1. Click **Tools** ....[Alt]+[T]
2. Click **Letters and Mailings** .[E]
3. Click **Envelopes and Labels** ....[E]
4. Click **Envelopes** tab ....[Alt]+[E]
5. Type **Delivery address** ....[Alt]+[D]
   ✓ *If inside address is already entered, skip to step 6.*
6. Type **Return address** ....[Alt]+[R]
   OR
   Select **Omit** check box ....[Alt]+[M]
   ✓ *If Omit check box is selected, you cannot type in Return address text box.*
7. Click **Print** button [Print] ....[Alt]+[P]
   OR
   Select **Add to Document** ....[Alt]+[A]

Create a Single Label

1. Click **Tools** ....[Alt]+[T]
2. Click **Letters and Mailings**. [E]
3. Click **Envelopes and Labels** ....[E]
4. Click **Labels** tab ....[Alt]+[L]
5. Click **Single label** option button ....[Alt]+[N]
6. Click **Options** ....[O]
7. Select option from **Label products** list ....[Alt]+[P]
8. Select option from **Product number** list.................[Alt]+[U]
   ✓ *Make sure correct printer and tray information is selected.*
9. Click **OK** ....[Enter]
10. Type **label text**.
    ✓ *If inside address is already entered, skip to 11.*
11. Make sure labels are loaded in printer.
12. Click **Print** button [Print] ....[Alt]+[P]

Create Return Address Labels

1. Click **Tools** ....[Alt]+[T]
2. Click **Letters and Mailings** .[E]
3. Click **Envelopes and Labels** ....[E]
4. Click **Labels** tab ....[Alt]+[L]
5. Select **Use return address** check box ....[Alt]+[R]
6. Click **Options** ....[Alt]+[O]
7. Select option from **Label products** list................[Alt]+[P]
8. Select option from **Product number** list.................[Alt]+[U]
   ✓ *Make sure the correct printer and tray information is selected.*
9. Click **OK** ....[Enter]
   ✓ *Make sure labels are loaded in printer.*
10. Click **Print** button [Print] ....[Alt]+[P]
    OR
    a. Click **New Document** ....[Alt]+[D]
    b. If prompted to save the return address, click **No** ...[N]
    c. Click **Save** button [💾] to save labels.

Exercise Directions

1. Start Word, if necessary.
2. Create a new document and save it as **REQUEST**.
3. Type the letter shown in Illustration A.
   - Use the full-block format for the letter.
   - Insert today's date using the Month Date, Year format. Make sure the date will not update automatically.
   - Use the default font and font size except where marked otherwise on the illustration.
4. Check the spelling and grammar.
5. Create an envelope for the letter.
   - Use your name and address as the return address.
6. Add the envelope to the document.
   - When prompted to save the new return address as the default, choose No.
7. Preview the document.
8. Print the document.
9. Save the changes to the document.
10. Create return address labels for the document.
    a. Use the return address in the document.
    b. Create a full page of the same label.
    c. Save the label document as **LABELS**.
    - ✓ *Do not save the return address as the default.*
11. Preview the new label document.
12. Print the label document.
    - ✓ *You can print the labels on standard letter-sized paper if you do not have labels available.*
13. Close the label document, saving all changes.
14. Close the letter document, saving all changes.
15. Create a new document and save it as **DESIGN**.
16. Apply font styles and alignments as shown in Illustration B.
17. Close the **DESIGN** document, saving all changes.

On Your Own

1. Create a new document in Word.
2. Save the file as **OWD07**.
3. Draft a personal business letter. For example, you might write a letter asking about summer job opportunities. If you have a job, you could write to your employer asking to take a vacation day in the coming month. You can also draft a personal letter to a company with whom you do business asking for a credit on returned merchandise, or to a college asking about application requirements. Record stores, clothing stores, or sporting goods stores are companies you might use.
   - ✓ *If smart tag indicators are displayed, you can ignore them or turn them off. To turn them off, Click Tools, and then click AutoCorrect Options. Click the Smart Tags tab and deselect the Label text with smart tags check box. Click OK to close the dialog box and continue working.*
4. Create an envelope for your letter and attach it to the document.
5. Create your own mailing labels using the return address from your letter, and save them in a separate document with the name **OWD07-2**.
6. Check the spelling and grammar before printing the documents.
7. Save your changes, close all open documents, and exit Word when you are finished.

Illustration A

Your Street Address
Your City, Your State Your Postal Code

Today's date

Ms. Emily DiNapoli
Vice President
Northwest Gear, Inc.
2749 Mission Street
Seattle, WA 98122

Dear Ms. DiNapoli:

I am writing to inquire about job opportunities in graphic design at Northwest Gear, Inc. Currently, I am employed as a sales associate at the Mergatroyd & Wren store in downtown Seattle. However, design is my true passion.

While studying graphic design at a local university, I worked as an assistant to a Web designer. I gained valuable experience working with other designers, creating designs of my own, and meeting deadlines. Now that I have a degree in graphic design, I would like to obtain a full-time position in design. Working at Northwest Gear would be a dream come true. I've enclosed a sample flyer that I did for a local CD shop.

In addition to my degree and experience, I believe that I have talent and style. Being young, I also have a good idea of the types of clothes that appeal to teens. I would be happy to meet you and show you my portfolio at any time.

I look forward to hearing from you soon.

Sincerely,

Your Name

Enc.

↓ *3x*

THE CD SPECIALIST
GRAND OPENING CELEBRATION

Words only underline

Arial Black, 12 pt.

**Announcing the Grand Opening of *The CD Specialist*
Saturday, June 9**

Copperplate Gothic Bold, 25 pt.

↓ *2x*

Specializing in:

Arial Black, 20 pt.

Classic Rock

Hip Hop

Techno

Jazz

Stop in for grand-opening specials:

Comic Sans Ms, 16 pt.

Arial Black, 12 pt.

CD Give Aways

Live Music

Free Food

And More . . .

Arial Black, 9 pt.

While you're in the store, take a moment to fill out a raffle entry form. The winner will receive an all-expenses paid trip to Mexico! Runners up will receive gift certificates redeemable any time.

Arial Black, 12 pt.

**The CD Specialist
321 Main Street
Hanover, NH 03755
603-555-9009
www.CDS.com**

◆ **Critical Thinking**

You are a party planner interested in developing a joint catering service venture with Coastline Gourmet Importers. In this exercise, you will start by creating a business letter proposing the idea to the owner of Coastline Gourmet. Next, you will create an envelope for the letter along with return address labels. Finally, you will create a flyer about the proposed service that you can attach to the letter. You will use alignments and font formatting to make the flyer visually exciting.

Exercise Directions

1. Start Word, if necessary.
2. Create a new document and save it as **PROPOSAL**.
3. Display nonprinting characters.
4. Make sure AutoCorrect is on.
5. Type the letter in Illustration A exactly as shown, including all circled errors.
6. Insert the date in the Month Date, Year format so that it does not update automatically.
7. Correct spelling and grammatical errors.
   - Add your name to the dictionary, if necessary.
   - Ignore all proper names.
   - Correct all other spelling errors that AutoCorrect did not automatically change.
8. Use the Thesaurus to find an appropriate replacement for the word **simply**.
9. Save the changes you have made to the document.
10. Display the document in Print Preview.
11. Display the document in Full Screen view.
12. Return the document to Normal view.
13. Create an envelope for the letter and add it to the document. Omit the return address.
14. Print the document.
15. Close the document, saving all changes.
16. Create return address mailing labels for your party planning business using the following information:

Your Name
Party Planner
P.O. Box 765
Miami, FL 33132

17. Save the labels document with the name **RETURN**.
18. Display the **RETURN** document in Print Preview, and then print it.
   ✓ *If you do not have labels available, print it on regular paper.*
19. Close the **RETURN** document, saving all changes.
20. Create a new document.
21. Save the document as **FLYER**.
22. Display nonprinting characters.
23. Type the document shown in Illustration B, using the specified alignments, font formatting, and tabs.
24. Check the spelling and grammar in the document.
25. Display the document in Print Preview.
26. If the document is longer than one page, shrink it to fit; if it is shorter than one page, adjust the vertical alignment to improve the appearance, as necessary.
27. Print the document.
28. Close the document, saving all changes.

[Today's date]   *Insert date in month,*
date, year format

Mr. Benjamin Boghosian
Owner
Coastline Gourmet Importers
7334 Sunshine Parkway, 12th Floor
Miami, FL 33132

Dear Mr. Boghosian:

Have you ever considered expanding your business? I have! As a party planner in the the Miami area,, I spend a great deal of time on the look out for reliable caterers. I finally realized that it would be alot easier to simply provide the service myself!

However; I am smart enough to know that I would benefit from a partner such as yourself. I think that together you and I have the knowldege, contacts, and resources to develop a sucessful catering service. My experience as a party planners, and your access to fine quality specialty foods make us uniqely positioned to pursue such a venture.

I has attached a flyer detailing my ideas for the new business. PLease call me to discuss the possibbillities.

Sincerely,

Your Name
Party Planner

Attachment

Illustration B

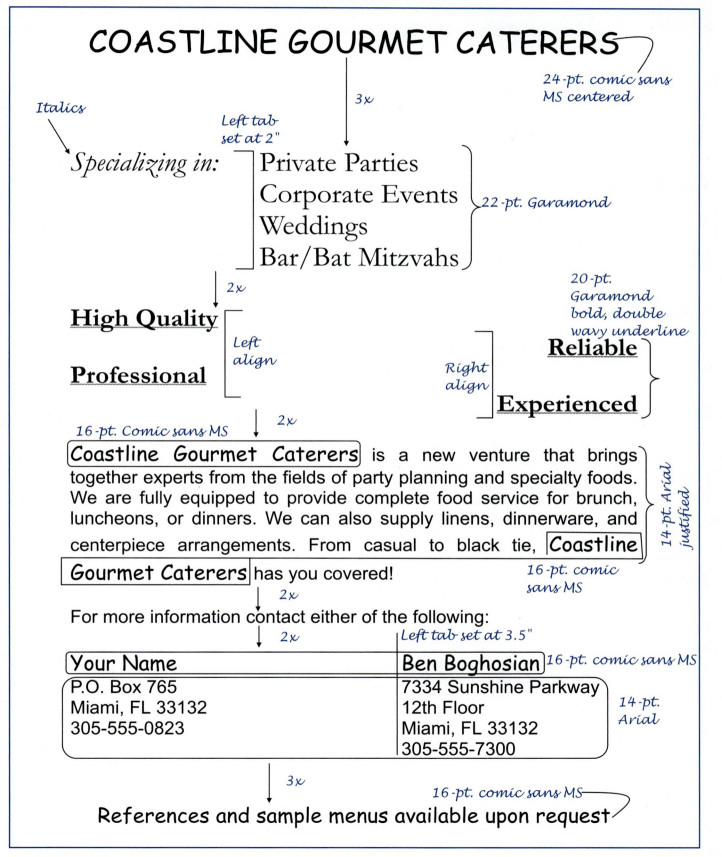

COASTLINE GOURMET CATERERS

24-pt. comic sans MS centered

Italics

Specializing in: Private Parties
Corporate Events
Weddings
Bar/Bat Mitzvahs

Left tab set at 2"

3x

22-pt. Garamond

2x

High Quality

Left align

Professional

20-pt. Garamond bold, double wavy underline

Right align

Reliable

Experienced

16-pt. Comic sans MS

2x

Coastline Gourmet Caterers is a new venture that brings together experts from the fields of party planning and specialty foods. We are fully equipped to provide complete food service for brunch, luncheons, or dinners. We can also supply linens, dinnerware, and centerpiece arrangements. From casual to black tie, Coastline Gourmet Caterers has you covered!

14-pt. Arial justified

16-pt. comic sans MS

2x

For more information contact either of the following:

2x

Left tab set at 3.5"

Your Name

Ben Boghosian

16-pt. comic sans MS

P.O. Box 765
Miami, FL 33132
305-555-0823

7334 Sunshine Parkway
12th Floor
Miami, FL 33132
305-555-7300

14-pt. Arial

3x

16-pt. comic sans MS

References and sample menus available upon request

Exercise 9

Skills Covered:

◆ **Use Proofreaders' Marks** ◆ **Open a Recently Saved Document**
◆ **Open a Document not Recently Saved** ◆ **Insert and Edit Text**
◆ **Use Overtype Mode** ◆ **Save a Document with a New Name**

On the Job

When you are ready to revise or improve a document that you've already created and saved—open it again in Word. Use the Save As command to save a copy of the document with a new name or in a new location. For example, you might need to write a letter that is similar to one you wrote earlier. Instead of starting from scratch, you can open the original letter, save it as a new document, then edit it.

As the office manager for California Cardiology, you have decided that you need to revise the press release that you wrote earlier regarding the new physician who has joined the practice. In this exercise, you will open the press release document and save it with a new name. You will then revise the document and save the changes. Finally, you will print the document.

Terms

Proofreaders' marks Symbols written on a printed document by a copyeditor or proofreader to indicate where revisions are required.

Places Bar A strip of buttons on the left side of certain dialog boxes used to open common folders quickly.

Insert mode The method of operation used for inserting new text within existing text in a document. Insert mode is the default.

Overtype mode The method of operation used to replace existing text in a document with new text.

Notes

Proofreaders' Marks

■ Often, you may need to revise a Word document based on a marked-up printed copy of the document. **Proofreaders' marks** on printed documents are written symbols that indicate where to make revisions.

■ Following is a list of common proofreaders' marks:

- ⌇⌇⌇⌇ indicates text to be bold.
- ∧ indicates where new text should be inserted.
- ⸋ indicates text to be deleted.

- ⌗ indicates where a new paragraph should be inserted.
- ≡ indicates that a letter should be capitalized.
- ———— or ⓘⓣⓐⓛ indicates text to be italicized.
- ⟨highlight⟩ indicates text to highlight.
-][indicates text to center.

  ✓ There are many other common proofreading symbols. You can find a list in *Webster's Collegiate Dictionary*, or *The Chicago Manual of Style*.

74

Open a Recently Saved Document

- To revise a document that has been saved and closed, open it in Word.

- The four most recently used documents are listed at the bottom of the File menu and at the top of the New Document Task Pane.

  ✓ *The listed file names may also include the complete path to the file, which means the folder and/or disk where the file is stored. Since you can have a file with the same name stored in different locations, be sure you select the one you really want to open.*

Open saved documents from the File menu

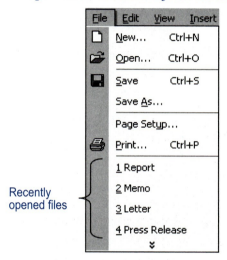

Recently opened files

Open saved documents from the New Document Task Pane

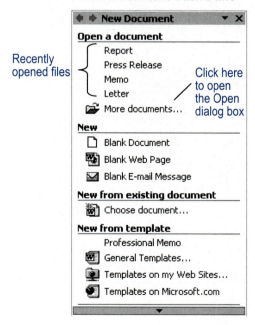

Recently opened files

Click here to open the Open dialog box

- Click on a document to open it.

Open a Document not Recently Saved

- Any document stored on disk can be opened from Word, no matter when it was last used.

- Use the Open dialog box to locate files that you want to open.

Open dialog box

Current folder

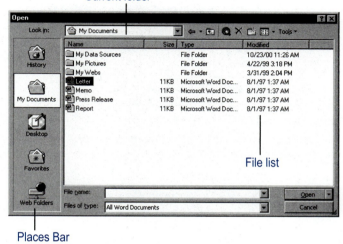

File list

Places Bar

Insert and Edit Text

- By default, you insert new text in a document in **Insert mode**. Existing text moves to the right as you type to make room for new text.

- You can insert text anywhere in a document.

- You can also insert nonprinting characters, including paragraph marks to start a new paragraph, tabs, and spaces.

Use Overtype Mode

- To replace text as you type, use **Overtype mode**.

- In Overtype mode, existing characters do not shift right to make room for new characters. Instead, new characters replace existing characters as you type, deleting existing characters.

- Most editing should be done in Insert mode, so you do not accidentally type over text that you need.

Save a Document with a New Name

- The Save As feature lets you save a copy of a document in a different location or with a different file name.
- Use the Save As command to leave the original document unchanged while you edit the new copy.

Save As dialog box

Procedures

Open a Recently Saved Document

1. Click **File** .... <kbd>Alt</kbd>+<kbd>F</kbd>
2. Click document name at bottom of menu.

OR

1. Click **View** .... <kbd>Alt</kbd>+<kbd>V</kbd>
2. Click **Task Pane** .... <kbd>K</kbd>

  ✓ *If the New Document Task Pane is not displayed, select it from the Other Task Panes drop-down list.*

3. Click document name at top of Task Pane.

Open a Document not Recently Saved *(Ctrl+O)*

1. Click **Open** button 📂.

  OR

  a. Click **File** .... <kbd>Alt</kbd>+<kbd>F</kbd>

  b. Click **Open** .... <kbd>O</kbd>

2. Click **Look in** drop-down arrow .... <kbd>Alt</kbd>+<kbd>I</kbd>
3. Select drive or folder.

  ✓ *If necessary double-click folder name.*

  OR

  Click folder in Places Bar to open it.

4. Double-click document name.

  OR

  a. Click document name.

  b. Click **Open** .... <kbd>O</kbd>

Insert Text

1. Position insertion point to right of character where you want to insert new text.
2. Type new text.

Overtype mode

1. Position insertion point to left of first character you want to replace.
2. Press **Insert** key .... <kbd>Ins</kbd>

  OR

  Double-click **OVR** indicator <kbd>OVR</kbd> on Status bar.

  ✓ *OVR indicator appears in bold when active.*

3. Type new text.

To turn off Overtype mode:

- Press **Insert** key again .... <kbd>Ins</kbd>

  OR

- Double-click **OVR** indicator <kbd>OVR</kbd> again.

  ✓ *OVR indicator appears dimmed when inactive.*

Save a Document with a New Name

1. Click **File** .... <kbd>Alt</kbd>+<kbd>F</kbd>
2. Click **Save As** .... <kbd>A</kbd>
3. Type new file name.
4. Select new drive and/or folder.
5. Click **Save** button 💾 Save .... <kbd>Alt</kbd>+<kbd>S</kbd>

Exercise Directions

1. Start Word, if necessary.

2. Open ⌨**PRESS** or open 💿**09PRESS**.

   ✓ *If necessary, ask your instructor where this file is located.*

3. Save the file as **NEWPRESS**.

4. Make the revisions as indicated by the proofreaders' marks in Illustration A.

   a. Insert new text as marked.

   b. Replace text as marked.

   c. Apply font styles as marked.

5. Check the spelling and grammar.

6. Print the document.

7. Close the document, saving all changes.

Illustration A

Cynthia Ramirez, M.D. Joins California Cardiology, Inc.

Bold

Los Angeles, CA -- California Cardiology, Inc. is pleased to announce that Dr. Cynthia Ramirez has joined our practice. Dr. Ramirez received a BS degree from Stanford University in 1991 and an MD from the University of California at Los Angeles College of Medicine in 1995. She completed a residency at UCLA Medical Center and is board certified in cardiology. Dr. Ramirez is fluent in Spanish. In her spare time she enjoys skiing, biking, and hiking.

California Cardiology provides high-quality cardiac care to patients in the metro Los Angeles area. With the addition of Dr. Ramirez, we now have six ten full-time physicians supported by an exceptional staff of nurses and physician's assistants. Our offices are thoroughly up-to-date with the most current technologies, and we have admitting privileges at most major numerous hospitals in L.A.

For more information about Dr. Ramirez or about California Cardiology, please call 310-555-2922, or visit us on the Web at www.ddcpub.com/calcardiology. We accept most major insurance policies.

On Your Own

1. Open ⌨**OWD06**, the document you created in the On Your Own section of Exercise 6, or open 💿**09LETTER**.

2. Save the file as **OWD09**.

3. Make revisions to the document using Insert mode and Overtype mode.

4. Print the document.

5. Close the document, saving all changes.

Exercise 10

On the Job

Move text to rearrange a document quickly without retyping existing information. You can move any amount of text, from a single character to an entire page.

The employees at the law firm of Perry, Hawkins, Martinez, and Klein have been asking a lot of questions regarding "Casual Fridays." The personnel director has asked you to edit a document that lists guidelines for the new policy. In this exercise, you will open the existing document, edit and format the text, and rearrange the guidelines into a more suitable order.

Terms

Cut To delete a selection from its original location and move it to the Clipboard.

Paste To insert a selection from the Clipboard into a document.

Clipboard A temporary storage area that can hold up to 24 selections at a time.

Drag-and-drop editing The action of using a mouse to drag a selection from its original location and drop it in a new location.

Notes

Move Text

- While editing, you may decide you need to move text that is already typed in a document to a new location.
- Word's move commands can save you from deleting and retyping text.
- Be sure to consider nonprinting characters when you select text to move:
  - Select the space following a word or sentence to move along with text.
  - Select the paragraph mark following a paragraph or line to move paragraph formatting with text.
- Use Undo to reverse a move that you made unintentionally.

✓ *When you paste text into a new location, Word may display the Paste Options button, which allows you to select the way formatting is pasted along with the text. For now, ignore the Paste Options button. It is explained in Exercise 15. You can turn off the display of the Paste Options button if you want. Click Tools, Options, Edit. Deselect the Show Paste Options button check box, then click OK.*

Use Cut and Paste

- Use the **Cut** and **Paste** commands to move text in a document.
- The Cut command deletes selected text from its original location and moves it to the **Clipboard**.
- The Paste command copies the selection from the Clipboard to the insertion point location.

- Up to 24 selections can remain in the Clipboard at one time.

- You can access the Cut and Paste commands from the Edit menu, from the Standard toolbar, from a shortcut menu, or with keyboard shortcuts.

Use the Clipboard

- Use the Clipboard Task Pane to access selections for pasting.

- The last 24 items cut or copied are displayed in the Clipboard.

- You can paste or delete one or all of the items.

- You can turn the following Clipboard options off or on:

  - Show Office Clipboard Automatically. Sets the Clipboard Task Pane to open automatically when you cut or copy a selection.

  - Collect Without Showing Office Clipboard. Sets the Clipboard Task Pane so it does not open automatically when you cut or copy data.

  - Show Office Clipboard Icon on Taskbar. Displays a Clipboard icon at the right end of the Taskbar if there are selections on the Clipboard. Double-click the icon to open the Task Pane.

  - Show Status Near Taskbar When Copying. Displays a ScreenTip with the number of items on the Clipboard when you cut or copy a selection.

Clipboard Task Pane

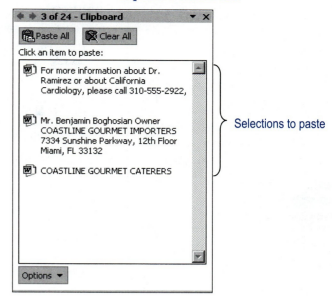

Selections to paste

Use Drag-and-Drop Editing

- Use **drag-and-drop editing** to move text with the mouse.

- Drag-and-drop editing is convenient when you can see the text to move and the new location on the screen at the same time.

Move a Paragraph

- You can quickly move an entire paragraph up or down in a document.

Procedures

Move Text

1. Select text to move.
2. Press **F2** key F2
3. Position insertion point at new location.
4. Press **Enter** .... Enter

Use Cut and Paste to Move Text *(Ctrl+X, Cltr+V)*

1. Select text to move.

2. Click **Cut** button ✂.
   OR
   a. Click **Edit** .... Alt + E

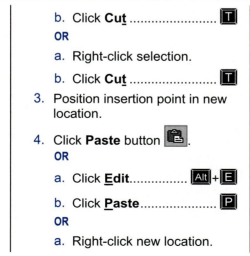

b. Click **Cut** .... T
OR
a. Right-click selection.

b. Click **Cut** .... T

3. Position insertion point in new location.

4. Click **Paste** button 📋.
   OR
   a. Click **Edit** .... Alt + E
   b. Click **Paste** .... P
   OR
   a. Right-click new location.

b. Click **Paste** .... P

Paste a Selection from the Clipboard Task Pane

1. Click **View** .... Alt + V
2. Click **Task Pane** .... K
3. Click **Other Task Panes** drop-down arrow New Document ▾.
4. Click **Clipboard**.
5. Click item to paste.
   OR
   Click **Paste All** button

   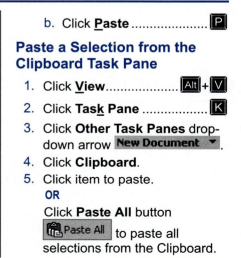 to paste all selections from the Clipboard.

Set Clipboard Options

1. Display Clipboard Task Pane.
2. Click **Options** drop-down button `Options ▼`.
3. Click desired options:
   - **Show Office Clipboard Automatically** .... `A`
   - **Collect Without Showing Office Clipboard** .... `C`
   - **Show Office Clipboard Icon on Taskbar** .... `T`
   - **Show Status Near Taskbar When Copying** .... `S`

   ✓ *A check mark indicates the option is selected.*

Delete Selections from the Clipboard

1. Right-click selection to delete.
2. Click **Delete** .... `D`
   on context menu
   OR
   Click **Clear All** button
   `🗙 Clear All` to delete all selections from the Clipboard.

Use Drag-and-Drop Editing to Move Text

1. Select text to move.
2. Move mouse pointer anywhere over selected text and click, continuing to hold down the left mouse button.
3. Drag selection to new location.

✓ *As you drag, the mouse pointer changes to a box with a dotted shadow attached to an arrow; selection does not move until you drop it in step 4.*

4. Release mouse button when insertion point is in new location.

Move a Paragraph

1. Position insertion point anywhere within paragraph to move.
2. Press .... `Alt` + `Shift` + `↑`
   OR
   Press .... `Alt` + `Shift` + `↓`
3. Repeat step 2 until paragraph is in desired location.

Exercise Directions

1. Start Word, if necessary.
2. Open ⊙ **10POLICY**.
3. Save the file as **POLICY**.
4. Revise the document so it resembles the document shown in Illustration A.
   - Apply alignments as marked.
   - Apply fonts, font sizes, and font styles as marked.
   - Insert blank lines by pressing the Enter key as marked.
   - Move text to rearrange the document as marked.
5. Check the spelling and grammar in the document.
6. Display the document in Print Preview.
7. Print the document.
8. Close the document, saving all changes.

On Your Own

1. Create a new document in Word.
2. Save the file as **OWD10**.
3. Create a list of things you have accomplished in the past year. For each item in the list, describe what you accomplished, how you accomplished it, and when it was done.
4. Rearrange the listed items using cut-and-paste and drag-and-drop techniques. For example, you might want to arrange the list by importance of what you accomplished or by date.
5. Print the document.
6. Close the document, saving all changes.

Illustration A

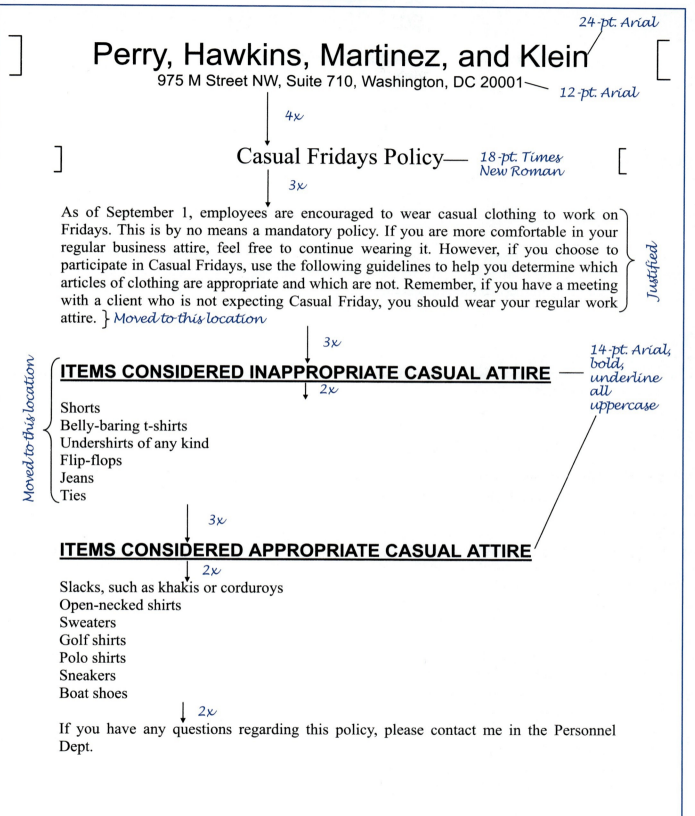

Perry, Hawkins, Martinez, and Klein
24-pt. Arial

975 M Street NW, Suite 710, Washington, DC 20001 — *12-pt. Arial*

4x

Casual Fridays Policy — *18-pt. Times New Roman*

3x

As of September 1, employees are encouraged to wear casual clothing to work on Fridays. This is by no means a mandatory policy. If you are more comfortable in your regular business attire, feel free to continue wearing it. However, if you choose to participate in Casual Fridays, use the following guidelines to help you determine which articles of clothing are appropriate and which are not. Remember, if you have a meeting with a client who is not expecting Casual Friday, you should wear your regular work attire. } *Moved to this location* — *Justified*

3x

ITEMS CONSIDERED INAPPROPRIATE CASUAL ATTIRE — *14-pt. Arial, bold, underline all uppercase*

2x

Moved to this location

Shorts
Belly-baring t-shirts
Undershirts of any kind
Flip-flops
Jeans
Ties

3x

ITEMS CONSIDERED APPROPRIATE CASUAL ATTIRE

2x

Slacks, such as khakis or corduroys
Open-necked shirts
Sweaters
Golf shirts
Polo shirts
Sneakers
Boat shoes

2x

If you have any questions regarding this policy, please contact me in the Personnel Dept.

Exercise 11

◆ **Use Copy and Paste**

◆ **Use the Drag-and-Drop Feature to Copy**

On the Job

Copy or move text from one location to another to speed up your work and avoid repetitive typing. You can copy or move any amount of text, from a single character to an entire document.

The personnel director of Perry, Hawkins, Martinez, and Klein wants you to enhance the Casual Fridays policy document. In this exercise, you will revise the guidelines using some of the editing and formatting techniques you have learned so far in this book.

Terms

Copy To create a duplicate of a selection and move it to the Clipboard.

Notes

Use Copy and Paste

- Use the Copy and Paste feature to copy existing text from one location in a document and paste it to another location.

- The **Copy** command stores a duplicate of selected text on the Clipboard, leaving the original selection unchanged.

- The Paste command pastes the selection from the Clipboard to the insertion point location.

- You can access the Copy and Paste commands from the Edit menu, the Standard toolbar, from a shortcut menu, or with keyboard shortcuts.

- You can store up to 24 selections on the Clipboard at one time.

- Use the Clipboard Task Pane to choose which selection to paste into the document.

  ✓ *The same Clipboard used for moving is used for copying. For more information, refer to Exercise 10.*

Use the Drag-and-Drop Feature to Copy

- Use drag-and-drop editing to copy text with the mouse.

- The Drag-and-Drop feature is convenient when you can see the text to copy and the new location on the screen at the same time.

Procedures

Use Copy and Paste
(Ctrl+C, Ctrl+V)

1. Select the text to copy.
2. Click **Copy** button 📋.
   OR
   a. Click **Edit** .... Alt+E
   b. Click **Copy** C
   OR
   a. Right-click selection.
   b. Click **Copy** C
3. Position insertion point in new location.
4. Click **Paste** button 📋.
   OR
   a. Click **Edit** .... Alt+E
   b. Click **Paste** .... P
   OR
   a. Right-click new location.
   b. Click **Paste** .... P

Paste a Selection from the Clipboard Task Pane

1. Click **View** .... Alt+V
2. Click **Task Pane** .... K
3. Click **Other Task Panes** drop-down arrow New Document ▼.
4. Click **Clipboard**.
5. Click item to paste.
   OR
   Click **Paste All** button
   📋 Paste All to paste all selections from the Clipboard.

   ✓ *The actions for pasting a copied item from the Task Pane are the same as for pasting a cut item. For more information on using the Clipboard Task Pane, refer to Exercise 10.*

Use Drag-and-Drop to Copy Text

1. Select text to copy.
2. Move mouse pointer anywhere over selected text and click, continuing to hold down the left mouse button.
3. Press and hold the **Ctrl** key .... Ctrl
4. Drag selection to new location.
   ✓ *As you drag, the mouse pointer changes to a box with a dotted shadow and a plus sign attached to an arrow; the selection does not move until you drop it in step 5.*
5. Release mouse button.
6. Release the **Ctrl** key........... Ctrl

Exercise Directions

1. Start Word, if necessary.
2. Open 📖**POLICY** or open 💿**11POLICY**.
3. Save the file as **POLICY**.
4. Use the following steps to revise the document so it looks like the one in Illustration A.
5. Delete blank lines above and below the headline **Casual Fridays Policy**.
6. Copy the second sentence of the document to the beginning of the last paragraph, and format it bold.
7. Insert the sentence at the end of the last paragraph.
8. Start a new paragraph at the end of the document, leaving one blank line.
9. Type the heading **Dos**; apply Words only underlining.
10. Copy the list of appropriate attire to the new location under the heading **Dos**.
11. Set a Left tab stop at 4" on the horizontal ruler for all lines from the heading **Dos** to the end of the document.
12. Position the insertion point at the end of the word **Dos**, press Tab, and type the heading **Don'ts**, underlined.
    - One by one, copy the items from the list of inappropriate attire under the heading **Don'ts**. Use the tab stop to align them.
    - Copy the text to the Clipboard being sure not to copy the paragraph mark with it.
    - Position insertion point at the end of the current line, press Tab, paste the item at the tab stop location.
13. Check the spelling and grammar in the document.
14. Display the document in Print Preview. It should look similar to the one in the Illustration.
    ✓ *If necessary, use Shrink to Fit to fit the document on a single page.*
15. Print the document.
16. Close the document, saving all changes.

Perry, Hawkins, Martinez, and Klein

975 M Street NW, Suite 710, Washington, DC 20001

↓ *2x*

Casual Fridays Policy

↓ *2x*

As of September 1, employees are encouraged to wear casual clothing to work on Fridays. This is by no means a mandatory policy. If you are more comfortable in your regular business attire, feel free to continue wearing it. However, if you choose to participate in Casual Fridays, use the following guidelines to help you determine which articles of clothing are appropriate and which are not. Remember, if you have a meeting with a client who is not expecting Casual Friday, you should wear your regular work attire.

Copy sentence

ITEMS CONSIDERED INAPPROPRIATE CASUAL ATTIRE

Shorts
Belly-baring t-shirts
Undershirts of any kind
Flip-flops
Jeans
Ties

ITEMS CONSIDERED APPROPRIATE CASUAL ATTIRE

Slacks, such as khakis or corduroys
Open-necked shirts
Sweaters
Golf shirts
Polo shirts
Sneakers
Boat shoes

This is by no means a mandatory policy. If you have any questions regarding this policy, please contact me in the Personnel Dept. Use the following for quick reference:

↓ *2x*

Copy list

Dos	Don'ts
Slacks, such as khakis or corduroys	Shorts
Open-necked shirts	Belly-baring t-shirts
Sweaters	Undershirts of any kind
Golf shirts	Flip-flops
Polo shirts	Jeans
Sneakers	Ties
Boat shoes	

Copy items

Set left tab stop at 4" on horizontal ruler

On Your Own

1. Create a new document in Word.

2. Save the file as **OWD11**.

3. Create a letter in which you apply for an officer's position of a group or organization to which you might belong. For example, the group could be a school club. The officer's position could be secretary, treasurer, or president. Mention that you have accomplished many things in the past year.

4. Open the document ⌨**OWD10**, the list of your personal accomplishments for the past year, which you created in the On Your Own section of Exercise 10, or open ◉**11LIST**.

5. Save the file as **OWD11-2**.

6. Copy some of the items from **OWD11-2** to the **OWD11** document.
   - First, copy an item from **OWD11-2** to the Clipboard. Next position the insertion point in the **OWD11** document. Finally, paste the item from the Clipboard into the **OWD11** document.

7. Complete the letter.

8. Display the document in Print Preview. Make editing or formatting changes as necessary.

9. Print the document.

10. Close the document, saving all changes.

Exercise 12

Skills Covered:

◆ **Open a Document as Read-Only** ◆ **Open a Document from Windows**
◆ **Document Properties** ◆ **File Types**
◆ **Use Basic Search to Find a File**

On the Job

Word offers many options for opening a document. For example, open a document as read-only when you do not want to allow changes made to the original file. (You must save the file with a new name in order to save changes.) You can use Windows features to open a document and start Word at the same time, and you can use Word to open files created with different word processing programs. You can even locate and open a file when you don't know the file name. And you can use document properties to identify important information about a file, such as the name of the author and the main topic.

Northwest Gear, Inc., a maker of clothes for teenagers, is sponsoring an essay contest. The marketing director stored a text file with the information you need to create a press release on your computer without telling you the folder location. In this exercise, you will search for the text file, open it, and save it as a Word document. You will apply formatting to the document and add document properties. You will then close the file and open it again as read-only.

Terms

Read-only A mode of operation in which revisions cannot be saved in the original document.

Document Properties Categories of information about a document.

Keywords Important words found in a document. Keywords can be used to classify a document.

File type The format in which the file is stored. Usually, the file type corresponds to the program used to create the file.

File extension A dot followed by three or four characters at the end of a file name, used to indicate the file type. For example, a *.doc* file extension indicates a Word document file.

File icon The icon used to represent a file in a file list, such as Windows Explorer or Word's Open dialog box.

Compatible file type A file type that Word can open, even though it was created and saved using a different program.

Notes

Open a Document as Read-Only

- Opening a document as **read-only** is a safeguard against accidentally making changes.

- Word prompts you to use Save As to save revisions made to a document opened as read-only in a new document with a different file name.

- The words *Read-Only* appear in the title bar of a document opened as read-only.

Open a Document from Windows

- Use the Windows Start Menu to open a document and start Word at the same time.

  - Click Documents on the Start menu to select from a list of recently used files.

  - Locate and open any document using Windows Explorer.

  ✓ *You can also open a Word document using the Open Office Document dialog box accessed from the Windows Start menu or from the Office Shortcut Bar. See "Getting Started with Office XP", Exercise 1 for more information.*

Document Properties

- With the **Document Properties** feature you can save information that is unique to a particular document.

- Document Properties lets you enter information in five categories.

- Three of the more useful categories are:

  - General properties: Include the type of document, its size, its location, when it was created, last accessed, and last modified.

    ◆ Use General properties to check file storage and access information.

  - Summary properties: Include a document title, subject, author, **keywords**, and comments.

    ◆ Use Summary properties to save summary information with a document.

  - Statistics properties: Include the number of pages, paragraphs, lines, words, characters, and bytes in the document.

    ◆ Use Statistics properties to create documents of a specific length or word count.

- You can set Word to display the Properties dialog box automatically each time you save a document.

The Summary page of the Properties dialog box

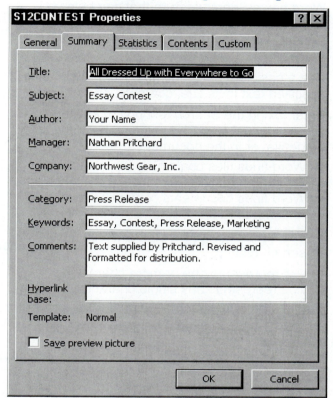

File Types

- Files are saved in different **file types**, depending on the application used to create, save, and open the file.

- In Windows and Windows applications, file types can be identified by the **file extension** and by the **file icon**.

- Word 2002 can open documents saved in **compatible file types**. For example, Word can open text files, Web page files, and files created with other versions of Word.

- You can save a compatible file in its original file type or as a Word document file.

- Some common file types include the following:
  - Word document files   .doc
  - Word template files   .dot

- Text files   .txt
- Web pages   .htm
- Excel workbooks   .xls
- Access databases   .mdb
- PowerPoint presentations   .ppt

Use Basic Search to Find a File

■ Word has a Search feature that can help you find a file stored anywhere on your computer system, even if you can't remember the file name.

■ Use a basic search to locate a file that contains specified text in its title, contents, or properties.

■ Enter text in the Search text box to locate files containing that text. The text may be in the body of the file, or in the document properties.

- Word finds files containing various forms of the search text. For example, if you enter *run*, Word finds documents containing *run*, *running*, or *ran*.

- You can use wildcard characters in the search text.

  ◆ * represents one or more characters.
  ◆ ? represents any single character.

■ Before starting a search, select the disks or folders to search, as well as the types of files to search for.

- If you know the folder to search, type it in the Search in box.

- Alternatively, select the check box beside the folder(s) to search.

■ In the *Results should be* box, select the types of files to find:

- Anything. Finds all file types.

- Office Files. Finds all files created with Office programs. You can select the specific program type.

- Outlook Items. Finds only files created with Microsoft Outlook.

- Web Pages. Finds only Web page files.

■ You can search using the Search Task Pane, or by opening the Search dialog box from the Open dialog box. Both methods offer you the same options.

Search Task Pane

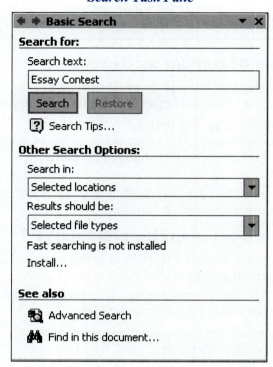

■ Word displays files matching your criteria in the Search Results list.

Search Results in Task Pane

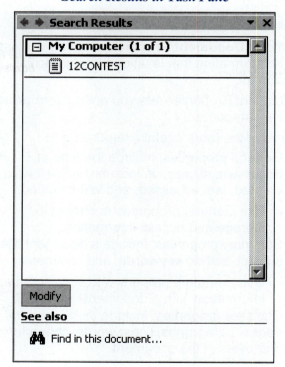

Procedures

Open a Document as Read-Only (Ctrl+O)

1. Click **Open** button 📂.
   OR
   a. Click **File**.................`Alt`+`F`
   b. Click **Open**.....................`O`
2. Click document name.
3. Click **Open** drop-down arrow
   📂 `Open` ▾.
4. Click **Open Read-Only**........`R`

Open a Word Document from the Documents Menu

1. Click **Start** button
   `Start`......................`Ctrl`+`Esc`
2. Select **Documents**..............`D`
3. Click document name.

Open a Word Document From Windows Explorer

1. Right-click **Start**
   button `Start`.
2. Click **Explore**.......................`X`
3. Select drive where folder/file is located.
4. Open folder.
5. Double-click document name that you want to open.

Use Document Properties

1. Click **File**....................`Alt`+`F`
2. Click **Properties**.................`I`
3. Select desired tab.......`Ctrl`+`Tab`
   For example:
   • Click **Summary** tab and type summary information.
   • Click **Statistics** tab to see statistical information.
   • Click **General** tab to see file storage and access information.
4. Click **OK**...........................`Enter`

Automatically Display Properties Dialog Box

1. Click **Tools**..................`Alt`+`T`
2. Click **Options**......................`O`
3. Click **Save** tab ....`Ctrl`+`Tab`
4. Select **Prompt for document properties** check box...`Alt`+`I`
5. Click **OK**..........................`Enter`

Open a Compatible File Type (Ctrl+O)

1. Click **File** ....`Alt`+`F`
2. Click **Open** ....`O`
3. Click the **Look in** drop-down arrow ....`Alt`+`I`
4. Select the disk or folder.
   ✓ Alternatively, click the folder you want to open in the Places Bar.
5. Click the **Files of type** drop-down arrow ....`Alt`+`T`
6. Click the file type.
7. Click the desired file name.
8. Click **Open** ....`Alt`+`O`
   ✓ If the File Conversion dialog box is displayed, click OK.

Save a Compatible File (Ctrl+S)

1. Open the compatible file.
2. Click **File** ....`Alt`+`F`
3. Click **Save** ....`S`
4. Click **Yes** ....`Y`
   to save the file in its original format.
   OR
   Click **No** ....`N`
   to save the file as a Word document.

Save a Compatible File as a New File in Word Format

1. Open the compatible file.
2. Click **File** ....`Alt`+`F`
3. Click **Save As** ....`A`
4. Click the **Save as type** drop-down arrow ....`Alt`+`T`

5. Click **Word document (*.doc)**.
6. Click the **File name** text box ....`Alt`+`N`
7. Type the new file name.
8. Click **Save** ....`Alt`+`S`

Search for Files from the Search Task Pane

1. Click **View**....................`Alt`+`V`
2. Click **Task Pane** ....`K`
3. Click **Other Task Panes** drop-down arrow
   `New Document` ▾ ....`Ctrl`+`↓`
4. Click **Search**............`↓`, `Enter`
5. Type search text in **Search text** box.
6. If necessary, delete existing text first.
7. Click **Search in**: drop-down arrow.
8. Select folders as follows:
   • Click **plus sign** to expand list ....`+`
   • Click check box to select folder ....`Space`
9. Click **Results should be:** drop-down arrow.....`Tab`, `Space`
10. Click **plus sign** to expand list ....`+`
11. Click desired file type(s)..............`↑`, `↓`, `Space`
12. Click **Search** button `Search`.
13. Click file to open.
    OR
    Click **Modify** button `Modify` to display Basic Search Task Pane again.
    ✓ To interrupt a search before it is complete, click the Stop button `Stop`.

Search for Files from the Open Dialog Box

1. Click **File** .... `Alt`+`F`
2. Click **Open** .... `O`
3. Click the **Look in** drop-down arrow .... `Alt`+`I`
4. Select the disk or folder.
   - ✓ *Alternatively, click the folder you want to open in the Places Look in bar.*
5. Click **Tools** drop-down arrow `Tools ▾` .... `Alt`+`L`
6. Click **Search** .... `S`
7. Click **Basic** tab, if necessary .... `Ctrl`+`Tab`
8. Type search text in **Search text** box.
   - ✓ *If necessary, delete existing text first.*
9. Click **Search in**: drop-down arrow .... `Alt`+`I`
10. Select folders as follows:
    - Click **plus sign** to expand list .... `+`
    - Click check box to select folder .... `Space`, `Enter`
11. Click **Results should be:** drop-down arrow .... `Alt`+`B`
12. Click **plus sign** to expand list .... `+`
13. Click desired file type(s).... `↑`, `↓`, `Space`, `Enter`
14. Click **Search** .... `Alt`+`S`
15. Double-click file to open.
    OR
    Click file to open.
16. Click **OK** .... `Enter`
17. Word displays Open dialog box.
18. Click **Open** .... `Alt`+`O`

Exercise Directions

- ✓ *Before beginning this exercise, make sure that the*
  ⊛ **12CONTEST** *file is stored somewhere on your computer. Ask your instructor for more information.*

1. Start Word, if necessary.
2. Search your computer for the file about the essay contest using the following steps:
   a. Open the Search Task Pane or the Search dialog box.
   b. Enter the Search text **Essay Contest**.
   c. Select the folder(s) to search. For example, if the file is stored locally, choose to search drive C, or My Computer. If the file is stored on a network, choose the network drive. The more you can narrow down the location, the faster the search will be.
   d. Select Word Files in the Files Should be list.
   e. Start the search.
3. Open the document from the Search Results list.
4. Save the file as **CONTEST**.
5. Using the Document Properties dialog box, check the number of words in the document.
6. Enter the following summary information:
   Title: **All Dressed Up with Everywhere to Go**

   Subject: **Essay Contest**
   Author: **Your name**
   Manager: **Nathan Pritchard**
   Company: **Northwest Gear, Inc.**
   Category: **Press Release**
   Keywords: **Essay, Contest, Press Release, Marketing**
   Comments: **Text supplied by Pritchard. Revised and formatted for distribution**.

7. Check the spelling and grammar in the document.
8. Display the document in Print Preview.
9. Print the document.
10. Close the document.
11. Open the document as read-only.
12. Change the headline to **All Dressed Up with Everywhere to Go**.
13. Save the changes.
    - ✓ *Word will display the Save As dialog box.*
14. Save the document in plain text format, with the name **CONTEST2**.
15. Close the document, saving all changes. If prompted, remember to save the file in text format, not Word format.
16. Open the **CONTEST2.TXT** document in Word. The text file should look similar to the one in the illustration.
17. Close the file, saving all changes.

Illustration A

All Dressed Up with Everywhere to Go

Seattle, WA – Northwest Gear, Inc., a maker of clothing for teenagers, has announced that it is sponsoring an essay contest. Prizes include scholarship money, trips, computers, and gift certificates.

The topic of the essay contest is "All Dressed Up with Everywhere to Go." According to Northwest's Marketing Director, Nathan Pritchard, the object of the contest is to get teens thinking about the opportunities available to them in the 21st century.

"We live in an exciting time. We want to encourage teens to explore their own potential," said Mr. Pritchard.

The rules for the contest are as follows:

Students aged 12 through 18 are eligible.
Essays must be between 1,000 and 1,500 words.
Essays may be typed or handwritten.
Original copies will not be returned, and will become the property of Northwest Gear, Inc.
All entries must be postmarked by March 1. Winners will be announced on June 1.

The essays will be judged based on originality, creativity, grammar, and spelling. The judges will be employees of Northwest Gear, Inc.

For more information, contact Mr. Pritchard at 206-555-3922, or consult the company's Web site: northwestgear.com.

On Your Own

1. Search for the **OWD11**, the file you created in the On Your Own section of Exercise 11, or search for 🌐 **12LETTER**.

2. Open the file as read-only.

3. Check the number of words in the document.

4. Note the file size, date created, and date last modified.

5. Enter document properties, including Title, Subject, Manager, Company, Category, Keywords, and Comments.

6. Try saving the document.

7. Save the file as **OWD12**.

8. Save the file in text format as **OWD12-2**.

9. Print the file.

10. Close the document, saving all changes.

Exercise 13

◆ **Preview a Closed Document**
◆ **Print Files without Opening Them**

On the Job

Preview a document before opening it or printing it to make sure it is the correct file. Print files without opening them to save time or to print more than one document at once.

As the assistant to the marketing director at Northwest Gear, Inc., you have been asked to find employees willing to serve as judges for the essay contest. In this exercise, you will preview, open, and revise the press release about the contest. Then you will create a memo to employees. Finally, you will print both documents.

Notes

Preview a Closed Document

- By default, Word displays a list of files in the Open dialog box.

- You can change the display in the dialog box to show a preview of the document selected in the file list.

- Previewing is useful for making sure a document is the one you want before you open it or print it.

- Most documents are too large to be displayed completely in the dialog box; use the scroll arrows in the preview area to scroll up and down.

- If you don't want to display a preview, you can set the Open dialog box to display large or small file icons, the default file list, file details, such as size, type, and date last saved, or document properties.

Preview a document in the Open dialog box

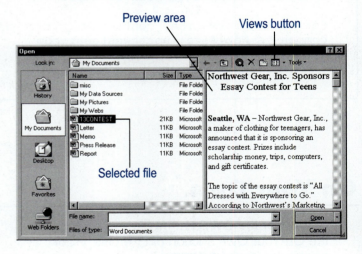

Print Files without Opening Them

- To save time, you can print a document from the Open dialog box without opening it.

- Print without opening when you are certain the document is ready for printing.

  ✓ *You can also print a document without opening it from the Open Office dialog box or from Windows Explorer.*

- You can select more than one file at a time for printing in the Open dialog box.

- Selecting multiple files for printing sends them all to the printer, where they will be printed one after the other.

- All selected files must be in the same folder.

Procedures

Preview a Closed Document

1. Click **File** .... Alt + F
2. Click **Open** .... O
3. Click **Views** button drop-down arrow  .
4. Click **Preview** V
5. Click document name to preview.

   ✓ *If necessary, select drive and/or folder to locate document.*

To turn Preview off:

1. Click **File** .... Alt + F
2. Click **Open** .... O
3. Click **Views** button drop-down arrow  .

4. Select another view:

   - Click **Large Icons** .... G
   - Click **Small Icons** .... M
   - Click **List** L
   - Click **Details** .... D
   - Click **Properties** .... R

   ✓ *Or click the Views button repeatedly to cycle through the Views options.*

Print a File without Opening It

1. Click **File** .... Alt + F
2. Click **Open** .... O

   ✓ *If necessary, select drive and/or folder to locate document.*

3. Click **Tools** button .... Alt + L
4. Click **Print** .... P

Print Multiple Files

1. Click **File** .... Alt + F
2. Click **Open** .... O
3. Click the first document name.
4. Press and hold **Ctrl**. .... Ctrl
5. Click each additional document name.
6. Click **Tools** button .... Alt + L
7. Click **Print** .... P

Exercise Directions

1. Start Word, if necessary.
2. In the Open dialog box, preview ⌨**CONTEST**, the document you created in Exercise 12, or preview ◉**13CONTEST**.
3. This should be a press release announcing the essay contest sponsored by Northwest Gear, Inc.
4. Change the Open dialog box to display document properties instead of the preview.
5. Open the document and save it as **PRESS**.
6. Make revisions as indicated in Illustration A.
7. Check the spelling and grammar in the document.
8. Close the document, saving all changes.
9. Create a new document and type the memo shown in Illustration B, or open ◉**13MEMO**.
10. Save the document as **MEMO**, then close it.
11. Preview the document **MEMO** in the Open dialog box.
12. Print both the **PRESS** and **MEMO** documents without opening them.

~~Northwest Gear, Inc. Sponsors Essay Contest for Teens~~

Seattle, WA – Northwest Gear, Inc., a maker of clothing for teenagers, has announced that it is sponsoring an essay contest. Prizes include scholarship money, trips, computers, and gift certificates. *on the topic of "All Dressed Up with Everywhere to Go."*

~~The topic of the essay contest is "All Dressed Up with Everywhere to Go."~~ According to Northwest's Marketing Director, Nathan Pritchard, the object of the contest is to get teens thinking about the opportunities available to them in the 21st century.

Northwest Gear selected the topic because

"We live in an exciting time. We want to encourage teens to explore their own potential," said Mr. Pritchard.

The rules for the contest are as follows:

Students aged 12 through 18 are eligible.
Essays must be between 1,000 and 1,500 words.
Essays may be typed or handwritten.
Original copies will not be returned, and will become the property of Northwest Gear, Inc.
All entries must be postmarked by March 1. Winners will be announced on June 1.

The essays will be judged based on originality, creativity, grammar, and spelling. The judges will be employees of Northwest Gear, Inc.

For more information, contact Mr. Pritchard at 206-555-3922, or consult the company's Web site: northwestgear.com.

Illustration B

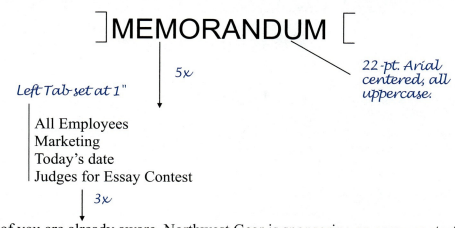

]MEMORANDUM [

22-pt. Arial centered, all uppercase.

5x

Left Tab set at 1"

12-pt. Times New Roman Flush left

To:	All Employees
From:	Marketing
Date:	Today's date
Subject:	Judges for Essay Contest

3x

As many of you are already aware, Northwest Gear is sponsoring an essay contest for teens (see attached press release). We are looking for volunteers interested in acting as judges for the contest. No previous judging experience is required, but a basic understanding of spelling, grammar, and other writing skills would be an asset.

2x

We hope to assemble a panel of ten judges and two alternates. We will provide training to help you understand the goals of the contest. There will be no compensation, but it could be a lot of fun.

2x

If you are interested, pick up a form in the Marketing Department and return it as soon as possible. The form is also available on the company Intranet.

On Your Own

1. Start Word.

2. Preview some of the documents that you have created for the On Your Own sections of previous exercises, or preview ☯ **13LETTER**, ☯ **13MISSION** and ☯ **13LIST**.

3. Display file properties instead of the preview.

4. Display the preview again.

5. Print at least two of the documents without opening them.

6. When you are finished, exit Word.

Exercise 14

◆ **Critical Thinking**

The owner of Coastline Gourmet Importers has received a new lead on someone who may be able to help him procure Russian caviar. In this exercise, you will search for and open the existing letter to Mr. Volfson regarding the caviar. You will save it with a new name, revise it using the techniques you have learned so far, and add document properties. Finally, you will preview and print the new letter.

Exercise Directions

1. Start Word, if necessary.

2. Open ⌨**CAVIAR** or 💿**14CAVIAR** as read-only.

3. Save the file as **CAVIAR**.

4. Insert, delete, and replace text as marked on Illustration A.

5. Copy and move text as marked on the illustration.

6. Apply formatting as marked on the illustration.

7. Enter Document Properties summary information as follows:

   Title: **Romanov Brothers**
   Subject: **Russian Caviar**
   Company: **Coastline Gourmet**
   Author: **Your name**
   Category: **Letter**
   Keywords: **Caviar, Russian, Romanov**.
   Comments: **Letter of inquiry regarding importing caviar**.

8. Check the spelling and grammar.

9. Save the changes.

10. Close the document.

11. Use a basic search to locate and open 💿**14FLYER**.

12. Save the document as **FLYER** in Rich Text Format.

   ✓ *Rich Text Format preserves some of the font formatting that Plain Text format does not preserve. It adds an .rtf file extension to the file name.*

13. Close the document.

14. Preview the **CAVIAR** and **FLYER** documents without opening them.

   ✓ *Remember, to display the FLYER document in the Open dialog box you will have to select All Files to display all file types.*

15. Print both the **CAVIAR** and **FLYER** documents without opening them.

16. Exit Word.

Illustration A

~~Today's date~~ *Replace with today's date*

~~CERTIFIED MAIL~~ *Delete mail notation and extra blank lines*

Mr. Alex Volfson
District Representative
Imperial Products, Inc.
62 Beaumont Street
Brooklyn, NY 11235

Mr. Boris Kolchenko
Proprietor
Romanov Brothers Food Company
1922 Beacon Street
Boston, MA 02115

Replace with new inside name and address. Format company name in bold.

Dear Mr. ~~Volfson~~: *Kolchenko*

Subject: Procuring Russian Caviar

Mr. Jake Pierson of the Fine Foods Emporium in Boca Raton, Florida.
Recently, I was talking to ~~Ms. Katherine Sanders, the proprietor of a fine dining establishment here in Miami.~~ When I mentioned that I have been having a difficult time procuring high-quality Russian caviar for COASTLINE GOURMET IMPORTERS, my chain of retail food stores, *s*he suggested that I try contacting you.

COASTLINE GOURMET carries high-quality specialty items imported from around the world. If, in fact, you can provide caviar that meets our standards, I would be very interested in discussing terms and availability. I have enclosed a brochure that describes ~~COASTLINE GOURMET~~ *the new catering service,* or you may want to look us up on the Web at coastlinegourmet.com.

We have also recently started a catering service.

Sincerely,

Mr. Benjamin Boghosian
Owner
COASTLINE GOURMET IMPORTERS
7334 Sunshine Parkway, 12th Floor
Miami, FL 33132

Bb/yo

Enclosure

Copy to: ~~Ms. Katharine Sanders~~ *Mr. Jake Pierson*

Skills Covered:

◆ **Apply Font and Text Effects** ◆ **Font Color**
◆ **Highlight Text** ◆ **Format Painter**

On the Job

You can enhance text using font effects, text effects, and colors. You can highlight text to change the color around the text without changing the font color. Highlighting is useful for calling attention to text and for making text stand out on the page. Use the Format Painter to quickly copy formatting from one location to another. The Format Painter saves you time and makes it easy to duplicate formatting throughout a document.

You have been asked to design a document advertising the essay contest for Northwest Gear, Inc. If the company approves of the document, it will be made available at retail stores and posted as a Web page on the company Web site. In this exercise, you will create the document using font effects, text effects, and color. You will also highlight text, and use the Format Painter to copy formatting.

Terms

Text effects Effects used to animate text on-screen.

Font effects Formatting features used to enhance or emphasize text.

Highlight formatting Applying a color background to selected text.

Notes

Apply Font and Text Effects

■ Font and **text effects** are used to enhance and emphasize text in a document.

■ Word includes numerous **font effects** for enhancing and emphasizing text, including the ones available in the Font dialog box:

• ~~Strikethrough~~

• ~~Double strikethrough~~

• Superscript

• Subscript

• Shadow

• Outline

• Emboss

• Engrave

• SMALL CAPS

• ALL CAPS

✓ Hidden is also an option in the Effects area of the font dialog box. Hidden text is not displayed on-screen or printed unless you select to display it.

■ Text effects are animations used in documents that will be viewed on-screen. They cannot be printed.

■ Select font and text effects in the Font dialog box.

The Font dialog box

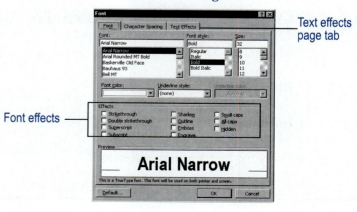

Text effects page tab

Font effects

Font Color

- Use color to enhance text in documents that will be viewed on-screen or printed on a color printer.

- You can change the color of an underline independently from the color of the font.

Highlight Text

- Highlighting calls attention to text by placing a color background on the text just like using a highlighter pen on paper.

- Yellow is the default highlight color, but you can change the color of **highlight formatting**.

  ✓ *Color highlighting will print in color when printed on a color printer and print in gray when printed on a black and white printer.*

Format Painter

- Use the Format Painter to copy formatting from existing formatted text to existing unformatted text.

Procedures

Apply Font Effects

1. Select text.
   OR
   Position insertion point where new text will be typed.
2. Click **Format**...............Alt+O
3. Click **Font** ....F
4. Select check box for desired effect(s).
   ✓ *Clear check mark to remove effect.*
5. Click **OK**...........................Enter
   ✓ *Select text and press Ctrl+Spacebar to remove all character formatting.*

Apply Text Effects

1. Select text.
   OR
   Position insertion point where new text will be typed.
2. Click **Format**...............Alt+O
3. Click **Font** ....F
4. Click **Text Effects** page tab.......................Alt+X
5. Click desired **Animation** .....Alt+A, ↑/↓
   ✓ *View a sample of the effect in the Preview area.*
6. Click **OK**...........................Enter

Apply Font Color

1. Select text.
   OR
   Position insertion point where new text will be typed.
2. Click **Format** ....Alt+O
3. Click **Font**...........................F
4. Click **Font color** drop-down arrow ....Alt+C
5. Click desired **color**.., Enter
   ✓ *Click Auto to select default color.*
6. Click **OK** ....Enter
   OR
1. Select text.
   OR
   Position insertion point where new text will be typed.
2. Click **Font Color** button drop-down arrow ▲ ▾.
3. Click desired color.

Apply Color to Underlines

1. Select underlined text.
   OR
   Position insertion point where new underlined text will be typed.
2. Click **Format** ....Alt+O
3. Click **Font**...........................F
4. Click **Underline color** drop-down arrow ....Alt+I
5. Click desired **color**.
   ✓ *Click Auto to select default color.*
6. Click **OK** ....Enter

Apply Highlights

Highlight existing text:

1. Select text.
2. Click **Highlight** button 🖊.
   ✓ *Repeat steps to remove highlight.*
   OR
1. Click **Highlight** button 🖊.
   ✓ *Mouse pointer changes to look like an I-beam with a pen attached to it.*
2. Drag across text to highlight.
3. Click **Highlight** button 🖊 again to turn off Highlight feature.

Change highlight color:

1. Click **Highlight** button drop-down arrow 🖊 ▾.
2. Click new color.
   ✓ *Click None to select the automatic background color.*

Copy Formatting

Copy formatting once;

1. Select formatted text.
2. Click **Format Painter** button .
   ✓ *The mouse pointer looks like an I-beam with a paintbrush:*
   🖌I
3. Select text to format.
   ✓ *Click a word to quickly copy the formatting to that word.*

Copy formatting repeatedly:

1. Select formatted text.
2. Double-click **Format Painter** button 🖌.
3. Select text to format.
4. Repeat step 3 until all text is formatted.
5. Click **Format Painter** button 🖌 to turn off Format Painter.

Exercise Directions

1. Start Word, if necessary.
2. Open 💿 **15ANNOUNCE**.
3. Save the document as **ANNOUNCE**.
4. Apply the formatting shown in the illustration.
   a. Change the font and font size as marked.
   ✓ *If the specified font is not available on your computer, select a different font.*
   b. Set horizontal alignments as marked.
   c. Apply font and text effects as marked.
   d. Change font color as marked.
   e. Apply highlighting as marked.
   ✓ *Use the Format Painter to copy formatting whenever possible.*
5. Check the spelling and grammar.
6. Display the document in Print Preview. It should look similar to the illustration.
   ✓ *The animated effects do not appear in Print Preview or in a printed document.*
   ✓ *If the document is longer or shorter than the one shown, check to see if you inadvertently formatted the blank lines between paragraphs. In the illustration, all blank lines have the default 12-pt. Times New Roman formatting.*
7. Save the changes.
8. Print the document.
9. Close the document, saving all changes.

On Your Own

1. Create an invitation to an event such as a birthday party, graduation, or meeting.
2. Save the document as **OWD15**.
3. Format the document using the techniques you have learned so far, including fonts, alignment options, and font effects.
4. Change the font color for some text.
5. Try some text effects.
6. Try different underline styles.
7. Copy the formatting from one location to another.
8. Preview the document and print it.
9. Save your changes, close the document, and exit Word.

Illustration A

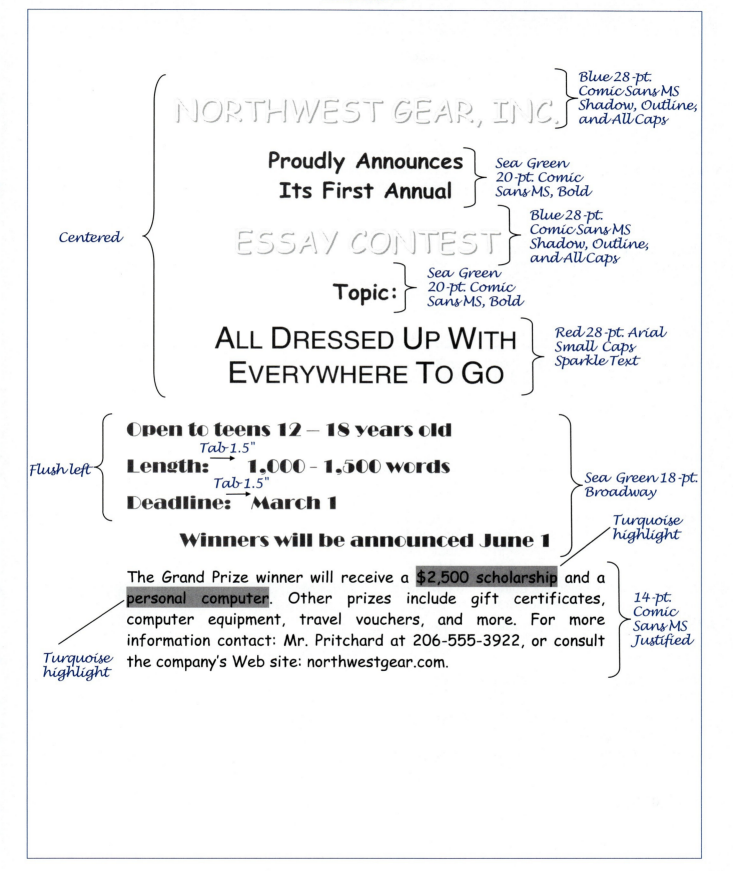

NORTHWEST GEAR, INC.
Blue 28-pt. Comic Sans MS Shadow, Outline, and All Caps

Proudly Announces
Its First Annual
Sea Green 20-pt. Comic Sans MS, Bold

ESSAY CONTEST
Blue 28-pt. Comic Sans MS Shadow, Outline, and All Caps

Topic:
Sea Green 20-pt. Comic Sans MS, Bold

ALL DRESSED UP WITH EVERYWHERE TO GO
Red 28-pt. Arial Small Caps Sparkle Text

Centered

Open to teens 12 – 18 years old
Tab 1.5"
Length: **1,000 – 1,500 words**
Tab 1.5"
Deadline: **March 1**

Flush left

Sea Green 18-pt. Broadway

Winners will be announced June 1

Turquoise highlight

The Grand Prize winner will receive a $2,500 scholarship and a personal computer. Other prizes include gift certificates, computer equipment, travel vouchers, and more. For more information contact: Mr. Pritchard at 206-555-3922, or consult the company's Web site: northwestgear.com.

14-pt. Comic Sans MS Justified

Turquoise highlight

Exercise 16

Skills Covered:

◆ Use Symbols

On the Job

Use symbols to supplement the standard characters available on the keyboard and to add visual interest to documents. For example, you can insert shapes such as hearts and stars into documents as borders or separators.

The owner of Coastline Gourmet Importers has asked you to create a flyer announcing the grand opening of a new store. In this exercise, you will create the flyer using the formatting techniques you have learned so far. You will also insert symbols to enhance the flyer.

Terms

Symbol Shapes, mathematical and scientific notations, currency signs, and other visual elements you can insert in documents by using the Symbol dialog box.

Notes

Use Symbols

- **Symbols** are characters that cannot be typed from the keyboard, such as hearts, stars, and other shapes, as well as foreign alphabet characters.

- Symbols can be selected, edited, and formatted in a document just like regular text characters.

- Several symbol fonts come with Office XP and others are available through vendors and shareware.

- Many regular character fonts also include some symbol characters.

- You select a font, then select the desired symbol in the Symbol dialog box.

- You can also select from a list of recently used symbols.

- When you insert symbols, the symbol font formatting is applied to the character. You can change the font style and effects just as you can for regular text characters.

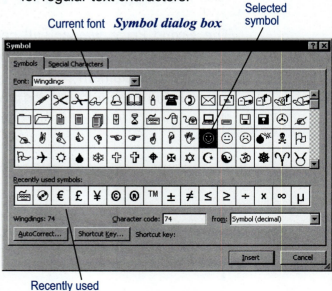

Current font   *Symbol dialog box*   Selected symbol

Recently used symbols

Procedures

Insert Symbols

1. Position insertion point where you want to insert a symbol.
2. Click **Insert**..................`Alt`+`I`
3. Click **Symbol**. ....`S`
4. Click **Font** drop-down arrow................`Alt`+`F`
5. Select any symbol **font**............`↓`, `Enter`
6. Click desired **symbol**......................`Tab`, `→`
7. Click **Insert**..................`Alt`+`I`

✓ *Repeat the steps to insert additional symbols without closing the Symbol dialog box.*

8. Click **Close**........................`Esc`

Exercise Directions

1. Start Word, if necessary.
2. Open ⊙**16GRAND**.
3. Save the document as **GRAND**.
4. Format the text as marked in the illustration.
   a. Use a serif font for the entire document. (Perpetua is used in Illustration A.)
   b. Apply font sizes, colors, and effects as shown.
      ✓ *Be careful not to change the font size and formatting of the blank lines in the document. They should remain at 12-point Times New Roman.*
   c. Apply alignments as shown.

5. Use the Wingdings font to insert symbols as marked in the illustration.
   ✓ *Leave spaces between each snowflake symbol. Adjust the font size and formatting of symbol characters the same way you adjust the font size and formatting of text characters.*
   ✓ *Hint: Use Copy and Paste to copy a symbol from one location to another, or use the Repeat command (Ctrl+Y) to repeat the insertion. Use the Format Painter to copy formatting.*
6. Display the document in Print Preview. It should look similar to the illustration.
7. Print the document.
8. Close the document, saving the changes.

On Your Own

1. Open the document **OWD15**, the document you created in exercise 15, or open ⊙**16INVITE**.
2. Save the document as **OWD16**.
3. Use symbols to enhance the document. For example, use symbols as separators between words or paragraphs, or use them to decorate or emphasize the document.
4. Try different symbol fonts.
5. Try changing the font size for a symbol inserted in a document.
6. Try repeating a symbol to create a line across the page.
7. Preview and print the document.
8. Close the document, saving all changes

Grand Opening *26-pt., red*

*34-pt., red,
Engrave,
Small Caps*

COASTLINE GOURMET IMPORTERS

Announces *18-pt., red*

The Grand Opening of its Newest Retail Outlet *20-pt.
Turquoise*

✸ ✸ ✸ ✸ ✸ ✸ ✸ ✸ ✸ ✸ ✸ ✸ ✸ ✸ ✸ *Wingdings
Symbol (#175)*

16509 NORTHEAST 26TH AVENUE

NORTH MIAMI BEACH, FL 33160

*34-pt., red,
Engrave
Small Caps*

✸ ✸ ✸ ✸ ✸ ✸ ✸ ✸ ✸ ✸ ✸ ✸ ✸ ✸ ✸ *Wingdings
Symbol (#175)*

Centered

Stop in to share our grand opening celebration
Saturday, April 13 and Sunday, April 14

24-pt. black

*Wingdings
Symbol (#70)*

→ ☞ → **PRODUCT SAMPLES**

Left tab 1" → ☞ → **DEMONSTRATIONS**

→ ☞ → **AND MORE…**

Left tab 2"

*34-pt., red,
Engrave
Small Caps*

Coastline Gourmet Importers is well known as a
specialty food store featuring items imported
from around the world.

*24-pt.
Justified*

Exercise 17

On the Job

Lists are an effective way to present items of information. Use a bulleted list when the items do not have to be in any particular order, like a grocery list or a list of objectives. Use a numbered list when the order of the items is important, such as directions or instructions. Use Sort to organize a list into alphabetical or numerical order.

As a personnel assistant at Electron Consumer Industries, Inc., a manufacturer of computer electronics, you have been asked to issue a memo about a change in emergency procedures. In this exercise, you will edit and format a memo document using a bulleted list and a numbered list. You will also sort the bulleted list into alphabetical order.

Terms

Bullet A dot or symbol that marks an important line of information or designates items in a list.

Sort To organize items into a specified order.

Notes

Bulleted Lists

- Use **bullets** to mark lists when the order of items does not matter.

- Word has seven built-in bullet symbols, but uses a simple black dot by default.

- A variety of bullet styles are available in the Bullets and Numbering dialog box, or you can create a customized bullet using a symbol.

- Word automatically carries bullet formatting forward to new paragraphs in a list.

Select a bullet style in the Bullets and Numbering dialog box

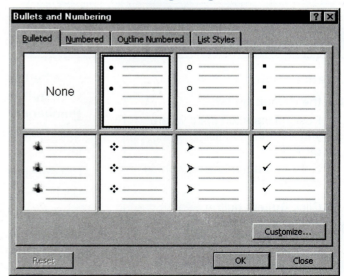

Numbered Lists

- Use numbers to mark lists when the order of items matters, such as directions or how-to steps.

- Word automatically renumbers a list when you add or delete items.

- Word comes with seven numbering styles, but the default numbering style is an Arabic numeral followed by a period.

- You can select a different number style in the Bullets and Numbering dialog box.

- Word automatically carries number formatting forward to new paragraphs in a list.

Select a number style in the Bullets and Numbering dialog box

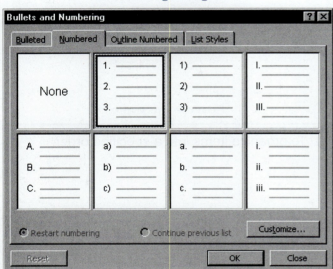

Sort

- Word can automatically **sort** items into alphabetical, numerical, or chronological order.

- A sort can be ascending (A to Z or 0 to 9) or descending (Z to A or 9 to 0).

- The default sort order is alphabetical ascending.

- Although the Sort command is on the Table menu, sorting is available for arranging lists, paragraphs, or rows in regular text as well as a table.

Options for a default sort

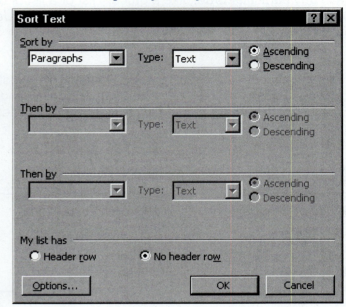

Procedures

Create Bulleted List

Use the default bullet:

1. Position insertion point where you want to start list.
   OR
   Select paragraphs you want in the list.
2. Click **Bullets** button ▦ .

Select a different bullet style:

1. Position insertion point where you want to start list.
   OR
   Select paragraphs you want in the list.

2. Click **F**ormat .... `Alt`+`O`
3. Click **Bullets and Numbering** .... `N`
4. Click **B**ulleted page tab .... `Alt`+`B`
5. Click desired Bullet style ... `↔`
6. Click **OK** .... `Enter`

Customize bullet:

1. Position insertion point where you want to start list.
   OR
   Select paragraphs you want in list.

2. Click **F**ormat............... `Alt`+`O`
3. Click **Bullets and Numbering**........................ `N`
4. Click **B**ulleted page tab............................. `Alt`+`B`
5. Click desired **Bullet style**..................... `↓`|`↑`|`→`|`←`
6. Click **Cus**tomize.......... `Alt`+`T`
7. Click desired **Bullet character**.......... `Alt`+`U`, `→`|`←`

Use a symbol as a bullet:

1. Position insertion point where you want to start list.
   OR
   Select paragraphs you want in list.
2. Click **Format** .... `Alt`+`O`
3. Click **Bullets and Numbering** .... `N`
4. Click **Bulleted** page tab .... `Alt`+`B`
5. Click desired **Bullet style** .... `↓``↑``→``←`
6. Click **Customize** .... `Alt`+`T`
7. Click **Character** .... `C`
8. Click desired symbol .... `Tab`, `↓``↑``→``←`
9. Click **OK** .... `Enter`
10. Click **OK** .... `Enter`

Turn off bullets:

- Click **Bullets** button `▤`.
  ✓ *To remove existing bullets, select bulleted list then click Bullets button.*

Create Numbered List

Use default number style:

1. Position insertion point where you want to start list.
   OR
   Select paragraphs you want in list.
2. Click **Numbering** button `▤`.

Select different number style:

1. Position insertion point where you want to start list.
   OR
   Select paragraphs you want in list.
2. Click **Format** .... `Alt`+`O`
3. Click **Bullets and Numbering** .... `N`
4. Click **Numbered** page tab .... `Alt`+`N`
5. Click **Number style** .... `↔`
6. Click **OK** .... `Enter`

Turn off numbering:

- Click **Numbering** button `▤`.
  ✓ *To remove numbers, select numbered list, then click Numbering button.*

Sort a List

Use default sort order:

1. Select the paragraphs you want sorted.
2. Click **Table** .... `Alt`+`A`
3. Click **Sort** .... `S`
4. Click **OK** .... `Enter`

Use a numerical or chronological sort:

1. Select the paragraphs you want sorted.
2. Click **Table** .... `Alt`+`A`
3. Click **Sort** .... `S`
4. Click **Type** drop-down arrow .... `Alt`+`Y`
5. Click **Number** .... `↓`, `Enter`
   OR
   Click **Date** .... `↓`, `Enter`
6. Click **OK** .... `Enter`

Reverse the sort order:

1. Select the paragraphs you want sorted.
2. Click **Table** .... `Alt`+`A`
3. Click **Sort** .... `S`
4. Click **Descending** .... `Alt`+`D`
5. Click **OK** .... `Enter`

Exercise Directions

1. Start Word, if necessary.
2. Open ⊙**17FIREDRILL**.
3. Save the document as **FIREDRIL**.
4. Edit and format the document as shown in Illustration A.
   a. Set fonts, font sizes, and alignments as shown.
   b. Insert symbols as shown.
   c. Use the default bullet style to turn the five guidelines into a bulleted list.
   d. Select a different bullet style.
   e. Use the default number style to turn the four steps for evacuation into a numbered list.
   f. Select a different number style.
   g. Change back to the default number style.
   h. Sort the bulleted list into ascending alphabetical order.
5. Check the spelling and grammar.
6. Display the document in Print Preview. It should look similar to the one in the Illustration, depending on the bullet and number styles you selected.
7. Print the document.
8. Close the document, saving all changes.

22 pts.

Electron Consumer Industries, Inc.

8740 S. Crawford Rd. ✦ Chicago, IL 60619

Arial Black

Phone: (312) 555-7700 ✦ **Fax: (312) 555-7800** ✦ **e-mail: electron@ddcpub.com**

16 pts.

Insert Wingdings Symbol

8 pts.

Left Tab 1"

Memo To: → All employees

From: → Your name

Date: → Today's date

Subject: → Emergency procedures

Recently, we invited professionals in the field of emergency evacuations to evaluate our emergency procedure policies. While most of our policies received high marks, we have made some changes to our fire emergency procedure. Please review the following information, and then post this memo within clear sight of your desk. We will have a drill sometime in the near future.

Numbered list

1. Alarm sounds.
2. Proceed calmly to one of the fire exits.
3. Walk out of the building.
4. Convene with your department in the designated meeting area.

Adhere to the following guidelines:

Bulleted list in alphabetical order

➢ Avoid the elevators.
➢ Do not ignore the alarm.
➢ Leave personal belongings behind.
➢ Use the closest fire exit.
➢ Walk! Do not run.

If you have any questions about the new procedures, please contact me in the Personnel Department at ext. 344. Thank you for your cooperation.

On Your Own

1. Create a new document in Word.

2. Save the file as **OWD17**.

3. Type a bulleted list of five things you'd like to accomplish in the next year. These can be goals for school, work, or personal development. Examples might include earning a better grade in math, completing a project on the job, or getting in better shape by exercising and eating right.

4. Sort the list in alphabetical order.

5. Type a numbered list that includes at least five steps describing how you expect to accomplish one of the items in the bulleted list.

6. Change the sort order of the bulleted list to descending order.

7. Save your changes, close the document, and exit Word.

Exercise 18

Skills Covered:
◆ **Line Spacing** ◆ **Paragraph Spacing** ◆ **Indent Text**

On the Job

Format documents using the right amount of space between lines, paragraphs, and words to make the pages look better and the text easier to read. Use indents to call attention to a paragraph, to achieve a particular visual effect, or to leave white space along the margins for notes or illustrations.

Coastline Gourmet is instituting a few new programs in response to a marketing survey. In this exercise, you will format a document explaining the new programs using line and paragraph spacing and indents. You will also use other formatting techniques, such as font formatting, alignments, and tabs.

Terms

Line spacing The amount of white space between lines of text in a paragraph.

Leading Line spacing measured in points.

Paragraph spacing The amount of white space between paragraphs.

Indent A temporary left and/or right margin for lines or paragraphs.

Notes

Line Spacing

- **Line spacing** sets the amount of vertical space between lines. By default, line spacing in Word is set to single space. Line spacing can be measured in either lines (single, double, etc.) or in points.

- When line spacing is measured in points, it is called **leading** (pronounced *ledding*).

By default, Word uses leading that is 120% of the current font size. For a 10-point font, that means 12-point leading. This paragraph is formatted with the default leading for a 12-point font (14.4 pts.).

Increase leading to make text easier to read. In this paragraph, the font is still 12 points, but the leading has been increased to exactly 16 points.

Decrease leading to fit more lines on a page. In this paragraph, the leading has been set to exactly 10 points, while the font size is still 12 points. Keep in mind that decreasing leading makes text harder to read.

- Line spacing measured in lines can be set to single spaced, 1.5 spaced, or double spaced.

Paragraph Spacing

- **Paragraph spacing** affects space before or after paragraphs.

- Amount of space can be specified in lines or in points. The default is points.

- Use increased paragraph spacing in place of extra returns or blank lines.

Indent Text

- There are five types of **indents**:
  - *Left* indents text from the left margin.
  - *Right* indents text from the right margin.
  - *Double* indents text from both the left and right margins.
  - First line indents just the first line of a paragraph from the left margin.
  - *Hanging* indents all lines but the first line from the left margin.

- Indent markers on the horizontal ruler show where current indents are set.

Indents in a document

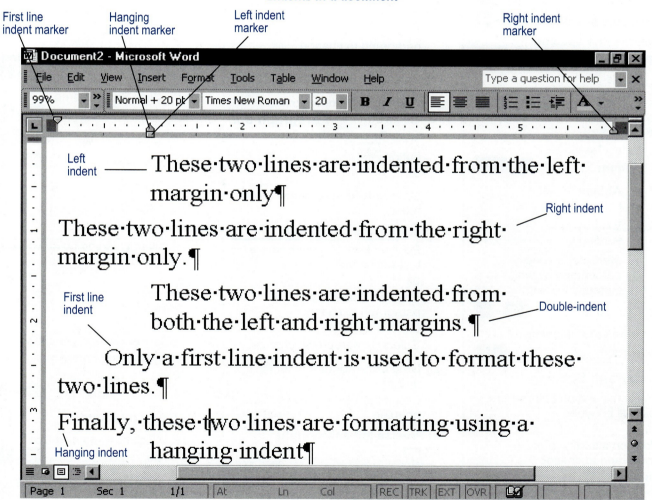

Procedures

Set Line Spacing
(Ctrl+1, Ctrl+2, Ctrl+5)

1. Position insertion point where text will be typed.
   OR
   Position insertion point in paragraph to change.
   OR
   Select paragraphs to change.
2. Click **Format** .... `Alt`+`O`
3. Click **Paragraph** .... `P`
4. Click **Indents and Spacing** page tab .... `Alt`+`I`
5. Click **Line spacing** ..... `Alt`+`N`
6. Select a **line spacing option:** .... `↓`, `Enter`
   - Single
   - 1.5 lines
   - Double
   OR
   a. Select **leading option:** .... `↓`, `Enter`
      - **At least** to set a minimum leading.
      - **Exactly** to set an exact leading.
      - **Multiple** to specify a percentage by which to increase leading.
   b. Click **At** box .... `Alt`+`A`
   c. Type value in points.
7. Click **OK** .... `Enter`

Set Paragraph Spacing

1. Position insertion point where text will be typed.
   OR
   Position insertion point in paragraph to change.
   OR
   Select paragraphs to change.
2. Click **Format** .... `Alt`+`O`
3. Click **Paragraph** .... `P`
   ✓ *To open the Paragraph dialog box quickly, right-click paragraph to format, then click Paragraph.*

4. Click **Indents and Spacing** page tab .... `Alt`+`I`
5. Click **Before** text box... `Alt`+`B`
   OR
   Click **After** text box ..... `Alt`+`E`
6. Type amount of space to leave.
   ✓ *Type li after value to specify lines.*
7. Click **OK** .... `Enter`

Indent Text

Quickly Indent from the left:

1. Position insertion point where text will be typed.
   OR
   Position insertion point in paragraph to change.
   OR
   Select paragraphs to change.
2. Click **Increase Indent** button.
   OR
   Click **Decrease Indent** button.
   OR
   Drag **Left-indent** marker on ruler.

Indent from the left and/or right:

1. Position insertion point where text will be typed.
   OR
   Position insertion point in paragraph to change.
   OR
   Select paragraphs to change.
2. Drag **Left-indent** marker on ruler.
3. Drag **Right-indent** marker on ruler.

Set Precise left and/or right indents:

1. Click **Format** .... `Alt`+`O`
2. Click **Paragraph** .... `P`
3. Click **Indents and Spacing** page tab .... `Alt`+`I`
4. Click **Left** text box .... `Alt`+`L`
5. Type distance from left margin.
6. Click **Right** text box ..... `Alt`+`R`

7. Type distance from right margin.
8. Click **OK** .... `Enter`

Indent first line only *(Tab)*:

1. Position insertion point where text will be typed.
   OR
   Position insertion point in paragraph to change.
   OR
   Select paragraphs to change.
2. Drag **First Line indent** marker.
   OR
   a. Click **Format** .... `Alt`+`O`
   b. Click **Paragraph** .... `P`
   c. Click **Indents and Spacing** page tab .... `Alt`+`I`
   d. Click **Special** drop-down arrow .... `Alt`+`S`
   e. Click **First line** ..... `↓`, `Enter`
   f. Click **By** text box ..... `Alt`+`Y`
   g. Type amount to indent.
   h. Click **OK** .... `Enter`

Hanging indent *(Ctrl+T)*:

1. Position insertion point where text will be typed.
   OR
   Position insertion point in paragraph to change.
   OR
   Select paragraphs to change.
2. Drag **Hanging indent** marker.
   OR
   a. Click **Format** .... `Alt`+`O`
   b. Click **Paragraph** .... `P`
   c. Click **Indents and Spacing** page tab .... `Alt`+`I`
   d. Click **Special** drop-down arrow .... `Alt`+`S`
   e. Click **Hanging** ..... `↓`, `Enter`
   f. Click **By** text box ..... `Alt`+`Y`
   g. Type amount to indent.
   h. Click **OK** .... `Enter`

Exercise Directions

1. Start Word, if necessary.
2. Open ⊙ **18PROGRAMS**.
3. Save the document as **PROGRAMS**.
4. Follow steps 5 through 9 to achieve the results shown in the illustration.
5. Remember, you can use the Format Painter to copy formatting from one paragraph to another.
6. Apply font formatting as shown.
   - ✓ *Unless otherwise specified, all text is 12-point sans serif. (Arial is used in Illustration A.)*
7. Insert symbols as marked in the illustration.
8. Set alignments and tabs as marked in the illustration.
   - ✓ *Unless otherwise noted, all paragraphs are justified.*
9. Set line spacing, paragraph spacing, and indents as shown in the illustration.
10. Check spelling and grammar.
11. Display the document in Print Preview. It should look similar to the illustration.
12. Print the document.
13. Close the document, saving all changes.

On Your Own

1. Create a new document in Word.
2. Save the file as **OWD18**.
3. Think of some documents that could benefit from line spacing, paragraph spacing, and indent formatting. For example, many instructors require reports and papers to be double spaced. First drafts of documents that will be read by others should be double spaced so reviewers can jot notes or make corrections. A resume can be set up neatly using spacing and indent features, as can a reference list.
4. Create a resume describing your school experience, outside activities such as clubs or athletic teams, and any work experience.
5. Use spacing and indent features to format the resume.
6. Use alignments and font formatting to enhance the text and to call attention to important items.
7. Use lists and symbols if appropriate.
8. Save your changes, close the document, and exit Word.

Flush left

28-pt. Harlow Solid Italic Underlined

<u>*Coastline Gourmet Importers*</u>

7334 Sunshine Parkway ✿12ᵗʰ Floor Miami, FL 33132 — 10-pt. Arial

Phone: (305) 555-7300 ✿ Fax: (305) 555-7301 ✿ e-mail: coastlinegourmet@ddcpub.com — 8-pt. Arial

Insert Wingdings Symbol

Leave 24 pts. of space after

Contact: ⟶ Marissa Hernandez

Left Tab 1" ⟶ Ext. 245 — *Leave 24 pts. of space after*

First line indent .5"

Double-spaced

⟶ Coastline Gourmet Importers recently conducted a marketing survey in an attempt to determine how best to boost sales. The results of the survey have been compiled, and the key point can be summarized in a few lines:

6 pts. of space before; 6 pts. of space after

Indent 1.5" from left and right

Set leading to at least 12 pts.

"Coastline Gourmet Importers faces challenges from numerous other retail stores in the Southern Florida area. To boost sales, Coastline Gourmet must make every effort to bring more customers into each store, and to keep them in the store for a longer period of time in order to maximize buying potential."

10-pt. Arial

6 pts. of space before; 0 pts. of space after

Indent 3" from left ———— Survey Results

10-pt. Arial 0 pts. before 18 pts. after

In response to the survey results, the company has decided to implement the following programs in selected stores. If the programs are successful, the company will expand them into all stores.

Same as first paragraph above

<u>Product demos</u>. Coastline Gourmet will invite customers to attend demonstrations for using small appliances and utensils such as espresso and cappuccino machines, pasta makers, and food processors.

Hanging indent set at 1.5"

<u>Cooking classes</u>. Coastline Gourmet will sponsor hands-on cooking classes in which customers can learn how to make simple, yet elegant dishes such as salads, appetizers, and desserts.

<u>Singles parties</u>. Coastline Gourmet will invite customers to meet and mingle while sampling some of the imported cheeses, crackers, and sweets. Door prizes will be offered, and shopping will be encouraged.

6 pts. of space before; 6 pts of space after

Set leading to exactly 16 pts.

Exercise 19

Skills Covered:

◆ **Apply Styles** ◆ **Create a Style** ◆ **Edit a Style**
◆ **Reapply Direct Formatting** ◆ **Check Formatting**
◆ **Select Paste Formatting Options** ◆ **Clear Formatting**

On the Job

Word provides many ways to apply and remove formatting in documents. Use styles to apply a collection of formatting settings to characters or paragraphs. Styles help ensure continuity in formatting throughout a document. You can also set Word to check for formatting inconsistencies in much the same way it checks for spelling and grammatical errors.

Murray Hill Marketing, an advertising and public relations firm, has contracted with a training company to provide computer training for employees. You have been asked to prepare a document listing the courses that will be available for the first three months of the year. In this exercise, you will use styles and direct formatting to apply consistent formatting to the document.

Terms

Style A collection of formatting settings that can be applied to characters or paragraphs.

Style sheet A list of available styles.

Direct formatting Individual font or paragraph formatting settings applied directly to text, as opposed to a collection of settings applied with a style.

Notes

Apply Styles

- **Styles** make it easy to apply a collection of formatting settings to characters or paragraphs all at once.

- Word includes built-in styles for formatting body text, headings, lists, and other parts of documents.

- Different Word templates have different **style sheets** depending on formatting required for the document. For example, the default Normal template uses only five styles, while the Resume template includes 25 styles.

The Style list for the Normal template style sheet

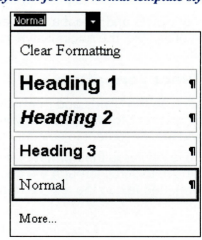

- You can apply a style to existing text, or select a style before you type new text.
- You can select a style from the drop-down style list or from the Styles and Formatting Task Pane.

Styles and Formatting Task Pane

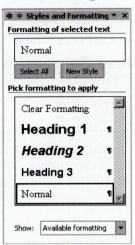

Create a Style

- You can create new styles for formatting your documents.
- Styles can contain font and/or paragraph formatting.
- Style names should be short and descriptive.
- The style will be added to the style sheet for the current document.

Edit a Style

- You can modify an existing style.
- When you modify a style that has already been applied to text in the document, the formatted text automatically changes to the new style.
- If you modify a style and give it a new name, it becomes a new style; the original style remains unchanged.

Reapply Direct Formatting

- You can also use the Styles and Formatting Task Pane to apply **direct formatting** that you have already used in a document to selected text.
- This feature is similar to the Format Painter, but you do not have to scroll through the document from the formatted text to the text you want to format.

Check Formatting

- Use Word's Format Checker to insure consistent formatting throughout a document.
- As with the spelling checker and the grammar checker, you can have Word check formatting while you work. Word underlines formatting inconsistencies with a wavy blue underline.

Use the Format Checker

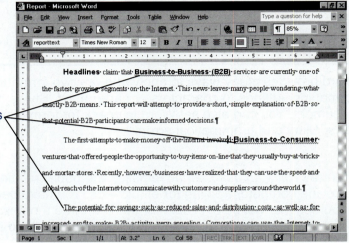

Blue wavy lines

- You can ignore the blue lines and keep typing, or correct the error.
- The automatic format checker is off by default; you must turn it on to use it.
- If the wavy underlines distract you from your work, you can turn off the automatic formatting checker.
- You can also have Word check the formatting immediately after you check the spelling and grammar in a document.

Select Paste Formatting Options

- When you use the Clipboard to paste text from one location to another, Word automatically displays the Paste Options button.
- Click the Paste Options button to display a list of options for formatting the text in the new location.

The Paste Options button

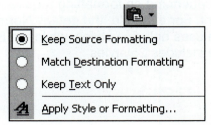

Clear Formatting

- You can quickly remove all formatting from selected text. This returns text to the default font.

- Clearing the formatting from text removes both direct formatting and styles.

  ✓ *To quickly remove direct character formatting from selected text, press Ctrl+Spacebar; to remove direct paragraph formatting, press Ctrl+Q.*

- You can clear formatting using the Style list, or the Styles and Formatting Task Pane.

- After you clear the formatting, text is displayed in the default normal style for the current document. For the default document, that means single spaced 12-point Times New Roman, flush left.

Procedures

Apply a Style

1. Click in the paragraph.
   OR
   Select the text.
2. Click the **Style** drop-down arrow on the Formatting toolbar.
3. Select style to apply .... ⬆, ⬇, Enter

Apply a Style Using the Task Pane

1. Click in the paragraph.
   OR
   Select the text.
2. Click the **Styles and Formatting** button 🄰 on the Formatting toolbar
   OR
   a. Click **F**ormat.......... Alt + O
   b. Click **S**tyles and Formatting .... S
3. Click style to apply in **Pick formatting to apply** list.

   ✓ *If necessary, scroll through the list to find the desired formatting.*

Create a Style

1. Format text or paragraph.
2. Click in the **Style** box Normal on the Formatting toolbar.
3. Type style name.
4. Press **Enter**..................... Enter

Edit a Style

1. Change formatting of text or paragraph formatted with the style.
2. Click in **Style** box on the Formatting toolbar.
3. Press **Enter**..................... Enter
4. Click **Update the style to reflect recent changes?** .... Alt + U
5. Click **OK** .... Enter

Reapply Direct Formatting

1. Select text to format.
2. Click the **Styles and Formatting** button 🄰 on the Formatting toolbar.
   OR
   a. Click **F**ormat .... Alt + O
   b. Click **S**tyles and Formatting .... S
3. Click style to apply in **Pick formatting to apply** list.

   ✓ *If necessary, scroll through the list to find the desired formatting.*

Turn on Automatic Format Checking

1. Click **T**ools .... Alt + T
2. Click **O**ptions .... O
3. Click the **Edit** tab........ Ctrl + Tab
4. Select **Mark formatting inconsistencies** check box .... Alt + F
5. Click **OK** .... Enter

Check Formatting as You Type

1. Right-click formatting inconsistency marked with blue, wavy underline.
2. Click desired correct formatting option on context menu.
   OR
   Click **I**gnore Once to hide this occurrence I
   OR
   Click **Ignore Ru**le to hide all occurrences .... U

Check Formatting

1. Run Spelling and Grammar checker.

   ✓ *Refer to Exercise 3 for information on checking the spelling and grammar in a document.*

2. When check is complete, click **Check Formatting**.
3. Choose from the following options:

   - Click **C**hange .... Alt + C to accept the recommended formatting.
   - Click **I**gnore to continue without changing formatting .... Alt + I
   - Click **Ignore Rule** to continue without changing formatting and without highlighting inconsistency if it occurs anywhere else in document............... Alt + G

Select Paste Formatting Options

1. Paste text at new location.
   - ✓ *Refer to Exercises 10 and 11 for information on pasting.*
2. Click **Paste Options** button 📋.
3. Select one of the following:
   - **Keep Source Formatting** .... K
     to maintain formatting from original location.
   - **Match Destination Formatting** .... D
     to apply existing formatting to new text.
   - **Keep Text Only** .... T
     to remove all applied formatting.

- **Apply Styles or Formatting** .... A
  to open Styles and Formatting Task Pane.

If Paste Options button is not displayed:

1. Click **Tools** .... Alt + T
2. Click **Options** .... O
3. Click the **Edit** tab .... Ctrl + Tab
4. Select **Show Paste Options buttons** check box ...... Alt + O
5. Click **OK** .... Enter

Clear Formatting

1. Select text.
2. Click the **Style** drop-down arrow [Normal ▾] on the Formatting toolbar.

OR

Click the **Styles and Formatting** button 🔲 on the Formatting toolbar.

OR

a. Click **Format** .... Alt + O
b. Click **Styles and Formatting** .... S
3. Select **Clear Formatting** .... ↑, ↓, Enter
   - ✓ *Clear Formatting is usually found at the top of the drop-down style list or at the top of the Formatting to Apply list.*

Exercise Directions

1. Start Word, if necessary.
2. Open 💿 **19COURSE**.
3. Save the document as **COURSE**.
4. Apply the Heading 1 style to the company name.
5. Apply the Heading 3 style to the names of the months.
6. Increase the font size of the company name to 26 points, center it, and increase the amount of space after it to 12 points.
7. Modify the Heading 1 style to include the changes.
8. Apply the new Heading 1 style to the text **Training Schedule**.
9. Insert Wingding symbols to separate the parts of the company address, then format the address as follows:
   a. Increase the font size to 14 points.
   b. Center the line horizontally.
   c. Apply italics.
   d. Add 6 points of space before and after the line.
10. Reapply the formatting you have just applied to the company address to the names of the three courses.
11. Format the paragraph describing the Word 1 course as follows:
    a. Change the font to 14-point Arial.
    b. Justify the alignment.
    c. Indent the paragraph 1" from both the left and the right.
    d. Leave 12 points of space before and after the paragraph.
12. Create a style named *Course* based on the formatting of the course description.
13. Apply the *Course* style to the paragraphs describing the Word 2 and Word 3 courses.
14. Add a new line to the end of the document.
15. Clear all formatting from the new line, then type: **For more information, call:**
16. Copy the phone number from the company address line near the top of the document and paste it at the end of the new last line of the document.
17. Select to paste only the text, without any formatting.
18. Complete the line by typing **ext. 343** after the pasted phone number.
19. Set Word to automatically check formatting.

20. Format the text **Training Schedule** in 13-point bold Arial, then move the insertion point to a different location in the document. The format checker should display a wavy blue underline under the text Training Schedule.

21. Right-click the wavy blue underline to see what Word suggests.

22. Ignore the rule, then reapply the Heading 1 style to the text.

23. Check the spelling, grammar, and formatting in the document.

24. Display the document in Print Preview. It should look similar to the one in the illustration.

25. Print the document.

26. Close the file saving all changes.

On Your Own

1. Start Word and open **OWD18**, the document you created in the On Your Own section of Exercise 18, or open ⊙ **19RESUME**.

2. Save the document as **OWD19**.

3. Clear all formatting from the document.

4. Use styles to format the document. You can use existing styles, modify existing styles, or create new styles.

5. Apply some direct formatting for emphasis, then reapply the formatting to other text in the document.

6. If you want, try pasting text and selecting different Paste Options for formatting.

7. Check the spelling, grammar, and formatting in the document.

8. Close the document, saving all changes.

Murray Hill Marketing, LLC *Heading 1*

285 Madison Avenue ✦ New York, NY 10016 ✦ 212-555-4444 *14-pt. Italics, centered, 6 pts. before, 6 pts. after*

Heading 1 ## Training Schedule

January

Microsoft Word 1 *Same as address*

This introductory course will cover the basics of using Microsoft Word to create common business documents. By the end of the course you will know how to: create and print text-based documents such as letters and envelopes, and apply formatting.

February

Microsoft Word 2 *Same as address*

A continuation of the Word I course, this introductory level class will delve into some of the more intriguing features of Microsoft Word. By the end of the course you will know how to conduct a mail merge, set up a document in columns, include headers and footers, and insert pictures.

March

Microsoft Word 3 *Same as address*

This final course in the Microsoft Word series covers the advanced features. By the end of this course you will know how to work with tables, create and modify outlines, use e-mail and Internet features in Word, and share documents with other users.

Heading 3

Course

For more information call: 212-555-4444, ext. 343. *Normal*

Exercise 20

Skills Covered:

◆ **Format a One-Page Report** ◆ **Set Margins** ◆ **Set Page Orientation**

On the Job

Format a one-page report so that it is attractive and professional. Set margins to meet expected requirements and to improve the document's appearance and readability. For example, leave a wider margin in a report if you expect a reader to make notes or comments; leave a narrower margin to fit more text on a page.

Regency General, Inc. has realized that many people are not sure what *business-to-business*—"B2B"—means. In this exercise, you are responsible for formatting a one-page report explaining how business-to-business services work. The report can be included in marketing packets given to prospective clients.

Terms

Gutter Space added to the margin to leave room for binding.

Margins The amount of white space between the text and the edge of the page on all four sides.

Section In Word, a segment of a document defined by a section break. A section may have different page formatting from the rest of the document.

Portrait orientation The default position for displaying and printing text horizontally across the shorter side of a page.

Landscape orientation Rotating document text so it displays and prints horizontally across the longer side of a page.

Notes

Format a One-Page Report

■ Traditionally, a one-page report is set up as follows:

- Text starts 1" or 2" from the top of the page.
- Text is justified.
- Lines are double spaced.
- First-line indents are .5" or 1".
- The report title is centered and all uppercase.
- Spacing following the title ranges from ¾" (54 pts.) to 1" (72 pts.).
- Unbound reports have left and right margins of 1".

- A **gutter** on bound reports makes the left margin wider than the right margin.
- ✓ *Use the Mirror margins option to set gutter width on inside margin of each page.*

Set Margins

■ **Margins** are measured in inches.

■ Default margins are 1.25" on the left and right and 1" on the top and bottom.

■ Margin settings affect an entire document, or the current **section**.

- ✓ *To set margins for a paragraph that are different from the page margins, use indents as described in Exercise 18.*

- On the rulers, areas outside the margins are shaded gray, while areas inside the margins are white.

  ✓ *To see both vertical and horizontal rulers, use Print Layout view.*

- Light gray bars mark the margins on the rulers.

Set Page Orientation

- There are two page orientations available:
  - **Portrait**
  - **Landscape**

- Portrait is the default orientation, and is used for most documents, including letters, memos, and reports.

- Use landscape orientation to display a document across the wider length of the page. For example, if a document contains a table that is wider than the standard 8.5" page, Word will split it across two pages. When you change to landscape orientation, the table may fit on the 11" page.

Procedures

Set Margins in Print Layout View

1. Move the mouse pointer over the margin marker on the ruler.

   ✓ *The mouse pointer changes to a double-headed arrow, and the ScreenTip identifies the margin.*

2. Drag the margin marker to a new location.

   ✓ *Press and hold the Alt key while you drag to see the margin width.*

Set Margins in any View

1. Click **File** .... `Alt`+`F`
2. Click **Page Setup** .... `U`
3. Click **Margins** tab .... `Alt`+`M`
4. Click **Top** text box .... `Alt`+`T`
5. Type top margin width.
6. Click **Bottom** text box............................... `Alt`+`B`
7. Type bottom margin width.
8. Click **Left** text box .... `Alt`+`F`
9. Type left margin width.
10. Click **Right** text box............................... `Alt`+`H`
11. Type right margin width.
12. Click the **Apply to** drop-down arrow .... `Alt`+`Y`
13. Select **This point forward**.
    OR
    Select **Whole document**.
14. Click **OK** .... `Enter`

Set Page Orientation

1. Click **File**..................... `Alt`+`F`
2. Click **Page Setup** .... `U`
3. Click **Margins** tab.
4. Click **Portrait** .... `P`
   OR
   Click **Landscape** .... `S`
5. Click **OK**.......................... `Enter`

Exercise Directions

1. Start Word, if necessary.
2. Open ⊙ **20BUSINESS**.
3. Save the document as **BUSINESS**.
4. Change the margins to 1" on all sides of the page.
5. Format the report as shown in the illustration.
6. Use a 16-point sans serif font in all uppercase for the title. (Arial is used in the illustration.)
7. Center the title and leave 54-points of space after it.
8. Use a 12-point serif font for the body text. (Times New Roman is used in the illustration.)
9. Justify and double-space all body text paragraphs.
10. Leave 6 points of space before and after each paragraph.
11. Indent the first line of each body text paragraph by .5".
12. If the document extends onto a second page, change the top and bottom margins to .75".
13. Check the spelling and grammar.
14. Change the page orientation to Landscape.
15. Display the document in Print Preview.
16. Print the document.
17. Change the page orientation back to Portrait.
18. Print the document.
19. Close the document, saving all changes.

On Your Own

1. Create a new document in Word.
2. Save the file as **OWD20**.
3. In the third person, draft a one-page report about yourself. For example, draft a document that you could include in a directory for an organization of which you are a member. Think of the *About the Author* paragraphs found in books and magazines, or the *About the Performers* paragraphs found in a theater program.
4. Double space the report.
5. Use correct document formatting for a one-page report.
6. Use other formatting effects, including fonts, lists, and symbols.
7. Check the spelling and grammar, then print the document.
8. Save your changes and close the document.

BUSINESS-TO-BUSINESS: MAKING THE INTERNET WORK

16-pt. Arial Centered

54 pts.

Headlines claim that Business-to-Business (B2B) services are currently one of the fastest growing segments on the Internet. This news leaves many people wondering what exactly B2B means. This report will attempt to provide a short, simple explanation of B2B so that potential B2B participants can make informed decisions.

The first attempts to make money off the Internet involved Business-to-Consumer ventures that offered people the opportunity to buy items on-line that they usually buy at "bricks-and–mortar" stores. Recently, however, businesses have realized that they can use the speed and global reach of the Internet to communicate with customers and suppliers around the world.

The potential for savings such as reduced sales and distribution costs, as well as for increased profits make B2B activity very appealing. Corporations can use the Internet to communicate more effectively with their current strategic partners, but they can also use it to locate new partners. This increase in competition promotes additional savings in terms of lower prices and better service.

One obstacle in achieving B2B Internet interaction has been locating and implementing the links between companies. As a result, a new order of Internet service company has emerged. These companies specialize in providing the hardware, software, and consulting services that help businesses locate and communicate with suppliers, customers, strategic partners, and distributors. By assuming the responsibility for maintaining databases and tracking orders and shipments, this new segment of Internet service companies is making it possible for corporations of all sizes to successfully implement B2B ventures on-line.

1"

1"

1"

1"

Double spaced 12-pt. Times New Roman, Justified .5" 1st line indent, 6 pts. Before, 6 pts. after

Exercise 21

◆ **Critical Thinking**

You are responsible for preparing a document for Murray Hill Marketing employees who are participating in the in-house training program. In this exercise, you will format the document using font formatting, symbols, lists, line and paragraph spacing, indents, styles, and margins.

Directions

1. Start Word, if necessary.
2. Open ☞ **21TRAIN**.
3. Save the file as **TRAIN**.
4. Set the margins to 1" on all sides.
5. Format the title with a 20-point blue, sans serif font in all uppercase letters, centered, with 48 points of space after.
6. Apply the Heading 3 style to the headings **Introduction**, **Come Prepared**, and **Behavior in Class**.
7. Modify the Heading 3 style so it is a 16-point plum colored, sans serif font, small caps, with a solid underline. Apply 12 points of space before and after.
8. Insert an appropriate Wingding symbol at the beginning of each heading.
9. Format the remaining Normal text in a 14-point serif font with a leading of exactly 17 points. Justify the alignment.
10. Format the three items in the list under the heading **Introduction** as a numbered list, using letters instead of numbers.

11. Apply a different color highlight to each item in the list.
12. Change the indents of the list so the left indent is .5" and the hanging indent is .5".
13. Create two bulleted lists under the heading **Come Prepared** (refer to the illustration) using an appropriate Wingding symbol as a bullet.
14. Sort all three lists into descending alphabetical order.
15. Emphasize the text **come prepared** at the end of first sentence under the heading **Come Prepared** by applying font formatting and color.
16. Reapply the formatting you applied in step 15 to the text **maintain a professional attitude** in the last paragraph.
17. Check the spelling, grammar, and formatting in the document.
18. Display the document in Print Preview. It should look similar to the one in the illustration.
19. Print the document.
20. Close the document, saving all changes.

WHAT TO EXPECT FROM IN-HOUSE TRAINING

🖹 INTRODUCTION

In-house training courses are offered to insure that employees have the opportunity to stay current in their selected fields, or to provide instruction that the employer requires. In general, you can expect the following from most in-house training courses:

A.   Hands-on training
B.   Focused content
C.   Experienced teachers

🖹 COME PREPARED

One of the most important things you can do to insure your success in any in-house training course is to *come prepared*. If there is any homework or outside reading to complete, be sure it is done on time. Also, there are a few basic items you should always bring to class:

- ✒ Pencil
- ✒ Pen
- ✒ Notebook

In addition, there may be items that are specific to the course as well as optional items. For example:

- ✒ Water bottle
- ✒ Pencil sharpener
- ✒ Calculator

🖹 BEHAVIOR IN CLASS

Keep in mind that although in-house training classes may feel like a day off, you are still at work. You should *maintain a professional attitude* at all times. The other members of the class are your co-workers, who you will see every day. The information you are learning is designed to enhance your job performance. With that said, you should make every effort to be relaxed, to have fun, and to get as much as possible out of the course. If you pay attention, ask questions, and complete the assignments, you will find that in-house training is a positive, enjoyable experience.

Exercise 22

Skills Covered:

◆ **Send E-Mail from Word**
◆ **Attach a Word Document to an E-Mail Message**
◆ **Send a Word Document as E-Mail**
◆ **Receive E-Mail Messages in Outlook or Outlook Express**

On the Job

E-mail is suitable for jotting quick notes such as an appointment confirmation. You can create and format e-mail messages and then send the messages via Outlook or Outlook Express directly from Word. When you need to communicate in more depth, you can attach a Word document to the message, or simply send a document as the message itself. You can exchange e-mail messages via the Internet or an intranet with anyone who has an e-mail account, including coworkers located down the hall, in a different state, or halfway around the world. To receive e-mail, you can use Outlook or Outlook Express.

As the assistant to the marketing director at Northwest Gear, you have been compiling a list of employees willing to be judges for an essay contest. In this exercise, you will use e-mail to communicate with the marketing director about the contest. First, you will create and send a brief e-mail message about the list of judges. Then, you will follow up with a second message to which you will attach the list of prospective judges. You will then send a copy of a memo you plan to distribute to the prospective judges. Finally, you will launch Outlook Express and check to see if you have received any e-mail messages.

Terms

E-mail (electronic mail) A method of sending information from one computer to another across the Internet or intranet.

HTML (Hypertext Markup Language) A universal file format used for files displayed on the World Wide Web.

Internet A global network of computers.

Intranet A network of computers within a business or organization.

Mail service provider A company that maintains and controls e-mail accounts.

Outlook A personal information management program that includes e-mail features that comes with the Office suite.

Outlook Express An e-mail program that is included as part of the Microsoft Internet Explorer Web browser.

E-mail address The string of characters that identifies the name and location of an e-mail user.

To Mail notation that indicates to whom an e-mail message is addressed.

Cc (carbon copy) Mail notation that indicates to whom you are sending a copy of the message.

Subject The title of an e-mail message.

Message window The area in an e-mail message where the message body is typed.

Online Actively connected to the Internet.

Attachment A document attached to an e-mail message and sent in its original file format.

Offline Not connected to the Internet.

Notes

Send E-mail from Word

- You can create and send **e-mail** messages directly from Word.

- You can edit and format the messages with Word's editing and formatting features, including the spelling and grammar checkers, and AutoCorrect.

- Messages created in Word are sent in **HTML** format so they can be read by almost all e-mail applications.

- To send e-mail messages you must have the following:
  - A connection to the **Internet** or to an **intranet**.
  - An account with a **mail service provider**.
  - An e-mail program such as **Outlook** or **Outlook Express**.
  - ✓ *To exchange e-mail, the e-mail program must be correctly configured with your e-mail account information.*

- To send an e-mail message you must know the recipient's **e-mail address**.

- E-mail messages have four basic parts:
  - The recipient's address is entered in the **To**: text box.
  - The addresses of other people receiving copies of the message are entered in the **Cc**: text box.
  - A title for the message is entered in the **Subject** text box.
  - The body of the message is typed in the **message window**.

- When you send the message, Word automatically accesses the Internet using your Internet connection settings.

- The Internet connection remains **online** in the background until you disconnect.

Attach a Word Document to an E-mail Message

- You can attach a Word document to an e-mail message.

- The original document remains stored on your computer, and a copy is transmitted as the **attachment**.

- An attached message is sent in its original file format.

- The message recipient can open the attached Word document on his or her computer in Word, or in another application that is compatible with Word.

Send a Word Document as E-mail

- You can send an entire Word document as an e-mail message without attaching it to another message.

- Word adds an Introduction text box to the message header when you send a Word document as e-mail. This text box gives you more room to enter information about the document.

- The original document remains stored on your computer, and a copy is transmitted as e-mail.

- The transmitted document is sent in HTML format so it retains its original formatting when opened in the recipient's e-mail application.

  - ✓ *If you don't want to send or attach an entire document, you can paste a selection from the document into the e-mail message. Simply copy the text from the Word document, make the message window active, and then paste the text into the message.*

E-mail created in Word

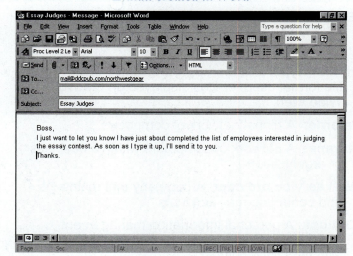

Receive E-mail Messages in Outlook or Outlook Express

■ To receive electronic mail (e-mail) messages with Microsoft Outlook or Outlook Express, you must have a connection to the Internet or to an intranet and an account with a mail service provider.

  ✓ *To exchange e-mail, Outlook or Outlook Express must be correctly configured with your e-mail account information.*

■ When you connect to the Internet, the e-mail application downloads new messages into a folder called *Inbox*.

■ You can read the downloaded messages at any time.

■ You can read downloaded messages **offline**.

■ Messages remain in the Inbox until you move them or delete them.

■ You can save e-mail messages in HTML format to open in Word.

  ✓ *See Exercise 24 for information on opening HTML documents in Word.*

Procedures

Send an E-mail Message from Word

1. Click **E-mail** button .

  ✓ *Use a ScreenTip to identify the button; it looks a lot like the E-mail button used to send a document as e-mail* 📧.

  OR

  a. Click **F**ile .... Alt + F
  b. Click **N**ew .... N
  c. Click **Blank E-mail**

  ✉
  E-mail
  Message icon Message in Task Pane.

2. Fill in **To**: information: type recipient's address

3. Press **Tab** .... Tab

4. Fill in **Cc**: information: type additional recipients' addresses.

5. Press **Tab** .... Tab

6. Fill in **Subject** information: type subject title.

7. Press **Tab** .... Tab

8. Type and format **message text**.

9. Click **S**end button
   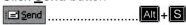 .... Alt + S

  ✓ *Log on to transmit message as necessary.*

  ✓ *If you change your mind about sending the message, simply click the **New E-Mail Message** button 📧 again. Word removes the message heading.*

Attach a Word Document to an E-mail Message

1. Compose an e-mail message.

2. Click **Insert File** button 📎.

3. Select **file to attach**.

  ✓ *Select disk or folder from Look in drop-down list, then double-click folder name to locate file.*

4. Click **Ins**ert .... Alt + S

  ✓ *Word adds a new text box to the message heading called Attach: and enters the document name.*

5. Click **S**end button .... Alt + S

  OR

1. Open or create the document to attach.

2. Click **F**ile .... Alt + F

3. Highlight **Sen**d To .... D

4. Click **M**ail Recipient (as Attachment) .... A

5. Compose e-mail message.

  ✓ *By default, Word enters the document name in the Attach text box.*

6. Click **S**end button 📧 Send .... Alt + S

Send an Existing Word Document as E-mail

1. Open document to send.

2. Click **E-Mail** button 📧.

  OR

  a. Click **F**ile .... Alt + F
  b. Select **Sen**d To .... D
  c. Click **M**ail Recipient ...... M

3. Fill in **To**: information: type recipient's address.

4. Press **Tab** .... Tab

5. Fill in **Cc**: information: type additional recipients' addresses.

6. Press **Tab** .... Tab

7. Fill in **Subject** information: type subject title.

  ✓ *By default, Word enters the document name in the Subject text box. You can edit it if necessary.*

8. Press **Tab** .... Tab

9. Fill in **Introduction** information type introductory text.

10. Click **S**end a Copy
    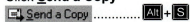 .... Alt + S

  ✓ *If you change your mind about sending the document as e-mail, simply click the **E-Mail** button 📧 again. Word removes the message heading and displays the document.*

Receive E-mail Messages in Outlook or Outlook Express

In Outlook:

1. Click **Start** ..... `Ctrl`+`Esc`
2. Click **P**rograms................... `P`
3. Select **Microsoft Outlook**.
   - ✓ Outlook may automatically connect to your mail service provider and download new messages. Enter account name and password if prompted.
4. Click **Send/Re**_c_**eive** button .... `Alt`+`C`
   - ✓ You may read messages online, or disconnect from Internet to read messages offline.
5. Click **Inbox** folder.
6. With Preview Pane displayed, click message to open and read.
   - ✓ To open the message in its own window, double-click it.

In Outlook Express:

1. Click **Start** ..... `Ctrl`+`Esc`
2. Click **P**rograms................... `P`
3. Select **Outlook Express**.
   - ✓ Outlook Express may automatically connect to your mail service provider and download new messages. Enter account name and password if prompted.
4. Click **Send/Recv** button .
5. Click **Inbox** folder.
6. With Preview Pane displayed, click message to read.
   - ✓ To open the message in its own window, double-click it.

Disconnect Outlook Express from the Internet

1. Click **F**ile.....................`Alt`+`F`
2. Click **W**ork Offline.............`W`
3. Click **Y**es...........................`Y`

Disconnect Outlook from the Internet

1. Click **F**ile.....................`Alt`+`F`
2. Click **Wor**_k_ Offline.............`K`
3. Click **Y**es...........................`Y`

Exercise Directions

- ✓ If you do not have access to the Internet, you may still complete the steps in this exercise. However, when you try to send the e-mail, you will receive an error message.

1. Start Word, if necessary.
2. Compose an e-mail message as follows:
   a. Enter the address:
      northwestgear@ddcpub.com
   b. Enter the subject: **Essay Judges**
   c. Enter the message: **Boss, I just want to let you know I have just about completed the list of employees interested in judging the essay contest. As soon as I type it up, I'll send it to you. Thanks**.
3. Send the message.
   - Enter your user name and password if prompted.
4. Open the document ⊙ **22LIST**.
5. Save the document as **LIST**.
6. Sort the names listed in the document alphabetically in ascending order.
7. Apply a numbered list format to the names.
8. Change paragraph formatting to leave 6 pts. of space before and after each paragraph.
9. Check the spelling and grammar in the document.
10. Save the file and close it.
11. Compose another e-mail message as follows:
    a. Enter the address:
       northwestgear@ddcpub.com
       - ✓ Don't be surprised if Word automatically completes the address as you type it!
    b. Enter the subject: **List of Judges**
    c. Enter the message: **Boss, I've attached the list of potential judges. Let me know if there's anyone you think we should omit. I'll send you a copy of the memo I plan to distribute to the people on the list. Thanks, again.**
12. Attach the document **LIST** to the e-mail message. The message should look similar to the one in Illustration A.
13. Send the message.
14. Open the document ⊙ **22RULES**.
15. Save the document as **RULES**.

16. Prepare to send the **RULES** document as e-mail by creating an e-mail message and entering the following message heading information:

    a. Enter the address: **northwestgear@ddcpub.com**

    b. Enter the subject: **Memo About Judging Rules**

    c. Enter the introduction: **As promised, here's a copy of the memo I plan to send to the employees interested in judging the essay contest. Let me know what you think.**

17. The message should look similar to the one in Illustration B.

18. Send the document.

19. Close all open documents, saving all changes.

20. Launch Outlook Express.

    ✓ *If Outlook Express is not installed on your computer, use Outlook, or any other mail program.*

21. Check for new messages.

    ✓ *The northwestgear@ddcpub.com site is set to automatically return messages to you.*

22. Disconnect from the Internet.

23. Read the new message(s) offline, then exit Outlook Express.

Illustration A

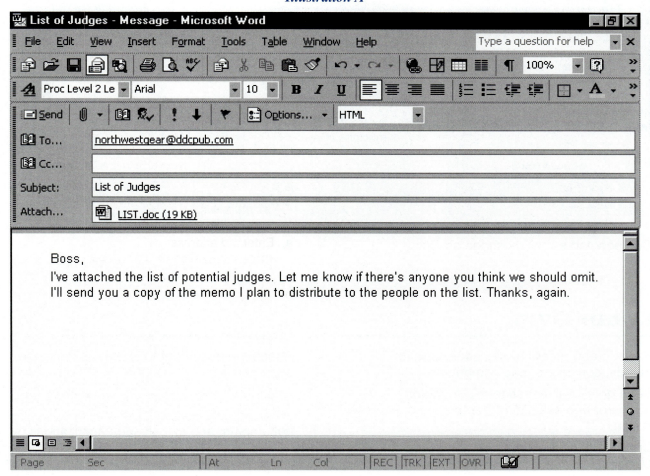

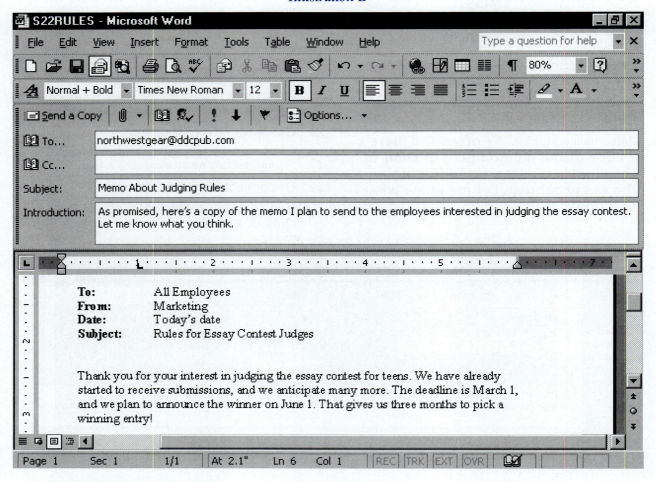

On Your Own

1. Look up and record e-mail addresses for friends, coworkers, and companies.

2. Send an e-mail message to a friend or coworker and ask him or her to send one back to you.

3. Create a new document and save it as **OWD22**.

4. Type a letter to someone else whose e-mail address you have. For example, type a letter to a teacher requesting a missed homework assignment, or to your employer.

5. Attach the document to an e-mail message and send it.

6. Check your e-mail to see if you received a reply.

7. When you are finished, close all open documents, and exit all open applications.

Exercise 23

◆ **Internet Basics** ◆ **Use Internet Features in Word**
◆ **Save a Web Page Locally** ◆ **The Favorites Folder**

On the Job

Log on to the Internet to access information on any subject and to communicate with other people. Use Word's Internet features to make using the Internet easy and familiar.

Your supervisor at Murray Hill marketing is going to meet a client in Cleveland, Ohio. She is interested in visiting the Rock and Roll Hall of Fame while she is there and has asked you to locate some basic information, such as what exhibits will be there, what the hours are, and how much it costs. In this exercise, you will use the Internet to locate the Rock and Roll Hall of Fame site. You will add the site to your Favorites folder, and save the page that has the information you need locally so you can read it offline in Word.

Terms

Modem A hardware device that controls communication connections between computers.

Internet A worldwide network of computers.

World Wide Web A system for finding information on the Internet through the use of linked documents.

Internet Service Provider (ISP) A company that provides access to the Internet for a fee.

Web browser Software that makes it easy to locate and view information stored on the Internet. Common browsers include Internet Explorer and Netscape Navigator.

Shareware Software that can be downloaded from the Internet for free or for a nominal fee.

Web site A set of linked Web pages.

Web page A document stored on the World Wide Web.

Uniform Resource Locator (URL) A Web site's address on the Internet.

Hyperlinks or links Text or graphics in a document set up to provide a direct connection with a destination location or document. When you click a hyperlink, the destination displays.

Notes

Internet Basics

■ Anyone with a computer, a **modem**, communications software, and a standard phone line can access the **Internet** and the **World Wide Web**.

■ For a fee, **Internet Service Providers (ISP)** provide you with an e-mail account, **Web browser** software, and Internet access.

■ Office XP comes with the Internet Explorer Web browser, although your computer may be set up to use a different browser.

■ Some things available via the Internet and the World Wide Web include e-mail communication, product information and support, reference material, shopping, stock quotes, travel arrangements, real estate information, **shareware,** and games.

Use Internet Features in Word

■ If you have a connection to the Internet and Web browser software, you can use Word's Web toolbar to access the Internet.

The Web toolbar

■ Word remains running while you use the Internet, so you can go back and forth from Word to the Internet sites that you have opened on your browser.

■ To locate a **Web site**, **Web page**, or document, you enter its Internet address, or **Uniform Resource Locator (URL)**, in the Address field on the Web toolbar.

■ If you don't know the URL of a site, you can search the Web for the site you want using an Internet search engine.

■ Most sites provide **hyperlinks**, also called **links**, to related pages or sites. Text links are usually a different color and underlined to stand out from the surrounding text. Graphics may also be links.

■ When the mouse pointer rests on a link, the pointer changes to a hand with a pointing finger, and a ScreenTip shows the destination.

■ Word tracks the Web sites you have visited during the current Internet session so you can move back and forth through them.

Save a Web Page Locally

■ You use your browser's Save As command to save a Web page on your computer.

■ Once you save a Web page, you can access it while you are working offline.

■ When you save a Web page you can select from four file types:

• Web page, complete. This saves all of the associated files needed to display the Web page, including graphics in a separate folder in the same location as the HTML file.

• Web Archive. Saves a snapshot of the current Web page in a single file.

• Web Page, HTML only. Saves the information on the Web page but does not save the associated files.

• Text Only. Saves the information in plain text format.

■ If you don't need to save an entire Web page, you can paste selected information into a Word document.

■ You can also use your browser to print a Web page.

The Favorites Folder

■ Use the Favorites folder on your computer to store the URLs of Web sites you like to access frequently.

■ You can also add locally stored files and folders to your Favorites folder.

■ The easiest way to add a URL to the Favorites folder is by using your Web browser.

■ Access the Favorites folder from Word or from Windows when you want to go directly to one of your favorite sites.

The Favorites Folder

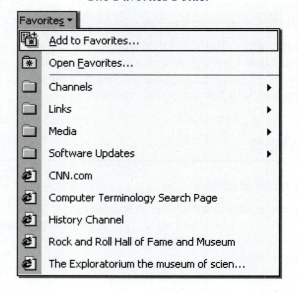

Procedures

Use Internet Features in Word

To display the Web toolbar:

1. Click **View** .... `Alt`+`V`
2. Select **Toolbars** .... `T`
3. Click **Web** .... `↑`, `↓` `Enter`

    OR

    Right-click on any toolbar and select **Web**.

    ✓ *Be sure to select the Web toolbar, and not the Web Tools toolbar.*

To search the Web:

✓ *You must have an Internet connection and an account with an ISP in order to search the Web.*

1. Click **Search the Web** button `Q`.

    OR

    a. Click **Go** `Go ▾` .... `Alt`+`G`
    b. Click **Search the Web** .... `W`

    ✓ *The default search site will vary depending on ISP. Common Search sites include Yahoo!, AltaVista, and Excite.*

2. Type search topic in Search text box.
3. Click **Search** button.

    ✓ *The name on the search button (Find It, Go Get It, etc.) will vary depending on the search site.*

4. Click a hyperlink on the Search Results page to go to that site.

To go to a specific URL:

1. Type URL in Address drop-down list box on Web toolbar
2. Press **Enter** .... `Enter`

    OR

1. Click **Go** `Go ▾` .... `Alt`+`G`
2. Click **Open Hyperlink** `📁` ... `O`

3. Type the URL in the **A**ddress list box.
4. Click **OK** .... `Enter`

To go to a previously visited URL:

1. Click Address list drop-down arrow on Web toolbar.
2. Click URL.

To use a hyperlink:

1. Move mouse pointer to touch link.
2. Click left mouse button.

To display the previously displayed page or document:

• Click **Back** button `Back` on the Browser's toolbar.

    OR

• Click **Back** button `⇦` on Web toolbar

    OR

1. Click **Go** `Go ▾` .... `Alt`+`G` on the Web toolbar.
2. Click **B**ack .... `B`

To display the next Web page:

• Click **Forward** button `Forward` on the Browser's toolbar.

    ✓ *If the Back or Forward button is dimmed on the toolbar, there is no page to go to.*

    OR

• Click **Forward** button `⇨` on Web toolbar

    OR

1. Click **Go** `Go ▾` .... `Alt`+`G` on the Web toolbar.
2. Click **F**orward .... `F`

Save a Web page locally:

1. Open Web page in browser.
2. Click **F**ile .... `Alt`+`F`
3. Click **Save A**s .... `A`
4. Type file name.

5. Select disk or folder.
6. Click **Save as type** .... `T` drop-down arrow.
7. Click desired file type.
8. Click **S**ave .... `Alt`+`S`

The Favorites Folder

To use Internet Explorer to add a site to your Favorites folder:

1. Open Internet site to add to Favorites.
2. Click **F**avorites .... `Alt`+`A`
3. Click **A**dd to Favorites .... `A`
4. Type site name if necessary .... `Alt`+`N`

    ✓ *Your browser automatically enters a site name; you can edit it if you want.*

5. Click **OK** .... `Enter`

To use Word to add a file to your Favorites folder:

1. Open file to add to Favorites.
2. Click **Favorites** button `Favorites ▾` provided ..... `Alt`+`S` on Web toolbar.
3. Click **A**dd to Favorites .... `A`

    ✓ *The Add to Favorites dialog box is similar to the Save As dialog box.*

4. Type a name.
5. Click **A**dd `💾 Add` .... `Enter`

To go to a site from your Favorites folder:

1. Click **Favorites** button `Favorites ▾` .... `Alt`+`S`
2. Click site name.

    ✓ *If necessary, Word starts your Web browser to connect to the Internet and display the site.*

Exercise Directions

✓ Use the Internet simulation provided on the CD that accompanies this book to complete this exercise.

1. Start Word, if necessary.

2. Display the Web toolbar.

3. On the Address line, type the following and press Enter:
   D:/Internet/Word/Ex23/altavista.htm

   ✓ *If you've copied the Internet simulation files to your hard drive or your CD-ROM drive is not D:, substitute the correct drive letter for D.*

4. In the Search text box type **What is the address of the Rock and Roll Hall of Fame**.

   ✓ *The simulation uses the search site AltaVista. If you are using a live Internet connection instead of the simulation, the results of the search will vary depending on the search site used.*

5. Click the **Search** button.

6. Scroll down the search results page, and click the number 1 link.

7. A Welcome page for the Rock and Roll Hall of Fame opens in your browser.

8. Click the **Back** button to return to the search results page.

9. Click the **Forward** button.

10. Click the enter link on the Welcome page.

11. Use your Web browser to add the Rock and Roll Hall of Fame Home Page to your Favorites folder.

12. Scroll down the page and click the explore link under the heading **Calendar**.

13. Click the March link.

14. Scroll through the page to see what events are scheduled in March.

15. Click the visitor information link.

16. Save the Visitor Information page in Web archive format with the name **VISITOR**.

17. Close the Internet simulation by clicking the Close button ⊠.

18. Open the **VISITOR** document in Word. It should look similar to the one in the Illustration.

    ✓ *If the document is not listed in the Open dialog box, change the list to display all file types.*

19. Use Word to add the **VISITOR** document to your Favorites folder.

20. Close the document, saving all changes.

Illustration A

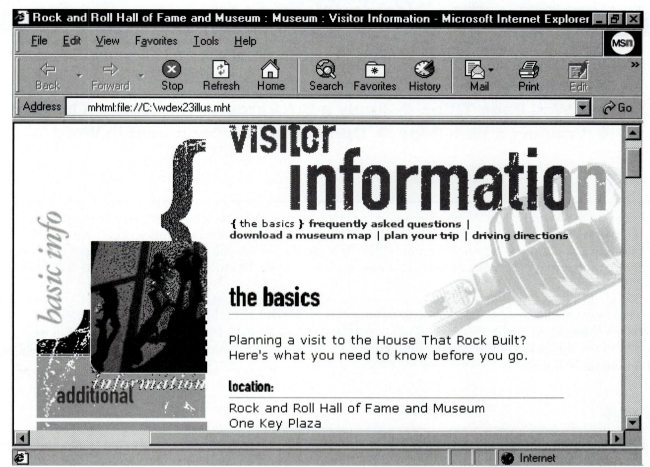

On Your Own

1. If you have access to the Internet, use it to locate a Web site about something that interests you. For example, search for information about your hometown, a sports team that you follow, or a writer, musician, or artist you admire.

2. When you find a site you like, add it to your Favorites folder.

3. Save one of the pages you find as a Web archive document so you can spend more time reading it offline. Save it as **OWD23**.

4. Disconnect from the Internet.

5. In Word, open **OWD23** or open ✪ **23WEB**.

6. Read the document in Word.

7. Close the document and exit Word.

Exercise 24

Skills Covered:

◆ **Create a Web Page Document in Word** ◆ **Use Web Layout View**
◆ **Use Web Page Titles** ◆ **Apply a Background** ◆ **Apply a Theme**
◆ **Preview a Web Page** ◆ **Open an HTML Document in Word**

On the Job

Documents on the World Wide Web are created in HTML format. With Word, you can easily save documents in HTML format. You can save existing documents in HTML format, and you can use all of Word's features and tools to edit and format HTML documents. When you complete a document in HTML format, you can store it on a **Web server**, so everyone with access to the Web can access the document.

You have been asked to post the in-house training course schedule for Murray Hill Marketing on the company's intranet. In this exercise, you will open the existing training course document, format it with color, a theme, and a background, and then save it as a Web page. You will view it in your browser, close it, and then open it again to make some additional changes. Finally, you will print it.

Terms

Web server A computer connected to the Internet used to store Web page documents.

HTML Hypertext Markup Language. It is the file format used for files accessed on the World Wide Web.

htm An extension given to files saved in HTML format.

Background The color, pattern, or fill displayed on the page behind data in a document.

Fill effect A texture, shading, picture, or pattern used as a background.

Theme A unified set of design elements and colors that can be applied to a document.

Web bullets Graphics files inserted as bullet markers.

Graphics lines Graphics files inserted as horizontal rules or dividers.

Graphics object A picture, chart, shape, or other element that can be inserted into a Word document.

Clip art Picture files that can be inserted into a document.

Notes

Create a Web Page Document in Word

- You can save an existing Word document in **HTML** format. Word preserves the formatting in the new document.

- You can also create a new blank Web page document.

- When you save a Web page document, Word abbreviates the file extension to **htm**.

■ Word automatically creates a folder to store graphics files such as bullets, lines, and pictures that are associated with the Web page. The folder has the same name as the file, followed by an underscore and the word *files*, like this: *Filename_files*

✓ *Use caution when moving or renaming the graphics files or the folder they are stored in. The graphics files are linked to the HTML document; if they are not available, the page will display without graphics elements.*

The Save As Web Page dialog box

Use Web Layout View

■ Web Layout view displays documents in Word as they will look on the Web.

■ Word automatically switches to Web Layout view when you save a document as a Web page, when you create a new Web page document, or when you open an existing Web page document.

■ You can also switch to Web Layout view using the View menu or the View buttons.

■ Web Layout view lets you edit a document for viewing on screen, instead of for printing on a page.

■ Features of Web Layout view include:

• Wordwrapping to fit the window, not a page.

• Graphics positioned as they would be in a Web browser.

• Backgrounds (if there are any) displayed as they would be in a browser.

Use Web Page Titles

■ Web page titles are displayed in the Web browser title bar.

■ By default, Word uses the file name or the first line of document text as the Web page title.

■ You can set or change the page title name from the Save As dialog box.

Apply a Background

■ By default, Word documents—including HTML documents—have a plain white **background**.

■ Add visual interest or create an effect by applying a color, pattern, **fill effect,** or picture to a document background.

■ You should coordinate backgrounds for pages in a Web site to establish continuity.

Apply a Theme

■ Word comes with built-in **themes** you can use to format any Word document.

■ Each theme includes a background, font formatting, and graphics elements such as **Web bullets** and **graphics lines**.

■ You can select a theme to apply consistent formatting to a document.

■ Themes can be used with any Word document, but they are particularly useful for formatting Web pages.

Preview a Web Page

■ Use Web Page Preview to see how a Word document will look in a Web browser.

■ You can display regular Word documents or HTML documents in Web Page Preview.

■ When you preview a Web page document, Word opens the document in your default browser.

■ You cannot edit a document in Web Page Preview.

Open an HTML Document in Word

■ You open an HTML document in Word the same way you open a regular Word document.

■ The document displays in Web Layout view.

■ When you save the document, it remains in HTML format.

✓ *By default, if you try to open an HTML document from Windows, the document displays in your Web browser, not in Word.*

Procedures

Save a Document as a Web Page

1. Open the document.
2. Click **File** .... Alt + F
3. Click **Save as Web Page** .... G
4. Type file name.
   - ✓ *If necessary, open the folder, disk, or server where the file will be stored.*
5. Click **Save**
    .... Alt + S

Create a New Blank Web Page Document

1. Click **File** .... Alt + F
2. Click **New** .... N
3. Click **Blank Web Page** in New Document Task Pane.
4. Click **File** .... Alt + F
5. Click **Save as** .... A
6. Type file name.
   - ✓ *If necessary, open the folder, disk, or server where the file will be stored.*
7. Click **Save**
   Save .... Alt + S

Change to Web Layout View

- Open Web page document in Word.

OR

- Click **Web Layout View** button
  .

OR

1. Click **View** .... Alt + V
2. Click **Web Layout** .... W

Set a Web Page Title to a Saved Web Page

1. Click **File** .... Alt + F
2. Click **Save As** .... A
3. Click **Change Title** button
   Change Title... .... Alt + C
4. Type new title.
5. Click **OK**
6. Click **Save**
   Save .... Alt + S

Apply a Background

1. Open file to format.
2. Click **Format** .... Alt + O
3. Click **Background** .... K
4. Click desired color.

OR

a. Click **Fill Effects** .... F
b. Click desired
   page tab .... Ctrl + Tab
c. Select desired **effect**.
d. Click **OK** .... Enter

Apply a Theme

1. Open file to format.
2. Click **Format** .... Alt + O
3. Click **Theme** .... H
4. Select desired
   Theme .... Alt + T, ↑, ↓
5. Click **OK** .... Enter
   - ✓ *Not all themes are installed automatically; if a theme you select is not installed, use the Setup disk to install it, or select a different theme.*

Use Web Page Preview

1. Click **File** .... Alt + F
2. Click **Web Page Preview** .... B

Close Web Page Preview

1. Click **File** .... Alt + F
2. Click **Close** C

Open an HTML Document in Word

1. Click **File** .... Alt + F
2. Click **Open** .... O
3. Click **file name**.
   - ✓ *If necessary, open the folder or disk where the file is stored.*
4. Click **Open** .... Alt + O

Exercise Directions

1. Start Word, if necessary.
2. Open ⌨**COURSE** or open 💿**24COURSE**.
3. Save the file as **COURSE**.
4. Use the following steps to format the document as shown in the illustration.
5. Apply the Pixel Theme to the document.
6. Highlight each of the three months/course/course descriptions by using a different font color. Change the **January** information to Blue, the **February** information to Red, and the **March** information to Green.
7. Change the month names to bullet items.
8. Apply the Newsprint Texture fill effect background to the document.
9. Save the document as a Web page with the name **COURSE2** and the Web page title MHM Training Schedule.
10. Display it in Web Page Preview.
11. Close Web Page Preview.
12. Close the file, saving all changes.
13. Open the **COURSE2** document in Word.
14. Change the color of the font for the first three lines to Plum.
15. Change the color of the font for the last line in the document to Plum.
16. Display the document in Web Page Preview again. It should look similar to the one in the illustration.
17. Close Web Page Preview.
18. Check the spelling and grammar in the document.
19. Print the document.
20. Close the file, saving all changes.

On Your Own

1. Create a new document in Word.
2. Save the file as **OWD24**.
3. Use this document to create your own personal Web page. You should include your name and other information about yourself—what you like to do, who your favorite musicians and sports teams are, where you go to school or where you work.
4. Add some other information you think will be interesting: favorite sayings, upcoming events in your life, or fun things your family or friends plan to do.
5. Save the document as a Web page in HTML format with the name **OWD24-2**.
6. Applying formatting to improve the appearance of your Web page. For example, change the font formatting, apply a theme or background, create lists, and so on.
7. View the document in Web Layout view.
8. Use Web Page Preview to look at your new Web page in your browser software.
9. Close Web Page Preview.
10. Close the document and exit Word.

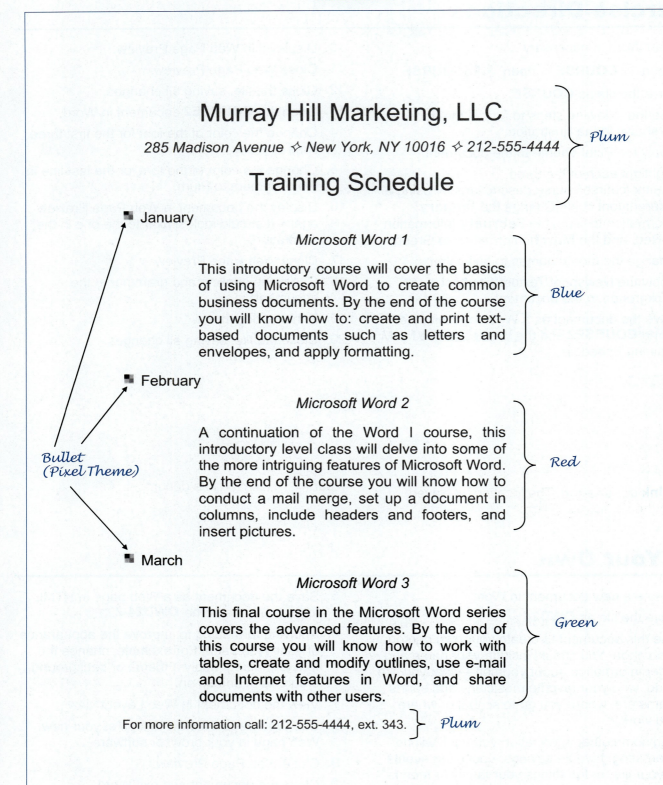

Murray Hill Marketing, LLC

285 Madison Avenue ✧ New York, NY 10016 ✧ 212-555-4444

Training Schedule

Plum

■ January

Microsoft Word 1

This introductory course will cover the basics of using Microsoft Word to create common business documents. By the end of the course you will know how to: create and print text-based documents such as letters and envelopes, and apply formatting.

Blue

■ February

Microsoft Word 2

A continuation of the Word I course, this introductory level class will delve into some of the more intriguing features of Microsoft Word. By the end of the course you will know how to conduct a mail merge, set up a document in columns, include headers and footers, and insert pictures.

Red

Bullet (Pixel Theme)

■ March

Microsoft Word 3

This final course in the Microsoft Word series covers the advanced features. By the end of this course you will know how to work with tables, create and modify outlines, use e-mail and Internet features in Word, and share documents with other users.

Green

For more information call: 212-555-4444, ext. 343.　**Plum**

Exercise 25

◆ **Create Hyperlinks**

On the Job

Create a hyperlink to connect related documents to each other, to connect a Word document to a Web site, or to connect one location in a document to another location in the same document. For example, create hyperlinks from a report topic to an Internet site where more information can be found. Hyperlinks let you expand the boundaries among documents and among computers because, in effect, you can link to information stored anywhere on the Internet.

You have created a Web page document listing training courses for Murray Hill Marketing. In this exercise, you will insert hyperlinks to help readers navigate through the Web page. You will also link the Web page to a Word document describing what employees should expect from in-house training, and to a Web site that provides more information about Microsoft Office products.

Terms

Hyperlink Text or graphics linked to a destination file or location. Click the link to jump to the destination.

Hypertext Text formatted as a hyperlink.

Hyperlink destination The location displayed when the hyperlink is clicked.

Hyperlink source The document where the hyperlink is inserted.

Bookmark A nonprinting character that you insert and name so that you can quickly find a particular location in a document.

Notes

Create Hyperlinks

- **Hyperlinks** can be used to link locations within a single document, to link two documents, or to link a document to an e-mail address.

- Hyperlinks can be created in any Word document, including HTML files.

- A **hyperlink destination** does not have to be in the same file format as the **hyperlink source** document. For example, you can link a Word document file to an HTML file or to an Excel file, and the like.

- The hyperlink destination can be a file stored on your computer, on your company intranet, or a site on the Internet.

- When you click a hyperlink to an e-mail address, Word starts your e-mail program and displays a new e-mail message. The address and subject are filled in with the hyperlink information.

- You can create a hyperlink within a document for moving to the top of the document, to a specific heading, or to a **bookmark**.

The Insert Hyperlink dialog box

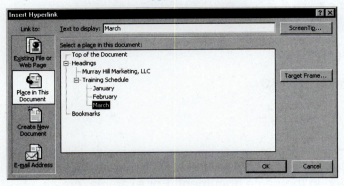

- By default, in Word documents (including those saved in HTML) you must press Ctrl and click the hyperlink in order to go to the hyperlink destination.
- You can change the setting so that you don't have to press Ctrl.
- You can edit and format hyperlink text the same way you edit and format regular text.
  - ✓ *If you change the setting so that you don't have to press Ctrl to follow a hyperlink, you must select the hyperlink before you can edit it or format it.*
- You can change a hyperlink destination.
- You can remove a hyperlink completely.

Procedures

Insert a Hyperlink within a Document

1. Position insertion point where you want to insert hyperlink.
   OR
   Select text to change to a hyperlink.
2. Click **Insert Hyperlink** button 🔗.
   OR
   a. Click **Insert** .... `Alt`+`I`
   b. Click **Hyperlink**.............. `I`
3. Click **Place in this document** in Link to bar.......................... `Alt`+`A`
4. In the **Select a place in this document list**, click hyperlink destination............ `Alt`+`C`, `↓`
   - ✓ *If necessary click the expand symbol ＋ to expand the list to show additional headings and/or bookmarks.*
5. Click **OK**........................... `Enter`
   - ✓ *If existing text is not selected, Word uses the destination name as the hyperlink text.*

Insert a Hyperlink to a Different Document

1. Position insertion point where you want to insert hyperlink.
   OR
   Select text to change to a hyperlink.
2. Click **Insert Hyperlink** button 🔗.
   OR
   a. Click **Insert**............ `Alt`+`I`
   b. Click **Hyperlink**.............. `I`
3. Click **Existing File or Web Page** in the Link to bar.................... `Alt`+`X`
4. In the **Address** text box, type the hyperlink destination file name .. `Alt`+`E`, *type file name*
   - ✓ *Word automatically completes the file name as you type based on recently used file names; stop typing to accept the entry or keep typing to enter the name you want.*
   OR
   a. Click **Current Folder** in the Look in bar .... `Alt`+`U` to display a list of files stored in the current folder
   b. Click the file name in the list of files.

OR
a. Click **Browsed Pages** to display a list of recently viewed Web pages.....................`Alt`+`B`
b. Locate and click file name.
c. Click **OK** .... `Enter`

OR
a. Click **Recent Files**.. `Alt`+`C` to display a list of recently used files.
b. Click the file name in the list of files.
5. Edit **Text to display**............ `Alt`+`T`
   - ✓ *Word displays this text as the hyperlink in the document.*
6. Click **OK**.......................... `Enter`

Insert a Hyperlink to a Web Page

1. Position insertion point where you want to insert the hyperlink.
   OR
   Select text to change to a hyperlink.
2. Click **Insert Hyperlink** button 🔗.
   OR
   a. Click **Insert**............. `Alt`+`I`
   b. Click **Hyperlink** .... `I`

3. Click **Existing File or Web Page** in Link to bar.......[Alt]+[X]

4. In the **Address** text box, type the hyperlink destination URL.............[Alt]+[E], *type URL*

   ✓ *Word automatically completes the URL as you type based on other URLs you have typed in the past. Stop typing to accept the entry, or keep typing to enter the URL you want.*

   OR

   a. Click **Browsed Pages** ....[Alt]+[B] to display a list of Web pages you have recently accessed.

   b. Click the URL or site name you want in the list of files.

5. Edit **Text to display**.........................[Alt]+[T]

   ✓ *Type the text you want displayed for the hyperlink. Word displays this text as the hyperlink.*

6. Click **OK**...........................[Enter]

Insert a Hyperlink to an E-Mail Address

1. Position insertion point where you want to insert the hyperlink.
   OR
   Select text to change to a hyperlink.

2. Click **Insert Hyperlink** button [icon].
   OR
   a. Click **Insert** ....[Alt]+[I]
   b. Click **Hyperlink**..............[I]

3. Click **E-mail Address** in Link to in bar...........[Alt]+[M]

4. In the **E-mail address** text box, type the e-mail address ....[Alt]+[E], *type address*

   ✓ *This address will be inserted in the to line of the e-mail message.*

   OR

   a. Click the address in the **Recently** used e-mail addresses list.......[Alt]+[C], [↑↓], [Enter]

   b. In the **Subject** text box, type the text you want displayed in the e-mail Subject text box. ....[Alt]+[U], *type text*

5. Click **OK**...........................[Enter]

Remove a Hyperlink

1. Right-click hyperlink text.

2. Click **Remove Hyperlink** ....[R]

   ✓ *This removes hyperlink, not the text.*

Change a Hyperlink Destination

1. Right-click hyperlink text.

2. Click **Edit Hyperlink**...........[H]

3. Select new destination.

4. Click **OK** ....[Enter]

Set Word to Follow Hyperlink On Click

1. Click **Tools** ....[Alt]+[T]

2. Click **Options** ....[O]

3. Click **Edit** tab ....[Ctrl]+[Tab]

4. Deselect **Use CTRL+Click to follow hyperlink** check box ....[H]

5. Click **OK** ....[Enter]

Select a Hyperlink

1. Right-click hyperlink text.

2. Click **Select Hyperlink**........[S]

Exercise Directions

✓ *Use the Internet simulation provided on the CD that accompanies this book to complete this exercise.*

1. Start Word, if necessary.

2. Open ⌨**TRAIN** or open 💿**25TRAIN**.

3. Save the file as **TRAIN**.

4. Insert a new line at the top of the document and clear all formatting from it.

5. Type the text **Return**, and then press **Enter**.

6. Display the document in Print Preview.

7. If the document extends on to two pages, use the Shrink to Fit command to fit it on one page.

8. Close Print Preview, and then close the document, saving all changes.

9. Open the file ⌨**COURSE2** or open 💿**25COURSE**.

   ✓ *Remember, this is an HTML document. If you try to open it from Windows, it will open in your browser, not in Word.*

10. Save the file as **COURSE3**.

11. Edit and format the document using the following steps.

    ✓ *Refer to Illustration A to see the completed document.*

12. Position the insertion point at the end of the heading **Training Schedule** and press **Enter**.

13. Type **January** and press **Enter**.

14. Type **February** and press **Enter**.

15. Type **March** and press **Enter** twice.

16. Type the following: **Questions?** and press **Enter** twice.

17. Type **Click here to read about in-house training** and press **Enter**.

18. Type **Click here to learn more about Microsoft Office**.

19. Insert a hyperlink from the text **January** that you typed in step 13 to the heading **January**.

20. Insert a hyperlink from the text **February** that you typed in step 14 to the heading **February**.

21. Insert a hyperlink from the text **March** that you typed in step 15 to the heading **March**.

22. At the end of each course description paragraph, press **Enter** and type **Back to Top**.

23. Insert hyperlinks from each occurrence of **Back to Top** to the top of the document.

24. Insert a hyperlink from the text you typed in step 17 to the **TRAIN** document.

25. Insert a hyperlink from the text you typed in step 18 to the URL **D:/Internet/Word/Ex25/microsoft.htm**

    ✓ *If you've copied the Internet simulation files to your hard drive or your CD-ROM drive is not D:, substitute the correct drive letter for D.*

    ✓ *If you have an Internet connection, point the hyperlink to the URL www.microsoft.com/office/ instead.*

26. Increase the font size of all hyperlink text to 16 points.

27. Test the hyperlinks to navigate through the **COURSE3** document.

    ✓ *Use the hyperlinks to go to each month heading, then to return to the top of the document.*

28. Test the hyperlink to go to the **TRAIN** document.

29. Insert a hyperlink from the text **Return** at the top of the **TRAIN** document, back to the **COURSE3** document.

30. Test the hyperlink to return to the **COURSE3** document.

31. Test the hyperlink to go to the Microsoft Office Web site.

    ✓ *You may be prompted to sign on to your ISP.*

32. Click the Back button on your browser's toolbar to return to the **COURSE3** document.

33. Disconnect from the Internet, if necessary.

34. Close all open documents, saving all changes.

Murray Hill Marketing, LLC

285 Madison Avenue ✧ New York, NY 10016 ✧ 212-555-4444

Training Schedule

<u>January</u> ——— *Hyperlink to heading January*
<u>February</u> ——— *Hyperlink to heading February*
<u>March</u> ——— *Hyperlink to heading March*

Questions?

<u>Click here to read about in-house training.</u> ——— *Hyperlink to TRAIN.DOC*
<u>Click here to learn more about Microsoft Office.</u>

Hyperlink to www.microsoft.com\office

■ January

Microsoft Word 1

This introductory course will cover the basics of using Microsoft Word to create common business documents. By the end of the course you will know how to: create and print text-based documents such as letters and envelopes, and apply formatting.

<u>Back to top.</u> ——— *Hyperlink to top of document*

■ February

Microsoft Word 2

A continuation of the Word I course, this introductory level class will delve into some of the more intriguing features of Microsoft Word. By the end of the course you will know how to conduct a mail merge, set up a document in columns, include headers and footers, and insert pictures.

Back to Top ——————— *Hyperlink to top of document*

■ March

Microsoft Word 3

This final course in the Microsoft Word series covers the advanced features. By the end of this course you will know how to work with tables, create and modify outlines, use e-mail and Internet features in Word, and share documents with other users.

Back to Top ——————— *Hyperlink to top of document*

For more information call: 212-555-4444, ext. 343.

On Your Own

1. Open the document **OWD20**, your personal Web page, or open ☉ **25WEB**.

2. Save the file as **OWD25**.

3. Think of ways you can link the Web page to documents you have created in the On Your Own sections of previous exercises. For example, you could link the Web page to the list of things you'd like to accomplish, to your resume, or to the announcement of the upcoming event.

4. Open the document **OWD19**, your resume, or open ☉ **25RESUME**.

5. Save the file as **OWD25-2**.

6. Create a hyperlink from **OWD25** to **OWD25-2**. You can create new hyperlink text, or use text that is already entered in the document.

7. Create a link back to the Web page from the resume.

8. Open the document **OWD17**, your list of personal goals, or open ☉ **25GOALS.**

9. Save the file as **OWD25-3**.

10. Create a hyperlink from **OWD25** to **OWD25-3**. Again, you can create new hyperlink text, or use text that is already entered in the document.

11. Create a link back to the Web page from the list of goals.

12. If you have access to the Internet, try linking your Web page to a Web site that you like.

13. Test the links.

14. Save your changes to all documents, then close the documents.

Exercise 26

◆ Critical Thinking

You have been hired to develop a Web site for Coastline Gourmet Importers. In this exercise, you will use e-mail to communicate with your supervisor. You will also browse the Internet looking at gourmet food sites, and save a Web page that you like. You will create and format a Web page document, and you will insert hyperlinks linking the Web page to a regular Word document.

Exercise Directions

1. Start Word, if necessary.

2. Create a new e-mail message with the following header information:
   To: **coastlinegourmet@ddcpub.com**
   Subject: **Company Web page**
   Message text: **Dear Mr. Boghosian, I am delighted that you asked me to design the company Web site. Look for future e-mail including sample page designs. Thanks**.

3. Send the message.

4. Start the browser of your choice.
   ✓ *If you don't have Internet access, choose to work offline.*

5. On the address line of your browser, type the following and press Enter:
   D:/Internet/Word/Ex26/harryanddavid.htm
   ✓ *If necessary, substitute the correct drive letter for D.*

6. Go back to Word.

7. Display the Web toolbar.

8. On the Address line, type the following and press Enter:
   D:/Internet/Word/Ex26/cardullos.htm

9. Go back to Word.

10. On the Address line, type the following and press Enter:
    D:/Internet/Word/Ex26/altavista.htm

11. Type **gourmet food** in the search text box and click the **Search** button.

12. Scroll down and click the link to GourmetUSA.

   ✓ *The simulation uses the Altavista search engine. If you are using a different search engine, the results may vary. The URL is www.freshcaviar.com.*

13. Save the Web page in Web archive format with the name **GOURMET**.

14. Close Internet Explorer.

15. Create a new e-mail message with the following header information:
    To: **coastlinegourmet@ddcpub.com**
    Subject: **Company Web page**
    Message text: **Dear Mr. Boghosian, I've been browsing the Web looking at gourmet food site home pages. What do you think of the attached page? Thanks**.

16. Attach the **GOURMET** file to the message and send it.

17. Create a new blank Web page document in Word.

18. Save the file as **WEBCOAST**, with the page title **COASTLINE GOURMET HOME PAGE**.

19. Apply the Edge theme to the document.

20. Type and format the document shown in Illustration A.

21. Check the spelling and grammar in the document.

22. Display the file in Web Page Preview. It should look similar to the one in the illustration.

23. Open the file ⊛ **26SPECIALS**.

24. Save the file as **SPECIALS**.

25. At the beginning of the line of text beginning **Coastline Importers is running**… type **Return to Home Page**, and then press **Enter** twice.

26. Insert a hyperlink from the text **Return to Home Page** to the **WEBCOAST** document.

27. At the end of the document, following the phone number, type the following sentence. **Or, click here to request information via e-mail**.

28. Select the new sentence and insert a hyperlink to *coastlinegourmet@ddcpub.com,* with the subject **Info about special programs**.

29. Test the *Return to Home Page* hyperlink.

30. Insert a hyperlink from the text **Special Programs** to the **SPECIALS** document.

31. Test the hyperlink.

32. Close the **SPECIALS** document, saving all changes.

33. Send a copy of the **WEBCOAST** document as an e-mail using the following message header information:

    To: **coastlinegourmet@ddcpub.com**

    Subject: Company Web page

    Introduction: **Here's my first stab at a Home Page. Click the link to see a document stored on the company intranet**.

34. Send the document.

35. Disconnect from the Internet, if necessary.

36. Close the **WEBCOAST** document, saving all changes.

Illustration A

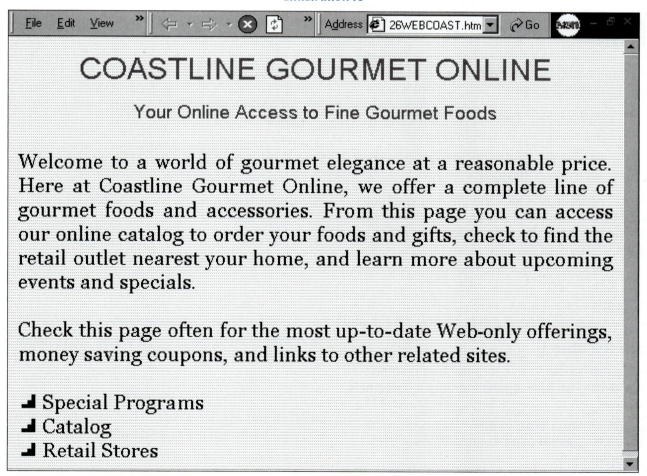

Exercise 27

Skills Covered:

◆ **Create a Table** ◆ **Enter Data in a Table** ◆ **Select in a Table**
◆ **Change Table Structure** ◆ **Format a Table**

On the Job

Create tables to organize data into columns and rows. Any information that needs to be presented in side-by-side columns can be set up in a table. For example, a price list, an invoice, and a resume are all types of documents for which you should use a table. The table format lets you align information side by side and across the page so the information is easy to read.

Murray Hill Marketing is offering the staff training courses. In this exercise, you will create a memo that includes a list of courses being offered. You will set up the course list in a table.

Terms

Table A grid comprised of horizontal rows and vertical columns into which you can enter data.

Column A vertical series of cells in a table.

Row A horizontal series of cells in a table.

Column markers Markers on the horizontal ruler that indicate column dividers.

Dividers The lines that indicate the edges of cells in a table. Dividers do not print, although they are indicated on-screen by either gridlines or borders.

Border A line drawn around the edges of an element, such as a table or a table cell. Borders can also be drawn around paragraphs and pages.

Cell The rectangular area at the intersection of a column and a row in a table, into which you enter data or graphics.

Gridlines Nonprinting lines that can be displayed around cells in a table.

End of row/cell marks Nonprinting characters used to mark the end of a cell or a row in a table.

Notes

Create a Table

- **Tables** are easier to use than tabbed columns when setting up and organizing data in **columns** and **rows**.
- You can create a table in any Word document; they are frequently used to align data on Web page documents.
- You select the number of columns and rows you want in the table.
- Word creates the table at the insertion point location.
- By default, Word sizes the columns equally across the width of the page.
- **Column markers** on the horizontal ruler show the location of the right **divider** of each column.
- By default, Word places a ½-pt. **border** around all **cells** in a table.

A table with four columns and four rows

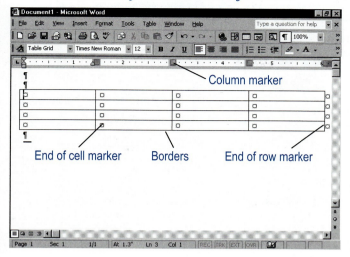

- Tables have three unique nonprinting elements:
  - **Gridlines**
  - **End of cell markers**
  - **End of row markers**

Enter Data in a Table

- You enter data in the cells of a table.
- Row height increases automatically to accommodate as much data as you type.
- Column width does not change automatically. Text wraps at the right margin of a cell the same way it wraps at the right margin of a page.
- To move from cell to cell you press Tab, or click in another cell with the mouse.
- When you press Enter in a cell, Word starts a new paragraph within the cell.
- You can edit and format text within a cell the same way you do outside a table.

Select in a Table

- As with other Word features, you must select table components before you can affect them with commands.
- You select text within a cell using the standard selection commands.
- You can select one or more columns, one or more rows, one or more cells, or the entire table.
- Selected table components appear highlighted.

Change Table Structure

- Change a table's structure by inserting and deleting columns, rows, or cells.
- You can insert components anywhere in a table.
- **You** can delete any component.
  - ✓ *Data entered in a deleted column or row is deleted as well.*
- You choose which way to shift existing cells when cells are inserted or deleted.

Format a Table

- You can format text within a table using standard Word formatting techniques. For example, use font formatting, alignments, spacing, indents, and tabs to enhance text in a table.
- You can apply formatting to selected text, or to selected cells, columns, or rows.
- Use Table AutoFormat to quickly apply formatting effects to an existing table.
- AutoFormat styles include border lines, shading, color, fonts, and other formatting.

Table AutoFormat dialog box

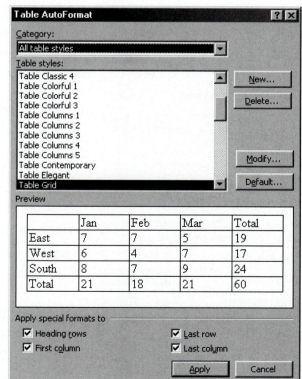

- AutoFormat overrides existing formatting. Therefore, you should apply AutoFormat first, then apply additional formatting as needed.

Procedures

Create a Table

To use the toolbar button:

1. Position insertion point.
2. Click **Insert Table** button ▦.
3. Drag the mouse pointer across the grid to select desired number of columns and rows.
4. Release the mouse button.

To use menu commands:

1. Position the insertion point.
2. Click **Table** .... `Alt`+`A`
3. Select **Insert** .... `I`
4. Click **Table** .... `T`
5. Type **number of columns** .... `Alt`+`C`
6. Press **Tab** .... `Tab`
7. Type **number of rows** .... `Alt`+`R`
8. Click **OK** .... `Enter`

To show/hide gridlines:

1. Click **Table** .... `Alt`+`A`
2. Click **Show Gridlines** .... `G`

   OR

   Click **Hide Gridlines** .... `G`

   ✓ *The default border is not hidden when you select to hide gridlines.*

To move the insertion point in a table:

With the mouse

- Click mouse pointer where you want to position insertion point.

With the keyboard

- One cell left .... `Shift`+`Tab`
- One cell right .... `Tab`
- One cell up .... ↑
- One cell down .... ↓
- First cell in column ..... `Alt`+`Page Up`
- Last cell in column ...... `Alt`+`Page Down`
- First cell in row .... `Alt`+`Home`
- Last cell in row .... `Alt`+`End`

Enter Data in a Table

1. Click in desired cell.
2. Type data.
3. Press **Tab** .... `Tab`
4. Type data in next cell.
5. Repeat until all data is entered.

Select in a Table

1. Position insertion point within table component to select.

   ✓ *For example, click in cell if selecting cell; click anywhere in row if selecting row, etc.*

2. Click **Table** .... `Alt`+`A`
3. Select **Select** .... `C`
4. Click one of the following:
   - **Table** .... `T`
   - **Column** .... `C`
   - **Row** .... `R`
   - **Cell** .... `E`

Select Adjacent Components

1. Select first component.
2. Press and hold **Shift** .... `Shift`
3. Click in last component to select.

   ✓ *This method enables you to select adjacent columns, adjacent rows, or adjacent cells.*

Change Table Structure

Insert columns or rows:

1. Position insertion point within table.

   ✓ *To insert more than one component, select as many as you want to insert. For example, to insert two columns, select two columns.*

2. Click **Table** .... `Alt`+`A`
3. Click **Insert** .... `I`
4. Click one of the following:
   - **Columns to the Left** ..... `L`
   - **Columns to the Right** ... `R`
   - **Rows Above** .... `A`
   - **Rows Below** .... `B`
   - **Cells** .... `E`

   ✓ *Select option for shifting existing cells to make room for new cells, then click OK.*

Delete entire table, columns, rows, or cells:

1. Select or click in the row or column to delete.
2. Click **Table** .... `Alt`+`A`
3. Select **Delete** .... `D`
4. Click one of the following:
   - **Table** .... `T`
   - **Columns** .... `C`
   - **Rows** .... `R`
   - **Cells** .... `E`

   ✓ *Select option for shifting existing cells to fill in deleted cell area, then click OK.*

Apply AutoFormat

1. Click **Table** .... `Alt`+`A`
2. Click **Table AutoFormat** ..... `F`
3. Select table style .. `Alt`+`T`, ↓
4. Click **Apply** ... `Alt`+`A` or `Enter`

Format Text in a Table

1. Select text or cell(s) to format.
2. Apply formatting as with regular document text.

Exercise Directions

1. Start Word, if necessary.
2. Create a new document.
3. Save the file as **SCHEDULE**.
4. Move the insertion point to the last line of the document.
5. Type the document shown in Illustration A.
   - Create the table as follows:
   a. Insert a table with three columns and four rows.
   b. Enter the data as shown.
      ✓ To enter an en dash between the times, simply type a space, a hyphen, and a space. By default, AutoFormat automatically replaces the hyphen and spaces with an en dash after the second number is typed.
6. Select the last two rows.
7. Insert two new rows above the selected rows.
8. Enter the following data in the new rows:

   Advanced Word Conference
   Room A   8:30 – 11:45

   Excel for Beginners Conference
   Room B   1:30 – 3:30

9. Insert a new column to the left of the Time Column.

10. Enter the following data in the new column:
    Days
    Tuesday, Thursday
    Monday, Wednesday
    Tuesday, Wednesday
    Monday, Thursday
    Friday
11. Delete the row for the Beginner's Word course.
12. Apply the Table Contemporary AutoFormat to the table.
13. Apply italics to all of the course names.
    ✓ Select the text, then apply the formatting.
14. Check the spelling and grammar in the document.
15. Preview the document. It should look similar to the one in Illustration B.
16. Save the changes and print the document
17. Close the document and exit Word.

On Your Own

1. Think of documents that would benefit from table formatting. Some examples include a weekly schedule, meeting agenda, travel itinerary, sales report, telephone/address list, and roster.
2. Create a new document in Word.
3. Save the file as **OWD27**.
4. Use a table to set up the document as a telephone list. The list could include friends, family members, or members of a club or organization to which you belong.
5. Use at least three columns—one for the first name, one for the last name and one for the telephone number. You may use more columns if you want to include mailing addresses, e-mail addresses, cell phone numbers, or other information.
6. Include at least eight names in the list.
7. Apply an AutoFormat to the table. If you are not satisfied with the results, try a different AutoFormat.
8. Check the spelling and grammar in the document, then print it.
9. Close the document, saving all changes.

MEMO

To: All Employees
From: Your Name
Date: Today's date
Subject: Training Schedule

Here is the schedule of courses being offered next week. If you haven't signed up, see me immediately.

Insert column

Course Name	Location	Time
Word for Beginners	Conference Room A	8:30 – 11:45
Advanced Excel	Conference Room B	8:30 – 11:45
Introduction to the Internet	Media Lab	1:30 – 3:30

Insert two new rows

Illustration B

MEMO

To: All Employees
From: Your Name
Date: Today's date
Subject: Training Schedule

Here is the schedule of courses being offered next week. If you haven't signed up, see me immediately.

Course Name	Location	Days	Time
Advanced Word	Conference Room A	Monday, Wednesday	8:30 – 11:45
Excel for Beginners	Conference Room B	Tuesday, Wednesday	1:30 – 3:30
Advanced Excel	Conference Room B	Monday, Thursday	8:30 – 11:45
Introduction to the Internet	Media Lab	Friday	1:30 – 3:30

On the Job

Use alignment options and tabs to make tables easy to read. Numbers are usually aligned flush right in a cell, while text can be flush left, centered, justified, or rotated to appear vertical. You can vertically align data in a cell as well. Decimal tabs are especially useful in tables for aligning dollar values. Other ways to improve the appearance of a table include aligning the table horizontally on the page, and adjusting column width and row height.

Northwest Gear, Inc. is offering employees special savings on selected items from its inventory. In this exercise, you will create a memo that includes information about the available items. You will use alignment options to set up the data in the table. You will also set row heights and column widths, and you will align the table horizontally on the page.

Terms

Column width The width of a column in a table, measured in inches.

Row height The height of a row in a table, measured in inches.

Notes

Set Alignments within Table Cells

- You can set horizontal alignment within a cell the same way you set alignment in a document by using paragraph formatting and tabs.

- In a table, numbers are usually right aligned, and text is either left aligned or centered.

- All tab stops can be used within a table cell, but the most useful is the decimal tab stop.

- Decimal tab stops automatically align numbers such as dollar values within a cell or a column.

- You can vertically align data at the top of the cell, centered in the cell, or at the bottom of the cell. The default is at the top.

Text aligned in a table

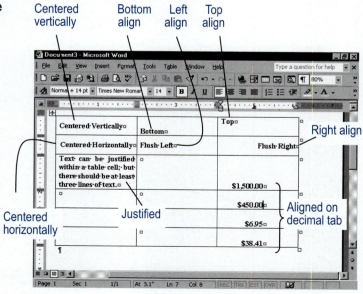

Align Table on the Page

- You can left align, right align, or center a table on the page.

Table tab of the Table Properties dialog box

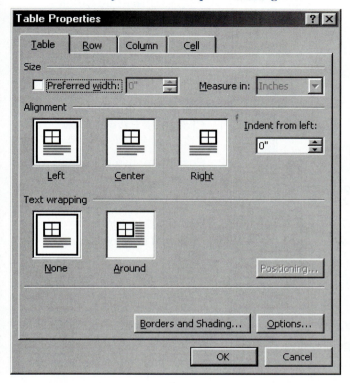

Column Width and Row Height

- By default, Word creates columns of equal **column width**, sized so the table extends from the left margin to the right margin.

- Rows are sized according to the line spacing on the line where the table is inserted.

- By default, **row height** automatically increases to accommodate lines of text typed in a cell.

- You can drag column dividers to increase or decrease column width.

  ✓ *Press and hold the Alt key as you drag to see the column width measurements displayed on the ruler.*

- In Print Layout view, you can drag row dividers to increase or decrease row height.

  ✓ *You cannot drag row dividers in Normal view.*

- You can set precise measurements for columns, rows, cells, and entire tables in the Table Properties dialog box.

Column tab of the Table Properties dialog box

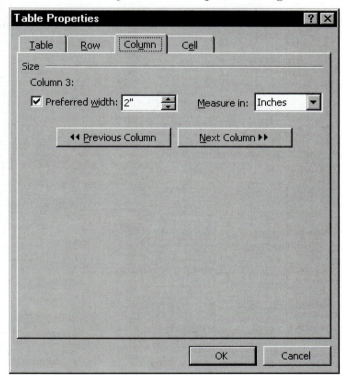

Procedures

Set Alignments within Table Cells

To change horizontal alignment:

1. Position insertion point in cell.
   OR
   Select component to format.
2. Click desired alignment button on Formatting toolbar:
   - **Align Left** ⊟ .
   - **Center** ⊟ .
   - **Align Right** ⊟ .
   - **Justify** ⊟ .

To set tabs in a cell:

1. Position insertion point in cell.
   OR
   Select component(s) to format.
2. Click Tab box at left end of horizontal ruler to select tab stop type.
3. Click desired position on horizontal ruler.
   ✓ For more information on tabs, refer to exercise 6.

To advance insertion point one tab stop within a cell:

- Press.......................... `Ctrl` + `Tab`

To change vertical alignment:

1. Position insertion point in cell.
   OR
   Select component to format.
2. Click **Table** .... `Alt` + `A`
3. Click **Table Properties** .... `R`
4. Click the **Cell** tab .... `Alt` + `E`
5. Click desired Vertical Alignment option:
   - **Top** ☐ .... `Alt` + `P`
   - **Center** ▤ .... `Alt` + `C`
   - **Bottom** ▤ .... `Alt` + `B`
6. Click **OK** .... `Enter`

Align Table Horizontally in Document

1. Select **table**.

---

2. Click desired alignment button on Formatting toolbar:
   - **Center** ⊟ .
   - **Align Right** ⊟ .
   - **Align Left** ⊟ .

OR

1. Click anywhere in table.
2. Click **Table** .... `Alt` + `A`
3. Click **Table Properties** .... `R`
4. Click the **Table** tab ...... `Alt` + `T`
5. Click desired Alignment option:
   - **Left** ⊞ .... `Alt` + `L`
   - **Center** ⊞ .... `Alt` + `C`
   - **Right** ⊞ .... `Alt` + `H`
6. Click **OK** .... `Enter`

Change Column Width

1. Position mouse pointer on column divider.
   ✓ Pointer changes to a double-vertical line with arrows pointing left and right.
2. Click and drag divider left or right.
   ✓ Press `Alt` at the same time that you drag the divider to see the width displayed on the horizontal ruler.

OR

a. Click in column.
b. Click **Table** .... `Alt` + `A`
c. Click **Table Properties**... `R`
d. Click **Column** tab ... `Alt` + `U`
e. Select **Preferred Width** check box .... `Alt` + `W`
f. Press **Tab** .... `Tab`
g. Type column width.
h. Click **OK** .... `Enter`

   OR

Click **Next Column**
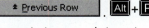 ... `Alt` + `N`

OR

Click **Previous Column**
⏪ Previous Column .. `Alt` + `P`

i. Repeat steps e – h to set additional column widths.
j. Click **OK** .... `Enter`

Change Row Height

1. Click **Print Layout View** button ▤ .
2. Position mouse pointer on row divider.
   ✓ Pointer changes to a double-horizontal line with arrows pointing up and down.
3. Click and drag divider up or down.
   ✓ Press `Alt` at the same time that you drag the divider to see the height displayed on the vertical ruler.

OR

a. Click in row.
b. Click **Table** .... `Alt` + `A`
c. Click **Table Properties** .. `R`
d. Click **Row** tab .... `Alt` + `R`
e. Select **Specify Height** check box .... `Alt` + `S`
f. Press **Tab** .... `Tab`
g. Type row height in inches.
   ✓ Select Exactly in Row height is box to fix row height at specified size.

   OR

Click **Next Row**
Next Row ⏷ . `Alt` + `N`

   OR

Click **Previous Row**
⏶ Previous Row . `Alt` + `P`

h. Repeat steps e – h to set additional row heights.
i. Click **OK** .... `Enter`

Exercise Directions

1. Start Word, if necessary.
2. Create a new document.
3. Save the file as **SALE**.
4. Use the following steps to create the document shown in Illustration A.
5. Type the memo text.
6. Create a table with five columns and eight rows and enter the data as shown.
   - ✓ *You can enter the data before setting alignments in step 7, or after.*
7. Set alignment as follows:
   a. Align the data in the first column flush right horizontally and on the top vertically.
   b. Align the data in columns 2, 3, 4, and 5 flush left horizontally and on the bottom vertically.
   c. Center the data in the first row horizontally and vertically.
   d. Set a left tab within column 4 at approximately .7" and use it to align the sizes (press Ctrl+Tab to move the insertion point to the tab stop).
      - ✓ *To see the location of the tab, insert the tab stop, then press and hold the Alt key as you drag the tab stop marker.*
   e. Use a decimal tab to align the prices in the fifth column.
      - ✓ *Try to set the tab stop at about .5" to match the illustration. Also, notice that the numbers align automatically as soon as you set the tab.*
8. Make the text in the first row bold.
9. Set preferred column widths as follows:
   - Column 1: .8"
   - Column 2: .7"
   - Column 3: 1.25"
   - Column 4: 1.5"
   - Column 5: .6"
10. Set all rows to be at least .5" high.
11. Center the entire table horizontally on the page.
12. Check the spelling and grammar.
13. Display the document in Print Preview. It should look similar to the one in Illustration A.
    - ✓ *If necessary, adjust the column widths so your document looks like the illustration.*
14. Print the document.
15. Close the document, saving all changes.

On Your Own

1. Create a new document in Word.
2. Save the file as **OWD28**.
3. Use a table to set up the document as a weekly schedule. The schedule might include your classes, things you do at work, afternoon or evening activities, or activities you do on the weekends
4. Set up the table so that times are listed in the first column and the days of the week are listed in the first row.
5. Set the first row to exactly .25" high.
6. Set the first column to exactly .5" wide and set the remaining columns to 1" wide.
7. If necessary, adjust other columns and rows by dragging the table dividers.
8. Use different alignments in the table. For example, center the names of the days but right-align the times.
9. Center the table on the page.
10. Save the changes, close the document, and exit Word.

↓4x

MEMO

↓4x

Tab to 1"

To: →   All employees
From: Your name — *Type your name*
Date: Today's date — *Insert today's date*
Subject: Special Pricing on Selected Items

↓3x

We are pleased to announce that we are making some of our most popular items available to you at special discounted prices.

↓2x

You may order the items on the company Intranet, or pick up an order form from the receptionist in the Fulfillment department.

↓2x

	Item No.	Description	Sizes		Price
Clothing					
	R-242V	Fleece Vest	Men:	M, L, XL	$12.99
			Women:	S, L	
	S-966X	Hiker's convertible pants	Men:	29 – 38	$15.99
			Women:	6, 10, 12	
	R-244P	Fleece Pullover	Men:	S, M, L	$15.99
			Women:	S, M, L	
	R-246L	Fleece Pants	Men:	S, M, L	$16.99
			Women:	S, M, L	
Accessories					
	A-567H	Baseball cap			$5.99
	G-459C	Daypack			$10.99
	B-980L	Web belt		S, M, L	$4.99

Exercise 29

Skills Covered:

◆ **Tables and Borders Toolbar**
◆ **Draw a Table** ◆ **Move and Resize Tables**
◆ **Merge and Split Cells** ◆ **Rotate Text** ◆ **Wrap Text**

On the Job

Word's Draw Table tool gives you great flexibility to organize tables the way you want them, not necessarily in rigid columns and rows. You can lay out the table cells exactly as you want them in order to organize text and data. You can then move and resize the table, if necessary, merge and split cells, and rotate the text to achieve the exact effect you need.

Your supervisor at Coastline Gourmet Importers has asked you to design a flyer announcing a series of cooking classes. In this exercise, you will open and format a document describing the classes. You will then create a table listing the schedule of classes, and integrate it into the flyer.

Terms

Merge Combine multiple adjacent cells together to create one large cell.

Split Divide one cell into multiple cells, either vertically to create columns or horizontally to create rows.

Notes

Tables and Borders toolbar

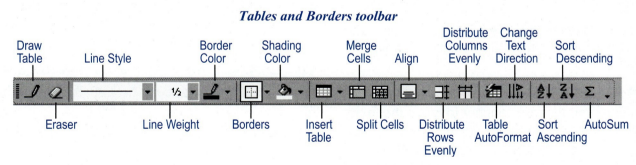

Tables and Borders Toolbar

- Use the buttons on the Tables and Borders toolbar to create and format tables.

  ✓ *If the toolbar is in your way while working, move it or dock it across the top of the document window.*

Draw a Table

- Word's Draw Table feature lets you create tables with uneven or irregular columns and rows.

A table drawn with uneven columns and rows

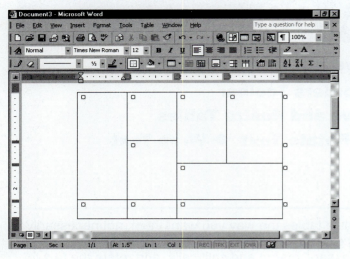

Table anchor and sizing handle

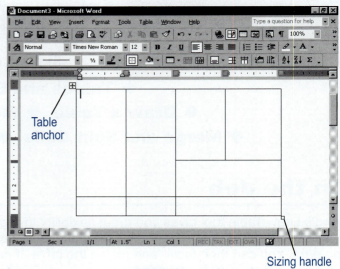

Table anchor

Sizing handle

- You must use Print Layout view to draw a table.
- When you draw a table, the mouse pointer functions as a pencil.

- You drag the pointer to draw lines vertically or horizontally to create cell dividers.
  - ✓ *Word creates straight lines at 90 degree angles to existing cell dividers, even if you do not drag in a straight line.*
- You can draw a diagonal line across a cell as a visual element or border, not to split the cell diagonally.
- New cells can be drawn anywhere. Rows and columns do not have to extend across the entire table.
- You can combine the Insert Table command with the Draw Table command to customize any table.

Move and Resize Tables

- You can drag the table anchor to move the table anywhere on the page.
- You can drag the sizing handle to change the table size.

Merge and Split Cells

- You can **merge** horizontally adjacent cells or vertically adjacent cells.
- You can use the eraser tool to erase dividers between cells, thus merging the cells.
  - ✓ *If you erase a divider on the outer edge of the table, you simply erase the border line, not the divider itself.*
- Merging is useful for creating a heading row across a table.
- **Split** a cell to insert dividers to create additional columns or rows.

Rotate Text

- Rotate text direction within a cell so text runs from left to right, from top to bottom, or from bottom to top.

Rotate text in a table

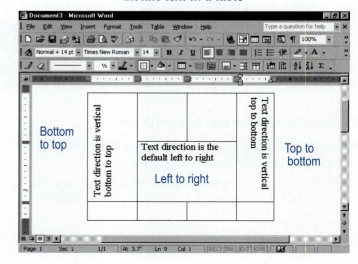

Wrap Text

■ By default, tables are inserted on a blank line above or below existing text.

■ You can set Word to wrap text around the table.

■ Wrapping text around a table integrates the table object into the text so text appears above, below, and on either side of the table.

Procedures

Display Tables and Borders Toolbar

- Click **Tables and Borders** button 🔲 on the Standard toolbar.

OR

1. Click **V**iew .... Alt + V
2. Click **T**oolbars .... T
3. Click **Tables and Borders**.

OR

1. Right-click any toolbar.
2. Click **Tables and Borders**.

Draw a Table

1. Click **T**able .... Alt + A
2. Click **Dra**w **Table** .... W

   OR

   Click **Draw Table** button 🖉 on Tables and Borders toolbar.

   ✓ *The mouse pointer resembles a pencil.*

3. Click where you want to position upper-left corner of the table.
4. Drag diagonally down and to the right.
5. Release mouse button where you want to position lower-right corner of the table.

   ✓ *This draws one cell.*

6. Click and drag mouse pointer to draw horizontal borders and vertical borders.

   ✓ *As you drag, Word displays a dotted line where the border will be. Once you drag far enough, Word completes the line when you release the mouse button.*

7. Press **Esc** .... Esc to turn off Draw Table.

   OR

   Click **Draw Table** button 🖉.

Move a Table

1. Rest mouse pointer on table so handles are displayed.
2. Click and drag table anchor to new location.

   ✓ *A dotted outline moves with the mouse pointer to show new location.*

3. Release mouse button to drop table in new location

Resize a Table

1. Rest mouse pointer on table so handles are displayed.
2. Click and drag sizing handle to increase or decrease table size.

   ✓ *A dotted outline moves with the mouse pointer to show new size.*

3. Release mouse button to resize table.

Merge Cells

1. Select cells to merge.
2. Click **Merge Cells** button 🔲 on Tables and Borders toolbar.

   OR

   a. Click **T**able .... Alt + A
   b. Click **Merge Cells** .... M

Merge Cells and Erase Table Dividers

1. Click **Eraser** button 🖉 on Tables and Borders toolbar.
2. Drag over borders to erase.

Split a Cell

1. Select cell to split.
2. Click **Split Cells** button 🔲 on Tables and Borders toolbar.

   OR

   a. Click **T**able .... Alt + A
   b. Click **S**plit Cells .... P

3. Enter **Number of columns** to create .... Alt + C, *number*
4. Enter **Number of rows** to create .... Alt + R, *number*
5. Click **OK** .... Enter

Rotate Text

1. Click in cell to format.

   OR

   Select components to format.

2. Click **Change Text Direction** button 🔲 on Tables and Borders toolbar.

   ✓ *Click the button to toggle through the three available directions.*

Wrap Text

1. Click in table.
2. Click **T**able .... Alt + A
3. Click Table **P**roperties .... R
4. Click **T**able .... T
5. Click **A**round .... Alt + A
6. Click **OK** .... Enter

Exercise Directions

1. Start Word, if necessary.
2. Open ⊙ **29COOKING**.
3. Save the file as **COOKING**.
4. On the first line of the document, use the Draw Table tool to draw a cell approximately 4" wide and 4" high.
   - ✓ *Use the rulers as guides to measure the height and width of cells as you draw, but don't worry if the table components are not sized exactly.*
5. Create three columns by drawing vertical lines through the cell. Try to size the columns as follows:
   Column 1: 1" wide
   Columns 2 and 3: 1.5" wide
6. Leave the first column intact, and create five rows across the second and third columns as follows:
   Row 1: .5" high
   Rows 2, 3, and 4: 1" high
   Row 5: .5" high
7. Merge the cells in the top row of the right two columns, and then merge the corresponding cells in the bottom row.
8. Leaving the top and bottom rows intact, use the Split Cells tool to create three rows within each of the cells in the third column (refer to Illustration A to see the desired result).
9. Enter the text in the table as shown in Illustration A, using the following formatting and alignments to achieve the desired result:
   a. Column 1 (program name): 26-pt. serif, rotated so it runs from bottom to top, centered horizontally and vertically.
   b. Row 1 (table title): 16-pt. serif, centered horizontally and vertically.
   c. Dates: 12-pt. serif, aligned left, and centered vertically.
   d. Menus: 12-pt. serif, aligned left horizontally, and aligned with the cell bottom vertically.
   e. Bottom row: 10-pt. serif, centered horizontally, and aligned with the cell bottom vertically.
10. Format the text that is not in the table in a 14-point sans serif font (Comic Sans MS is used in the illustration).
11. Center the first three lines of text below the table.
12. Leave 30 points of space after the third line.
13. Leave 6 points of space after the three paragraphs of text in the document.
14. Set text to wrap around the table.
15. Position the table flush right on the page, with its top at about 2" on the vertical ruler.
16. Resize the table to decrease its height to about 3.5".
17. Check the spelling and grammar in the document.
18. Display the document in Print Preview. It should look similar to the one in the illustration.
19. Print the document.
20. Close the document, saving all changes.

On Your Own

1. Create a new document in Word.
2. Save the file as **OWD29**.
3. Type a personal business letter to an employer or to your parents explaining why you need a raise. Write at least two paragraphs about why you deserve the raise and what you plan to do with the additional funds. Include information about how you spend the money you receive now.
4. To illustrate your point, draw a table in the letter and list items that you have purchased in the past two weeks. For example, include CDs, books, meals, movie tickets, and other expenses. The table should have at least three columns—for the date, the item, and the cost. List at least four items.
5. Merge a row across the top of the table and type in a title.
6. Try rotating text in some of the cells.
7. Use different alignments in the table cells.
8. Set the text in the letter to wrap around the table.
9. Try moving and resizing the table to improve the appearance of the letter.
10. When you are satisfied with the appearance of the table and the letter, check the spelling and grammar and print the document.
11. Close the document, saving all changes.

Illustration A

Cooking with Coastline
A new series of cooking classes sponsored by
Coastline Gourmet Importers

Cooking with Coastline is a series of hands-on cooking classes designed to introduce customers to a complete dinner menu. Each two-hour class will cover preparation of an appetizer, an entrée, and a dessert. Some classes will have themes, such as Valentine's Day, and St. Patrick's Day.

Classes will also include information such as shopping tips, selecting the right beverage, and how to set the table.

Cooking with Coastline

Scheduled Dates and Menus	
January 23	Antipasto
	Pasta Primavera
	Crème Brulee
February 11	Oysters on the half shell
	Rosemary Lamb Chops
	Chocolate Fondue
March 16	Baked Potato Skins
	Corned Beef and Cabbage
	Apple Crisp
Space is limited. Reservations are required.	

The first series of classes will begin in January. The classes will be held at our flagship store in Miami Beach.

Space is limited, so please make your reservations early.

Coastline Gourmet Importers
7334 Sunshine Parkway
12th Floor
Miami, FL 33132
305.555.7300
coastlinegourmet@ddcpub.com

Exercise 30

Skills Covered:

◆ **Calculations in a Table** ◆ **Number Formats**
◆ **Cell Borders and Shading** ◆ **Sort Rows**

On the Job

Perform basic calculations in tables to total values in a column or row. If the values change, you can update the result without redoing the math. At the same time, you can format the calculation results with one of Word's built-in number formats. Sorting rows helps you keep your tables in order, while cell borders and shading let you dress up your tables to make them look good as well as to highlight important information.

Coastline Gourmet is offering a special gift basket for Valentine's Day. In this exercise, you will create a document to advertise the gift basket. You will use a table to organize the information and to calculate costs. You will format the table using cell borders and shading.

Terms

Spreadsheet An application, such as Microsoft's Excel 2002, used for setting up mathematical calculations.

Function A built-in **formula** for performing calculations, such as addition, in a table.

Formula A mathematical equation.

Field A placeholder used to insert information that changes, such as the date, the time, a page number, or the results of a calculation.

Line style The appearance of a line.

Line weight The thickness of a line.

Shading A color or pattern used to fill the background of a cell.

Notes

Calculate in a Table

- Word tables include basic **spreadsheet functions** so you can perform calculations on data entered in tables.

- By default, Word assumes you want to add the values entered in the column above the current cell, or in the row beside the current cell.

- Word enters the calculation result in a **field**, so it can be updated if the values in the table change.

- For anything other than basic calculations, use an Excel worksheet, not a Word table.

The Formula dialog box set up to total the column

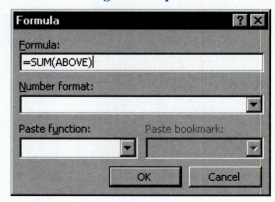

Number Formats

- When you set up a calculation in a table, you can select a number format to use for the result.
- Number formats include dollar signs, commas, percent signs, and decimal points.

Number formats

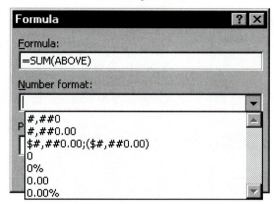

Cell Borders and Shading

- By default, Word applies a ½-pt. black solid line border around all table cells.
- Use the Tables and Borders toolbar buttons to change the borders and shading of table cells.
- You can select borders and shading before you draw new cells, or apply them to selected cells.

- Select a different **line style**.
- Select a different **line weight**.
- Change the border color.
- Erase or add border lines.
- Add color or **shading**.

- Selected border and shading formatting remains in effect until new formatting is selected.
  - ✓ *When table borders are removed, you can see table cells on-screen by displaying gridlines.*

Sort Rows

- Sort rows in a table the same way you sort lists or paragraphs.
  - ✓ *See Word, Exercise 17.*
- Rows can be sorted according to the data in any column.
- For example, in a table of names and addresses, rows can be sorted alphabetically by name or by city, or numerically by ZIP Code.
- Word rearranges the rows in the table but does not rearrange the columns.

Procedures

Total Values in a Column or Row

1. Click in cell where you want the total to be displayed.
2. Click **Table**.................. Alt + A
3. Click **Formula**...................... O
   - ✓ *By default, Word enters the formula for totaling the values in the cells in the column above or the row to the left.*
4. Click **Number format** .. Alt + N
5. Click desired format ...... ↑, ↓
6. Click **OK**.......................... Enter

Update the Total

1. Select the text in the cell where the total is displayed.
2. Press **F9**.............................. F9

✓ *You must update the total each time one of the values used in the formula is changed. The total is not updated automatically.*

Sort Rows

1. Select the data in the column by which you want to sort.
2. Click **Sort Ascending** button to sort from A to Z or from 0 to 9.
   OR
   Sort **Descending** button to sort from Z to A or from 9 to 0.
   - ✓ *If the sort should not include the first row, click Table, Sort and select the My list has Header row option button, then click OK.*

OR
1. Click **Table**................. Alt + A
2. Click **Sort**........................... S
3. Click **Sort by**.............. Alt + S
4. Click desired column.
5. Click **Type**.................. Alt + Y
6. Click either:
   - **Text**
   - **Number**
   - **Date**
7. Click either:
   - **Ascending** .... Alt + A
   - **Descending** .... Alt + D
   - ✓ *If the sort should not include the first row, make sure the My list has Header row option button is selected.*
8. Click **OK**.......................... Enter

Sort by Multiple Columns

1. Click **Table** .... Alt + A
2. Click **Sort** .... S
3. Click **Sort by** .... Alt + S
4. Click desired column.
5. Click **Type** .... Alt + Y
6. Click either:
   - **Text**
   - **Number**
   - **Date**
7. Click either:
   - **Ascending** .... Alt + A
   - **Descending** .... Alt + D
8. Click **Then by** .... Alt + T
9. Click desired column.
10. Click **Type** .... Alt + P
11. Click either:
    - **Text**
    - **Number**
    - **Date**
12. Click either:
    - **Ascending** .... Alt + C
    - **Descending** .... Alt + N
13. Click **Then by** .... Alt + B
14. Click desired column.
15. Click **Type** .... Alt + E
16. Click either:
    - **Text**
    - **Number**
    - **Date**
17. Click either:
    - **Ascending** .... Alt + I
    - **Descending** .... Alt + G

    ✓ *If the sort should not include the first row, make sure the My list has Header row option button is selected.*

18. Click **OK** .... Enter

Apply Cell Borders

1. Select cell(s) to format.
2. Click **Borders** drop-down arrow ▢ ▾.
3. Click Border style.

   ✓ *Border buttons are toggles— click on to display border, click off to hide border.*

Select Line Style

1. Click **Line Style** drop-down arrow ▭ ▾.
2. Click desired line style.

   ✓ *Click No Border to remove border lines.*

3. Click on a border line to apply the style.

Select Line Weight

1. Click **Line Weight** drop-down arrow ¼ ▾.
2. Click desired line weight.
3. Click on a border line to apply the style.

Select Line Color

1. Click **Border Color** button ✏.
2. Click desired color.
3. Click on a border line to apply the style.

Select Cell Shading

1. Click in cell to shade.
2. Click **Shading Color** drop-down arrow ▵ ▾.
3. Click desired color.
4. Click **No Fill** to remove shading or color.

Exercise Directions

1. Start Word, if necessary.
2. Open ⊙ **30BASKET**.
3. Save the file as **BASKET**.
4. Move the insertion point to the last line of the document.
5. Use either the Draw Table tool or the Insert Table command to create a table with two columns and five rows.
6. Enter the data shown in Illustration A.
7. Align all dollar values with a decimal tab.
8. Preview the document. It should look similar to the one in Illustration A.
9. Sort the rows in descending order according to the values in the Price column.

   ✓ *Remember not to sort the header row.*

10. Insert a new row at the end of the table.
11. In the first cell in the new row, type **Total**.
12. In the last cell of the new row, insert a formula to calculate the total cost.

    ✓ *Select the currency format showing two decimal places.*

13. Insert a row above the total.
14. In the left column, type **1 bottle sparkling white grape juice**.
15. In the right column type **$4.59**.
16. Update the calculation result.
17. Apply the Table Grid 8 AutoFormat to the table.
18. Apply a dark blue double-line border around all of the cells in the bottom row.

    ✓ *If you have trouble seeing the change on-screen, try zooming in to a higher magnification.*

19. Remove the borders between columns in the bottom row.

    ✓ *Do not merge the cells. Just remove the printing border lines.*

20. Apply a 12.5% gray shading to all of the cells in the bottom row.

    ✓ *ScreenTips display the % Gray Shading.*

21. Resize the table so it is approximately 4" wide by 3½" high.

22. Set column 1 to be approximately 2.5" wide and column 2 to be approximately 1.5" wide

23. Vertically center the text in the bottom row.

24. Center the table horizontally on the page.

25. Check the spelling and grammar.

26. Preview the document. It should look similar to the one in Illustration B.

27. Print the document.

28. Close the document, saving all changes.

Illustration A

Coastline Gourmet

$49.99 Gift Basket Valentine's Day Special

This specially priced package includes all of the items listed below, artfully arranged in a delightful wicker basket and wrapped in red cellophane with a bow. Attached to the handle is a Mylar heart-shaped balloon, and your own personalized card.

Basket includes:	Regularly priced:
8 oz. box of premium chocolate	$12.99
Teddy bear	$9.99
1 dozen red roses	$32.99
1 dozen chocolate chip cookies	$14.99

Coastline Gourmet

$49.99 Gift Basket Valentine's Day Special

This specially priced package includes all of the items listed below, artfully arranged in a delightful wicker basket and wrapped in red cellophane with a bow. Attached to the handle are a Mylar heart-shaped balloon and your own personalized card.

Basket includes:	Regularly priced:
1 dozen red roses	$32.99
1 dozen chocolate chip cookies	$14.99
8 oz. box of premium chocolate	$12.99
Teddy bear	$9.99
1 bottle sparkling white grape juice	$4.59
Total	$ 75.55

On Your Own

1. Open the document **OWD29**, the letter asking for a raise that you wrote in the On Your Own section of Exercise 29, or open **30RAISE**.

2. Save the file as **OWD30**.

3. Sort the rows in the table into descending numerical order, according to the amount of the expenses.

4. Add a row to the bottom of the table.

5. Label the row **Total**.

6. Calculate the total amount of expenses in the table. Make sure the result is displayed in dollar format.

7. Change one or more of the values in the table.

8. Update the calculation.

9. Format the table using cell borders and shading. For example, use borders and shading to highlight the cell in which the total is displayed.

10. Check the spelling and grammar, then print the document.

11. Close the document, saving all changes.

Exercise 31

◆ **Critical Thinking**

Coastline Gourmet has been collecting demographic information about customers who come into its stores. In this exercise, you will create a memo to the marketing director listing some of the interesting demographics in table form.

Exercise Directions

1. Start Word, if necessary.
2. Open ✪ **31DEMOS**.
3. Save the document as **DEMOS**.
4. Complete the memo heading information as follows, tabbing in to the 1" mark to enter the data:

   To: **Marketing Director**
   From: **your own name**
   Date: **Today's date**
   Subject: Customer Demographics

5. Between the first two paragraphs of the memo, insert a table with three columns and seven rows.
6. Set all columns to be 1" wide and all rows to be .25" high.
7. Enter the following data:

Age	18 – 25	5%
	26 – 35	22%
	36 – 45	23%
	46 – 55	28%
	55 +	22%
Gender	Male	54%
	Female	46%

8. Vertically align all data on the bottom.
9. Left align the data in columns 1 and 2.
10. Right align the data in column 3.
11. Insert a new row at the top of the table.
12. Merge the cells in the new row.
13. In the new row, type the table title: **CUSTOMER DEMOGRAPHICS**.
14. Center the table title horizontally and vertically.

15. Insert another blank row above the row labeled **Gender**.
16. Apply the Table Contemporary AutoFormat to the table.
17. Apply a single line ¾-pt. outside border to the entire table.
18. Between the second and third paragraphs of the memo, insert a table with two columns and five rows.
19. Set column 1 to be 1.5" wide and column 2 to be .5" wide.
20. Set all rows to be .25" high.
21. Enter the following data:

Naples	42
Miami Beach	36
Fort Lauderdale	47
Fort Meyers	8
North Miami	21

22. Align column 2 flush right.
23. Delete the cells containing the label and data for Fort Meyers, shifting the cells up.
24. Insert a blank row at the bottom of the table.
25. In the blank cell at the bottom of column 1, type **Total**, and right align it.
26. In the blank cell at the bottom of column 2, insert a formula to calculate the total number of respondents.
27. Sort the rows in ascending alphabetical order by city.
28. Insert a new column at the left side of the table.
29. Merge the cells in the first column.

30. Type **Respondents by Store** in column 1.

31. Rotate the text in column 1 so it reads from the bottom of the table to the top, and center it vertically.

32. Apply a 1-pt. Indigo border around the inside and outside of all cells in the table.

33. Apply a 10% gray shading to column 1.

34. Apply a 20% gray shading to rows 1, 3, and 5. Reduce the width of the column as necessary.

35. Center the table on the page.

36. Change the number of respondents in the North Miami store to **24**.

37. Update the result of the calculation.

38. Check the spelling and grammar in the document.

39. Display the document in Print Preview. It should look similar to the illustration.

40. Print the document.

41. Close the document, saving all changes.

Illustration A

MEMO

To: Marketing Director
From: Your Name
Date: Today's date
Subject: Customer Demographics

I thought you might like a preview of the customer demographic data we have been collecting. I find the age breakdowns quite interesting. Based on what we know of spending patterns, I think we should pursue promotions that will attract some younger consumers.

CUSTOMER DEMOGRAPHICS		
Age	18 – 25	5%
	26 – 35	22%
	36 – 45	23%
	46 – 55	28%
	55 +	22%
Gender	Male	54%
	Female	46%

Customers were surprisingly eager to fill out our questionnaire, as you can see from the numbers in the table below.

Respondents by Store	Fort Lauderdale	47
	Miami Beach	36
	Naples	42
	North Miami	24
	Total	149

We should have the complete report by the end of next week. We'll meet then to go over the results.

Exercise 32

On the Job

Use Mail Merge to customize mass mailings. For example, with Mail Merge you can store a document with standard text, such as a form letter, and then insert personalized names and addresses on each copy that you generate or print. You can also use Mail Merge to generate envelopes, labels, e-mail messages, and directories, such as a telephone list.

A letter thanking those people who submitted essays to Northwest Gear's contest becomes a simple task using the Mail Merge feature. The form letter will be personalized with each person's name and address. In this exercise, you will create the letter document and the data source address list, and you will merge them to generate the letters.

Terms

Mail Merge A process that inserts variable information into a standardized document to produce a personalized or customized document.

Main document The document containing the standardized text that will be printed on all documents.

Merge field A placeholder in the main document that marks where and what will be inserted from the data source document.

Merge block A set of merge fields stored as one unit. For example, the Address block contains all of the name and address information.

Data source The document containing the variable data that will be inserted during the merge.

Office address list A simple data source file stored in Access file format, which includes the information needed for an address list, such as first name, last name, street, city, state, and so on.

Outlook contact list The names, addresses, and other information stored as contacts for use in the Microsoft Outlook personal information manager program.

Microsoft Access database A file created with the Microsoft Access program, used for storing information.

Merge document The customized document resulting from a merge.

Field One item of variable data, such as a first name, a last name, or a ZIP Code.

Record A collection of variable data about one person or thing. In a form letter merge for example, each record contains variable data, for each person receiving the letter: first name, last name, address, city, state, and ZIP Code.

Address list form A dialog box used to enter mailing list information for a data source file.

Notes

Mail Merge Basics

- Use **Mail Merge** to create mass mailings, envelopes, or labels.

- To create a mail merge, you must have two files:

  - A **main document**, which contains information that won't change, as well as **merge fields** and **merge blocks**, which act as placeholders for variable information. For example, you might have a form letter that has merge fields where the address and greeting should be.

  - A **data source** file, which contains variable information such as names and addresses. Word lets you use many types of data source files for a merge, including an **Office address list**, an **Outlook contact list**, or a **Microsoft Access database**.

- During the merge, Word generates a series of **merge documents** in which the variable information from the data source replaces the merge fields entered in the main document.

- You can print the merge documents or save them in a file for future use.

- You can use the Mail Merge Wizard or the buttons on the Mail Merge toolbar to access Mail Merge features and command.

A main document

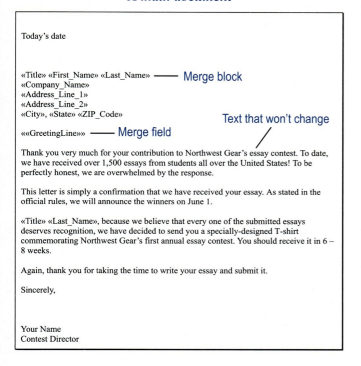

Today's date

«Title» «First_Name» «Last_Name» —— Merge block
«Company_Name»
«Address_Line_1»
«Address_Line_2»
«City», «State» «ZIP_Code»
                                    Text that won't change
««GreetingLine»» —— Merge field

Thank you very much for your contribution to Northwest Gear's essay contest. To date, we have received over 1,500 essays from students all over the United States! To be perfectly honest, we are overwhelmed by the response.

This letter is simply a confirmation that we have received your essay. As stated in the official rules, we will announce the winners on June 1.

«Title» «Last_Name», because we believe that every one of the submitted essays deserves recognition, we have decided to send you a specially-designed T-shirt commemorating Northwest Gear's first annual essay contest. You should receive it in 6 – 8 weeks.

Again, thank you for taking the time to write your essay and submit it.

Sincerely,

Your Name
Contest Director

Mail Merge Toolbar

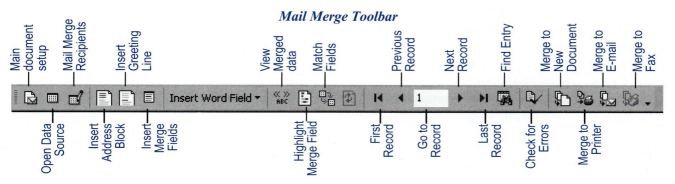

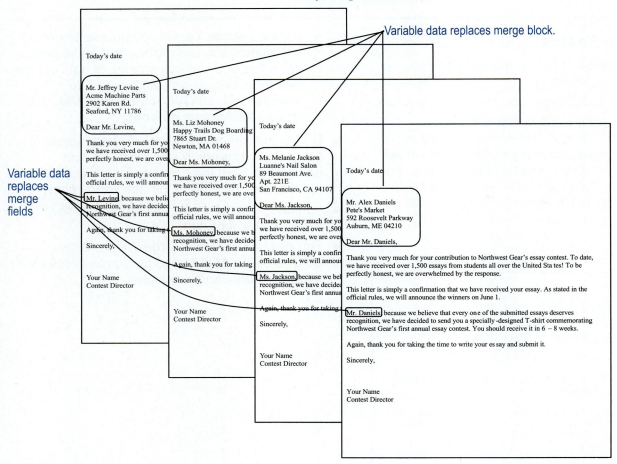

A series of merge documents

Variable data replaces merge block.

Variable data replaces merge fields

Use the Mail Merge Wizard

- The Mail Merge Wizard steps you through the process of conducting a merge.
- There are six steps in the Mail Merge Wizard:
  - The first step is to select the type of main document you want to create:

Letters	used for letters or other regular Word documents such as reports, flyers, or memos.
E-mail messages	used to create messages to send via e-mail.
Envelopes	used to create personalized envelopes.
Labels	used to create personalized labels.
Directory	used for lists such as rosters, or telephone lists.

- The second step is to select a starting document. You may select to start from the current document, an existing document, or a new document based on a template.

- The third step in the Mail Merge Wizard is to select recipients. In this step, you locate or create the data source file, and then select the individual recipients to include in the merge.

  - ✓ *If you select to create a new list, the Mail Merge Wizard prompts you through the steps for creating the data source file by entering the variable data for each recipient.*

- The fourth step is to create the main document. In this step, you type and format the data you want included in each merge document, and you insert the merge fields or merge blocks where Word will insert the variable data.

Step 4 of the Mail Merge Wizard

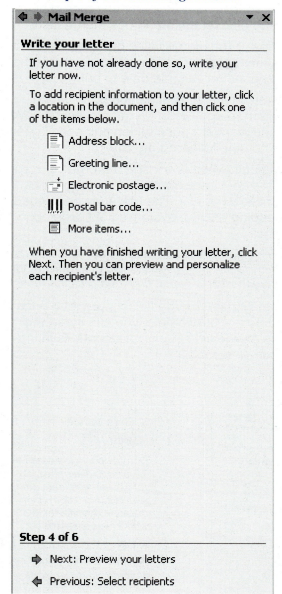

- The fifth step is to preview the merge documents. In this step, you have the opportunity to see the merge documents before you print them.

- The final step is to complete the merge. You have the option of printing the merge documents, or saving them in a new file for later use.

Create a New Address List

- An Office address list is a simple data source file used to store all of the variable information required to complete a mail merge.

- The data is stored in a table format, with each column containing one **field** of information and each row containing the **record** for one recipient.

- One merge document is created for each record in the data source document.

The list of recipients stored in an address list

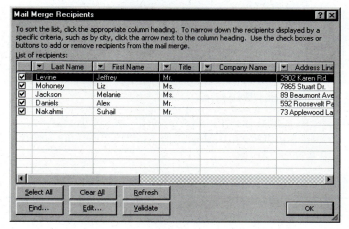

- You enter the data in an **address list form** that has already been set up to include the necessary fields.

- You must save the file the same way you save any Office file—by giving it a name and selecting a storage location.

- By default, Word stores the file in the My Data Sources folder, which is a subfolder of My Documents.

- If a field in the data source is blank, the information is left out of the merge document for that record.

- You can use an address list file many times, with different main documents.

- You can sort the list, and you can select the specific recipients you want to include in the merge.

An address list form Type data here

New Address List

Enter Address information

Field names {
Title
First Name
Last Name
Company Name
Address Line 1
Address Line 2
City
State
}

New Entry | Delete Entry | Find Entry ... | Filter and Sort... | Customize...

View Entries

View Entry Number | First | Previous | 1 | Next | Last

Total entries in list 1

Cancel

Use Merge Fields

- Word has a preset list of merge fields that correspond to variable information typically used in a mail merge.

- It also creates merge blocks combining several fields so that you can insert one merge block instead of inserting numerous merge fields.

- You insert the merge fields or blocks in the main document at the location where you want the corresponding variable data to print.

- You must type all spaces and punctuation between merge fields. Merge blocks, however, include standard punctuation and spacing, such as a comma following the city.

- By default, when you insert a merge field, you see the field name enclosed in merge field characters (<< >>). The field may be shaded, depending on your system's field code option settings.

   ✓ The field code option settings are found on the View tab in the Options dialog box. Select Options from the Tools menu, and then click the View tab.

- You may insert merge fields more than once in a document. For example, you can insert the name merge field in multiple locations in order to personalize a letter.

Procedures

Use the Mail Merge Wizard to Generate a Form Letter Using a New Address List Data Source File

Select the main document:

1. Open a new blank document.
2. Click **Tools**.................. Alt + T
3. Select **Letters and Mailings**........................... E
4. Click **Mail Merge Wizard** .... M
5. Click the **Letters** options button.
6. Click **Next: Starting document**.
7. Click the **Use Current Document** option button.
8. Click **Next: Select recipients**.

Create an address list data source file:

1. Click the **Type a new list** option button.
2. Click **Create**.
3. Type the title for the first person you want to add to the address list.

4. Press **Enter**..................... Enter

   or **Tab** .... Tab

   ✓ Press Shift+Tab to move to previous field.
5. Type the person's first name.
6. Press **Enter**..................... Enter

   or **Tab** .... Tab
7. Continue typing variable data until record is complete.

   ✓ You may leave blank any fields for which information is not available or necessary.
8. Click **New Entry** .... Alt + N

   ✓ Word displays next blank address form.
9. Repeat steps 3–8 until you have entered the information for all recipients.

   ✓ You can edit the data source file in the future. For example, you can add and delete records. For more information, refer to exercise 40.
10. Click **Close** .... Esc

   ✓ Word displays the Save Address List dialog box.
11. Type file name.

12. Click **Save** button

   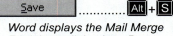 .... Alt + S

   ✓ Word displays the Mail Merge Recipients dialog box. By default, all recipients are selected. For information on selecting specific recipients, refer to exercise 40.
13. Click **OK**........................... Enter
14. Click **Next: Write your letter**.

   ✓ Word displays the starting document, and a list of available merge blocks.

Create a form letter document:

1. Begin typing the letter, including all text and formatting as you want it to appear on each merge document. For example, insert the date and move the insertion point down four lines.
2. At the location where you want the recipient's address displayed, click **Address block**

   OR

Click **Insert Address Block**
button 🖺 on Mail Merge
toolbar.

✓ *Word displays the Insert
Address Block dialog box.*

3. Select desired options.

4. Click **OK**..........................Enter

OR

a. Click **More items** 🗐 in
the Task Pane.

OR

Click **Insert Merge Fields**
button 🗐 on Mail Merge
toolbar.

✓ *Word displays the Insert Merge
Field dialog box.*

b. Click field to insert.... ↑,↓

c. Click **I**nsert .... Alt + I

d. Click **Close** .... Esc

5. Continue typing and formatting
letter, repeating steps to insert
merge fields or merge blocks
at desired location(s).

6. Save the document.

7. Click **Next: Preview your
letters**.

✓ *Word displays the first merge
document.*

Preview merge documents:

1. Click the **Next recipient** button
>> in the Mail Merge Wizard
Task Pane.

OR

Click the **Next recipient** button
▶ on the Mail Merge toolbar.

OR

Click the **Previous recipient**
button << in the Mail Merge
Wizard Task Pane.

OR

Click the **Previous recipient**
button ◀ on the Mail Merge
toolbar.

2. Click **Next: Complete the
Merge**.

Complete the merge:

• Click **Print** button 📇 to open
the Print dialog box to print the
merged documents

OR

1. Click **Edit individual letters**
button 📑 to create a new file
containing all merged letters.

✓ *Word displays the Merge to
File dialog box.*

2. Click **OK** .... Enter
to merge all letters to a new
file.

✓ *You can make changes to
individual letters, and/or save
the document to print later.*

Exercise Directions

1. Start Word, if necessary.

2. Create a new blank document.

3. Save the file as **FORM**.

4. Start the Mail Merge Wizard.

5. Select to create a letter, using the current
document.

6. Create a new address list to use as a data
source document.

7. Enter the recipients from the table below into
the data source file.

8. Save the data source file as **SOURCE**.

9. Select to use all recipients in the merge, then
close the Mail Merge Recipients dialog box.

10. Type the document shown in Illustration A,
inserting the merge fields and merge blocks as
marked.

11. Check the spelling and grammar in the
document.

12. Preview the merged documents.

13. Complete the merge by generating a file
containing all of the individual records.

14. Save the file as **LETTERS**.

15. Print the file.

16. Close all open documents, saving all changes.

Title	First Name	Last Name	Address Line 1	Address Line 2	City	State	ZIP Code
Mr.	Jeffrey	Levine	2902 Karen Road		Seaford	NY	11786
Ms.	Liz	Mohoney	7865 Stuart Drive		Newton	MA	01468
Ms.	Melanie	Jackson	89 Beaumont Avenue	Apt 221E	San Francisco	CA	94107
Mr.	Alex	Daniels	592 Roosevelt Parkway		Auburn	ME	04210
Mr.	Suhail	Nakahmi	73 Applewood Lane		Jenkintown	PA	19046

Today's date

«‹«AddressBlock»›» ⎤
⎬ *Insert merge blocks*
«‹«GreetingLine»›» ⎦

Thank you very much for your contribution to Northwest Gear's essay contest. To date, we have received over 1,500 essays from students all over the United States! To be perfectly honest, we are overwhelmed by the response.

This letter is simply a confirmation that we have received your essay. As stated in the official rules, we will announce the winners on June 1.

Insert merge fields — «Title» «Last_Name», because we believe that every one of the submitted essays deserves recognition, we have decided to send you a specially-designed T-shirt commemorating Northwest Gear's first annual essay contest. You should receive it in 6 – 8 weeks.

Again, thank you for taking the time to write your essay and submit it.

Sincerely,

Your Name
Contest Director

On Your Own

1. Think of ways Mail Merge would be useful to you. For example, are you involved in any clubs or organizations that send out mass mailings? Do you send out "Holiday Letters" every year? Are you responsible for regular reports that contain variable data, such as sales reports or forecasts?

2. Use the Mail Merge Wizard to create a form letter.

3. Save the main document as **OWD32-1**.

4. Create an address list data source file that includes at least five records.

5. Save the data source file as **OWD32-2**.

6. Type the letter, inserting merge fields and merge blocks as necessary.

7. Check the spelling and grammar in the document.

8. Merge the documents into a new file.

9. Save the merge document file as **OWD32-3**.

10. Print the letters.

11. Close all open documents, saving all changes.

Exercise 33

Skills Covered:

◆ **Merge with an Existing Address List**
◆ **Edit an Address List** ◆ **Customize Merge Fields**
◆ **Merge Envelopes and Labels**

On the Job

If you have an existing data source document, you can merge it with any main document to create new merge documents. This saves you from retyping repetitive data. For example, using an existing Address List data source makes it easy to create envelopes and labels to accompany a form letter merge that you created previously. You can edit the data source to add or remove records, or to customize merge fields to include specialized information not included in the default Address List data source file.

To mail out the form letters for Northwest Gear, you need to print envelopes. In this exercise, you will create an envelope main document and merge it with the same Address List file you used in exercise 38. You will then edit the Address List and customize the merge fields. Finally, you will use the Address List to print labels to use on the packages containing the T-shirts promised to every person who submitted an essay.

Terms

There is no new vocabulary in this exercise.

Notes

Merge with an Existing Address List

- Once you create and save an Office Address List data source file, you can use it with different main documents.

- In Step 3 of the Mail Merge Wizard you can locate and open the data source file you want to use.

  ✓ *You can also click the Open Data Source button*

  ![icon] *on the Mail Merge toolbar to display the Select Data Source dialog box.*

The Select Data Source dialog box

- You can also use existing data source files created with other applications, including Microsoft Access.

184

✓ *If you select a data source created with Access, you must specify which table or query to use, and the merge fields inserted in the Word document must match the fields used in the Access file.*

■ Using an existing data source saves you the time and trouble of retyping existing data.

Edit an Address List

■ You can easily edit an existing Address List.

■ You can change information that is already entered.

■ You can add or delete information, including entire records.

Customize Merge Fields

■ Customize merge fields to change field names, delete unused fields, or add fields specific to your needs. For example, you might want to add a field for entering a job title.

■ You can also move fields up or down in the field list.

The Customize Address List dialog box

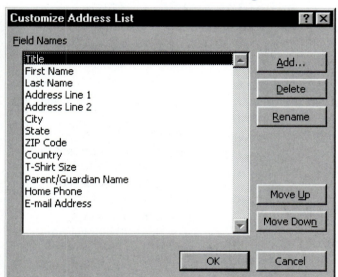

Merge Envelopes and Labels

■ To create envelopes using Mail Merge, select Envelopes as the main document type.

■ To create labels using Mail Merge, select Labels as the main document type.

■ The Mail Merge Wizard prompts you to select envelope options so that the main document is laid out just like the actual paper envelopes on which you will print.

The Envelope Options dialog box

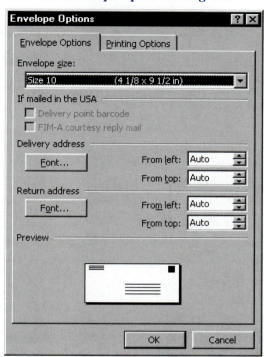

■ Likewise, you must select label options so that the label layout on-screen is the same as the actual labels.

✓ *When you select the size and format of the envelopes or labels, Word changes the layout of the current document to match. Any existing data in the document is deleted.*

The Label Options dialog box

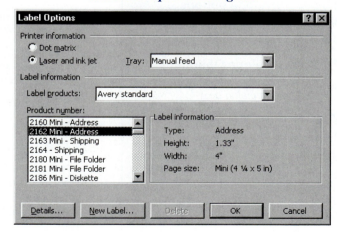

■ You can create a new data source file as covered in Exercise 32, or use an existing data source file.

■ You can merge the envelopes or labels to a printer or to a new document to save, edit, or use at a later time.

Procedures

Use the Mail Merge Wizard to Generate Envelopes or Labels Using an Existing Address List Data Source File

Select the main document:

1. Open a new blank document.
2. Click **Tools**.................. `Alt`+`T`
3. Select **Letters and Mailings**............................ `E`
4. Click **Mail Merge Wizard**.... `M`
5. Click the **Envelopes** option button to create envelopes.
   OR
   Click the **Labels** option button to create labels.
6. Click **Next: Starting document**.
   - ✓ *The next step depends on whether you are merging envelopes or labels. To merge envelopes, continue with the procedures for selecting envelope options. To merge labels, continue with the procedures for selecting label options. Once the options are selected, both continue with the procedures for selecting recipients.*

To select envelope options:

1. Click the **Change Document Layout** option button.
2. Click **Envelope Options** .
   - ✓ *Word displays the Envelope Options dialog box.*
3. Click **Envelope size**.... `Alt`+`S`
4. Click desired size.................... `↑`, `↓`, `Enter`
5. Click **OK**........................... `Enter`
   - ✓ *Word changes the layout of the current document. If a warning is displayed, click OK to continue or Cancel to cancel the change.*
6. Click **Next: Select recipients**.

To select label options:

1. Click the **Change Document Layout** option button.
2. Click **Label Options** .
   - ✓ *Word displays the Label Options dialog box.*
3. Select label options.
4. Click **OK** .... `Enter`
   - ✓ *Word changes the layout of the current document. If a warning is displayed, click OK to continue or Cancel to cancel the change.*
5. Click **Next: Select recipients**.

Select an existing Address List data source file:

1. Click the **Use an existing list** option button.
2. Click **Browse** .
   - ✓ *Word opens the Select Data Source dialog box.*
3. Locate and select the desired data source file.
4. Click **Open** ...... Open
5. Word displays the Mail Merge Recipients dialog box.
   - ✓ *By default, all recipients are selected. For information on selecting specific recipients, refer to Exercise 34.*
6. Click **OK** .... `Enter`
7. Click **Next: Arrange your envelope/labels**.
   - ✓ *Word displays the starting document, and a list of available merge blocks.*

Arrange the envelope:

1. Type any text you want to appear on each printed envelope. For example, type a return address in the upper-left corner.
2. Position the insertion point at the location where you want the recipient's address displayed.
   - ✓ *By default, Word creates a text box on the envelope document where the address should print.*
3. Click **Address block** .
   OR
   Click **Insert Address Block** button on Mail Merge toolbar.
   - ✓ *Word displays the Insert Address Block dialog box.*
4. Select desired options.
5. Click **OK**........................... `Enter`
   OR
   a. Click **More items** in the Task Pane.
      OR
      Click **Insert Merge Fields** button ▤ on Mail Merge toolbar.
      - ✓ *Word displays the Insert Merge Field dialog box.*
   b. Click field to insert ... `↑`, `↓`
   c. Click **Insert**............. `Alt`+`I`
   d. Click **Close** .... `Esc`
6. Type any other standard text required on the envelope.
7. Insert additional fields or blocks as necessary.
8. Save the document.
9. Click **Next: Preview your envelopes**.
   - ✓ *Word displays the first merge document.*

Arrange the labels:

1. In the first label, position the insertion point at the location where you want the recipient's address displayed.
2. Click **Address block** ▤.
   OR
   Click **Insert Address Block** button ▤ on Mail Merge toolbar.

✓ *Word displays the Insert Address Block dialog box.*

3. Select desired options.
4. Click **OK**...........................Enter

OR

Click **More items** 📄 in the Task Pane.

OR

Click **Insert Merge Fields** button 📄 on Mail Merge toolbar.

✓ *Word displays the Insert Merge Field dialog box.*

a. Click field to insert....↑, ↓

b. Click **Insert**.............Alt + I

c. Click **Close**..................Esc

5. Type any other standard text and/or punctuation required on the label.
6. Insert additional fields or blocks as necessary.
7. Click **Update all labels**

Update all labels in the Task Pane to copy the layout from the first label to all other labels.

✓ *Alternatively, click **Propagate Labels** 🔁 on the Mail Merge toolbar.*

8. Save the document.
9. Click **Next: Preview your labels**.

✓ *Word displays the first merge document.*

Preview merge documents:

1. Click the **Next recipient** button >> in the Mail Merge Wizard Task Pane.

OR

Click the **Next recipient** button ▶ on the Mail Merge toolbar.

OR

Click the **Previous recipient** button << in the Mail Merge Wizard Task Pane.

OR

Click the **Previous recipient** button ◀ on the Mail Merge toolbar.

2. Click **Next: Complete the merge**.

Complete the merge:

• Click **Print** 🖨 to open the Print dialog box and print the merged documents.

OR

1. Click **Edit individual envelopes** 📑 to create a new file containing all merged envelopes.

OR

Click **Edit individual labels** 📑 to create a new file containing all merged labels.

✓ *Word displays the Merge to New Document dialog box.*

2. Click **OK**...........................Enter to complete the merge.

✓ *You can make changes to individual envelopes or labels, and/or save the document to print later.*

Edit an Existing Address List

1. Click **Mail Merge Recipients** button 📇 on Mail Merge toolbar.

OR

In Step 3 or Step 5 of Mail Merge Wizard, click **Edit recipient list** 📇.

2. Click **Edit**......................Alt + E

✓ *Word displays the Address List dialog box, with the record for the first recipient displayed.*

3. Do any the following:

To add a new record:

a. Click **New Entry**.....Alt + N

b. Enter variable information as covered in Exercise 38.

To delete a record:

a. Click **Delete Entry**. Alt + D to delete the entry currently displayed.

b. Click **Yes**................Alt + Y to delete the entry.

OR

• Click **No**.................Alt + N to cancel the deletion.

✓ *You cannot undo an entry deletion.*

To edit a record:

a. Display record to edit.

✓ *Use the Next, Previous, First, and Last buttons to scroll through the records.*

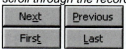

b. Edit variable data as desired.

4. Click **Close**....................Enter

5. Click **OK**.........................Enter

Customize Merge Fields

1. Click **Mail Merge Recipients** button 📇 on Mail Merge toolbar.

OR

In Step 3 or Step 5 of Mail Merge Wizard, click **Edit recipient list** 📇.

2. Click **Edit**....................Alt + E

✓ *Word displays the Address List dialog box, with the record for the first recipient displayed.*

3. Click **Customize**..........Alt + Z

✓ *Word displays the Customize Address List dialog box.*

4. Do any of the following:

To add a field:

a. Click **Add**...............Alt + A

b. Type field name.

c. Click **OK**....................Enter

To delete a field:

a. Click field to delete............↑, ↓, Enter

b. Click **Delete**...........Alt + D

c. Click **Yes**...............Alt + Y to delete the field and all data entered in the field.

OR

• Click **No**..................Alt + N to cancel the deletion.

To change the order of fields in the field list:

a. Click field to
move .... ⬆, ⬇, `Enter`

b. Click **Move Up** .... `Alt`+`U`
to move the field up one line in list.
OR

- Click **Move Down** .. `Alt`+`N`
to move field down one line in list.

5. Click **OK**.......................... `Enter`
6. Click **Close** .... `Enter`
7. Click **OK**.......................... `Enter`

Exercise Directions

✓ In this exercise you will use **SOURCE** the Office Address List file you created in Exercise 32. If that file is not available on your system, prior to starting the exercise copy the file 💿 **33SOURCE** and save the copy as **SOURCE**.

✓ To copy the file, right-click the file name and select Copy. Right-click the destination folder and select Paste. Right-click the copied file name and select Rename. Type the new file name and press Enter.

1. Start Word if necessary.
2. Create a new blank document.
3. Save the document as **MAINENV**.
4. Start the Mail Merge Wizard.
5. Select to create envelopes.
6. Select Change document layout.
7. Select envelope size 10.
8. Select to use an existing address list file as a data source document.
9. Locate and open **SOURCE**.
10. Close the Mail Merge Recipients dialog box.
11. Set up the envelope main document as shown in Illustration A.
    a. Type the return address.
    b. Insert the Address merge block.
12. Check the spelling and grammar in the document.
13. Preview the merged documents.
14. Complete the merge by generating a file containing all of the individual envelopes.
15. Save the file as **ENVELOPES**.
16. If requested by your instructor, print the merge documents.
    ✓ If you do not have actual envelopes, you can print the merge documents on regular paper.
17. Close all open files, saving all changes.
18. Create a new blank document.

19. Save the file as **MAINLABE**.
20. Start the Mail Merge Wizard.
21. Select to create labels.
22. Select Change document layout.
23. Select Avery standard number 2163 Mini-Shipping labels.
24. Select to use an existing address list file as a data source document.
25. Locate and open **SOURCE**.
26. Customize the merge fields as follows:
    a. Delete the Company Name field.
    b. Delete the Work Phone field.
    c. Add a T-Shirt Size field.
    d. Move the new field down between the Country and the Home Phone fields.
    e. Add a Parent/Guardian Name field.
    f. Move the new field down between the T-Shirt Size and the Home Phone fields.
27. Add a new record to the address list using the following information:
    Ms. Janine Flaherty
    39621 Gardendale Drive
    Tampa, FL 33624
    T-Shirt Size: L
    Parents: Mr. and Mrs. Jake Flaherty
28. Fill in the new fields for all existing records using the information in the following table:

	Size	Parent/Guardian
Jeffrey Levine	XL	Mr. and Mrs. Keith Levine
Liz Mohoney	S	Mrs. Delia Smith
Melanie Jackson	M	Mr. and Mrs. Ronald Jackson
Alex Daniels	M	Mr. and Mrs. Robert Daniels
Suhail Nakhami	L	Mr. Sam Nakhami

29. Close the Mail Merge Recipients dialog box.
30. Set up the labels main document as shown in Illustration B.
    a. Insert the individual merge fields as shown.
       ✓ *Don't worry if the field names wrap onto multiple lines.*
    b. Type text, punctuation, and spacing as shown.
    c. Once you set up the first label, use Update all labels to set up the other labels.
31. Check the spelling and grammar in the document.
32. Preview the merged documents.
33. Complete the merge by generating a file containing all of the individual labels.
34. Save the file as **LABELS**.
35. Close all open files, saving all changes.

Illustration A

```
Northwest Gear, Inc.
2749 Mission St.
Seattle, WA 98122




                              ««AddressBlock»»


```

Illustration B

```
«Title» «First_Name» «Last_Name» or
«ParentGuardian_Name»
«Address_Line_1»
«Address_Line_2»
«City», «State» «ZIP_Code»

Enclosed shirt size: «TShirt_Size»
```

On Your Own

1. Create a new document in Word.
2. Save it as **OWD33-1**.
3. Use the Mail Merge Wizard to create envelopes, using **OWD32-2** (the data source document you used in Exercise 32) as the data source.

   ✓ If **OWD32-2** *is not available, use* ⊙ **33DATA**.

4. Add at least one new record to the data source.
5. Delete at least one field.
6. Add at least one field.
7. Fill in all missing information for the existing records.
8. Merge the envelopes to a new document.
9. Save the merge document as **OWD33-3**.
10. Close all open documents, saving all changes.

Exercise 34

Skills Covered:

◆ **Sort Recipients in an Address List** ◆ **Select Specific Recipients**
◆ **Filter Recipients** ◆ **Create a Directory with Merge**

On the Job

You can use Mail Merge to create a directory, such as a telephone directory, an address list, or a customer directory. Mail Merge makes it easy to select records in your data source file so you can include only specific recipients in a merge. You can also sort the data source file so that the merge documents are generated in alphabetical or numerical order.

California Cardiology has asked you to create a directory of its doctors to give out to patients. You have an existing Office Address List file that lists all doctors and nurses. In this exercise, you will use the existing Address List data source file, which you will filter in order to select the records you need. You will also sort the list before generating the directory.

Terms

Column heading The label displayed at the top of a column.

Filter To display records based on whether or not they match specified criteria.

Criteria Specific data used to match a record or entry in a data source file or list.

Directory A single document listing data source file entries

Notes

Sort Recipients in an Address List

- You can quickly change the order of records in an address list based on the data entered in any column in the list.
- Simply click any **column heading** in the Mail Merge Recipients dialog box to sort the records into ascending order.
- Click the column heading again to sort the records into descending order.

Select Specific Recipients

- By default, all recipients in an Address List are selected to be included in a merge.
- You can select the specific recipients you want to include. For example, you might want to send letters only to the people who live in a specific town.
- To indicate that a recipient is selected, Word displays a check in the checkbox at the left end of the recipient's row in the Mail Merge Recipients dialog box.
- You click the checkbox to clear the check, or click the empty box to select the recipient again.

An Address List with only some recipients selected

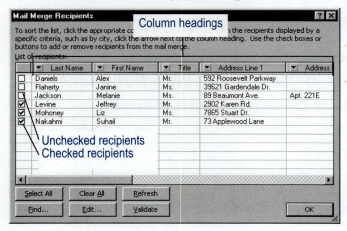

An Address List with only some recipients selected

- When you merge to a directory, Word creates a single document that includes the variable data for all selected recipients.

- You arrange the layout for the first entry in the directory; Mail Merge uses that layout for all entries.

- You may type text, spacing, and punctuation, and you can include formatting. For example, you might want to include labels such as *Name:*, *Home Phone:*, and *E-Mail:*.

- The Mail Merge Wizard does not give you the option of printing the directory in step 6; however, you may print the merged document the same way you would print any document.

Filter Recipients

- You can **filter** the records in an Address List in order to display records that match specific **criteria**.

- The records that match the criteria are displayed, while those that don't match are hidden.

- Filtering can help make it easier to select the specific records you want to include in a merge. For example, if you want to include only the people who live in the state of California, you can deselect all records, filter the list to display only those that have CA entered in the State field, then select the displayed records.

The layout for a directory

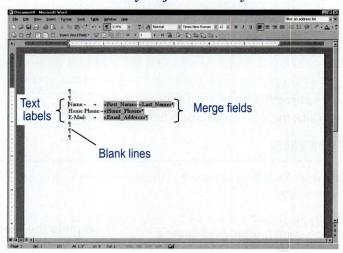

The merged directory

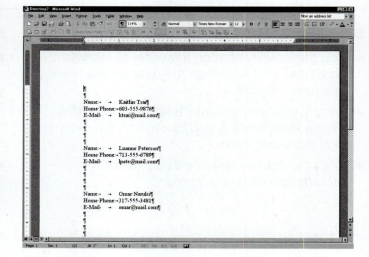

A filtered list

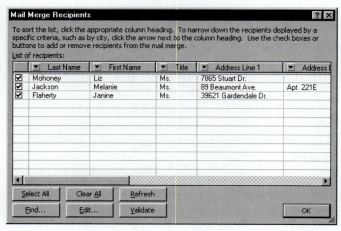

Create a Directory with Mail Merge

- Use Mail Merge to create a **directory**, such as a catalog, an inventory list, or a membership address list.

Procedures

Use the Mail Merge Wizard to Generate a Directory Using an Existing Address List Data Source File

Select the main document:

1. Open a new blank document.
2. Click **Tools**.................. **Alt** + **T**
3. Select **Letters and Mailings**............................ **E**
4. Click **Mail Merge Wizard**..... **M**
5. Click the **Directory** option button.
6. Click **Next: Starting document**.
7. Click the **Use the current document** option button.
8. Click **Next: Select recipients**.

Select an existing Address List data source file:

1. Click the **Use an existing list** option button.
2. Click **Browse** button ☷.
   ✓ Word opens the Select Data Source dialog box.
3. Locate and select the desired data source file.
4. Click **Open** [Open].
   ✓ Word displays the Mail Merge Recipients dialog box.
5. Click **OK**.......................... **Enter**
6. Click **Next: Arrange your directory**.
   ✓ Word displays the starting document, and a list of available merge blocks.

Arrange the directory:

1. In the current document, position the insertion point at the location where you want the first entry in the directory displayed.
2. Insert the merge fields or merge blocks as necessary to set up the first entry.
3. Type any additional text, spacing, or punctuation you want in the first entry.

✓ Typed data will be repeated as part of each entry in the directory.

4. Save the document.
5. Click **Next: Preview your directory**.
   ✓ Word displays the first entry in the document.

Preview merge documents:

1. Click the **Next recipient** button [>>] in the Mail Merge Wizard Task Pane.
   OR
   Click the **Next recipient** button [▶] on the Mail Merge toolbar.
   OR
   Click the **Previous recipient** button [<<] in the Mail Merge Wizard Task Pane.
   OR
   Click the **Previous recipient** button [◀] on the Mail Merge toolbar.
2. Click **Next: Complete the merge**.

Complete the merge:

1. Click **To New Document** button [🗐] to create the directory document.
   ✓ Word displays the Merge to New Document dialog box.
2. Click **OK** .... **Enter**
   ✓ You can make changes to the document and/or save the document to print later.

Sort Recipients in an Address List

1. Click **Mail Merge Recipients** button [☷] on Mail Merge toolbar.
   OR
   In Step 3 or Step 5 of Mail Merge Wizard, click **Edit recipient list** [☷].
2. Click **column heading** by which you want to sort.

✓ To sort in descending order, click column heading again.

3. Click **OK** .... **Enter**
   ✓ Records will be merged in current sort order.

Select Specific Recipients

1. Click **Mail Merge Recipients** button [☷] on Mail Merge toolbar.
   OR
   In Step 3 or Step 5 of Mail Merge Wizard, click **Edit recipient list** button [☷].
2. Do one of the following:
   • Click **checkbox** at left of row to deselect recipient..................... [☑]
   • Click **blank checkbox** to select recipient .... [☐]
   • Click **Clear All** .... **Alt** + **A** to deselect all recipients.
   • Click **Select All** ...... **Alt** + **S** to select all recipients.
3. Click **OK** .... **Enter**

Filter Recipients

1. Click **Mail Merge Recipients** button [☷] on Mail Merge toolbar.
   OR
   In Step 3 or Step 5 of Mail Merge Wizard, click **Edit recipient list** [☷].
2. Click **filter arrow** [▼] on column heading by which you want to filter.
   ✓ Word displays a list of data.
3. Select data to filter by.
   ✓ Word displays only those entries that match the selected data.
   OR
   Select one of the following:
   • **[All]** to display all entries.
     ✓ Use this option to remove an existing filter.
   • **[Blanks]** to display entries in which the current field is blank.

- **[Nonblanks]** to display entries in which the current field is not blank.

✓ *The filter arrow on the column heading changes to blue so you know which column is used for the filter.*

4. Click **OK**......................... Enter

Exercise Directions

1. Make a copy of the Office Address List file ⊙**34CALDATA**, and name the copy **CALDATA**.

   ✓ *To copy the file, right-click the file name and select Copy. Right-click the destination folder and select Paste. Right-click the copied file name and select Rename. Type the new file name and press Enter.*

2. Start Word if necessary.
3. Create a new blank document.
4. Save the document as **MAINDIR**.
5. Start the Mail Merge Wizard.
6. Select to create a directory, using the current document.
7. Select to use an existing address list file as a data source document.
8. Locate and open **CALDATA**.
9. Filter the list to display only the nurses.
   a. Click the filter arrow on the Title column heading.
   b. Click Ms.
10. Deselect all of the nurses.
11. Remove the filter.
    a. Click the filter arrow on the Title column heading.
    b. Click [All].
12. Sort the list in ascending order by Last Name.
13. Close the Mail Merge Recipients dialog box.

14. Set up the directory main document as shown in Illustration A.
15. Complete the merge by generating a new directory document.
16. Preview the directory.
17. Save the directory document in a new file, named **DIRECTORY**.
18. Edit the file as shown in Illustration B.
    a. Insert five new lines at the beginning of the document.
    b. Centered on line 1, type **California Cardiology, Inc**. in a 26-point serif font.
    c. Centered on line 2, type the address as shown in a 12-point serif font.
    d. Leave line 3 blank.
    e. Centered on line 4, type **Directory of Physicians** in a 20-point serif font.
    f. Leave line 5 blank.
19. Check the spelling and grammar in the document.
20. Display the document in Print Preview. It should look similar to the one shown in Illustration B.
21. Print the directory.
22. Close all open files, saving all changes.

On Your Own

1. Create a new document in Word.
2. Save it as **OWD34-1**.
3. Use the Mail Merge Wizard to create a directory, using **OWD32-2** (the data source document you used in Exercise 32) as the data source.

   ✓ *If **OWD32-2** is not available, use ⊙**34DATA**.*

4. Filter the list.
5. Select to include only certain entries.

6. Sort the list.
7. Merge the directory to a new document.
8. Save the directory as **OWD34-3**.
9. Edit the directory document to include a title.
10. Check the spelling and grammar.
11. Complete the merge by generating a new document.
12. Print the directory.
13. Close all open documents, saving all changes.

Illustration A

Typed text;
14-pt. serif   *Tab to 1.5"*
font

Name: →   «Title» «First_Name» «Last_Name»   *Merge fields*

Phone: →   «Work_Phone»

E-Mail →   «Email_Address»

Specialty: → «Specialty»

California Cardiology, Inc.

10101 Santa Monica Blvd., Suite 1200, Los Angeles, CA 90067

Directory of Physicians

Name:	**Dr. Finn Broderbund**
Phone:	**310-555-2928**
E-Mail	**finn@calcardiology.com**
Specialty:	**Prevention**

Name:	**Dr. Francis Dorsky**
Phone:	**310-555-2924**
E-Mail	**dorsky@calcardiology.com**
Specialty:	**Cardiovascular Disease**

Name:	**Dr. William Doyle**
Phone:	**310-555-2927**
E-Mail	**wdoyle@calcardiology.com**
Specialty:	**Cardiovascular Surgery**

Name:	**Dr. Amanda Josephson**
Phone:	**310-555-2923**
E-Mail	**josephson@calcardiology.com**
Specialty:	**Geriatric Care**

Name:	**Dr. Clarissa Joubert**
Phone:	**310-555-2929**
E-Mail	**cjoubert@calcardiology.com**
Specialty:	**Cardiovascular Disease**

Exercise 35

◆ Critical Thinking

Murray Hill Marketing wants you to create class lists for three upcoming in-house training courses so the instructors know how many people to expect. In addition, you need to send out memos to all enrollees confirming their course selection. In this exercise, you will use Mail Merge to create the memos and the directories. You will create a new data source file that you can use for all merges. The file will need to be customized to include fields specific to your needs. It will also need to be filtered and sorted to complete each merge.

Exercise Directions

1. Start Word, if necessary.
2. Create a new blank document.
3. Save the file as **CONFIRM**.
4. Start the Mail Merge Wizard.
5. Select to create a letter, using the current document.
6. Create a new address list to use as a data source document.
7. Customize the address list as follows:
   a. Rename the Company field to **Department**.
   b. Delete all of the fields pertaining to address (Address Line 1, Address Line 2, City, State, ZIP Code, and Country).
   c. Add a field named **Course**.
   d. Delete the Home Phone field.
8. Enter the recipients from the table on the following page into the data source file.
9. Save the data source file as **NAMES**.
10. Sort the data source file by Department.
11. Select to use all recipients in the merge, then close the Mail Merge Recipients dialog box.
12. Type the document shown in Illustration A, inserting the merge fields as marked.
13. Check the spelling and grammar in the document.
14. Preview the merged documents.
15. Complete the merge by generating a new file containing all merged records.

16. Save the file as **MEMOS**.
17. Print the file.
18. Close all open documents, saving all changes.
19. Create a new blank document.
20. Save the file as **ENROLLED**.
21. Start the Mail Merge Wizard.
22. Select to create a directory, using the current document.
23. Use the **NAMES** address list as the data source file.
24. Sort the list alphabetically by last name.
25. Filter the list to display only the people enrolled in the Word 1 course.
26. Set up the directory as shown in Illustration B.
27. Preview the directory.
28. Generate the directory and save it in a new file named **Word 1**.
29. Add the title **Word 1 Class List** in a 24-point sans serif font at the top of the Word 1 directory.
30. Check the spelling and grammar in the document.
31. Print the document.
32. Close the document, saving all changes.
   ✓ *The Enrolled document should still be open on-screen, with the Mail Merge Wizard displaying Step 6.*
33. Go back through the Mail Merge Wizard to step 5.

34. Edit the Recipient list to change the filter from Word 1 to Word 2.

35. Preview the directory.

36. Generate the directory and save it in a new file named **Word 2**.

37. Add the title **Word 2 Class List** in a 24-point sans serif font at the top of the Word 2 directory.

38. Check the spelling and grammar in the document.

39. Print the document.

40. Close the document, saving all changes.

41. Repeat steps 33–40 to create a directory for the Word 3 class.

42. Close the **ENROLLED** document, saving all changes.

Mr. Gary Dubin	Human Resources	Word 3	555-3232	gdubin@murrayhill.com
Ms. Elizabeth Doone	Graphic Design	Word 1	555-3233	lizdoone@murrayhill.com
Ms. Janice Loring	Accounting	Word 2	555-3234	jloring@murrayhill.com
Mr. Antonio DiBuono	Marketing	Word 1	555-3235	Antonio@murrayhill.com
Ms. Katharine Peterson	Human Resources	Word 2	555-3236	kpeterson@murrayhill.com
Ms. Marianne Flagg	Graphic Design	Word 3	555-3237	mflagg@murrayhill.com
Mr. Howard Jefferson	Customer Support	Word 2	555-3238	hjefferson@murrayhill.com
Mr. Julian Lovett	Graphic Design	Word 3	555-3239	jullovett@murrayhill.com
Ms. Christina Bottecelli	Accounting	Word 1	555-3240	chrisbott@murrayhill.com
Ms. Rose Mekalian	Marketing	Word 3	555-3241	rosemekalian@murrayhill.com
Mr. Dana Teng	Copywriting	Word 2	555-3242	dteng@murrayhill.com
Mr. Luis Martinez	Accounting	Word 1	555-3243	lmartinez@murrayhill.com

Illustration A

MEMO

↓4x

Insert merge fields

To: 「«Title» «First_Name» «Last_Name», «Department»」
From: Your name
Date: Today's date
Subject: In-house Training Confirmation

↓3x

Insert merge field

This memo confirms that you have enrolled in the in-house training course 「«Course»」.
Classes start the second week of April. You will receive additional information
concerning class materials and the meeting location from your instructor a few days
before the first class.

↓2x

If you have any questions 「«Title» «Last_Name»」, please contact me and I will do my best
to answer them.

Insert merge fields

↓3x

«Title» «First_Name» «Last_Name»
«Department»
«Work_Phone»
«EMail_Address»
↓4x

On the Job

Create an outline to organize ideas for any document that covers more than one topic, such as an article, a report, a presentation, or a speech. For example, you might create an outline to list the chapters or headings in a report or to arrange main subjects for a presentation. The outline serves as a map you can follow as you complete the entire document.

California Cardiology, Inc. wants to publish a document describing some of the things patients can do to insure good cardiovascular health. In this exercise, you will create an outline for that document.

Terms

Outline A document that lists levels of topics.

Style A set of formatting features that can be applied to text.

Promote To move up one level in an outline.

Demote To move down one level in an outline.

Collapse To hide subtopics in an outline.

Expand To show subtopics in an outline.

Notes

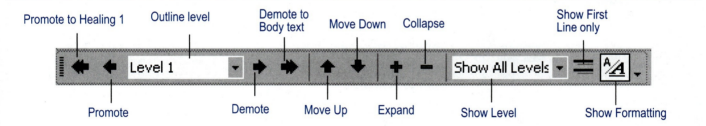

Create an Outline

- Use Outline view to create and edit **outlines**.
- Outline topics are set up in levels, which are sometimes called headings: Level 1 is a main heading, Level 2 is a subheading, Level 3 is a sub-subheading, and so on up to 9 heading levels.
- Word automatically applies different **styles** to different levels in an outline.

- Levels that have sublevels under them are preceded by an Expand Outline symbol ⊕.
- Levels that do not have sublevels are preceded by a Collapse Outline symbol ▭.
- Regular document text is called Body text.

Edit an Outline

- You can edit an outline using the same techniques you use to edit regular document text. For example, you can insert and delete text at any location.

- To reorganize an outline, you can **promote** or **demote** heading levels. For example, you can demote a Level 1 paragraph to a Level 2 paragraph.

- You can also move headings and subheadings up or down the outline to reorganize the outline.

Collapse and Expand Outlines

- When you want to work with only some heading levels at a time, you can **collapse** the outline using the Collapse button █ .

- Collapsing an outline hides lower level headings.

- To see hidden or collapsed levels, you can **expand** the outline using the Expand button ✚ .

Number an Outline

- Traditional outlines are numbered with different number and letter styles used to represent different levels.

- Word comes with seven built-in outline numbering styles.

- You can select a numbering style before or after typing the outline.

Select an outline numbering style in the Bullets and Numbering dialog box

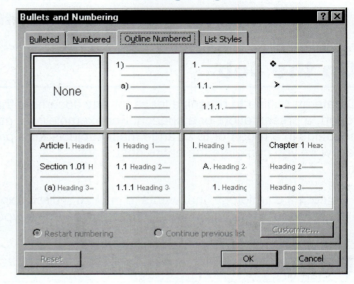

Procedures

Create an Outline

1. Click the **Outline View** button ▤ .
   OR
   a. Click **View** .... Alt + V
   b. Click **Outline** .... O
2. Type Heading 1 text.
3. Press **Enter** .... Enter
   ✓ *Heading level is carried forward to the new paragraph.*
4. Type more Heading 1 text.
   OR
   a. Click the **Demote** button ➡ .... Tab
   b. Type Heading 2 text.
5. Press **Enter** .... Enter
6. Type Heading 2 text.
   OR

Click the **Demote** button ➡ to type text for the next lower level .... Tab
OR
Click the **Promote** button ⬅ to type text for the next higher level .... Shift + Tab
7. Press **Enter** .... Enter
8. Continue until outline is complete.

Type body text:
1. Position insertion point where you want to type Body text.
2. Click **Demote to Body Text** button ➡ .... Ctrl + Shift + N
3. Type text.

Edit an Outline

Select headings:
1. Click outline symbol preceding the heading ✚ or █ .
   ✓ *The heading and all subheadings are selected.*
2. Make desired changes.

Change heading levels:
1. Position insertion point anywhere on heading line.
   OR
   Select heading.
2. Click **Promote** button ⬅ .... Shift + Tab to promote heading one level.
   OR
   - Click **Demote** button ➡ .... Tab to demote heading one level.

OR

a. Click **Outline Level** drop-

down arrow `Level 1 ▾`.

b. Click desired level.

Move headings:

1. Position insertion point anywhere on the heading line.

OR

Select heading to move.

2. Drag **outline symbol** up `+` or

down `–` to a new location.

OR

Click **Move Up** `↑` to move heading up one line.

OR

Click **Move Down** `↓` to move heading down one line.

Collapse and expand an outline:

- Click **Show Level** drop-

down arrow `Show All Levels ▾`.

- Click desired level.

OR

Double-click **outline symbol**

`+` or `–` preceding heading.

Change Outline Numbering Style

1. Position the insertion point where the outline will begin.

OR

Select headings to number.

2. Click **Format**...............`Alt`+`O`

3. Click **Bullets and Numbering**.........................`N`

4. Click **Outline Numbered** page tab.....................`Alt`+`U`

5. Select numbering style.

✓ *Select None to remove numbering.*

6. Click **OK** ....`Enter`

Exercise Directions

1. Start Word, if necessary.

2. Create a new document and save it as **HEART**.

3. Change to Outline view.

4. Select the Numbering style used in the illustration.

5. Type the outline shown in the illustration.

   a. Press Tab or click Demote to demote a level.

   b. Press Shift+Tab, or click Promote to promote a level.

   c. Press Ctrl+Shift+N or click Demote to Body Text to type regular text.

6. Collapse the outline to show only levels 1 and 2.

7. Display all levels.

8. Move the heading **Symptoms** and its subheading down so it is the third subheading under **What is Coronary Heart Disease?**.

   ✓ *Notice that Word renumbers the outline automatically.*

9. Promote the heading **Will You Have a Heart Attack?**.

10. Move **Lack of Exercise** up under **Obesity**, and demote it to level 4.

11. Check the spelling in the document.

12. Print the document.

13. Close the document, saving all changes.

On Your Own

1. Create a new document in Word.

2. Save the file as **OWD36**.

3. Draft an outline for a speech or presentation you'd like to give. Include at least three levels. For example, draft an outline for a presentation you have to give to a class, to an organization, or for a speech to a family member about a household issue that has been on your mind.

4. Examine the outline and make sure all headings are at the correct level. Change the levels if necessary.

5. Try rearranging the headings to see if you can improve the organization.

6. Close the document, saving all changes.

I. Caring for Your Heart *Level 1*

    A. What is Coronary Heart Disease? *Level 2*

        1. **Symptoms** *Level 3*

            a) **Range of severity** *Level 4*

Move down

            It is possible to suffer from CHD without exhibiting any symptoms. Symptoms range from intermittent chest pain that may be confused with indigestion, to severe pain and difficulty breathing. *Body text*

        2. **Angina**

            a) **Clogged arteries**

            b) **Reduced oxygen flow**

        3. **Heart attack**

            a) **Blocked arteries**

            b) **No oxygen flow**

Promote →

    B. Will You Have a Heart Attack?

    C. Uncontrollable Risk Factors

        1. **Age**

        2. **Gender**

            a) **Male vs. Female**

        3. **Genes**

            a) **Heredity counts**

    D. Controllable Risk Factors

        1. **Smoking**

            a) **Doubles risk**

        2. **High blood pressure**

            a) **High cholesterol**

        3. **Obesity**

Move and Demote

        4. **Stress**

        5. **Lack of Exercise**

II. What You Can Do to Maintain a Healthy Heart

    A. Healthy Diet

        1. **Lose weight**

        2. **Lower cholesterol levels**

            a) **Eat more fruit and vegetables**

            b) **Eat less fat**

    B. Exercise

    C. Quit Smoking

        Quitting smoking significantly lowers the risk of a heart attack.

    D. See Your Doctor Regularly

Exercise 37

Skills Covered:

◆ **Insert Page Breaks** ◆ **Insert Section Breaks**
◆ **Create Headers and Footers** ◆ **Insert Page Numbers**
◆ **View the Word Count**

On the Job

Make a long document easier to read and work in by inserting page breaks and section breaks, page numbers, and headers and footers. Page breaks let you control where a new page should start, avoiding page layout problems such as headings at the bottom of a page. Section breaks let you apply different page formatting to different areas of your document. Headers and footers let you print information on the top or bottom of every page.

In this exercise, you will work with a version of the heart care report you outlined in Exercise 27 for California Cardiology. You will insert page breaks and section breaks, apply formatting, and insert headers and footers. When the report is complete, you will print it.

Terms

Soft page break The place where Word automatically starts a new page when the current page is filled with text.

Hard page break A nonprinting character that tells Word to start a new page, even if the current page is not filled with text.

Section A portion of a document that can be formatted independently from other sections.

Section break A nonprinting character that tells Word to start a new section within a document.

Header Repetitive text or graphics printed at the top of pages in a document.

Footer Repetitive text or graphics printed at the bottom of pages in a document.

Notes

Insert Page Breaks

- A standard 8.5" by 11" sheet of paper with 1" top and bottom margins has 9" of vertical space for entering text.
    - ✓ *The number of lines depends on the font size and spacing settings.*
- Word inserts a **soft page break** to start a new page when the current page is full.
- Soft page breaks adjust automatically if text is inserted or deleted, so a break always occurs when the current page is full.

- Insert a **hard page break** to start a new page before the current page is full. For example, insert a hard page break before a heading that falls at the bottom of a page; the break forces the heading to the top of the next page.

- Breaks move like characters when you insert and delete text. Therefore, you should insert hard page breaks after all editing is complete to avoid having a break occur at an awkward position on the page.

- In Normal view, a soft page break is marked by a dotted line across the page.

- By default, in Print Layout view page breaks are indicated by a space between the bottom of one page and the top of the next page; if you have nonprinting characters displayed, the space where you insert a hard page break is marked by a dotted line with the words Page Break centered in it.

  - ✓ *You can hide the space between pages in Print Layout view. If you do, page breaks are marked by a solid black line. Simply click on the space between pages to hide it, or click on the solid line between pages to show the space again.*

- In Normal view, a hard page break is marked by a dotted line with the words Page Break centered in it.

Page breaks in Normal view

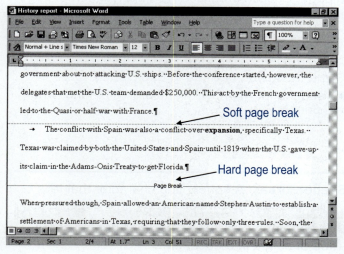

Page breaks in Print Layout view

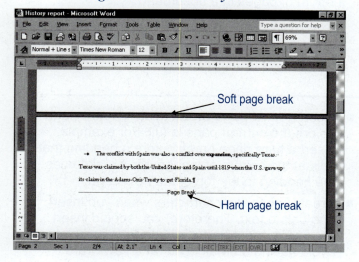

Insert Section Breaks

- A default Word document contains one **section**.

- You can divide a document into multiple sections to apply different formatting to each section. For example, you can set different margins, headers, or footers for each section.

- There are four types of **section breaks**:

  - Next page: inserts a section break and a page break so that the new section will start on the next page.

  - Continuous: inserts a section break so that the new section will start at the insertion point.

  - Even page: inserts a section break and page breaks so the new section will start on the next even-numbered page.

  - Odd page: inserts a section break and page breaks so the new section will start on the next odd-numbered page.

- In Normal view, section breaks are displayed as solid double lines across the width of the page with the words Section Break in the middle, followed by the type of break in parentheses.

  - ✓ *In Print Layout view section breaks are displayed only if nonprinting characters are displayed.*

Section breaks in Normal view

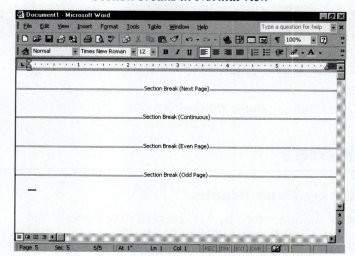

Create Headers/Footers

- Create a **header** and/or **footer** to print repetitive information such as page numbers, dates, author, or subject on every page of a document.

- Headers and footers are not displayed in Normal view; use Print Preview or Print Layout view to see them on the screen.

- By default, headers print .5" from the top of the page; footers print .5" from the bottom of the page.

- You can apply headers and footers to the entire document or to the current section.

- Set options to control which pages headers/footers print on:
  - Different odd and even lets you print different headers and/or footers on odd and even pages.
  - Different first page lets you print a different header and/or footer on the first page.
    - ✓ *Leave first page header/footer blank to print no header/footer on first page.*

The Layout tab of the Page Setup dialog box

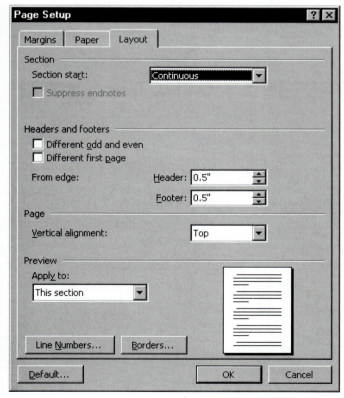

- Use Header/Footer toolbar buttons to customize headers and footers.

Header and Footer toolbar

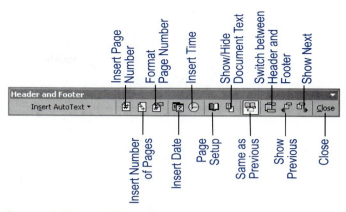

Insert Page Numbers

- You can insert page numbers in a header or footer using either the Header and Footer toolbar, or the Insert, Page Numbers command.

- Use the Header and Footer toolbar when you are inserting page numbers as part of a more complete header or footer.

- Use the Insert, Page Numbers command when you don't want to create an entire header or footer. The command provides additional options for formatting and positioning the numbers on the page.

Page Numbers dialog box

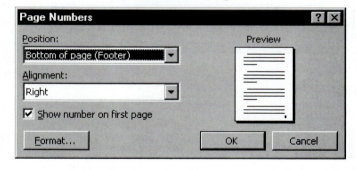

- Position: sets numbers at the top or bottom of the page.

- Alignment: sets numbers left, right, centered, inside, or outside of the page.

- Show number on first page: shows or suppresses the page number on the first page.

- Regardless of which method you use to insert the page number, you can use the Page Number Format dialog box to select a different number style, to include chapter numbers, or to restart numbering in a new section.

✓ *Restarting the numbering is useful when your document has a title page that you do not want numbered. Insert a Next Page section break between the title page and the first page of the document. That makes the title page the first section. Then, click the Format button in the Page Numbers dialog box to display the Page Number Format dialog box. Select the option to restart the page numbers for the second section, then click OK to return to the Page Numbers dialog box.*

✓ *If you originally inserted the page number using the Header and Footer toolbar, you should click the **Close** button in the Page Numbers dialog box instead of the OK button in order to prevent inserting two page numbers on each page.*

Page Number Format dialog box

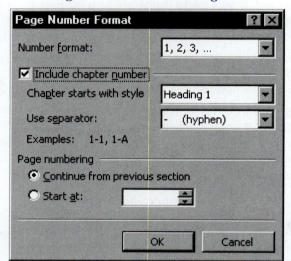

View the Word Count

- Word keeps track of statistics, such as how many words you have typed in a document.

- There are three ways to view the word count:
  - Use the Word Count command on the Tools menu to check the document statistics.

Word Count dialog box

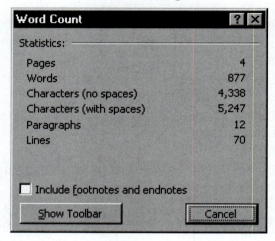

- Use the Word Count toolbar to have access to the current word count while you work.

Word Count toolbar

- Use the Statistics page of the Properties dialog box.

  ✓ *See Exercise 12 for information about Document Properties.*

Procedures

Insert a Hard Page Break (Ctrl+Enter)

1. Click **Insert** .... `Alt`+`I`
2. Click **Break** .... `B`
3. Click the **Page break** option button .... `Alt`+`P`
4. Click **OK** .... `Enter`

Delete a Hard Page Break

1. In Normal view, position insertion point on hard page break.

2. Press **Delete** .... `Del`

Insert a Section Break

1. Click **Insert** .... `Alt`+`I`
2. Click **Break** .... `B`
3. Click the option button for desired break:
   - **Next page** .... `Alt`+`N`
   - **Con**t**inuous** .... `Alt`+`T`
   - **Even page** .... `Alt`+`E`
   - **Odd page** .... `Alt`+`O`

4. Click **OK** .... `Enter`

Delete a Section Break

1. In Normal view, position insertion point on section break.
2. Press **Delete** .... `Del`

Create Headers/Footers

To create a header on every page:

1. Click **View** .... `Alt`+`V`
2. Click **Header and Footer** .... `H`

3. In the **Header box**, type header text.

   ✓ *Use formatting options as desired, including fonts, font effects, alignment, tabs, and spacing.*

4. Click **Close** button Close on the Header/Footer toolbar.

To create a footer on every page:

1. Click **View** .... Alt + V
2. Click **Header and Footer** .... H
3. Click the **Switch Between Header and Footer** button 🖹.
4. In the **Footer box**, type footer text.

   ✓ *Use formatting options as desired, including fonts, font effects, alignment, and tabs.*

5. Click **Close** button Close on the Header/Footer toolbar.

Insert page numbers, date, and/or time in a header/footer:

1. Click **View** .... Alt + V
2. Click **Header and Footer** .... H
3. Click the **Switch Between Header and Footer** button 🖹 as needed.
4. Click desired toolbar button(s):

   • **Insert Page Number** #
   • **Insert Date** 📅
   • **Insert Time** 🕐

5. Click **Close** button Close on the Header/Footer toolbar.

   ✓ *Combine text and page numbers, date, or time in any combination. For example, type Page, press the spacebar once to leave a space, then insert page number.*

Create first page header/footer:

1. Click **View** .... Alt + V
2. Click **Header and Footer** .... H
3. Click the **Page Setup** button 📖.
4. Select the **Different first page** check box .... Alt + P

---

5. Click **OK** .... Enter
6. In **First Page Header box**, type first page header text.

   ✓ *Leave blank to suppress header on first page.*

7. Click **Switch Between Header and Footer** button 🖹.
8. In **First Page Footer** box, type first page footer text.

   ✓ *Leave blank to suppress footer on first page.*

9. Click **Show Next** button 🔽 to display the header/footer for the next section.
10. In the **Footer** box, type footer text.
11. Click **Switch Between Header and Footer** button 🖹.
12. In the **Header** box, type header text.
13. Click **Close** button Close on Header/Footer toolbar.

Create different odd and even headers/footers:

1. Click **View** .... Alt + V
2. Click **Header and Footer** .... H
3. Click the **Page Setup** button 📖.
4. Click the **Different odd and even** check box .... Alt + O
5. Click **OK** .... Enter
6. In **Even Page Header box**, type even page header text.

   ✓ *If Odd Page Header box displays first, click Show Next or Show Previous button to display Even Page Header.*

7. Click the **Switch Between Header and Footer** button 🖹.
8. In **Even Page Footer** box, type even page footer text.
9. Click the **Show Next** button 🔽 or **Show Previous** button 🔼.
10. In **Odd Page Footer box**, type odd page footer text.

---

11. Click the **Switch Between Header and Footer** button 🖹.
12. In **Odd Page Header** box, type odd page header text.
13. Click **Close** button Close on Header/Footer toolbar.

Insert Page Numbers Only

1. Click **Insert** .... Alt + I
2. Click **Page Numbers** .... U
3. Click the **Position** drop-down arrow .... Alt + P
4. Select **Bottom of page (Footer)** .... Enter
   OR
   Top of page (Header) .... ⬆, Enter
5. Click the **Alignment** drop-down arrow .... Alt + A
6. Select alignment option:...................... ⬆, Enter

   • **Right**
   • **Left**
   • **Center**
   • **Inside**
   • **Outside**

7. Select **Show number on first page** if desired............. Alt + S
8. Click **OK** .... Enter

Change Page Number Formatting

1. Click **Insert** .... Alt + I
2. Click **Page Numbers** .... U
3. Click **Format** Format... .... Alt + F
4. Click the **Number format** drop-down arrow .... Alt + F
5. Select **format** .... ⬇, Enter

   • Arabic numerals.... 1, 2, 3, 4, 5, etc.
   • Arabic numerals with dashes........ -1-, -2-, -3-, etc.
   • Lowercase letters...... a, b, c, d, e, f, etc.

- Uppercase letters . A, B, C, D, E, F, etc.
- Lowercase roman numerals .....i, ii, iii, iv, v, etc.
- Uppercase roman numerals . I, II, III, IV, V, etc.

6. Click **OK** ....『Enter』
   to close formatting box.

7. Click **OK** ....『Enter』
   to close Page number box and insert page numbers.
   OR

Click **Close** 『Close』 to close Page number box without inserting additional page numbers.

View Word Count

1. Click **Tools** ....『Alt』+『T』
2. Click **Word Count** ....『W』
3. Click **Close** button 『Close』 to close dialog box when done. ....『Esc』
   OR

1. Click **View** ....『Alt』+『V』
2. Click **Toolbars** ....『T』
3. Click **Word Count**.
4. Click **Recount** 『Recount』 ....『Alt』+『C』
   to update word count calculation.

Exercise Directions

1. Start Word, if necessary.
2. Open ☺ **37HEART**.
3. Save the file as **HEART**.
4. Format the document as follows (refer to the illustration to see the finished result):
   a. Format the title **Caring for Your Heart** in 26-point Arial, centered, with 12 points of space after.
   b. Justify the first paragraph.
   c. Align the text **California Cardiology, Inc.** with a left tab set at 3.5" on the horizontal ruler.
   d. Leave 12 points of space after the text **California Cardiology, Inc**.
   e. Insert a continuous section break between the text **California Cardiology, Inc.** and the heading **What is Coronary Heart Disease?**.
   f. Format the headings **What is Coronary Heart Disease? Am I at Risk?** and **What Can I Do?** with the Heading 1 style, modified to leave 12 points of space after.
   g. Format the paragraph text under all the headings double-spaced, with a first line indent, and justified.
   h. Insert a page break at the beginning of the second paragraph under the heading **Am I at Risk?** to move it to the top of the second page.
5. Insert a page number flush left at the top of both pages in the document.
6. Preview the document to see how the page numbers look.
7. Use Undo to remove the page number.

8. Create headers and footers as follows:
   a. Create a different first page header and footer in the whole document.
   b. Leave the header on the first page blank.
      ✓ *Note that the first page header and footer areas also indicate that they are for section 1, while the second page header and footer areas indicate that they are for section 2.*
   c. In the first page footer, press Tab to center the insertion point, then type the word **Page**, a space, and insert the page number.
   d. In the second page header, type the report title—**Caring for Your Heart**—flush left, and insert today's date in the center.
   e. In the second page footer, type the company name—**California Cardiology, Inc.**—flush left, and the word Page, a space, and the page number in the center.
      ✓ *If Word automatically inserts the same header or footer on both pages, you did not correctly change the Page Setup options. Make sure you make the change for the whole document, not just section 1 or section 2. If you still have a problem, try repeating the steps with the insertion point in the header, and then with the insertion point in the footer.*
9. Change the margins for the second section to 1.5" on the left and right.
10. Check the spelling and grammar in the document.
11. Check the word count.
12. Display the document in Print Preview. It should look similar to the illustration (2 pages).
13. Print the document.
14. Close the document, saving all changes.

Caring for Your Heart

In response to inquiries from our patients, we are providing this report to help you better understand the nature of coronary heart disease. Most importantly, we are including information about steps you can take to minimize your risks. Please keep in mind that no report can substitute for an open and honest discussion with your physician. If you have any questions, please call, or schedule an appointment.

California Cardiology, Inc.

What is Coronary Heart Disease?

Coronary heart disease (CHD) is the most common form of heart disease. It is caused by a thickening of the inside walls of the coronary arteries, called atherosclerosis. The coronary arteries are responsible for carrying blood to the heart. If they become clogged, the flow of blood to the heart is slowed. As a result the heart is deprived of oxygen and other vital nutrients. Usually – but not always – a patient with atherosclerosis will experience symptoms such as pain and shortness of breath, called angina.

If the condition progresses, the arteries become blocked and the blood supply is cut off completely. The result is a heart attack. The part of the heart that does not receive oxygen begins to die, and some of the heart muscle may be damaged beyond repair.

Am I at Risk?

In most people, cholesterol and fat circulate in the blood and build up on the walls of the coronary arteries. Atherosclerosis usually occurs when a person has unusually high levels of cholesterol in the blood.

Caring for Your Heart   Today's Date

While CHD can strike anyone, there are certain factors that can help doctors identify patients who may be at a higher risk than others. Some of these factors are uncontrollable, such as your age, but some are directly controllable by lifestyle choices, such as diet and exercise.

What Can I Do?

The major controllable risk factors are cigarette smoking, high blood pressure, high cholesterol levels, obesity, and an inactive lifestyle. As you may notice, many of these factors are related. For example, high blood pressure, high cholesterol, and obesity are all potentially the result of an unhealthy diet and a lack of exercise.

Although there are medical and surgical treatments available to control CHD, clearly it is in your best interest to reduce your risk factors as soon as possible. First and foremost, quit smoking. Smoking is thought to double your risk of heart attack, and when combined with the other risk factors, it may raise your chances by eight or ten times.

Other steps to take include changing your diet to reduce or eliminate saturated fats and sodium. In other words, eat more fruits and vegetables and less candy and potato chips. This will help lower your blood pressure and cholesterol, and will promote weight loss. Finally, you should increase the amount of exercise you get each day. Exercise does not have to be strenuous, but it should be consistent. A simple walk around the block will help get your body moving and your heart pumping.

On Your Own

1. Start Word and draft and format a multiple page document, or open ⊙ **37GUIDES**. The document might be a letter, a report, a short story, an outline, or an autobiography. Try to include at least three pages. If necessary, double-space the document and increase the width of the margins.

2. Save the file as **OWD37**.

3. Create headers and footers for the document. Include your name and the date in the header, and center the page numbers in the footer.

4. Insert page breaks if necessary so that headings or paragraphs start at the top of a page instead of at the bottom of one.

5. Insert at least one section break. Change the header for section 2 so it includes the page number, and change the footer so it includes your name and the date.

6. Print the document.

7. Close the document, saving all changes.

Exercise 38

Skills Covered:

◆ **Footnotes and Endnotes** ◆ **Find and Replace**
◆ **Create Bookmarks** ◆ **Select Browse Object**

On the Job

Include footnotes or endnotes in documents to provide information about the source of quoted material, or to supplement the main text. Use the Find, Bookmark, and Browse Object features to locate specific parts of a document, including text, graphics, paragraph marks, etc. Use Find and Replace when you want to automatically replace existing text or formatting with something different.

You have been working to complete the report on heart care for California Cardiology, Inc. In this exercise, you will edit the document using Find and Replace. You will also insert footnotes, endnotes, and bookmarks into the document, browse through the document, and modify the formatting.

Terms

Footnote An explanation or reference to additional material printed at the bottom of a page.

Endnote An explanation or reference to additional material printed at the end of a document.

Citation A reference to the source of quoted material.

Note reference mark A number or character inserted in the document to refer to footnote or endnote text.

Note text The text of the footnote or endnote citation.

Bookmark A nonprinting character that you insert and name so that you can quickly find a particular location in a document.

Browse object A specified element that Word locates and displays when you scroll through a document.

Notes

Footnotes and Endnotes

- **Footnotes** or **endnotes** are required in documents that include quoted material, such as research papers.
- Standard footnotes and endnotes include the following **citation** information:
  - The author of the quoted material (first name first) followed by a comma.
  - The title of the book, article, or Web page (in quotation marks), followed by a comma.

- The publication volume and/or date (in parentheses) followed by a colon.
- The page number(s) where the material is located, followed by a period.
- If the source is a Web page, the citation should also include the URL address, enclosed in brackets <>.

  ✓ *There are other styles used for footnotes and endnotes. For example, some use periods between parts instead of commas. If you are unsure which style to use, ask your instructor for more information.*

- Footnotes or endnotes can also provide explanations or supplement text. For example, an asterisk footnote might provide information about where to purchase a product mentioned in the text.

- When you insert a footnote, Word first inserts a **note reference mark** in the text, then a separator line following the last line of text on the page, and finally inserts the note number corresponding to the note mark below the separator line. You then type and format the **note text**.

Footnotes at the bottom of a page

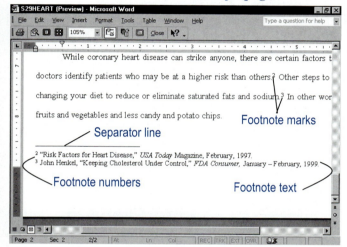

- Endnotes include the same parts as footnotes but are printed on the last page of a document.

- Footnotes and endnotes are not displayed in Normal view; to see them, use Print Preview or Print Layout view.

- Notes can be displayed in a ScreenTip by resting the mouse pointer on the note mark.

- It is easiest to insert footnotes or endnotes in Print Layout view.

- Word uses arabic numerals for footnote marks; if endnotes are used in the same document, the endnote marks are roman numerals.

- You can select a different number format or a symbol for the note mark.

  ✓ *By default, numbering is consecutive from the beginning of the document. You can set Word to restart numbering on each page or each section. You can also change the starting number if you want.*

- Word automatically updates numbering if you add or delete footnotes or endnotes, or rearrange the document text.

Footnote and Endnote dialog box

Find and Replace

- Use Word's Find command to locate specific text, nonprinting characters, formatting, graphics, objects, and other items in a document.

- You can use Find to scroll one by one through each occurrence of the Find text, or you can find and replace all occurrences at once.

Find tab of the Find and Replace dialog box

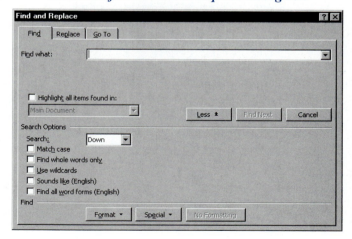

- Combine Find with Replace to replace items.

- The Find and Replace commands are useful for correcting errors that occur several times in a document, such as a misspelled name.
- In addition to text, you can find and replace formatting, symbols, and special characters such as paragraph marks.

Replace tab of the Find and Replace dialog box

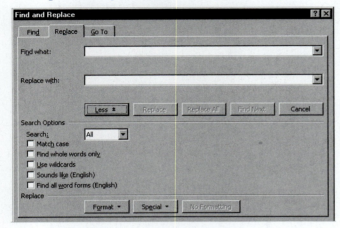

Create Bookmarks

- Use a **bookmark** to mark a specific location in a document, such as where you stopped working or where you need to insert information.
- You can use many bookmarks in one document.
- Use descriptive bookmark names to make it easier to find the bookmark location that you want.
- Use the Go To feature to go directly to a bookmark.

Go To tab of Find and Replace dialog box

Select Browse Object

- Use **browse object** to scroll to specific points in a document.
- There are twelve browse objects from which to choose; rest the mouse pointer on an object to see its name across the top of the object pallet.
  - When you choose the Go To browse object, you must specify the object to go to.
  - When you choose the Find browse object, you must enter text to Find and/or Replace.

The available browse objects

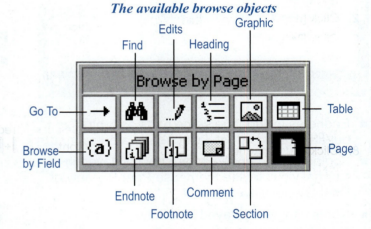

Procedures

Footnotes and Endnotes

To insert footnotes in Print Layout view:

1. Position insertion point after text to footnote.
2. Click **Insert** ....`Alt`+`I`
3. Click **Reference**...................`N`
4. Click **Footnote**......................`N`
5. Click the **Footnote** option button ....`Alt`+`F`
6. Click **Insert** ....`Alt`+`I`
7. Type note text.
8. Click in document text ....`Shift`+`F5`

To insert endnotes in Print Layout view:

1. Position insertion point after text to endnote.
2. Click **Insert** ....`Alt`+`I`
3. Click **Reference**...................`N`
4. Click **Footnote**......................`N`
5. Click the **Endnote** option button ....`Alt`+`E`
6. Click **Insert** ....`Alt`+`I`
7. Type note text.
8. Click in document text ....`Shift`+`F5`

Display Note Text in ScreenTip

1. Click **Tools**...................`Alt`+`T`
2. Click **Options**.......................`O`
3. Click **View** tab ....`Ctrl`+`Tab`
4. Select **ScreenTips** check box...................`Alt`+`N`
5. Click **OK**...........................`Enter`
6. Rest mouse pointer on note reference mark in text.

Edit a Footnote or Endnote

1. Double-click note reference mark in text.
   ✓ The insertion point automatically moves to the note text.
2. Edit footnote or endnote text.
3. Click in document text...`Shift`+`F5`

Delete a Footnote or Endnote

1. Position insertion point to the right of note reference mark in text.
2. Press **Backspace** ......`Backspace`
   ✓ Mark is selected.
3. Press **Backspace** ......`Backspace`
   ✓ Note is deleted.

Change the Footnote or Endnote Mark in Print Layout View

1. Position insertion point after text to footnote.
2. Click **Insert**..................`Alt`+`I`
3. Click **Reference** ....`N`
4. Click **Footnote** ....`N`
5. Click the **Footnote** ......`Alt`+`F` or **Endnote** ....`Alt`+`E` option button.
6. Click in the **Custom Mark** text box....................`Alt`+`C`
7. Type character in text box.
   OR
   a. Click **Symbol** ....`Alt`+`S`
   b. Select desired font ......`Alt`+`F`, `↓`, `Enter`
   c. Click symbol to use.
   d. Click **OK**....................`Enter`
8. Click **Insert**..................`Alt`+`I`
9. Type note text.
10. Click in document text ....`Shift`+`F5`

Find Text *(Ctrl+F))*

1. Position the insertion point at the beginning of the document ....`Ctrl`+`Home`
   ✓ You may start searching at any point in the document, or you may search selected text. However, to be sure to search the entire document, start at the top.
2. Click **Edit**....................`Alt`+`E`
3. Click **Find**...........................`F`
4. Click **Find what**...........`Alt`+`N`

5. Type text to find.
6. Click **More**  (if necessary) ....`Alt`+`M`
7. Select options:
   - **Match case** ....`Alt`+`H` to find only words in same case as text to find.
   - **Find whole words only** ....`Alt`+`Y` to find text as a whole word, not as part of a longer word.
   - **Use wildcards** ......`Alt`+`U` to find words specified with wildcard characters.
   - **Sounds like** ....`Alt`+`K` to find homonyms.
   - **Find all word forms** ....`Alt`+`W` to find all grammatical forms of text.
8. Click **Find Next** `Find Next` ....`Alt`+`F`
   ✓ Word highlights first occurrence of text in document. You can click in the document to edit or format the text, while leaving the Find and Replace dialog box open.
9. Repeat step 8 until finished.
   ✓ Click Cancel at any time to close the dialog box.
10. Click **OK** ....`Enter`
11. Click **Cancel** `Cancel` ....`Esc`

Find and Select Text

1. Click **Edit**....................`Alt`+`E`
2. Click **Find** ....`F`
3. Click **Find what**...........`Alt`+`N`
4. Type text to find.
5. Click **Highlight all items found in:** ....`Alt`+`T`
   ✓ Default is to highlight items in main document only; you may select Headers and Footers from the drop-down list if desired.

6. Click **F̲ind All**

    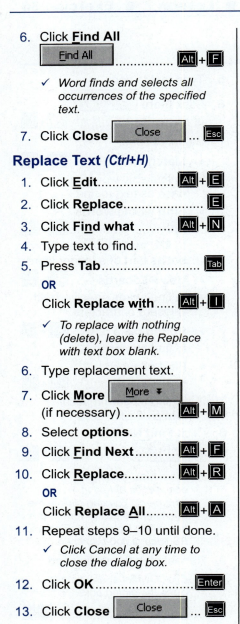

    F̲ind All .... `Alt`+`F`

    ✓ *Word finds and selects all occurrences of the specified text.*

7. Click **Close** `Close` ... `Esc`

Replace Text *(Ctrl+H)*

1. Click **E̲dit** .... `Alt`+`E`
2. Click **R̲eplace** .... `E`
3. Click **Fi̲nd what** .... `Alt`+`N`
4. Type text to find.
5. Press **Tab** .... `Tab`

    OR

    Click **Replace wi̲th** ..... `Alt`+`I`

    ✓ *To replace with nothing (delete), leave the Replace with text box blank.*

6. Type replacement text.
7. Click **M̲ore** `More ▼`

    (if necessary) .... `Alt`+`M`

8. Select **options**.
9. Click **F̲ind Next** .... `Alt`+`F`
10. Click **R̲eplace** .... `Alt`+`R`

    OR

    Click **Replace A̲ll** .... `Alt`+`A`

11. Repeat steps 9–10 until done.

    ✓ *Click Cancel at any time to close the dialog box.*

12. Click **OK** .... `Enter`
13. Click **Close** `Close` ... `Esc`

Find and Replace Special Characters *(Ctrl+H)*

1. Click **E̲dit** .... `Alt`+`E`
2. Click **R̲eplace** .... `R`
3. Click **Fi̲nd what** .... `Alt`+`N`
4. Click **Special** .... `Alt`+`E`
5. Select special character.
6. Press **Tab** .... `Tab`

    OR

    Click **Replace wi̲th** ..... `Alt`+`I`

    ✓ *To replace with nothing (delete), leave Replace with text box blank.*

7. Click **M̲ore** .... `Alt`+`M`
8. Click **Special** .... `Alt`+`E`
9. Select special character.
10. Click **F̲ind Next** .... `Alt`+`F`
11. Click **R̲eplace** .... `R`

    OR

    Click **Replace A̲ll** .... `Alt`+`A`

12. Repeat steps 10–11 until done.

    ✓ *Click Cancel at any time to close the dialog box.*

13. Click **OK** .... `Enter`
14. Click **Close** `Close` .... `Esc`

Create a Bookmark

1. Position the insertion point where you want the bookmark.
2. Click **I̲nsert** .... `Alt`+`I`
3. Click **Boo̲kmark** .... `K`
4. Click in the **Bookmark name** text box .... `Alt`+`B`
5. Type bookmark name.
6. Click **A̲dd** `Add` .. `Alt`+`A`

Go To Bookmark *(Ctrl+G)*

1. Press **F5** .... `F5`

    OR

    a. Click **E̲dit** .... `Alt`+`E`
    b. Click **Go To** .... `G`

2. Click Bookmark in the **Go to what** list .... `Alt`+`O`

    ✓ *Select any object in the Go to what list to browse directly to that object.*

3. Click **Enter bookmark name** .... `Alt`+`E`
4. Type bookmark name.

    OR

    Select bookmark name from drop-down list.

5. Click **Go T̲o** .... `Alt`+`T`
6. Click **Close** `Close` .... `Esc`

Browse by Object

1. Click the **Select Browse Object** button `○`.
2. Click the desired browse object.

    ✓ *If you select Find or Go To, the Find and Replace dialog box is displayed.*

3. Click the **Previous** button `⬆` to scroll up to the previous browse object.

    OR

    Click the **Next** button `⬇` to scroll down to the next browse object.

Exercise Directions

1. Start Word, if necessary.

2. Open 🖾**HEART** or open 💿**38HEART**.

3. Save the file as **HEART**.

4. Use the Find command to locate the first occurrence of **CHD**, the acronym for Coronary Heart Disease.

5. Delete the acronym and the parentheses around it.

6. Use the Replace command to replace all remaining occurrences of the acronym **CHD** with the full text **coronary heart disease**. Use the Match Case option so that the text is not in all uppercase letters.

7. Use the Find command to select all occurrences of the company name—**California Cardiology, Inc.**—in the main document and format it with italics.

8. Repeat step 7 for the headers and footers.

9. Delete the last sentence of the first paragraph in the body of the report (beginning with the word **Usually**…).

10. Delete the last sentence of the second paragraph (beginning with the words **The part**…) and replace it with the following:

    The most common symptoms of a heart attack include a heavy, squeezing pain or discomfort in the center of the chest which may last for several minutes and pain which may radiate to the shoulder, arm, neck, or jaw.

11. Insert a footnote at the end of the new sentence as follows:

    U.S. Department of Health, Education, and Welfare, "The Warning Signals of a Heart Attack," *How Doctors Diagnose Heart Disease, Today's date,* **<http://www.atlcard.com/ hddhd.html>**.

    ✓ *You can remove the hyperlink if you want.*

12. At the end of the first sentence of the fourth paragraph (beginning with the words **While coronary**…), insert the following footnote:

    "Risk Factors for Heart Disease," *USA Today Magazine*, **February, 1997**.

13. At the end of the first sentence of the seventh paragraph (beginning with the words **Other steps**…), insert the following footnote:

    John Henkel, "Keeping Cholesterol Under Control," *FDA Consumer*, **January – February, 1999**.

14. At the end of the first heading in the document—**What is Coronary Heart Disease?**—insert the following endnote:

    For more information, write to the National Heart, Lung, and Blood Institute (NHLBI) Information Center, P.O. Box 30105, Bethesda, MD 20824-0105.

15. Move the insertion point to the beginning of the document and then use Find to locate the first occurrence of the word **cigarette**.

    ✓ *You may have to clear the option for highlighting all occurrences.*

16. Insert a bookmark at the found location, named CIG.

17. Use Browse by Object to go to the first footnote.

18. Use Browse by Object to go to the CIG bookmark.

19. Change the left and right margins of the second section to 1.25".

20. Check the spelling and grammar in the document and correct errors as necessary.

21. Display the document in Print Preview. It should look similar to the one in the illustration.

22. Close Print Preview.

23. Print the document.

24. Close the document, saving all changes.

Caring for Your Heart

In response to inquiries from our patients, we are providing this report to help you better understand the nature of coronary heart disease. Most importantly, we are including information about steps you can take to minimize your risks. Please keep in mind that no report can substitute for an open and honest discussion with your physician. If you have any questions, please call, or schedule an appointment.

California Cardiology, Inc.

What is Coronary Heart Disease?[i]

Coronary heart disease is the most common form of heart disease. It is caused by a thickening of the inside walls of the coronary arteries, called atherosclerosis. The coronary arteries are responsible for carrying blood to the heart. If they become clogged, the flow of blood to the heart is slowed. As a result the heart is deprived of oxygen and other vital nutrients.

If the condition progresses, the arteries become blocked and the blood supply is cut off completely. The result is a heart attack. The most common symptoms of a heart attack include a heavy, squeezing pain or discomfort in the center of the chest which may last for several minutes and pain which may radiate to the shoulder, arm, neck, or jaw.[1]

Am I at Risk?

In most people, cholesterol and fat circulate in the blood and build up on the walls of the coronary arteries. Atherosclerosis usually occurs when a person has unusually high levels of cholesterol in the blood.

---

[1] U.S. Department of Health, Education, and Welfare, "The Warning Signals of a Heart Attack," *How Doctors Diagnose Heart Disease, Today's Date,* <http://www.atlcard.com/hddhd.html>.

Page 1

Caring for Your Heart   Today's Date

While coronary heart disease can strike anyone, there are certain factors that can help doctors identify patients who may be at a higher risk than others[2]. Some of these factors are uncontrollable, such as your age, but some are directly controllable by lifestyle choices such as diet and exercise.

What Can I Do?

The major controllable risk factors are cigarette smoking, high blood pressure, high cholesterol levels, obesity, and an inactive lifestyle. As you may notice, many of these factors are related. For example, high blood pressure, high cholesterol, and obesity are all potentially the result of an unhealthy diet and a lack of exercise.

Although there are medical and surgical treatments available to control coronary heart disease, clearly it is in your best interest to reduce your risk factors as soon as possible. First and foremost, quit smoking. Smoking is thought to double your risk of heart attack, and when combined with the other risk factors, it may raise your chances by eight or ten times.

Other steps to take include changing your diet to reduce or eliminate saturated fats and sodium[3]. In other words, eat more fruits and vegetables and less candy and potato chips. This will help lower your blood pressure and cholesterol, and will promote weight loss. Finally, you should increase the amount of exercise you get each day. Exercise does not have to be strenuous, but it should be consistent. A simple walk around the block will help get your body moving and your heart pumping.

---

[i] For more information, write to the National Heart, Lung, and Blood Institute (NHLBI) Information Center, P.O. Box 30105, Bethesda, MD 20824-0105.

---

[2] "Risk Factors for Heart Disease," *USA Today Magazine*, February, 1997.
[3] John Henkel, "Keeping Cholesterol Under Control," *FDA Consumer*, January – February, 1999.

California Cardiology, Inc.   Page 2

On Your Own

1. Open the document **OWD37** that you used in the On Your Own section of Exercise 37, or open ⊘ **38GUIDES**.

2. Save the document as **OWD38**.

3. Insert at least three footnotes to provide citations, or to supplement text with additional information.

4. Insert at least three endnotes.

5. Browse to the footnotes.

6. Browse to the endnotes.

7. Use Find to locate specific text, such as your own name.

8. Use Find and Replace to locate and replace specific text, such as an abbreviation or acronym.

9. Print the document.

10. Close the document, saving all changes.

Exercise 39

Skills Covered:

◆ **Preview Multiple Pages** ◆ **Use Document Map**
◆ **Copy and Move Text from One Page to Another**
◆ **Print Specific Pages**

On the Job

Preview multiple pages to see how an entire multi-page document will look when it is printed. For example, when you preview more than one page at a time, you can see headers and footers on every page and determine whether the text flow from one page to the next looks professional. The Document Map helps you quickly locate sections of a long document without spending time scrolling through pages. Printing specific pages or selected text is an option that can save paper and time if you find that you only need hard copies of parts of a document.

California Cardiology has expanded the patient report on coronary heart disease. In this exercise, you will preview, proofread, and edit the document. You will use the Document Map to navigate through the document to find headings and paragraphs. You will move text from one page to another. You will preview multiple pages to determine whether page breaks are in the correct locations. Finally, you will print selected pages of the document.

Terms

Document Map A vertical pane that opens on the left side of the document window to show the major headings and sections in a document; click a topic in the pane to go to it.

Heading A paragraph formatted in one of Word's built-in Heading styles or a paragraph formatted like a heading. For example, a paragraph formatted in a larger font size than normal text, and/or with bold or italic font styles.

Notes

Preview Multiple Pages

- By default, Print Preview displays one page at a time.
- You can change the Print Preview to display multiple pages at one time.
- Preview multiple pages to get an overall view of the document, not to edit or format text.
  - ✓ *You can edit in Print Preview, but it is difficult if the pages appear small.*

- You can select the number of pages you want to display using the Multiple Pages button on the Print Preview toolbar.
  - ✓ *You can also select a setting from the Zoom drop-down list. For more on the Zoom feature, refer to "Getting Started with Office XP", Exercise 3.*

- The more pages displayed, the smaller the pages appear on the screen, so the harder it is to read the text.
- Use the Magnifier tool 🔍 to zoom in on a page to get a better look.

A six-page document in Print Preview

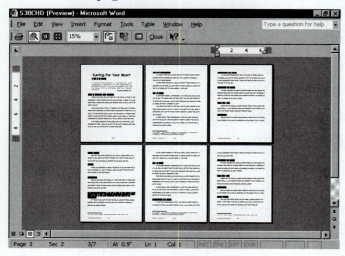

Use Document Map

- **Document Map** is useful for navigating through long documents.

- Word displays the Document Map in a pane on the left side of the document window.

The Document Map

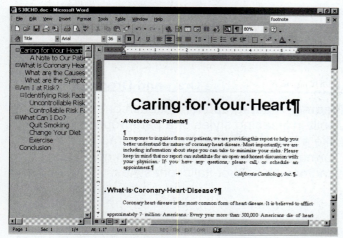

- The Document Map shows **headings** and major topics in an outline format.

  ✓ *Outlines are covered in Exercise 36.*

- If there are no headings or major topics, the Document Map is empty.

- You can expand and collapse the Document Map as you would an outline to show the headings you need.

Copy or Move Text from One Page to Another

- Use standard copy and move techniques to copy or move text from one page in a document to another page.

  ✓ *Moving text is covered in Word Exercise 10; Copying text is covered in Word Exercise 11.*

- Use Cut and Paste to move text.

- Use Copy and Paste to copy text.

- If you can see both locations on the screen at the same time, use the drag-and-drop method.

  ✓ *Use Print Preview to see more than one page at a time.*

- Copying and/or moving text may affect hard page breaks already inserted in a document.

Print Specific Pages

- Select Print options to print a specific page, several pages, selected text, or the current page.

- In the Print dialog box, you can specify consecutive pages or nonconsecutive pages. You can also specify pages to print by page number.

Set print options in the Print dialog box

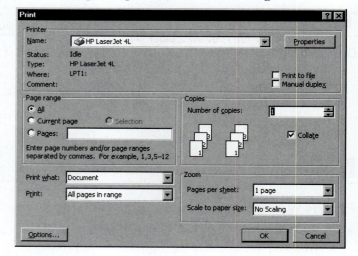

Procedures

Preview Multiple Pages

1. Click **Print Preview** button 🔲.
   OR
   a. Click **File**.................Alt+F
   b. Click **Print Preview**........V
2. Click **Multiple Pages** button 🔲.
3. Drag across number of rows and pages to display.
4. Release mouse button.

Change Back to One Page Preview

- Click **One Page** button 🔲.

Zoom In in Print Preview

1. If necessary, click in document to position the insertion point on the desired page.
2. Position the magnifier mouse pointer over the area to enlarge 🔍.
   ✓ *The magnifier is selected by default. If the magnifier pointer is not displayed, click Magnifier button on Print Preview toolbar to toggle the option on.*
3. Click mouse once.
4. Click again to zoom out 🔍.
   ✓ *To cancel the magnifier so you can edit a document, click the Magnifier button on Print Preview toolbar to toggle the option off.*

Use Document Map

To display Document Map:

1. Click **View**.................Alt+V
2. Click **Document Map**..........D
   OR
- Click **Document Map** button 🔲.

To hide Document Map:

1. Click **View**.................Alt+V
2. Click **Document Map**..........D
   OR

- Click **Document Map** button .

To jump to a heading:

- Click desired heading in Document Map.

To expand/collapse heading:

1. Right-click anywhere in **Document Map**.
2. Click level of heading to Expand/Collapse.
   OR
   Click **Expand** ➕ or **Collapse** ➖ button next to headings in Document Map.

Use Copy and Paste to Copy Text from One Page to Another *(Ctrl+C, Ctrl+V)*

1. Select the text to copy.
2. Click **Copy** button 🔲.
   OR
   a. Click **Edit** ....Alt+E
   b. Click **Copy** C
3. Display other page and position insertion point in new location.
4. Click **Paste** button 🔲.
   OR
   a. Click **Edit** ....Alt+E
   b. Click **Paste**....................P

Use Drag-and-Drop Editing to Copy Text

1. Display multiple pages in Print Preview.
   ✓ *If necessary, click Magnifier button to turn off zoom feature.*
2. Select text to copy.
3. Move mouse pointer anywhere over selected text.
4. Press and hold **Ctrl** ....Ctrl
5. Drag selection to new location 🔲.
6. Release mouse button.
7. Release **Ctrl**......................Ctrl

Move Text from One Page to Another

1. Select text to move.
2. Press **F2** F2
3. Display other page and position insertion point at new location.
4. Press **Enter** ....Enter

Use Cut and Paste to Move Text *(Ctrl+X, Cltr+V)*

1. Select text to move.
2. Click **Cut** button 🔲.
   OR
   a. Click **Edit**...............Alt+E
   b. Click **Cut**.........................T
3. Display other page and position insertion point at new location.
4. Click **Paste** button 🔲.
   OR
   a. Click **Edit**...............Alt+E
   b. Click **Paste** ....P

Use Drag-and-Drop Editing to Move Text

1. Display multiple pages in Print Preview.
2. Select text to move.
   ✓ *If necessary, click Magnifier button to turn off zoom feature.*
3. Move mouse pointer anywhere over selected text.
4. Drag selection to new location.
5. Release mouse button when the insertion point is in new location.

Print Specified Pages *(Cltr+P)*

To print a single page:

1. Click **File**....................Alt+F
2. Click **Print**..........................P
3. Click **Pages** ....Alt+G
4. Type page number.
5. Click **OK** ....Enter

To print consecutive page:

1. Click **File** .... Alt + F
2. Click **Print** .... P
3. Click **Pages** .... Alt + G
4. Type page range as follows: first page number, hyphen, last page number. For example: 3-5.
   - ✓ *Do not type spaces.*
5. Click **OK** .... Enter

To print nonconsecutive pages:

1. Click **File** .... Alt + F
2. Click **Print** .... P
3. Click **Pages** .... Alt + G
4. Type each page number separated by commas. For example: 3,5,7.
   - ✓ *Do not type spaces.*
5. Click **OK** .... Enter
   - ✓ *You can combine consecutive and nonconsecutive pages. For example, 2-5,7,10.*

To print current page:

1. Click **File** .... Alt + F
2. Click **Print** .... P
3. Click **Current Page** ..... Alt + E
4. Click **OK** .... Enter

To print selected text:

1. Select text to print.
2. Click **File** .... Alt + F
3. Click **Print** .... P
4. Click **Selection** .... Alt + S
5. Click **OK** .... Enter

Exercise Directions

1. Start Word, if necessary.
2. Open 💿 **39CHD**.
   - ✓ *This is an expanded version of the report used in Exercises 37 and 38.*
3. Save the file as **CHD**.
4. Display the Document Map.
5. Using the Document Map to navigate through the document, move the first paragraph under the heading **Identifying Risk Factors** so that it is the first paragraph under the heading **Conclusion**.
6. Create a header for all pages but the first. Include the report title, **Coronary Heart Disease**, flush left and the current date flush right.
7. Create a centered footer for all pages with the word **Page**, followed by the page number.
8. Use Print Preview to display all pages of the document on-screen at the same time.
9. Zoom in on the bottom of page 3.
10. Toggle the magnifier option off, then insert a hard page break to move the heading **Quit Smoking** to the top of page 4.
11. Toggle the magnifier option on, then zoom back out to view all four pages at once.
12. Close Print Preview.
13. Use the Document Map to go to the heading **What are the Symptoms?**.
14. Print the current page.
15. Use the Document Map to go to the heading **A Note to Our Patients**.
16. Select the heading and the paragraph under it, and print the selection.
17. Print pages 1, 3, and 4.
18. Close the Document Map.
19. Close the document, saving all changes.

On Your Own

1. Open the document 🖴 **OWD38** that you used in the On Your Own section of Exercise 38, or open 💿 **39GUIDES**.
2. Save the document as **OWD39**.
3. Use the Document Map to navigate through the document.
4. Preview multiple pages of the document at one time.
5. Move or copy text from one page in the document to another. (You can always use Undo to revert back, if necessary.)
6. Preview all pages at once.
7. If necessary, adjust page and section breaks breaks.
8. Print the last page of the document.
9. Print the first paragraph of the document.
10. Close the document, saving all changes.

Caring for Your Heart

A Note to Our Patients

In response to inquiries from our patients, we are providing this report to help you better understand the nature of coronary heart disease. Most importantly, we are including information about steps you can take to minimize your risks. Please keep in mind that no report can substitute for an open and honest discussion with your physician. If you have any questions, please call, or schedule an appointment.

California Cardiology, Inc.

What is Coronary Heart Disease?

Coronary heart disease is the most common form of heart disease. It is believed to afflict approximately 7 million Americans. Every year more than 500,000 Americans die of heart attacks caused by coronary heart disease, which makes it the number one killer of both men and women in the U.S.

What are the Causes?

Coronary heart disease is caused by a thickening of the inside walls of the coronary arteries, called atherosclerosis. The coronary arteries are responsible for carrying blood to the heart. If they become clogged, the flow of blood to the heart is slowed. As a result the heart is deprived of oxygen and other vital nutrients. Usually – but not always – a patient with atherosclerosis will experience symptoms such as pain and shortness of breath, called angina.

If the condition progresses, the arteries become blocked and the blood supply is cut off completely. The result is a heart attack. The part of the heart that does not receive oxygen begins to die, and some of the heart muscle may be damaged beyond repair.

Coronary Heart Disease   Today's Date

What are the Symptoms?

It is possible to suffer from CHD without exhibiting any symptoms. However, typically symptoms range from intermittent chest pain -- which may be confused with indigestion to severe pain and difficulty breathing.

The most common symptoms of a heart attack include a heavy, squeezing pain or discomfort in the chest that lasts for several minutes, and pain that radiates to the shoulder, arm, neck, or jaw.[1] Stabbing pain is not usually indicative of a heart attack.

Am I at Risk?

In most people, cholesterol, a fat-like substance, and fat circulate in the blood and build up on the walls of the coronary arteries. This process begins in most people during childhood and the teenage years, and gets worse as they get older. Atherosclerosis usually occurs when a person has unusually high levels of cholesterol in the blood.

Identifying Risk Factors

While coronary heart disease can strike anyone, there are certain factors that can help doctors identify patients who may be at a higher risk than others.[2] Some of these factors are uncontrollable, such as your age, but some are directly controllable by lifestyle choices such as diet and exercise.

Of course, without a crystal ball it is impossible to predict with absolute certainty who will and who will not have a heart attack. However, the chances of suffering a heart

---

[1] U.S. Department of Health, Education, and Welfare, "The Warning Signals of a Heart Attack," *How Doctors Diagnose Heart Disease*, Today's date, <http://www.atlcard.com/hddhd.html>.
[2] "Risk Factors for Heart Disease," *USA Today Magazine*, February, 1997.

Coronary Heart Disease   Today's Date

attack are certainly increased by the presence of the any of the risk factors, and the more

risk factors an individual has, the greater the chance.

Uncontrollable Risk Factors

The three major uncontrollable risk factors are age, gender, and heredity. Because

CHD is progressive, the older you get, the more susceptible you are. It has also become

clear that men are more susceptible than women. Finally, if others in your family have

suffered from CHD, it is more likely that you will, also.

Controllable Risk Factors

The major controllable risk factors are cigarette smoking, high blood pressure,

high cholesterol levels, obesity, and an inactive lifestyle. As you may notice, many of

these factors are related. For example, high blood pressure, high cholesterol, and obesity

are all potentially the result of an unhealthy diet and a lack of exercise.

What Can I Do?

Although there are medical and surgical treatments available to control coronary

heart disease, clearly it is in your best interest to reduce your risk factors as soon as

possible. This may require some significant behavior modification and lifestyle changes.

Coronary Heart Disease   Today's Date

Quit Smoking

First and foremost, quit smoking. Smoking is thought to double your risk of heart attack, and when combined with the other risk factors, it may raise your chances by eight or ten times.

Change Your Diet

Other steps to take include changing your diet to reduce or eliminate saturated fats and sodium.[3] In other words, eat more fruits and vegetables and less candy and potato chips. This will help lower your blood pressure and cholesterol, and will promote weight loss.

Exercise

Finally, you should increase the amount of exercise you get each day. Exercise does not have to be strenuous, but it should be consistent. A simple walk around the block will help get your body moving and your heart pumping.

Conclusion

There are many factors that contribute to a healthy heart. There is no reason people cannot develop habits to care for their hearts the same way they do their teeth. Of course, it is very important to discuss any lifestyle changes with your physician. Sudden changes in diet or exercise can put stress on your heart.

As mentioned earlier, there is no way to know for sure whether or not you are going to have a heart attack. It is possible, however, to asses your risk, and to take steps to minimize that risk.

---

[3] John Henkel, "Keeping Cholesterol Under Control," *FDA Consumer,* January – February, 1999.

Exercise 40

Skills Covered:

◆ **Insert Comments** ◆ **Track Changes** ◆ **Customize Revision Marks**
◆ **Compare and Merge Documents** ◆ **Accept/Reject Changes**

On the Job

Insert comments in a document when you want to include a private note to the author, another reader, or to yourself, in much the same way you might attach a slip of paper to a hard copy print out. Track changes made to a document to monitor when and how edits are made. Tracking changes lets you consider revisions before incorporating them into a document. If you agree with the change, you can accept it, but if you disagree with the change, you can reject it. You can track changes made by one person, or by many people, which is useful when you are collaborating on a document with others. When you compare and merge documents, differences between the two are marked as revisions.

The Director of Training at Murray Hill Marketing has asked you to revise a document listing in-house training courses. In this exercise, you will use the track changes feature while you edit the document and insert comments. You will then review the document to accept or reject the changes. Finally, you will compare the document to an earlier version, then print it.

Terms

Comment A hidden note attached to a document for reference.

Comment balloon An area in the right margin in which comment text is displayed.

Reviewing pane A window where revisions and comments are displayed.

Comment mark A color-coded I-beam that marks the location in the document where a comment was inserted.

Revision marks Formatting applied to text in a document to identify where insertions, deletions, and formatting changes have been made.

Revision balloon An area in the right margin in which revisions are displayed.

Notes

The Reviewing toolbar

Display for Review

Previous

Accept Change

New Comment

Reviewing Pane

Final Showing Markup | Show ▾

Show menu

Next

Reject Change/ Delete Comment

Track Changes

Insert Comments

- Insert **comments** to annotate text, communicate with readers, or to attach reminders or questions.

- By default, in Print Layout and Web Layout views you can type and edit comments in either the **comment balloon** or in the **Reviewing pane**. In Normal view, you must use the Reviewing pane.

- When you create a comment, Word inserts a **comment mark**. In Print Layout and Web Layout views, the mark is connected to the comment balloon by a dashed line.

- Both the comment mark and comment balloons are color coded by author.

- You can choose to hide or show comments on-screen.

- Comments can be printed with a document.

A comment in Print Layout view

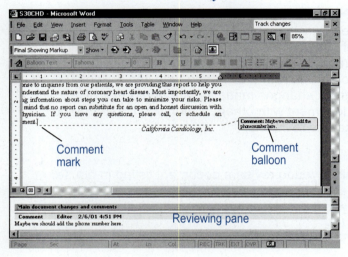

Track Changes

- Turn on Word's Track Changes feature to apply **revision marks** to all insertions, deletions, and formatting changes in a document.

- When Track Changes is active, the TRK button on the status bar is bold and Word applies revision marks as you edit a document.

- The way that revisions are marked on-screen depends on the current view and on the selected Display for Review option:

  - Final Showing Markup (default). This option displays inserted text in color with an underline, and all formatting changes are applied. In Print Layout and Web Layout views, deleted text is moved into a **revision balloon**, while in Normal view, deleted text is marked in color with a strikethrough effect.

  - Final. In all views, this option displays the document as it would look if all of the revisions that had been entered were incorporated in the document.

- Original Showing Markup. This option displays deleted text in color with a strikethrough effect. In Print Layout and Web Layout views, inserted text and formatting are displayed in a revision balloon, while in Normal view, inserted text is marked in color with an underline.

- Original. In all views, this option displays the document as it would look if no revisions had been made.

- Like comments, revisions are color coded by author.

- By default, Word also inserts a vertical line to the left of any changed line to indicate where revisions occur in the document.

- In any view, you can view descriptions of all revisions in the Reviewing pane.

- You can select which changes you want displayed on-screen. For example, you can display insertions and deletions, but not formatting.

- You can even set Word to show only the changes made by one reviewer at a time.

Tracking changes in Normal view

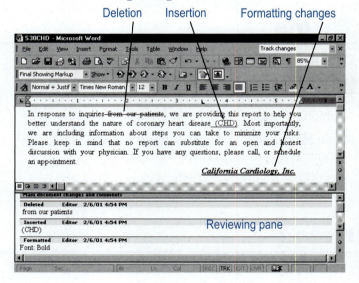

Customize Revision Marks

- You can customize revision marks in the Track Changes dialog box as follows:
  - You can select the color you want to use.

- You can select the formatting used to indicate changes. For example, you can mark formatting changes with a double-underline, or insertions with color only instead of color and an underline.

- You can customize the location vertical bar used to mark lines that have been changed.

- You can also customize the way balloons are displayed in a document.

Track Changes Options dialog box

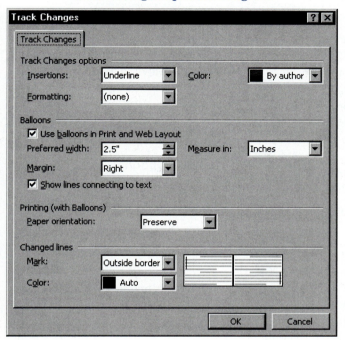

Compare and Merge Documents

- You can compare two or more documents to mark the differences between them.

- When you compare documents, Word uses revision marks to indicate where text has been inserted, deleted, or formatted.

- Comparing and merging documents is useful if you have more than one version of a document and need to see what changes have been made, if more than one person has edited a document, or if someone has edited a document without using the track changes features.

- You can merge the documents into the original document, the current document, or into a new document.

Accept/Reject Changes

- Revision marks remain stored as part of a document until the changes are either accepted or rejected.

- To incorporate edits into a document file, accept the changes.

- To cancel the edits and erase them from the file, reject the changes.

- You can also reject comments to delete them from the file.

Procedures

Display Reviewing Toolbar
1. Click **View**.................. `Alt`+`V`
2. Select **Toolbars**.................. `T`
   OR
   Right-click any toolbar.
3. Click **Reviewing.**

Display Reviewing Pane
- Click **Reviewing Pane** button 📤 on Reviewing toolbar.

OR
1. Click **Show** drop-down arrow.......... `Alt`+`S` on Reviewing toolbar.
2. Click **Reviewing Pane**......... `P`

✓ *Repeat steps to hide reviewing pane.*

OR
1. Right-click **TRK** button `TRK` on status bar.
2. Click **Reviewing Pane** button 📤.

Display Balloons in Print Layout or Web Layout View
1. Click **View** .... `Alt`+`V`
2. Click **Markup**....................... `A`

✓ *Repeat steps to hide balloons.*

Insert a Comment
1. Position insertion point where you want to insert comment.

2. Click **New Comment** button 📝 on Reviewing toolbar.
   OR
   a. Click **Insert**............. `Alt`+`I`
   b. Click **Comment**............. `M`
3. Type comment text.

Edit a Comment
1. Click in comment balloon.
   OR
   a. Display Reviewing pane.
   b. Scroll up or down to locate comment.
2. Edit comment text.

Delete a Comment

1. Right-click comment balloon.
   OR
   Right-click comment in Reviewing pane.
2. Click **Delete Comment** .... M
   OR
1. Click anywhere in comment text.
2. Click **New Comment** drop-down arrow 🖱 on the Reviewing toolbar.
3. Click Delete **Comment** .... M
   OR
1. Click anywhere in comment text.
2. Click **Reject Change/Delete Comment** drop-down arrow 🔖▾ on the Reviewing toolbar.
3. Click **Reject Change/Delete Comment** .... R

Turn Track Changes On or Off
(Ctrl+Shift+E)

* Double-click **TRK** button TRK on status bar to toggle feature on and off.
   OR
* Click **Track Changes** button 🖱 on Reviewing toolbar.
   OR
1. Right-click **TRK** button TRK on status bar.
2. Click **Track Changes** button 🖱.
   OR
1. Click **Tools** .... Alt+T
2. Click **Track Changes** .... T

   ✓ *Repeat steps to turn feature off.*

Select a Display for Review

1. Click Display for Review drop-down arrow on Reviewing toolbar.
2. Click desired option: .... 🔽, Enter
   * Final Showing Markup
   * Final
   * Original Showing Markup
   * Original

Compare and Merge Documents

1. Open edited document.
2. Click **Tools** .... Alt+T
3. Click **Compare and Merge Documents** .... D
4. Locate and select original document.
5. Click **Merge** drop-down arrow .... Alt+M
6. Click desired option:
   * **Merge** .... M
     to merge changes into original document.
   * **Merge into current document** C
     to merge changes into document opened in step 1.
   * **Merge into new document** .... N
     to merge changes into a new document.

Print Comments and Revisions

1. Click **File** .... Alt+F
2. Click **Print** .... P
3. Click **Print what** drop-down arrow .... Alt+W
4. Click **Document showing markup** to print comment and revision balloons with the document.
   OR
   Click **List of markup** to print a list of comments and revisions separately.
5. Click **OK** .... Enter

Select Revision Display Options

1. Click **Show** drop-down arrow on Reviewing toolbar ... Alt+S
2. Select Desired option:
   * **Comments** C
   * **Insertions and Deletions** I
   * **Formatting** .... F

   ✓ *Repeat to select additional options.*

To select which reviewers' marks to display:

1. Click **Show** drop-down arrow on Reviewing toolbar ... Alt+S
2. Select **Reviewers** .... R
3. Click **All Reviewers** .... A
   to display marks for all reviewers.
   OR
   Click desired reviewer name.

   ✓ *Repeat to select additional reviewers.*

Customize Revision Marks

1. Click **Show** drop-down arrow on Reviewing toolbar ... Alt+S
   OR
   Right-click **TRK** button TRK on status bar.
   OR
2. Click **Options** .... O
   OR
   a. Click **Tools** .... Alt+T
   b. Click **Options** .... O
   c. Click **Track Changes** tab .... Ctrl+Tab
3. Select options as desired.
4. Click **OK** .... Enter

Accept/Reject Changes One by One

1. Right-click revision in document.
   OR
   Right-click revision in balloon.
2. Click **Accept Insertion (or Deletion)** .... E
   OR
   Click **Reject Insertion (or Deletion)** .... R
   OR
1. Click **Next** button 🔁 on Reviewing toolbar to browse forward from insertion point.
   OR
   Click **Previous** button 🔁 to browse back from insertion point.

2. Click **Accept Change** button 🔖 to incorporate highlighted change into document.

OR

Click **Reject Change** button 🔖 to delete highlighted change from document.

Accept Changes All At Once

1. Click **Accept Change** drop-down arrow 🔄 ▾ on Reviewing toolbar

2. Click **Accept All Changes Shown** .... 🅂

OR

Click **Accept All Changes in Document** .... 🅷

Reject Changes All At Once

1. Click **Reject Change/Delete Comment** drop-down arrow 🔄 ▾ on Reviewing toolbar

2. Click **Reject All Changes Shown** .... 🅂

OR

Click **Reject All Changes in Document** .... 🅷

Exercise Directions

1. Start Word, if necessary.
2. Open 💿 **40INHOUSE**.
   ✓ *This is a version of the course list document you worked with earlier in this book.*
3. Save the file as **INHOUSE**.
4. Insert the comment shown in Illustration A.
5. Turn on the Track Changes feature.
6. Make sure Word is set to display comments, insertions, deletions, and formatting changes.
7. Customize the marks to show formatting changes with a double-underline and set the Changed lines color to blue.
8. Switch to Normal view.
9. Make the insertions, deletions, and formatting changes shown in Illustration A.
10. Switch to Print Layout view.
11. Display the document as Final.
12. Display the Document as Original Showing Markup.
13. Display the Document as Final Showing Markup.

14. Print the document with the comments and changes.
15. Delete the comment.
16. Accept the insertion of the word **Spring**.
17. Accept the changes to the names of the months.
18. Reject the formatting changes.
19. Accept the changes to the last sentence in the document.
20. Turn off the Track Changes feature.
21. Save the changes.
22. Compare the document to the original 💿 **40INHOUSE**, merging the changes into the current document.
23. Accept all changes.
24. Check the spelling and grammar in the document.
25. Print the document.
26. Close the document, saving all changes.

On Your Own

1. Open **OWD19**, the resume you created earlier, or open 💿 **40RESUME**.
2. Save the document as **OWD40**.
3. Insert at least one comment.
4. Turn on the Track Changes feature.
5. Customize revision marks.
6. Make changes to the document.
7. Save the changes.

8. Print the document with revision marks.
9. Save the document **OWD40-2**.
10. Review the changes, accepting some, and rejecting others.
11. If the document is more than one page, add a footer to the second page, including your name, a document title, and the page number.
12. Close the document, saving all changes.

Murray Hill Marketing, LLC

285 Madison Avenue ✧ New York, NY 10016 ✧ 212-555-4444

Comment: Should we add the Web site URL?

Spring

^Training Schedule

~~January~~

April

Microsoft Word 1 ———— *Underline*

This introductory course will cover the basics of using Microsoft Word 2000 to create common business documents. By the end of the course you will know how to: create and print text-based documents such as letters and envelopes, and apply formatting.

~~February~~

May

Microsoft Word 2 ———— *Underline*

A continuation of the Word I course, this introductory level class will delve into some of the more intriguing features of Microsoft Word 2000. By the end of the course you will know how to conduct a mail merge, set up a document in columns, include headers and footers, and insert pictures.

~~March~~

June

Microsoft Word 3 ———— *Underline*

This final course in the Microsoft Word series covers the advanced features. By the end of this course you will know how to work with tables, create and modify outlines, use e-mail and Internet features in Word, and share documents with other users.

For more information call: 212-555-4444, ext. 343.

contact Lisa Ungarro at   or murrayhill@ddcpub

Exercise 41

Your supervisor at Regency General, Inc., a Web startup specializing in business-to-business Internet services, has asked you to edit and format a multi-page document. The document is provided without formatting. It is up to you to edit the document, apply formatting, set spacing and margins, insert footnotes and comments, insert breaks as necessary, and add a header and a footer.

Exercise Directions

Use Find and Replace

1. Start Word, if necessary.
2. Open ⊙ **41B2B**.
3. Save the document as **B2B**.
4. Find and replace all occurrences of the abbreviation **B2B** with the text **Business-to-Business**.
   - ✓ *Remember to use the Match Case option so the replacement is not in all uppercase letters.*

Insert a Bookmark and Use the Outline Feature

1. Insert a bookmark named **Intro** at the beginning of the text **Introduction**.
2. Insert footnotes and comments as shown on Illustration A.
3. Change to Outline view.
4. Promote the headings as shown on Illustration A.
5. Change to Print Layout view.
6. Format the paragraph of text under the heading Introduction using double-spacing, a first line indent, and justified alignment. Leave 6 points of space before and after.

Create a Style and Format Text

1. Create a style named *Report Text* based on the paragraph formatting you just applied, and apply the new style as indicated on the illustration.
2. Create a bullet list from the five industries as marked on the illustration.
3. Increase the spacing after the last item in the list to 18 points.

4. Change the margins for the entire document to 1.25" top and bottom and 1.5" left and right.

Create a Cover Page and Use Headers/Footers

1. Create a cover page as follows:
   a. Go to the bookmark Intro and insert a Next page section break between the title and the heading Introduction.
   b. Center the title vertically and horizontally on the first page.
   c. Leave 54 points of space after the title.
   d. Using the Heading 2 style, centered, type the text **Prepared by** then press Enter.
   e. In 14-point Arial, centered, with 12 points of space before and after, type the following lines:

      Your Name
      Today's Date
      Regency General, Inc.
      1500 W. High Tech Boulevard
      Suite 700
      Austin, TX 73301

2. Create a header on all pages except the cover page. Put the text **Business-to-Business** flush left, and today's date flush with the new right margin.
   - ✓ *If necessary, move the right tab stop in the header to align with the margin.*

3. Insert page numbers starting on the first page of the report, not on the cover page.
   - ✓ *Be sure to set options so that page numbering starts in the second section, and to suppress numbers on the cover page.*

BREAKING AWAY
BICYCLE SHOP

Volume 4, Number 3   Summer/Fall

Bicycle Safety Day

Breaking Away is pleased to sponsor the third annual Bicycle Safety Day! The event is organized and managed by LIMBO, the Long Island Mountain Biking Organization. In past years the event has drawn more than 1,000 people of all ages. We expect this year to be even more successful.

Some of the activities that will be offered include workshops on road rules and etiquette, helmet fitting, and bike maintenance.

Summer Sale

Our semi-annual sale event is just getting underway. Almost every item in the store has been marked down. Discounts range from 10% to 50% off regular sales prices.

Many floor models and samples are now being offered at near cost prices. If you've been thinking about upgrading, now's the time!

Expanded Store Hours

As of August 1st, Breaking Away is staying open longer!

Our new, expanded store hours are 10 a.m. until 9 p.m. Monday through Saturday.

Upcoming Events

The fall is a great time to take to the roads and trails. The air is cooler, the sky is bluer, and the leaves are bright. Many area biking clubs and organizations are planning outings in and around the Island.

Breaking Away works closely with LIMBO, the Long Island Mountain Biking Organization, to plan events for all levels of riders. Two of the most popular trips are currently planned for September and October.

On 9/30, join LIMBO members on a day trip to Shelter Island. Then, on October 24th and 25th, pack up for an overnight out to Montauk Point. For more information about these two great rides, contact LIMBO, at 555-3344.

Raffle Update

Don't forget to fill out an entry form for our monthly raffle drawings. Prizes range from Breaking Away water bottles to brand new bikes!

Drawings are held on the 25th of every month, at 6 p.m. No purchase is necessary, and you do not have to be present to win.

Illustration A

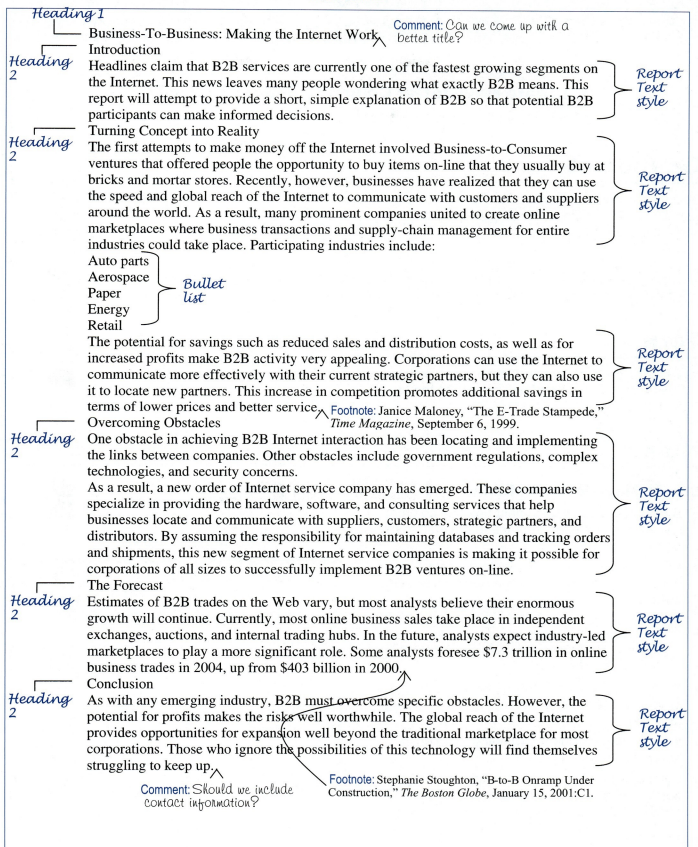

Heading 1

Business-To-Business: Making the Internet Work

Comment: *Can we come up with a better title?*

Introduction

Heading 2

Headlines claim that B2B services are currently one of the fastest growing segments on the Internet. This news leaves many people wondering what exactly B2B means. This report will attempt to provide a short, simple explanation of B2B so that potential B2B participants can make informed decisions.

Report Text style

Turning Concept into Reality

Heading 2

The first attempts to make money off the Internet involved Business-to-Consumer ventures that offered people the opportunity to buy items on-line that they usually buy at bricks and mortar stores. Recently, however, businesses have realized that they can use the speed and global reach of the Internet to communicate with customers and suppliers around the world. As a result, many prominent companies united to create online marketplaces where business transactions and supply-chain management for entire industries could take place. Participating industries include:

Report Text style

Auto parts
Aerospace
Paper
Energy
Retail

Bullet list

The potential for savings such as reduced sales and distribution costs, as well as for increased profits make B2B activity very appealing. Corporations can use the Internet to communicate more effectively with their current strategic partners, but they can also use it to locate new partners. This increase in competition promotes additional savings in terms of lower prices and better service.

Report Text style

Footnote: Janice Maloney, "The E-Trade Stampede," *Time Magazine*, September 6, 1999.

Overcoming Obstacles

Heading 2

One obstacle in achieving B2B Internet interaction has been locating and implementing the links between companies. Other obstacles include government regulations, complex technologies, and security concerns.

As a result, a new order of Internet service company has emerged. These companies specialize in providing the hardware, software, and consulting services that help businesses locate and communicate with suppliers, customers, strategic partners, and distributors. By assuming the responsibility for maintaining databases and tracking orders and shipments, this new segment of Internet service companies is making it possible for corporations of all sizes to successfully implement B2B ventures on-line.

Report Text style

The Forecast

Heading 2

Estimates of B2B trades on the Web vary, but most analysts believe their enormous growth will continue. Currently, most online business sales take place in independent exchanges, auctions, and internal trading hubs. In the future, analysts expect industry-led marketplaces to play a more significant role. Some analysts foresee $7.3 trillion in online business trades in 2004, up from $403 billion in 2000.

Report Text style

Conclusion

Heading 2

As with any emerging industry, B2B must overcome specific obstacles. However, the potential for profits makes the risks well worthwhile. The global reach of the Internet provides opportunities for expansion well beyond the traditional marketplace for most corporations. Those who ignore the possibilities of this technology will find themselves struggling to keep up.

Report Text style

Comment: *Should we include contact information?*

Footnote: Stephanie Stoughton, "B-to-B Onramp Under Construction," *The Boston Globe*, January 15, 2001:C1.

Exercise 42

Skills Covered:

◆ **Create Newsletter Columns** ◆ **Set Column Width**
◆ **Insert Column Breaks** ◆ **Balance Columns**

On the Job

Designing a document with columns lets you present more information on a page, as well as create a visually interesting page. Newsletter-style columns are useful for creating documents such as newsletters, pamphlets, articles, or brochures.

As the marketing director at Coastline Gourmet Importers, you are responsible for designing newsletters. In this exercise, you will create a newsletter to send to customers who have signed a store register.

Terms

Newsletter-style columns Columns in which text flows from the bottom of one column to the top of the next column.

Gutter The space between column margins.

Notes

Create Newsletter Columns

- By default, a Word document has one column, the width of the page from the left margin to the right margin.

- Use Word's Columns feature to divide a document into more than one **newsletter-style column**.

  ✓ *Use tables to create side-by-side columns; use the Columns feature to create newsletter-style columns; use tabs to align data along a single line in a document.*

- You can apply column formatting to existing text or you can set column formatting before typing new text.

- You can apply column formatting to an entire document or to the current section.

- By dividing a document into sections using section breaks, you can combine different numbers of columns within a single document.

- Multiple columns are not displayed in Normal view. Switch to Print Layout view or Print Preview to see the column formatting in a document.

Newsletter columns

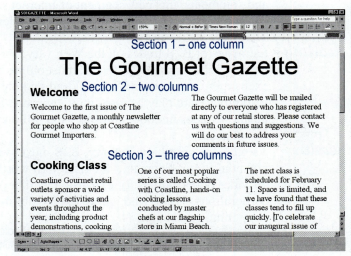

Notes

Graphics Objects

- **Graphics objects** created with other applications or with Word features can be inserted into Word documents.

- Some common graphics objects are shapes, drawings, **clip art**, charts, and **text boxes**. Horizontal lines and bullets may also be graphics objects.

Graphics objects in Word document

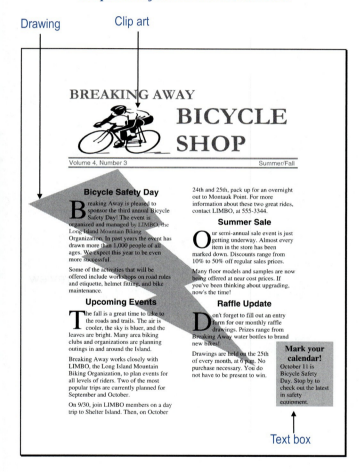

- **Floating objects** can be positioned anywhere on a page.

- Floating objects do not display in Normal view. You must use Print Layout view.

- Graphics objects can be integrated with text in five ways:

  - **In line** with text: Object is positioned on a line with text characters.

  - Wrapped square: Text is wrapped on all four sides of the object's **bounding box**.

  - Wrapped tight: Text is wrapped to the contours of the image.

  - Behind text: Text continues in lines over the object, obscuring the object.

  - In front of text: Text continues in lines behind the object, which may obscure the text.

Select a wrapping style to integrate objects with document text

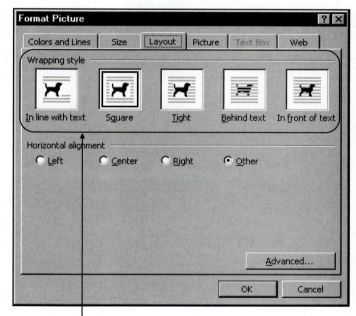

- Graphics objects can be formatted using border lines and shading.

Procedures

Create Columns of Equal Width

1. Click the **Columns** button ▦.
2. Drag across the number of columns to create.
3. Release mouse button.

OR

1. Click **F**ormat .... `Alt`+`O`
2. Click **C**olumns .... `C`
3. Click **N**umber of columns .... `Alt`+`N`
4. Type the number of columns to create.
5. Click **OK** .... `Enter`

Select a Preset Column Format

1. Click **F**ormat .... `Alt`+`O`
2. Click **C**olumns .... `C`
3. Click the desired Preset option:
   - **One** ▦ .... `Alt`+`O`
   - **Tw**o ▦ .... `Alt`+`W`
   - **Three** ▦ .... `Alt`+`T`
   - **Left** ▦ .... `Alt`+`L`
   - **Right** ▦ .... `Alt`+`R`
4. Click **OK** .... `Enter`

Return to One Column Formatting

1. Click the **Columns** button ▦.
2. Drag across one column only.
3. Release mouse button.

OR

1. Click **F**ormat .... `Alt`+`O`
2. Click **C**olumns .... `C`
3. Click **O**ne ▦ .... `Alt`+`O`

   OR

   a. Click **N**umber of columns .... `Alt`+`N`
   b. Type **1** *1*
4. Click **OK** .... `Enter`

Create Columns of Any Width

1. Click **F**ormat .... `Alt`+`O`
2. Click **C**olumns .... `C`
3. Click **N**umber of columns .... `Alt`+`N`
4. Type the number of columns to create.
5. For column 1, do the following:
   a. Type column **W**idth .... `Alt`+`I` in inches.
   b. Type gutter **S**pacing .... `Alt`+`S` in inches.
6. Deselect **Equal column width** check box .... `Alt`+`E`
7. Repeat step 5 for additional columns.
8. Click **OK** .... `Enter`

Adjust Gutter Spacing

1. Position mouse pointer on column margin marker.
   ✓ *When positioned correctly, the ScreenTip shows either Left Margin or Right Margin.*
2. Drag left or right.

Insert Column Break

1. Position insertion point where you want the break.
2. Click **I**nsert .... `Alt`+`I`
3. Click **B**reak .... `B`
4. Click **C**olumn break .... `C`
5. Click **OK** .... `Enter`

Balance Columns

1. Position insertion point at end of last column.
2. Click **I**nsert .... `Alt`+`I`
3. Click **B**reak .... `B`
4. Click **C**ontinuous .... `T`
5. Click **OK** .... `Enter`

Exercise Directions

1. Start Word, if necessary.
2. Open 💿**42GAZETTE**.
3. Save the file as **GAZETTE**.
4. Format the document as follows:
   a. Center the title in 36-point sans serif.
   b. Center the company name and address (lines 2 and 3) in 12-point sans serif.
   c. Leave 12 points of space after address.
   d. Format the three headlines (**Welcome**, **Cooking with Coastline**, and **Recipe Showcase**) using the Heading 1 style
   e. Format all occurrences of **The Gourmet Gazette** in the body of the newsletter in italics.
   f. Create a bulleted list out of the menu items listed in the **Cooking with Coastline** article.
   g. Insert 6 points of space before and 6 points of space after all body text paragraphs in the first two articles.
   h. Format the recipe title and serving information (**Eggplant Fritters** and **Yield: Six Servings**) with the Heading 2 style.
   i. Insert a right tab stop on that line to align the serving information at the 5" mark on the horizontal ruler.
   j. Apply the Heading 3 style to the text **Ingredients** and **Directions**.
   k. Format the directions as a numbered list.
5. Format the entire document into three columns of equal width.
6. Preview the document.
7. Return to one column formatting.
8. Insert a continuous section break before the headline **Welcome**.
   ✓ *There are now two sections in the document.*

9. Format the second section (from the headline **Welcome** to the end of the document) into two columns of equal width.
10. Preview the document.
11. Insert another continuous section break before the headline **Recipe Showcase**.
    ✓ *There are now three sections in the document.*
12. Insert another continuous section break before the heading **Ingredients**.
    ✓ *There are now four sections in the document.*
13. Apply one-column formatting to the third section (the section containing the headline **Recipe Showcase**).
14. Format the fourth section (from the heading **Ingredients** to the end of the document) using the Left Preset arrangement.
15. Decrease the gutter spacing between the columns in the fourth section to .25".
16. Preview the document.
17. Insert a column break before the headline **Cooking with Coastline**.
    ✓ *This moves the headline to the top of the second column.*
18. Preview the document. It should look similar to the one in Illustration A.
19. Check the spelling and grammar in the document.
20. Print the document.
21. Close the document, saving all changes.

The Gourmet Gazette

Published by Coastline Gourmet Importers, Inc.
7334 Sunshine Parkway Miami, FL 33132

Welcome

Welcome to the first issue of *The Gourmet Gazette*, a monthly newsletter for people who shop at Coastline Gourmet Importers. The primary goal of this publication is to provide you with news and information about activities and events occurring at Coastline stores. In addition, we plan to print recipes, tips, and product reviews that we think you will enjoy.

The Gourmet Gazette will be mailed directly to everyone who has registered at any of our retail stores. Please contact us with questions and suggestions. We will do our best to address your comments in future issues.

Cooking with Coastline

Coastline Gourmet retail outlets sponsor a wide variety of activities and events throughout the year, including product demonstrations, cooking classes, and social gatherings. One of our most popular series is called Cooking with Coastline, hands-on cooking lessons conducted by master chefs at our flagship store in Miami Beach.

The next class is scheduled for February 11. The menu is:

- Oysters on the half shell
- Rosemary Lamb Chops
- Chocolate Fondue

Space is limited, and we have found that these classes tend to fill up quickly. To celebrate our inaugural issue of *The Gourmet Gazette*, we are pleased to offer early registration to our readers. Please call 305-555-7300 for more information, or to reserve a place.

Recipe Showcase

Eggplant Fritters   ### *Yield: Six Servings*

Ingredients

1 small eggplant
1 teaspoon vinegar
1 egg
3 tablespoons flour
½ tablespoon salt
½ teaspoon baking powder
7 cups oil

Directions

1. Heat oil in deep fryer to 365 degrees.
2. Pare and slice eggplant.
3. Boil eggplant until tender; then add vinegar.
4. Drain eggplant and mash it.
5. Beat in the egg, flour, salt, and baking powder.
6. Place rounded spoonfuls into fryer basket.
7. Cook for 3 – 4 minutes or until light golden brown.

On Your Own

1. Start Word and create a new document.
2. Save the document as **OWD42**.
3. Create a newsletter about yourself.
4. Set the newsletter up so it has a one-column title at the top.
5. Divide the rest of the document into either two or three columns, and include two or three articles about things happening in your life. For example, write an article about classes you are taking, jobs you have, trips you have taken or are going to take, or movies or T.V. shows you have watched recently.
6. Try adjusting the widths of the columns.
7. Try changing the number of columns.
8. Insert column breaks as necessary.
9. Balance the columns if necessary.
10. Check the spelling and grammar in the document.
11. Print the document.
12. Close the document, saving all changes.

Exercise 43

Skills Covered:

◆ **Use Dropped Capitals**

◆ **Enhance a Document with Borders and Shading**

On the Job

Dropped capital letters, borders, and shading can call attention to a single word, a line, a paragraph, or an entire page. They make a document visually appealing and interesting to the reader, so the reader will be more likely to take the time to read and remember the text.

California Cardiology has asked you to create a one-page flyer to distribute to its patients. You'll use newsletter-style columns for the flyer, and you will enhance the document with dropped capitals, borders, and shading.

Terms

Dropped capital An enlarged capital letter that drops below the first line of body text in the paragraph.

Border A line placed on one or more sides of a paragraph(s), page, or text box.

Shading A color or pattern applied to a paragraph(s), page, or text box.

3D A perspective added to a border to give the appearance of three dimensions.

Shadow An effect designed to give the appearance of a shadow behind a border.

Notes

Use Dropped Capitals

- **Dropped capital** letters, called *drop caps,* are used to call attention to opening paragraphs.

- Drop caps can be placed in the margin to the left of the paragraph, or within the paragraph.

Drop Cap dialog box

- Drop caps can be in the same font as the surrounding text or in a different font.

- Selecting a different, more decorative font can enhance the drop cap effect.

✓ *In Normal view, drop caps will not appear exactly as they will in a printed document. Use Print Layout view or Print Preview to display the drop cap correctly.*

Enhance a Document with Borders and Shading

- You can apply **borders** and/or **shading** to a paragraph, selected paragraphs, or an entire page.

- Basic border and shading options are similar to those for tables, including line style, line weight (width), and line color.

- Additional border options include **3D** or **Shadow** effects.

- You can apply page borders to the whole document or to specified section(s).

- In addition to using basic border options, Word has a built-in list of artwork designed for page borders. Art borders are useful for stationery, invitations, and other informal, decorative documents.

- You can apply paragraph and page borders and shading using the Borders and Shading dialog box; you can also apply paragraph borders and shading using the Tables and Borders toolbar.

Borders and Shading dialog box: Page Border tab

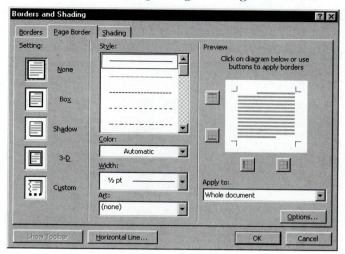

Borders and Shading dialog box: Shading tab

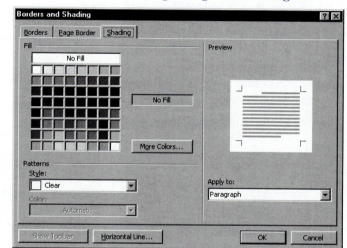

Borders and Shading dialog box: Borders tab

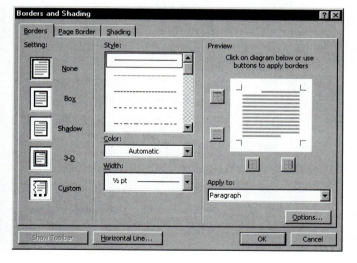

Procedures

Dropped Capital

1. Position insertion point in the paragraph.
2. Click **F**ormat .... `Alt`+`O`
3. Click **D**rop Cap .... `D`
4. Select one of the following:
   - **Dropped** `W≡` ...... `Alt`+`D`
   - **In margin** `W≡` ..... `Alt`+`M`
     - ✓ *Click None `≡` to remove an existing drop cap.*
5. If desired, do the following:
   a. Click the **Font** drop-down arrow .... `Alt`+`F`
   b. Select font to apply.
   c. Click **L**ines to drop .... `Alt`+`L`
   d. Type the **number of lines** to drop capital letter.
      - ✓ *The default is three.*
   e. Click **Distance from te**x**t** .... `Alt`+`X`
   f. Type the distance from text to position dropped capital (in inches).
      - ✓ *The default is zero.*
6. Click **OK** .... `Enter`

Paragraph Borders

1. Position insertion point in the paragraph.
   OR
   Select paragraphs.
2. Click **F**ormat .... `Alt`+`O`
3. Click **B**orders and **S**hading .... `B`
4. Click the **B**orders tab.......... `B`
5. Click a Setting option:
   - **Bo**x .... `Alt`+`X`
   - **Sh**adow .... `Alt`+`A`

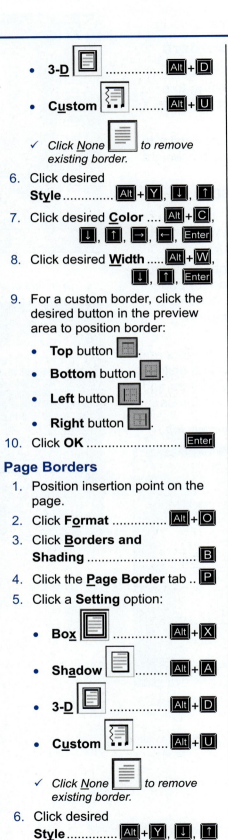

- **3-D** .... `Alt`+`D`
- **Cu**stom .... `Alt`+`U`
  - ✓ *Click None `≡` to remove existing border.*

6. Click desired **Style** .... `Alt`+`Y`, `↓`, `↑`
7. Click desired **Color** .... `Alt`+`C`, `↓`, `↑`, `→`, `←`, `Enter`
8. Click desired **Width** ..... `Alt`+`W`, `↓`, `↑`, `Enter`
9. For a custom border, click the desired button in the preview area to position border:
   - **Top** button `▢`.
   - **Bottom** button `▢`.
   - **Left** button `▢`.
   - **Right** button `▢`.
10. Click **OK** .... `Enter`

Page Borders

1. Position insertion point on the page.
2. Click **F**ormat .... `Alt`+`O`
3. Click **B**orders and **S**hading .... `B`
4. Click the **P**age Border tab .. `P`
5. Click a **Setting** option:
   - **Bo**x .... `Alt`+`X`
   - **Sh**adow .... `Alt`+`A`
   - **3-D** .... `Alt`+`D`
   - **Cu**stom .... `Alt`+`U`
     - ✓ *Click None `≡` to remove existing border.*
6. Click desired **Style** .... `Alt`+`Y`, `↓`, `↑`

7. Click desired **Color** ..... `Alt`+`C`, `↓`, `↑`, `→`, `←`, `Enter`
8. Click desired **Width** .. `Alt`+`W`, `↓`, `↑`, `Enter`
   OR
   Select desired **Art** ...... `Alt`+`R`, `↓`, `↑`, `Enter`
   - ✓ *If the art borders are not installed on your system, Word prompts you to insert the setup disk.*
9. For a custom border, click the desired button in preview area to position border:
   - **Top** button `▢`.
   - **Bottom** button `▢`.
   - **Left** button `▢`.
   - **Right** button `▢`.
10. Select section(s) to **Apply to** .... `Alt`+`L`, `↓`, `↑`, `Enter`
11. Click **OK** .... `Enter`

Shading

1. Position insertion point in paragraph.
   OR
   Select paragraphs.
2. Click **F**ormat .... `Alt`+`O`
3. Click **B**orders and **S**hading.................. `B`
4. Click the **S**hading tab .... `S`
5. Click desired **Fill color** .... `Tab`, `↓`, `↑`, `→`, `←`
6. If desired:
   - Select Patterns **St**y**le** .... `Alt`+`Y`, `↓`, `↑`, `Enter`
   - Select Patterns **Color** .... `Alt`+`C`, `↓`, `↑`, `→`, `←`, `Enter`
7. Click **OK** .... `Enter`

Exercise Directions

1. Start Word, if necessary.
2. Open ⊘ **43PATIENT**.
3. Save the file as **PATIENT**.
4. Apply a 26-point sans serif font to lines 1 and 2.
5. Apply formatting to leave 6 points of space after line 3.
6. On line 4, set a right tab stop flush with the right page margin (6" on the horizontal ruler). This will right-align the date, **Fall/Winter**, while leaving the text **Patient News** flush left.
7. Apply formatting to leave 12 points of space after line 4.
8. Apply the Heading 1 style to the headlines: **Healthy Heart Symposium**, **New Associate**, **Expanded Office Hours**, and **Report Available**.
9. Modify the formatting of the headlines **Healthy Heart Symposium** and **Report Available** so that there is no space left before.
10. Leave 6 points of space before and after all body text paragraphs.
11. Insert a continuous section break before the headline **Healthy Heart Symposium**.
12. Format section 2 into three newsletter-style columns of equal width.
13. Apply the default dropped capital formatting to the first character under the headlines **Healthy Heart Symposium**, **New Associate**, and **Report Available**.
14. Select the headline **Expanded Office Hours**, and the paragraph following it, and apply a 1½-point solid line shadow border and a 12.5% gray shading.
15. In the third article (**Report Available**), italicize every occurrence of the report title **Caring for Your Heart**.
16. Apply bullet list formatting to the sections listed as being included in the report (if necessary, change the paragraph formatting so there is no space before or after the bulleted items).
17. Select the bulleted list and apply a ½-point solid line outside border.
18. Display the Tables and Borders toolbar.
19. Apply the border shown in Illustration A along the top of line 4.
    a. Select the line style (unequal double-line with the thinner line on the bottom).
    b. Select the line weight (3 points).
    c. Select Top Border from the Border drop-down palette.
20. Apply the border shown in Illustration A along the bottom of line 4.
    a. Select the line style (unequal double-line with the thinner line on the top).
    b. Select the line weight (3 points).
    c. Select Bottom Border from the Border drop-down palette.
21. Apply a 10% gray shading to line 4, as shown in Illustration A.
22. Apply the Hearts page border (select the border from the Art drop-down list) to the entire document.
23. Check the spelling and grammar.
24. Display the document in Print Preview. It should look similar to the one in Illustration A.
25. Print the document.
26. Close the document, saving all changes.

CALIFORNIA CARDIOLOGY, INC.

10101 Santa Monica Boulevard, Suite 1200, Los Angeles, CA 90067

Patient News   Fall/Winter

Healthy Heart Symposium

On Sunday, February 14, our very own Dr. Finn Broderbund will be the featured speaker at the LA County Healthy Heart Breakfast Symposium.

The Healthy Heart Breakfast Symposium is held every year on St. Valentine's Day. It is sponsored by a consortium of cardiac care providers, and is intended to foster cardiac awareness throughout the community.

Tickets are still available. If you are interested in attending, call the office as soon as possible

New Associate

California Cardiology is pleased to welcome Dr. Cynthia Ramirez to our practice.

Expanded Office Hours

As of January 1, California Cardiology will be open until 8:30 p.m. on Mondays, Tuesdays, and Thursdays.

Dr. Ramirez received a B.S. degree from Stanford University in 1991 and an M.D. from the University of California at Los Angeles College of Medicine in 1995. Dr. Ramirez completed a residency at UCLA Medical Center and is board certified in cardiology. She is fluent in English, Spanish, and Portuguese.

We know that Dr. Ramirez will be an excellent addition to our staff. Please call the office for more information, or to schedule an appointment.

Report Available

The associates at California Cardiology have been hard at work researching and writing *Caring for Your Heart,* a four-page report that we hope offers useful information.

The report takes a question-and-answer approach to providing information in regards to cardiac care.

In addition to pointing out risk factors and recommending positive actions you can take to improve the health of your heart, *Caring for Your Heart* includes the following sections:

- What is coronary heart disease?
- What are the causes?
- What are the symptoms?
- Am I at risk?

The report is now available. Call the office for more information or to request a copy.

On Your Own

1. Open **OWD42**, the newsletter document you created in the On Your Own section of Exercise 42, or open ⊘ **43NEWS**.

2. Save the file as **OWD43**.

3. Apply dropped capitals to the first paragraph of each article.

4. Use borders to call attention to paragraphs. Try different effects, including different line styles, shadows, and 3-D. You might want to insert a border between the single column section and the multi-column section.

5. Apply a page border.

6. If necessary, adjust column breaks and balance columns to improve the appearance of the newsletter.

7. Check the spelling and grammar in the document.

8. Preview the document.

9. Print the document.

10. Close the document, saving all changes.

Exercise 44

Skills Covered:

◆ **Insert Drawing Objects** ◆ **Use the Drawing Canvas**
◆ **Use Text Boxes** ◆ **Use Diagrams and Organization Chart**
◆ **Resize Drawing Objects** ◆ **Move Drawing Objects**
◆ **Format Drawing Objects**

On the Job

Use graphics such as shapes and text boxes to illustrate and enhance text documents. You can position, size, and format the graphics to integrate them into the document, making the document easier to read and more interesting for the reader.

The owner of Coastline Gourmet has asked you to improve a flyer announcing the grand opening of a new store. In this exercise, you will enhance the document using AutoShapes and text boxes.

Terms

Graphics object A picture, chart, shape, or other element that can be inserted into a Word document.

Drawing object A shape or line created in Word and saved as part of the Word document.

Picture object A graphics object created using a different application and then inserted into a Word document.

Text box A rectangular drawing object in which text or graphics images can be inserted and positioned anywhere on a page.

Bitmap A picture made from a series of small dots. Bitmaps are created with and edited in paint programs, such as Microsoft Paint, and usually have the file extension .bmp, .png, .jpg, or .gif.

Clip art Picture files that can be inserted into a document.

Floating object A graphics object that is positioned independently from the document text.

Drawing canvas A drawing object that defines an area in a document in which you can insert other drawing objects.

Diagram A chart or graph usually used to illustrate a concept or describe the relationship of parts to a whole.

Organization chart A chart that depicts hierarchical relationships, such as a family tree or corporate management.

Sizing handles Rectangular boxes around the edges of a selected object that you use to resize the object.

Scale To change the size of an object by a percentage of the original size. For example, to double the size of an object, you would set the scale to 200%.

In line A graphics object that is positioned as a text character along with other text characters in the document.

Notes

Insert Drawing Objects

- You can insert two types of **graphics objects** into a Word document: **drawing objects** and **pictures**.

  - Common drawing objects include AutoShapes (including closed shapes, such as ovals and rectangles, as well as lines, such as curves and arrows), diagrams, and **text boxes**.

  - Common pictures include **bitmaps** and **clip art.**

    ✓ *Using clip art is covered in Exercise 45.*

  - Use Word's Drawing toolbar to insert drawing objects into a document.

The Basic Shapes AutoShapes palette

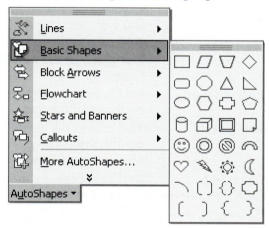

- You can insert a single drawing object, or combine multiple objects to create a larger drawing.

- By default, Word inserts drawings as **floating objects** in a document so they can be positioned anywhere on a page.

- Floating objects cannot be displayed in Normal view. Use Print Layout view to insert and edit drawing objects.

Use the Drawing Canvas

- Word automatically inserts a **drawing canvas** around objects you draw in a document.

- You can move and resize the entire canvas, which is useful if your drawing includes multiple objects that you want to keep together.

- If you want to work with a single object at a time, you can drag the object off the canvas.

  ✓ *If you create the object outside the canvas area, Word removes the canvas.*

- By default, the canvas has no border or fill; you can apply formatting if you want the canvas to be visible in the finished document.

- You can delete an unused canvas from a document.

- You can create a blank canvas.

Drawing Objects on a Drawing Canvas

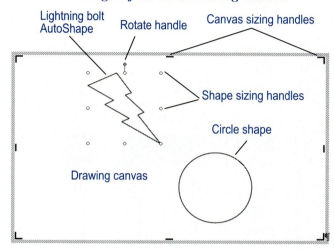

Use Text Boxes

- Insert a text box to position several blocks of text on a page or to give text a different orientation from other text in the document.

Text box in a Word document

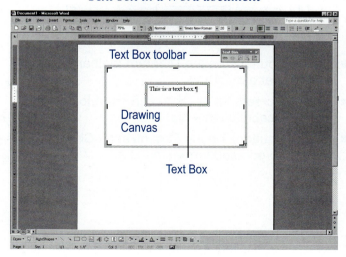

- You can insert a new text box, and then type in text, or you can insert a text box around existing text.

- You can format text within a text box using the same commands as you would to format regular text.

- When a text box is selected, the Text Box toolbar is displayed.

Use Diagrams and Organization Chart

- Word includes a selection of five **diagrams** and an **organization chart** that you can insert in a document as drawing objects:
  - Organization Chart
  - Cycle Diagram
  - Target Diagram
  - Radial Diagram
  - Venn Diagram
  - Pyramid Diagram

The Diagram Gallery

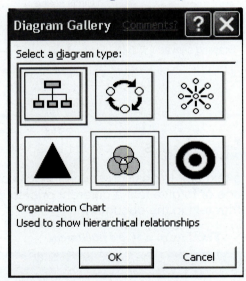

- Use the buttons on the Diagram toolbar to edit and format a diagram.

- You can create an organization chart to illustrate hierarchical relationships.

- Use the buttons on the Organization Chart toolbar to edit and format the chart.

Resize Drawing Objects

- You can resize graphics objects evenly so the height and width remain proportional, or you can resize objects unevenly, distorting the image.

- Drag the **sizing handles** to resize an object.

- **Scale** an object to increase or decrease the size proportionally.

Move Drawing Objects

- You can drag an object to move it to a new location.

- You can use alignment options to right align or center an object on the page.

- You can rotate an object around its center axis.

- You can change an object's wrapping style to affect the way the object is integrated into the document text. Select from seven wrapping options:

  - **In line** with text: Object is positioned on a line with text characters.

  - Wrapped square: Text is wrapped on all four sides of the object's bounding box.

  - Wrapped tight: Text is wrapped to the contours of the image.

  - Behind text: Text continues in lines over the object, obscuring the object.

  - In front of text: Text continues in lines behind the object, which may obscure the text.

  - Top and bottom: Text is displayed above and below object but not on left or right sides.

  - Through: Text runs through object.

  ✓ *You cannot set wrapping options for individual objects on a drawing canvas.*

Format Drawing Objects

- By default, drawing objects have a solid .75-pt. single line border on all sides.

- Drawing objects can be formatted using border lines and shading.

- You can also apply shadows and 3-D effects.

- The line and shading options are similar to those used for tables and paragraphs. For example, you can select a line style, line weight, and line color.

- You can use the buttons on the Drawing toolbar to apply formatting to drawing objects, or you can use the Format dialog box.

- The Format dialog box changes depending on the type of object you are formatting. For example, if you select a text box, the Format Text Box dialog box is available. If you select an AutoShape, the Format AutoShape dialog box is available.

Format AutoShape dialog box

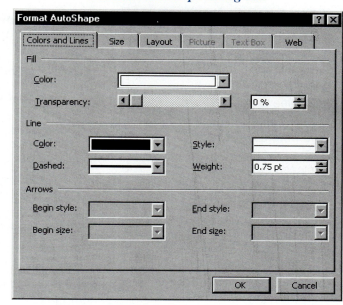

Procedures

Insert Blank Drawing Canvas

1. Click **Insert** .... Alt + I
2. Click **Picture** .... P
3. Click **New Drawing** .... D

Select AutoShape

1. Click **AutoShapes** button
   AutoShapes ▾ on Drawing toolbar.
2. Select desired AutoShapes palette:
   - **Lines** L
   - **Connectors** .... N
   - **Basic Shapes** .... B
   - **Block Arrows** .... A
   - **Flowchart** .... F
   - **Stars and Banners** .... S
   - **Callouts** C
3. Click desired AutoShape.
   - ✓ *Word inserts the Drawing canvas.*

Insert Closed Shape

1. Select desired AutoShape.
   OR
   Click **Rectangle** button on Drawing toolbar.
   OR
   Click **Oval** button on Drawing toolbar.
   - ✓ *Mouse pointer changes to crosshair.*
2. Click on canvas where you want to insert shape.
   OR
   Click and drag to draw shape.
   - ✓ *Press and hold Shift while dragging to draw perfect square or circle.*

Insert Line or Arrow

1. Select desired AutoShape.
   OR
   Click **Line** button on Drawing toolbar.
   OR
   Click **Arrow** button on Drawing toolbar.
   - ✓ *Mouse pointer changes to crosshair.*

2. Click on canvas where you want line or arrow to begin.
3. Drag to point where you want line or arrow to end.
4. Release mouse button.

Insert Curve

1. Select **Curve** AutoShape from Lines palette.
   - ✓ *Mouse pointer changes to crosshair.*
2. Click on canvas where you want line to begin.
3. Release mouse button.
4. Click at point where you want line to curve.
5. Repeat step 4 at each point where you want line to curve,
6. Double-click to end line.

Insert Freeform Line

1. Select **Freeform** AutoShape from Lines palette ⬜.
   - ✓ *Mouse pointer changes to pencil icon.*
2. Click on canvas where you want line to begin.
3. Drag to draw freehand as if you were using a pencil.
   OR
   Release mouse button and click to draw straight lines.
4. Double-click to end line.

Insert Scribble Line

1. Select **Scribble** AutoShape from Lines palette ⬜.
   - ✓ *Mouse pointer changes to pencil icon.*
2. Click on canvas where you want line to begin.
3. Drag to draw freehand as if you were using a pencil.
4. Release mouse button to end line.

Insert a Diagram or Organization Chart

1. Click **Insert Diagram or Organization Chart** button ⬜ on Drawing toolbar.
   OR
   a. Click **I**nsert .... `Alt`+`I`
   b. Click **Dia**gram .... `G`
2. Click desired diagram type .... `→`,`←`
3. Click **OK** .... `Enter`
   - ✓ *Word inserts the diagram on the Drawing Canvas.*
4. Use toolbar buttons to edit and format diagram as desired.

Insert a Text Box

1. Click **Text Box** button ⬜ on Drawing toolbar.
   OR
   a. Click **I**nsert .... `Alt`+`I`
   b. Click **Te**xt Box .... `X`
   - ✓ *Word inserts the Drawing Canvas and the mouse pointer changes to a cross hair.*
2. Position the mouse pointer where you want the upper-left corner of the text box to be.
3. Click and drag diagonally to draw the text box.
4. Release the mouse button.
5. Type text.

Insert a text box around existing text:

1. Select paragraph(s).
2. Click **Text Box** button ⬜ on Drawing toolbar.
   OR
   a. Click **I**nsert .... `Alt`+`I`
   b. Click **Te**xt Box .... `X`

Change direction of text in text box:

1. Select text box.
2. Click **Change Text Direction** button ⬜ on Text Box toolbar.
3. Type text.
   - ✓ *Click Change Text Direction button again to cycle through available text directions.*

Add a text box to an AutoShape:

1. Insert AutoShape.
2. Right-click shape.
3. Click **Add Te**xt .... `X`
4. Type text.

Resize an Object

1. Click object to select it.
2. Drag a corner sizing handle to resize both height and width proportionally.
   OR
   Drag a side sizing handle to resize height or width only.

   OR
1. Select object.
2. Click **F**ormat .... `Alt`+`O`
3. Click object type:
   - **Text Bo**x .... `O`
   - **Aut**o**Shape** .... `O`
   - **Drawing Canvas** .... `D`
4. Click the **Size** tab .... `Ctrl`+`Tab`
5. Click **H**eight .... `Alt`+`E`
6. Type new height measurement.
   - ✓ *If the Lock aspect ratio check box is selected, Word automatically enters the appropriate Width measurement to keep the object proportioned.*
7. Click **Wi**dth .... `Alt`+`D`
8. Type new width measurement.
9. Click **OK** .... `Enter`

Scale an Object

1. Select object.
2. Click **F**ormat .... `Alt`+`O`
3. Click object type:
   - **Text Bo**x .... `O`
   - **Aut**o**Shape** .... `O`
   - **Drawing Canvas** .... `D`
4. Click the **Size** tab .... `Ctrl`+`Tab`
5. Click **H**eight .... `Alt`+`H`
6. Type height percentage.
   - ✓ *If the Lock aspect ratio check box is selected, Word automatically enters the appropriate Width size to keep the object proportioned.*
7. Click **W**idth .... `Alt`+`W`
8. Type new width percentage.
9. Click **OK** .... `Enter`

Move an Object

1. Click object to select it.
2. Position the mouse pointer over object until it becomes a four-headed arrow.
3. Drag object to new location.
   - ✓ *Use this method to move an object off the Drawing Canvas.*

Rotate an Object

1. Click object to select it.
2. Position the mouse pointer over green rotation handle.
   - ✓ *When pointer is positioned correctly, it resembles a circular arrow* ⟳ .
3. Drag handle clockwise or counterclockwise.
4. Release mouse button when object is positioned as desired.

Wrap Text Around an Object

1. Click object.
2. Click **D**raw .... D on Drawing toolbar.
3. Click **Text Wrapping** button .... T
4. Click desired wrapping option.
   - **In line with text**............ I
   - **S**quare........................... S
   - **T**ight............................... T
   - **Behin**d text .... D

- **In** front of text............... N
- **T**op and bottom........... O
- **Th**rough .... H

OR

1. Click object.
2. Click **F**ormat .... Alt + O
3. Click object type:
   - **Text B**ox .... O
   - **Aut**o**S**hape .... O
   - **Drawing Canvas** .... D
4. Click **Layout** tab......... Ctrl + Tab
5. Click desired Wrapping style:
   - **In line with text** ..... Alt + I
   - **S**quare................... Alt + Q
   - **T**ight .... Alt + T
   - **Behind text** .... Alt + B
   - **In f**ront of text....... Alt + F
6. Click **OK** .... Enter

Format Drawing Objects

Select line color:

1. Click object.
2. Click **Line Color** drop-down arrow .... on Drawing toolbar.
3. Click desired color.
   - ✓ *To quickly apply color displayed on Line Color button, simply click the button.*

Select line style:

1. Click object.
2. Click **Line Style** button ≡ on Drawing toolbar.
3. Click desired style.

Select dash style:

1. Click object.
2. Click **Dash Style** button on Drawing toolbar.
3. Click desired style.

Select arrow style:

1. Click object.
2. Click **Arrow Style** button ⇄ on Drawing toolbar.
3. Click desired style.

Apply fill:

1. Click object.
2. Click **Fill Color** drop-down arrow on Drawing toolbar.
3. Click desired color.
   - ✓ *To quickly apply color displayed on Fill Color button, simply click the button.*

Delete an Object

1. Select the object.
2. Press **Del**........................... Del
   - ✓ *When you delete a Drawing Canvas, all objects on the canvas are deleted as well.*

Exercise Directions

1. Start Word, if necessary.

2. Open 44OPEN.

3. Save the file as **OPEN**.

4. Insert a Lightning Bolt AutoShape from the Basic Shapes palettes.

5. Drag the shape off the Drawing Canvas, then delete the canvas.

   ✓ *When you drag the object off the canvas, the canvas is no longer selected. Click it to select it, then press Del.*

6. Resize the shape so it is 2.5" by 2.5".

7. Fill the shape with the color yellow.

8. Apply a 3-pt. double-line border around the shape, in light orange.

9. Move the shape so its top-left corner is about 1" from the top of the page and ½" from the left edge of the page.

10. Set text wrapping for the shape so it is displayed behind the text.

    ✓ *Once the shape is behind the text, you may have trouble selecting it. Try positioning the pointer near the top of the shape, where it is not behind any text. When the pointer looks like a double-headed arrow, click to select the shape.*

11. Copy and paste the shape to create another Lightning Bolt. Alternatively, repeat steps 4 through 8.

12. Rotate the second shape clockwise 90 degrees (1/4 turn) (refer to Illustration A).

13. Move the shape so its top point is about 1" from the right edge of the page and about ½" from the top of the page.

14. Set text wrapping so the shape is displayed behind the text.

15. Select the last paragraph in the document and insert a text box around it.

16. Resize the text box so it is 2" high by 4" wide.

17. Apply the third line style from the bottom (a 4.5-pt. unequal double-line), in blue, to the text box.

18. Apply a pale blue fill to the text box.

19. Insert an Explosion 1 AutoShape from the Stars and Banners palette.

20. Drag it off the canvas and delete the canvas.

21. Size it to 2.5" by 2".

22. Fill it with the color Rose.

23. Add the text **Product Demos!** to the shape, in 18-pt. Comic Sans MS, centered.

24. Set text wrapping so the shape is in front of the text.

25. Move the shape so it overlaps the top-left corner of the text box, as shown in the illustration.

26. Copy and paste the explosion shape to create a duplicate, replacing the text with **Fun for All!**. Alternatively, repeat steps 22 through 27, this time typing the text **Fun for All!**.

27. Move this shape so it overlaps the top-right corner of the text box.

28. Copy and paste the explosion shape to create a duplicate, replacing the text with **Raffles!**. Alternatively, repeat steps 22 through 27, this time with the text **Raffles!**.

29. Position the third shape to overlap the bottom right side of the text box.

30. Create a fourth explosion with the text **Tasty Treats!** to position over the lower-left side of the text box.

31. Rotate the fourth explosion counterclockwise a little to about the 350 degree point, so its points fit between the words in the text box.

32. Preview the document. It should look similar to Illustration A.

33. Check the spelling and grammar in the document.

34. Print the document.

35. Close the file, saving all changes.

Illustration A

COASTLINE GOURMET IMPORTERS

Announces

THE GRAND OPENING

of its

Newest Retail Outlet

16509 NORTHEAST 26TH AVENUE
NORTH MIAMI BEACH, FL 33160

Stop in to share our grand opening celebration
Saturday April 13 and Sunday April 14

Product Demos!

Coastline Gourmet Importers is well known as a specialty food store featuring items imported from around the world.

Fun for All!

Tasty Treats!

Raffles!

On Your Own

1. Open **OWD43**, the newsletter document you used in the On Your Own section of Exercise 43, or open **44NEWS**.

2. Save the file as **OWD44**.

3. Insert a text box between the two columns and type in a headline, quotation, or other important information you want to stand out in the document.

4. Format the text box using borders and shading.

5. Select a text wrapping option that enhances the appearance of the document.

6. Insert an AutoShape in the newsletter title.

7. Resize and position the shape for the best effect.

8. Try different text wrapping options.

9. Check spelling and grammar in the document.

10. Preview the document.

11. Adjust column breaks and balance columns as necessary.

12. Print the document.

13. Close the document, save all changes

Skills Covered:

◆ **Insert Clip Art** ◆ **Use the Clip Organizer**

On the Job

Insert clip art into documents to illustrate and enhance your text. In addition to pictures, such as drawings and cartoons, you can insert sound, video, and photograph clips.

The associates at California Cardiology have asked you to embellish the flyer you created using graphics. In this exercise, you insert clip art pictures into the existing flyer.

Terms

Clip art Files, such as pictures, sounds, and videos, that can be inserted into an Office document.

Clip collection A folder used to store clip files.

Microsoft Clip Organizer A folder that comes with Office. It contains drawings, photographs, sounds, videos, and other media files that you can insert and use in Office documents.

Notes

Insert Clip Art

- Office comes with a selection of **clip art** that you can insert into your Office documents.

- Clip art files include pictures, sounds, and videos created in different programs—but fully supported and editable in Word.

- You can edit and format clip art pictures using many of the same commands you use for editing and formatting drawing objects. For example, you can resize, move, and set text wrapping options.

  ✓ *Refer to Word, Exercise 44 for information on editing and formatting drawing objects.*

- You can also use the buttons on the Picture toolbar to edit and format clip art. For example, you can change the brightness and contrast of colors, and you can crop the pictures to remove edges you don't need.

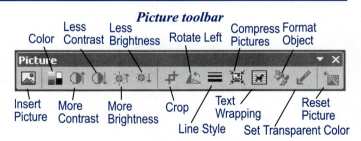

- By default, clip art pictures are inserted inline with text; you must change the text wrapping settings if you want them to float.

- Use the Insert Clip Art Task Pane to locate and insert clip art.

- The Insert Clip Art Task pane is similar to the Basic Search Task Pane.

  ✓ *Using the Basic Search Task Pane is covered in Word, Exercise 12.*

✓ You can also use the Insert Picture From File command to insert clip art. This is useful when you know where the file you need is stored on your system.

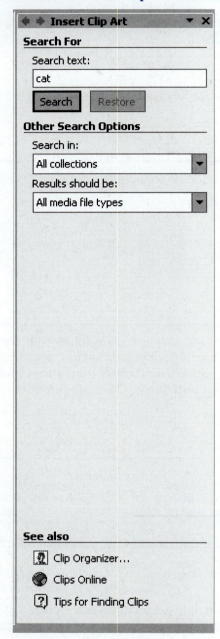

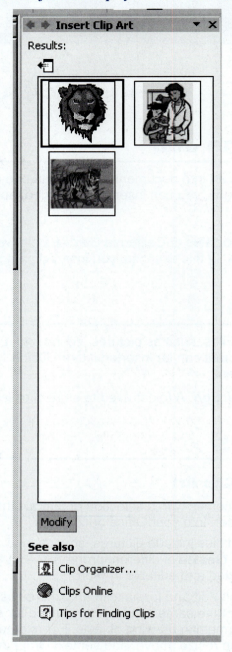

Insert Picture dialog box

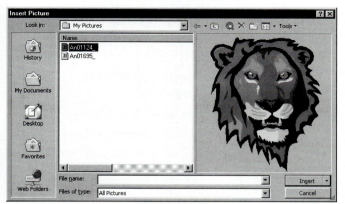

Use the Clip Organizer

- To make it easy to find the clips you want, Office sorts the files into **clip collections** and stores them in the **Microsoft Clip Organizer**.
- By default, the Clip Organizer includes the following clip collections:
  - *My Collections*, which includes clips that you have stored on your system and sorted into folders such as *Favorites*. It may also include a Windows folder containing clips that come with Windows, other Windows programs, or clips that you had installed before you installed Office XP.

- *Office Collections*, which includes the clips that come with Office and sorted into folders such as *People, Animals, Emotions, and Food.*
- *Web Collections*, which automatically uses an open Internet link to access clips stored on Microsoft's Clips Online Web site.

- You can use the Clip Organizer to browse through clip collections, create new collections, add clips from other locations, and copy or move clips from one collection to another.

The Clip Organizer

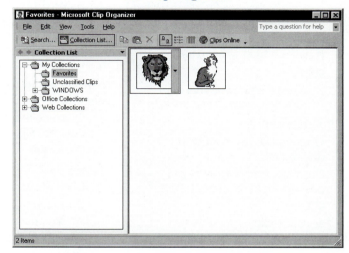

Procedures

Insert Clip Art

Using the Task Pane:

1. Click **Insert Clip Art** button
   [icon] on Drawing toolbar.

   OR

   a. Click **I**nsert .... `Alt`+`I`
   b. Select **P**icture .... `P`
   c. Click **C**lip Art .... `C`
   ✓ *The Insert Clip Art Task Pane opens.*

2. Type search text in Search text box.
   ✓ *If necessary, delete existing text, first.*

3. Click **Search in**: drop-down arrow.

4. Select and deselect collection folders as necessary, using the follows methods:
   - Click **plus sign** to expand list .... `→`
   - Click check box to select folder .... `↑`, `↓`, `Space`

5. Click outside expanded list to close list .... `Tab`

6. Click **Results should be:** drop-down arrow .... `Tab`, `Space`

7. Click **plus sign** to expand list .... `↓`, `←`

8. Deselect clip type(s) you don't need .... `↑`, `↓`, `Space`

9. Click **Search** button `Search`.
   ✓ *Word displays clips that match your criteria.*

10. Click clip to insert.

    OR

    Click **Modify** button `Modify` to display Insert Clip Art Task Pane again and start a new search.

Using the Insert Picture dialog box:

1. Click **I**nsert .... `Alt`+`I`
2. Select **P**icture .... `P`
3. Click **F**rom File .... `F`
   ✓ *Word displays the Insert Picture dialog box, with the contents of the My Pictures folder displayed.*
4. Locate and select desired clip file.
5. Click In**s**ert .... `S`

Use the Clip Organizer

1. Click **Insert Clip Art** button 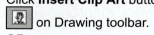 on Drawing toolbar.

   OR

   a. Click **I**nsert .... `Alt`+`I`

   b. Select **P**icture .... `P`

   c. Click **C**lip Art .... `C`

   ✓ *The Insert Clip Art Task Pane opens.*

2. Click **Clip Organizer** .

   ✓ *The Microsoft Clip Organizer window opens, with the My Favorites Collection displayed.*

3. Click desired folder in Collection List to view its contents.

   ✓ *If necessary, click **plus sign** next to a folder to expand list.*

To insert a clip:

1. Open collection containing desired clip.

2. Drag clip from Organizer to desired location in document.

   OR

   a. Click clip.

   b. Click clip's drop–down arrow.

   c. Click **C**opy .... `C`

   d. Position insertion point in document where you want to insert clip.

   ✓ *Move organizer out of the way if necessary.*

   e. Click **E**dit .... `Alt`+`E`

   f. Click **P**aste .... `P`

To copy a clip to a different collection:

1. Open collection containing desired clip.

2. Click clip.

3. Click clip's drop-down arrow.

4. Click Cop**y** to Collection .... `Y`

   ✓ *The Copy to Collection dialog box opens.*

5. Select collection to copy to.

   OR

   a. Click **N**ew .... `Alt`+`N` to create a new collection.

   b. Type new collection name.

   c. Click OK .... `Enter`

6. Click OK .... `Enter`

To move a clip to a different collection:

1. Open collection containing desired clip.

2. Click clip.

3. Click clip's drop-down arrow.

4. Click **M**ove to Collection .... `M`

   ✓ *The Move to Collection dialog box opens.*

5. Select collection to move to.

   OR

   a. Click **N**ew .... `Alt`+`N` to create a new collection.

   b. Type new collection name.

   c. Click OK .... `Enter`

6. Click OK .... `Enter`

To add a clip to the Clip Organizer:

1. Open collection in which you want to store clip.

2. Click **F**ile .... `Alt`+`F`

3. Select **A**dd Clips to Organizer .... `A`

4. Do one of the following:

   a. Click Auto**m**atically .... `M` to have Word automatically locate and add clips stored on your system.

   b. Click OK to begin .... `Enter`

   OR

   a. Click **O**n My Own .... `O` to manually select clips to add.

   b. Locate and select desired clip file(s).

   c. Click **A**dd .... `Alt`+`A`

   OR

   • Click From **S**canner or Camera .... `S` to upload a clip from a scanner device or camera device attached to your system.

To delete a clip from the current folder:

1. Open collection containing desired clip.

2. Click clip.

3. Click clip's drop-down arrow.

4. Click **Delete from** "Collection Name" .... `F`

To delete a clip from the Clip Organizer:

1. Open collection containing desired clip.

2. Click clip.

3. Click clip's drop-down arrow.

4. Click **Delete from Clip Organizer** .... `D`

5. Word asks if you are sure.

6. Click **Y**es .... `Y`

Exercise Directions

1. Start Word, if necessary.
2. Open ▨**PATIENT** or open ◉ **45PATIENT**
3. Save the file as **PATIENT**.
4. Change the left and right page margins to 1".
5. Remove the page border from the document.
    a. Open the Borders and Shading dialog box.
    b. Switch to the Page Borders tab.
    c. Select None in the Settings list.
    d. Click OK.
6. Position the insertion point at the beginning of the first line in the document.
7. Use the Insert Clip Art Task Pane to search for clips with the keyword *Heart*.
8. Insert the clip shown in Illustration A.
    ✓ *If you cannot locate the same clip, use the Insert Picture From File command to insert the file* ◉*HEART1.WMF supplied with this book.*
9. Change the text wrapping setting for the picture to Square.
10. Change the font size of the line of text displaying the address from 12 points to 10 points.
11. Move the picture up just a bit so that the shaded paragraph with the issue name and date extends across the page (refer to illustration).
12. If necessary, move the picture to the right also so that it is does not extend into the left margin.
13. Move the insertion point to the headline **New Associate**.
14. Use the Insert Clip Art Task Pane to search for clips with the keyword *Doctor*.
15. Insert the clip shown in the illustration.
    ✓ *If you cannot locate the same clip, use the Insert Picture From File command to insert the file* ◉ *DOCTOR1.WMF supplied with this book.*
16. Set the text wrapping to Square.
17. Resize the clip so it is 1" wide (the height will adjust automatically).
18. Position the picture to the right of the headline, as shown in the illustration.
19. Check the spelling and grammar in the document.
20. Display the document in Print Preview. It should look similar to the one in Illustration A.
21. Print the document.
22. Close the file, saving all changes.

On Your Own

1. Start Word and open ▨**OWD44**, the newsletter you have used in previous exercises, or open ◉ **45NEWS**.
2. Save the document as **OWD45**.
3. Insert one or more clip art pictures into the newsletter.
4. Select text wrapping that integrates the pictures effectively with the document text.
5. Size and position the pictures so they enhance the document.
6. Preview the document.
7. Adjust column breaks and text formatting as necessary.
8. Check the spelling and grammar in the document.
9. Preview the document again.
10. Print the document.
11. Close the document, saving all changes.

CALIFORNIA CARDIOLOGY, INC.

10101 Santa Monica Boulevard, Suite 1200, Los Angeles, CA 90067

Patient News　　　　　　　　　　　　　　　　**Fall/Winter**

Healthy Heart Symposium

On Sunday, February 14, our very own Dr. Finn Broderbund will be the featured speaker at the LA County Healthy Heart Breakfast Symposium.

The Healthy Heart Breakfast Symposium is held every year on St. Valentine's Day. It is sponsored by a consortium of cardiac care providers, and is intended to foster cardiac awareness throughout the community.

Tickets are still available. If you are interested in attending, call the office as soon as possible

New Associate

California Cardiology is pleased to welcome Dr. Cynthia Ramirez to our practice.

Expanded Office Hours

As of January 1, California Cardiology will be open until 8:30 p.m. on Mondays, Tuesdays, and Thursdays.

Dr. Ramirez received a B.S. degree from Stanford University in 1991 and an M.D. from the University of California at Los Angeles College of Medicine in 1995. Dr. Ramirez completed a residency at UCLA Medical Center and is board certified in cardiology. She is fluent in English, Spanish, and Portuguese.

We know that Dr. Ramirez will be an excellent addition to our staff. Please call the office for more information, or to schedule an appointment.

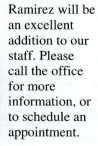

Report Available

The associates at California Cardiology have been hard at work researching and writing *Caring for Your Heart,* a four-page report that we hope offers useful information.

The report takes a question-and-answer approach to providing information in regards to cardiac care.

In addition to pointing out risk factors and recommending positive actions you can take to improve the health of your heart, *Caring for Your Heart* includes the following sections:

- What is coronary heart disease?
- What are the causes?
- What are the symptoms?
- Am I at risk?

The report is now available. Call the office for more information or to request a copy.

Skills Covered:

◆ Templates ◆ Wizards

On the Job

Templates and wizards help you create similar documents efficiently—and time after time. Templates include page setup and formatting settings to insure that new documents will be uniform. In many cases they include standard text and graphics as well. Wizards are automated templates that prompt you to provide information that can be used to customize the resulting document.

Samantha Parsons, a vice president at Regency General, Inc., is planning a business trip to a new client. As an administrative assistant at Regency General, you are in charge or coordinating the travel arrangements. In this exercise, you will use a template to create a memo document to the client, detailing the itinerary. You will then use a Wizard to create a fax cover sheet which you could use when transmitting the memo to the client.

Terms

Template A Word document on which new documents are based. Templates include formatting settings, text, and graphics used to create the new documents.

Dot extension The file extension assigned by Word to template files.

Normal.dot The default template used to create new documents in Word.

Wizard An automated template.

Notes

Templates

- All new Word documents are based on a **template**.
- Templates include formatting settings, such as margins, font, and font size.
- Some templates include boilerplate text and graphics that are part of new documents.

Memo template

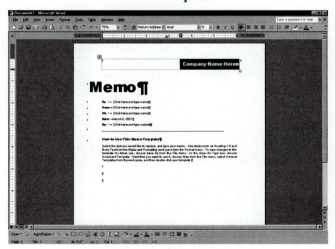

- All new documents based on the same template will have the same default formatting settings and will display any boilerplate text and graphics.

- Some templates include editing directions or sample text for completing the document. You replace sample text, fill in missing information, and customize the document using standard editing and formatting commands.

- Word comes with built-in templates for creating common documents, such as memos, letters, Web pages, and resumes.

- Built-in templates are usually available in several styles, which means different formatting settings for different situations. For example, a letter in the Professional template may be suitable for business correspondence, while the Elegant, template may be more suitable for personal correspondence.

- You can preview built-in templates in the Templates dialog box.

- Recently used templates are listed in the New Documents Task Pane.

- Template files have a **.dot extension**. The default template for creating a blank document is called **Normal.dot**.

Templates dialog box

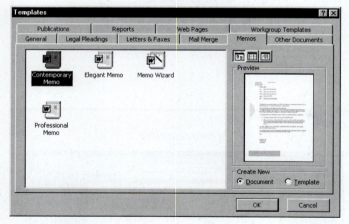

Wizards

- You can use **Wizards** to create customized new documents.

- Wizards prompt you through a series of dialog boxes to enter information that can be incorporated into the document.

  ✓ *The flowchart in the first dialog box indicates how many dialog boxes there are.*

Memo Wizard

- For example, a memo Wizard might prompt you for the recipient's name and the memo subject. When Word creates the document, the recipient's name and the memo subject will be entered automatically.

- You can customize documents created with a Wizard using standard editing and formatting commands.

- Wizards are listed along with templates in the Templates dialog box; recently used Wizards are listed in the New Documents Task Pane.

Procedures

Create a Document Using a Template

1. Click **File** .... Alt + F
2. Click **New** .... N

   ✓ *The New Document Task Pane opens.*

3. Click **General Templates** ⊞ .

   ✓ *If desired template is listed in the New Document Task Pane, click it and skip to step 8.*

4. Click the desired tab ... Ctrl + Tab
5. Select the desired
   template icon .... ↑ , ↓
6. Click **OK** .... Enter
7. Replace directions and prompts with text.

8. Edit and format document as desired.
9. Name and save
   document .... Ctrl + S

Create a Document Using a Wizard

1. Click **File** .... Alt + F
2. Click **New** .... N

   ✓ *The New Document Task Pane opens.*

3. Click **General Templates** ⊞ .

   ✓ *If desired wizard is listed in the New Document Task Pane, click it and skip to step 8.*

4. Click the desired tab... Ctrl + Tab

5. Click the desired
   Wizard icon .... ↑ , ↓
6. Click **OK** .... Enter
7. Respond to prompts in dialog box.
8. Click **Next** .... Alt + N

   ✓ *Click Back to return to previous dialog box to change responses. Click Finish to create document with default settings.*

9. Repeat steps 7 and 8 until last dialog box is displayed.
10. Click **Finish** .... Alt + F
11. Edit and format document as desired.
12. Save document .... Ctrl + S

Exercise Directions

1. Start Word, if necessary.
2. Use the Professional Memo template to create a new document.
3. Save the file as **TRAVEL**.
4. Replace the sample text with the following information as shown in Illustration A:

   Company Name: Regency General, Inc.
   To: Bonnie Margolis
   From: Your Name
   CC: Samantha Parsons
   Date: Today's date
   Re: Travel Plans.
5. Delete the text **How to Use This Memo Template**.
6. Replace the remaining paragraph of explanatory text with the paragraphs shown in Illustration A.
7. Check the spelling and grammar in the document.
8. Display the document in Print Preview. It should look similar to the one in Illustration A.
9. Print the document.
10. Close the document, saving all changes.
11. Use the Fax Wizard to create a fax cover sheet.

12. Complete the prompts in the Wizard dialog boxes as follows:
    - In the document to fax screen, select the option to create just a cover sheet with a note.
    - Specify that you want to print the document and send it from a separate fax machine.
    - Use the following information:

      Recipient's name: Bonnie Margolis

      Recipient's fax number: 801-555-2598

      Use the Professional style.

      Sender: Your Name

      Sender's company: Regency General, Inc.

      Mailing address: 1500 W. High Tech Blvd., Suite 700, Austin, TX 73301

      Phone: 512-555-3900

      Fax: 512-555-3910
13. Replace all remaining sample text in the document as shown in Illustration B.

    ✓ *Double-click in the Please Reply box to insert the check mark.*
14. Save the document as **FAXCOVER**.
15. Check the spelling and grammar in the document.
16. Display the document in Print Preview. It should look similar to the one in Illustration A.
17. Print the document.
18. Close the document, saving all changes.

On Your Own

1. Start Word and use the Letter Wizard to create a new document.
2. Save the document as **OWD46-1**.
3. In the document, type a letter to a friend or relative explaining some of the documents you have learned to create with Word.
4. Check the spelling and grammar in the document.

5. Display the document in Print Preview.
6. Print the document.
7. Use the Envelope Wizard to create an envelope for the letter.
8. Add the envelope to a new document.
9. Save the document as **OWD46-2**.
10. Close the documents, saving all changes.

Regency General, Inc.

Memo

To: Bonnie Margolis

From: Your Name

CC: Samantha Parsons

Date: Today's date

Re: Travel plans

I have finalized the travel plans for Ms. Parsons' visit to Wasatch Communications next week. She will be arriving at the airport in Salt Lake City at 8:40 a.m., via Southwest Airlines. I have arranged for a car service to pick her up and take her directly to your corporate office. Assuming the flight is on time, she should be there in time for the 10:00 a.m. meeting.

She is scheduled to depart Salt Lake City airport on a Southwest flight at 4:10 p.m. The same car service will pick her up at your office at 3:00 p.m., to insure that she is on time for departure.

Please notify me as soon as possible if there are any problems or conflict with these arrangements. In addition, could you please send me the meeting agenda, and any other information about activities that you have scheduled for Ms. Parsons. She likes to be prepared.

Thank you for your assistance.

1

1500 W. High Tech Blvd.
Suite 700
Austin, TX 73301
Phone: 512-555-3900
Fax: 512-555-3910

Regency General, Inc.

To:	Bonnie Margolis	**From:**	Your Name
Fax:	801-555-2598	**Date:**	Today's date
Phone:	801-555-2500 ext. 101	**Pages:**	2 (including cover)
Re:	Travel plans	**CC:**	

☐ **Urgent**   ☐ **For Review**   ☐ **Please Comment**   ☑ **Please Reply**   ☐ **Please Recycle**

•**Comments:** Bonnie – Here's a memo with some information about Ms. Parsons' visit later this week.

Thanks,

Your Name

Exercise 47

◆ **Insert a File in a Document** ◆ **Use AutoText**

On the Job

Insert a file into another file to save time retyping existing text. When you insert a file, the entire contents of the file become part of the current document, while the original file remains unchanged. Use AutoText to quickly insert words or phrases you type often, such as the closing to a letter.

As an administrative assistant at Northwest Gear, you want to show that you are resourceful. In this exercise, you will design a letterhead that you will save as AutoText. You can then insert it at the top of a press release you will write announcing the winners of the essay contest. You also need to include the company's mission statement in the press release. Since you already have a document containing the mission statement, you can simply insert it directly into the press release.

Terms

AutoText A feature of Word that lets you automatically insert a selection of stored text and graphics.

Notes

Insert a File in a Document

- You can insert one file into another file to incorporate the first file's contents into the second file.

- The entire contents are saved as part of the second file.

- The first file remains unchanged.

- Inserting a file is different from copying and pasting, because you do not have to open the file to insert it and the entire file contents are inserted—no selecting is necessary.

  ✓ *To mark where a file is inserted into an existing document, turn on the Track Changes feature before the insertion.*

Use AutoText

- **AutoText** is part of Word's AutoCorrect feature.

  ✓ *Using AutoCorrect is covered in Word, Exercise 4.*

- AutoText eliminates repetitive typing by automatically inserting saved blocks of text or graphics.

- An unlimited amount of text or graphics may be stored in an AutoText entry.

- Word comes with a built-in list of AutoText entries, including standard letter closings and salutations.

- You can add entries to the AutoText list.

- You can delete an entry when you don't need it anymore.

The AutoText tab of the AutoCorrect dialog box

Procedures

Insert a File

1. Position the insertion point where you want file inserted.
2. Click **Insert** .... `Alt`+`I`
3. Click **File** .... `L`
4. Select file to insert .... `↓`, `↑`
5. Click **Insert** button
    .... `Alt`+`S`

Use AutoText

To create an AutoText entry:
(Alt+F3)

1. Select text or graphics.
2. Click **Insert** .... `Alt`+`I`
3. Select **AutoText** .... `A`
4. Click **New** .... `N`
5. Type the entry name
   - ✓ *AutoText entry names can have 31 characters including spaces. Use descriptive names.*
6. Click **OK** .... `Enter`

To insert an AutoText entry:

1. Type entry name.
   - ✓ *Notice a ScreenTip appears as soon as Word recognizes the AutoText entry. If entry name is unique, you can type just the first three characters.*
2. Press **F3** .... `F3`
   OR
   Press **Enter** .... `Enter`

   OR

1. Click **Insert** .... `Alt`+`I`
2. Select **AutoText** .... `A`
   - ✓ *Recently used AutoText entries are displayed on the AutoText submenu.*
3. Click desired AutoText entry on submenu.

   OR

1. Click **Insert** .... `Alt`+`I`
2. Select **AutoText** .... `A`
3. Click **AutoText** .... `X`
4. Select desired AutoText entry.
5. Click **Insert** .... `Alt`+`I`

Delete an AutoText entry:

1. Click **Insert** .... `Alt`+`I`
2. Select **AutoText** .... `A`
3. Click **AutoText** .... `X`
   - ✓ *The AutoCorrect dialog box is displayed, with the AutoText tab active.*
4. Locate and select entry to delete in list of entries.
   - ✓ *You can type the entry in the text box at the top of the list to quickly scroll to it.*
5. Click **Delete** .... `Alt`+`D`
6. Click **OK** .... `Enter`

Exercise Directions

1. Start Word, and create a new document.

2. Design the letterhead shown in Illustration A.

   a. Type the company name in a 36-pt. serif font (Garamond is used in the illustration), flush right.

   b. Type the address in the same font in 16 pts., also flush right.

   c. Insert a clip art picture of a tree.

      ✓ *If you cannot locate the picture shown, insert the file* ◉ ***TREE.WMF*** *providing with this book.*

   d. Set the text wrapping for the picture to In front of text, and position it as shown.

3. Save the letterhead as an AutoText entry named letterhead.

   a. Press Ctrl+A to select everything in the document.

   b. Click Insert, AutoText, New.

   c. Type the name **letterhead** in the Create AutoText dialog box.

   d. Click OK.

4. Close the document without saving any changes.

5. Open ◉ **47WINNERS**.

6. Save the file as **WINNERS.**

7. Position the insertion point at the beginning of the document, and then insert the letterhead AutoText entry.

8. Move the insertion point to the end of the document and insert the file ◉ **47MISSION**.

9. Check the spelling and grammar in the document.

10. Display the document in Print Preview. It should look similar to the one in Illustration B.

11. Print the document.

12. Close the file, saving all changes.

On Your Own

1. Start Word and create a new document.

2. Design a letterhead for yourself.

3. Save the letterhead as an AutoText entry, with a descriptive name, such as **MYNAME**.

4. Close the document without saving the changes.

5. Create another new document.

6. Save the document as **OWD47-1**.

7. Type a brief biography. The biography should be no more than two paragraphs, and it should be appropriate for inclusion in a document such as a yearbook, a team or club roster, or a theater program.

8. Check the spelling and grammar in the document.

9. Close the document, saving all changes.

10. Create another new document and save it as **OWD47-2**.

11. Type a letter to the yearbook editor, or the club president, or whoever is responsible for printing the collection of biographies. Leave space above the closing to insert the **OWD47-1** document.

12. Insert the **OWD47-1** biography into the **OWD47-2** letter.

13. Check the spelling and grammar in the document.

14. Display the document in Print Preview.

15. Print the document.

16. Close the document, saving all changes.

Illustration B

FOR IMMEDIATE RELEASE

SEATTLE, WA – Northwest Gear, Inc. is pleased to announce the winners of its first annual essay contest. The theme of the contest this year was "All Dressed Up with Everywhere to Go." Over 150 entries were received, and the judges were hard pressed to pick a winner. After much deliberation, the winners are as follows:

Grand Prize: Kristen Montegna, Silver Spring, MD
First Place: Vincent Jackson, Indianapolis, IN
Second Place: Bailey Hartmann, Atlanta, GA
Third Place: Peter King, Provo, UT

All participants received commemorative T-Shirts and discount coupons for use in any Northwest Gear retail outlet. Due to the success of the program, Northwest Gear anticipates sponsoring an essay contest every year. Information about the next contest will be made available in the fall.

Northwest Gear, Inc. is committed to excellence. In order to meet the needs of our clientele, we encourage and support creativity at every level of our organization from our president, Mr. Khourie, to Bob on the loading dock. We vow to maintain the highest standards, pursue the extraordinary, and guarantee customer satisfaction.

The employees at Northwest Gear are encouraged to set personal and professional goals. Following the leadership of Mr. Khourie, we respect all employees as individuals and believe that fostering a strong community within the workplace strengthens our position in the marketplace. We are confident that our commitment to quality will make us leaders in our industry.

Exercise 48

◆ **Record a Macro** ◆ **Run a Macro**

On the Job

Macros let you simplify tasks that ordinarily require many keystrokes or commands, such as creating a header or footer, or changing line spacing and indents for a paragraph. Once you record a macro, you can run it at any time to repeat the recorded actions. You can use macros for tasks as simple as opening and printing a document, or for more complicated tasks such as creating a new document, inserting a table, entering text, and applying an AutoFormat.

As a marketing assistant at Regency General, Inc., you frequently have to format reports by changing the margins to 1" on all sides and by inserting a standard header and footer. In this exercise, you will create macros for setting the margins and creating a header and footer. You will then use the macros to format a one-page report.

Terms

Macro A series of commands and keystrokes that you record and save together. You can run the macro to replay the series.

Normal template A document that stores the default settings for new Word documents.

Shortcut key A combination of keys (including Alt, Ctrl, and/or Shift, and a regular keyboard key) that you assign to run a macro.

Notes

Record a Macro

- Record a **macro** to automate tasks or actions that you perform frequently.

- By default, new macros are stored in the **Normal template**, so they are available for use in all new documents created with the Normal template.

- Macros can save time and help eliminate errors.

- A single macro can store an unlimited number of keystrokes or mouse actions.

- You can record mouse actions that select commands in menus and dialog boxes; however, you cannot record mouse actions that select text or position the insertion point.

- Recording a macro is similar to recording on a cassette tape. As soon as you start recording, everything you input into your computer is stored in the macro, just as everything you input into a cassette recorder is stored on a tape.

  ✓ *When recording a macro, the mouse pointer changes to an arrow with a cassette tape icon.*

- A macro is different from AutoText because a macro can store actions and commands as well as text and graphics.

- You can assign a **shortcut key** combination including Alt, Ctrl, and/or Shift and a regular keyboard key to a macro when you record it to use to play the macro back at any time.

Customize Keyboard dialog box

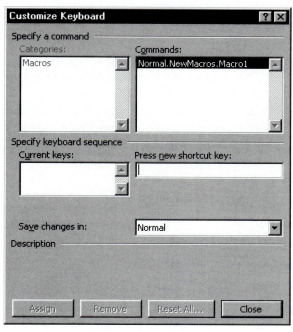

✓ You can also create a toolbar button to assign to the macro.

■ If a macro doesn't work the way you want, you can delete it and record it again.

Run a Macro

■ Once you have recorded a macro, you can run it at any time.

■ When you run a macro, Word executes the recorded commands and actions in the current document.

■ Use the key combination you assigned when you recorded the macro to run the macro.

■ To perform the macro on part of a document, be sure to select the part first.

Procedures

Record a Macro

1. Position the insertion point where you want it to be when you start recording the macro.

2. Double-click **REC** button `REC` on Status bar.

   OR

   a. Click **Tools** .... `Alt`+`T`

   b. Click **Macro** .... `M`

   c. Click **Record New Macro** .... `R`

3. Type a macro name.

4. Click **Description** .... `Alt`+`D`

5. Type a description of the macro.

6. Click **Keyboard** .... `Alt`+`K`

7. Press a shortcut key combination.

✓ Word displays a message indicating whether the combination is unassigned or already assigned to a Word command. If you use a combination that is already assigned, the original purpose of the combination is replaced. For example, if you assign the combination Ctrl+S, you will no longer be able to use that combination to save a file.

8. Click **Assign** .... `Tab`, `Alt`+`A`

9. Click **Close** `Close` ...... `Enter`

10. Perform actions to record.

To stop recording a macro:

● Click the **Stop** button `■` on the Macro Control box.

OR

1. Click **Tools** .... `Alt`+`T`

2. Click **Macro** .... `M`

3. Click **Stop Recording** .... `R`

   OR

   Double-click **REC** button `REC` on Status bar.

Run a Macro *(Alt+F8)*

● Press assigned key combination.

OR

1. Click **Tools** .... `Alt`+`T`

2. Select **Macro** .... `M`

3. Click **Macros** .... `M`

4. Click the name of macro to run .... `↑`, `↓`

5. Click **Run** .... `Alt`+`R`

Delete a Macro *(Alt+F8)*

1. Click **Tools** .... `Alt`+`T`

2. Click **Macro** .... `M`

3. Click **Macros** .... `M`

4. Click the name of macro to delete .... `↑`, `↓`

5. Click **Delete** button `Delete` .... `Alt`+`D`

6. Click **Yes** button `Yes` .... `Y`

7. Click **Close** button `Close` .... `Enter`

Exercise Directions

1. Start Word, if necessary.

2. Open the Record Macro dialog box.

   a. Name the macro **Margins**.

   b. Enter the description: **Sets all margins to 1"**.

   c. Assign the macro to the key combination Alt+Shift+G.

   d. Click Assign and then Close to begin recording the macro keystrokes.

   e. Set all page margins to 1".

   f. Stop recording the macro.

3. Open the Record Macro dialog box and create a second macro as follows:

   a. Name the macro **Header**.

   b. Include the description: **Creates a header and footer in Regency General documents**.

   c. Assign the macro to the key combination Alt+Shift+H.

   d. Click Assign and then Close to begin recording the macro keystrokes using Illustration A as a guide.

   e. Create a header with the company name flush left and today's date flush right.

      ✓ *If necessary, move the right tab stop so that the date is flush with the right margin.*

   f. Create a footer with your name flush left and the word **Page** followed by a space then the page number flush right.

   g. Close the Header/Footer dialog box.

   h. Stop recording the macro.

4. Close the blank document without saving any changes.

5. Open ⊚ **48BUSINESS**.

6. Save the file as **BUSINESS**.

7. Run the Header macro.

8. Run the Margins macro.

9. Preview the document. It should look similar to the one in Illustration A.

10. Check the spelling and grammar in the document.

11. Print the document.

12. Close the document, saving all changes.

Illustration A

Regency General, Inc.   Today's date

BUSINESS-TO-BUSINESS: MAKING THE INTERNET WORK

Headlines claim that Business-to-Business (B2B) services are currently one of the fastest growing segments on the Internet. This news leaves many people wondering what exactly B2B means. This report will attempt to provide a short, simple explanation of B2B so that potential B2B participants can make informed decisions.

The first attempts to make money off the Internet involved Business-to-Consumer ventures that offered people the opportunity to buy items on-line that they usually buy at bricks-and-mortar stores. Recently, however, businesses have realized that they can use the speed and global reach of the Internet to communicate with customers and suppliers around the world.

The potential for savings such as reduced sales and distribution costs, as well as for increased profits make B2B activity very appealing. Corporations can use the Internet to communicate more effectively with their current strategic partners, but they can also use it to locate new partners. This increase in competition promotes additional savings in terms of lower prices and better service.

One obstacle in achieving B2B Internet interaction has been locating and implementing the links between companies. As a result, a new order of Internet service company has emerged. These companies specialize in providing the hardware, software, and consulting services that help businesses locate and communicate with suppliers, customers, strategic partners, and distributors. By assuming the responsibility for maintaining databases and tracking orders and shipments, this new segment of Internet service companies is making it possible for corporations of all sizes to successfully implement B2B ventures online.

Your Name   Page 1

On Your Own

1. Start Word and open **OWD47-1**, the brief biography you created in the On Your Own section of Exercise 47, or open ⊚ **48BIO**.

2. Save the document as **OWD48-1**, and then close it.

3. Create a new blank document.

4. Create a new macro named **Insertbio** and assign it to a shortcut key combination, such as Shift+Alt+B.

5. Record the keystrokes for inserting the **OWD48-1** file into the open document.

6. After you stop recording the macro, close the current document without saving the changes.

7. Create a new blank document and save it as **OWD48-2**.

8. Type a document in which you can include your biography. You might type a letter to someone other than the person you wrote to in Exercise 47, or you might type part of a program or yearbook page.

9. At the appropriate location, use the Insertbio macro to insert the **OWD48-1** file into the **OWD48-2** document.

10. Check the spelling and grammar in the document.

11. Preview the document.

12. Print the document.

13. Close the document, saving all changes

◆ Critical Thinking

Enrollment in the in-house training courses at Murray Hill Marketing, LLC has been low. Caroline Gagas, the director of training has asked you to design a one-page flyer advertising the benefits of in-house training. She has supplied you with a file containing the information she wants included in the file. In this exercise, you will use a Wizard to create a memo to Ms. Gagas. You will then create the flyer by using an AutoText entry and inserting a file. To make the document appealing you will need to use desktop publishing features, such as newsletter columns and graphics.

Exercise Directions

1. Start Word, if necessary.
2. Create a new document.
3. Record a macro, as follows:
   - Name the new macro **Columns**.
   - Type the description: **Inserts a section break and divides the new section into two columns**.
   - Assign the key combination Alt+Shift+B.
   - Record the keystrokes for inserting a continuous section break and formatting the new section into two columns, then stop recording.
4. Close the current document without saving it.
5. Create a new document using the Memo Wizard.
6. Provide the following information in the Wizard dialog boxes:
   - Contemporary style
   - Title: Murray Hill Marketing, LLC.
   - Date: Default
   - From: Your Name
   - Subject: Training Flyer
   - To: Ms. Caroline Gagas
   - Include: Attachments
   - Header/Footer: Accept all of the defaults, except Confidential.
7. Save the document with the name **MHMMEMO**.
8. Delete the CC: line.
9. Enhance the title by inserting the clip art image as shown in Illustration A.

   ✓ To locate the image, try searching for the keyterm Business. If you cannot locate the image, insert the picture file ⊙**IDEA1.wmf** supplied with this book.

10. Leave the text wrap inline.
11. Use the Color button on the picture toolbar to change the color to Grayscale.
12. Apply a 3-pt. triple-line border along the bottom of the title line as shown in Illustration A.
13. Create an AutoText entry from the letterhead, including the clip art picture. Save the entry with a descriptive name, such as **mhmtitle**.

    ✓ Note that the Memo Wizard inserts graphics elements, called a watermark, as part of the background image. Do not try to select those elements for the AutoText entry. You can only select them when you are working in the header/footer area.

14. Complete the document by typing the text shown in Illustration A.
15. Check the spelling and grammar in the document.
16. Display the document in Print Preview. It should look similar to the one in Illustration A.
17. Print the document.
18. Close the document, saving all changes.
19. Create a new blank document.
20. Save the document as **TRAINAD**.
21. Insert the file ⊙**49ADINFO**.
22. Move the insertion point to the beginning of the document.
23. Run the Columns macro.

24. Move the insertion point to the beginning of the document again.

25. Insert the MHMTITLE AutoText entry.

26. Modify the title by removing the left indent and centering the line horizontally.

27. Format the three main headlines in a bold, 16-pt. sans serif font, with 3 pts. of space before and 3 pts. of space after.

28. Format the three course title headlines in a bold, 14-pt. sans serif font with 3 pts. of space before and 3 pts. of space after.

29. Format the article text in a regular 14-pt. serif font.

30. Create a bulleted list from the three items in the first article beginning with the word **Increase**.

31. Format the first letter in each of the three main articles as a dropped capital.

32. Insert the clip art picture as shown in Illustration B.

✓ *To locate the picture, search using the keyterm computer. If you cannot locate the picture, insert the file* ✐ ***COMPUTER1.WMF*** *provided with this book.*

33. Change the text wrap for the picture to square.

34. Resize the picture so it is 2.25" high (the width will adjust automatically).

35. Position the picture in the center of the page as shown.

36. Insert a continuous section break at the beginning of the last sentence in the document.

37. Format the new third section in one column.

38. Change the text formatting for the last sentence in the document to a 12-pt. serif font, centered, leaving 6 pts. of space before.

39. Check the spelling and grammar in the document.

40. Display the document in Print Preview. It should look similar to the one in Illustration B.

41. Print the document.

42. Close the document, saving all changes.

Illustration A

murray hill marketing, llc.

Date:	Today's date
To:	Ms. Caroline Gagas
From:	Your Name
RE:	Training Flyer

In order to effectively market the in-house training courses to employees, I have decided to create a flyer using many exciting graphics elements. Once we catch their attention, I believe we will be able to convince a significant number of employees to enroll in the upcoming training session.

With that in mind, I have attached a copy of the proposed flyer to this memo. Notice the use of columns, borders, shading, and graphics elements. These features are designed to draw the reader's eyes to specific paragraphs. In addition, I can easily keep the document up-to-date in case of changes in schedule, location, etc.

Please let me know what you think. With your approval, I can have this flyer ready for distribution by the end of the day.

Attachments

Today's date   1

murray hill marketing, llc.

Climb the Ladder to Success

In-house training provides immediate benefits! You know you will learn new skills, but did you know you will also:

- Increase your productivity.
- Increase your value to the company.
- Increase your chances of promotion.

Customize Your Course Load

MHM Training offers a wide variety of courses designed to improve your computer skills. Courses range from introductory word processing to advanced database design. Courses are offered at intervals throughout the year at different locations, insuring that all employees have access.

Stay In Tune with the Times

We know that the skills you need today may not be the same as the ones you relied on yesterday. That's why we regularly evaluate our courses to keep them up to date. Check out our current schedule:

Microsoft Word

This series covers everything from basic document creation to integration with other programs.

Introduction to the Internet

Learn to navigate the World Wide Web, locate useful information, and avoid common on-line pitfalls.

Everyday Excel

Make the most of your spreadsheets by learning how to simplify data entry, automate calculations, and understand basic analysis.

For more information, or to register, call 212-555-4444, ext. 343.

Excel 2002

Lesson 1

Getting Started with Excel 2002
Exercises 1-6

Lesson 2

Working with Formulas and Formatting
Exercises 7-12

Lesson 3

Working with Functions, Formulas, and Charts
Exercises 13-19

Lesson 4

Advanced Printing, Formatting, and Editing
Exercises 20-27

Lesson 5

Advanced Chart Techniques
Exercises 28-31

Lesson 6

Working with Lookup Functions, PivotCharts, and PivotTables
Exercises 32-35

Lesson 7

Internet and Integration with Excel
Exercises 36-39

Exercise #	File Name	Page #
1	N/A	N/A
2	N/A	N/A
3	03DEMOS, 03PLAYSETS	304
4	04OVERDUE	310
5	05OVERDUE	313
6	06CHANG, 06CGIORDER	315
7	07DBQUOTE	319
8	08CASHTOPS	323
9	09CASHTOPS	327
10	10DRUGINV	331
11	11ORGANIC	335
12	12OVERDUE	337
13	13COMPETE	343
14	14CHIPSALES	347
15	15NWGNEW	351
16	16CGISALES	357
17	17NWGNEW	363
18	18COMPETE	368
19	19SALESCONT	370
20	20COMPETE, murray hill marketing logo.gif	375
21	21YTDCHIPS	380
22	22SALESCONT	384
23	23ORGANIC	388
24	24FOODYTD	392
25	25AUGINV	396
26	26CHIPCOSTS	400
27	27PAYROLL 27PAYHOURS 27NEWRATES	402
28	28SALESCONT	407
29	29CHIPCOSTS, 29PROFITRPT.doc	413
30	30CHIPCOSTS	418
31	31TOFU, 31TOFU.doc	421
32	32TOFUCOST	427
33	33CGIINVOICE	432
34	34PHARMACY	437
35	35NWGEAR	440
36	36NWGEAR	445
37	37TRIALS, COURTTV.htm, FINDLAW.htm	450
38	38TRIALS, 38WKTRIALS.doc, 38NXTTRIALS	455
39	39PHARMACY, HEARTFORUM.htm	457

Exercise 1

◆ **Start Excel** ◆ **The Excel Window** ◆ **Excel Menu and Toolbars**
◆ **Explore the Worksheet Using the Mouse and Keyboard**
◆ **Change Between Worksheets** ◆ **The View Menu** ◆ **Exit Excel**

On the Job

When you want to analyze business, personal, or financial data and create reports in a table format consisting of rows and columns, use the Microsoft Excel spreadsheet application in the Office suite.

You've just been hired as a legal aide for Perry, Hawkins, Martinez, and Klein, and you've enrolled yourself in a class to learn to use Excel. In this exercise, you will start Excel, familiarize yourself with the Excel window, change your view of the worksheet, and practice moving around the worksheet using the mouse and the keyboard.

Terms

Workbook An Excel file with one or more worksheets.

Worksheet The work area for entering and calculating data made up of columns and rows separated by gridlines (light gray lines). Also called a *spreadsheet.*

Cell A cell is the intersection of a column and a row on a worksheet. You enter data into cells to create a worksheet.

Active cell The active cell contains the cell pointer—a dark outline around the cell.

Formula bar As you enter data into a cell, it simultaneously appears in the Formula bar, which is located above the worksheet frame.

Cell reference The location of a cell in a worksheet identified by its column letter and row number. This is also known as the cell's *address.*

Scroll A way to view locations on the worksheet without changing the active cell.

Sheet tabs Tabs that appear at the bottom of the workbook window, which display the name of each worksheet.

Tab scrolling buttons Buttons that appear just to the left of the sheet tabs, which allow you to scroll hidden tabs into view.

Notes

Start Excel

■ Start Excel using the Start menu.

The Excel Window

■ When the program starts up, the Microsoft Excel window displays an empty **workbook** with three worksheets.

● A **worksheet** contains rows and columns that intersect to form **cells**.

✓ *You may see the New Workbook Task Pane briefly on the right-hand side of the Excel window when you first start the program. You use this Task Pane to create new workbooks and open existing ones. You'll learn more about this Task Pane in Exercise 2.*

- A black border appears around the **active cell**.
- The name box, located on the left side of the **Formula bar**, displays the cell reference (also known as the address) of the active cell (its column letter and row number).

Name box

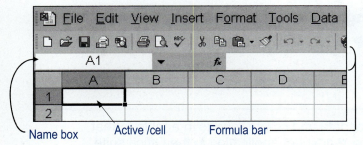

Name box — Active /cell — Formula bar

- To help you identify the **cell reference** for the active cell, Excel highlights its column label (above the worksheet) and row number (to the left of the worksheet).

✓ *Notice, for example, that the active cell shown in the Name box figure is surrounded by a dark outline. The active cell's address or cell reference, A1, appears in the Name box just to the left of the Formula bar. Notice also that the column label A, and the row label 1, are highlighted in blue gray in order to make it easier for you to decipher the address of the current cell.*

- You can change the active cell using the mouse or the keyboard.

Excel Menu and Toolbars

- The menu bar, Standard toolbar, Formatting toolbar, formula bar, and Ask a Question box appear at the top of the workbook window while the status bar appears at the bottom.

- The Standard and Formatting toolbars share one row but you can use the View, Toolbars, Customize command, Options tab to change this option.

- The menu bar, toolbars (except for the Formula bar), and the Ask a Question box are similar to those used in Word and are covered in Exercise 1 of the Word section of this text.

Excel window

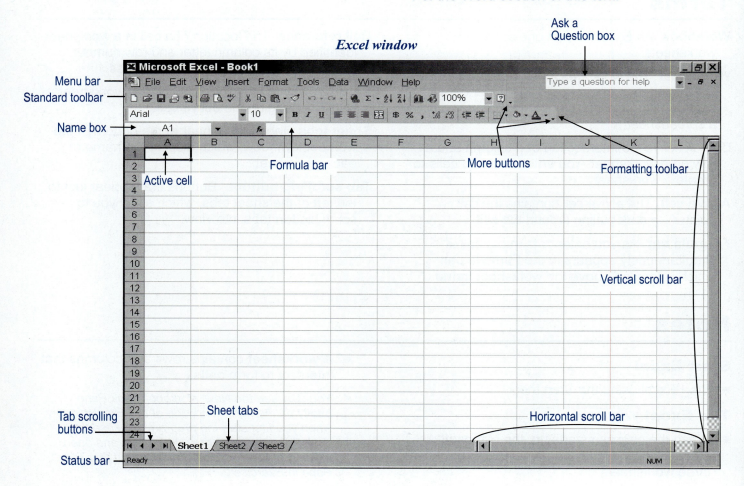

Ask a Question box

Menu bar

Standard toolbar

Name box

Formula bar

More buttons

Formatting toolbar

Active cell

Vertical scroll bar

Tab scrolling buttons

Sheet tabs

Horizontal scroll bar

Status bar

Explore the Worksheet Using the Mouse and Keyboard

- Since the workbook window displays only a part of a worksheet, you **scroll** through the worksheet to view another location.

- Use the mouse or keyboard to scroll to different locations in a worksheet without changing the active cell.

- With the mouse, you can scroll using the horizontal or vertical scroll bars.

- With the keyboard, you can scroll by pressing specific keys or key combinations.

- There are 256 columns and 65,536 rows available in a worksheet, but you don't need to fill the entire worksheet in order to use it—just type data into the cells you need.

Active cell in bottom-left corner of worksheet

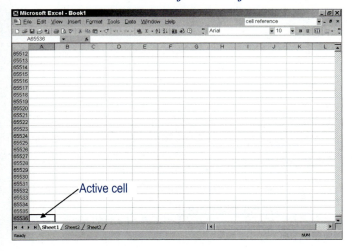

Active cell in bottom-right corner of worksheet

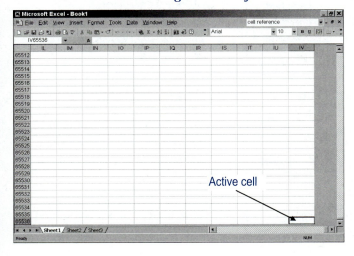

Change Between Worksheets

- Normally, each workbook comes with three worksheets. You can add or delete worksheets as needed.

  ✓ *You'll learn how to add and remove worksheets in Exercise 11.*

- You can enter related data on different worksheets within the same workbook.

  ✓ *For example, you can enter January, February, and March sales data on different worksheets within the same workbook.*

- Change between worksheets using the **sheet tabs** located at the bottom of the Excel window.

  ✓ *If a particular worksheet tab is not visible, use the **tab scrolling buttons** to display it.*

The View Menu

- To view or hide the Formula bar, Status bar, or Task Pane, select or deselect them from the View menu.

  ✓ *When you click the View menu several options are hidden. Wait a few seconds for the menu to expand automatically, or click the arrows at the bottom of the menu.*

- The Toolbar command from the View menu displays a submenu with a list of available toolbars.

Available toolbars

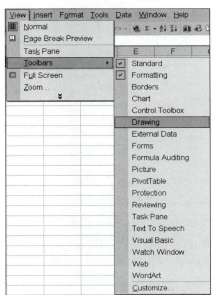

- If you need to expand the worksheet to fill the screen, choose Full Screen. The menu bar is still displayed for commands and a Close Full Screen dialog box appears in order to return to the default view.

- The Zoom command magnifies cells in a worksheet by choosing from a list of magnification options or setting a specific zoom percentage from 10%–400%.
  - ✓ *You can also change the Zoom by selecting the Zoom level you want from the Zoom button, located on the Standard toolbar.*

Zoom dialog box

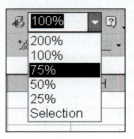

Exit Excel

- When your worksheet is complete and you want to close the Excel application, use the Exit command from the File menu.

Procedures

Start Excel

1. Click **Start** [Start] ... Ctrl + Esc
2. Select **Programs** .... P
3. Click **Microsoft Excel 2002** .... ↓, Enter

Change Active Cell Using Keyboard

- One cell right .... →
- One cell left .... ←
- One cell down .... ↓
- One cell up .... ↑
- One screen up .... Page Up
- One screen down.............. Page Down
- One screen right .... Alt + Page Down
- One screen left .... Alt + Page Up
- First cell in current row.... Home
- First cell in worksheet .... Ctrl + Home
- Last used cell in worksheet .... Ctrl + End

Change Active Cell Using Mouse

- Click desired cell.

Change Active Cell Using Go To (Ctrl+G)

1. Press **F5** F5

   OR

   a. Click **Edit**............... Alt + E
   b. Click **Go To** .... G
   - ✓ ***Go To** list box displays last four references that you accessed.*
2. Type cell reference in **Reference** text box.
3. Click **OK** .... Enter

Change Active Cell Using Name Box

1. Click in Name box.
2. Type cell reference.
3. Press **Enter** .... Enter

Scroll Using Mouse

To scroll one row up or down:

- Click up or down scroll arrow, located at the top or bottom of the vertical scroll bar.

To scroll one column left or right:

- Click left or right scroll arrow, located at either end of the horizontal scroll bar.

To scroll one screen right or left:

- Click horizontal scroll bar to right or left of scroll box.

To scroll one screen up or down:

- Click vertical scroll bar above or below scroll box.

To scroll to beginning rows:

- Drag vertical scroll box to top of scroll bar.

To scroll to beginning columns:

- Drag horizontal scroll box to extreme left of scroll bar.

To scroll to last row containing data:

- Press Ctrl and drag vertical scroll box to bottom of scroll bar.

Change to a Different Worksheet

- Click the tab of the worksheet you want to display.

✓ *If the worksheet tab you need is not displayed, click the appropriate tab scrolling button. The first or last buttons display the first or last worksheet tab. The middle tab scrolling buttons move the sheet tabs one sheet in the direction of the arrow.*

Customize View of Standard and Formatting Toolbars

1. Click **View** .... `Alt`+`V`
2. Click **Toolbars** .... `T`
   OR
   Right-click on toolbar.
3. Click **Customize** .... `C`
4. Click **Options** tab .... `Ctrl`+`Tab`
   ✓ *Press Ctrl+Tab until Options page displays.*
5. Select **Show Standard and Formatting toolbars on two rows** check box. .... `Alt`+`S`
   ✓ *Removes check mark from option.*
6. Click **Close** button
   `Close` .... `Enter`

Display or Hide Task Pane

1. Click **View** .... `Alt`+`V`
2. Click **Task Pane** .... `K`
   ✓ *The New Workbook task pane appears by default. You can scroll to recently displayed task panes by clicking the left or right arrows.*

Display or Hide Formula Bar

1. Click **View** .... `Alt`+`V`
2. Click **Formula Bar** .... `F`

Display or Hide Status Bar

1. Click **View** .... `Alt`+`V`
2. Click **Status Bar** .... `S`

Display or Hide Toolbar

1. Click **View** .... `Alt`+`V`
2. Click **Toolbars** .... `T`
3. Select toolbar name .... `↓`
4. Click toolbar name .... `Enter`

Set Zoom Percentage

1. Click **View** .... `Alt`+`V`
2. Click **Zoom** .... `Z`
3. Set percentage .... `↓``↑`
4. Click **OK** .... `Enter`

Set Zoom Percentage with Zoom Button

1. Click arrow on Zoom button.
2. Select Zoom level.
   ✓ *You can also type the zoom percentage you want to use in the box on the Zoom button, and press Enter.*

Exit Excel

1. Click **File** .... `Alt`+`F`
2. Click **Exit** .... `X`
   OR
   Click **Application Close** button `X`.

Exercise Directions

1. Follow these steps to start Excel from the taskbar.
   a. Click Start.
   b. Select Programs, Microsoft Excel 2002.
2. Move the active cell pointer to cell A1 using the keyboard:
   a. Press the down arrow key four times until cell A5 is highlighted.
   b. Press the right arrow key twice until cell C5 is highlighted.
   ✓ *View the cell references in the name box.*
3. Click cell B3 to make it the active cell.
   ✓ *View the cell reference in the name box.*
4. Point to the horizontal scroll bar and click the right scroll arrow.
   ✓ *The worksheet moves right by one column but the active cell does not change.*
5. Point to the horizontal scroll bar and click to the left of the scroll box.
   ✓ *The worksheet moves left by one screen but the active cell does not change.*
6. Point to the horizontal scroll bar, then drag the scroll box all the way to the right.
   ✓ *The view of the worksheet has changed again but the active cell does not change.*
7. Click the down scroll arrow on the vertical scroll bar.
   ✓ *The worksheet moves down two rows but the active cell does not change.*
8. Press F5 to activate the Go To command.
9. In the Reference text box, type **M41**.
10. Click OK.
    ✓ *The active cell changes to M41.*
11. Click in the name box to change the active cell to the following, pressing Enter after each new cell address:
    • M1200 (Row 1200, column M)
    • A65536 (Bottom left of worksheet)
    • IV65536 (Bottom right of worksheet)
    • A1 (Home)
12. Click the tab for Sheet 2 to display it.
13. Click the tab for Sheet 1 to redisplay it.

14. Rest the mouse pointer on each visible button on the Standard and Formatting toolbars until the ScreenTip appears.

    ✓ *A ScreenTip appears under the button with the name of the button.*

15. Click the More Buttons button next to the Microsoft Excel Help button, located on the Standard toolbar.

    ✓ *The More Buttons menu appears, displaying the hidden buttons from both toolbars.*

16. Point to the Zoom button and click its down arrow.

    ✓ *The Zoom menu appears.*

17. Select 200% from the Zoom menu.

    ✓ *The Zoom changes to 200%, so cells appear much larger. Also, the Zoom button is added to the Standard toolbar.*

18. Select View, Zoom to display the Zoom dialog box.

19. Select 100%, then click OK.

    ✓ *Cells are restored to their normal size as you return to 100% magnification.*

20. Click View, Status Bar to remove the Status bar from the screen.

21. Click View, Status Bar to restore the Status bar to the screen.

22. Click View, Toolbars, Drawing to display the Drawing toolbar.

23. Right-click the Drawing toolbar and select Drawing from the menu that appears to remove the Drawing toolbar.

24. Click the Close button ⊠ to exit Excel.

On Your Own

1. Use the New Office Document command on the Start menu to start Excel and create a new workbook document.

2. Click cell G7.

    ✓ *View the cell reference in the name box.*

3. Move the active cell pointer to cell D21 using the keyboard.

4. Click below the scroll box in the vertical scroll bar.

    ✓ *The worksheet moves down one screen but the active cell does not change.*

5. Drag the scroll box all the way to the top of the vertical scroll bar.

    ✓ *The view of the worksheet changes but the active cell does not change.*

6. Use the horizontal scroll bar to scroll one screen to the right.

7. Use the horizontal scroll bar to scroll one screen to the left.

8. Change to Sheet 3.

9. Use the Go To command to make V20 the active cell.

10. Use the Name box to make AA1000 the active cell.

11. Make A1 the active cell.

12. Return to Sheet 1.

13. Display the Standard and Formatting toolbars in two rows.

14. Hide the Formula bar.

15. Redisplay the Formula bar.

16. Change the View, Toolbar, Customize options so that the Standard and Formatting toolbars will once again appear on the same row.

17. Change the Zoom percentage to 155%.

18. Return the Zoom percentage to 100%.

19. Exit Excel without saving the current workbook document.

Exercise 2

Skills Covered:

◆ **Create a New (Blank) Workbook**
◆ **Create a Workbook from a Template**
◆ **Enter Labels** ◆ **Make Simple Corrections** ◆ **Undo and Redo**
◆ **Delete (Clear) Cell Contents** ◆ **Save a Workbook**
◆ **Document Recovery** ◆ **Close a Workbook**

On the Job

To create your first worksheet, you begin by entering the column and row titles (labels) for a report. Next, you enter the numeric data, using the row and column labels to help you enter each amount into the correct cell. As you enter data, you may make a few mistakes and then find out how easy it is to correct them. Finally, you save your workbook before exiting Excel so that the entries are not lost.

You are an invoice clerk for California Cardiology, Inc., and it is your job to send overdue notices to insurance companies that have not made payments on their patients' behalf. You'll create a report that lists overdue amounts for the Healthcare HMO and then complete the report in a later exercise.

Terms

Blank workbook The Excel default workbook contains three worksheet tabs or sheets.

Template A workbook with certain labels, formulas, and formatting preset, saving you time in creating commonly used forms, such as invoices or purchase orders.

Label Text in the first row or column of a spreadsheet that identifies the type of data contained there.

Defaults The standard settings Excel uses in its software, such as column width or number of pages in a workbook.

Undo The command used to reverse one or a series of editing actions.

Redo The command used to redo an action you have undone.

Notes

Create a New (Blank) Workbook

- Excel displays a **blank workbook** when you open the Excel application.

- A blank workbook initially contains three blank worksheets into which you can enter data.

- When you need to create a new, blank workbook, click the New button on the Standard toolbar, or select that option from the New Workbook task pane.

Create new workbooks using the Task Pane

Create a Workbook from a Template

- To save time when creating a new workbook from scratch, select an Excel **template** from the New Workbook Task Pane.

- Excel provides a small number of templates for use in creating common forms, such as balance sheets, sales invoices, expense statements, and time cards. There's even a template for comparing loans.

  ✓ *If a template for the type of report you want to create is not available, you can base your new workbook on a copy of an existing workbook by selecting that option from the Task Pane. You can also go on the Internet and select a template from Microsoft's Web site by clicking **Templates on Microsoft.com**.*

- When you select a template for a new workbook, a lot of the work is already done for you, including most of the formatting, formulas, and layout design.

- After the new workbook is created from the template, simply enter your data.

  ✓ *For example, enter your company's name and address where indicated, then type the actual data for the report (such as the individual items you want to appear on an invoice).*

Enter Labels

- The first character entered into a cell determines the status of a cell.

- If you enter an alphabetical character or a symbol (` ~! # % ^ & *( ) _ \ | { } ; : ' " < > ,?) as the first character in a cell, you are entering a **label**.

- A label generally represents text data, such as the labels: Blue, Sally Smith, Ohio, or Above Average.

- The **default** width of each cell is 8.43 characters wide in the standard font (Arial, 10 point); therefore, a label longer than the cell width will display fully only if the cell to the right is blank, or if the column is made wider to accommodate the long entry.

- Excel supports up to 32,000 characters in a cell entry.

- As you type a label into a cell, it appears in the cell and the Formula bar.

- To enter the label in the cell, type the text, and then do any of the following to finalize the entry: press the Enter key, an arrow key, or the Tab key, click another cell, or click the Enter button (the green check mark) on the Formula bar.

- A label automatically aligns to the left of the cell, making it a left-justified entry.

Entry in cell and Formula bar

Make Simple Corrections

- As you type data into a cell, if you notice a mistake before you press Enter (or any of the other keys that finalize an entry), you can press the Backspace key to erase characters to the left of the insertion point.

- Before you finalize an entry, you can press the Escape key or click the Cancel button (the red X) on the Formula bar to cancel it.

- After you enter data, you can make the cell active (by clicking it, pressing an arrow key, etc.) and then type a new entry to replace the old one.

- You can also double-click a cell in which the entry has been finalized to enable cell editing and then make changes to only part of the entry.

Undo and Redo

- Use the **Undo** command from the Edit menu or the Undo button on the Standard toolbar to reverse any editing action.

- With the Undo command, you can reverse up to 16 previous editing actions.

- The Undo command names the last editing action to be reversed.

- You can also redo (reinstate any action you've undone in error) up to 16 reversed actions using the **Redo** command.

Delete (Clear) Cell Contents

- Press the Escape key or click the Cancel box on the Formula bar to clear a cell's contents before finalizing any cell entry.

- To erase a single cell entry or a range of cell entries after you enter data, use the Clear, Contents command from the Edit menu or the Delete key on the keyboard.

Save a Workbook

- After entering data into a workbook, you must save it, or that data will be lost when you exit Excel.

- A workbook may be saved on a hard drive or a removable disk for future use. A saved workbook is referred to as a file.

- You must provide a name for the file when you save it. File names should be descriptive, with a limit of 255 characters for the name, drive, and path.

- A file name may contain letters, numbers, and spaces, but not \ / : * ? " < > or | .

- Excel automatically adds a period and a file type extension (usually .xls) to the end of a file name when you save it.

Save As command

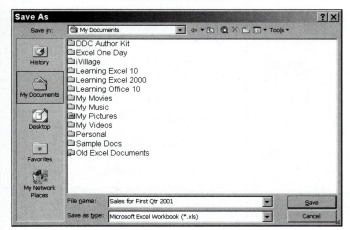

- Workbooks are saved in the My Documents folder by default, although you may select another location if you like. You can even create new folders in which to store your workbooks.

- Data can also be saved in other formats, such as Lotus 1-2-3 or older versions of Excel.

  ✓ *You might want to save data in a different format in order to share that data with someone who uses a different version of Excel, or a different spreadsheet program, such as Lotus 1-2-3.*

- Once you've saved a workbook, you need only click the Save button to resave any changes made since the last save action. You will not need to reenter the file name.

Document Recovery

- Even after saving your workbook data in a file, you must periodically resave it in order to avoid accidental loss of new data you are entering in an open workbook.

- You can lose changes that you have not yet saved if Excel locks up for some reason (refuses to respond), or you suddenly lose power.

- To avoid accidental loss of data, click the Save button periodically to resave new changes.

- If you forget to resave a workbook, your data may not be lost if Excel has saved it for you using its AutoRecovery feature.

- By default, AutoRecovery automatically saves changes made to a file every 10 minutes. You can have AutoRecovery save changes more often or turn it off completely if you want.

Document Recovery Task Pane

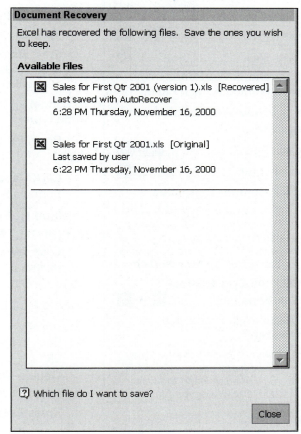

- If AutoRecovery is on and Excel is restarted after a power loss or program crash, the Document Recovery task pane will automatically appear.

- Manually saved workbooks are listed as [Original], while versions created by AutoRecovery are listed as [Recovered].
- Use the Document Recovery Task Pane to view each version of a workbook and to select the version you want to save.
  - ✓ *AutoRecovery is not a perfect process, so don't be tempted to select that version of a workbook after a crash. Review each version listed and select the one that contains the most complete version of your document. To avoid critical data loss, your best bet is to manually save open workbooks as often as you can.*

Close a Workbook

- Save a workbook before you close it or you will lose the current data or updated entries that you made.
- If you attempt to close a workbook or close Excel before saving, you will be prompted to save the changes.
- If you have more than one file open, Excel allows you to close and save all of the files before you exit the program.

Procedures

Create a New, Blank Workbook (Ctrl+N)

- Click **New** button 🗋 .

OR

1. Click **File** .... Alt + F
2. Click **New** .... N
3. Click **Blank Workbook** in the New Workbook Task Pane.

Create a New Workbook from a Template

1. Click **File** .... Alt + F
2. Click **New** .... N
3. Click **General Templates**.
   - ✓ *If you have a connection to the Internet, you can download additional templates from Microsoft's Web site by clicking* **Templates on Microsoft.com**.
4. Click the **Spreadsheet Solutions** tab .... Ctrl + Tab
5. Double-click the desired template.
   - ✓ *Some of these templates may not be installed, in which case, you'll need to insert the Office CD-ROM when prompted.*

Enter Labels

1. Click cell for data entry. ...... ⬍
2. Type label text.
3. Press **Enter** .... Enter
   OR
   Press any arrow key to enter label and move to next cell.

OR

Click **Enter** button ✔ on Formula bar.

Correct Data while Typing

1. Type character(s) in cell.
2. Press **Backspace** key .. Backspace to erase characters to left of insertion point.

To cancel all characters while typing:

- Press **Escape** key .... Esc
OR
- Click **Cancel** button ✖ on Formula bar.

Replace Cell Contents in Typeover Mode

1. Click cell with data to be replaced.
2. Type new data.

Enable Cell Editing

1. Select cell.
2. Click in Formula bar.
   OR
   Double-click cell.
3. Make correction.
4. Press **Enter** .... Enter
   - ✓ *To replace an entry with something else, simply select the cell and type the new entry.*

Undo Last Action (Ctrl+Z)

- Click **Undo** button ↺ .
OR

1. Click **Edit** .... Alt + E
2. Click **Undo** action name ...... U

Redo Last Reversed Action (Ctrl+Z)

- Click **Redo** button ↻ .
OR
1. Click **Edit** .... Alt + E
2. Click **Redo** action name ...... R

Undo Multiple Actions

1. Click **Undo** arrow ▾ .
2. Drag through actions to undo, and then click.
   - ✓ *You can only undo consecutive actions, beginning with the action at the top of the list.*

Delete (Clear) Cell Contents

1. Select desired cell(s).
2. Press **Delete** key. .... Del
   OR
   a. Click **Edit** .... Alt + E
   b. Click **Clear** .... A
   c. Click **Contents** C

Save Workbook (Ctrl+S)

1. Click **File** .... Alt + F
2. Click **Save** .... S
   OR
- Click **Save** button 💾 .
3. Type name in **File name** text box .... Alt + N

4. Click **Save in**
   drop-down arrow. .... `Alt`+`I`

5. Select drive and folder in which
   to save workbook.

   ✓ *You can skip steps 4 and 5 and
   click a folder on the Places bar,
   such as My Documents.*

6. Click **Save** .... `Enter`

   ✓ *To save the workbook in a
   different file format such as
   Lotus 1-2-3, select that format
   from the **Save as type** list
   before you click Save.*

Recover a Workbook

✓ *After a program crash, or power
outage, the Document Recovery
Task Pane automatically appears.*

1. In the Document Recovery
   Task Pane, click the entry for
   any version of the workbook
   you're looking to recover.

   ✓ *The contents of that version of
   the workbook appears.*

2. Select another version of the
   same workbook to view it.

3. Once you've decided on the
   version you wish to keep, close
   all other versions of the
   workbook (if open).

4. In the Document Recovery list,
   point to the entry for the
   workbook version you want to
   save.

   ✓ *An outline surrounds the entry
   you point to, and a drop-down
   list arrow appears to the right.*

5. Click the arrow on the
   drop-down list and select
   Save As .... `S`

6. If needed, change the file
   name to match the workbook's
   original file name.

   ✓ *If you selected one of the
   [Recovered] versions of the
   workbook, the file name will not
   be the same as the original file
   name, so you'll need to edit it
   slightly to make it match.*

7. Click **Save** .... `Enter`

8. Click **Yes** to save changes. . `Y`

Close Workbook

1. Click **File** .... `Alt`+`F`

2. Click **Close** .... `C`

3. Click **Yes** to save changes .. `Y`
   OR
   Click **No** to cancel changes ... `N`

Exit Excel and Save Files

1. Click **File** .... `Alt`+`F`

2. Click **Exit** .... `X`

3. Click **Yes to All** to save
   all changes .... `A`
   OR
   Click **No** to exit without
   saving changes .... `N`

Exercise Directions

1. Start Excel, if necessary.

2. Save the file as **OVERDUE**.

3. Using the arrow keys, or by clicking, move the
   active cell pointer to cell B3.

4. Type **California Cardiology, Inc.** and press
   Enter.

5. Go to cell B5.

6. Type **Healthcare HMO**, but do *not* press
   Enter.

7. Press Backspace to erase characters as
   needed, and change the entry to read,
   Healthman HMO, and then click the Enter
   button on the Formula bar.

   ✓ *The Cancel and Enter buttons are to the left of
   the formula bar.*

8. Go to cell B7.

9. Type **Invoice Number**, but instead of
   pressing Enter, cancel the entry by clicking the
   Cancel box or pressing the Escape key.

10. Type **Patient** in cell B7 instead.

11. Enter the rest of the data as shown in
    Illustration A.

12. Correct any errors using Backspace, or if the
    entry has been finalized, by retyping it. You can
    also try in-cell editing if you like, by double-
    clicking a cell and editing its contents.

13. Go to cell B11.

14. Erase the entry by pressing Delete.

15. Undo the erasure by clicking Undo, and the
    entry reappears.

16. Click Redo to redo the erasure so that cell B11
    is empty.

17. Close the file and exit Excel, saving all changes.

	A	B	C	D	E
1					
2					
3		California Cardiology, Inc.			
4					
5		Healthman HMO			
6					
7		Patient	Amount	Invoice Number	
8		J. Thomas Wilson			
9		Carlos Riveria			
10		Alice Thomson			
11		Ricky Valdez			
12					

On Your Own

1. Create a new workbook using the template Timecard.

   ✓ *After you select the General Templates link in the New Workbook Task Pane, the Templates dialog box is displayed. You'll find the Time Card template on the Spreadsheet Solutions tab.*

2. Save the file as **OXL02**.

3. Enter your information in the Employee section.

   ✓ *Your employee number is 12345, and you're an Invoice Clerk working in the Accounting Department under Ms. Shaledra Gamble.*

4. The pay period begins 5/8/01 and ends 5/14/01.

5. Enter your hours on different rows, as shown.

6. Save the changes, close the file, and exit Excel.

Illustration B

Account Description	Account Code	M	T	W	Th	F
Regular Hours	REG	8.00	8.00	8.00		
Sick Time	SICK				8.00	
Holiday	HOL					8.00

Exercise 3

◆ **Open Files** ◆ **Change from Workbook to Workbook**
◆ **Arrange Workbooks** ◆ **AutoComplete** ◆ **Pick From List**
◆ **AutoCorrect** ◆ **Spell Check**

On the Job

When you've saved and closed a workbook, if you need to view it again or make changes, you must open it first. After opening several workbooks, you may want to arrange them on-screen so you can view their contents at the same time. When entering data, take advantage of the many time-saving features Excel offers: Excel's AutoComplete feature, for example, automatically completes certain entries based on previous entries that you've made. AutoCorrect automatically corrects common spelling errors as you type, while the spelling checker checks your worksheet for any additional errors.

You're a marketing manager for a mid-sized advertising and PR firm, and you've recently been assigned the Penguin Play Sets account. To increase public awareness of these high quality play sets, you've decided to arrange for a series of demonstrations at various children's shows, home shows, and festivals. In this exercise, you'll use Excel to create a worksheet that tracks upcoming demos.

Terms

AutoComplete A feature used to complete an entry based on previous entries made in the column containing the active cell.

Pick From List A shortcut used to insert repeated information.

AutoCorrect A feature used to automate the correction of common typing errors.

Spelling checker A tool used to assist you in finding and correcting typographical or spelling errors.

Notes

Open Files

- When you have saved and closed a workbook you can open it from the same drive, folder, and file name you used during the save process.

- In the Open dialog box, click the Look in text box arrow to display a drop-down list with the drives or folders.

- If the location of the workbook is shown on the Places bar, click its icon to display that location's contents.

✓ *You can customize the Places bar with buttons that point to the folders you use often, making it easier to open and save files to them.*

- Click the Views button in the Open dialog box to preview a file, change the list to display file details, or display the properties of a file.

- You can access a recently used file more quickly by clicking its file name from the list displayed at the top of the New Workbook Task Pane, or at the bottom of the File menu.

- A newly opened workbook becomes the active workbook and hides any other open workbook.

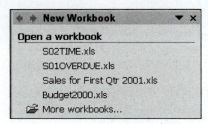

Places bar   *Open dialog box*

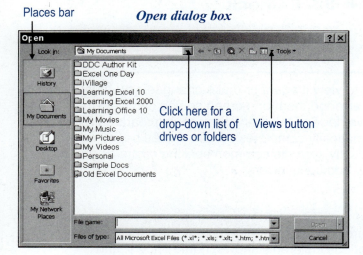

Click here for a drop-down list of drives or folders   Views button

Change from Workbook to Workbook

■ When more than one workbook is open, use the Window menu to change to a different workbook by selecting it from the displayed list of names.

Window menu displays list of open files

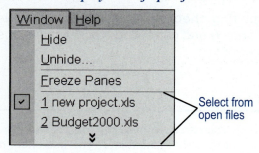

Select from open files

■ You can also change between workbooks by clicking a workbook's button on the Windows taskbar.

Windows taskbar

Arrange Workbooks

■ Arrange workbooks on-screen if you want to view their contents simultaneously.

■ You can arrange workbooks in four ways:
- Tiled: arranges windows in small, even rectangles to fill the screen.
- Horizontal: arranges windows one on top of the other.
- Vertical: arranges windows side by side.
- Cascade: creates a stack of windows with only the title bar in view.

Arrange Windows dialog box

AutoComplete

■ When you need to repeat a label that has already been typed in the same column, the **AutoComplete** feature allows you to enter the label automatically.

AutoComplete a label entry

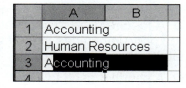

Pick From List

■ If several labels are entered in a list and the next items to be typed are repeated information, click the right mouse button to display the **Pick From List** command on the shortcut menu.

List of labels for next entry in column

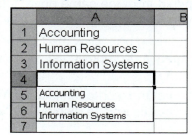

✓ The cells in the list and the cell to be typed must be contiguous and in the same column.

AutoCorrect

- If you type a word incorrectly and it is in the **AutoCorrect** list, Excel automatically changes the word as you type.

- You can add words to the AutoCorrect list that you often type incorrectly.

- AutoCorrect automatically capitalizes the first letter of a sentence and names of days of the week, corrects incorrectly capitalized letters in the first two positions in a word, and undoes accidental use of the Caps Lock key.

- When certain autocorrections are made, you're given an option to remove the corrections by clicking the arrow on the AutoCorrect button that appears, and selecting the action you want to take.

AutoCorrect dialog box

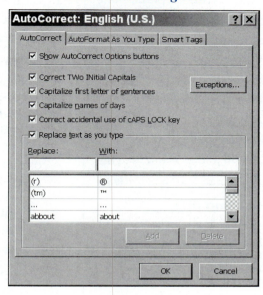

AutoCorrect Button

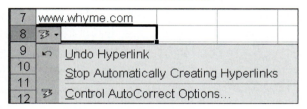

Spell Check

- To check the spelling of text in a worksheet and obtain replacement word suggestions, use the **spelling checker** feature.

Procedures

Open Recent Workbook

1. Click **File** .... Alt + F
2. Click the workbook you want to open from the list at the bottom of the menu.

Open Workbook *(Ctrl+O)*

1. Click **Open** button 📂.

   OR

   a. Click **View** .... Alt + V
   b. Click **Task Pane** .... K
   c. Click the workbook you want to open, or if it is not listed in the task pane, click **More Workbooks**.

2. If the workbook you want to open is not listed in the current folder, perform one of the following:

   a. Click **Look in** .... Alt + I
   b. Select desired
      drive .... ⬆⬇ , Enter

   OR
   Double-click folder
   name .... Tab , ⬆⬇ , Enter
   OR
   Click the appropriate button on the Places bar.

3. Click the file you want to open.
4. Click **Open** .... Enter

Change to Different Open Workbook

1. Click **Window** .... Alt + W
2. Click workbook name in list at bottom of menu ...... ⬆⬇ , Enter

   OR

   - Click anywhere in open workbook window.

   OR

   - Click workbook's button on Window's taskbar.

Arrange Open Workbooks

1. Click **Window** .... Alt + W
2. Click **Arrange** .... A

3. Select from four options:

   - **Tiled** .... Alt + T
   - **Horizontal** .... Alt + O
   - **Vertical** .... Alt + V
   - **Cascade** .... Alt + C

4. Click **OK** .... Enter

AutoComplete

1. Type part of label.

   ✓ *Repetitive text is highlighted as you type label.*

2. Press **Enter** .... Enter

   ✓ *Just continue typing if you do not want to repeat label.*

Pick From List

1. Right-click cell to receive entry.
2. Click **Pick From List** .... K
3. Click desired text.

Create AutoCorrect Replacement

1. Click **Tools** .... Alt + T
2. Click **AutoCorrect Options** .... A
3. Click **Replace** .... Alt + R
4. Type misspelled word.
5. Click **With** .... Alt + W
6. Type replacement characters.
7. Click **Add** .... A
8. Click **OK** .... Enter

Check Spelling *(F7)*

1. Select a cell.
   - ✓ *If you don't start the spell check from the beginning of the worksheet, Excel completes the spell check then displays "Do you want to continue checking at the beginning of the sheet?"*

2. Click **Spelling** button [ABC ✓].

   OR
   a. Click **Tools** .... Alt + T
   b. Click **Spelling** .... S

3. To change the spelling of a word:
   - Click correctly spelled word in **Suggestions** list. .... Alt + N

   OR
   - Change the misspelled word manually in the **Not in Dictionary:** text box .... Alt + D

4. Select an option:
   - Click **Change** .... Alt + C

- Click **Change All** to change the word everywhere in document .... Alt + L
- Click **Ignore Once** to continue without changing word .... Alt + I
- Click **Ignore All** to continue without changing word and without highlighting it anywhere else in document .... Alt + G
- Click **Add to Dictionary** to add word to dictionary .... Alt + A

5. Repeat steps 3 and 4 for every misspelled word.
6. Click **OK** when Excel completes check. .... Enter

Exercise Directions

1. Start Excel, if necessary.
2. Open ⊙ **03DEMOS**.
3. Save the file as **DEMOS**.
4. Open ⊙ **03PLAYSETS**.
5. Using the Windows, Arrange command, arrange the two workbooks on-screen in a tiled fashion.
6. Arrange the workbooks again, this time horizontally.
7. Click within the window of the **DEMOS** workbook to activate it.
   - ✓ *Notice that the title bar of the active workbook's window is dark blue, while the inactive workbook's title bar is gray.*
8. Maximize the **DEMOS** workbook.
   - ✓ *The 03PLAYSETS workbook is no longer visible.*
9. Change to the **03PLAYSETS** workbook by clicking its button on the taskbar.
10. Close **03PLAYSETS**.

11. Double-click cell E10 to enable cell editing, then type **(r)** at the end of the entry, after **Princess Playhouse**.
    - ✓ *After you press Enter to finalize the entry, notice that AutoCorrect has changed Princess Playhouse (r) to Princess Playhouse®.*
12. Type the data as shown in Illustration A.
    a. As you type the names of the play sets for Haywood and Lyton, use the AutoComplete feature to speed up the process.
    b. Use the Pick From List feature to enter the play sets for Claymore.
13. Click cell B3.
14. Use the spelling checker to check your worksheet.
    a. At the first error, select **play sets** from the Suggestions list, then click Change All to change playsets to play sets throughout.
    b. Click Ignore All to ignore the error for Lyton.
    c. Click Yes to continue the spell check at the beginning of the worksheet.
15. Close the **DEMOS** workbook, saving all changes.

Illustration A

Date	Event	City	Playsets We'll Demo
7/14/2001	Kids Day	Chicago	Mountain Climber ®
			King of the Hill ®
			Princess Playhouse ®
7/21/2001	Haywood Home Show	Haywood	King of the Hill ®
			King's Castle ®
7/21/2001	Children's Fair	Lyton	Mountain Climber ®
			Princess Playhouse ®
7/21/2001	Claymore Kids Carnival	Claymore	King of the Hill ®
			Princess Playhouse ®
			Mountain Climber ®
			King's Castle ®

On Your Own

1. Start Excel, if necessary.

2. Open 💿 **03TEACHERS**.

3. Start a new workbook, and save the file as **OXL03**.

   ✓ *Here you'll create a report to track homework assignments. You'll start by entering information about each assignment—in later lessons, you'll add the dates when the assignments are due and make other adjustments.*

4. Type a title for the report in row 2.

5. Label column A: **ASSIGNMENTS**.

6. Label column C: **SUBJECT**.

7. Label column E: **ASSIGNED BY**.

8. In column A, type a list of assignments, such as a book report, term paper, chapters to read, or a topic report (such as a report on China).

9. In column C, type the name of the class in which the assignment was given. If you repeat names, use AutoComplete and Pick From List to complete the entries.

10. Arrange the two open workbooks vertically.

11. Using the list of teachers in **03TEACHERS**, type the name of the teacher who assigned each homework assignment.

12. Close **03TEACHERS** and maximize the **OXL03** window.

13. Type your school's Web address in cell G2, like this: **www.coolschool.org**.

   ✓ *If your school doesn't have a Web site, make up an appropriate Web address.*

   ✓ *Notice that AutoCorrect automatically creates a hyperlink from the entry by underlining it and making it blue. If you click this link, Internet Explorer starts, and displays the Web address. You don't want this to happen, so you'll change the link back into ordinary text.*

14. Revert the Web address back to simple text by moving the active cell pointer to cell F2 (use the arrow keys and do not click the cell). Click the AutoCorrect button that appears in the left-hand corner of the cell when you point to it, and select the Undo Hyperlink option.

15. Spell check the workbook.

16. Close the workbook, saving all changes.

Exercise 4

On the Job

Because Excel allows you to work with numbers so easily, numeric values are one of the most common Excel entry types. After typing numbers and labels into a worksheet, you can improve its appearance by changing the alignment of data and the widths of columns. If entering a series of labels (such as Monday, Tuesday, Wednesday) or values (such as 1, 2, 3), use Excel's AutoFill feature to save data-entry time and reduce errors.

As the invoice clerk for California Cardiology, Inc., you started a report that listed overdue amounts for the Healthman HMO. In this exercise, you'll add invoice numbers, dates, and amounts to the report.

Terms

Value A number entered in the worksheet.

Numeric label A number entered in the worksheet as a label, not as a value—such as the year 2002 used as a column label.

Label prefix An apostrophe (') used to indicate that a number is really a label and not a value.

Series A list of sequential numbers, dates, times, or text.

Standard column width The default number of characters that display in a column based on the default font.

Notes

Numeric Labels and Values

- A cell contains a **value** when its first character begins with either a number or one of the following symbols (+, − , =, $).

- Type the value, and then do one of the following to enter it into the cell:
  - Press the Enter key.
  - Press an arrow key.
  - Click the Enter box on the Formula bar.
  - Click another cell.

- If you enter a value that contains more than 11 digits into a cell that uses the default format, Excel will display the number in scientific notation.

  ✓ *For example, the entry 123,456,789,012 is displayed as 1.234567E11.*

  ✓ *To display the number in a different format, apply the number format you want to use, as explained in Exercise 8.*

- If you see pound signs displayed in a cell instead of a number, simply widen the column to display the value.

  ✓ *If a number is displayed in scientific notation, widen the column and apply a different format to the cell as explained in Exercise 8.*

- A **numeric label**, such as a Social Security number, is a number that will not be used in calculation.

- Begin the entry of a numeric label with an apostrophe (') as a **label prefix** to indicate that the number should be treated as a label (text) and not as a value.

- Although the label prefix (') is shown on the Formula bar, it is not displayed on the worksheet or printed.

- When you enter a value with an apostrophe, Excel displays a green triangle in the upper left-hand corner of the cell. Select the cell again, and an error button appears. Click the button and confirm that the number is really a label (Ignore Error), or that the value was entered in error and should be treated as a number (Convert to Number).

Error button appears after you enter a numeric label

	A	B	C	D	E
1	Text				
2	1200		Error button		
3	2001	◇ ▾			
4			Number Stored as Text		
5			Convert to Number		
6			Help on this error		
7					
8			Ignore Error		
9			Edit in Formula Bar		
10			Error Checking Options...		
11			Show Formula Auditing Toolbar		
12					

Enter Dates

- You can enter a date using one of these date formats:
  - mm/dd/yy, as in 1/14/02 or 01/14/02
  - mm/dd, as in 3/14
  - dd-mmm-yy, as in 14-Jan-02
  - dd-mmm, as in 14-Jan
    - ✓ *The current year is assumed.*
  - mmm-yy, as in Jan-02
    - ✓ *The first day of the month is assumed.*

- After entering a date, you can change its display to suit your needs.
  - ✓ *For example, you can change the date 1/14/02 to display as January 14, 2002.*

- To enter time, follow a number with **a** or **p** to indicate AM or PM, like this:
  10:43 p

- You can enter a date and time in the same cell, like this:
  10/16/99 2:31 p

Create a Series

- A series is a sequence of numbers (such as 1, 2, 3), dates (such as 10/21/02, 10/22/02, 10/23/02), times (such as 2:30, 2:45, 3:00) or text (such as January, February, March).

- To enter a series based on the active cell, drag the fill handle, a small square in lower-right corner of the active cell that turns into a plus sign (+), over the range of cells you want to fill with the series.
  - ✓ *For example, type January into a cell, then drag the fill handle down or to the left to create the series January, February, March, and so on.*

Drag the fill handle of the active cell to create a series

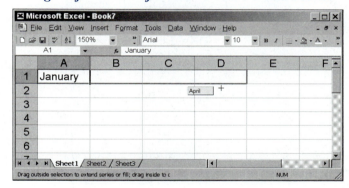

- ✓ *A SmartTag appears under the mouse pointer, displaying the values of the series you're creating. The series values appear in the cells after you release the mouse button.*

- To create an incremental series (i.e., 1, 3, 5, 7), enter the data for the first and second cells of a series, select the two cells, then drag the fill handle for the selection over the range of cells to fill.

- You can also use the fill handle to copy formatting (such as bold, italics, and so on) from one cell to adjacent cells, and not its value.

Data Alignment

- When a label is typed in a cell, it automatically aligns to the left of the cell. Values are automatically right aligned.

- To improve the appearance of a worksheet, you can change the alignment of column labels, row labels, and other data.

Example of how data is aligned in cells

	A	B
1	Text	Text is aligned to the left
2	1200	Values are aligned to the right
3	2001	Numeric labels entered with an apostrophe are aligned left

- To align data, use the alignment buttons on the Formatting toolbar or choose other alignment options through the Format Cells dialog box.

Format Cells dialog box

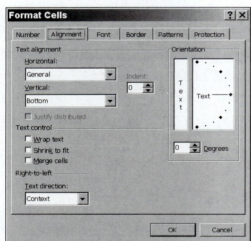

Alignment buttons on Formatting toolbar

Align left — Center — Align Right — Merge and Center

- To center a label across the columns use the Merge and Center button on the Formatting toolbar.

  - ✓ You most often use this option to center a worksheet title within a range of cells. The Merge and Center button actually merges the selected cells into one large cell and then centers the data in the newly merged cell.

  - ✓ To get Merge and Center to work properly, enter the data into the first cell in a range, then select adjacent cells to the right.

Change Column Width

- The default Excel workbook is set for a **standard column width** (80 pixels or 8.43 characters in the standard font of Arial, 10 point).

- You can change (widen or narrow) the column widths individually so that text or values fit the longest entry or be arranged more neatly on the page.

- Changing column width changes the width of an entire column or a group of columns—not the width of a single cell.

- You can quickly adjust a column to fit the longest entry in that column, or you can set the column to any width you like.

- You can also shrink text to fit in a cell (the Shrink to fit option on the Alignment tab of the Format Cells dialog box), regardless of its width. (The text size readjusts automatically if the column width is changed.)

Procedures

Enter Numeric Label

  - ✓ A number entered as a numeric label is left aligned and cannot be calculated.

1. Select cell............................
2. Type **apostrophe**................ `'`
3. Type number.
4. Press **Enter**....................... `Enter`

  - ✓ If a green triangle appears in a the cell, select it again to display the error button, then click its down arrow and select the option **Ignore Error** from its list.

  - ✓ You can select multiple cells prior to choosing Ignore Error.

Enter Value

  - ✓ A number entered as a value is right-aligned and can be calculated.

1. Select cell ....
2. Type number.
  - ✓ Start the entry with a number from zero to nine, a decimal point, or a dollar sign ($). Enclose a negative number in parentheses() or precede it with a minus sign (-).

3. Press **Enter**....................... |Enter|

✓ *If Excel displays pound signs (######), the column needs to be widened. Double-click the right border of the column heading to display the value.*

Create a Series Using Mouse

1. Enter the value to copy in active cell.

2. Select the cell, and then point to its fill handle.

✓ *The mouse changes to* **+** .

3. Drag the fill handle down, up, left, or right to copy the value.

4. Click arrow on AutoFill button and select an option:

✓ *If you don't select an option from the AutoFill button, then the range is filled with a series as explained below. Also, the button disappears after you enter data into any other cell.*

✓ *You can select multiple cells at once, and choose the same option for all of them.*

● **Copy Cells**

✓ *Copies the contents of the first cell into the fill range.*

● **Fill Series**

✓ *Increases the value in the first cell by one to fill each cell in the fill range.*

● **Copy Formatting Only**

✓ *Copies the formatting of the first cell, but not its value.*

● **Fill Without Formatting**

✓ *Same as Fill Series option, but this does not copy the formatting of the first cell to the cells in the fill range.*

● **Fill Days**

✓ *Fills cells in the range with dates one day apart.*

● **Fill Weekdays**

✓ *Fills cells in the range with dates one day apart, skipping over dates that fall on weekends.*

● **Fill Months**

✓ *Fills cells in the range with dates one month apart.*

● **Fill Years**

✓ *Fills cells in the range with dates one year apart.*

Create an Incremental Series Using Mouse

1. Enter first and second data in adjacent cells.

✓ *The text can be numbers, dates, or times, such as 2:45 and 3:00.*

2. Select the two cells containing series data.

3. Point to fill handle.

4. Drag fill handle down, up, left, or right.

✓ *Using the two cells as a sample, cells in the range are filled with values that increase or decrease by that same amount.*

✓ *If desired, click the arrow on the AutoFill button that appears and select an option as explained in the previous procedure. However, if you select any of the date options, the dates in the fill range will still be incremented based on the two sample cells.*

Align Entry Using Formatting Toolbar

1. Select cell(s) containing label(s) ....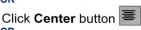

2. Click **Align Left** button ▤ .
   OR
   Click **Center** button ▤ .
   OR
   Click **Align Right** button ▤ .

Merge and Center Entry Using Formatting Toolbar

1. Drag across the cell with entry and adjacent cells to select them.

2. Click **Merge and Center** button .

✓ *Data is centered within the selected range. If you want, you can left- or right-align data within the merged cell by clicking the Align Left or Align Right buttons on the Formatting toolbar.*

✓ *To unmerge the cells (and create separate cells again), click the **Merge and Center** button to turn it off.*

Align Labels Using Format Cells Dialog Box

1. Select cell(s) containing label(s).............................. |↕|

2. Click **Format**............... |Alt|+|O|

3. Click **Cells** .... |E|

4. Click **Alignment** tab ... |Ctrl|+|Tab|

5. Click **Horizontal** .... |Alt|+|H|

6. Click **Left (Indent)** .... |L|, |Enter|
   OR
   Click **Center** .... |C|, |Enter|
   OR
   Click **Right** .... |R|, |Enter|

✓ *You can also select two lesser used options: **Fill** (repeats data in cell to fill cell completely, regardless of its width) or **Justify** (adds spaces between characters as needed to fill the cell completely).*

7. Click **OK** .... |Enter|

Change Column Width Using Menu

1. Select any cell in column to change.

2. Click **Format**............... |Alt|+|O|

3. Click **Column** .... |C|

4. Click **Width**......................... |W|

5. Type number (0-255) in Column Width text box.

✓ *This value represents the number of characters wide you want the column to be, using the standard font.*

6. Click **OK** .... |Enter|

Change Column Width Using Mouse

1. Point to right border of column heading to be sized.

2. Pointer becomes ↔ .

3. Drag ↔ left or right to desired width.

✓ *Excel displays column width above and to the right of the mouse pointer as you drag.*

Set Column Width to Fit Longest Entry

- Double-click right border of column heading.

OR

1. Select column
   to size .... [↔], [Ctrl]+[Space]
2. Click **Format** .... [Alt]+[O]
3. Click **Column**. .... [C]
4. Click **AutoFit Selection** ...... [A]

Set Standard Column Width

✓ *This command will adjust column widths that have not been previously changed in a worksheet.*

1. Click **Format** .... [Alt]+[O]
2. Click **Column**. .... [C]
3. Click **Standard Width** .... [S]
4. Type new number (0-255) .... in Standard Column Width text box.

   ✓ *This number represents number of characters to be displayed in cell using the standard font.*

5. Click **OK** .... [Enter]

Exercise Directions

1. Start Excel, if necessary.
2. Open ⌨**OVERDUE** or 💿**04OVERDUE**.
3. Save the file as **OVERDUE**.
4. Enter the values in columns C and D as shown in Illustration A.

   ✓ *Make sure the invoice numbers in column D are entered as numeric labels.*
   ✓ *Select Ignore Error from the Error button list for each entry in column D.*

5. Enter the label **Date Due** and the date shown in cell E8.
6. Copy the date in cell E8 to cells E9 and E10 by dragging its fill handle.

   ✓ *Select the option, Copy Cells from the AutoFill button menu.*

7. Set the width of column D to fit the longest entry.
8. Change column B to a width of 16.0.
9. Drag across cells B3, C3, D3, and E3 to select them, then merge and center the worksheet title as shown in Illustration A.
10. Center the **Amount**, **Invoice Number**, and **Date Due** column labels.
11. Spell check the worksheet.
12. Close the workbook, saving all changes.

Illustration A

	A	B	C	D	E	F
1						
2						
3		California Cardiology, Inc.				
4						
5		Healthman HMO				
6						
7		Patient	Amount	Invoice Number	Date Due	
8		J. Thomas Wilson	2147.48	2145801	4/21/2001	
9		Carlos Riveria	375.97	2189357	4/21/2001	
10		Alice Thomson	1281.72	2049462	4/21/2001	

On Your Own

1. Open a new workbook in Excel and save it as **OXL04**.

2. Create a worksheet to track inventory. For example, you might want to track your CD collection, or your books. For a business, club, or organization, you might want to track office supplies or equipment.

3. In row 1, type a title for your inventory report.

4. Enter the following labels as column headings starting in column A:

   ITEM
   DESCRIPTION
   COST

5. In the rows below each column heading, enter the appropriate data for at least five items.

   ✓ *If you enter numeric labels, be sure to include the label prefix (').*

6. Adjust the column width so you can read all of the data entered in the report.

7. Center the column heading labels.

8. Right align all number values.

9. Left align all text (except the column headings).

10. Merge the cells in row 1 and center the report title over the worksheet.

11. Save the worksheet, close the file, and exit Excel.

Exercise 5

On the Job

One of the benefits of Excel is its ability to create formulas within a worksheet that perform calculations. When you make a change to a cell that is referenced in a formula, Excel performs the recalculation, and the formula result is automatically updated to reflect the change.

As the invoice clerk for California Cardiology, Inc., you're glad that the invoice for Healthman HMO is almost ready. However, you know that there are still a few things you need to do to the report before you print it, such as adding formulas to calculate the total invoice amount and late fees.

Terms

Formula An instruction Excel uses to calculate a number.

Mathematical operators Symbols used in mathematical operations: **+** for addition, **-** for subtraction, ***** for multiplication, **/** for division, and **^** for exponentiation.

Order of mathematical operations The order in which Excel performs the calculations specified in a formula.

Notes

Enter a Formula

■ A **formula** is a worksheet instruction that performs a calculation.

■ You enter a formula in the cell where the answer should display.

■ As you type a formula, it displays in the cell and in the Formula bar.

■ After you enter a formula into the cell, the answer displays in the cell while the formula appears in the formula bar.

■ When creating formulas, you use cell references, values, and **mathematical operators**.

✓ *A formula can also contain Excel's predefined "functions," which are covered in Exercise 13.*

■ The following are standard mathematical operators used in formulas:

+ Addition
- Subtraction
* Multiplication
/ Division
^ Exponentiation

■ The equal sign (=) must be typed at the beginning of a formula. For example, the formula =B2+B4+B6 adds the values in these cell locations together.

■ When you make a change to a value in a cell that is referenced in a formula, the answer in the formula cell automatically changes.

■ The **order of mathematical operations** is important to remember when creating formulas.

- When calculating a formula, Excel performs operations enclosed in parentheses first.

- Exponential calculations have the next priority.

- Moving left to right within the formula, multiplication and division operations are then calculated before the addition and subtraction operations.

■ When typing a percentage as a value in a formula, you can enter it with the percent symbol or as a decimal.

■ Excel automatically provides assistance in correcting common mistakes in a formula (for example, omitting a parenthesis).

Procedures

Enter Formula Using Mathematical Operators

1. Click cell where answer should display ....
2. Press **Equal** [=] ....
3. Type formula.
   - ✓ *Example: =(C2+C10)/2*
4. Press **Enter** .... [Enter]
   - ✓ *Instead of typing a cell reference into a formula, you can simply click the appropriate cell.*

Exercise Directions

1. Start Excel, if necessary.

2. Open 🖴**OVERDUE** or 💿**05OVERDUE**.

3. Save the file as **OVERDUE**.

4. In cells B12, B13, B14, and B16, type the labels shown in Illustration A.

5. Right align the labels entered in step 4.

6. In cell C12, type a formula to calculate the total amount that Healthman owes you:
   =C8+C9+C10
   - ✓ *Click the cells in the formula instead of typing their addresses. For example, type = then click cell C8. Type + then click C9. Type another + and click C10.*

7. In cell C13, calculate a 2% late fee by entering this formula: **=C12*2%**

8. In cell C14, calculate the current amount due, (the old total plus the 2% late fee) by entering this formula: **=C12+C13**

9. In cell C16, type the new amount that will be due if the current amount is not paid on time (the current amount plus another 2%):
   =C14+(C14*2%)
   - ✓ *In this formula, you must use parentheses to get the correct answer. If you type =C14+C14*2%, then Excel will add cell C14 to cell C14, then take that total times 2%. If you didn't want to use parentheses, you could type this formula instead: =C14*102%.*

10. Spell check the workbook.

11. Close the file, saving all changes.

	A	B	C	D	E	F
3		California Cardiology, Inc.				
4						
5		Healthman HMO				
6						
7		Patient	Amount	Invoice Number	Date Due	
8		J. Thomas Wilson	2147.48	2145801	4/21/2001	
9		Carlos Riveria	375.97	2189357	4/21/2001	
10		Alice Thomson	1281.72	2049462	4/21/2001	
11						
12		Overdue amount:	3805.17			
13		Late charge:	76.1034			
14		Current amount due:	3881.273			
15						
16	Amount due if paid after 5/16:		3958.899			
17						

On Your Own

1. Start Excel, if necessary.

2. Start a new workbook in Excel and save it as **OXL05**.

   ✓ *As the treasurer of the Art Club, you'll use Excel to set up a worksheet for tracking the total weekly candy sales for your current fundraiser.*

3. Enter a title for the worksheet in row 2.

4. Label the columns as follows:
   Member Name
   Candy
   Price
   Number Sold
   Total Sales

5. Type sales data for the first member, using multiple rows to list each type of candy sold by that person.

   ✓ *For example, the first row might be: Jane Brown, Milk chocolate candy bars, price 1.50, 10 sold. The next line might be: Tamika Brown, Toffee bars, price 2.25, 17 sold.*

   ✓ *Enter at least three people, with each person selling at least two types of candy. In the Member Name column, use the fill handle to copy the person's name to additional rows as needed.*

6. In the Total Sales column for the first item, enter a formula that multiples the value in the Price column by the value in the Number Sold column.

7. Repeat step 6 for each item.

8. Below the last item in the Total Sales column, enter a formula that adds the total sales for each item to compute a grand total for the week.

9. To the left of the cell that contains the grand total, type the label **Weekly Total**.

10. Adjust the width of columns so you can read all of the data.

11. Spell check the worksheet.

12. Close the worksheet, saving all changes.

Exercise 6

◆ Critical Thinking

You are the owner of a store in the Coastline Gourmet Importers food chain, and it's time to order some seafood from one of your best suppliers, Chang Lo Lee Oriental Seafood. Luckily, Coastline has supplied you with a template you can use to create your order form. All you need to do is to enter the items you want, the number of cases for each item, and the cost per case (which you'll look up in an Excel workbook you created using Chang Lo Lee's current price list).

Exercise Directions

1. Start Excel, if necessary.

2. Open 💿 **06CHANG**.

3. Start a workbook using the template 💿 **06CGIORDER**.

   ✓ *This template file is included with the data files. You will need to copy the file to the \Program Files\Microsoft Office\Templates folder. After you've copied the file, you'll see this template listed with the other General Templates.*

4. Save the file as **CHANGLEE**.

   ✓ *To save the template as an Excel workbook, select **Microsoft Excel Workbook** from the Save as type drop-down list. Otherwise, the file will remain a template.*

5. In cell B9, type the name of the supplier you're ordering from: **Chang Lo Lee Seafood**.

6. In cell B10, type their Web site address: **www.changlolee.com**.

   ✓ *Notice how AutoComplete creates an Internet link with your entry, underlining the text and making it blue.*

7. Enter particulars for this order in the **Item** and **No. of Cases** columns, as shown in Illustration A.

8. Arrange the two open workbooks horizontally.

9. Using the prices listed in **06CHANG**, enter appropriate data in the **Cost per Case** column of the **CHANGLEE** workbook for each item ordered.

10. Close **06CHANG**.

11. In cell E13, type a formula that calculates the total cost for the order of Mongolian Barbequed Shrimp.

    ✓ *Take the number of cases times the cost per case.*

12. In column E, type similar formulas that compute the total cost of the remaining items.

13. In cell E24, type a formula that calculates the total for the order.

    ✓ *Add cells E13, E14, E15, E16, and E17 together.*

    ✓ *Your worksheet should now look like the one in Illustration B.*

14. Spell check the workbook.

    ✓ *Be sure to correct the spelling of Florida.*

15. Close the workbook, saving all changes.

Illustration A

Item	No. of Cases
Mongolian Barbequed Shrimp	6
Crab Meat AA	10
Sesame Crab Claw	2
Squid Paste	7
Sea Bass Sushi	11

Illustration B

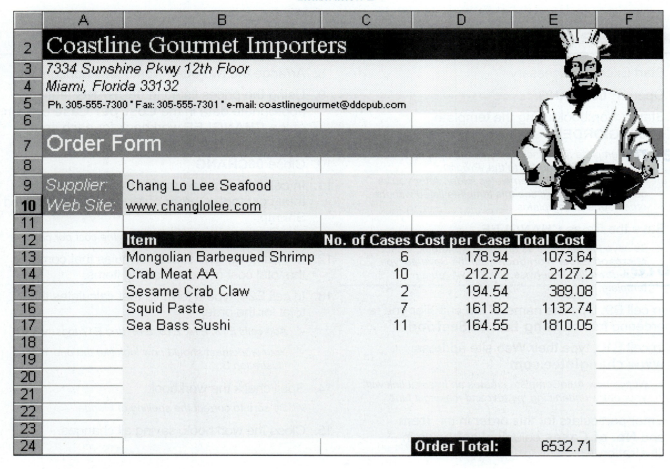

Coastline Gourmet Importers

7334 Sunshine Pkwy 12th Floor
Miami, Florida 33132
Ph. 305-555-7300 ˙ Fax: 305-555-7301 ˙ e-mail: coastlinegourmet@ddcpub.com

Order Form

Supplier: Chang Lo Lee Seafood
Web Site: www.changlolee.com

Item	No. of Cases	Cost per Case	Total Cost
Mongolian Barbequed Shrimp	6	178.94	1073.64
Crab Meat AA	10	212.72	2127.2
Sesame Crab Claw	2	194.54	389.08
Squid Paste	7	161.82	1132.74
Sea Bass Sushi	11	164.55	1810.05
		Order Total:	6532.71

Exercise 7

On the Job

Select a group of cells (a range) to copy, move, or erase them, or to quickly apply the same formatting throughout the range. You can also perform calculations on cell ranges—creating sums and averages, for example.

You're a salesperson with Regency General, Inc., a Web company that offers Internet-based database and inventory management services to other companies. Baylor Furniture is interested in putting their inventory online and offering Web-based sales to the general public, so they've asked for a price quote. In this exercise, you'll use Excel to make some final adjustments to the quote before you send a copy to your manager for her approval.

Terms

Range A block of cells in an Excel worksheet.

Contiguous range A block of adjacent cells in a worksheet.

Noncontiguous range A block of cells in a worksheet that is not necessarily adjacent to each other.

Notes

Use Ranges

- A **range** is an area made up of two or more cells.

- When you select cells A1, A2, and A3, for example, the range is indicated as A1:A3.

- The range A1:C5 is defined as a block of cells that includes all the cells in columns A through C in rows one through five.

- A range of cells can be **contiguous** (all cells are adjacent to each other) or **noncontiguous** (not all cells are adjacent to each other).

- When a range is selected, the active cell is displayed normally, but the rest of the cells appear highlighted, as shown.

Selected range of contiguous cells

	A	B	C
1	123	287	142
2	415	794	835
3	189	688	974

Selected range of noncontiguous cells

	A	B	C
1	123	287	142
2	415	794	835
3	189	688	974

Range Entry Using Collapse Button

- When you need to enter cell addresses or ranges in a dialog box, you may click the Collapse button on the right side of the text box to return to the worksheet temporarily and select the range.

- After selecting the range, click the Collapse button to return to the dialog box to finalize your selections.

Example of text box with Collapse button

Collapse button

Procedures

Use Keyboard to Select Range of Cells

To select range of adjacent cells:

1. Press arrow key(s)............. to move to first cell of range.
2. Press **Shift + arrow** key........................... Shift +

To select entire column containing active cell:

- Press **Ctrl + Spacebar**..... Ctrl + Space

To select entire row containing active cell:

- Press **Shift + Spacebar**.. Shift + Space

To select adjacent rows:

1. Press arrow keys .... to move to cell in first row to select.
2. Press and hold down **Shift**................ Shift , then press **spacebar**..... Space , to select first row.
3. While still pressing **Shift**, press up or down arrow key........ to select additional adjacent rows.

To select worksheet from top-left cell to bottom-right cell:

1. Press arrow keys .... to move to first cell in selection.
2. Press and hold down **Ctrl**, then press and hold down **Shift**, then press and release **End** .... Ctrl + Shift + End
3. Release **Ctrl** and **Shift** keys.

Use Mouse to Select Range of Cells

To select range of adjacent cells:

- Click and drag across cells.

To select noncontiguous cells and ranges:

- Click and drag across first selection of cells.
- Press and hold **Ctrl** as you click additional cells, and/or drag over additional ranges.

To select entire row:

- Click row heading.

To select entire column:

- Click column heading.

To select adjacent rows:

- Click and drag across row headings.

To select adjacent columns:

- Click and drag across column headings.

To select noncontiguous rows:

1. Click row heading.
2. Press and hold down **Ctrl** key and click additional row headings.

To select noncontiguous columns:

1. Click column heading.
2. Press and hold down **Ctrl** key and click additional column headings.

Range Entry Using Collapse Button

1. Click **Collapse** button 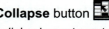 at right of text box.

   ✓ *The dialog box collapses to provide a better view of the worksheet.*

2. Select desired cell(s) by following either the keyboard or mouse method described here.

3. Press **Enter** .... Enter

   OR

   Click **Collapse** button .

   ✓ *The dialog box returns to normal size and the text box displays the cell reference(s). Continue making selections within the dialog box as needed.*

Exercise Directions

1. Start Excel, if necessary.
2. Open ⊙ **07DBQUOTE**.
3. Save the file as **DBQUOTE**.
4. Select the range D13:F19. (See Illustration A.)
5. Center-align the data in the range by clicking the Center button on the Formatting toolbar.
6. Select the range B8:B10.
7. Press Ctrl, and click cell E10 to create a non-contiguous selection. See Illustration A below.
8. Right-align the selected cells by clicking the Align Right button on the Formatting toolbar.
9. Click the heading for column G to select the entire column.
10. Erase the contents of column G by pressing Delete.
11. Spell check the workbook.
12. Close the workbook, saving all changes.

Illustration A

	A	B	C	D	E	F	G
1							
2							
3			Regency General, Inc.				
4							
5			Monthly Price Quote				
6							
7							
8		Name:	Baylor Furniture				
9		Address:	2143 Grand Ave. Austin, TX 73309				
10		Phone:	512-555-7989		Fax:	512-555-7941	
11							
12							
13			Service	Price per Unit	No. of Units	Total	
14			Database server	$ 0.50	1505	$ 752.50	
15			Remote administration	$ 0.35	1505	$ 526.75	
16			Shopping cart	$ 0.15	1505	$ 225.75	
17			Credit verification	$ 0.09	1505	$ 135.45	
18			Real-time inventory	$ 0.27	1505	$ 406.35	
19			Search-enabled	$ 0.05	1505	$ 75.25	
20						$ 2,046.80	
21							
22							

On Your Own

1. Open the file named **OXL05** that you created in the On Your Own section of Exercise 5, or open the file ⊙ **07CANDY**.
2. Save the file as **OXL07**.
3. Select the range of cells containing the column labels (Member Name, etc.), and change the cell alignment to center.
4. Select the range of cells containing the member names and candy names, and change the cell alignment to right.
5. Select the columns that contain the **Price**, **Number Sold**, and **Totals Sales** labels, and set the column widths to exactly 10.5.
6. Spell check the workbook.
7. Close the workbook, saving all changes.

Exercise 8

Skills Covered:

◆ **Format Data** ◆ **Fonts and Font Size**
◆ **Number Formats** ◆ **Percent Format** ◆ **Comma Format**
◆ **Currency** ◆ **Add Color to Cells**

On the Job

When you change the appearance of worksheet data by applying various formats, you also make that data more attractive and readable.

As the manager of the local Northwest Gear store, you've been asked by your regional office to track the sales fluctuations for a new item, a sleeveless cashmere sweater. You've entered the raw data, and in this exercise, you will format the worksheet using various number formats. You'll make font and font size changes as well and apply color to enhance the appearance of the report.

Terms

Format To apply attributes to cell data to change the appearance of the worksheet.

Font The typeface or design of the text.

Font size The measurement of the typeface in points ($1/72$ of an inch).

Number format A format that controls how numerical data is displayed, including the use of commas, dollar signs (or other symbols), and the number of decimal places.

Percent format A style that displays decimal numbers as a percentage.

Comma format A style that displays numbers with a thousands separator (,).

Currency format A style that displays dollar signs ($) immediately preceding the number and includes a thousands separator (,).

Accounting format A style that vertically aligns with dollar signs ($), thousands separators (,), and decimal points.

Fill A color that fills a cell, appearing behind the data.

Pattern A secondary color added to the background of a cell in a pattern.

Notes

Format Data

- **Format** data by selecting it and clicking the appropriate button on the Formatting toolbar or by choosing options from the Format Cells dialog box.

Fonts and Font Size

- A **font** is a set of characters with a specific design and name.
- The **font size** of a set of characters is based on its average height in points. One point is equal to 1/72 of an inch.

- Change the font and font size of your data to improve its appearance and to make it more readable.

- You can apply special effects—such as bold, italics, or underline—to any font you select.

- You make font, font size, and special effects changes through the Formatting toolbar or the Format Cells dialog box.

Font and font size changes from Formatting toolbar

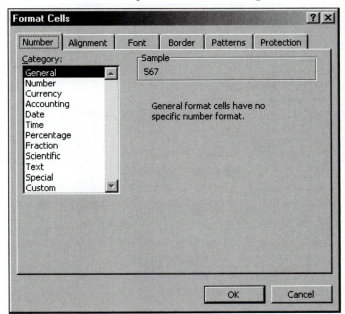

- The way in which your data appears after making font and font size changes is dependent on your monitor and printer.

  ✓ *If your monitor cannot display a particular font, it will choose a similar font to replace it with. However, when you print the data out, the actual font you picked may be used. To avoid this discrepancy between what you see on-screen and what is printed, use Windows TrueType fonts whenever possible.*

- Windows TrueType fonts are "true" to their on-screen appearance—what you see is what you will get when your data is printed.

  ✓ *TrueType fonts are identified with a small TT in front of their name in the Font drop-down list on the Formatting toolbar.*

- When you change the size of a font, Excel automatically adjusts the row height but does not adjust the column width.

- By default, data appears in Arial 10-point font. You can change the standard (default) font and font size if you want, or you can apply different fonts and font sizes to selected data.

Number Formats

- When formatting numerical data, you may want to change more than just the font and font size— you may want to also apply a **number format**.

- The number format determines the number of decimal places and the position of zeros (if any) before/after the decimal point. Number formats also place various symbols such as dollar signs or percentage signs with formatted numbers. You can also add dollar signs and commas with the number format you select.

- Changing the format of a cell does not affect the actual value stored there or used in calculations—it affects only the way in which that value is displayed.

- You can quickly apply Currency, Percent, or Comma format to numerical data using the buttons on the Formatting toolbar.

- You can also increase or decrease the number of decimal places displayed in a number with buttons on the Formatting toolbar.

- To apply other number formats, or to adjust the settings used by default with Currency, Percent, or Comma format, use the Number tab of the Format Cells dialog box.

Number tab of Format Cells dialog box

Percent Format

- To change data entered as decimals (such as .75) into percentages (75%), use the **percent format**.

Comma Format

- If you want to make large numbers easier to read, use the **comma format** to include commas in the number, as in 2,345,945.98.

Currency

- The currency and accounting formats may be used for formatting money values.

- **Currency format** displays numbers with currency symbols: dollar signs, commas, and decimals. For example, $21,456.83.

- **Accounting format** displays numbers in a style similar to currency format, but the dollar signs are aligned to the far left of the cell, with additional spaces inserted between the dollar sign and the first digit, depending on the column width. For example, $ 21,456.83.

  ✓ *When you use the Currency button on the Formatting toolbar to apply a number format, you're really applying Accounting format.*

Add Color to Cells

- To focus attention on particular areas of the worksheet, such as the column or row labels or important totals, fill the cell background with color. You can add color to your data as well.

- You can add color (called a **fill**) to a cell with the Fill Color button on the Formatting toolbar. Add color to the text in a cell with the Font Color button.

- With the Format Cells dialog box, you can select from a wider variety of color fills. You can also include a **pattern**.

Color or pattern added to cells

2001 Budget			
	January	**February**	**March**
Income	5654	6102	4987
Expenses	3102	3254	2795

Procedures

Change Font Using Font Box

1. Select cells or characters in cells to format.
2. Click **Font** list box arrow
   `Arial`
3. Select font .... `↑↓`, `Enter`

Change Font Size Using Font Size Box

1. Select cells or characters in cells to format.
2. Click **Font Size** list box arrow
   `10`
3. Select number
   in list .... `↑↓`, `Enter`
   OR
   a. Click **Font Size** box
      `10`
   b. Type desired number.
   c. Press **Enter** .... `Enter`

Percentage Number Format

1. Select cell(s) to format.
2. Click **Percent Style** button `%`
   OR
   a. Click **Format** .... `Alt`+`O`

b. Click **Cells** .... `E`
c. Select
   Number tab .... `Ctrl`+`Tab`
d. Click **Percentage**
   in **Category**
   list box .... `Alt`+`C`, `↑↓`
e. Click
   Decimal places ..... `Alt`+`D`
f. Set number of places.
g. Click **OK** .... `Enter`

Comma Number Format

1. Select cell(s) to format.
2. Click **Comma Style** button `,`
   OR
   a. Click **Format** .... `Alt`+`O`
   b. Click **Cells** .... `E`
   c. Select **Number** tab .. `Ctrl`+`Tab`
   d. Click **Number**
      in **Category**
      list box .... `Alt`+`C`, `↑↓`
   e. Click
      Decimal places ..... `Alt`+`D`
   f. Set number of places.

g. Click **Use**
   1000 Separator ...... `Alt`+`U`
h. Click **OK** .... `Enter`

Currency Number Format

1. Select cells(s) to format.
2. Click **Format** .... `Alt`+`O`
3. Click **Cells** .... `E`
4. Select **Number** tab ..... `Ctrl`+`Tab`
5. From the **Category**
   list box click
   Currency .... `Alt`+`C`, `↑↓`
6. Set decimal places and choose currency symbol.
7. Click **OK** .... `Enter`

Accounting Number Format

1. Select cell(s) to format.
2. Click **Format** .... `Alt`+`O`
3. Click **Cells** .... `E`
4. Select **Number** tab ..... `Ctrl`+`Tab`
5. From the **Category**
   list box click
   Accounting .... `Alt`+`C`, `↑↓`
6. Click **Decimal places** ... `Alt`+`D`

7. Set number of places.
   - ✓ *You can choose a symbol other than the US dollar and specify how negative numbers display in the cell.*
8. Click **OK**..........................[Enter]
   - ✓ *If you prefer, you can click the Currency Style button $ on the Formatting toolbar.*

Increase or Decrease Decimal Places

1. Select cell(s) to format.
2. Click **Increase Decimal** or **Decrease Decimal** buttons on the Formatting toolbar.

Add a Color Fill

1. Select cell(s) to format.
2. Click the arrow on the **Fill Color** button and select a color.
   - ✓ *You can also add a fill by choosing Format, Cells, clicking the Patterns tab and selecting a color.*
   - ✓ *Add a pattern to a fill by selecting its color from the Pattern list on the Patterns tab of the Format Cells dialog box. Be sure to choose a pattern for the second color from the top of the Pattern list.*

Add Text Color

1. Select cell(s) to format.
2. Click the arrow on the **Font Color** button and select a color.
   - ✓ *You can also add a color to text by choosing Format, Cells, clicking the Font tab and selecting a color from the Color list.*

Exercise Directions

1. Start Excel, if necessary.
2. Open **08CASHTOPS**.
3. Save the file as **CASHTOPS**.
4. Select the ranges B14:C19 and E14:E19.
5. Using the Comma Style button, format the data for two decimal places.
6. Click the Currency Style button to apply Accounting format to the selection.
7. Click the Decrease Decimal button twice to remove the decimal places.
8. Select the ranges D14:D19 and F14:F19.
9. Click the Percent Style button to apply the Percent format.
10. Click the Increase Decimal button three times to display three decimal places.
11. Apply these fonts to the following cells or ranges:
    - ✓ *If you don't have these exact same fonts, choose ones of your own, using Illustration A as an example.*
    a. A2: Chilada ICG Dos, 20 point
    b. A3:A5: Andy, 12 point
    c. A9: Chilada ICG Dos, 18 point
    d. A10: Andy, 14 point
    e. A14:A19: Andy 12 point, italic
    f. B13:F13: Andy 14 point

12. Apply the following color fills:
    a. A9:C9: Tan
    b. A10:C10: Pale Blue
    c. B13:F13: Aqua
    d. A14:A19: Red
13. Select the range A14:A19, and change its text color to white.
14. Widen any columns, if necessary. See Illustration A.
15. Spell check the workbook.
16. Close the workbook, saving all changes.

	A	B	C	D	E	F
2	**Northwest Gear, Inc.**					
3	2749 Mission St., Seattle, WA 98122					
4	Ph. 206-555-3922					
5	Fax: 206-555-3923					
6						
7						
8						
9	**New Item Tracker**					
10	Sleeveless, cashmere tops					
11						
12						
13		October	November	% Inc./Dec.	December	% Inc./Dec.
14	Red	$ 2,415	$ 2,694	11.553%	$ 2,421	-10.134%
15	Lt. Blue	$ 3,108	$ 3,278	5.470%	$ 4,386	33.801%
16	Brown	$ 978	$ 1,105	12.986%	$ 1,098	-0.633%
17	Burnt Umber	$ 1,027	$ 1,594	55.209%	$ 1,655	3.827%
18	Burgundy	$ 2,374	$ 3,497	47.304%	$ 4,297	22.877%
19	Cyan	$ 2,156	$ 3,387	57.096%	$ 4,092	20.815%
20						

On Your Own

1. Open the file 📁 **OXL07** that you created in the On Your Own section of Exercise 7, or open 💿 **08CANDY**.

2. Save the file as **OXL08**.

3. Apply the Comma format to the data in the Price and Total Sales columns.

4. Apply the Currency format with no decimal places to the data instead.

5. Finally, apply the Accounting format with two decimal places to the same data in the Price and Total Sales columns.

6. Change the font for all the data in B5:F12 to Verdana, and increase the font size to 11 points.

7. Increase the font size of the title to 18 points, and apply bold and italics effects. Select the cells that contain the title and fill them with yellow.

8. Increase the font size of the column labels to 14 points. Apply a light yellow color fill. Change the text color to green. Apply these same changes to cell E13.

9. Adjust the width of columns as necessary so that you can see all of the data in the worksheet.

10. Spell check the workbook.

11. Close the workbook, saving all changes.

Exercise 9

Skills Covered:

◆ **Copy and Paste Data** ◆ **Relative Reference**
◆ **Absolute Reference** ◆ **Preview and Print a Worksheet**

On the Job

Excel provides many shortcuts to save you time as you enter data and write formulas in your worksheets. For example, you can use the copy and paste features to reuse data and formulas in the same worksheet, in another worksheet, or in another workbook. The **AutoFill** handle bypasses the copy and paste features and allows you to copy data to adjacent cells. When you complete a report, you can preview and print a hard copy.

The worksheet you designed to track cashmere sweater sales was complete—that is, until the regional office called to tell you to add January sales data as well. In addition, they want you to add totals by month, a grand total, and the percentage of grand total sales by month. Luckily, all you need to do is create a few formulas and copy them throughout the worksheet.

Terms

AutoFill A method used to copy data from a cell or range of cells to an adjacent cell or range of cells by dragging the fill handle.

Clipboard A feature of Windows that holds data or graphics that you have cut or copied ready to be pasted into any document.

Fill handle Dragging this handle, located in the lower-right corner of the active cell, will copy cell contents, formatting, or a formula to adjacent cells.

Relative cell reference A cell address expressed in relation to another cell in a formula. For example, rather than naming a cell such as A3, a relative cell reference might identify a range of cells to the left of the cell containing the formula.

Absolute cell reference A cell address, such as E14, referenced in a formula that does not change based on the location of the formula.

Print Preview A feature used to display a document as it will appear when printed.

Notes

Copy and Paste Data

- Copying data involves two actions: copying and pasting.
  - When you copy data, the copy is placed on the **Clipboard**.
  - When you paste data, that data is copied from the Clipboard to the new location.

- Worksheet data (labels, values, and formulas) may be copied to another cell, a range of cells, another worksheet, or another workbook. Excel data can also be copied to documents created in other programs, such as Word.

- To copy a range of data to a new location, use the Copy and Paste buttons on the Standard toolbar or the Copy and Paste commands from the Edit menu.

- If the cells to which you want to copy data are adjacent to the original cell, you can use the **fill handle** to copy the data.

  ✓ *In Exercise 4, you learned how to use the fill handle to create a series. Here, you'll learn to use the fill handle to copy labels, values, and formulas to adjacent cells instead of creating a series.*

- When you copy data, its format is copied as well, and overrides any format in the destination cell.

  ✓ *You can override this and copy just the data without copying its formatting.*

- If data exists in the destination cell, that data will be overwritten.

Relative Reference

- When you copy a formula to another cell, Excel uses **relative cell referencing** to change the formula to reflect its new location.

  ✓ *For example, the formula =B4+B5 written in column B becomes =C4+C5 when copied to column C or =D4+D5 when copied to column D, etc.*

Absolute Reference

- Usually, you want the cell addresses in the original formula to change when you copy it. Sometimes, you don't want it to change, so you need to create an **absolute cell reference**.

- Absolute cell references do not change when a formula is copied.

- To make a cell reference absolute, enter a dollar sign ($) before both the column letter and row number of that cell in the formula.

  ✓ *For example, the formula =$B$4+$B$5 written in column B remains =$B$4+$B$5 when copied to column C. The cell addresses do not adjust based on the new formula location.*

- Sometimes, you may wish to copy a formula's result, and not the actual formula.

  ✓ *For example, if cell B10 contains the formula =B2-B3 with a result of $1200, and you copy that formula to cell C10, the formula will change to =C2-C3. The result of this copied formula would be based on the contents of cells C2 and C3. However, if all you want to do is to show the result, $1200, in another location of the worksheet, copy the value of cell B10 instead of its formula.*

Preview and Print a Worksheet

- You may print the selected worksheet(s), an entire workbook, or a selected data range.

- Use the Print command from the File menu to access the print options in the Print dialog box.

- To view the output before you print, use the **Print Preview** command, which appears on the File menu, in the Print dialog box, and as a button on the Standard toolbar.

Print dialog box

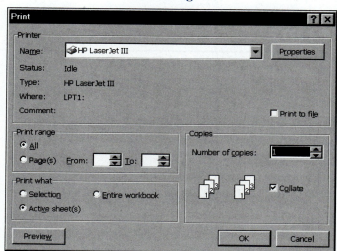

Procedures

Copy Data *(Ctrl+C)*

1. Select cell(s) to copy.

2. Click **Edit**..................... Alt +E

3. Click **Copy** C

   OR

   Click **Copy** button 📋.

   ✓ *A moving line (marquee) surrounds selected cell(s).*

4. Select cell(s) to receive data.

   ✓ *Click upper-left cell of destination range or select entire range of cells to receive data on current worksheet, another worksheet, or another workbook.*

Paste Data *(Ctrl+V)*

1. Click **Edit**..................... Alt +E

2. Click **Paste** .... P

OR

Click **Paste** button .

✓ *Press **Escape** key to remove marquee that surrounds original selected cell(s).*

✓ *If you paste formatting along with data and you don't want to do that, click the Paste Options button that appears and select the desired option.*

Paste Formula Result

1. Click arrow on **Paste** button
   [icon].
2. Select **Values**.

Copy Formula Using AutoFill

1. Select cell(s) to copy.
2. Point to fill handle.
   - ✓ *Mouse shape changes to crosshair.*
3. Drag fill handle across or down to adjacent cells to fill them.

Print Worksheet *(Ctrl+P)*

1. Select sheet(s) to print.
   - ✓ *To print a range of data instead of an entire sheet, select that range now.*
2. Click **File** .... [Alt]+[F]
3. Click **Print** .... [P]
4. Select appropriate print options.

OR

- Click **Print** button [icon].
  - ✓ *When you click the Print button on the Standard toolbar, the active worksheet is sent directly to the printer without displaying the Print dialog box.*

Print Preview a Worksheet

1. Click **File** .... [Alt]+[F]
2. Click **Print Preview** .... [V]

OR

Click **Print Preview** button [icon] on the toolbar.

3. Select options from the Print Preview toolbar.
4. Click **Close** button [Close] to close Print Preview.

Exercise Directions

1. Start Excel, if necessary.
2. Open [icon]**CASHTOPS** or open [icon] **09CASHTOPS**.
3. Save the file as **CASHTOPS**.
4. Select the range E13:F19.
5. Using the fill handle, copy the selection to the range G13:H19.
   - ✓ *Ignore the AutoFill Options box that appears.*
6. Change the data in column G to match the data shown in Illustration A.
7. In cell A21, type **Totals**.
   - ✓ *Notice that the formatting from cell A20 is copied automatically to cell A21. Excel repeats formatting from adjacent cells, on the assumption that's what you'll want nine times out of ten. You can, of course, modify this automatic formatting when needed to suit your own taste.*
8. Enter a formula in cell B21 that totals the sales for October.
9. Use the Copy and Paste buttons to copy this formula to cells C21, E21, and G21.
10. In cell A22, type **Grand Total**.
11. In cell B22, create a formula that totals the sales for October through January.
12. In cell A23, type **% of Grand Total**.

13. Type this formula in cell B23: **=B21/B22**.
14. Use the Copy and Paste buttons to copy this formula to cells C23, E23, and G23.
15. You've created an error because the relative cell addresses changed, and now Excel thinks you want to divide by zero. Change the original formula in cell B23 to read: **=B21/$B$22**.
    - ✓ *This change will cause each month's total to be divided by the grand total in cell B22, instead of some empty cell.*
16. Copy the formula again to cells C23, E23, and G23.
    - ✓ *Notice that this time, there is no error, because all the formulas divide that month's total by the grand total in cell B23.*
17. Apply Percent format, 3 decimal places, to cells B23, C23, E23 and G23.
18. Widen any columns as necessary.
19. Spell check the worksheet.
20. Preview the worksheet.
21. Print two copies of the completed worksheet.
    - ✓ *Each copy of the worksheet will print on two pages; in Exercise 20, you'll learn how to print the worksheet sideways on the paper, so that it prints on only one page.*
22. Close the workbook, saving all changes.

13		October	November	% Inc./Dec.	December	% Inc./Dec.	January	% Inc./Dec.
14	Red	$ 2,415	$ 2,694	11.553%	$ 2,421	-10.134%	$ 2,018	-16.646%
15	Lt. Blue	$ 3,108	$ 3,278	5.470%	$ 4,386	33.801%	$ 4,187	-4.537%
16	Brown	$ 978	$ 1,105	12.986%	$ 1,098	-0.633%	$ 955	-13.024%
17	Burnt Umber	$ 1,027	$ 1,594	55.209%	$ 1,655	3.827%	$ 1,459	-11.843%
18	Burgundy	$ 2,374	$ 3,497	47.304%	$ 4,297	22.877%	$ 4,299	0.047%
19	Cyan	$ 2,156	$ 3,387	57.096%	$ 4,092	20.815%	$ 3,975	-2.859%
20								
21	Totals	$ 12,058	$ 15,555		$ 17,949		$ 16,893	
22	Grand Total	$ 62,455						
23	% of Grand Total	19.307%	24.906%		28.739%		27.048%	

On Your Own

1. Open a new workbook in Excel.

2. Save the file as **OXL09**.

3. Imagine that you are general manager of CD Mania, a chain of music stores. Set up a worksheet showing the monthly sales for three stores in the first three months of the year.

4. In row 1, type a title for the worksheet.

5. Labels columns for: **Store**, **Jan**, **Feb**, and **Mar**.

6. List data for three different stores in the rows below the column labels. You can make up names for the stores, and sales totals.

   ✓ *For example, Store 1 might have had sales of $21,548 in January, $27,943 in February, and $25,418 in March.*

7. Apply the Accounting format, 2 decimal places, to the sales data.

8. In the row below the data for the third store, enter the label **Totals**.

9. In the Totals row for the Jan column, enter a formula to add the January sales for all three stores.

10. Copy the formula to the Totals row for Feb and Mar.

11. Add a column for the April sales data. Label the column **Apr**.

12. Copy the data for each store from the Jan column into the April column.

13. Copy the Totals formula from the Mar column to the Apr column.

14. Adjust the width of the columns so you can read all of the data in the worksheet.

15. Apply formatting such as font, font size, fill color, and text color changes to improve the appearance of the worksheet.

16. Spell check the workbook.

17. Preview then print the file.

18. Close the workbook, saving all changes.

Exercise 10

On the Job

After you create a worksheet, you may want to rearrange data or add additional information. For example, you may need to insert additional rows to a section of your worksheet because new employees have joined a department. With Excel's editing features, you can easily add, delete, and rearrange entire rows and columns. You can also move or drag and drop sections of the worksheet with ease.

As the head nurse at California Cardiology, Inc., it's your job to keep track of all the supplies, including the in-office pharmacy. You've designed a worksheet to help you perform a weekly inventory of the pharmacy. It still needs some work, but with Excel's powerful tools for inserting, deleting, and moving data, you'll be able to make changes quickly.

Terms

Cut The command used to remove data from a cell or range of cells and place it on the Clipboard.

Paste The command used to place data from the Clipboard to a location on the worksheet.

Drag-and-drop feature A method used to move or copy the contents of a range of cells by dragging the border of a selection from one location in a worksheet and dropping it in another location.

Notes

Insert and Delete Columns and Rows

- You can insert or delete columns or rows when necessary to change the arrangement of the data on the worksheet.

- When you insert column(s) into a worksheet, existing columns shift their position to the right.

  ✓ *For example, if you select column C and then insert two columns, the data that was in column C is shifted to the right, and becomes column E.*

- Likewise, if you insert row(s) into a worksheet, existing rows are shifted down to accommodate the newly inserted row(s).

  ✓ *For example, if you select row 8 and insert two rows, the data that was in row 8 is shifted down to row 10.*

- When you delete a column or row, existing columns and rows shift their positions to close the gap.

  ✓ *Any data in the rows or columns you select for deletion is erased.*

  ✓ *Data in existing columns is shifted back to the left to fill the gap left by deleted columns.*

  ✓ *In a similar manner, data in existing rows is shifted up to fill any gaps.*

- Instead of deleting columns or rows, you can hide them temporarily and then redisplay them as needed.

  ✓ *You might do this, for example, to hide data from a coworker who's not authorized to view it.*

Move Data (Cut/Paste)

- To move data from one location to another, you "cut" it out of the worksheet, then "paste" it in its new location.

- When you cut data from a location, it is temporarily stored on the Clipboard. That data is then copied from the Clipboard to the new location when you paste.

- If data already exists in the location you wish to paste to, Excel overwrites it.
  - Instead of overwriting data with the Paste command, you can insert the cut cells and have Excel shift cells with existing data down or to the right.

- To move data from one place in the worksheet to another, use the **Cut** and **Paste** commands from the Edit menu or the buttons on the Standard toolbar.

- When you move data, its format is moved as well.
  - ✓ You can override this and move just the data.

Drag-and-Drop Editing

- The **drag-and-drop feature** allows you to use the mouse to copy or move a range of cells simply by dragging them.

- The drag-and-drop process works like this: first, you select a range to copy or move, then you use the border surrounding the range to drag the data to a different location. When you release the mouse button, the data is "dropped" there.
  - ✓ An outline of the selection appears as you drag it to its new location on the worksheet.
  - ✓ Drag and drop normally moves data, but you can copy data instead by simply holding down the Ctrl key as you drag.

Example of drag-and-drop editing

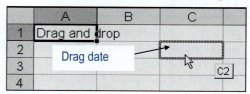

- Insert, delete, move, and copy operations may affect formulas, so you should check the formulas after you have made changes to be sure that they are correct.

- When a drag-and-drop action does not move data correctly, use the Undo feature to undo it.

Procedures

Insert Columns/Rows with Menu

1. Select as many adjacent columns or rows you need to insert.
   - ✓ Drag across column letters or row numbers to select entire column(s) or row(s).
2. Click **Insert**................ Alt + I
3. Click **Columns**.............. C
   OR
   Click **Rows**........................ R
   - ✓ New columns are inserted to the left of selected columns. New rows are inserted above selected rows.

Insert Columns/Rows with Mouse

1. Select as many adjacent columns or rows you need to insert.
   - ✓ Drag across column letters or row numbers to select entire column(s) or row(s).
2. Right-click selection.
3. Click **Insert**......................... I

Delete Columns/Rows with Menu

1. Select column(s) or row(s) to be removed.
2. Click **Edit**.................... Alt + E
3. Click **Delete**......................... D

Delete Columns/Rows with Mouse

1. Select column(s) or row(s) to be removed.
2. Right-click selection.
3. Click **Delete**........................ D

Hide Columns or Rows

1. Select the columns or rows you wish to hide.
2. Click **Format** .... Alt + F
3. Click **Column** C
   OR
   Click **Row** .... R
4. Click **Hide**........................... H

Unhide Columns or Rows

1. Select surrounding columns or rows.
2. Click **Format**...................... F
3. Click **Column**...................... C
   OR
   Click **Row** .... R
4. Click **Unhide**....................... U

Cut Data *(Ctrl+X)*

1. Select cell(s) to move.
2. Click **Edit** .... Alt + E
3. Click **Cut**............................. T
   OR
   Click **Cut** button ✂ .
   - ✓ A moving line (marquee) surrounds selected cell(s).
4. Select cell(s) to accept data.
   - ✓ You only need to select the top left cell of destination range. You can also move data to another worksheet or another workbook.

Paste Data (Ctrl+V)

1. Click **E**dit .... Alt + E
2. Click **P**aste.......................... P
   OR

   Click **Paste** button .
   ✓ *If you paste formatting along with data and you don't want to do that, click the Paste Options button that appears and select the desired option.*

Insert Data between Cells

1. Click **I**nsert .... Alt + I
2. Click C**e**lls........................... E
3. Click **Shift cells r**ight I
   OR

   Shift cells down .... D
4. Click OK.......................... Enter

Move Selection with Drag-and-Drop Editing

1. Select cell or range of cells to move.
2. Move mouse pointer to border of selection.

To move selection to destination cells and *overwrite* existing data:

a. Drag selection outline to new location.
b. Release mouse button.
c. Click OK. .... Enter

To move selection to destination cells and *insert* between existing data:

a. Press **Shift** while dragging selection outline to column or row gridline .... Shift
   ✓ *If you drag outline to column gridline, existing data shifts right. If you drag outline to a row gridline, existing data shifts down.*
b. Release mouse button and then Shift key.

Copy Selection with Drag-and-Drop Editing

1. Select cell or range of cells to copy.
2. Move mouse pointer to border of selection.

To copy selection to destination cells and *overwrite* existing data:

a. Press **Ctrl** while dragging selection outline to column or row gridline .... Ctrl
b. Release **Ctrl** key, then mouse button.

To copy selection to destination cells and *insert* between existing data:

a. Press **Ctrl+Shift** and drag selection outline to column or row gridline .... Ctrl + Shift
   ✓ *If you drag the outline to column gridline, existing cells shift right. If you drag outline to row gridline, existing cells shift down.*
b. Release mouse button, then **Ctrl** and **Shift** keys.

Exercise Directions

1. Start Excel, if necessary.
2. Open 💿 **10DRUGINV**.
3. Save the file as **DRUGINV**.
4. Type today's date in cell C5.
5. Insert two columns between columns E and F. Label the columns **Additions** and **Total**.
6. Since you received a shipment of some drugs during this period, type the following amounts in the Additions column, in the appropriate cells:
   • Dozehnaze: **200**
   • Mycolex: **350**
   • Zybox: **750**
7. To add a new drug, insert a row between rows 12 and 13.
   a. Type the label **Silease** in cell D13.
   b. In the Additions column for Silease, type **975**.
8. In cell G8, type a formula to calculate the total inventory on hand for the current period.
   ✓ *Take the previous count and add the additions that occurred during the period.*
9. Copy this formula to cells G9:G15.
10. Type these current inventory amounts in the appropriate cells in column H (Current Count):
    • Blador: **97**, Clumins: **203**, Clear All: **71**
    • Dozehnaze: **112**, Mycolex: **207**
    • Silease: **764**, Tempour: **57**, Zybox: **684**
11. In cell I8, type a formula that calculates the amount of Blador used during the period.
    ✓ *Take the Total for Blador minus the Current Count.*
    ✓ *Copy this formula to the range I9:I15*
12. Using the Cut and Paste buttons, move the contents of cells D7:I15 to the range beginning with cell D5.
13. Using drag and drop, move the contents of cells B3:D3 to the range F3:H3.
14. Widen columns, as necessary.
15. Spell check the worksheet.
16. Print the worksheet.
17. Close the file, saving all changes.

	A	B	C	D	E	F	G	H	I
1				California Cardiology, Inc.					
2									
3						Pharmacy Inventory			
4									
5		Date:	12/1/2000	Drug	Previous Count	Additions	Total	Current Count	Used
6				Blador	205		205	97	108
7				Clumins	312		312	203	109
8				Clear All	115		115	71	44
9				Dozehnaze	96	200	296	112	184
10				Mycolex	74	350	424	207	217
11				Silease		975	975	764	211
12				Tempour	187		187	57	130
13				Zybox	205	750	955	684	271
14									

On Your Own

1. Open the file **OXL09**, created in the On Your Own section of Exercise 9, or open ⊚ **10CDMANIA**.

2. Save the file as **OXL10**.

3. Insert two new rows above the Totals row, and enter sales data for two new stores.

4. Insert a column between March and April, and label the column **Qtr 1**.

5. In the Qtr 1 column, type formulas to total the first quarter sales (January through March) for each store.

6. Where the Totals row and the Qtr 1 column meet, type a formula that calculates the grand total for Qtr 1.

7. Using drag and drop, copy the store names (and the Store and Totals labels) to an area a few rows below the sales data—but in the same column.

   ✓ *You're creating a duplicate sales area below the current area that will eventually store the sales amounts for the second quarter—April, May, and June.*

8. Using Cut and Paste, move the April column totals to this new sales area, below the data for January.

9. Add labels for **May**, **June**, and **Qtr 2** in the columns to the right of the April column.

10. In the Qtr 2 column, type formulas to total the second quarter sales (May through June) for each store.

11. Spell check the workbook.

12. Print the worksheet.

13. Close the workbook, saving all changes.

Exercise 11

Skills Covered:

◆ **Work with Worksheets**

◆ **Group Sheets** ◆ **Format Sheets**

On the Job

Use workbook sheets to organize your reports. For example, instead of entering the data for an entire year on one worksheet, use multiple worksheets to represent each month's data. Excel gives you the freedom to add, delete, move and even rename your worksheets so you can keep a complex workbook organized. In addition, you can group multiple sheets and work on them simultaneously and quickly format an entire worksheet in one step.

You're the owner of an organic food chain called Golden Harvest, and you've asked Murray Hill Marketing to create a marketing campaign for you. They need to see your survey on people's buying habits, which you happen to have in Excel format. Before you print the survey for them, however, you want to add formatting and make a few adjustments.

Terms

Grouping Worksheets that are selected as a unit; any action performed on this unit will affect all the worksheets in the group.

Active sheet tab The selected worksheet; the tab name of an active sheet is bold.

Notes

Work with Worksheets

- The default workbook window contains three sheets named Sheet1 through Sheet3.

- The sheet tab displays the name of the sheet.

- Right-click a sheet tab to display a shortcut menu that allows you to insert, delete, rename move, and copy worksheets. You can also change the color of a worksheet's tab.

- You do not need to delete unused sheets from a workbook since they do not take up much room in the file; however, if you plan on sharing the file, you may want to remove unused sheets to create a more professional look.

- Renaming sheets and coloring sheet tabs make it easier to keep track of the data on individual sheets.

Sheet tab shortcut menu

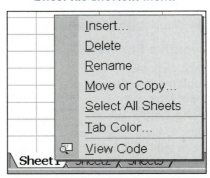

- Moving sheets allows you to place them in a logical order within the workbook.

- When you copy a worksheet, you copy all of its data and formatting. However, changes you later make to the copied sheet do not affect the original sheet.

333

- If you change the color of a sheet tab, that color appears when the tab is not selected. When a colored sheet tab is clicked, its color changes to white, with a small line of its original color at the bottom of the tab.
  - ✓ For example, an orange sheet tab changes to white with a thin orange line at the bottom when it is selected.

Group Sheets

- If you want to work on several worksheets simultaneously, select multiple worksheets and create a **grouping**.
- Grouped sheet tabs appear white when selected, and the name of the **active sheet tab** appears in bold.
- When you select a grouping, any editing, formatting, or new entries you make to the active sheet are simultaneously made to all the sheets in the group.

- ✓ For example, you can select a group of sheets and format, move, copy, or delete them in one step. You can also add, delete, change, or format the same entries into the same cells on every selected worksheet.
- ✓ Remember to deselect the grouping when you no longer want to make changes to all the sheets in the group.

Format Sheets

- One way in which you can quickly give your worksheets a professional look is to format them using AutoFormat.
- Using AutoFormat saves you time, because you won't have to format the column labels, row labels, and data manually.
- After you select an AutoFormat, Excel applies that format throughout the worksheet.
- You can select only part of an AutoFormat's attributes to apply.
  - ✓ For example, you could apply just the number formats and fonts, but not the alignments, patterns, borders, widths, and heights.

Procedures

Select One Sheet

1. If necessary, click tab scrolling buttons to view hidden sheet tabs.
2. Click sheet tab to select it.

Select All Sheets

1. Right-click any sheet tab.
2. Select **S**elect **All Sheets**............. , Enter

Select Consecutive Sheets

1. If necessary, click tab scrolling buttons to view hidden sheet tabs.
2. Click first sheet tab in group.
3. If necessary, to view additional hidden sheet tabs click tab scrolling buttons.
4. Press **Shift** and click last sheet tab in group.
   - ✓ The word [Group] appears in the title bar.

Select Nonconsecutive Sheets

1. If necessary, click tab scrolling buttons to view hidden sheet tabs.
2. Click first sheet tab in group.
3. If necessary, to view additional hidden sheet tabs click tab scrolling buttons.
4. Press **Ctrl** and click each subsequent sheet tab to be included in group.
   - ✓ The word [Group] appears in the title and task bars.

Ungroup Sheets

1. Right-click any sheet tab in group.
2. Click **U**ngroup Sheets........ U

OR

- Click any sheet tab not in group.

Delete Sheet(s)

1. Select sheet tab(s).
2. Right-click sheet tab.
3. Click **D**elete......................... D
4. Click **Delete** to confirm deletion of a sheet with data .... Enter

Rename Sheet

1. Double-click sheet tab.
   OR
   a. Right-click sheet tab.
   b. Select **R**ename.............. R
2. Type new name.
3. Press **Enter** .... Enter

Insert Sheet(s)

1. Select number of sheet tabs as sheets to be inserted.
2. Right-click sheet tab.
   - ✓ The new sheets will be inserted before the first sheet in the group.
3. Click **I**nsert I
4. Select **General tab** of Insert dialog box .... Ctrl + Tab
5. Select **Worksheet** ....
6. Click **OK**.......................... Enter

Move Sheet(s) within Workbook

1. If necessary, click tab scrolling buttons to view hidden sheet tabs.

2. Click and drag selected sheet tab(s) to new sheet tab position.

   ✓ *Mouse pointer shape changes to* 🔲. *Black triangle indicates where sheet will be inserted.*

Copy Sheet

1. If necessary, click tab scrolling buttons to view hidden sheet tabs.

2. Select sheet tab.

3. Press and hold **Ctrl**, as you click and drag selected sheet tab to its final position.

   ✓ *Mouse pointer shape changes to* 🔲 *with a plus sign. Black triangle indicates where sheet will be inserted.*

✓ *To copy multiple sheets at once, select them, then choose **Edit, Move** or **Copy Sheet**. Select a location to place the copies from the Move or Copy dialog box, choose **Create a copy**, and then click **OK**.*

Change Tab Color

1. Select the sheet tab(s) you wish to make the same color.

2. Right-click sheet tab in group.

3. Click **Tab Color**................... `T`

4. Select a color .... `↗↓`

5. Click **OK** .... `Enter`

   ✓ *You can remove the color on a tab by repeating these steps and choosing **No Color** in step 4.*

Use AutoFormat

1. Select the data range you want to format, or select multiple ranges if you like.

✓ *You can format the exact same range on multiple sheets by positioning the cursor within the data range, and selecting the tabs of the sheets you want to format.*

2. Click **Format**............... `Alt`+`O`

3. Click **AutoFormat** .... `A`

4. Select the format you want to apply.................... `↗↓`

5. To apply only selected parts of the format, click **Options** ..... `O`

6. From the expanded dialog box, select only the formats you want to apply:

   a. **Number** .... `N`

   b. **Border** .... `B`

   c. **Font** .... `F`

   d. **Patterns** .... `P`

   e. **Alignment** .... `A`

   f. **Width/Height** .... `W`

7. Click **OK** .... `Enter`

Exercise Directions

1. Start Excel if necessary.

2. Open 💿 **11ORGANIC**.

3. Save the file as **ORGANIC**.

4. Rename Sheet 1 **Frequency**. Rename Sheet 2 **Users**. Rename Sheet 3 **Buying Habits - Men**.

5. Make a copy of the Buying Habits – Men sheet, and place the copy in front of that sheet.

   a. Rename the copied sheet **Buying Habits – Women**.

   b. Change the percentages to match those shown in Illustration A.

   c. Change cell D9 to **Women**.

6. Move the Users worksheet in front of the Frequency sheet.

7. Insert a new worksheet in front of Users worksheet, and rename it **Basic Survey Info**.

8. Select the two Buying Habits worksheets to form a group.

9. Color the tabs of the worksheets in that group a light yellow.

10. Select the remaining worksheets, and color their tabs a light green.

11. Delete Sheet 4, since it contains duplicate data.

12. Group the two Buying Habits Worksheets.

13. Click cell C11 of the Buying Habits – Women worksheet, select the other Buying Habits worksheet, and apply the Colorful 2 AutoFormat.

14. Apply the Colorful 1 AutoFormat to the two Users and Frequency sheets.

   ✓ *Because the data on the Users and Frequency sheets is not laid out exactly the same, you must apply the AutoFormat to each sheet individually, by clicking within the data range and selecting the AutoFormat you want. You can't apply an AutoFormat to the Basic Survey Info sheet, since it does not contain any data.*

15. Select all four sheets, and apply these formats to the following ranges:

   ✓ *If you do not have these exact same fonts, choose your own, using Illustration A as an example.*

   a. D4:F4—Architect, 14, bold, tan fill

   b. D6:D7—Architect, 10, bold, tan fill

   c. E6—Light yellow fill

   d. E7:I7—Light yellow fill

16. Select the two Buying Habits worksheets, and apply Architect, 10, bold, tan fill to cell D9.

17. Adjust column widths as needed to fully display data.

18. Spell check the workbook.

19. Print the entire workbook.

20. Close the file, saving all changes.

Illustration A

Marketing Survey

Date:	8/21/2001						
Topic:	What types of organic foods do you buy?						

Women

	Fruits	Vegetables	Meats	Cheese	Eggs	Milk Products
Under 25	28%	32%	14%	18%	7%	1%
26-32	22%	42%	19%	8%	6%	3%
33-40	28%	41%	9%	5%	12%	5%
41-45	21%	38%	21%	2%	11%	7%
46-55	21%	24%	37%	2%	12%	4%
Over 55	18%	22%	48%	5%	5%	2%

Basic Survey Info / Users / Frequency \ Buying Habits - Women / Bu

On Your Own

1. Open a new workbook in Excel.

2. Save the file as **OXL11**.

3. Set up a worksheet for tracking weekly income.

   ✓ *For this exercise, assume that you receive income from a part-time job, along with a weekly allowance. Also, you've decided to sell some old CDs, so record the sales from that effort. In addition, your birthday falls during week 3 of this month, and you usually receive money gifts from several relatives.*

4. Delete Sheet 2 and Sheet 3.

5. On Sheet 1, enter a title for the worksheet in row 2.

6. Label columns B through H for the days of the week.

7. In the rows in column A, list your sources of income: **Job**, **Allowance**, **CD sales**, and **Gifts**.

8. Copy Sheet 1 three times, to create four worksheets.

9. Label the four sheets: **Week 1, Week 2, Week 3,** and **Week 4** respectively. Assign a unique color to each week's tab.

10. Enter data in all three worksheets. You may or may not have income for each day, or for each category (job, allowance, CD sales, or gifts).

11. Group the worksheets and enter formulas to calculate the total income for each category as well as for each day of the week.

    ✓ *Label the column and row where the results are displayed correctly.*

    ✓ *Select the data and totals, and apply the numeric format of your choice.*

12. Select the data range of one sheet, then group the worksheets and apply the AutoFormat of your choice—but do not apply the AutoFormat's Number format.

13. Spell check the workbook.

14. Print the entire workbook.

15. Close the file, saving all changes.

Exercise 12

◆ Critical Thinking

You're the invoice clerk for California Cardiology, Inc., and one of the insurance companies you work with has asked for a detailed summary of their client's initial bills, payments made, and overdue amounts. Since you need to summarize several months' worth of data, you'll place each month's unpaid invoices on a separate worksheet. You'll add formulas, formatting, insert sheets, and make several other changes before you're finished.

Exercise Directions

1. Start Excel, if necessary.

2. Open ⌨**OVERDUE** or 💿**12OVERDUE**.

3. Save the file as **OVERDUE**.

4. Apply the Classic 2 AutoFormat to the range B7:E10.

5. Add additional formatting:
   a. B8:B10—Right alignment.
   b. B12:B14 and A16:B16—Arial, 9 pt., violet fill, white text color, and adjust column widths as necessary.
   c. C8:C16—Currency format, 2 decimal places, and adjust column widths as necessary.
   d. B3:E3—Copperplate Gothic Bold, 14, pale blue fill.
   e. B5:E5—Arial, 11 pt., italic, light turquoise fill.

6. Make a copy of Sheet 1 and place that copy in front of Sheet 2.
   a. Rename Sheet 1 **April** and color its tab red.
   b. Rename Sheet 1 (2) **May** and color its tab blue.
   c. Delete Sheet 2 and Sheet 3.
   d. On the April sheet, change cell B5 to **Healthman HMO -- April Overdue Invoices**.
   e. On the May sheet, change cell B5 to **Healthman HMO – May Overdue Invoices**.

7. Select both worksheets.
   a. Insert two columns in front of column C.
   b. In cell C7, type **Original Amount**.
   c. In cell D7, type **Current Amount**.
   d. Change cell E7 to **% of Monthly Total**, and adjust the column width so all the text is visible.
   e. Using drag and drop, move the data in E8:E10 to D8:D10.
   f. Using Cut and Paste, move the data in E12:E16 to C12:C16.
   g. Select D12:D16, and remove the color fill.

8. With the sheets still selected, type a formula in cell E8 that computes the percentage of the total overdue amount (cell C14) the current amount due (cell D8) represents.
   ✓ In other words, how much of the total, $3,881.27, does the amount $2,147.48 represent? Is it 50%? 60%? Or something even higher?
   ✓ To calculate the percent, take the smaller number and divide by the bigger number.
   ✓ Since you want all the formulas to use the reference, C14, you'll need to make it an absolute cell address in the original formula.

9. Copy this formula to E9:E10, and apply Percent, 3 decimal place format.

10. Ungroup the worksheets, change to the April worksheet, and enter the following Original Amounts:
    a. J. Thomas Wilson: **$3,218.48**
    b. Carlos Riveria: **$375.97**
    c. Alice Thomson: **$4,893.21**
    d. Format the cells as currency with two decimals.

11. Change the information on the May worksheet to match Illustration A.
    ✓ Tell Excel to ignore the error that appears after you enter the invoice numbers as text.

12. Add a sheet after the May sheet, label it **Summary,** and color its tab yellow.

    a. Type the information shown in Illustration B.

    b. Copy the Current amount due and the Amount due if paid after 5/16 or 6/16 for April and May, and paste them in their appropriate spots on the Summary sheet as shown. Be sure to copy the values and number formats, and not the formulas.

    c. Apply the Classic 2 AutoFormat to the range B6:D8, and adjust the column widths as necessary.

    d. Apply Arial, 11 pt., italic, light turquoise fill to the range B4:E4.

    e. Apply Arial, 9 pt., right-align, violet fill, white text color to cell B10.

13. Adjust column widths to fit the data.

14. Spell check the workbook.

15. Preview each sheet, and print the workbook.

16. Close the file, saving all changes.

Illustration A

	A	B	C	D	E	F	G
1							
2							
3			CALIFORNIA CARDIOLOGY, INC.				
4							
5		Healthman HMO -- May Overdue Invoices					
6							
7		Patient	Original Amount	Current Amount	% of Monthly Total	Invoice Number	Date Due
8		Henry Lee	$4,975.65	$4,975.65	57.733%	2189558	5/15/2001
9		Sendal Gundra	$2,497.86	$2,497.86	28.983%	219776	5/15/2001
10		Alice Thomson	$4,893.21	$975.86	11.323%	2049462	4/21/2001
11							
12		Overdue amount:	$8,449.37				
13		Late charge:	$168.99				
14		Current amount due:	$8,618.36				
15							
16		Amount due if paid after 6/16:	$8,790.72				

Illustration B

	A	B	C	D	E
1					
2					
3					
4		Overdue Amounts for Healthman HMO - Summary			
5					
6			Current	If Paid Late	
7		April Overdue Amount	$3,881.27	$3,958.90	
8		May Overdue Amount	$8,618.36	$8,790.72	
9					
10		Grand Totals	$12,499.63	$12,749.62	
11					
12					
13					
14					
15					
16					

April / May / Summary /

Exercise 13

On the Job

Use an Excel function to help you write a formula to perform specific calculations in your worksheets. Excel's Paste Function feature provides a list of available functions with a wizard to assist you in "filling in the blanks" to complete a formula.

You work for Murray Hill Marketing, and you've just been assigned the account for Dan's Digital Camera Works, a new store that sells digital cameras exclusively. They are concerned about the competition, and they've asked you to create a report that lists the number of digital cameras sold and dollar sales by their four competitors for the last three years. You need to perform some analysis of this information, calculating averages, minimums, and maximums.

Terms

Function A predefined formula that depends on specific values to perform a specific calculation.

Function name The name given to Excel's predefined formulas.

Argument Part of a formula that contains the specific values necessary to perform the function.

Nest To insert a function into another function.

AutoCalculate A feature that temporarily performs the following calculations on a range of cells without making you write a formula: Average, Count, Count Nums, Max, Min, or Sum.

Notes

Use Functions

- Excel provides built-in formulas called **functions** to perform special calculations.
- A function contains these elements in the following order:
  - The equal symbol (=) starts the function.
  - The **function name** is entered in upper- or lowercase letters.
  - An open parenthesis separates the **arguments** from the function name.
  - The argument(s) identify the data required to perform the function.

- A closed parenthesis ends the argument.

  Example: =SUM(A1:A40)

  ✓ *This sum function adds the values listed in the argument, which in this case is a single range of cells A1 through A40.*

- Most functions allow multiple arguments, separated by commas.

  ✓ *For example, =SUM(A1:A40,C1:C40) adds the values in the ranges A1:A40 and C1:C40.*

- A function may be inserted into a formula.

  ✓ *For example, =B2/SUM(C3:C5)*

- When a function is used as an argument for other functions, it is **nested** within those functions.

Common Functions

- You'll find these functions to be the ones you use most often:
  - =SUM( ) adds the values in a range of cells.
  - =AVERAGE( ) returns the arithmetic mean of the values in a range of cells.
  - =COUNT( ) counts the cells containing numbers in a range of cells (blank cells or text entries are ignored).
  - =MAX( ) finds the highest value in a range of cells.
  - =MIN( ) finds the lowest value in a range of cells.
  - =ROUND( ) adjusts a value to a specific number of digits.

    ✓ *When a cell is formatted to a specified number of decimal places, only the display of that value is affected. The actual value in the cell is still used in all calculations. For example, if a cell contains the value 13.45687, and you decide to display only the last two decimal places, then the value 13.46 will display in the cell, but the value, 13.45687 will be used in all calculations.*

    ✓ *Let's say you have a long column of numbers such as this:*

    Sales Projections
    2147.8347
    2866.1633
    2593.0049
    Total: 7607.0029

    You're not interested in the extra digits past a penny, so you simply change the formatting, and the numbers appear like this:

    Sales Projections
    2147.83
    2866.16
    2593.00
    Total: 7607.00

    ✓ *So, if you plan on displaying a limited number of decimal places and not the whole number, you might want to use the ROUND function to adjust each value so that the displayed value is equal to the actual value used in calculations.*

    ✓ *For example, use the ROUND function to round the value 2147.8347 to 2147.8400, like this:*

Sales Projections
2147.8400
2866.1600
2593.0000
Total: 7607.0000

If you then display only two decimal places, the total will display correctly:

Sales Projections
2147.84
2866.16
2593.00
Total: 7607.00

✓ *Of course, if you are interested in every digit of the calculated sales projections, then display them fully so that your totals will add up.*

- Use the drop-down arrow on AutoSum button Σ ▾ on the Standard toolbar to quickly insert a SUM, AVERAGE, COUNT, MIN, or MAX function.

Insert a Function

- You can enter a function by typing it, or you can use the Insert Function dialog box to help you locate a specific function and enter the correct arguments.

- To insert a function instead of typing it, click the Insert Function button *fx* on the Formula bar; then type a brief description of the function you want help with (or type its name).

  ✓ *You can also display functions by category by choosing one from the Or select a category list.*

  ✓ *When you enter a formula using Insert Function, Excel automatically enters the equal sign in the formula.*

- After selecting a function, you're prompted to enter the appropriate arguments into a second dialog box—Function Arguments.
  - You can select cells instead of typing them by using the Collapse Dialog button located at the right of each text box.
  - Required arguments are displayed in bold.
  - As you enter the arguments, the value of that argument is displayed to the right of the text box.
  - Excel calculates the current result and displays it at the bottom of the dialog box.

- If you need help understanding a particular function's arguments, click the Help on this function link.

Insert Function dialog box

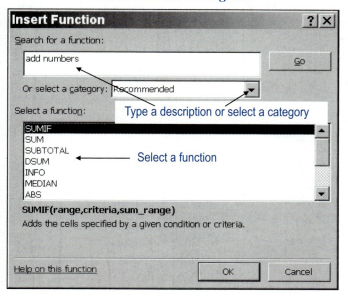

Function Arguments dialog box

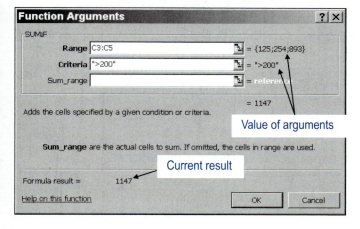

AutoCalculate

- When you want to quickly calculate the Average, Count, Count Nums, Max, Min, or Sum for a range of cells on your worksheet, without actually entering a formula, use **AutoCalculate**.

- Using the mouse, drag across a range of cells to display the auto calculation (default is SUM) on the Status bar.

- To use a different function with AutoCalculate, right-click the AutoCalculate result on the Status bar and pick from the list of functions.

AutoCalculate function list

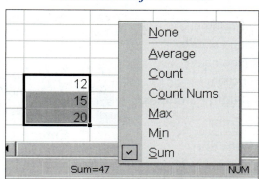

Procedures

Enter a Function Manually

1. Click cell where result should display .... ⬍
2. Type **Equal** .... =
3. Type function name.
4. Type **Left Parenthesis** ...... (
5. Enter arguments, separated by commas.
   You can enter:
   - Numeric value
   - Cell reference
   - Range of cells
   - Range name
   - Function
6. Press **Right Parenthesis** ...)
7. Press **Enter** .... Enter

Insert a Function

1. Click cell where result should display .... ⬍
2. Click **Insert Function** button ƒx.
   OR
   a. Click **I**nsert .... Alt + I
   b. Click **F**unction .... F
3. Type the function name or a brief description in the **S**earch for a function text box .... Alt + S
   OR
   Select category from **O**r select a **c**ategory list .... Alt + C , ⬍
4. Select function from **S**elect a functio**n** list ..... Alt + N , ⬍
5. Click **OK** .... Enter
   ✓ *The Function Arguments dialog box appears.*
6. Click argument text box ...... Tab

---

7. Type data.
   You can enter:
   - Numeric value
   - Cell reference
   - Range of cells
   - Range name
   - Function
   ✓ *To enter a cell reference or range of cells from the worksheet, click the Collapse button located to the right of the argument text box, select the cell(s), and then click the Collapse button again to expand the dialog box.*
8. Repeat steps 6 and 7 to complete arguments.
9. Click **OK** .... Enter

Enter a Common Function

1. Click cell where result should display .... ⬍
2. To enter SUM function, click **AutoSum** button Σ ▾ .
   OR
   To enter AVERAGE, COUNT, MAX, or MIN function, click the arrow on **AutoSum** button Σ ▾ and select the function you want.
   ✓ *Excel guesses the range you want to use with the function you selected.*
3. If the selected range is not the one you want to use, select the range you want by dragging over it with the mouse.
4. Press **Enter** .... Enter
   ✓ *You can display the Insert Function dialog box to enter any function by selecting **More Functions** from the AutoSum list.*

Edit a Function

1. Click result cell .... ⬍
2. Click in Formula bar.
3. Type correction.
   OR
   a. Click **Insert Function** button ƒx on Formula bar to redisplay Formula Arguments dialog box.
   b. Click argument text box.
   c. Type correction.
4. Click **OK** .... Enter

Enter a Function into a Formula

1. Click formula cell .... ⬍ where answer will display.
2. Type **Equal** .... =
3. Type the beginning part of the formula.
4. At the point in the formula where you wish to use a function, type the function name.
5. Type **Left Parenthesis** .... (
6. Type arguments(s).
7. Type **Right Parenthesis** .....)
8. Press **Enter** .... Enter

Use AutoCalculate

1. Select cells .... Shift + ⬍ you want to calculate.
2. View result of calculation on Status bar.
3. Right-click result.
4. Click desired function in list .... ⬍ , Enter

Exercise Directions

1. Start Excel, if necessary.
2. Open ✪ **13COMPETE**.
3. Save the file as **COMPETE**.
4. In cell G6, use the AutoSum button to enter a formula that calculates the total digital cameras sold over the last three years by Mike's Camera World.
5. Copy this formula to cells G9, G12, and G15.
   - ✓ Since you do not want to replace the formatting of the destination cells, you'll need to paste each cell one at a time, then select the Paste Option, Match Destination Formatting.
6. In cell G7, use the Insert Function button to enter a formula that calculates the total digital camera sales for Mike's Camera World.
7. Copy this formula to cells G10, G13, and G16. Do not overlay the formatting already in those cells.
8. In cell C20, use the AutoSum button to enter a formula that calculates the average number of units sold per year by all the competitors.
   - ✓ You'll need to select each of the 12 cells that contain units sold data. (Do not select the four cells that contain total units sold.) You can calculate the average of a group of ranges by entering them as separate arguments, with a comma between each one. Just press **Ctrl** and click each range.
9. In cell C21, use the Insert Function button to enter a function that calculates the average sales of the competitors' combined sales.
   - ✓ Again, select the 12 cells that contain the yearly sales data, not the total sales cells.
10. In cell C22, use the AutoSum button to enter a formula that calculates the minimum number of units sold during any one year by any competitor.
11. In cell C23, use the Insert Function button to enter a formula that calculates the maximum number of units sold during any one year by any competitor.
12. Widen any columns as necessary.
13. Use AutoCalculate to check your results.
    - ✓ Remember that to select non-contiguous ranges, press Ctrl and drag over each range. The sum of the selected ranges appears in the Status bar. To view the results using other functions (such as AVERAGE), right-click the word **Sum** on the Status bar and select a different function.
14. Spell check the worksheet.
15. Print the worksheet.
16. Close the file, saving all changes.

Illustration A

	A	B	C	D	E	F	G
2		**Murray Hill Marketing, LLC**					
3		*Survey of the Competition*					
5				1999	2000	2001	Totals
6		Mike's Camera World	Units Sold	632	2741	4595	7968
7			Sales	$ 287,000	$1,507,550	$2,986,750	$4,781,300
9		Enriz Photo	Units Sold	331	521	978	1830
10			Sales	$ 331,000	$ 208,400	$ 489,000	$1,028,400
12		Digital Den	Units Sold	1247	3125	4388	8760
13			Sales	$1,247,000	$1,953,125	$2,961,900	$6,162,025
15		Photos by Perez	Units Sold	681	756	1033	2470
16			Sales	$ 681,000	$ 378,000	$ 593,975	$1,652,975
18	**Summary**						
20		Average Units Sold each Year	1752.33333				
21		Average Sales each Year	$1,135,392				
22	Minimum Units Sold by Any Competitor in One Yr.		331				
23	Maximum Units Sold by Any Competitor in One Yr.		4595				

On Your Own

1. Open the **OXL10** file you created in the On Your Own section of Exercise 10, or open ⊘ **13CDMANIA**.

2. Save the file as **OXL13**.

3. Enter May and June sales data for each store.

4. Use the AutoSum button to enter formulas that calculate sales totals for May and June.

5. Apply Accounting Style, 2 decimal places, to the sales data and totals.

6. Widen any columns as needed.

7. Beginning in row 20, create a summary section that includes the following:

   a. In row 20, type the word **Summary**.

   b. In row 22, beginning in column B, enter the name of the months, January through June.

   c. In column A, beginning in row 23, type the labels **Average Sales**, **Maximum Sales by Any Store**, and **Minimum Sales by Any Store**.

   d. In row 23, enter formulas that calculate the average sales for each month—January through June.

   e. In row 24, enter formulas that display the sales total of the store that sold the most for that month.

   f. In row 25, enter formulas to display the total for the store that sold the least that month.

   g. In cell A27, type the label **Total number of times sales were over $25,000**.

   h. In cell B27, enter a formula that calculates the total number of times any store sold more than $25,000 in any given month.

      ✓ To calculate this, you'll need to use the COUNTIF function. Because COUNTIF only counts the valid cells in one range, you'll need to use two COUNTIF functions in one formula and add their results together.

      ✓ To use COUNTIF, select the range you want to analyze, then type the condition you want to compare against—which in this case, is >25000, which means "greater than 25000."

8. Use the AutoCalculate function to check the formula results.

9. Spell check the worksheet.

10. Apply formatting as you like, and print the worksheet.

11. Close the file, saving all changes.

Exercise 14

Skills Covered:
◆ **Natural Language Formulas** ◆ **Comments**

On the Job

Write natural language formulas and add comments to your worksheet to help you read the formulas or remember why you included certain information in your worksheet.

You're the Detroit plant manager for Electron Consumer Industries, and you've been asked to prepare a report detailing the sales of the company's new computer chip for automobiles, the Super G 2001. You've got a lot of data to summarize, so you weren't looking forward to entering a lot of tedious formulas—until you discovered Excel's natural language formula option. Using real words like "Ford" and "GMC" with Excel's SUM and AVERAGE functions will make the task of entering proper totals easier. When you're through, you'll use the Comment feature to add some notes that will help your boss interpret the data.

Terms

Natural language formula A formula that refers to column or row heading labels instead of a cell reference or range.

Comment A text note attached to a worksheet cell.

Notes

Natural Language Formulas

■ Excel allows you to create **natural language formulas** that refer to column and row labels in place of the cell reference or range.

✓ *When "natural language" is used in a formula the column or row label must be spelled exactly as the column or row label appears.*

■ For example, =SUM(Jan) totals the range of cells in the Jan column that are located either above or to the left of the formula.

Column heading in a natural language formula

	A	B	C
1	Jan	Feb	Mar
2	1500	1700	1500
3	600	1300	1000
4	800	1200	900
5	=SUM(Jan)	=SUM(Feb)	=SUM(Mar)

■ If you've used a label more than once in a worksheet, Excel may ask you to select the label to which you're referring in your natural language formula.

Identify Label dialog box

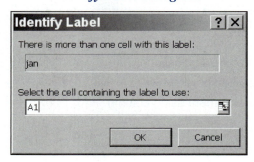

■ To use natural language formulas, you must first turn on that option on the Calculations tab of the Options dialog box, as explained in the Procedures.

Comments

- To attach a text note to a cell (maximum of 255 characters), use the Insert Comment command.

- A red triangle appears in the upper-right corner of any cell with an attached **comment**.

- To display the comment, simply rest the mouse pointer on the comment indicator (the red triangle).

- Comments help explain data, formulas, and labels used in a complex worksheet. You can insert comments as reminders to yourself, but they are especially useful for explaining a worksheet shared with others.

Comment displayed on worksheet

	A	B	C
1	Jan	Feb	Mar
2	1500	1700	1500
3	600	1300	1000
4	800	1300	900
5	=SUM(Jan)	**Jennifer Fulton:** This cell uses a natural language formula.	(Mar)
6			
7			
8			

- If you want, you can display all the comments on a worksheet with a single command.

Procedures

The following option must be checked for natural language formulas to work within a particular workbook:

1. Click **T**ools .... Alt + T
2. Click **O**ptions .... O
3. Click **Calculation** tab ... Ctrl + Tab
4. Select **Accept la**b**els in formulas** option .... B
5. **Click OK** .... Enter

Create Natural Language Formula

1. Click formula cell .... where answer will display.
2. Press equal symbol .... =
3. Type name of function.
4. Type open parenthesis .... (
5. Type argument using column or row labels instead of cell reference or range.
6. Type close parenthesis ....)
7. Press **Enter** .... Enter

Create Comment

1. Select cell to attach comment.
2. Click **I**nsert .... Alt + I
3. Click Co**m**ment .... M
4. Type text.
   ✓ *Note that handles appear around the box to resize or move it.*
5. Click outside box.
   ✓ *A red triangle now displays in the upper-right corner of the comment cell.*

Display Comment

- Move mouse pointer over cell that contains a comment.
   ✓ *Comment appears in a small yellow box beside the cell.*
   ✓ *To display all comments in a worksheet, choose **View**, **Comments**. Select **View**, **Comments** again to get rid of them.*

Edit Comment

1. Right-click cell with comment.
2. Click **E**dit **Comment** .... E
3. Make correction.
   ✓ *Drag a handle to increase or decrease the size of the box.*
4. Click outside of box.

Delete Comment

1. Right-click cell with comment.
2. Click **Delete Co**m**ment** .... M

Exercise Directions

1. Start Excel, if necessary.

2. Open 💿 **14CHIPSALES**.

3. Save the file as **CHIPSALES**.

4. Turn on the natural language feature for this workbook.

5. In cell C16, use the SUM function to create a natural language formula that calculates the total sales for April.

6. Use the fill handle to copy this formula to cells D16:E16.

   ✓ Notice that Excel creates a series from your formula. For example, in cell D16, Excel creates the formula, =SUM(May) and does not simply copy the formula =SUM(April) from cell C16.

7. In cell C17, use the AVERAGE function to create a natural language formula that calculates the average sales for April.

8. Copy this formula to cells D17:E17.

9. In cell F10, use the SUM function to create a natural language formula that calculates the total sales for the quarter to GMC.

10. Copy this formula to cell F11:F14.

11. Add a comment to cells E11 and E13 that indicates that these figures are not the final ones.

12. Using the mouse, view the comments one at a time.

13. Using the View, Comments command, display all the comments.

14. Delete the comment in cell E13.

15. Spell check the worksheet.

16. Print the worksheet.

17. Close the file, saving all changes.

Illustration A

	A	B	C	D	E	F	
1							
2		**Electron Consumer Industries**					
3							
4	SUPER G 2001 COMPUTER CHIP SALES						
5	PLANT #	5147					
6							
7	QUARTER 2, 2001						
8							
9			APRIL	MAY	JUNE	QTR 2 TOTAL	
10		GMC	14,506,789	17,894,511	15,684,791	48,086,091	
11		FORD	7,452,138	11,689,728	10,978,455	30,120,321	
12		DAIMLER-CHRYSLER	28,314,548	25,418,964	19,154,974	72,888,486	
13		TOYOTA	9,748,111	6,418,795	7,854,972	24,021,878	
14		HONDA	6,487,551	5,784,612	6,484,572	18,756,735	
15							
16		TOTAL UNITS SOLD	66,509,137	67,206,610	60,157,764		
17	AVERAGE # OF UNITS SOLD		13,301,827	13,441,322	12,031,553		
18							

On Your Own

1. Open a new workbook in Excel.
2. Save the file as **OXL14**.
3. Create a worksheet to estimate your anticipated college or school expenses for next year.
4. Enter a worksheet title in row 1.
5. Label column B **September** for September's expenses.
6. Use the fill handle to create the column labels for October through May.
7. Enter row labels for each different type of expense.
   - ✓ *Examples might include books, school supplies (such as notebooks, pens, and paper), computer supplies, gas and car maintenance, parking, and extras (such as concert tickets and dinners out).*
8. Enter values for the expense items in each month.
   - ✓ *If some expenses are the same for every month, copy and paste the data, or use the fill handle.*
9. Label the row below the last expense item **Totals**, and then create a natural language formula to sum September's expenses.
10. Copy the formula to the other columns.
11. Format the worksheet data as currency.
12. Apply other formatting to improve the worksheet's appearance.
13. Adjust column widths as needed.
14. Add comments to several cells explaining your estimates.
15. Spell check the workbook.
16. Print the workbook.
17. Close the file, saving all changes.

Illustration B

	A	B	C	D	E	F	G	H	I	J
1	**Estimated College Expenses for 2002**									
2										
3		September	October	November	December	January	February	March	April	May
4	Books	$ 185.00				$ 235.00				
5	Supplies	$ 100.00	$ 75.00	$ 35.00	$ 20.00	$ 125.00	$ 75.00	$ 45.00	$ 35.00	$ 15.00
6	Computer Stuff	$ 575.00	$ 45.00		$ 275.00	$ 50.00			$ 75.00	$ 55.00
7	Gas	$ 35.00	$ 25.00	$ 25.00	$ 45.00	$ 35.00	$ 25.00	$ 30.00	$ 25.00	$ 55.00
8	Repairs		$ 225.00	$ 75.00	$ 50.00	$ 125.00	$ 55.00			$ 35.00
9	Parking	$ 225.00				$ 225.00				
10	Extras	$ 100.00	$ 100.00	$ 100.00	$ 100.00	$ 100.00	$ 100.00	$ 100.00	$ 100.00	$ 100.00
11	Totals	$ 1,220.00	$ 470.00	$ 235.00	$ 490.00	$ 895.00	$ 255.00	$ 175.00	$ 235.00	$ 260.00
12										

Exercise 15

On the Job

At times it may be easier to reference a cell or range of cells with a descriptive name. For example, a range name can make the formulas in your worksheet easier to understand, and the formatting and printing easier to accomplish.

You are the manager of a local Northwest Gear store, and you did such a great job creating a worksheet to track the sales for your new sleeveless cashmere sweaters that you've been asked to expand the worksheet to include two other new items. You've entered the additional data, and now you need to add grand total and percent of grand total formulas for each new item, and to create a summary. Since there are so many formulas to add, you've decided to use range names to keep the data straight.

Terms

Range name An identification label assigned to a group of cells.

Name box The text box located to the left of the Formula bar.

Notes

Named Ranges

- A **range name** is a descriptive name assigned to two or more cells for identification.

- After naming a range, you can use the range name anyplace the range address might otherwise be entered—such as within a formula, defining the print range, selecting a range to format, and so on.

  ✓ *As you learned in Exercise 14, you don't have to name ranges to use your row and column labels in formulas. See Exercise 14 for more information.*

- Range names cannot be repeated within a workbook, even if they are located on different worksheets.

- Range names can be referenced across worksheets.

- A range name may use up to 255 characters, although short descriptive names are easier to read and remember.

- Some rules for naming ranges are:
  - Spaces are not allowed. Use the underscore character to simulate a space.
  - Do not use range names that could be interpreted as a cell address or a number, such as Q2 or Y2001.
  - A range name may include letters, numbers, underscores (_), backslashes (\), periods (.), and question marks (?).
  - You cannot begin a range name with a number.
  - Avoid using your column and row labels as range names, because they could confuse you when used with the natural language formula feature, should you turn that on.

✓ *For example, suppose you had a worksheet with column labels Jan, Feb, Mar and so on, and you created a range in the January column and named it Jan. Then suppose you forgot about that and turned on natural language formulas, typed the formula =SUM(Jan) at the end of the January column, and copied the formula to the Feb and Mar columns. If you hadn't created the range name Jan, then Excel would have created the formulas =SUM(Feb) and =SUM(Mar) as expected. But because you did, Excel treats the range name as an absolute reference and displays the formula =SUM(Jan) in both the February and March columns, resulting in errors.*

■ Use the Name, Define command or the **name box** to assign a name to a selected range.

Name box

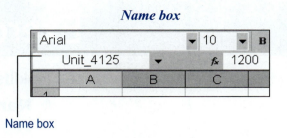

Name box

■ If you have a lot of named ranges in a workbook, you might want to have Excel insert a list of all your named ranges with their corresponding cell references into the worksheet.

Define Name dialog box

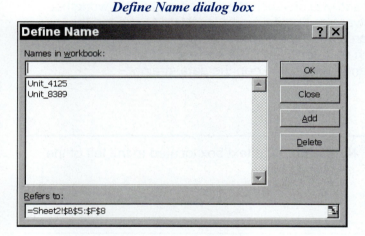

Procedures

Name Range with Menu

1. Select range to name.
2. Click **Insert**.................. Alt+I
3. Click **Name**.......................... N
4. Click **Define** .... D

   ✓ *Note that the selected range appears in **Refers to** text box and the nearest column or row label appears in **Names in workbook** text box.*

5. Type name in **Names in workbook** text box...... Alt+W
6. Click **Add** button [Add] ...... Alt+A
7. Click **OK**........................... Enter

Name Range with Name Box

1. Select range on worksheet to name.
2. Click in name box.
3. Type name.
4. Press **Enter**...................... Enter

Modify Named Range

1. Click **Insert**.................. Alt+I
2. Click **Name**.......................... N
3. Click **Define**.......................... D

   ✓ *Active cell reference appears in Refers to text box.*

To delete name:

a. Click name in list .... Tab, ↑↓

b. Click **Delete**............ Alt+D

To change name:

a. Click name in list.................... Tab, ↑↓

b. Double-click in **Names in workbook** .... Alt+W

c. Type new name for range.

d. Click **Add** button [Add] .... Alt+A

e. Click old name in list .... Tab, ↑↓

f. Click **Delete** button [Delete] .... Alt+D

To change range defined by a name:

a. Click name
   in list ....`Tab`, `↗`

b. Drag through reference in
   Refers to text box ...`Alt`+`R`

c. Use collapse button to
   select cells in worksheet.
   OR
   Type new cell reference.

4. Click **OK** ....`Enter`

Select Cells in a Named Range

Using name box:

1. Click drop-down arrow in
   name box.
2. Click desired named range.

Using Go To:

1. Press **F5** ....`F5`
2. Click name in
   Go to text box .... `Alt`+`G`, `↕`
3. Click **OK** ....`Enter`

Insert List of Named Ranges in Worksheet

1. Click in upper-left cell of range
   to receive list.
2. Click **Insert** ....`Alt`+`I`
3. Click **Name** ....`N`
4. Click **Paste** ....`P`
5. Select range to paste.
6. Click **Paste List**
   button ` Paste List ` ....`Alt`+`L`

   ✓ *List includes range name with
   corresponding sheet name
   and cell references.*

Set Print Area for Named Range

   ✓ *This option is useful when you
   want to print a specific area of
   the worksheet.*

1. Click **File** ....`Alt`+`F`
2. Click **Page Setup** ....`U`
3. Click **Sheet** tab ....`Ctrl`+`Tab`
4. Click **Print area** ....`Alt`+`A`
   text box.
5. Type name of range.
6. Click **Print**
   button ` Print... ` ....`Alt`+`P`

   ✓ *Choose print options
   as needed.*

7. Click **OK** ....`Enter`

Print Named Range

1. Follow steps to select
   named range.
2. Click **File** ....`Alt`+`F`
3. Click **Print** ....`P`
4. Click **OK** ....`Enter`

Exercise Directions

1. Start Excel, if necessary.
2. Open ◉ **15NWGNEW**.
3. Save the file as **NWGNEW**.
4. On the Cashmere Tops worksheet, select the range B14:D19, and name it **Cash_Tops**.
5. Name cell B23 **GTCash_Tops**.
6. On the Surfer Shorts worksheet, select the range B14:D17, and name it **Surf_Shorts**.
7. Name cell B21 **GTSurf_Shorts**.
8. On the Fleece Tops worksheet, select the range B14:D17, and name it **Fleece_Tops**.
9. Name cell B21 **GTFleece_Tops**.
10. On the Cashmere Tops worksheet, use the Cash_Tops range name to create a formula in cell B23 (total sales). See Illustration A.
11. Use the GTCash_Tops range name to create the formula for cell B24 (October percentage of total sales). Apply 2 Decimal, Percent format.

    ✓ *Take the monthly total for October and divide by the Grand Total to calculate the percentage of total sales for October.*

12. Copy the formula in cell B24 to C24:D24.

    ✓ *Notice that the range name acts as an absolute reference to cell B23—it's not adjusted as the formula is copied from cell to cell.*

13. Repeat steps 10 and 11 to create similar formulas on the Surfer Shorts and Fleece Tops worksheets.
14. On the Summary worksheet, in cells B13:B15, use your range names to enter formulas that calculate the total units sold.

    ✓ *In cell B13, for example, you could enter the formula =SUM(Cash_Tops) or =GTCash_Tops.*

15. Adjust column widths as needed.
16. Spell check the workbook.
17. Print the workbook.
18. Close the workbook, saving all changes.

13		October	November	December
14	Red	2415	2694	2421
15	Lt. Blue	3108	3278	4386
16	Brown	978	1105	1098
17	Burnt Umber	1027	1594	1655
18	Burgundy	2374	3497	4297
19	Cyan	2156	3387	4092
20				
21	Monthly Totals	=SUM(B14:B19)	=SUM(C14:C19)	=SUM(D14:D19)
22				
23	Grand Total	=SUM(Cash_Tops)		
24	% of Grand Total	=B21/GTCash_Tops	=C21/GTCash_Tops	=D21/GTCash_Tops

Illustration B

	A	B	C	D
1				
2	Northwest Gear, IN			
3	2749 Mission St., Seattle, WA 98122			
4	Ph. 206-555-3922			
5	Fax: 206-555-3923			
6				
7				
8				
9	New Item Tracker			
10	Qtr 4 Summary			
11				
12		Units Sold	Unit Price	Total Sales
13	Cashmere Tops	=GTCash_Tops	23.5	=B13*C13
14	Surfer Shorts	=GTSurf_Shorts	12.99	=B14*C14
15	Fleece Tops	=GTFleece_Tops	17.75	=B15*C15
16				

On Your Own

1. Open ⌨**OXL13**, created in the On Your Own section of Exercise 13, or open 💿**15CDMANIA**.

2. Save the file as **OXL15**.

3. Delete the data in the range B23:G27.

4. Name the range B4:B8 **JanTotal**.

5. Repeat step 4 for the Feb, Mar, Apr, May, and June data ranges.

   ✓ *For example, select the range C4:C8 and name it FebTotal.*

6. Using these new range names, reenter the formulas in cells B23:G25.

   ✓ *For example, in cell B23, enter =AVERAGE(JanTotal). In cell B24, enter MIN(JanTotal), and in cell B25, enter MAX(JanTotal).*

7. Name the range B4:E8 **Qtr1**. Name the range B13:E17 **Qtr2**.

8. Use these two range names to reenter the formula in cell B27, using the COUNTIF function.

9. Redefine the Qtr1 range to be A3:D8. Redefine the Qtr2 range to be A12:D17.

10. Print just the Qtr1 range, then print just the Qtr2 range.

11. Spell check the worksheet.

12. Print the worksheet.

13. Close the workbook, saving all changes.

Exercise 16

On the Job

IF functions allow you to test for values in your worksheet, and then perform specific actions based on the result. For example, with an IF function, you could calculate the bonuses for a group of salespeople on the premise that bonuses are only paid if a sale is over $1,000. With the SUMIF function, you could total up the sales in your Atlanta office, even if those sales figures are scattered through a long list of sales figures. And with the COUNTIF function, you could count the number of sales that resulted in a bonus being paid.

As the owner of Coastline Gourmet Importers, you're always concerned about your inventory, so you've decided to perform a little analysis on your product line to determine what items are your best sellers. You'll use this information to drop low-selling items from your inventory, and to add new ones.

Terms

Function A pre-programmed Excel formula for a complex calculation.

Condition A statement in an IF function that if true yields one result and if false yields another result.

Nesting Inserting one function within another one. For example, you could nest the AVERAGE function within the IF function like this:
=IF(G2="","",AVERAGE(G2:G21))
In this example, the IF function prevents the AVERAGE from occurring if G2 is blank("").

Argument A variable entered into a function. An argument can be a number, text, formula, or a cell reference. A comma separates each argument in a function.

Notes

Understand IF Functions

- With an IF **function**, you can tell Excel to perform one of two different calculations based on whether your data matches a certain **condition**.

  ✓ *For example, you can use an IF function to have Excel calculate a 10% bonus if total sales are over $500,000, and just a 3% bonus if they are not.*

- The format for an IF statement is:
  =IF(*condition,x,y*)
  - The *condition* is a True/False statement.

- If the condition is true, the result is *x*.
- If the condition is false, the result is *y*.

- To calculate the bonus described here, you would type =IF(B2>500000,B2*.10,B2*.03)

  ✓ *This function says, "If total sales (cell B2) are greater than 500,000, then take total sales times 10% to calculate the bonus. Otherwise, take total sales times 3%."*

  ✓ *Notice that in the IF function, the value, $500,000, is entered without the dollar sign or the comma.*

- You can have words appear in a cell instead of the result of a calculation.

    - ✓ *For example, you might type* **=IF(B2>500000,"We made it!","Good try.")** *to display the words* **We made it!** *if total sales are over 500,000, or the words* **Good try.** *if they are not.*

    - ✓ *Notice here that the words you want to use are surrounded by quotation marks " ".*

- IF statements may use the conditional operators below to state the condition:

=	Equals	<>	Not equal to
>	Greater than	>=	Greater than or equal to
<	Less than	<=	Less than or equal to
&	Used for joining text		

- For help in entering an IF function, Excel provides a screen tip that lists the IF function arguments in order.

- You can also type =IF(and click the Insert Function button to display the Function Arguments dialog box which provides a text box for each argument, making it easier to enter them correctly.

Function Arguments dialog box

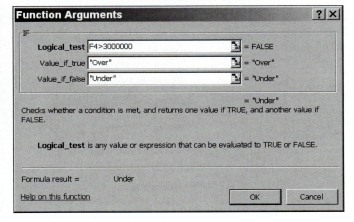

Nested IF Functions

- You can **nest** an IF function (or any other function) as one of the **arguments** in another function.

- For example, the formula:

    =IF(C3>92,"A",IF(C3>83,"B",IF(C3>73,"C",IF(C3>65,"D","F"))))

    - ✓ *If the average score is greater than 92, then the student gets an A, if the score is less than or equal to 92 but greater than 83, the student gets a B, if the score is less than or equal to 83 but greater than 73, the student gets a C, and so on.*

=SUMIF() Statements

- A SUMIF statement is a logical function that uses a condition to add certain data.

- If the condition is true, then data in a corresponding cell is added to the total; if it is false, then the corresponding data is skipped.

- The format for a SUMIF statement is =SUMIF(*range, condition, sum_range*)

    - The *range* is the range of cells you want to test.

    - The *condition* is a True/False statement that defines which cells should be added to the total.

    - If the condition is true, the corresponding cell in *sum_range* is added to the total.

    - If the condition is false, the corresponding cell in *sum_range* is skipped (not added to the total).

        - ✓ *The condition is written using the same symbols (such as >,<>, etc.) as listed in the IF section. However, here, you must enclose the condition in quotation marks "".*

- For example, if you had a worksheet listing sales for several different products, you could total the sales for widgets only by using this formula: =SUMIF(D2:D55,"Widget",G2:G55)

    - Column D contains the name of the product being sold and column G contains the total amount for that sale.

    - If column D contains the word "Widget" then the amount for that sale (located in column G) is added to the running total.

        - ✓ *Because Widget is a text label, you must enclose it in quotation marks (" ").*

- You can leave the last argument off if you want to sum the same range that you're testing. For example: =SUMIF(G2:G10,"<=500")

    - ✓ *This formula calculates the total of all values in the range G2 to G10 that are less than or equal to 500.*

=COUNTIF() Statements

- A COUNTIF statement is a logical function that uses a condition to count the number of items in a range.

- If the result of the condition is true, then the item is added to a running count; if it is false, then the item is skipped.

- The format for a COUNTIF statement is =COUNTIF(*range, condition*).
  - The *range* is the range of cells you want to test.
  - The *condition* is a True/False statement that defines which cells should be counted.
    - ✓ *The condition is written using the same symbols listed in the IF section. Again, enclose the condition in quotation marks " ".*

- For example, if you count the number of individual Widget sales, you could use this formula: =COUNTIF(D2:D55,"=Widget")
  - Column D contains the name of the product being sold.
  - If column D contains the word "Widget" then that sale is added to the running total.
    - ✓ *Because Widget is a text label, you must enclose it in quotation marks (" ").*

- You can combine functions to create complex calculations: =SUMIF(D3:D13,"PASS",C3:C13) /COUNTIF(D3:D13,"PASS")
  - This computes the average score of all the students who passed the course.
  - Column D contains the words "Pass" or "Fail" based on the student's final score. The final score is located in column C.

Procedures

Enter IF Function

1. Click desired cell.
2. Press **Equal** .... ▣
3. Type **IF**.
   - ✓ *You can click the Insert Functions button* *fx* *at this point to display the Function Arguments dialog box, which may make entering the IF function easier, or you can simply type the rest of the function by following these steps.*
4. Press **Left Parenthesis** ...... ▣
5. Type condition.
6. Press **Comma** .... ▣
7. Type argument if condition is true.
8. Press **Comma** .... ▣
9. Type argument if condition is false.
10. Press **Right** Parenthesis ..... ▣
11. Press **Enter** .... Enter

- ✓ *IF statements may be used in combination with OR, AND, and NOT statements to evaluate complex conditions. For example, =IF(OR(B3>C3,B3<1000),D4*1 .05,D4*1.03), which says "If B3 is greater than C3 or less than 1000, take D4 times 105%, otherwise, take D4 times 103%"*

Enter SUMIF Function

1. Click desired cell.
2. Press **Equal** .... ▣
3. Type **SUMIF**.
4. Press **Left Parenthesis** ...... ▣
5. Type range to test.
   - ✓ *You can select the range instead of typing it.*
6. Press **Comma** .... ▣
7. Type condition in quotation marks.
8. Press **Comma** .... ▣
9. Type range to sum if condition is true.

- ✓ *You can select the range instead of typing it.*
- ✓ *Skip steps 8-9 if the range you're testing is the same as the range you want to sum.*

10. Press **Right Parenthesis** .... ▣
11. Press **Enter** .... Enter

Enter COUNTIF Function

1. Click desired cell.
2. Press **Equal** .... ▣
3. Type **COUNTIF**.
4. Press **Left Parenthesis** .... ▣
5. Type range to count.
   - ✓ *You can select the range instead of typing it.*
6. Press **Comma** .... ▣
7. Type condition to test.
8. Press **Right Parenthesis** .... ▣
9. Press **Enter** .... Enter

Exercise Directions

1. Start Excel, if necessary.

2. Open ✏ **16CGISALES**.

3. Save the file as **CGISALES**.

4. In cell E11, use the IF function to enter a formula that displays the words "Best Seller" if cell D11 is greater than $7,000, and nothing (blank) if it is not.

   ✓ *Enclose the text in quotation marks. Use two quotations together "" to represent blank. Do not include the $ or , in the value $7,000.*

5. Copy this formula to E12:E25.

6. In cell C30, use the COUNTIF function to count the number of best selling items (items in which the sales value in column D is greater than $7,000).

   ✓ *Be sure to enclose the condition in "".*

7. In cell C31, use the SUMIF function to calculate total sales for best sellers.

8. In cell C32, use the SUMIF and COUNTIF functions to calculate the average sales for the best sellers (sales over $7,000).

   ✓ *You could type just =C31/C30, but for the purposes of this exercise, use SUMIF and COUNTIF in one formula.*

9. In cells C34:C36, use SUMIF to calculate the total sales for each of the different types of ethnic food.

   ✓ *For example, in cell C34, you could type =SUMIF(C11:C25,"Chang Lo Lee Oriental Seafood",D11:D25).*

   ✓ *If you want, instead of typing "Chang Lo Lee Oriental Seafood," you can simply click any cell that contains that value, such as cell C13.*

10. Spell check the worksheet.

11. Print the worksheet.

12. Close the workbook, saving all changes.

Illustration A

	A	B	C	D	E
20		Sea Bass Sushi	Chang Lo Lee Oriental Seafood	$ 4,312.89	
21		Seared Scallops with Haricot Verts and Truffle Oil	Al Dente Italian Gourmet Foods	$ 14,947.21	Best Seller
22		Sesame Crab Claw	Chang Lo Lee Oriental Seafood	$ 5,894.81	
23		Shrimp Chipotle	Tejano Terone Mexican Gourmet Food	$ 11,594.31	Best Seller
24		Squid Paste	Chang Lo Lee Oriental Seafood	$ 2,175.84	
25		Zabaglione Tart with Marsala-Lemon Sauce	Al Dente Italian Gourmet Foods	$ 6,134.95	
26			Total Sales for June	$ 113,850.43	
27					
28					
29	Summary				
30		No. of Best Selling Items	6		
31		Total Sales for Best Sellers	$72,201.90		
32		Average Sales for Best Sellers	$12,033.65		
33					
34		Total Sales--Oriental	$38,291.49		
35		Total Sales--Italian	$36,254.29		
36		Total Sales--Mexican	$39,304.65		
37					

On Your Own

1. Open **OXL14**, the school expenses workbook you created in the On Your Own section of Excel Exercise 14, or open **16COLEXP**.

2. Save the workbook as **OXL16**.

3. Below the expense data, add a row labeled **Income**, and input monthly income figures.

   ✓ *Your income should be only slightly above your monthly expenses.*

4. Enter a formula that calculates your total income for the school year.

5. Enter a formula for calculating the net income (total income minus total expenses) for each month, and for the school year.

6. Use an IF function to determine if you will have enough money left in the budget at the end of the year to purchase a new color printer for your computer. The printer costs $279. If you have enough, the formula should display **Yes!**. If you do not have enough, the formula should display **Maybe next year**.

7. Spell check the workbook.

8. Print the workbook.

9. Close the workbook, saving all changes.

Exercise 17

◆ **Chart Basics** ◆ **Select Chart Data** ◆ **Chart Elements**
◆ **Create Charts** ◆ **Change Chart Types** ◆ **Select a Chart**
◆ **Resize, Copy, Move, or Delete a Chart**

On the Job

A chart presents Excel data in a graphical format—making the relationship between data items easier to understand. To present your data in the best format, you must select the proper chart type. For example, if you wanted to highlight your department's recent reduction in overtime, you might use a column or bar chart. Whereas, to compare your division's sales with other divisions, you might use a pie chart instead.

In the fourth quarter, sales for a new product, cashmere tops, exceeded expectations—at least, certain colors did. Now it's up to you to analyze the sales data and decide which color tops to carry in your store for the rest of the season. You've decided that Excel's chart feature will help you make sense of all that data. You'll create some charts to analyze the sales of some of your other products as well.

Terms

Chart A graphic that allows you to compare and contrast data in a visual format.

Embedded chart A chart placed as an object within a worksheet.

Chart sheet A chart that occupies its own worksheet.

Plot To position data points on a graph.

Data series For most charts, a data series is the information in a worksheet column. If you select multiple columns of data for a chart, you'll create multiple data series.

Legend A key that identifies each of the data series in a chart.

X-axis The horizontal scale of a chart on which categories are plotted.

Y-axis The vertical scale of a chart on which the value of each category is plotted.

Categories For most charts, a category is information in a worksheet row. If you select multiple rows of data for a chart, you'll create multiple categories.

Notes

Chart Basics

- **Charts** provide a way of presenting and comparing data in a graphic format.
- You can create **embedded charts** or **chart sheets**.

- When you create an embedded chart, the chart exists as an object in the worksheet alongside the data.
    - ✓ *All illustrations in this exercise use embedded charts.*

- When you create a chart sheet, the chart exists on a separate sheet in the workbook.

- All charts are linked to the data they **plot**. When you change data in the plotted area of the worksheet, the chart changes automatically.

Select Chart Data

- To create a chart, you first select the data to plot. Following are some guidelines for selecting your chart data:

  - The selection should not contain blank columns or rows.

    - ✓ *Just press Ctrl and select each range separately, making sure not to select blank rows or columns that may separate the ranges.*

  - You can select multiple ranges to plot on a single chart.

  - You can hide columns or rows you do not wish to plot.

  - The selection should include the labels for the data when possible.

  - A blank cell in the upper-left corner of a selection tells Excel that the data below and to the right of the blank cell contains labels for the values to plot.

  - The selection determines the orientation of the data series (in columns or rows). However, you may change the orientation as desired.

Adjacent and nonadjacent selections

	B	C	D	E
3	**Profit and Loss Statement**			Adjacent selection
4	**Spring Quarter, 1997**			
5				
6	Income	January	February	March
7	Wholesale	$ 125,650	$122,645	$156,210
8	Retail Sales	$ 135,120	$125,645	$145,887
9	Special Sales	$ 10,255	$ 21,541	$ 15,647
10				
11	Totals by Month	$ 271,025	Non-adjacent selection	17,744
12				
13	Expenses	January	February	March
14	Disk Production	$ 15,642	$ 14,687	$ 18,741
15	Packaging	$ 2,564	$ 2,407	$ 3,071
16	Promotions	$ 4,525	$ 4,248	$ 5,420
17				
18	Totals by Month	$ 22,731	$ 21,342	$ 27,232
19				

Chart Elements

- The parts of a column chart are labeled in the illustration to the right.

- As you move your mouse over each part of a chart, the name of the object displays.

- Typically each chart includes the following parts:

  - **Data series**
    If you include data for more than one item (such as homes sold in the Oak Bend, River Knoll, and Glenview North communities), then you'll create a different **data series** for each item. Each series is represented on the chart by a different color bar, column, line, etc.

  - **Series labels**
    Labels identifying the charted values. These labels appear in the chart **legend**, which identifies each data series in the chart.

  - **Category labels**
    Labels identifying each data series shown on the horizontal or **x-axis**.

- For charts which use axes (all except pie charts):

  - The **y-axis** is the vertical scale, except on 3-D charts. The scale values are based on the values being charted.

  - The x-axis is the horizontal scale and typically represents the data series **categories**.

  - The x-axis title describes the x-axis (horizontal) data. (*Communities* in the illustration below.)

  - The y-axis title describes the y-axis (vertical) data. (*Homes Under Construction* in the illustration below.)

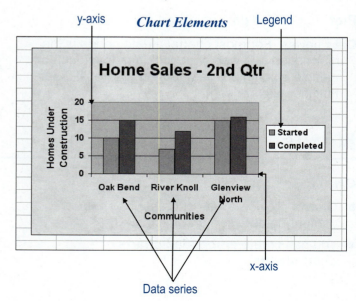

Create Charts

- You create charts with the Chart Wizard, which uses tabbed dialog boxes to step you through the entire process.

- As you make selections, the Chart Wizard shows you exactly how the chart will look.

  - ✓ *Previewing your chart enables you to select the chart type and other elements best suited to your data.*

- Each chart type contains chart subtypes, which are variations on the selected chart type.

- Excel also offers several customized chart types for specialized data.

Change Chart Types

- After creating a chart, you can easily change its chart type to something else.

- There are many chart types from which you can choose:

  - **Column charts** compare individual or sets of values. The height of each bar is proportional to its corresponding value in the worksheet.

    - ✓ *All of the chart types listed here are available in a 3-D format.*

  - **Bar charts** are basically column charts turned on their sides. Like column charts, bar charts compare the values of various items.

  - **Line charts** connect points of data and show changes over time effectively. Line charts are especially useful to plot trends.

  - **Area charts** are like "filled in" line charts; you use them to track changes over time.

  - **Pie charts** are circular graphs used to show the relationship of each value in a data range to the entire set of data. The size of each wedge represents the percentage each value contributes to the total.

    - ✓ *Only one numerical data range may be used in a pie chart. For example, if you have sales data for 2000 and 2001 for tricycles, offroad bikes, and helmets, you can only chart one year. If you select all the data, it will be lumped into one big pie, with each element (2000 tricycles, 2001 offroad bikes, etc.) representing a slice.*

    - ✓ *Pie charts may be formatted to indicate the percentage each piece of the pie represents of the whole.*

- A chart can be copied and then edited to produce a different chart that uses the same worksheet data.

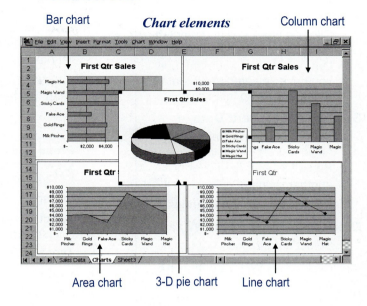

Chart elements

Bar chart / Column chart / Area chart / 3-D pie chart / Line chart

Select a Chart

- To resize, copy, or move a chart, you must first select it by clicking anywhere on the chart.

- A selected chart displays sizing handles. In addition, the Chart toolbar usually appears.

Resize, Copy, Move, or Delete a Chart

- You can resize, copy, or move an embedded chart as needed.

- You can't resize a chart on a chart sheet; however, you can copy or move it around on the sheet.

- You can move a chart on a chart sheet to another sheet, creating an embedded object. You can reverse the process when needed to change an embedded chart into a chart sheet.

- If you copy a chart, you can change the copied chart type to present data in a different way.

Procedures

Select Adjacent Data

1. Click on blank cell in upper left-hand corner of data range.
2. Drag downward and right, until you have selected entire data range, including label cells.

Select Nonadjacent Data

1. Click and drag over cells in first range you want to select.
2. Press **Ctrl** and drag over another range of cells.......... `Ctrl`
3. Repeat for additional ranges.

Create Chart with Chart Wizard

1. Select data to chart.
2. Click **Chart Wizard** button `📊`.
   OR
   a. Click **Insert** .... `Alt`+`I`
   b. Click **Chart**...................... `H`
3. Follow steps to create standard or custom chart type.
4. Click the **Finish** button
   `Finish` .... `Alt`+`F`

Select Embedded Chart

1. Click once on chart to select it.
2. To deselect chart, click anywhere in worksheet.

Select Chart Sheet

1. Click chart sheet's tab.
2. To deselect chart sheet, click different worksheet tab.

Change Chart's Type

1. Select chart or chart sheet.
2. Click **Chart**................. `Alt`+`C`
3. Click **Chart Type**................. `Y`
4. Select standard or custom chart type.

To select standard chart type:

a. Select chart type in **Chart type** list box .... `Alt`+`C`

b. Select sub-type for selected chart in **Chart sub-type** list box .... `Alt`+`T`

c. If desired, click and hold **Press and Hold to View Sample**
   `Press and Hold to View Sample`
   to display preview....... `Enter`

To select custom chart type:

a. Click **Custom Types** tab .... `Ctrl`+`Tab`

b. Select **User defined** .... `Alt`+`U`
   OR
   Select **Built-in**........ `Alt`+`B`

c. Select desired custom chart in **Chart type** list .... `Alt`+`C`

5. To set current chart type as default, click **Set as default chart**
   `Set as default chart` ...... `Alt`+`E`

6. Click **OK** .... `Enter`

Resize Embedded Chart

1. Select chart you want to resize.
2. Move mouse pointer to handle.

   ✓ Mouse pointer becomes 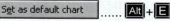 when positioned correctly.

   ✓ To size object proportionally, press Shift and point to corner handle.

3. Click handle and drag it outwards to make chart bigger, or inwards to make it smaller.

   ✓ To align edges of chart to worksheet gridlines, press Alt key as you drag.

4. Release mouse button and chart is resized.

Move Chart

1. Select chart you want to move.
2. Click chart and drag it to its new location.

   ✓ As you drag, outline of chart follows mouse pointer.

3. Release mouse button and chart is moved.

Switch from Embedded Chart to Chart Sheet or Vice-Versa

1. Right-click the chart.
2. Select **Location**. .... `Alt`+`L`
3. Select **As new sheet** .. `Alt`+`S`
   OR
   As object in .... `Alt`+`O`
4. Click **OK**..................... `Enter`

Copy Chart

1. Select chart you want to copy.
2. Click **Copy** button `📋`.
3. Click elsewhere in worksheet.
4. Click **Paste** button `📋`.

   ✓ You can change chart type of copied chart to view its data in a different way.

Delete Embedded Chart

1. Select chart you want to delete.
2. Press **Delete**..................... `Del`

Delete Chart Sheet

1. Click **Edit** .... `Alt`+`E`
2. Click **Delete Sheet** .... `L`
3. Click **OK**......................... `Enter`
   OR
1. Right-click sheet tab.
2. Select **Delete** .... `E`

Exercise Directions

1. Start Excel, if necessary.

2. Open ⌨**NWGNEW** or open 💿**17NWGNEW**.

3. Save it as **NWGNEW**.

4. On the Cashmere Tops worksheet, select the range A13:D19.

5. Use the Chart Wizard to create your first chart. Make the following selections:

   a. Select the Clustered Column chart type.

   b. Display the data series in columns.

   c. Enter the chart title **4th Qtr Sales by Month**.

   d. Enter the Category Axis title **Cashmere Tops**.

   e. Enter the Value Axis title **Units Sold**.

   f. Display the legend at the bottom center of the chart.

   g. Save the chart as an embedded object on the Cashmere Tops worksheet.

6. Size and move the chart so that the chart appears in A26:H51.

   ✓ *Some charts won't fully display their data no matter which you size you make them initially. Don't worry too much if this happens to you. You will format charts in the next exercise and learn how to achieve the effect you desire.*

7. To create a second chart that displays the data in a different format, copy the first chart to the worksheet range beginning at A53.

8. Change the chart type of the copied chart to Clustered bar with a 3-D visual effect. (See Illustration B. You'll learn how to fix the title in the next exercise.)

9. To create the third and last chart, change to the Surfer Shorts worksheet, and select the non-adjacent ranges B13:D13 and B19:D19.

10. Use the Chart Wizard to create the chart with the following selections:

    a. Select Exploded Pie with 3-D visual effect chart type.

    b. Display the series in rows.

    c. Add the chart title **4th Qtr Surfer Short Sales**.

    d. Don't show the legend.

    e. Select category name, value, and percentage data labels.

    f. Save the chart as a sheet titled **Surfer Short Chart**.

11. Spell check the workbook.

12. Print the workbook.

13. Close the workbook, saving all changes.

Illustration A

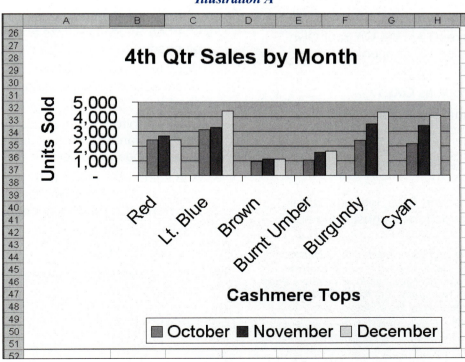

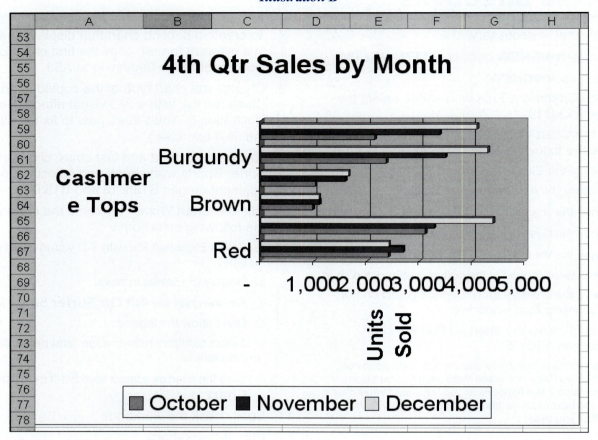

On Your Own

1. Start Excel, if necessary.

2. Open **OXL15**, created in the On Your Own section of Exercise 15, or open ⊙ **17CDMANIA**.

3. Save the workbook as **OXL17**.

4. Create two charts, stored on chart sheets, using the quarter 1 and quarter 2 totals, respectively.

   ✓ *Be sure to use two different chart types when creating the two charts.*

5. Add sheet titles, chart titles, legends, data labels, and other options as desired to each chart.

   ✓ *Some charts just won't look great until you format them, which you'll learn to do in the next exercise. So resize the charts as best you can to achieve a margin of respectability, then apply your formatting next exercise to create exactly the effect you want.*

6. Change the Quarter 1 chart to an embedded chart on Sheet 2. Resize and move the chart as needed to fully display its data.

7. Copy the Quarter 1 chart to another location on Sheet 2. Change the chart type of the copied chart.

8. Create a third chart that displays the average sales for January through June. Save the chart as an embedded object on Sheet 3.

9. Add sheet titles, chart titles, legends, data labels, and other options as desired. Resize and move the chart as needed.

10. Spell check the workbook.

11. Print the workbook.

12. Close the workbook, saving all changes.

Exercise 18

Skills Covered:

◆ **Use Chart Toolbar** ◆ **Resize, Move, or Delete a Chart Object**
◆ **Change Chart Text** ◆ **Enhance Chart Background**
◆ **Format Category and Value Axes**

On the Job

There are many ways in which you can enhance your chart: you can format the chart text, add color or pattern to the chart background, and format the value and category axes so that the numbers are easier to read.

Murray Hill Marketing has provided you with a pretty thorough analysis of your competition, but as the owner of Dan's Digital Camera Works, you're finding it hard to make sense of it all. So you've decided to take the data and chart it using Excel's charting feature. After the chart is created, you'll use your new Excel skills to apply formatting to the chart before printing it out.

Terms

Object An item that is treated separately from the main document. In the case of a chart, each chart element is an object that can be manipulated independently.

Chart area The total area occupied by a chart.

Plot area The area defined by the x and y axes.

Tick marks Lines of measurement along the value and category axes.

Notes

Use Chart Toolbar

Chart toolbar

- Chart Objects
- Chart Type
- Format Object Selected
- Data Table
- Legend
- By Row
- By Column
- Angle Clockwise
- Angle Counterclockwise

- Normally, when you select a chart or one of its parts, the Chart toolbar appears.

- If needed, you can access the Chart toolbar from the View menu.

- The Chart toolbar provides the following tools:

- Chart Objects allows you to select any part of a chart so you can delete or format it.

- Format Object presents format options for the selected chart object.

- Chart Type allows you to change the chart type associated with the selected chart.

- Legend hides or displays the chart legend.

- Data Table hides or displays data used in the chart.

- By Rows changes orientation of data series to rows.

- By Column changes orientation of data series to columns.

- Angle Clockwise angles selected text downward.

- Angle Counterclockwise angles selected text upward.

Resize, Move, or Delete a Chart Object

- Before you resize, move, or delete an **object**, you must select it first.

- By resizing, moving, or deleting the parts of your chart, you may make it more attractive and easier to read.

- If you resize an object that contains text, the font size of the text changes correspondingly.

- When you delete an object from a chart, the remaining parts of the chart are enlarged to fill the gap.

- You can change the value represented by a column or bar by resizing it.

Change Chart Text

- You can edit chart text or change its formatting. For example, you can change the size, font, and attributes of text.

Enhance Chart Background

- A chart actually has two backgrounds: the larger **chart area** and the smaller **plot area**, as shown in the figure to the right.

- You can format the chart area, the plot area, or both.

- To format either chart background, you can:
  - Add a border around the background area.
  - Apply a color to the background.
  - Apply a fill effect, such as gradient (a blend of two colors), texture (such as marble), pattern (such as diagonal stripes), or picture (a graphic file).
  - Add a shadow effect behind the border (chart area only).
  - Round the corners (chart area only).

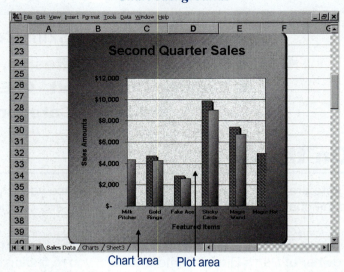

Chart backgrounds

Chart area   Plot area

Format Category and Value Axes

- The category axis, or x-axis, represents the horizontal axis for most charts. Categories and data series are plotted along the category axis.

- The value axis, or y-axis, represents the vertical axis for most charts. The values of various categories or data series are plotted along the value axis.

- You can change the font, size, color, attributes, alignment, and placement of text or numbers along both the category and value axes.

- You can also change the appearance of the **tick marks**.

- In addition, you can adjust the scale used along the value axis.

Procedures

Select Chart Object

- Click the object you wish to select.

OR

- Select the object's name from the Chart Object list on the Chart toolbar.

Resize Chart Object

1. Select object you want to resize.
2. Move mouse pointer over handle.

   ✓ *Mouse pointer becomes* ⬚ *when positioned correctly.*

   ✓ *To size object proportionally, press Shift and point to corner handle.*

3. Click handle and drag it outwards to make object bigger, or inwards to make it smaller.

4. Release mouse button and object is resized.

Move Chart Object

1. Select object you want to move.
2. Click object and drag it to its new location.

   ✓ *As you drag, outline of object follows mouse pointer.*

3. Release mouse button and object is moved.

Delete Chart Object

1. Select object you want to delete.
2. Press **Delete** .... `Del`

   ✓ *You can select the plot area, but your can't delete it.*

Change Chart Text

1. Click chart object that contains text you wish to change.
2. Edit the text using normal text editing techniques.
3. Click anywhere outside of chart text when finished.

   ✓ *You can apply any formatting you want to the selected text.*

Enhance Chart Background

1. Select either chart or plot area.
2. Click **Format Chart Area/Format Plot Area** button 🖼.
3. On the Patterns tab under Border, select **Automatic** to apply normal border style .... `Alt`+`A`

   OR

   a. Select **Custom**.
   b. Select border **Style** ... `Alt`+`S`
   c. Select border **Color** .... `Alt`+`C`
   d. Select border thickness, or **Weight** .... `Alt`+`W`

   To fill area with color:

   • On the Patterns tab under Area, select **Automatic** to apply normal background color (usually white) .... `Alt`+`U`

   OR

   • Select desired color from color palette .... `Alt`+`O`

   OR

   a. Click **Fill Effects**
      `Fill Effects..` .... `Alt`+`I`
   b. On Gradient tab, choose color option you want:

      • Select **One color** .... `Alt`+`O`

• Choose color you want to blend from **Color 1** drop-down list ... `Alt`+`1`

• Adjust transition from **Dark** to **Light** .... `Alt`+`K`

OR

• Select **Two colors** .... `Alt`+`T`

• Choose two colors you want to blend from **Color 1** and **Color 2** drop-down list boxes .. `Alt`+`1`, `Alt`+`2`

OR

• Select **Preset** .... `Alt`+`R`

• Choose **Preset colors** option you want .. `Alt`+`E`

   c. Select one of the **Shading styles**.
   d. Select one of the **Variants** .... `Alt`+`A`

To fill area with texture:

a. Click **Texture** tab.
b. Select texture you want.

To fill area with pattern:

a. Click **Pattern** tab.
b. Select **Foreground** color .. `Alt`+`F`
c. Select **Background** color . `Alt`+`B`
d. Click **Pattern** .... `Alt`+`T`

To fill area with a picture:

a. Click **Picture** tab.
b. Click **Select Picture** .... `Alt`+`L`
c. Select desired drive and folder from **Look in** drop-down list .... `Alt`+`I`
d. Double-click graphic file.

4. Click **OK** .... `Enter`
5. Click **OK** .... `Enter`

Format Category Axis

1. Select category axis.
2. Click **Format Axis** button 🖼.
3. If desired, on Patterns tab, select setting:

• Select **Automatic** to apply normal line style. .... `Alt`+`A`

OR

a. Select **Custom**.
b. Select border **Style** ... `Alt`+`S`
c. Select border **Color** .... `Alt`+`C`
d. Select border thickness, or **Weight** .... `Alt`+`W`

   OR

   Select **None** to remove the axis lines.

4. If desired, change **Major tick mark type** (change its location). .... `Alt`+`M`
5. If desired, change **Minor tick mark type** (change its location). .... `Alt`+`R`
6. If desired, change location of **Tick mark labels** .... `Alt`+`T`
7. Click **Scale** tab.

   a. To change point at which y-axis intersects category axis, enter category number in **Value (Y) axis crosses at category number** text box. .... `Alt`+`C`

   b. To change frequency of category labels, enter number in **Number of categories between tick-mark labels** text box. (Enter a 2 to display every other label, etc.) ...... `Alt`+`L`

   c. To change frequency of tick marks along category axis, enter number in **Number of categories between tick marks** text box........ `Alt`+`K`

   d. If you do not want first category to be placed right against y-axis, select **Value (Y) axis crosses between categories** .... `Alt`+`B`

   e. If desired, select **Categories in reverse order** ..... `Alt`+`R`

   f. To place y-axis on the right, select **Value (Y) axis crosses at maximum category** .... `Alt`+`M`

8. Click **Font** tab and make desired changes to font, size, and other attributes of data labels.

9. Click **Alignment** tab and angle label text:
   - Drag **Text** marker to set degree of rotation.

   OR

   a. Enter positive number in **Degrees** text box to angle text from lower left to upper right, or negative number to angle text from upper left to lower right .... `Alt`+`D`

   b. Select amount of space you want between data labels and x-axis by adjusting **Offset** value........... `Alt`+`O`

10. Click **OK**........................... `Enter`

Format Value Axis

1. Select value axis.

2. Click **Format Axis** button.

3. If desired, on Patterns tab, select setting:
   - Select **Automatic** to apply normal line style..... `Alt`+`A`

   OR

---

a. Select **Custom**.

b. Select border **Style**... `Alt`+`S`

c. Select border **Color** .... `Alt`+`C`

d. Select border thickness, or **Weight**. .... `Alt`+`W`

   OR

   Select **None** to remove the axis lines.

4. If desired, change **Major tick mark type** (location).... `Alt`+`M`

5. If desired, change **Minor tick mark type** (location).... `Alt`+`R`

6. If desired, change location of **Tick mark labels** .... `Alt`+`T`

7. Click **Scale** tab.

   a. Set **Minimum** and **Maximum** values used on y-axis .... `Alt`+`N`, `Alt`+`X`

   b. Adjust placement of major and minor tick marks along y-axis by changing values in **Major unit** and **Minor unit** text boxes .. `Alt`+`A`, `Alt`+`I`

---

c. To change point at which x-axis intersects value axis, enter value in **Category (X) axis crosses at** text box .... `Alt`+`C`

d. If desired, adjust **Display units** value.............. `Alt`+`U`

e. To display values as powers of 10, select **Logarithmic scale** option .... `Alt`+`L`

f. To display **Values in reverse order**, select that option .... `Alt`+`R`

g. To move category axis to top of plot area, select **Category (X) axis crosses at maximum value** ..... `Alt`+`M`

8. Click **Font** tab and make desired changes to font, size, and other attributes of value labels.

9. Click **Number** tab and select format you wish for your value labels.

10. Click **Alignment** tab and angle label text:
    - Drag **Text** marker to set degree of rotation.

11. Click **OK**.......................... `Enter`

Exercise Directions

1. Start Excel, if necessary.

2. Open **COMPETE** or **18COMPETE**.

3. Save the file as **COMPETE**.

4. Press Ctrl and select the following cells: B6, B9, B12, B15, F6, F9, F12, and F15.

5. Click the Chart Wizard button.

6. Follow the Chart Wizard steps and make the following selections:
   a. Select the Pie with 3-D visual effect chart type.
   b. Choose data series by columns.
   c. Add the title **Competitors' 2001 Sales**.
   d. Show percentage data value labels.
   e. Save the chart as an embedded object on Sheet 2.
   f. Resize the chart to fit in the range A1:H18.

7. Make the following improvements to the chart:
   a. Delete the Legend.

---

b. Add category name and value data labels. Turn on the Show leader lines option as well.
   ✓ *Select the chart and use the Chart, Chart Options command to make this change.*

c. Format the title in Architect, 24-point bold, green text.

d. Format the Series 1 Data Labels with Arial, 8-point green, bold font.

e. Select the plot area, and move it to the left, as shown in Illustration A. Resize the pie as shown.
   ✓ *To select the plot area, click right outside a slice. Then click on the plot area box and drag it to a new location.*

f. Drag the data labels to reposition them as shown. This will make the leader lines (the lines pointing to the associated pie slice) appear as well.

g. Apply Papyrus texture with a green rounded corner border of medium weight to the chart background.

8. Spell check the workbook.

9. Print the workbook.

10. Close the workbook, saving all changes.

Illustration A

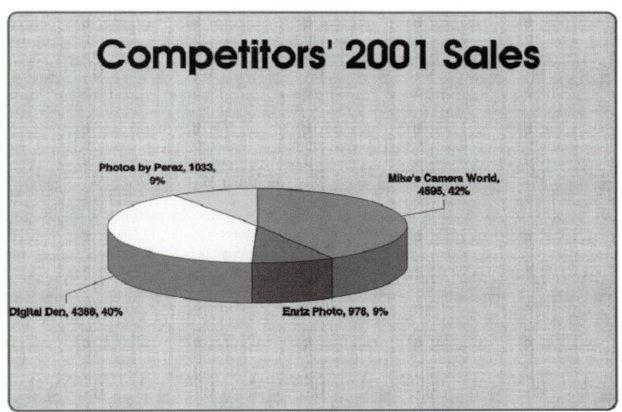

On Your Own

1. Open **OXL17**, the workbook you created in the On Your Own section of Exercise 17, or open ⊛**18CDMANIA**.

2. Save the file as **CDMANIA**.

3. Rename Sheet 2 **Quarter 1 Sales Charts**.

4. Apply formatting to the two charts on the Quarter 1 Sales Charts sheet.

   ✓ *Be sure to make different selections for the two charts, so that they are unique in appearance.*

   a. Select a small font size for the labels and a larger font size for the title.

   b. Apply formatting to the chart background, and a different format to the plot area.

   c. Adjust the scale used on the y-axis.

   ✓ *For example, you could set the minimum to 50,000, and the major unit to 10,000.*

5. Rename Sheet 3 **Average Sales Chart**.

6. Apply formatting as desired to the chart on the Average Sales Chart sheet.

7. Spell check the workbook.

8. Print the workbook.

9. Close the workbook, saving all changes.

Exercise 19

◆ **Critical Thinking**

You're the director of sales at Regency General, Inc., a Web-based company specializing in Internet services such as company database management and purchasing. Your company sponsored a sales contest for June, and now that it's July, it's up to you to organize the sales information and award prizes. You'll use various functions to help you analyze the data, and then you'll create a chart that will enable you to compare the contest results by city.

Exercise Directions

1. Start Excel, if necessary.
2. Open ⊚ **19SALESCONT**.
3. Save the file as **SALESCONT**.
4. Assign the range name **GOAL** to the cell C8.
5. In cell F12, type a formula that computes the average sales amount per client.
   - ✓ *Hint: Take the June Total and divide by the number of clients.*
6. Copy the formula to the range F13:F21.
7. In cell G12, type a formula that displays the word **Yes** if the person met the June sales goal, and nothing if he/she did not.
   - ✓ *Use the IF function, and compare the value in cell D12 to the range name, GOAL, and if it is greater than or equal to GOAL, display "Yes." Otherwise, display blank "".*
8. Copy this formula to the range G13:G21.
9. In cell D23, type a formula that computes the total sales.
10. In cell D24, type a formula that computes the average sales for all the salespeople.
11. Using the SUMIF function, type a formula in cell D26 that computes the total sales for the people in the Chicago office. Copy the formula to D27 and D28.
12. Apply Accounting style, zero decimal places, to the range D26:D28.
13. If necessary, adjust column widths to fit the data.
14. Create a clustered bar chart using the range, C26:D28.
    a. Use the title **June Sales**.
    b. Display minor gridlines along the Y axis.
    c. Remove the legend.
    d. Place the chart on its own sheet, titled **June Sales**.
    e. Format each bar with a unique color—South Bend=pale blue, Ft. Wayne=tan, and Chicago=lavender.
    f. Apply the Water droplets texture to the chart background.
    g. Apply blue-gray fill to the plot area.
    h. Apply Arial, bold, 28-point text to the title.
    i. Apply Arial, bold, 12-point text to the Category Axis labels.
15. Create a second chart using the range C11:D21.
    a. Choose the clustered column with 3-D effect chart type.
    b. Use the title **Contest Results**.
    c. Use the Value Axis title **$25,000 Goal**.
    d. Remove the legend.
    e. Place the chart on its own sheet, entitled **Contest Results**.
    f. Apply Arial, bold, 18-point type to the title.
    g. Apply 90 degrees Orientation alignment to the Value Axis title.
    h. Apply 45 degrees Orientation alignment to the Category Axis labels.
    i. Apply the Canvas texture to the chart background.
16. Spell check the workbook.
17. Print the workbook.
18. Close the file, saving all changes.

Illustration A

Illustration B

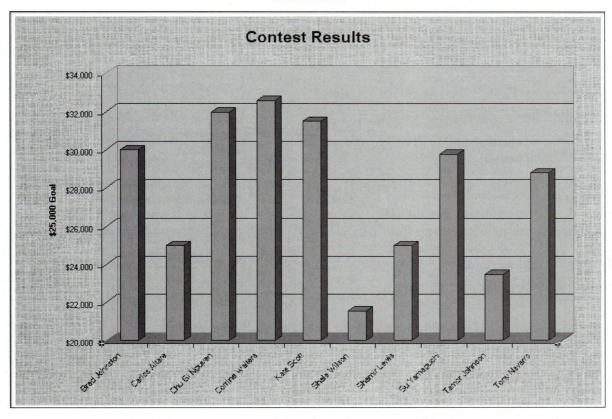

Exercise 20

Skills Covered:

◆ **Print a Workbook** ◆ **Print Multiple Copies**

◆ **Page Setup**

On the Job

Change the page setup of your worksheet and use the available print options to control the printed output of a report. For example, if you need to fit the worksheet on one page, you can change the margins, change the print orientation, change the paper size, and change the **scaling**. Add headers and footers to your report to repeat the same information at the top or bottom of each printed page.

> You work for Murray Hill Marketing, and as the account manager for the Dan's Digital Camera Works account, you've been asked to reprint the competitive survey you did for them last week. Before you do, however, you'll use many of your new printing skills in Excel to produce an even better looking report.

Terms

Scaling Reduces or enlarges information to fit on a specified number of pages.

Print options Selections that control what, where, how, and how many copies of the output to print.

Page Setup A dialog box that includes options to control the appearance of printed output.

Header Repeated information that appears in the top margin of a page.

Footer Repeated information that appears in the bottom margin of a page.

Notes

Print a Workbook

- The Print dialog box allows you to choose from a number of **print options**.

- As you learned in earlier lessons, normally only the active worksheet is printed when you choose File, Print or click the Print toolbar button.

  - If you select a range and choose Selection in the Print dialog box, that range will be the only data printed by default.

  - If you select multiple worksheets, those sheets will print by default.

- If you're using a number of worksheets within a single workbook and you want to print all of them, you don't need to select each sheet first. Just choose the Entire workbook option in the Print dialog box.

Print dialog box

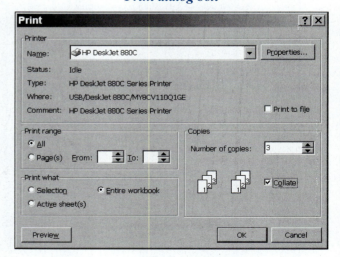

Print Multiple Copies

■ You can print multiple copies of your data by increasing the value in the Number of copies box.

■ If you print multiple copies of a multi-page document, select Collate so that each copy is printed in order: page 1, 2, 3, and so on.

Page Setup

■ Access the **Page Setup** dialog box from the Page Setup or Print Preview commands on the File menu to control printed output.

■ The following page tabs display in the Page Setup dialog box: Page, Margins, Header/Footer, and Sheet.

✓ *You'll learn about the Sheet tab in Exercise 21.*

Page Tab

Page tab of Page Setup dialog box

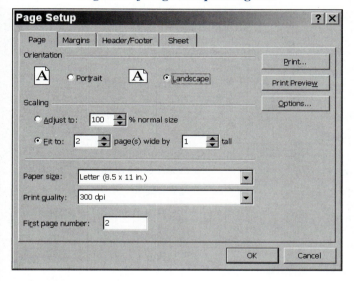

Orientation
• Print the worksheet in Portrait (vertical) or Landscape (horizontal) orientation.

Scaling
• Reduce or enlarge information through the Adjust to % normal size option. Use the Fit to pages option to compress worksheet data to fill a specific number of pages.

Paper size
• Change the paper size when printing on a paper size other than 8 ½" x 11".

Print quality
• Reduce the print quality to print draft output.

First page number
• Change the starting page number for the current worksheet.

Margins Tab

Margins tab of Page Setup dialog box

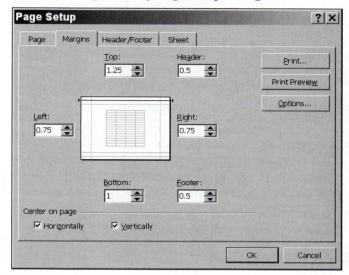

• Increase or decrease the Top, Bottom, Left, or Right margins to control the distance between your data and the edge of the paper.

• Increase or decrease the Header or Footer margins to specify the distance between the top/bottom of the page and the header/footer.

• Print the worksheet centered horizontally and/or vertically on the page.

Header/Footer Tab

Header/Footer tab of Page Setup dialog box

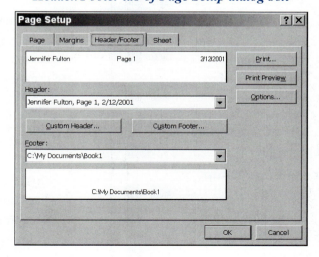

■ When you want to repeat the same information at the top of each page, create a **header**.

- When you want to repeat the same information at the bottom of each page, create a **footer**.
- You can select a pre-designed header or footer from those listed, or create customized ones.
- A customized header and footer is separated into three sections: left (text is left aligned), center (text is center aligned), and right (text is right aligned).
- When creating a custom header/footer, simply type the text you want to use into the appropriate section: left, center, or right.
- Text may be entered on multiple lines as needed.
- You can also click buttons to insert print codes for the current date, current time (both reset at time of printing), page number, file path, file name, sheet name into a custom header/footer.
- You can now insert a graphic (such as a company logo) into a custom header/footer.

- ✓ If you add graphics or additional lines of text, be sure to adjust the header/footer and top/bottom margins to allow enough space.

- The font, font style, and font size of the custom header/footer may also be changed.

- ✓ To change the font, style, or size of text in a pre-designed header or footer, just click the Custom Header or Custom Footer button after selecting the header/footer you want, and apply your font changes.

Custom Header/Footer dialog box

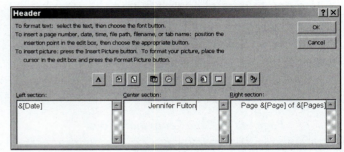

Procedures

Print Entire Workbook

1. Click **File** .... `Alt`+`F`
2. Click **Print** .... `P`
   OR
   Press .... `Ctrl`+`P`
3. Click **Entire workbook** .... `Alt`+`E`
4. Click **OK** .... `Enter`

Print Multiple Copies

1. Click **File** .... `Alt`+`F`
2. Click **Print** .... `P`
   OR
   Press .... `Ctrl`+`P`
3. Set **Number of copies** .... `Alt`+`C`
4. Print each copy in its own set by choosing **Collate** .... `Alt`+`O`
5. Click **OK** .... `Enter`

Access Page Setup

1. Click **File** .... `Alt`+`F`
2. Click **Page Setup** .... `U`
3. Select options.
4. Click **OK** .... `Enter`

Create Header or Footer

1. Click **File** .... `Alt`+`F`
2. Click **Page Setup** .... `U`
3. Click **Header/Footer** tab .... `Ctrl`+`Tab`

   To select built-in header or footer:
   a. Click **Header** drop-down arrow .... `Alt`+`A`
      OR
      Click **Footer** drop-down arrow..... `Alt`+`F`
   b. Click desired type in list .... `↓` `↑`, `Enter`

   To create custom header or footer:
   a. Click **Custom Header** ..... `Alt`+`C`
      OR
      Click **Custom Footer** ...... `Alt`+`U`
   b. Click appropriate section.
      - **Left section** ...... `Alt`+`L`
      - **Center section** . `Alt`+`C`
      - **Right section** ... `Alt`+`R`

   c. Type text to appear in header or footer.
      - ✓ Press Enter to insert text on another line.

   OR
   Click appropriate button to insert print code ... `Tab`, `Enter`
   - **Page Number** ...... `Alt`+`T`
   - **Total Pages** .... `Alt`+`U`
   - **Date** .... `Alt`+`D`
   - **Time** .... `Alt`+`M`
   - **Path and File name** .. `Alt`+`P`
   - **File name** ... `Alt`+`E`
   - **Sheet Name** .... `Alt`+`A`
   - **Picture** ...... `Alt`+`I`

   d. Choose **OK**.

To change font of custom header or footer text:

a. Select header or footer text.

b. Click **Font** button [A] .... [Tab] , [Enter]

   ✓ *Press Tab key until Font button is selected, then Enter.*

   OR

   Press...................... [Alt] + [F]

c. Choose from available font, font style, and font size options.

d. Click **OK**.................... [Enter]

To change format of picture

a. Select &[Picture] print code.

b. Click **Picture Format** button [icon] .... [Tab] , [Enter]

   ✓ *Press Tab key until Font button is selected, then Enter.*

   OR

   Press..................... [Alt] + [O]

c. Choose format options.

d. Click **OK**.................... [Enter]

4. Click **OK**.......................... [Enter]

Exercise Directions

1. Start Excel, if necessary.

2. Open 🖳**COMPETE** or open 💿**20COMPETE**.

3. Save the file as **COMPETE**.

4. Spell check the workbook.

5. Create a header and footer.

   a. Select Page 1 of ? from the Header list.

   b. To create the footer, click Custom Footer.

   c. Click inside the left hand section, then click the Date button to insert today's date. (See Illustration A.)

   d. Press Enter and click the Time button.

   e. Click inside the center section and type your name.

   f. Click inside the right section, and click the Picture button. Select the file 💿**murray hill marketing logo.gif**.

   g. Click the Format Picture button, and on the Size tab, set the Scale Height and Width to 25%.

6. Print the entire workbook, using the option in the Print dialog box.

7. Change to Sheet 2, select the chart, and copy it.

8. Change to Sheet 1, and place the copied chart within the range E19:K35 (do not resize the chart).

9. Click cell D6 so that the chart is no longer selected, then click Print Preview.

   ✓ *Notice that the sheet prints on two pages, and that the data is wider than it is long. In such a case, you may want to use Landscape orientation.*

10. Access Page Setup, and on the Page tab, change to Landscape orientation.

11. On the Margins tab, set the Bottom margin to 1.25". In addition, center the data on the page horizontally and vertically.

12. Preview the sheet again.

   ✓ *Everything's looking much better, except that the chart is printing on page one and two.*

13. Access Page Setup again, and on the Page tab, select the Fit to 1 page(s) wide by 1 tall option.

14. Print the result (see Illustration B).

15. Close the workbook, saving all changes.

Illustration A

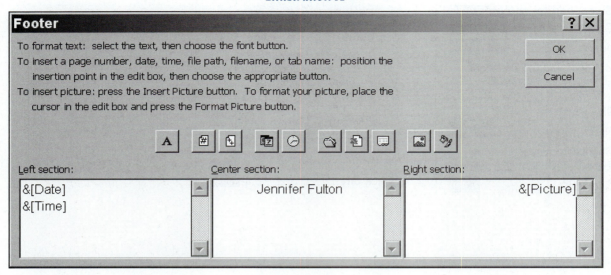

Footer

To format text: select the text, then choose the font button.

To insert a page number, date, time, file path, filename, or tab name: position the insertion point in the edit box, then choose the appropriate button.

To insert picture: press the Insert Picture button. To format your picture, place the cursor in the edit box and press the Format Picture button.

OK

Cancel

Left section:
&[Date]
&[Time]

Center section:
Jennifer Fulton

Right section:
&[Picture]

Illustration B

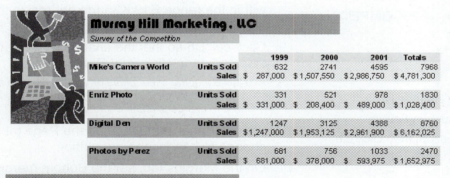

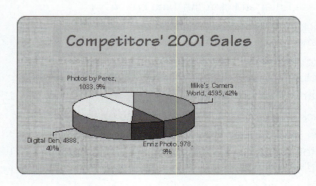

Page 1 of 1

Murray Hill Marketing, LLC
Survey of the Competition

		1999	2000	2001	Totals
Mike's Camera World	Units Sold	632	2741	4595	7968
	Sales	$ 287,000	$ 1,507,550	$ 2,986,750	$ 4,781,300
Enriz Photo	Units Sold	331	521	978	1830
	Sales	$ 331,000	$ 208,400	$ 489,000	$ 1,028,400
Digital Den	Units Sold	1247	3125	4388	8760
	Sales	$ 1,247,000	$ 1,953,125	$ 2,961,900	$ 6,162,025
Photos by Perez	Units Sold	681	756	1033	2470
	Sales	$ 681,000	$ 378,000	$ 593,975	$ 1,652,975

Summary

Average Units Sold each Year	1752.33333
Average Sales each Year	$ 1,135,392
Minimum Units Sold by Any Competitor in One Yr.	331
Maximum Units Sold by Any Competitor in One Yr.	4595

Competitors' 2001 Sales

Photos by Perez, 1033, 9%
Mike's Camera World, 4595, 42%
Digital Den, 4388, 40%
Enriz Photo, 978, 9%

2/12/2001
4:43 PM

Jennifer Fulton

On Your Own

1. Open the file **OXL16** that you created in the On Your Own section of Exercise 16, or open **20COLEXP**.

2. Save the file as **OXL20**.

3. Set the worksheet to print in Landscape mode.

4. Adjust the scaling so that the data is printed at 200% its normal size.

5. Create a custom header that includes your name, the current date, and the file name.

6. Format the header text using a font style and size you like.

7. Create a custom footer that lists your address and phone number.

8. Center the worksheet vertically on the page.

9. Spell check the worksheet.

10. Preview the worksheet.

11. Print two copies of the worksheet.

12. Close the workbook, saving all changes.

Exercise 21

Skills Covered:

◆ **Page Breaks** ◆ **Page Breaks Preview** ◆ **Set Print Area**
◆ **Repeat Row and Column Labels** ◆ **Other Sheet Tab Options**

On the Job

If you are not satisfied with the page layout defaults set in Excel, you can change them manually. For example, automatic page breaks are set if a worksheet doesn't fit on one page, but you can manually set your own page breaks before printing. If you need to print only part of a worksheet for a specific report, you can temporarily change the print area. When your printout includes multiple pages, you can reprint the row and column labels for your data on every page, making it easier for you to read the data. On large reports, gridlines may also help you interpret data correctly.

You're the accounting manager at Electron Consumer Industries, and it's time to print out the YTD (year-to-date) sales report. But before you do, you'll use your knowledge of Excel to insert page breaks where you want them, and to improve the overall look of the printout.

Terms

Page break A code inserted into a document that forces what follows to begin on a new page; a page break is represented in the document on your screen as a dashed line.

Page Break Preview A view that allows you to move and delete page breaks and redefine the print area.

Print area The specified range of cells to be printed.

Print titles Row and column labels that are reprinted on each page of a worksheet printout.

Gridlines Light gray lines that mark the cell borders.

Notes

Page Breaks

- When worksheet data will not fit on one page, Excel inserts automatic **page breaks** based on the paper size, margins, and scaling options.

- Automatic page breaks appear as dashed lines on the worksheet.

  ✓ *Page breaks appear on the worksheet in Normal view after you use Print Preview; they also appear in Page Break Preview.*

- If you prefer, you can override automatic page breaks and set manual page breaks before printing.

- While automatic page breaks (those created by Excel, based on your page setup options) appear as dashed lines, manual page breaks (those you create by either moving the automatic page breaks, or inserting new ones) display on the worksheet as bold dashed lines.

Page Break Preview

- **Page Break Preview** is a special view that displays both automatic and manual page breaks, and allows you to adjust them.

- In Page Break Preview, when you drag a dashed line (automatic page break) to move it, it changes to a solid line (manual page break).

- In Page Break Preview, drag a dashed line off the worksheet to remove a page break and reset the page breaks.

- You can also edit worksheet data and resize the **print area** from Page Break Preview.

- If you adjust a page break to include a few more columns or rows on a page, Excel automatically adjusts the scale (font size) to make that data fit on the page.

Set Print Area

- To print a selected area of data, adjust the print area.

- You can set the print area using Page Break Preview, the Print Area command on the File menu, or with a text box on the Sheet tab of the Page Setup dialog box.

- The print area appears on the worksheet with a dashed border and as a highlighted block in the Page Break Preview.

- You can define a unique print area for each worksheet in your workbook.

- To print the entire worksheet again, you must either clear the print area setting, or reset the print area to include all the data.

Repeat Row and Column Labels

- Using the Sheet tab of the Page Setup dialog box, you can select to reprint the **print titles** on each page of a worksheet printout.

- Without the row and column labels printed on each page, it might be difficult to decipher your data.

Other Sheet Tab Options

- The Sheet tab of the Page Setup dialog box provides an option for printing **gridlines** with your data.

- You can also print your worksheet in black and white (even if it includes color fills or graphics), in draft mode (faster printing, lower quality), with your comments, and with errors displayed.

- For large worksheets, you can specify the print order (the order in which data is selected to be printed on subsequent pages).

Sheet tab of Page Setup dialog box

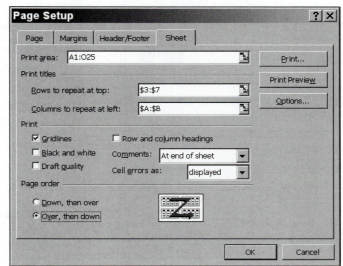

Procedures

Page Break Preview

1. Click **View** .... Alt+V
2. Click **Page Break Preview** ... P

OR

1. Click **Print Preview** button .
2. Click **Page Break Preview** ... V
   - ✓ If the Welcome to Page Break Preview dialog box displays, click **OK**.

To return to Normal view:

1. Click **View** .... Alt+V
2. Click **Normal** .... N

OR

1. Click **Print Preview** button .
2. Click **Normal View** V

   - ✓ When you are already in Page Break Preview, the Normal View Button appears on the Print Preview toolbar.

To move automatic or manual page break:

1. Switch to Page Break Preview.
2. Drag dashed or solid line to its new location.
   - ✓ The automatic page break dashed line changes to a solid line.

- ✓ When a manual page break is moved outside of the print area, the automatic page break is restored.

To remove all page breaks:

1. Switch to Page Break Preview.
2. Right-click cell on worksheet.
   - ✓ Shortcut menu appears.
3. Click **Reset All Page Breaks** .... A
   - ✓ Automatic page breaks are restored.

To adjust print area:

1. Switch to Page Break Preview.
2. Drag dark outline (border of print area) to resize it.

To restore print area:

1. Switch to Page Break Preview.
2. Right-click cell on worksheet.
   - ✓ *Shortcut menu appears.*
3. Click **Reset Print Area** .. `Alt`+`R`

Set Manual Page Breaks

- ✓ *Automatic page breaks that follow a manual page break will adjust automatically.*

To insert horizontal page break:

1. Click at beginning of row where new page should begin.
2. Click **Insert**.................. `Alt`+`I`
3. Click **Page Break**............... `B`

To insert vertical page break:

1. Click at beginning of column where new page should begin.
2. Click **Insert**.................. `Alt`+`I`
3. Click **Page Break**............... `B`

To insert both horizontal and vertical page breaks:

1. Click cell where new page should begin.
2. Click **Insert**.................. `Alt`+`I`
3. Click **Page Break**............... `B`

Set Print Area with File Menu

1. Select the worksheet area you wish to print.
2. Click **File** .... `Alt`+`F`
3. Click **Print Area** .... `T`
4. Click **Set Print Area**........... `S`

Clear Print Area with File Menu

1. Click **File** .... `Alt`+`F`
2. Click **Print Area** .... `T`
3. Click **Clear Print Area** .... `C`

Repeat Row and Column Labels

1. Click **File** .... `Alt`+`F`
2. Click **Page Setup** .... `U`
3. Click **Sheet** tab.......... `Ctrl`+`Tab`
4. Click **Rows to repeat at top**........................... `Alt`+`R`
5. Type the row numbers you wish to repeat at the top of each page.
   - ✓ *For example, to repeat the first seven rows, type 1:7.*
   - ✓ *You can also click the Collapse button and select the rows you wish to repeat.*

6. Click **Columns to repeat at left** .... `Alt`+`C`
7. Type the column letters you want to repeat to the left of each page.
   - ✓ *For example, to repeat the first three columns on the left, type A:C.*
   - ✓ *You can also click the Collapse button and select the columns you wish to repeat.*
8. Click **OK**............................. `Enter`

Print Gridlines

1. Click **File**..................... `Alt`+`F`
2. Click **Page Setup** .... `U`
3. Click **Sheet** tab.......... `Ctrl`+`Tab`
4. Click **Gridlines** .... `Alt`+`G`
5. Click **OK**.................................. `Enter`

Select Other Sheet Tab Options

1. Click **File**..................... `Alt`+`F`
2. Click **Page Setup** .... `U`
3. Click **Sheet** tab.......... `Ctrl`+`Tab`
4. Select options.
5. Click **OK**......................... `Enter`

Exercise Directions

1. Start Excel, if necessary.
2. Open 💿 **21YTDCHIPS**.
3. Save the file as **YTDCHIPS**.
4. Click Print Preview.
   - ✓ *Currently, the worksheet is set to print on three pages, but the chart is split and the design is confusing.*
5. Click Close to return to Normal view.
   - ✓ *Dashed lines appear, marking the automatic page breaks.*
6. Choose View, Page Break Preview. Click OK if prompted.
7. Insert a page break that places the chart on its own page:
   a. Click cell A18.
   b. Choose Insert, Page Break.

8. Use the Page tab of Page Setup to change to landscape orientation.
9. On the Sheet tab, change to Over, then down page order.
10. On the Sheet tab, enter 1:7 as the rows to repeat at top and A:B as the columns to repeat at left.
11. In the Page Break Preview, drag the automatic page break between columns I and J so that it resides between columns H and I.
    - ✓ *This will place six months of data on each page.*
12. Resize the chart so that it fits on page 3, without flowing over onto page 4 (Illustration A).
    - ✓ *You'll notice that I placed my chart with its left edge in column C, rather than columns A or B. The reason is that we've set up columns A and B to repeat on every page. If you place your chart there, the repeated headings in columns A and B will overlap it.*

13. Return to Normal view, spell check, then print the worksheet.

    ✓ *The worksheet prints on four pages, the last one blank. This is an Excel error. To get around this, you will print the worksheet data, then the chart.*

14. Select the range A1:N17, then choose File, Print Area, Set Print Area.

15. Print the worksheet again.

16. Click to select the chart, and print it.

17. Close the workbook, saving all changes.

Illustration A

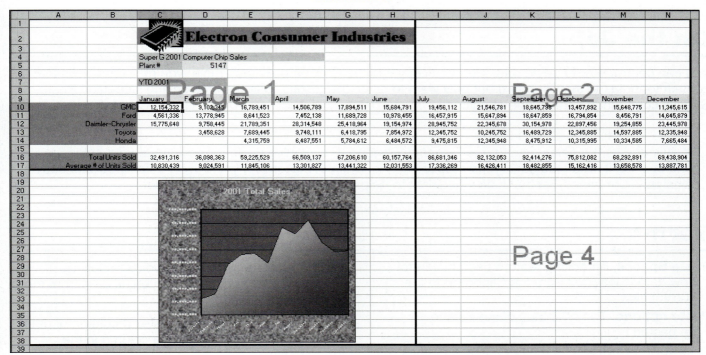

On Your Own

1. Open the **OXL18** file you used in the On Your Own section of Exercise 18, or open **21CDMANIA**.

2. Save the file as **OXL21**.

3. Change to Page Break Preview.

    ✓ *The print area, set in a prior lesson, is still active.*

4. Clear the print area settings.

5. Drag the print area border so that the Summary will not be printed.

6. Spell check, then print the worksheet.

7. Insert a page break between the Quarter 1 and Quarter 2 data.

8. Use Page Setup to print the row and column labels on each page of the printout.

9. Print the worksheet.

10. Print the worksheet again, this time with gridlines and in black and white.

11. Return to Normal view.

12. Close the workbook, saving all changes.

Exercise 22

Skills Covered:

◆ Copy and Paste Special ◆ Transpose Data

On the Job

You can control how to paste data after you copy it to the Clipboard. For example, you may copy cells that contain formulas to the Clipboard but only want to paste the results. Use the time-saving Copy and Paste Special commands for this type of editing.

It's July and as the sales manager at Regency General, Inc., you've decided to continue your sales contest since it produced such good results in June. So in this exercise, you'll use Paste Special to copy selected information from the June worksheet to help you set up the July Contest sheet.

Terms

Paste Special An editing feature used to control how data is inserted from the Clipboard to the current file.

Paste options The attributes of the data to be pasted.

Operation options The mathematical functions that can be applied to copied data.

Skip blanks An option that avoids replacing values in the paste area with blank cells from the copy area.

Transpose An option that pastes a column of data to a row or a row of data to a column in the current file.

Notes

Copy and Paste Special

- The **Paste Special** feature gives you control over how to insert data into a file from the Clipboard.
- The Paste Special dialog box contains the following options:
  - **Paste options** specify the attributes of the selection to be pasted.
    - All: pastes the contents and the formatting of the copied cells.
    - Formulas: pastes only the formulas as shown in the Formula bar.
    - Values: pastes only the values as shown in the cells.
    - Formats: pastes only the formats of the copied cells.

  ✓ *Copying formatting from one cell to another is a very common practice because it makes the process of formatting a worksheet so much easier. Because it's so popular, the Paste Special Formats command has its own toolbar button called the Format Painter.*

  - Comments: pastes only the comments attached to the copied cells.
  - Validation: pastes data validation rules for the copied cells.
  - All except borders: pastes the contents and formatting of the copied cells, except for borders.
  - Column widths: pastes the column widths of the selected cells.

◆ Formulas and number formats: pastes formulas (not results) and the number formats, but no additional formatting, such as color fills.

◆ Values and number formats: pastes the results of formulas (and not the formulas themselves), along with number formats. Additional formatting, such as text colors, is not copied.

- **Operation options** specifies the mathematical operation to use when data from the copy area is combined with data in the paste area.

  ✓ *You'll learn more about this option in Exercise 23.*

- **Skip blanks** in the copy area so they do not overwrite data in the paste area.

- **Transpose** pastes a column of data in the copy area to a row or a row of data in the copy area to a column.

  ✓ *You'll learn about the Paste Link option in Exercise 25.*

Paste Special dialog box

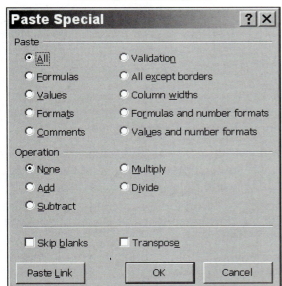

■ As you learned in Exercise 9, you can perform some of the Paste Special commands using the down arrow on the Paste button.

■ You can also change the formatting that's copied after a paste operation using the Paste Options button that appears on the worksheet next to the copied data.

  ✓ *By using the Paste button menu and the Paste Options button, you can perform many Paste Special functions without having to display the Paste Special dialog box. However, certain Paste Special functions, such as pasting validation rules only, skipping blanks, or performing a mathematical operation on data may only be done using the options in the Paste Special dialog box.*

Transpose Data

■ You can copy data in a column and then paste it into a row, or copy data in a row and then paste it into a column.

■ If you're transposing a group of cells containing formulas, Excel will adjust the cell references in the formulas so that they point to the correct transposed cells.

  ✓ *You can transpose data with formulas and paste the formula values only by selecting those options in the Paste Special dialog box.*

Row labels are transposed and pasted into the column

	A	B	C	D
1	1st Qtr	2nd Qtr	3rd Qtr	4th Qtr
2				
3				
4	1st Qtr			
5	2nd Qtr			
6	3rd Qtr			
7	4th Qtr			

Procedures

Paste Special Using Paste Special Dialog Box

1. Select range to copy.
2. Click **Edit**.................... `Alt`+`E`
3. Click **Copy** .... `C`
4. Click upper-left corner of range to receive data.
   a. Click **Edit** .... `Alt`+`E`
   b. Click **Paste Special** .... `S`
   OR
   a. Click down arrow on **Paste** button `📋▾`.
   b. Click **Paste Special** .... `S`
5. Select appropriate option from Paste Special dialog box.
6. Click **OK** .... `Enter`

Paste Special Using Paste Menu

1. Select range to copy.
2. Click **Edit**.................... `Alt`+`E`
3. Click **Copy** .... `C`
4. Click upper-left corner of range to receive data.
5. Click down arrow on **Paste** button `📋▾`.
6. Select Paste option.
   ✓ *The options that appear will vary, based on the contents of the data to be copied.*
   ✓ *After copying, if you need to adjust the pasted formatting, click the Paste Options button on the worksheet and select the option you want.*

Copying Formats with Format Painter

1. Click a cell that contains the formatting you wish to copy.
2. Click the **Format Painter** button `🖌`.
3. Drag the mouse pointer over the cells to which you want to paste the copied format.

✓ *If you double-click the Format Painter button, it stays on so you can drag the mouse pointer over several groups of cells. When you're through pasting formats, click the Format Painter button once to turn it off.*

Transpose Data

1. Select range to copy.
2. Click **Edit** .... `Alt`+`E`
3. Click **Copy** .... `C`
4. Click upper-left corner of range to receive data.
5. Click down arrow on **Paste** button `📋▾`.
6. Click **Transpose.**
   ✓ *The data is transposed. Formulas are adjusted so that cell references point to the correct cells.*
   ✓ *To transpose data with formulas and to paste only values, use the Paste Values and Transpose options in the Paste Special dialog box.*

Exercise Directions

1. Start Excel, if necessary.
2. Open ⌨**SALESCONT** or 💿**22SALESCONT**.
3. Save the file as **SALESCONT**.
4. Rename Sheet 1 **June Contest**.
5. Rename Sheet 2 **July Contest**.
6. On the June Contest sheet, select the range A1:G8 and click Copy.
   ✓ *Because of the location of the graphic, you might find it easier to select this range by clicking cell G8 and dragging up to cell A1.*
7. Click cell A1 on the July Contest sheet, then click Paste.
   ✓ *The data is copied, but the column widths are not right. To fix that, you'll use Paste Special to copy the column widths as well.*
8. Choose Edit, Paste Special.
9. Select Column widths, and click OK.
10. On the June Contest sheet, select the range C11:D21, and click Copy.
11. Click cell C11 on the July Contest sheet, then click the down arrow on the Paste button and select Transpose.
12. On the June Contest sheet, select the range F11:F21, and click Copy.
13. Click cell C13 on the July Contest sheet, and select Edit, Paste Special.
14. Choose Values and number formats and Transpose, then click OK.
15. Adjust the column widths to fit the data.
16. Change C5 to **July Sales Contest**.

17. Type the following in the designated cells:

    a. In cell C15, type **July Total**.

    b. In cell C16, type **No. of Clients**

    c. In cell C17, type **Average Sale per Client**

    d. In cell C18, type **Met Goal?**

18. Click cell C12, double-click the Format Painter button, then drag over cells C15:C18 to copy the format. Click the Format Painter button again to turn it off.

19. In cell D17, type a formula that computes the average July sale per client by dividing the July sales total in cell D15 by the total number of clients in cell D16.

    ✓ *Because cell D16 is currently empty (the July sales totals and number of clients for each representative have yet to be entered), this formula will result in an error. Click the error button and select Ignore Error. To avoid the error, you can use the formula, =IF(D16=0,"",D15/D16), which only performs the calculation if cell D16 contains data.*

20. In cell D18, type the formula, =IF(D15>$C$8,IF(D17>D13,"Yes",""),"")

    ✓ *This formula displays Yes in cell D18 only if the July Sales Total is greater than the goal, and if the average sale for July is greater than the average sale for June.*

21. Select cells D17:D18, then use the fill handle to copy the formulas to the range E17:M18.

22. Spell check the worksheet.

23. Print the worksheet.

24. Close the workbook, saving all changes.

Illustration A

	D17		▼	*fx*	=IF(D16=0,"",D15/D16)					
	A	B	C	D	E	F	G	H	I
1									
2									
3			Regency General, Inc.						
4									
5			June Sales Contest						
6									
7									
8		Sales Goal	$25,000						
9									
10									
11			Salesperson	Brad Johnston	Carlos Altare	Chu Gi Nguyen	Corrine Walters	Kate Scott	Shale Wilson Sha
12			June Total	$ 29,984	$ 24,975	$ 31,948	$ 32,548	$ 31,475	$ 21,556 $
13			Average Sale per Client	$ 2,998.40	$ 2,775.00	$ 3,993.50	$ 3,254.80	$3,497.22	$ 3,079.43 $
14									
15			July Total						
16			No. of Clients						
17			Average Sale per Client						
18			Met Goal?						
19									

On Your Own

1. Open the file **OXL20**, created in the On Your Own section of Exercise 20, or open ⊙ **22COLEXP**.

2. Save the file as **OXL22**.

3. In a cell below the data already entered in the worksheet, type the title: **Expense Analysis**.

4. Use Format Painter to copy the format from the worksheet title to this cell.

5. Label a column: **Months**; then label the column to the right of the Months column: **Totals**; and then label the column to the right of the Totals column: **% of Total**.

6. Use Format Painter to copy the format from your column labels above to this group of cells.

7. Select the range of cells at the top of the worksheet containing the labels for the months, and transpose it into the Months column you created in step 5.

   ✓ *Do not copy the formats—copy just the values.*

8. Select the range of cells in the worksheet data displaying the results of the formulas totaling the expenses for each month, and transpose the values into the Totals column you created in step 5.

   ✓ *Paste the values and the number formats, but not the formulas themselves.*

9. At the bottom of the new Totals columns, enter a formula to calculate the total annual expenses. Format the results as currency.

10. In the % of Total column, enter formulas to calculate each month's percent of the total annual expenses (use an absolute reference to the total annual expenses). Apply the Percentage format with two decimals to the results.

11. Adjust column width and apply formatting to improve the appearance of the worksheet.

12. Spell check the worksheet.

13. Print the worksheet.

14. Close the workbook, saving all changes.

Exercise 23

◆ **Combine Data**

On the Job

Use the Copy and Paste Special commands when you need to copy and combine data. For example, you may have individual worksheets containing the items sold each month and a summary sheet showing the total inventory. Use the Paste Special command, Subtract operation to reduce the inventory on the summary sheet by the number of items sold each month.

Your client Golden Harvest, has asked you, an account manager at Murray Hill Marketing, to prepare another report based on the data you collected on organic food users and their buying habits. Last time, the totals for men and women were separate. Now, Golden Harvest would like to see those figures combined. To create the totals you need for this new report, you'll use the Paste Special command and its Operation feature.

Terms

Copied cells Data copied to the Clipboard.

Destination cells The new location to receive the pasted data.

Notes

Combine Data

■ Using the Paste Special Operation commands, you can combine data when you paste it on top of existing data. Excel uses the mathematical operation (addition, subtraction, and so on) that you select to combine the data in the **copied cells** with the data in the **destination cells**.

■ Operations options include:

- None: replaces destination cells with copied cells. This is the default setting.

- Add: adds numeric data in copied cells to values in destination cells.

- Subtract: subtracts numeric data in copied cells from values in destination cells.

- Multiply: multiplies numeric data in copied cells by values in destination cells.

- Divide: divides numeric data in copied cells by values in destination cells.

Paste Special dialog box

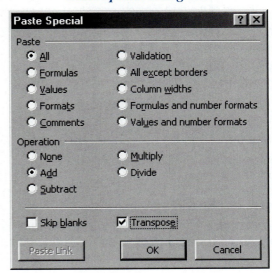

Procedures

Combine Data with Paste Special

1. Select range of cells to copy.
2. Click **Edit** .... Alt + E
3. Click **Copy** C
4. Select upper-left cell of destination area.
5. Click **Edit** .... Alt + E
6. Click **Paste Special** .... S
7. Select **Operation** option:
   - **None** .... O
   - **Add** .... D
   - **Subtract** .... S
   - **Multiply** .... M
   - **Divide** I
8. Select additional Paste Special options as desired.
9. Click **OK** .... Enter

Exercise Directions

1. Start Excel, if necessary.
2. Open 🖮**ORGANIC** or open 💿**23ORGANIC**.
3. Save the file as **ORGANIC**.
4. Insert a new worksheet after the Buying Habits – Men worksheet. Name it **Buying Habits – Totals**.

   ✓ *You'll need to select the Buying Habits – Men worksheet, then insert the new worksheet and move it into last position. The tab, by the way, will be yellow, like the Buying Habits – Men worksheet, which was selected at the time the new worksheet was inserted.*

5. On the Buying Habits – Women worksheet, select the range A1:K9, and click Copy.
6. Click cell A1 on the Buying Habits – Totals worksheet, and click Paste.
7. In cell D9 type **Total Percentages**.
8. On the Buying Habits – Women worksheet, select the range C11:I17, and click Copy.
9. Click cell D12 of the Buying Habits – Totals worksheet, click the button on the Paste button, and select Transpose. Adjust column widths as needed.
10. Select the range E12:J12 and add a Plum fill. Apply bold formatting to this range as well.
11. On the Buying Habits – Men worksheet, select the range D12:I17. Click Copy.
12. Click cell E13 on the Buying Habits – Totals worksheet, and choose Edit, Paste Special.
13. Under Operation, select Add. Choose the Transpose option and click OK.
14. Select the range D9:D18 and click Copy.
15. Click cell D21 and click Paste.
16. In cell D21 type **Total People**.
17. Select the range E12:J12 and click Copy.
18. Click cell E24 and click Paste.
19. In cell E25, type 1200. Use the fill handle to copy this value to the range E25:J30.
20. Select the range E13:J18 and click Copy.
21. Click cell E25, then choose Edit, Paste Special.
22. Under Operation, choose Multiply, then click OK.
23. Apply Comma style, two decimal places to the range E25:J30.
24. Spell check the worksheet.
25. Print the worksheet.
26. Close the workbook, saving all changes.

Illustration A

	D	E	F	G	H	I	J
11							
12		Under 25	26-32	33-40	41-45	46-55	Over 55
13	Fruits	35%	32%	40%	35%	34%	26%
14	Vegetables	57%	45%	62%	57%	41%	27%
15	Meats	28%	54%	31%	76%	75%	104%
16	Cheese	54%	50%	20%	4%	13%	19%
17	Eggs	24%	13%	25%	18%	20%	12%
18	Milk Products	2%	6%	22%	10%	17%	12%
19							
20							
21	Total People						
22							
23							
24		Under 25	26-32	33-40	41-45	46-55	Over 55
25	Fruits	420.00	384.00	480.00	420.00	408.00	312.00
26	Vegetables	684.00	540.00	744.00	684.00	492.00	324.00
27	Meats	336.00	648.00	372.00	912.00	900.00	1,248.00
28	Cheese	648.00	600.00	240.00	48.00	156.00	228.00
29	Eggs	288.00	156.00	300.00	216.00	240.00	144.00
30	Milk Products	24.00	72.00	264.00	120.00	204.00	144.00

On Your Own

1. Open the file **OXL22**, created in the previous On Your Own section, or open ⊚ **23COLEXP**.

2. Save the file as **OXL23**.

3. Create a semester summary by copying A1:A10 to Sheet 2.

4. For column labels, type **Semester 1** and **Semester 2**.

5. Copy the expenses for September to the Semester 1 column of Sheet 2.

6. Using Paste Special, add the expenses for October, November, and December to the Semester 1 column.

7. Copy the expenses for January to the Semester 2 column of Sheet 2.

8. Using Paste Special, add the expenses for February, March, April, and May to the Semester 2 column.

9. Create formulas that total the expenses for Semesters 1 and 2.

10. Format the Semester Expenses worksheet as you like.

11. Spell check the worksheet.

12. Print the worksheet.

13. Close the workbook, saving all changes.

Exercise 24

◆ **Freeze Labels** ◆ **Split Panes**

On the Job

When working with a large worksheet, you can freeze row and/or column labels to keep them in view and split the worksheet window into two or four panes. Freezing labels enables you to quickly identify a piece of data embedded within a large worksheet, while splitting a window into panes enables you to view multiple parts of a worksheet at the same time—in order to compare or copy data, for example.

You're the owner of Coastline Gourmet Importers, and last year you expanded your food line and experienced incredible growth. You're looking at the possibility of expanding again this year, but first you want to analyze last year's sales figures. Because the worksheet is large, you'll use the freeze labels and split window options to help you read the data correctly.

Terms

Freeze A method to keep labels in view when scrolling through a worksheet.

Panes Window sections that allow you to see different parts of the worksheet at one time.

Notes

Freeze Labels

- When you need to keep labels in view at the top or left edge of the worksheet as you scroll through it, you can **freeze** them in place.

- Position the insertion point in the column to the right or the row below the data to be frozen, then select the Freeze Panes command from the Windows menu.

- Thin lines indicate the borders of the frozen area. Within these borders, you can scroll using the arrow keys, and the frozen row/column labels will remain in view.

- To remove the freeze, use the Unfreeze Panes command.

Column A titles remain in view as you scroll the worksheet horizontally

	A	G	H	I	J	K	
1							
2	**Flying High**						
3							
4		June	July	August	September	October	Nove
5	Disk Production	$ 15,441	$ 23,147	$18,647	$ 16,214	$12,348	$ 1
6	Shipping	$ 1,544	$ 2,315	$ 1,865	$ 1,622	$ 1,235	$
7	Handling	$ 1,109	$ 1,662	$ 1,339	$ 1,164	$ 886	$
8	Packaging	$ 2,530	$ 3,793	$ 3,056	$ 2,657	$ 2,023	$
9	Promotions	$ 4,465	$ 6,694	$ 5,393	$ 4,689	$ 3,570	$
10							
11	Total Expenses for the Month	$ 25,089	$ 37,611	$30,300	$ 26,346	$20,062	$ 3
12							
13	Percentage of Total Expenses	16%	23%	19%	16%	12%	

Split Panes

- When you need to view different parts of a large worksheet at the same time, split the worksheet horizontally or vertically into **panes** using the Window menu.

390

- When you position the insertion point in a cell in Row 1 and use the Split command, the vertical panes scroll together when scrolling up and down, and independently when scrolling left to right.

- When you position the insertion point in a cell in Column A and use the Split command, the horizontal panes scroll together when scrolling left to right, and independently when scrolling up and down.

■ With the mouse, drag the horizontal or vertical split box to split the window into panes.

■ When you need to cancel the split, use the Remove Split command from the Window menu.

Window split into four panes

	A	B	C	D	I	J	K	L	M	N
2	**Flying High Sales - Expens**									
3										
4		January	February	March	August	September	October	November	December	Totals
5	Disk Production	$ 15,642	$ 14,687	$18,741	$18,647	$ 16,214	$12,348	$ 19,478	$ 21,548	$ 99,380
6	Shipping	$ 1,564	$ 1,469	$ 1,874	$ 1,865	$ 1,622	$ 1,235	$ 1,948	$ 2,155	$ 9,938
7	Handling	$ 1,125	$ 1,056	$ 1,347	$ 1,339	$ 1,164	$ 886	$ 1,398	$ 1,547	$ 7,142
5	Disk Production	$ 15,642	$ 14,687	$18,741	$18,647	$ 16,214	$12,348	$ 19,478	$ 21,548	$ 99,380
6	Shipping	$ 1,564	$ 1,469	$ 1,874	$ 1,865	$ 1,622	$ 1,235	$ 1,948	$ 2,155	$ 9,938
7	Handling	$ 1,125	$ 1,056	$ 1,347	$ 1,339	$ 1,164	$ 886	$ 1,398	$ 1,547	$ 7,142
8	Packaging	$ 2,564	$ 2,407	$ 3,071	$ 3,056	$ 2,657	$ 2,023	$ 3,191	$ 3,530	$ 16,285
9	Promotions	$ 4,525	$ 4,248	$ 5,420	$ 5,393	$ 4,689	$ 3,570	$ 5,631	$ 6,229	$ 28,740
10										
11	Total Expenses for the Month	$ 25,420	23,867	$30,453	$30,300	$ 26,346	$20,062	$ 31,646	$ 35,009	$161,485
12										
13	Percentage of Total Expenses	16%	15%	19%	19%	16%	12%	20%	22%	
14										
15										

Procedures

Freeze Labels

1. Select the row below horizontal labels to freeze.
   OR
   Select column to the right of vertical labels to freeze.
   OR
   Select cell located in row below horizontal labels and column to right of vertical labels to freeze both row and column labels.
2. Click **Window** .... Alt + W
3. Click **Freeze Panes** .... F
   - ✓ Use this feature if window is not split into panes.

Unfreeze Labels

1. Click **Window** .... Alt + W
2. Click **Unfreeze Panes** .... F

Split Worksheet into Panes with Menu

- ✓ This feature provides simultaneous pane scrolling.

1. Select row below desired horizontal split.
   OR
   Select column to right of desired vertical split.
   OR
   Select a cell located below and to right of desired horizontal and vertical split.
2. Click **Window** .... Alt + W
3. Click **Split** .... S

Split Worksheet into Panes with Split Boxes

- ✓ This feature provides simultaneous pane scrolling.

1. Point to horizontal split box ▶ on scroll bar.
   OR

Point to vertical split box ▲ on scroll bar.

2. Click and drag mouse split pointer ↔ along horizontal scroll bar until split bar is positioned.
   OR
   Click and drag mouse split pointer ↕ along vertical scroll bar until split bar is positioned.

Remove Split

- Double-click split bar.
OR
1. Click **Window** .... Alt + W
2. Click **Remove Split** .... S

Adjust Panes

1. Place mouse over split bar until cursor changes to up and down pointing or right and left pointing arrows ↕.
2. Click and drag the bar to a new position.

Move Between Panes

- Click in desired pane.

OR

- Press **F6 key**...................... `F6`
  until active cell is positioned in
  desired pane.

Freeze Panes in Split Window

✓ *This procedure is used to lock top
  or left pane when scrolling.*

1. Click **Window**.............. `Alt`+`W`
2. Click **Freeze Panes**............. `F`

Unfreeze Panes in Split Window

1. Click **Window** .... `Alt`+`W`
2. Click **Unfreeze Panes** .... `F`

Exercise Directions

1. Start Excel, if necessary.

2. Open ⊙ **24FOODYTD**.

3. Save the file as **FOODYTD**.

4. Click cell B11, and choose Window, Freeze Panes to freeze the row and column labels.

5. Use the arrow keys to scroll down to row 35 and over to the August column.

   ✓ *Note how the row and column labels are frozen so that you can still read the item names and the month label.*

6. Unfreeze the labels by choosing Window, Unfreeze Panes.

7. Click cell H11, and split the window into four panes by choosing Window, Split.

8. Click cell H9, then use the arrow keys to scroll up to row 1.

   ✓ *Notice that the two upper panes remain in synch, while the two lower panes are frozen.*

9. Use the arrow keys to scroll down to row 10, so that the column labels are once again visible in the upper panes.

10. Click cell D13, then use the arrow keys to scroll left until column A is visible.

    ✓ *Notice that the two left panes scroll in synch, while the two right panes are frozen.*

11. Use the arrow keys to scroll down to row 32.

    ✓ *This time, the two bottom panes scroll in synch.*

12. Remove the panes by choosing Window, Remove Split.

13. Spell check the worksheet.

14. Print the worksheet.

15. Close the workbook, saving all changes.

Illustration A

	A	B	C	H	I	J	K	
1								
2	COASTLINE GOURMET IMPORTERS							
3	7334 Sunshine Pkwy 12th Floor							
4	Miami, Florida 33132							
5	Ph. 305-555-7300 * Fax: 305-555-7301 * e-mail: mail@ddcpub.com/coastlinegourmet							
6								
7	YTD Food Sales							
8								
9								
10	Item	January	February	July	August	September	October	No
32	Farfalle with Butternut Squash, Mushrooms & Spinach	$ 6,458.97	$ 6,362.09	$ 5,573.81	$ 6,409.89	$ 6,166.31	$ 5,931.99	$
33	Almond Raspberry Clafoutis	$ 13,465.98	$ 13,263.99	$ 11,620.56	$ 13,363.65	$ 12,855.83	$ 12,367.31	$
34	Orange Roughy with Tomato-Cilantro Salsa	$ 11,546.94	$ 11,373.74	$ 9,964.51	$ 11,459.19	$ 11,023.74	$ 10,604.84	$
35	Chocolate Chili	$ 16,458.97	$ 17,775.69	$ 14,203.39	$ 16,333.89	$ 15,713.21	$ 15,116.10	$
36	Grilled Victoria Trout	$ 17,994.56	$ 19,434.12	$ 15,528.54	$ 17,857.82	$ 17,179.22	$ 16,526.41	$
37	Sea Bass Sushi	$ 4,312.89	$ 4,097.25	$ 5,322.06	$ 4,635.42	$ 4,310.87	$ 5,216.15	$
38	Seared Scallops with Haricot Verts and Truffle Oil	$ 14,947.21	$ 14,199.85	$ 18,444.68	$ 16,065.00	$ 14,940.19	$ 18,077.63	$
39	Sesame Crab Claw	$ 5,894.81	$ 5,600.07	$ 7,274.13	$ 6,335.64	$ 5,892.04	$ 7,129.37	$
40	Shrimp Chipotle	$ 11,594.31	$ 11,014.59	$ 14,307.24	$ 12,461.36	$ 11,588.87	$ 14,022.53	$
41	Squid Paste	$ 2,175.84	$ 2,067.05	$ 2,684.96	$ 2,338.55	$ 2,174.82	$ 2,631.53	$
42	Zabaglione Tart with Marsala-Lemon Sauce	$ 6,134.95	$ 5,828.20	$ 7,570.46	$ 6,593.74	$ 6,132.07	$ 7,419.80	$
43		$ 113,850.43	$ 108,157.91	$140,490.09	$122,364.45	$113,796.98	$137,694.34	$1
44								

On Your Own

1. Start Excel, if necessary.

   ✓ *Pretend you are a teacher, and that you need to create a worksheet to track your students test scores and grades.*

2. Save the workbook as **OXL24**.

3. In row 2, type a title for the worksheet.

4. Enter students' names in column A, beginning in row 5. Enter at least 25 names.

5. In row 4, beginning in column B, enter the labels for the tests and quizzes you need to track.

   ✓ *For example, type* **Test 1**, **Test 2**, **Quiz 1**, **Test 3**, **Quiz 2**, *and so on. Enter labels for a total of at least 12 tests and quizzes.*

6. Split the screen to the right of the student names and below the column labels.

7. Use the split windows to help you enter scores for all the tests and quizzes.

   a. Enter scores as whole numbers, such as 78.

   b. If you want to speed up your data entry, enter a range of scores and then copy those scores to another part of the worksheet.

8. Apply formatting to the worksheet.

9. Spell check the worksheet.

10. Print the worksheet.

11. Close the workbook, saving all changes.

Illustration B

	A	B	C	D	E	F	G	H	I	J	K	L	M
1													
2		Student Grades - Spring Semester, 2001											
3													
4		Test 1	Test 2	Quiz 1	Test 3	Quiz 2	Test 4	Quiz 3	Quiz 4	Quiz 5	Test 5	Quiz 6	Test 6
5	Antonia Whitney	83	100	72	97	85	93	79	91	94	89	100	
6	Bonnie Sferruzzi	59	71	82	98	82	79	91	59	59	65	89	
7	Carlos Altare	76	86	74	71	95	84	100	76	76	59	84	10
8	Chu Gi Nguyen	55	98	85	68	82	71	95	55	55	76	71	
9	Chu Lee	82	100	59	84	74	59	95	82	82	55	68	
10	Corrine Walters	67	82	76	71	85	76	59	67	67	82	99	
11	Eram Hassan	95	71	55	68	82	55	76	86	68	67	89	
12	Jan Borough	61	65	42	71	61	59	55	54	61	48	20	
13	Jewel Vidito	76	98	67	89	85	67	82	100	89	84	93	
14	Joshua Fedor	84	100	74	71	95	84	67	95	98	71	61	
15	Juan Nuniez	71	95	85	68	82	71	95	82	93	68	81	
16	Jyoti Shaw	68	55	61	59	64	42	36	70	58	61	41	
17	Kate Scott	99	85	76	81	98	76	89	85	81	89	85	
18	Katerina Flynn	89	74	55	95	84	55	98	98	59	98	98	
19	Maria Navarro	98	85	82	82	71	82	74	71	76	84	100	
20	Meghan Ryan	93	71	99	85	82	55	85	68	55	71	95	
21	Michael Jordain	61	65	89	85	67	82	81	98	82	81	98	
22	Rafiquil Damir	81	98	84	100	86	91	59	76	67	100	59	
23	Shakur Brown	84	74	71	95	74	71	76	84	100	95	76	
24	Shale Wilson	100	85	68	82	85	68	55	71	95	82	55	
25	Shamir Lewis	89	73	99	85	68	82	82	96	99	85	82	
26	Shiree Wilson	98	95	89	85	99	85	67	82	89	85	67	
27	Su Yamaguchi	76	91	98	98	89	85	98	70	98	98	82	

Exercise 25

◆ Drag-and-Drop Editing between Workbooks
◆ Link Workbooks

On the Job

Arrange open files on the screen so you can see the worksheets as you work on them. For example, you may want to copy or move information across worksheets using the drag-and-drop procedure. You may want to consolidate information from several workbooks into a single summary workbook using the link feature. With the source and destination workbooks open on the screen, you can see the linked information update as source data changes.

You're the inventory manager at Coastline Gourmet Importers, and it's time to take the August inventory so you can calculate food sales. At the same time, you want to create a workbook to track the September inventory, so you'll use drag and drop to copy data from the August inventory workbook. Since you often find mistakes in the closing inventory numbers after they are taken, you'll use the link workbooks feature to link the ending inventory figures for August to the beginning inventory column in the September workbook, ensuring that any changes you make in the August workbook after the fact will be automatically updated to the September workbook.

Terms

Drag-and-drop To use the mouse to copy or move information from one location to another on a worksheet, across worksheets, or across workbooks.

Link A reference in a dependent workbook to a cell or cells in the source workbook.

Source The workbook that contains the data being referenced.

Dependent The workbook that references the data in the source.

External references References to cells in other workbooks.

Notes

Drag-and-Drop Editing between Workbooks

- If you arrange open workbooks on the screen, you can use the **drag-and-drop** procedure to copy or move data across workbooks.

- To copy data, press the Ctrl key while dragging the border of the selected range from the source to the destination workbook.

- To move data, drag the border of the selected range from the source to the destination workbook.

Link Workbooks

- When you need to consolidate information from one or more workbooks into a summary workbook, create a **link**.

- The **source** workbook provides the data.

- The **dependent** workbook contains the link to the **external references** in the source workbook.

- The default setting for linking is to update workbook links automatically. This means that, as data in the source workbook is changed, the linked data in the destination workbook is updated as well.

- If the dependent workbook is not open when data in the source workbook is changed, then the data in the dependent workbook will be changed later, when that workbook is opened.

  ✓ *If you open a dependent workbook without opening a source workbook first, you'll be asked if you want to update your dependent workbook. You can choose to update at that time, or not to update at all.*

- You can link a file in one of three ways:

  • Copy data from the source workbook and paste it into the dependent workbook using the Paste Special, Paste Link command to create an external reference that links the workbooks.

  • Type the external reference as a formula using the following format:

=drive:\path\[file.xls]sheetname!reference

Example:

=c:\excel\mydocuments\[report.xls]\sheet1!H5

  ✓ *You may omit the path if the source and dependent files are saved in the same directory (folder).*

  • While editing or creating a formula in the dependent workbook, you can include an external reference by selecting a cell(s) in the source workbook.

- When a cell in an external reference includes a formula, only the formula result displays in the dependent workbook.

  ✓ *In the figure, the typed formulas are displayed in the dependent workbook, but normally, only the results would appear.*

- If possible, save linked workbooks in the same directory (folder). You should save source workbooks first, then save the dependent workbook.

The source workbook contains the data being referenced in the dependent workbook

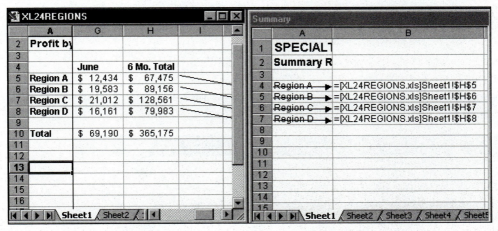

Source workbook   *Dependent workbook*

Procedures

Use Drag-and-Drop Editing between Workbooks

• Select range.

  To copy data:

  a. Press **Ctrl** while dragging border of selected range to new location in current worksheet, new worksheet, or new workbook.

  b. Release mouse, then **Ctrl** key.

To move data:

• Drag border of selected range to new location in current worksheet, new worksheet, or new workbook.

Link Workbooks Using Paste Link

1. Open source and dependent workbooks.
2. Arrange workbooks on screen.

3. Select cells to reference in source workbook.
4. Click **Edit** .... Alt +E
5. Click **Copy** C
6. Select cells in dependent workbook to receive cell references.
7. Click **Edit** .... Alt +E
8. Click **Paste Special** .... S
9. Click **Paste Link**

   [Paste Link] .... Alt +L

Exercise Directions

1. Start Excel, if necessary.

2. Open 💿 **25AUGINV**.

3. Save the file as **AUGINV**.

4. Open a new workbook and save it as **SEPTINV**.

5. Arrange the two open workbook windows, using the Tiled option.

6. Copy data to the new workbook by doing the following:

   a. In the **AUGINV** workbook, select the range, A1:G42.

   b. Press and hold the Ctrl key as you drag this data to the **SEPINV** workbook.

   c. Drop the data by releasing the mouse button when the cursor is over cell A1. Then release the Ctrl key.

7. Maximize the **SEPTINV** window, and adjust the columns to fit the data.

8. Change cell A7 to **Food Inventory – September**.

9. Select the range B11:D42, and clear its data by pressing Delete. Clear the data from the range F11:F42 as well.

10. Rename Sheet 1 **September**. Remove Sheet 2 and Sheet 3.

11. Switch to the **AUGINV** workbook, select the range F11:F42, then click Copy.

12. Change to the **SEPTINV** workbook, click cell B11, and choose Edit, Paste Special.

13. Choose Paste Link, then click OK.

14. Switch to the AUGINV workbook, and make the following changes:

    a. Cell F15: **42**

    b. Cell F23: **854**

    c. Cell F31: **864**

    d. Cell F40: **518**

15. Spell check both workbooks.

16. Print both workbooks.

17. Close **AUGINV**, saving all changes.

18. Close **SEPTINV**, saving all changes.

Illustration A

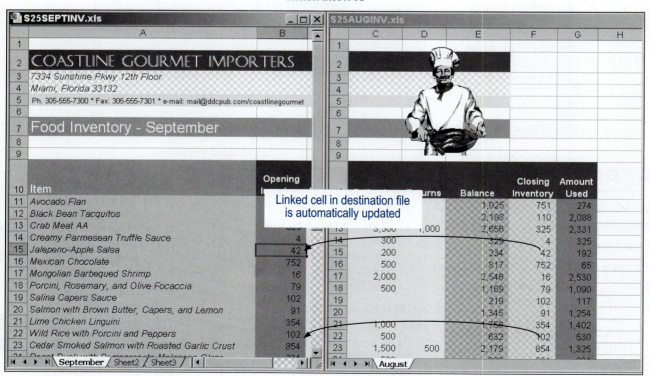

396

On Your Own

1. Open the file **OXL23**, created in the On Your Own of Exercise 23, or open ⊙ **25COLEXP**.

2. Save the file as **OXL25**. This will be your source document.

3. Create a new workbook and save it as **OXL25-2**. This will be your dependent document.

4. Set up the **OXL25-2** worksheet to show the semester totals for expenses:

   a. Enter a title in row 1.

   b. Enter four column labels for 2002 and 2003, semesters 1 and 2.

5. Tile the two files on the screen.

6. Use the Paste Link command to copy the 2002 semester totals from the **OXL25** source workbook to the appropriate cells below the column labels in the **OXL25-2** dependent workbook.

7. Enter estimated expenses for 2003.

8. Close the workbooks, saving all changes.

Illustration B

Exercise 26

◆ 3-D Formulas ◆ Duplicate Workbook Window

On the Job

Write a 3-D formula to reference values across worksheets. For example, you may want to total data from several worksheets into a summary worksheet. When you need to look at more than one of the worksheets in a workbook, create a duplicate workbook window.

Your boss at Electron Consumer Industries has asked you to compile the second quarter sales report. Luckily, the sales figures for each month have already been entered into several worksheets. All you need to do is to create a summary worksheet, using 3-D formulas to add the totals for each month together.

Terms

3-D formula An equation that references values across worksheets.

3-D reference A reference to a value from any sheet or range of sheets used in a 3-D formula.

Duplicate workbook window An option that allows you to view an exact copy of the active workbook.

Notes

3-D Formulas

- Create a **3-D formula** when you want to summarize data from several worksheets into a summary worksheet.

- A 3-D formula contains references to the same cell or range of cells on several worksheets in the same workbook. These cell references are called **3-D references**.

- You can refer to the same cell/range on consecutive (Sheet 1, Sheet 2, Sheet 3) or non-consecutive (Sheet 1 and Sheet 4) worksheets.

    =Sheet1!G24+Sheet4!G24

    =SUM(Sheet1:Sheet3!G24)

  - When typing a 3-D formula, use an exclamation point to separate the sheet name(s) from the cell reference(s).

- Use a colon (:) between sheet names to indicate a range of worksheets.

    April!G41+September!G41

    April:June!B23:D45

    Sheet2:Sheet3!C21

  - Quotation marks surround a sheet name that contains a space.

    "NW Region"D14+"SW Region"D14

    "Tax 2001":"Tax 2003"G23

  - Combine a 3-D reference with a function to create a formula that references data on different worksheets.

    =SUM(Exp2000:Exp2002!C14:C22)

  - As you create or edit a formula, you can select the cells of a 3-D reference in the worksheets or type them into the formula.

Use 3-D formulas to summarize data located on other worksheets

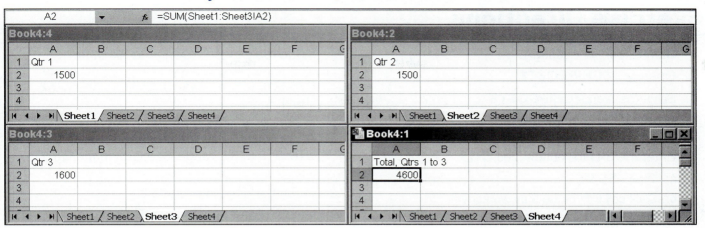

Duplicate Workbook Window

■ To view more than one worksheet of the active workbook at the same time on the screen, use the New Window command from the Window menu to make a **duplicate workbook window**.

✓ *When the new workbook window appears it is maximized; to see both workbooks you must arrange them on-screen.*

• Use the Arrange command from the Window menu to view the duplicate windows on the screen at the same time.

• In each window, click the sheet tab of the sheet you want to view.

• The number of duplicate windows that can be opened is determined by the amount of your system memory.

• You can add or edit data in the original or the duplicate window. All edits will be reflected in the other workbook automatically.

• If you close a duplicate window, the workbook remains open.

Procedures

Create 3-D Formula

To type 3-D reference in formula:

1. Position insertion point in formula where cell reference should be typed.

2. Type **=** and any function you wish to use in the formula, such as SUM.

3. Type sheet name.

   ✓ *Remember to type single or double quotation marks surrounding sheet names that contains spaces.*

   To type 3-D reference for range of worksheets in formula:

   a. Type **colon** (:) .... `:`

   b. Type last sheet name in range.

4. Type **exclamation point** (!) .. `!`

5. Type cell reference or range.

✓ *Some examples are:*
   Sheet2:Sheet6!C4:C10
   'Quarter1'!C4:C10

6. Press **Enter** .... `Enter`

To insert 3-D reference in formula:

1. Position insertion point in formula where cell referenced should be typed.

2. Click sheet tab containing cell(s) to reference.

   ✓ *The name of sheet will appear in Formula bar.*

3. Select cell(s) to reference.

   ✓ *The complete 3-D reference appears in Formula bar when you selected the cell(s).*

To enter 3-D reference for range of worksheets:

1. Press **Shift** and click last sheet tab in range to reference.

2. Type or insert remainder of formula.

3. Press **Enter** .... `Enter`

✓ *The formula is completed and Excel returns to starting worksheet.*

Open Duplicate Workbook Window

1. Open window to duplicate.

2. Click **Window** .... `Alt`+`W`

3. Click **New Window** .... `N`

4. Click **Window** .... `Alt`+`W`

5. Click **Arrange** .... `A`

6. Select the arrangement you prefer:

   Tiled .... `T`

   Horizontal .... `O`

   Vertical .... `V`

   Cascade .... `C`

7. Select **Windows of active workbook** .... `Alt`+`W`

8. Press **Enter**. .... `Enter`

Exercise Directions

1. Start Excel, if necessary.

2. Open ⊙ **26CHIPCOSTS**.

3. Save the file as **CHIPCOSTS**.

4. Type the formula, =SUM(May:July!C10) into cell C10 of the Qtr 2 workbook.

5. Enter the 3-D formula in cell C11:

   a. Type **=SUM(**

   b. Click cell C11 of the May worksheet.

   c. Press Shift, and click the tab of the July worksheet.

   d. Press Enter to complete the formula.

6. Copy the formula from cell C11 to the range C12:C14. Copy these formulas to the range D10:G14.

7. Adjust column widths to fit the data.

8. Duplicate the workbook window, and arrange them horizontally.

9. Display the May worksheet in the top window, and the Qtr 2 worksheet in the bottom window.

10. Use Edit, Paste Special to link the values in the range C16:G16 on the May worksheet to the range C21:G21 on the Qtr 2 sheet.

11. In the top window, change to the June worksheet, and link the values in the range C16:G16 to the range C22:G22 in the Qtr 2 sheet.

12. In the top window, change to the July worksheet, and link the values in the range C16:G16 to the range C23:G23 in the Qtr 2 sheet.

13. Close the duplicate window.

14. In cell C25 of the Qtr 2 worksheet, enter a 3-D formula to calculate the total sales:

    a. Type **=SUM(**

    b. Click cell C16 of the May worksheet.

    c. Press Shift, and click the tab of the July worksheet.

    d. Press Enter to complete the formula.

15. Copy this formula to the range D25:G25.

16. Spell check the workbook.

17. Print the workbook.

18. Close the workbook, saving all changes.

Illustration A

	A	B	C	D	E	F	G	H	I
1									
2				**Electron Consumer Industries**					
3									
4				SUPER G 2001 COMPUTER CHIP SALES					
5				PLANT #	5147				
6									
7				QTR 2 NET PROFIT					
8									
9				SALES	MATERIALS	LABOR	SHIPPING	NET PROFIT	
10		GMC		$ 53,035,414	$ 10,076,729	$ 20,153,457	$ 6,364,250	$ 16,440,978	
11		FORD		$ 39,126,098	$ 7,433,959	$ 14,867,917	$ 4,695,132	$ 12,129,090	
12		DAIMLER-CHRYSLER		$ 73,519,690	$ 13,968,741	$ 27,937,482	$ 8,822,363	$ 22,791,104	
13		TOYOTA		$ 26,619,519	$ 5,057,709	$ 10,115,417	$ 3,194,342	$ 8,252,051	
14		HONDA		$ 21,744,999	$ 4,131,550	$ 8,263,100	$ 2,609,400	$ 6,740,950	
15									
16		TOTALS		$ 214,045,720	$ 40,668,687	$ 81,337,374	$ 25,685,486	$ 66,354,173	
17									
18									
19									
20				SALES	MATERIALS	LABOR	SHIPPING	NET PROFIT	
21		MAY		$ 67,206,610	$ 12,769,256	$ 25,538,512	$ 8,064,793	$ 20,834,049	
22		JUNE		$ 60,157,764	$ 11,429,975	$ 22,859,950	$ 7,218,932	$ 18,648,907	
23		JULY		$ 86,681,346	$ 16,469,456	$ 32,938,911	$ 10,401,762	$ 26,871,217	
24									
25		TOTALS		$ 214,045,720	$ 40,668,687	$ 81,337,374	$ 25,685,486	$ 66,354,173	
26									
27									

May / June / July / Qtr 2

On Your Own

1. Open the file **OXL24**, created in the On Your Own of Exercise 24, or open ⊙**26GRADES**.

2. Save the file as **OXL26**.

3. Remove the window split bars.

4. Rename Sheet 1 **Sem 1**. Rename Sheet 2 **Grades**.

5. Insert a copy of the Sem 1 sheet between the two sheets, and rename it **Sem 2**.

6. Enter new scores on the Sem 2 sheet.
   ✓ You do not have to change every score.

7. Copy the worksheet title and the children's names from one of the semester sheets to the Grades worksheet.

8. On the Grades sheet, enter the column labels **Tests**, **Quizzes**, and **Final Grade**.

9. In the Tests column, for the first student, enter a 3-D formula that averages the test scores for both semesters. Copy this formula down the column.

10. Use a 3-D formula to average the quiz scores for both semesters.

11. Compute the final grades however you like.
    ✓ For example, I averaged the test and quiz scores together, rounded to zero decimal places.

12. Widen columns as needed to display data.

13. Apply formatting as desired.

14. Spell check the worksheet.

15. Print the worksheet.

16. Close the workbook, saving all changes.

Exercise 27

◆ Critical Thinking

As the payroll supervisor for Murray Hill Marketing, you know that you must get the payroll checks out quickly, and that they must be accurate. Luckily, Excel provides you with the tools you need to do the job. In this exercise, you'll use Paste Special, linking, 3-D formulas, Page Setup, and Page Break Preview to get the job done.

Exercise Directions

1. Start Excel, if necessary.
2. Open ⊙ **27PAYROLL**.
3. Save the file as **PAYROLL**.
4. Open ⊙ **27PAYHOURS**.
5. Arrange the two workbooks on-screen in a tiled fashion.
6. In the **27PAYHOURS** workbook, select the range E18:AA18, and click Copy.
7. In the **PAYROLL** workbook, click cell F6 on the Aug 31 worksheet, and choose Edit, Paste Special.
8. Choose Values, Transpose, and click OK.
9. Adjust the column widths as needed, and close the **27PAYHOURS** workbook.
10. Open ⊙ **27NEWRATES**. Save the file as **NEWRATES**. Tile both windows.
11. Select the range G6:G28 in the **NEWRATES** workbook, and click Copy.
12. In the **PAYROLL** workbook, on the Aug 31 sheet, click cell E6.
13. Click the arrow on the Paste button, and select Paste Link.
14. Switch back to the **NEWRATES** workbook, and add some last minute review scores:
    a. Karen Hernandez: **7.25**
    b. Kayla Blues: **6.75**
    c. Suardo Taura: **10**
    d. Wei Xu: **9.25**
    e. Tsu-Hua Wang: **8.75**
    f. Duanne Honn: **10**
    g. Lu Chen: **9.75**
    h. Ni Wu Gogin: **7.75**

15. Close **NEWRATES**, saving all changes.
16. Change to the Monthly Totals sheet of the **PAYROLL** workbook.
17. In cell E6, enter a 3-D formula to calculate the total Gross for Che Lopez:
    a. Type **=SUM(**
    b. Click cell G6 on the Aug 15 sheet.
    c. Press Shift and click the tab for the Aug 31 sheet.
    d. Type **)** and press Enter.
    e. Copy this formula to the range E6:E28.
    f. Use the fill handle to copy the range E6:E28 to F6:M28. Use the AutoFill Options button to fill without copying the formats.
    g. Adjust column widths to fit the data.
18. Spell check the workbook.
19. Print the Aug 31 worksheet:
    a. On the Page tab of the Page Setup dialog box, change to Landscape orientation.
    b. On the Header/Footer tab, select the standard header that displays your name, the page number, and date.
    c. On the Sheet tab, select columns A:E to repeat at left.
    d. Turn on Page Break Preview.
    e. Drag the page break so that it's between columns J and K.
    f. Apply Arial Narrow, 14 point, bold formatting to cell D2, and adjust column D so that the company name just fits within columns D and E.
    g. Print two copies of the worksheet.
20. Close the file, saving all changes.

Illustration A

Murray Hill Marketing, LLC

Name	Gross	Fed	Fica	State	Med	Dental	401k	LTD	Net Pay
Che Lopez	$1,023.70	$166.35	$150.48	$ 66.54	$ 14.50	$ 5.00	$ 81.90	$ 2.20	$ 536.73
Tyrone Robbins	$1,709.37	$277.77	$251.28	$111.11	$ 17.00	$ -	$119.66	$ 4.20	$ 928.35
Jim Banks	$2,384.05	$387.41	$350.45	$154.96	$ -	$ -	$143.04	$ 6.20	$1,341.98
Karen Hernandez	$1,838.57	$298.77	$270.27	$119.51	$ 17.00	$ 5.00	$110.31	$ 8.20	$1,009.51
Diomonico Suarez	$1,503.23	$244.27	$220.97	$ 97.71	$ 17.00	$ 5.00	$120.26	$ 10.20	$ 787.81
Katerina Wilson	$2,301.81	$374.04	$338.37	$149.62	$ 17.00	$ -	$138.11	$ 12.20	$1,272.48
Suzaii Suyut	$2,206.49	$358.55	$324.35	$143.42	$ 14.50	$ -	$132.39	$ 14.20	$1,219.07
Kayla Blues	$1,399.44	$227.41	$205.72	$ 90.96	$ 14.50	$ 5.00	$111.96	$ 16.20	$ 727.69
Yuin Wang	$ 966.81	$157.11	$142.12	$ 62.84	$ 17.00	$ 5.00	$ 58.01	$ 18.20	$ 506.53
Suardo Taura	$2,558.75	$415.80	$376.14	$166.32	$ 14.50	$ 5.00	$179.11	$ 20.20	$1,381.69
Kiria Metans	$1,287.24	$209.18	$189.22	$ 83.67	$ -	$ -	$ 77.23	$ 22.20	$ 705.74
LaJar Burton	$1,477.11	$240.03	$217.13	$ 96.01	$ 17.00	$ 5.00	$ 88.63	$ 24.20	$ 789.10
Liborio Garza	$1,320.85	$214.64	$194.17	$ 85.86	$ 17.00	$ 5.00	$ 79.25	$ 26.20	$ 698.74
Terry Crickmore	$ 982.39	$159.64	$144.41	$ 63.86	$ 14.50	$ -	$ 58.94	$ 28.20	$ 512.84
Wei Xu	$1,463.46	$237.81	$215.13	$ 95.13	$ 17.00	$ 5.00	$ 87.81	$ 30.20	$ 775.39
Tsu-Huai Wang	$1,535.68	$249.55	$225.75	$ 99.82	$ 14.50	$ 5.00	$122.85	$ 32.20	$ 786.02
Duanne Honn	$2,512.19	$408.23	$369.29	$163.29	$ -	$ -	$175.85	$ 34.20	$1,361.32
Jia Yankai	$2,146.73	$348.84	$315.57	$139.54	$ 17.00	$ 5.00	$150.27	$ 36.20	$1,134.31
Rodolfo Tavarez	$1,733.16	$281.64	$254.77	$112.66	$ 14.50	$ 5.00	$103.99	$ 38.20	$ 922.40
Lu Chen	$1,435.63	$233.29	$211.04	$ 93.32	$ 17.00	$ 5.00	$ 86.14	$ 40.20	$ 749.65
Maira Guarado	$1,599.19	$259.87	$235.08	$103.95	$ 17.00	$ 5.00	$127.94	$ 42.20	$ 808.16
Sabrina Thoesen	$1,594.13	$259.05	$234.34	$103.62	$ 14.50	$ -	$ 95.65	$ 44.20	$ 842.78
Ni Wu Gogin	$ 987.56	$160.48	$145.17	$ 64.19	$ 17.00	$ 5.00	$ 79.01	$ 46.20	$ 470.52

Illustration B

E6 ƒx ='C:\My Documents\Learning Office 10\Data and Solutions\[S27NEWRATES.xls]Sheet1'!G6

Murray Hill Marketing, LLC

Name	Rate	Hours	Gross	Fed	Fica	State	Med	Dental	401k	LTD	Net Pay
Che Lopez	$ 7.98	77.00	$ 614.08	$ 99.79	$ 90.27	$ 39.91	$ 7.25	$ 2.50	$ 49.13	$ 1.10	$324.13
Tyrone Robbins	$ 12.90	58.75	$ 757.62	$ 123.11	$ 111.37	$ 49.25	$ 8.50		$ 53.03	$ 2.10	$410.26
Jim Banks	$ 13.56	96.75	$ 1,312.17	$ 213.23	$ 192.89	$ 85.29			$ 78.73	$ 3.10	$738.93
Karen Hernandez	$ 10.99	81.00	$ 890.44	$ 144.70	$ 130.90	$ 57.88	$ 8.50	$ 2.50	$ 53.43	$ 4.10	$488.45
Diomonico Suarez	$ 9.35	96.00	$ 897.60	$ 145.86	$ 131.95	$ 58.34	$ 8.50	$ 2.50	$ 71.81	$ 5.10	$473.54
Katerina Wilson	$ 13.44	88.75	$ 1,193.19	$ 193.89	$ 175.40	$ 77.56	$ 8.50		$ 71.59	$ 6.10	$660.15
Suzaii Suyut	$ 12.87	97.75	$ 1,257.68	$ 204.37	$ 184.88	$ 81.75	$ 7.25		$ 75.46	$ 7.10	$696.87
Kayla Blues	$ 10.14	71.25	$ 722.56	$ 117.42	$ 106.22	$ 46.97	$ 7.25	$ 2.50	$ 57.81	$ 8.10	$376.31
Yuin Wang	$ 7.74	64.50	$ 499.19	$ 81.12	$ 73.38	$ 32.45	$ 8.50	$ 2.50	$ 29.95	$ 9.10	$262.19
Suardo Taura	$ 13.75	97.00	$ 1,333.75	$ 216.73	$ 196.06	$ 86.69	$ 7.25	$ 2.50	$ 93.36	$ 10.10	$721.05
Kiria Metans	$ 10.73	60.25	$ 646.18	$ 105.00	$ 94.99	$ 42.00			$ 38.77	$ 11.10	$354.32
LaJar Burton	$ 7.94	97.25	$ 772.04	$ 125.46	$ 113.49	$ 50.18	$ 8.50	$ 2.50	$ 46.32	$ 12.10	$413.49
Liborio Garza	$ 11.12	80.75	$ 898.04	$ 145.93	$ 132.01	$ 58.37	$ 8.50	$ 2.50	$ 53.88	$ 13.10	$483.74
Terry Crickmore	$ 7.85	72.75	$ 570.95	$ 92.78	$ 83.93	$ 37.11	$ 7.25		$ 34.26	$ 14.10	$301.52
Wei Xu	$ 10.38	73.50	$ 762.84	$ 123.96	$ 112.14	$ 49.58	$ 8.50	$ 2.50	$ 45.77	$ 15.10	$405.28
Tsu-Huai Wang	$ 9.24	90.50	$ 836.56	$ 135.94	$ 122.97	$ 54.38	$ 7.25	$ 2.50	$ 66.92	$ 16.10	$430.49
Duanne Honn	$ 13.75	99.75	$ 1,371.56	$ 222.88	$ 201.62	$ 89.15			$ 96.01	$ 17.10	$744.80
Jia Yankai	$ 12.93	87.00	$ 1,124.48	$ 182.73	$ 165.30	$ 73.09	$ 8.50	$ 2.50	$ 78.71	$ 18.10	$595.55
Rodolfo Tavarez	$ 10.31	87.50	$ 901.91	$ 146.56	$ 132.58	$ 58.62	$ 7.25	$ 2.50	$ 54.11	$ 19.10	$481.18
Lu Chen	$ 9.33	70.75	$ 660.01	$ 107.25	$ 97.02	$ 42.90	$ 8.50	$ 2.50	$ 39.60	$ 20.10	$342.14
Maira Guarado	$ 10.70	82.25	$ 880.13	$ 143.02	$ 129.38	$ 57.21	$ 8.50	$ 2.50	$ 70.41	$ 21.10	$448.01
Sabrina Thoesen	$ 11.28	82.75	$ 933.01	$ 151.61	$ 137.15	$ 60.65	$ 7.25		$ 55.98	$ 22.10	$498.27
Ni Wu Gogin	$ 7.81	73.75	$ 576.13	$ 93.62	$ 84.69	$ 37.45	$ 8.50	$ 2.50	$ 46.09	$ 23.10	$280.18

Exercise 28

On the Job

After creating a chart, you may want to print it out so you can share your data with others. You can print the chart with the rest of the worksheet data, or simply print just the chart. Another way to share your information is to publish your chart to the Internet, or to your company's intranet. You can even make your chart interactive, so that users can change the data in the chart as well as view it. This is especially useful when the data for the chart comes from several different sources, such as several different departments in your company.

Your salespeople at Regency General are quite anxious to see the results of the June Sales contest. Rather than print out multiple copies of your worksheet, you've decided to publish the results to your company's Web site. That way, the results can be viewed almost instantaneously by anyone who's interested, regardless of where they may be. This is a nice plus, since most of the sales force is typically out selling and not in the office. Also, you can easily make changes to the results if needed. Your boss, however, doesn't like computers much, so he wants to see the results printed out in a nice chart.

Terms

Chart sheet A chart that occupies its own worksheet.

Embedded chart A chart placed as an object within a worksheet, typically on a sheet that contains the data used to make the chart.

Intranet A private network of computers within a business or organization.

Publishing The process of saving data to an intranet or Internet.

Static data Information that, once published online, can not be changed by the viewer.

Interactive data Information that, once published online, can be changed by the viewer through their Web browser.

Notes

Print a Chart

- **Chart sheets** can be printed with the rest of the workbook or as separate sheets.
- **Embedded charts** typically print with the worksheet on which they are located.

- When printing a chart, you can select from various options that allow you to adjust the size of the chart.

Change Chart Location

- You can easily change the location of a chart by switching a chart from a Chart sheet to an embedded object on a sheet and vice-versa.

Publish Chart to the Internet/intranet

- The process of saving worksheet data to the Internet or your company's **intranet** is called **publishing**.

- To publish your chart on the Internet or an intranet, Excel converts it to HTML format.

- Once your data is published, you can republish it when needed to update the data.

- You can save the chart as **static data** or as **interactive data**.

- To publish interactive data, you make selections from the Publish as Web Page dialog box, shown below.

The Publish as Web Page dialog box

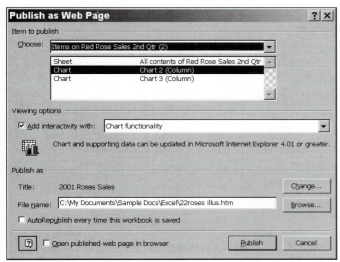

- Changing interactive data in your Web browser is similar to changing that same data within Excel. Simply click in the individual cells and the changes are reflected in the chart automatically, just as they would in a workbook.

An interactive chart

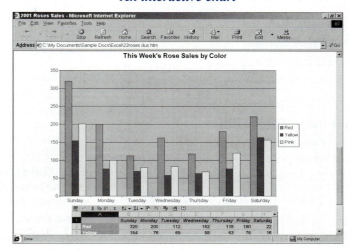

- Prior to publishing your data, you may want to save it to a local hard drive first. Using an HTML editor, such as FrontPage 2002, you can make any changes to the Web page as needed to improve its appearance.

Procedures

Print Embedded Chart and Worksheet or Chart Sheet

1. Select worksheet or chart sheet containing chart to print.
2. Click **Print** button .

Print Embedded Chart Separately

1. Select embedded chart.
2. Click **Print** button .

Set Chart Print Options

1. Select embedded chart or chart sheet.
2. Click **File** .... `Alt`+`F`
3. Click **Page Setup**............... `U`
4. Click **Chart** tab.
5. Set printed chart size:
   - **Use full page**......... `Alt`+`U`
   - **Scale to fit page** ... `Alt`+`F`
   - **Custom**.................. `Alt`+`C`

   ✓ *With Custom selected, the actual size of the embedded chart is used. If you are printing a chart sheet, you can adjust its size manually when Custom is selected.*

6. If desired, select **Draft quality** option to print chart more quickly but with less quality .... `Alt`+`Q`
7. To print each data series using pattern rather than color or shades of gray, select **Print in black and white** option.......................... `Alt`+`B`
8. Click **OK**.......................... `Enter`

Change Location of Chart

1. Select embedded chart or chart sheet.
2. Click **Chart**.......................... `C`
3. Click **Location** .... `L`
4. Change location of chart:
   a. Select **As new sheet**.............. `Alt`+`S`
   b. Type name for new sheet in text box.

OR

a. Select **As object in** .... `Alt`+`O`
b. Select sheet on which you want to place chart from drop-down list.
5. Click **OK** .... `Enter`

Publish Chart as Static Data

1. Select embedded chart or chart sheet.
2. Click **File** .... `Alt`+`F`
3. Click **Save as Web Page** .... `G`
4. From **Save in** list, type (or select) Internet or intranet location on which you want to save chart................ `Alt`+`I`
5. Type name for HTML file in the **File name** text box. ..... `Alt`+`N`
6. If desired, click **Change Title** and then change title for Web page (HTML file)........... `Alt`+`C`

   ✓ *Title appears in title bar of Web browser when viewed online.*

7. Click **OK** .... `Enter`
8. Choose **Selection:Chart**.......... `Alt`+`E`
9. Click **Publish**............... `Alt`+`P`
10. If desired, select **Open published web page in browser** to launch your Web browser so you can view HTML file .... `Alt`+`O`
11. If desired, select **AutoRepublish every time this workbook is saved** to automatically update the chart each time you save the workbook .... `Alt`+`U`

    ✓ *If you don't select this option, and you later make changes to a chart, you'll need to follow the steps under "Republish Data" to republish the chart manually.*

12. Click **Publish**............... `Alt`+`P`

Publish Chart as Interactive Data

1. Select embedded chart or the chart sheet.
2. Click **File**..................... `Alt`+`F`
3. Click **Save as Web Page** .... `G`
4. From **Save in** list, type (or select) Internet or intranet location on which you want to save chart .... `Alt`+`I`
5. Type name for HTML file in **File name** text box....... `Alt`+`N`
6. If desired, click **Change Title** and then change title for Web page (HTML file).......... `Alt`+`C`

   ✓ *Title appears in title bar of Web browser when viewed online.*

7. Click **OK**.......................... `Enter`
8. Choose **Selection:Chart** .... `Alt`+`E`
9. Click **Publish**............... `Alt`+`P`
10. Choose **Add interactivity with** .... `Alt`+`A`
11. If desired, select **Open published web page in browser** to launch your Web browser so you can view HTML file .... `Alt`+`O`
12. If desired, select **AutoRepublish every time this workbook is saved** to automatically update the chart each time you save the workbook .... `Alt`+`U`
13. Click **Publish**............... `Alt`+`P`

Republish Chart

1. Open original workbook.
2. Make changes to chart as needed.
3. Click **File**.................... `Alt`+`F`
4. Click **Save as Web Page** .... `G`
5. Click **Publish**............... `Alt`+`P`
6. Open **Choose** list and select **Previously published items**. .... `Alt`+`C`
7. Choose item you want to republish from those listed.
8. Click **Publish**. .... `Alt`+`P`

Exercise Directions

1. Start Excel, if necessary.
2. Open 📇**SALESCONT** or open 💿**28SALESCONT**.
3. Save the file as **SALESCONT**.
4. Move the chart on the June Sales sheet to the June Contest sheet as an embedded object.
   - ✓ *Copy the chart and complete step 5, then save the workbook, then delete the June Sales worksheet.*
5. Move and resize the chart so that it occupies the range I12:R36.
6. Change the category axis to Arial, bold, 12 point. Change the value axis to Arial, bold, 9 point.
7. Publish the chart to the Web:
   a. Click the chart to select it.
   b. Choose File, Save as Web Page.
   c. Select the location to save the chart from the Save In list.
   d. Type the file name **JUNESALES** in the File name box.
   e. Click Change Title, type **June Sales**, and click OK.
   f. Choose Selection:Chart and click Publish.
   g. Choose Open published Web page in browser.
   h. Click Publish.
   i. Switch back to Excel, but leave the browser open.
8. Republish the chart with interactivity:
   a. Click the chart and choose File, Save as Web Page.
   b. Choose Republish: Chart.
   c. Type **JUNESALES** in the File name box.
   d. Click Add interactivity.
   e. Click Publish.
   f. Make sure that the option Open web page in browser is selected, and click Publish.

9. In the browser, change Shale Wilson's sales total to $25,021.
   - ✓ *A "Yes" appears in the "Met Goal?" column, and the South Bend sales total on the chart is adjusted.*
10. Close the Web browser and return to Excel.
    - ✓ *Note that changes made on the Web do not affect the original Excel worksheet from which the data was published.*
11. In the June Contest sheet, change Shale Wilson's total to $25,021. See Illustration A.
12. Republish the chart:
    a. Click the chart and choose File, Save as Web Page.
    b. Choose Republish: Chart.
    c. Type **JUNESALES** in the File name box.
    d. Click Add interactivity.
    e. Click Publish.
    f. Make sure that the option Open web page in browser is selected, and click Publish.
13. After viewing your Web page, close the browser and return to Excel.
14. Spell check the worksheet.
15. Print the June Contest sheet and its chart.
16. Print just the chart:
    a. Use Page Setup to change the chart size so that it's scaled to fit the page.
    b. Print the chart in draft quality.
    c. Reprint the chart using the Print in black and white option, non-draft quality.
17. Close the workbook, saving all changes.

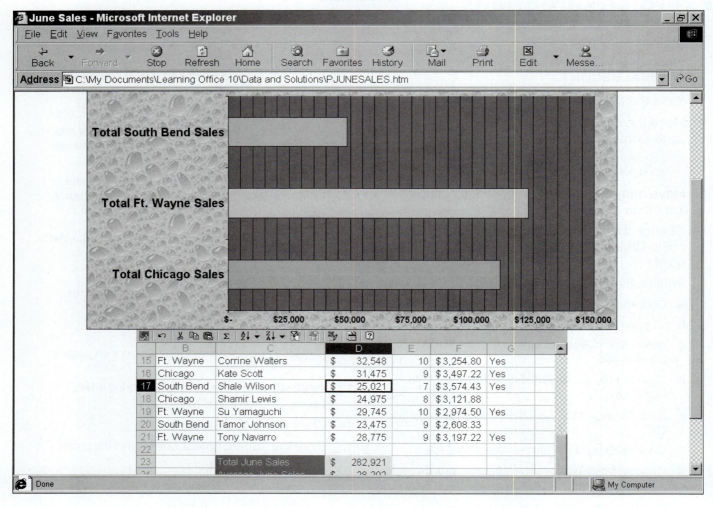

On Your Own

1. Start Excel, if necessary.
2. Open ⌨OXL25, created in the On Your Own section of Exercise 25, or open ⊘28COLEXP.
3. Save the file as **OXL28**.
4. Create a chart using the Semester 1 and Semester 2 expense amounts.
   a. Use a chart style of your own choice.
   b. Embed the chart as an object in Sheet 2.
   c. Apply whatever formatting you want.
5. Spell check the worksheet.
6. Print the chart in black and white.
7. Publish the chart interactively:
   a. Use the file name **COLEXP**.
   b. Use the title 2001 Estimated College Expenses.
   c. Turn on the option AutoRepublish every time the workbook is saved.
   d. View the results in your Web browser.
   e. In the workbook, change the value of one of the expenses.
   f. Save the changes, and view the updated results in your browser by clicking the Refresh button.
8. Close your Web browser.
9. Close the workbook, saving all changes.

Illustration B

	A	B	C
1	Estimated College Expenses by Semester for 2002		
2			
3		Semester 1	Semester 2
4	Books	$ 185.00	$ 235.00
5	Supplies	$ 230.00	$ 295.00
6	Computer Stuff	$ 895.00	$ 180.00
7	Gas	$ 150.00	$ 170.00
8	Repairs	$ 350.00	$ 215.00
9	Parking	$ 225.00	$ 225.00
10	Extras	$ 400.00	$ 500.00
11	Totals	$2,435.00	$1,820.00

Exercise 29

Skills Covered:

◆ **Pasting a Picture of a Chart** ◆ **Link a Chart**
◆ **Embed a Chart into a Word Document**
◆ **Edit a Linked or Embedded Chart**

On the Job

You can link or embed an Excel chart into another document, such as a Word document. If the source data is likely to change, you should link the data to its source, so that your chart will automatically update. This is especially useful when the source data is updated by several different people in your organization. You can also embed the chart in your Word document in order to ensure that your changes will not effect the original data.

You are the plant manager at Plant #5147 of Electron Consumer Industries. The accounting manager at the home office has asked you to produce a report detailing your plant's expenses and net profit for the last three months. Since you already have the necessary figures loaded in Excel, you'll use it to quickly create the charts you'll need and then link and embed them into a letter you've created using Word.

Terms

Link A reference in a destination document to an object (such as a chart) in a source document. When a linked objected is changed, the object is updated in the destination document through the link.

Embed A process that inserts an object into a destination document so that it can still be edited by the source application. When you double-click an embedded object, the source application (or its tools) appear, so you can edit the object. However, the original data is unchanged by this process.

Notes

Paste a Picture of a Chart

- The simplest way in which you can display an Excel chart within another document, such as a Word document, is to paste its picture.

- The advantage of using a picture of a chart is that it will not affect the size of your Word file very much.

- The disadvantage of using a chart picture is that the data is static—meaning if the data changes, the picture of the chart is not updated.

- To update the picture, you would need to change the data in Excel and paste a new picture.

Link a Chart

- If you don't want to paste a picture of your chart into another document, you can either **link** to that data, or **embed** it.

- When you link a chart to a destination file, such as a Word document, the chart is not copied into the document. Instead, a link to the chart is created.

  - The linked data is still displayed in the destination file, but it is not stored there—instead, the data is stored in the source file (the Excel workbook).

- Because the linked data is not stored in the destination file, the file's size is much smaller than a file in which data has been embedded.

- Linked data in the destination file may also be displayed as an icon.

■ When you change the data in a linked chart and open the destination file again, the link causes the data displayed in the destination document to be updated as well.

- The link also allows you to start Excel from within the destination file (from within Word, for example), display the chart, and make your changes.

- Changes are made to the actual Excel chart and then copied through the link to the destination file.

■ In order to maintain the link, the files must remain in their original locations.

■ By default, linked data is updated automatically, but you can choose manual updating if you like.

- If manual, you control when the chart data is updated into your destination document.

- If automatic, you need only open the destination document to update it.

■ You can link to an embedded chart, or a chart sheet.

   ✓ Although we're only talking about charts in this section, you could use these same procedures to link worksheet data to an external file, such as a Word document.

Embed a Chart into a Word Document

■ When you **embed** a chart in a Word document, the data is copied into the Word file and stored there.

■ Making changes to an embedded chart does not affect the original data, since there is no link to that data.

   ✓ Although we're only talking about charts in this section, you could use these same procedures to embed worksheet data to an external file, such as a Word document.

- Embedded data in the destination file may also be displayed as an icon.

■ When you link or embed a chart, you may use the Paste toolbar button and the Paste Options button to perform the task. You can also use the program's Paste Special dialog box, similar to the one shown here, which is from Word.

Paste Special dialog box

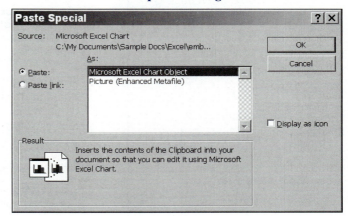

Edit a Linked or Embedded Chart

■ Since linked data is stored in the source document, you simply open Excel to edit a linked chart.

- You can open Excel from within the destination document if you like, rather than starting Excel separately.

- When you change the worksheet data in Excel, the corresponding chart is updated.

- When you save the worksheet file, the link is updated.

- Open the destination document and the chart is either updated automatically or when you manually update the link.

■ Embedded data is stored within the destination document.

- To edit the embedded chart, you must work within the destination document.

- When you open the chart for editing, Excel menus and tools appear to help you make your changes.

- When you edit embedded data, the original data (in an Excel workbook) is not changed.

Procedures

Link, Embed, or Paste Chart as Picture

✓ *Use this procedure when pasting data to another Office XP program.*

1. Click chart to select it.
2. Click **Copy** button 📋.
3. Switch to the other Office XP program, such as Word.
4. Click **Paste** button 📋.
5. Click arrow on Paste Options button, and select the option you desire:
   - **Picture of Chart**
   - **Excel Chart**
     ✓ *This option embeds the chart.*
   - **Link to Excel Chart**

Paste a Chart Picture

1. Click chart to select it.
2. Press and hold **Shift** as you click **E**dit .... `Shift`+`Alt`+`E`
3. Click **C**opy Picture .... `C`
4. Select appearance:
   - **As shown on s**creen .... `S`
   - **As shown when printed** .... `P`
5. Select format:
   - **Pic**ture .... `T`
   - **B**itmap .... `B`
     ✓ *Select Picture (Windows metafile) in most instances—the Bitmap option results in a smaller file size, but lower quality, and may not appear correctly if the destination file is viewed with a different resolution than yours.*
6. Switch to destination document.
7. Click **E**dit .... `Alt`+`E`
8. Click **P**aste .... `P`

Link Chart

✓ *For automatic links to update data properly, make sure that the **Update remote references** option is turned on in Excel's **Tools**, **Options**, **Calculation** tab.*

1. Click chart to select it.
2. Click **Copy** button 📋.
3. Switch to destination file and position cursor where you want chart inserted.
4. Click **E**dit .... `Alt`+`E`
5. Click Paste **S**pecial .... `S`
6. Click Paste **l**ink .... `L`
7. Select Microsoft Excel Chart Object.
8. If you want to display chart as an icon in your Word document, select **D**isplay as icon option .... `D`
   ✓ *To change the icon that's displayed, click **Change Icon** and select one from those listed.*
9. Click **OK** .... `Enter`
   ✓ *When you create a link, it is updated automatically. However, you can change updating to manual if you like.*

Change Link Information

1. Click **E**dit .... `Alt`+`E`
2. Click Lin**k**s .... `K`
3. Select link you want to update.
4. To change location of linked file, click Cha**n**ge Source .... `N`
   a. From **Look in** list folder in which file is currently located ..... `Alt`+`I`
   b. Select name of file you want to link to in File **n**ame text box... `Alt`+`N`
   c. Click **Open** button 📂.
5. To remove link, click **B**reak Link .... `B`

6. To change way in which link is updated, select option:
   - **A**utomatic update .... `A`
   - **M**anual update .... `M`
   - Loc**k**ed .... `K`
     ✓ *Locked option prevents linked object from being updated.*
7. Click **OK** .... `Enter`

Update Manual Link

1. Open destination file.
2. Click **E**dit .... `Alt`+`E`
3. Click Lin**k**s .... `K`
4. Select link you want to update.
5. Click **U**pdate Now .... `U`
   ✓ *You can also press F9 after selecting object to update it.*

Embed Chart in Word Document

1. Click chart to select it.
2. Click **Copy** button 📋.
3. Switch to destination document and position cursor where you want chart inserted.
4. Click **E**dit .... `Alt`+`E`
5. Click Paste **S**pecial .... `S`
6. Click **P**aste .... `P`
7. Select Microsoft Excel Chart Object.
8. If you want to display chart as an icon in your Word document, select **D**isplay as icon option .... `D`
9. Click **OK** .... `Enter`

Edit Linked Chart

1. Double-click linked chart or icon.
   ✓ *Excel starts and displays chart.*
2. Make desired changes.
3. Click **F**ile .... `Alt`+`F`
4. Click E**x**it .... `X`
5. When prompted, select **Y**es to save your changes .... `Y`

Edit Embedded Chart

1. Double-click embedded chart or icon.
   - ✓ Chart is surrounded by thick gray border, and Excel's menus and Chart toolbar appear.

2. Make changes as needed.
   - ✓ To change chart data, click tab for worksheet that contains data, and make your changes.
   - ✓ Be sure to redisplay chart tab before you end editing session.

3. Click outside chart border.

Exercise Directions

1. Start Excel, if necessary.

2. Open 📠**CHIPCOSTS** or open 💿**29CHIPCOSTS**.

3. Save the file as **CHIPCOSTS**.

4. On the Qtr 2 sheet, select the ranges B21:B23 and G21:G23, and create a clustered column chart.

   a. Use the title **Net Profits – May to June**.

   b. Do not include a legend.

   c. Embed the chart on the Qtr 2 sheet. Resize the chart to fit the range C27:G46.

   d. Format the title with Verdana, 18 pt., bold. Format the Value axis with Verdana, 8 pt. Format the Category axis with Verdana, 12 pt.
      - ✓ If you don't have this font select another font.

   e. Apply Ivory fill to the Plot Area.

   f. Apply the Fog preset fill, From center, to the Chart Area. Use the second variant.

   g. Apply the Cork texture to "Series 1".
      - ✓ See Illustration A.

5. Make a copy of the chart:

   a. Click the chart, then click Copy.

   b. Click cell C49, then click Paste.

   c. Click this second chart, and choose Chart, Source Data.

   d. On the Data Range tab, click the Collapse Dialog button at the end of the Data range text box, select the ranges, B20:B23 and D20:F23. Click the Expand Dialog box button to return to the dialog box. Click OK.
      - ✓ Cell B20 may be blank, but you need to select it in order to have equal sized-ranges.

   e. Change the title of the second chart to **Expenses – May to June**.

   f. Click the Legend button on the Chart toolbar to display the legend.

   g. Click the legend, and format it with Verdana 9 pt.

   h. Apply Denim texture to Series "Shipping".

6. Open 💿**29PROFITRPT.doc**.

7. Save the file as **PROFITRPT.doc**.

8. Select the first chart on the Qtr 2 sheet, and click Copy.

9. In the **PROFITRPT.doc** file, select the text **[embed chart here]** and delete it.

10. Click Paste.

11. Click the Paste Options button, and select Excel Chart (entire workbook).

12. Switch back to the **CHIPCOSTS** workbook, select the second chart on the QTR 2 worksheet, and click Copy.

13. Change to the **PROFITRPT.doc** file, select the text **[link chart here]** and press Delete.

14. Choose Edit, Paste Special. Choose Paste link, then click OK.

15. Make changes to the first chart:

    a. Within the **PROFITRPT.doc** file, double-click the Net Profits chart.

    b. Switch to the Qtr 2 sheet, and change the Sales figure for June (cell C22) to 62,157,764.

    c. Click the Chart 1 tab.

    d. Click outside the edit window.

16. Make changes to the second chart:

    a. Double-click the Expenses chart.
       - ✓ Excel displays the workbook.

    b. Change the Shipping costs for June (cell F22) to 7,018,931.68.
       - ✓ Notice that the June sales figure was not changed previously in the Excel file, since you made that change (in step 15) to an embedded chart.

    c. Save the workbook.

17. Spell check the workbook and the Word document.

18. Print the Word document.

19. Close the Word document and the Excel workbook, saving all changes.

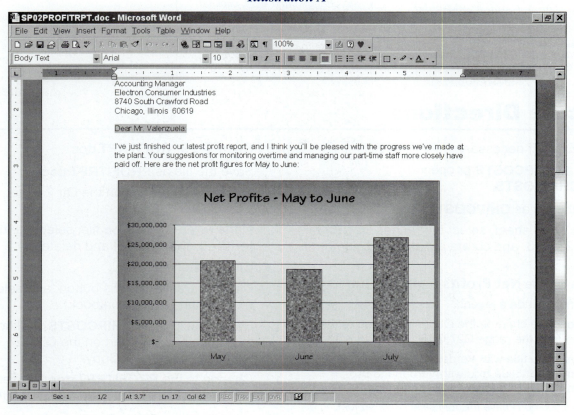

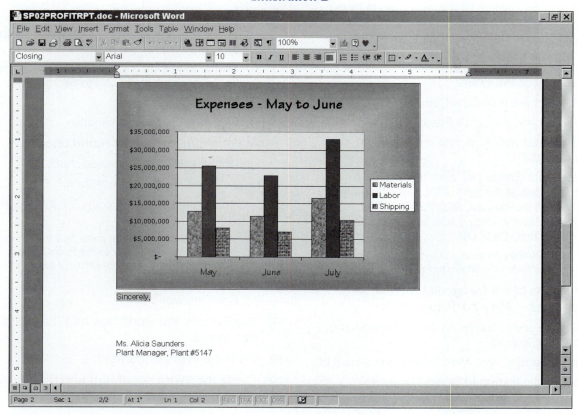

On Your Own

1. Open **OXL28**, the college expenses workbook you used in the On Your Own in Exercise 28, or open ⊙**29COLEXP**.
   - Disable the AutoRepublish feature for this exercise.

2. Save the workbook as **OXL29**.

3. Start Word and type a letter to a family member, who is interested in your estimated college expenses because he or she could possibly provide you with some assistance. Include a paragraph explaining the expense figures and how you came up with your estimates. Let her or him know that you are including an Excel chart in the letter for reference.

4. Save the letter as **OXL29-2.doc**.

5. Embed the chart from the **OXL29.xls** workbook in the letter.

6. Make a change to one of your estimates.

7. Spell check the letter.

8. Print the letter.

9. Close the letter, saving all changes.

10. Close the workbook, saving all changes.

Exercise 30

On the Job

With an organization chart, you can easily show the relationship between objects or people. For example, you could show how your department is organized. With other conceptual charts, you could show the progress of a project—from conception to completion, areas of overlapping responsibility within a department or on a group project, or the cycle of events with a school or calendar year.

As the plant manager at Plant #5147 of Electron Consumer Industries, you're in charge of the reorganization of your plant. The goal is to maximize profits while still producing quality chips. Easier said than done, however, you think you've come up with a great plan. In this exercise, you'll use Excel to create the new organization chart. You'll also create a chart listing the various stages in the production of each chip.

Terms

Organization chart Displays the relationships within an organization, such as the managers in an office, the people they manage, and who they report to.

Superior A person in an organization whose power and responsibilities are above those of other people. Typically, these responsibilities include managing other people.

Assistant A person in an organization whose chief responsibility is to assist a superior in his/her work.

Subordinate A person who reports to a superior, and thus, is subordinate to them.

Coworker A person within an organization who reports to the same superior as someone else.

Notes

Create Organization Charts

- To show relationships within a group such as an office, the government, or a school, create an **organization chart**.

- When you start an organization chart, Excel provides a chart showing several basic relationships: **superior, assistant, subordinate,** and **coworker.**

- Using the Insert Shape button on the Organization Chart toolbar, you can easily add relationships to this starting chart.

- Shapes (relationships) you don't need for your chart may be easily removed as well.

Organization Chart toolbar

AutoFormat button

- You can use the Autoformat button on the Organization Chart toolbar to quickly format an entire organization chart.

- You can also apply your own formatting (borders, fills, textures, or patterns) to individual shapes and the background.

■ With the Layout button on the Organization Chart toolbar, you can change the way in which relationships are displayed within the chart.

✓ *Your ability to create an organization chart within Excel is limited—for example, you will not be able to change the relationships between people easily. If you have PowerPoint installed and you're familiar with the program, you may want to use it's organization chart builder, and then paste the chart onto an Excel worksheet.*

Create Diagrams

■ Besides organization charts, Excel allows you to create other conceptual charts (diagrams) as well.

■ You can choose from among these diagram types:

● Cycle: Charts a cyclical process (such as the changing seasons, or the life cycle of a butterfly).

● Radial: Charts the relationships of several items to a single item.

● Pyramid: Charts items that build upon one another, as upon a foundation—for example, the Food Pyramid.

● Venn: Charts items of overlapping characteristics, such as two jobs with overlapping responsibilities.

● Target: Charts items that build upon each other, such as the steps towards a goal.

■ Excel provides the Diagram toolbar, similar to the Organization Chart toolbar, for building and formatting your conceptual chart.

Procedures

Create an Organization Chart

1. Click **Insert** .... `Alt`+`I`
2. Click **Diagram** .... `G`

   ✓ *You can also click the Diagram button on the Drawing toolbar to create a conceptual chart.*

3. Click **OK** .... `Enter`

Add Relationships to an Organization Chart

1. Click shape to which you want to add a relationship.
2. Click **Insert Shape** button on the Organization Chart toolbar .... `Alt`+`N`
3. Select relationship to add:
   ● **Subordinate** .... `S`
   ● **Coworker** .... `C`
   ● **Assistant** .... `A`

Add Text to a Shape

1. Click shape to which you want to add text.
2. Type text.
3. Click outside the shape when done.

Remove Shape

1. Click the shape you wish to remove.
2. Press **Delete** .... `Del`

Change Organization Layout

1. Click the shape superior to the group of shapes whose layout you wish to change.
2. Click **Layout** button on the Organization Chart toolbar .... `Alt`+`L`
3. Select the layout desired:
   ● **Standard** .... `S`

     ✓ *Coworkers appear horizontally.*

   ● **Both Hanging** .... `B`

     ✓ *Coworkers appear on either side of a vertical line.*

   ● **Left Hanging** .... `L`

     ✓ *Coworkers appear on the left side of a vertical line.*

   ● **Right Hanging** .... `R`

     ✓ *Coworkers appear on the right side of a vertical line.*

   ✓ *If the AutoLayout button is pressed, any shapes you add to the chart will automatically use the selected layout.*

Resize an Organization Chart

1. Click chart.
2. Click **Layout** button on the Organization Chart toolbar .... `Alt`+`L`
3. Select the option desired:
   ● **Fit Organization Chart to Contents** .... `F`

     ✓ *Resize background to fit the size of the chart.*

   ● **Expand Organization Chart** .... `E`

     ✓ *Expand background without resizing chart.*

   ● **Scale Organization Chart** .... `C`

     ✓ *As you drag outer border of background, chart and background retain their proportions to each other.*

     ✓ *You can also drag the outer border to scale the chart, without selecting this command.*

Apply AutoFormat	**Create a Conceptual Diagram**
1. Click chart.	1. Click **Insert** .... `Alt`+`I`
2. Click **Autoformat** button .	2. Click **Diagram** .... `G`
3. Select an AutoFormat .... `↑↓←→`	✓ *You can also click the Diagram button on the Drawing toolbar to create a conceptual chart.*
4. Click **Apply** .... `Enter`	3. Select chart type .... `↑↓←→`
	4. Click **OK** .... `Enter`

Exercise Directions

1. Start Excel, if necessary.

2. Open ⌨**CHIPCOSTS** or open 💿**30CHIPCOSTS**.

3. Save the file as **CHIPCOSTS**.

4. Add a new worksheet after the Qtr2 sheet, and name it **Org Chart**.

5. Create an organization chart:

   a. Select Insert, Diagram.

   b. Click OK.

   c. Click the top-most shape and type **Alicia Saunders**. Press Enter and type her title: **Plant Manager**.

   d. Enter her subordinates, as shown in Illustration A.

6. Apply various layout styles:

   a. Click Roberto Guzman's box, click the Layout button, and select Right Hanging.

   b. Click Christine Noblitt's box, click the Layout button, and select Right Hanging.

   c. Click Michael Ryan's box, click the Layout button, and select Both Hanging.

7. Apply an AutoFormat:

   a. Click the Autoformat button.

   b. Select Bookend Fills and click Apply.

8. Resize the chart using the Scale Organization Chart option so that it occupies the range A1:M27.

9. Apply Arial, 7 pt. to each shape.

10. Insert a new worksheet after the Org Chart sheet and name it **Life of a Chip**.

11. Create a conceptual diagram:

    a. Select Insert, Diagram.

    b. Choose Cycle Diagram and click OK.

12. Click the Insert Shape button two times, then click each shape and enter its text, as shown in Illustration B.

13. Apply an AutoFormat:

    a. Click the Autoformat button.

    b. Select Fire and click OK.

14. Using the Scale Diagram command, resize the diagram so that it occupies the range A1:I27.

15. Format each shape with Arial Narrow, 14 pt., bold.

16. Spell check each chart.

17. Print both charts.

18. Close the workbook, saving all changes.

Illustration A

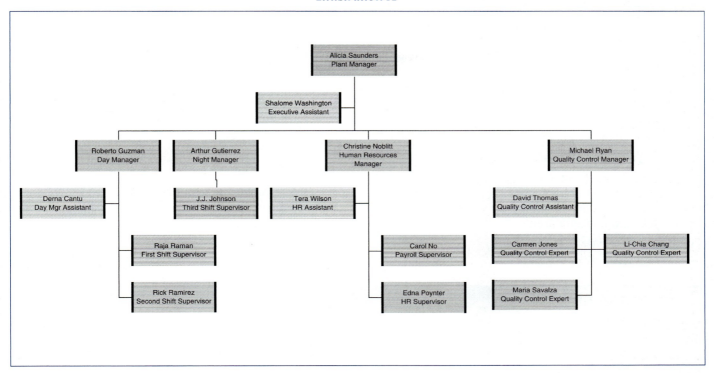

Illustration B

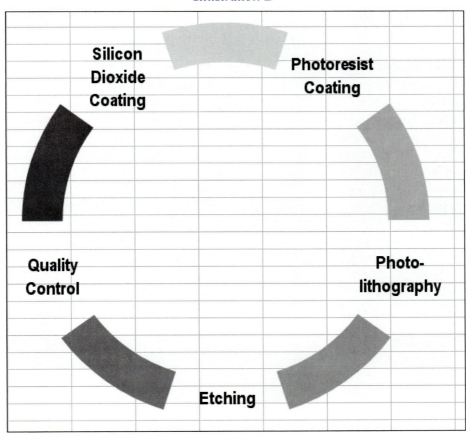

On Your Own

1. Create a new workbook.

2. Save the workbook as **OXL03**.

3. Create an organization chart that lists your family tree.

   a. Start with yourself in the top box.

      ✓ If you don't know everyone's name, you can substitute fake data for this exercise

   b. On the next level down, list your parents, and below them, their parents. (See Illustration C.) Continue in this manner, until you've reached your great-grandparents.

      ✓ Do not list the your parents, grandparents, or great-parents' siblings, since that will take up too much room.

   c. Apply an Autoformat.

   d. Apply other formatting to the text and the diagram background.

4. Spell check the chart.

5. Print the chart.

6. Close the workbook, saving all changes.

Illustration C

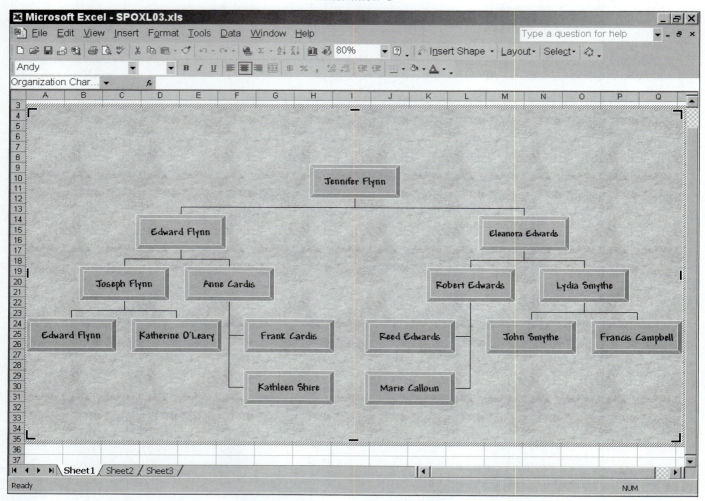

Exercise 31

◆ Critical Thinking

You're a marketing manager at Murray Hill Marketing, and you need to update your client Penguin Frozen Foods on the results of a survey about their new product line, a series of tofu-based frozen dinners. In this exercise, you'll create a chart detailing the survey results and create a diagram listing the marketing steps to product rollout. Then you'll paste both charts into a Word document you've already prepared. You'll also update your marketing team by publishing the survey results on your company's intranet.

Exercise Directions

1. Start Excel, if necessary.
2. Open ☻ **31TOFU**.
3. Save the file as **TOFU**.
4. Make a chart:
   a. Select the ranges C22:D28, G22:G28, I22:I28.
   b. Create a stacked bar chart.
   c. Enter the title **Preferences by Age**.
   d. Resize the chart to fit the range A34:J56.
   e. Change the title font to Arial Black, 20 pt.
   f. Change the Category axis font to Arial Narrow, 12 pt., bold.
   g. Change the Value axis font to Arial Narrow, 12 pt., bold.
   h. Change the Legend font to Arial Narrow, 9 pt., bold.
   i. Apply a Tan fill to the background, and a Recycled Paper texture to the plot area.
5. Spell check the workbook.
6. Print the chart:
   a. Use the Chart tab of the Page Setup dialog box to scale the chart to fit the page.
   b. Add a header that includes your name, page number, and the date.
   c. Print the chart in black and white.
7. Publish the chart to the Internet:
   a. Change the title of the Web page to **Popularity of Tofu Frozen Dinners**.
   b. Add interactivity.
   c. Use the file name **TOFU.htm**.
   d. Turn on the AutoRepublish option.
   e. Display the result in your Web browser.

8. In the browser, change the number of participants in the 33-40 age group (cell B15) to 63.
9. Make this same change to the Excel worksheet. Also change the number of participants in the Under 25 age group to 63.
10. Save the workbook but do not close it. (If prompted, be sure to enable the AutoRepublish feature.)
11. Change back to the browser, click Refresh, and notice that the additional change you made in Excel is now reflected on the Web page as well. (See Illustration A.) Close the Web browser.
12. Create a conceptual chart:
    a. Rename Sheet 2 **Marketing Plan**.
    b. Create a pyramid diagram, as shown in Illustration B.
    c. Apply the Primary Colors AutoFormat. Apply the Bouquet texture to the background.
13. Open ☻ **31TOFU.doc.**
14. Save the file as **TOFU.doc**.
15. Link and embed various charts in a Word document:
    a. Link the chart on the Survey Results worksheet to the place in **TOFU.doc** marked **[link chart here]**.
    b. Paste a picture of the pyramid chart to the place in **TOFU.doc** marked **[picture of chart here]**.
       ✓ Resize the charts as needed to fit in the margins. (See Illustrations C and D.)
    c. Spell check and print the Word document.
16. Close all open files, saving all changes.

Illustration A

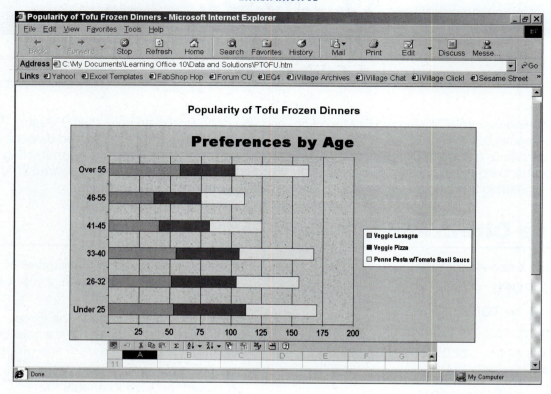

Illustration B

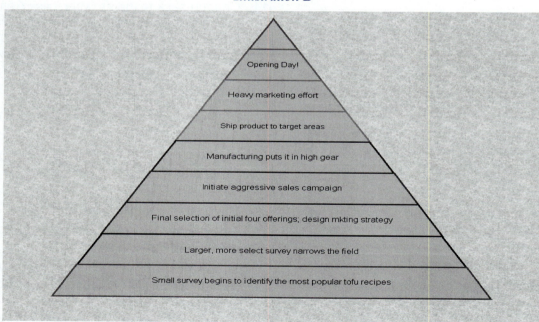

Illustration C

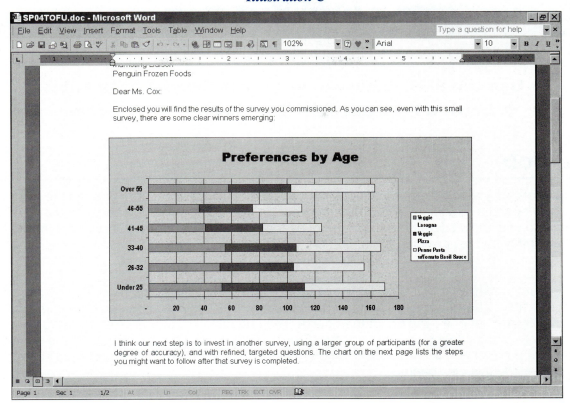

Illustration D

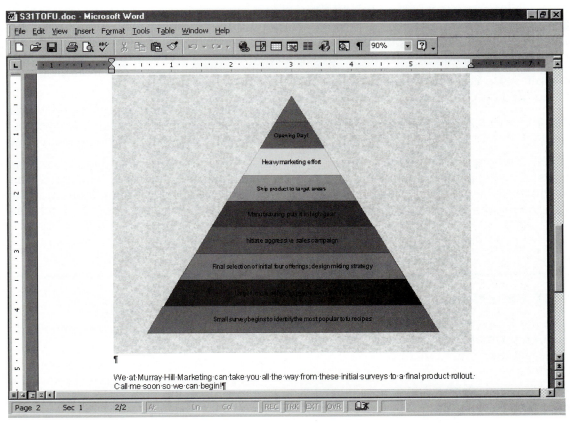

Exercise 32

Skills Covered:

◆ **Use the PMT Function** ◆ **Create What-If Data Tables**
◆ **Solve a Problem with Goal Seek** ◆ **Use Solver**

On the Job

What-if analysis allows you to determine the optimal values for a given situation. For example, if you know that you can only spend a maximum of $32,000 this year on new computers, you could adjust the monthly budget amount so you could spend the total amount by the end of the year and yet still remain within your department's monthly budgetary constraints.

You're an account manager at Murray Hill Marketing, and your client Penguin Frozen Foods has asked for more of your help. They want to go ahead with the plan to sell tofu-based frozen food items, but have decided to initially market one—the vegetarian pizza. They need your expertise with Excel to help them determine likely revenues based on your surveys. From that, they would like your input on a good price point for the new product and some information on getting a loan to cover the initial startup costs and first month's expenses on this new venture.

Terms

What-if analysis Excel's term for a series of tools that you can use to create calculations that involve one or more variable.

Variable An input value that changes depending on the desired outcome.

Substitution values A special name given to the variables used in a data table.

Input cell A cell in a data table to which your formula refers. Excel copies a variable into this cell, solves the formula, and then goes on to the next variable to create a series of answers.

Data table A method of performing what-if analysis, involving a column (and possibly a row) of variables and a formula that Excel solves over and over, using each of the variables. The result is a table of answers.

Goal Seek A method of performing what-if analysis in which the result is known, but the value of a dependant variable is unknown.

Solver A method of performing what-if analysis in which the result is known, but more than a single variable is unknown. Also, there may be additional constraints upon the final result.

Notes

Use the PMT Function

- You can use the PMT (payment) function to calculate a loan payment amount given the principal, interest rate, and number of payment periods.

- The arguments for the PMT function are:
  =PMT(rate,nper,pv)

- rate: Interest rate per period (for example, annual interest rate/12).

- nper: Number of payment periods (for example, years*12).

- pv (present value): The total amount that a series of future payments is worth now (for example, the principal).

- You must express the rate and the number of payment periods (nper) for the same period, such as monthly or annually.

- For example, if you wish to calculate a monthly payment at a 9% rate of interest for 25 years, you must enter .09/12 as the monthly rate and enter 25*12 to get the number of monthly payment periods (nper) per year.

- You must enter the present value as a negative if you want the result to be displayed as a positive number.

Create What-if Data Tables

- With a **what-if analysis**, you can evaluate different situations based on certain variables and find the best solution.

- For example, if you want to purchase a home and can only afford $1,000 per month, a what-if data table could determine the maximum mortgage amount you can afford.

- The **variables** used in a data table are called **substitution values**, because Excel substitutes each value in the given formula when evaluating the what-if situation.

- The **input cell** is the cell to which your what-if formula refers. Excel uses this cell as a working area during the analysis—it can be blank, or it contain one of the variables (typically, the first one in the variables list).

- Excel places each variable into the input cell as it solves each equation.

  ✓ *The what-if formula must refer to this input cell.*

- **Data tables** come in two types: one-input data tables and two-input data tables.

- In a one-input data table, you enter one series of variables, which are then substituted in a formula to come up with a series of answers.

- For example, you can enter a series of loan rates to determine the varying payment amounts on a 30-year fixed loan.

- In a two-input data table, you enter two series of variables, thus increasing the number of possible solutions.

- For example, you can enter both the loan rates and several different loan terms (15-, 20-, 25-, or 30-year) to determine what amounts you can afford under varying plans.

One-input data table

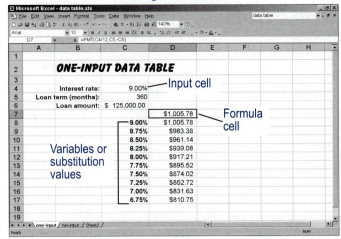

Two-input data table

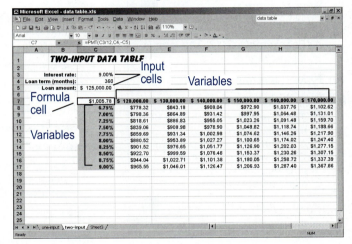

Solve a Problem with Goal Seek

- With **Goal Seek**, you can solve a problem when you know the desired result, but not one of the input variables.

- Goal Seek tests possible variables until it finds the input value that produces the desired result.

- For example, you could use Goal Seek to determine the exact amount you could borrow with a payment of $1,000 a month and a specific interest rate, such as 9.25%.

Use Solver

- With **Solver**, you can resolve problems involving more than one variable, with a known result.

- For example, you could use Solver to determine the exact amount you could borrow, spending $1,000 a month, using various interest rates and various down payments.

  ✓ *You can also solve multiple variables problems with a pivot table, which you'll learn about in Exercise 34.*

Procedures

Use PMT Function

1. Click cell where answer should appear...................⊞
2. Type = (equal sign) .... ▣
3. Type *PMT*.
4. Press ((open parenthesis).... ▣
5. Type rate *divided by 12.*
   - ✓ *For example, .09/12. This gives you the monthly equivalent rate. The rate is a percentage, so you would enter 9% or .09.*
6. Type **,** (comma) ....▣
7. Type term times 12.
   - ✓ *For example, 3*12. The term is the number of years.*
8. Type **,** (comma) ....▣
9. Type the principal.
   - ✓ *The principal is the amount of the loan, minus any down payment amount. If you want the answer expressed as a positive number, type a minus sign before the principal.*
10. Press) (close parenthesis) ... ▣
    - ✓ *For example, to compute the monthly payment on a $100,000, 20-year loan at 6%: =PMT(.06/12,20*12,-100000)*
    - ✓ *You can use cell references instead of typing values, as in: =PMT(A1/12,A2*12,-A3)*
11. Press **Enter**.....................Enter

Create One-Input Data Table

1. Enter variables in a column.
2. Type formula.
   - ✓ *You must enter formula in a cell one row above and one column to right of first column variable.*
   - ✓ *For example, if you entered your variables in cells C8:C17, then type the formula in cell D7.*

- ✓ *The formula refers to a cell, which acts as an input cell. The input cell is NOT located within the range formed by the formula cell, the variables column, and the blank cells below the formula cell but to the right of the variables.*
- ✓ *To enter additional formulas, type them in the cells to the right of the formula cell. All formulas must refer to the same input cell, and thus use the same list of substitution values.*

3. Select all cells in data table range.
   - ✓ *Select cells containing formula and substitution values. For example, select C7:D17.*
   - ✓ *Do not select the input cell.*
4. Click **Data**....................Alt+D
5. Click **Table** ....T
6. Select **Column input cell**:....................Alt+C
   - ✓ *Select input cell referred to by the formula, in which column variables should be used.*
7. Click **OK** ....Enter

Create Two-Input Data Table

1. Enter one set of variables in column.
2. Enter second set of variables in row.
   - ✓ *Enter first row variable one row above, and one column to right of column of variables.*
   - ✓ *For example, if you entered your column variables in cells C11:C19, then enter your row variables in cells D10, E10, etc.*
3. Click upper-left cell in table ....⊞
   - ✓ *For example, click in cell C10, just to left of first row variable.*
4. Type formula.
   - ✓ *Formula refers to two blank cells, which act as input cells.*

---

5. Select all cells in data table range.
   - ✓ *Select cells containing formula and substitution values. For example, select C10:H19.*
   - ✓ *Do not select input cells.*
6. Click **Data** ....Alt+D
7. Click **Table**..........................T
8. Select **Row input cell** in worksheet................Alt+R
   - ✓ *Select input cell referred to by formula, in which row variables should be used.*
9. Select **Column input cell**: ....Alt+C
   - ✓ *Select input cell referred to by formula, in which column variables should be used.*
10. Click **OK**..........................Enter

Use Goal Seek

1. Click **Tools** ....Alt+T
2. Click **Goal Seek**...................G
3. In **Set Cell** box, select cell that contains formula you want to solve.
4. In **To value** text box, type result you desire.
5. In **By changing** cell box, select cell that contains value you want adjusted.
6. Click **OK**..........................Enter

Use Solver

1. Click **Tools** ....Alt+T
2. Click **Solver** V
   - ✓ *If Solver is not installed, you can install it with Tools, Add-Ins command.*
3. In **Set Target Cell** box, select cell that contains formula you want to solve.
4. Select option:
   - • Select **Max**..............Alt+M
   - • Select **Min** ....Alt+N
   - • Select **Value of**.......Alt+V
5. Type value you want.

6. In **By Changing Cells** box, select cell that contains values you want adjusted.

7. Add any constraints:

   a. Click **Add** .... `Alt`+`A`

   b. Select **Cell Reference** .... `Alt`+`R`

c. Select comparison operator ...... `▬`

d. Type or select **Constraint**... `Alt`+`C`

e. Click **OK** .... `Enter`

8. Click **Solve** button `Solve` .... `Enter`

   ✓ *You can save the scenario, restore your previous values, or print reports from dialog box that appears.*

Exercise Directions

1. Start Excel, if necessary.

2. Open ⊙ **32TOFUCOST**.

3. Save the file as **TOFUCOST**.

4. Create a two-input table on the Price-Point Pizza worksheet:

   a. Type the following formula in cell B23: =(D18*D15)*F18.

      ✓ *This calculates the weekly revenues if the minimum number of units are sold (71% of 37,500) at $4.50 each.*

   b. Select the range B23:I45.

   c. Choose Data, Table.

   d. For the Row Input cell, select F18.

   e. For the Column Input cell, select D18. Click OK.

      ✓ *Widen the columns if necessary.*

      ✓ *See Illustration A.*

5. Use Solver to decide on a good price point for you new product:

   a. Change to the Profit Margin worksheet.

   b. Choose Tools, Solver.

   c. Set the Target cell to D19.

   d. After Solver resolves the problem, the value in cell D19 must equal 25000.

   e. Allow Solver to change the value in cell D16.

   f. Enter constraints that keep the value in cell D16 between 4.50 and 6.00.

      ✓ *See Illustration B.*

6. Create a one-input data table:

   a. Change to the Loan Costs worksheet.

   b. In cell D22, enter PMT formula using the values in cells G12, G13, and D20.

      ✓ *Be sure to enter D20 as –D20, so the result will display as a positive number.*

   c. Select the range C22:D33.

   d. Choose Data, Table.

   e. For the Column Input cell, select G12. Click OK.

      ✓ *See Illustration C.*

7. Spell check the workbook.

8. Print the workbook.

9. Close the workbook, saving all changes.

Illustration A

	A	B	C	D	E	F	G	H	I
21		**Weekly revenues from sales, using various price points and sales percentages**							
23		$119,812.50	$ 4.50	$ 4.75	$ 5.00	$ 5.25	$ 5.50	$ 5.75	$ 6.00
24		71%	$ 119,812.50	$126,468.75	$ 133,125.00	$ 139,781.25	$146,437.50	$153,093.75	$159,750.00
25		72%	$ 121,500.00	$128,250.00	$ 135,000.00	$ 141,750.00	$148,500.00	$155,250.00	$162,000.00
26		73%	$ 123,187.50	$130,031.25	$ 136,875.00	$ 143,718.75	$150,562.50	$157,406.25	$164,250.00
27		74%	$ 124,875.00	$131,812.50	$ 138,750.00	$ 145,687.50	$152,625.00	$159,562.50	$166,500.00
28		75%	$ 126,562.50	$133,593.75	$ 140,625.00	$ 147,656.25	$154,687.50	$161,718.75	$168,750.00
29		76%	$ 128,250.00	$135,375.00	$ 142,500.00	$ 149,625.00	$156,750.00	$163,875.00	$171,000.00
30		77%	$ 129,937.50	$137,156.25	$ 144,375.00	$ 151,593.75	$158,812.50	$166,031.25	$173,250.00
31		78%	$ 131,625.00	$138,937.50	$ 146,250.00	$ 153,562.50	$160,875.00	$168,187.50	$175,500.00
32		79%	$ 133,312.50	$140,718.75	$ 148,125.00	$ 155,531.25	$162,937.50	$170,343.75	$177,750.00
33		80%	$ 135,000.00	$142,500.00	$ 150,000.00	$ 157,500.00	$165,000.00	$172,500.00	$180,000.00
34		81%	$ 136,687.50	$144,281.25	$ 151,875.00	$ 159,468.75	$167,062.50	$174,656.25	$182,250.00
35		82%	$ 138,375.00	$146,062.50	$ 153,750.00	$ 161,437.50	$169,125.00	$176,812.50	$184,500.00
36		83%	$ 140,062.50	$147,843.75	$ 155,625.00	$ 163,406.25	$171,187.50	$178,968.75	$186,750.00
37		84%	$ 141,750.00	$149,625.00	$ 157,500.00	$ 165,375.00	$173,250.00	$181,125.00	$189,000.00
38		85%	$ 143,437.50	$151,406.25	$ 159,375.00	$ 167,343.75	$175,312.50	$183,281.25	$191,250.00
39		86%	$ 145,125.00	$153,187.50	$ 161,250.00	$ 169,312.50	$177,375.00	$185,437.50	$193,500.00
40		87%	$ 146,812.50	$154,968.75	$ 163,125.00	$ 171,281.25	$179,437.50	$187,593.75	$195,750.00
41		88%	$ 148,500.00	$156,750.00	$ 165,000.00	$ 173,250.00	$181,500.00	$189,750.00	$198,000.00
42		89%	$ 150,187.50	$158,531.25	$ 166,875.00	$ 175,218.75	$183,562.50	$191,906.25	$200,250.00
43		90%	$ 151,875.00	$160,312.50	$ 168,750.00	$ 177,187.50	$185,625.00	$194,062.50	$202,500.00
44		91%	$ 153,562.50	$162,093.75	$ 170,625.00	$ 179,156.25	$187,687.50	$196,218.75	$204,750.00
45		92%	$ 155,250.00	$163,875.00	$ 172,500.00	$ 181,125.00	$189,750.00	$198,375.00	$207,000.00

Sheet tabs: Market Survey | **Price Point-Pizza** | Profit Margin | Loan Costs

Illustration B

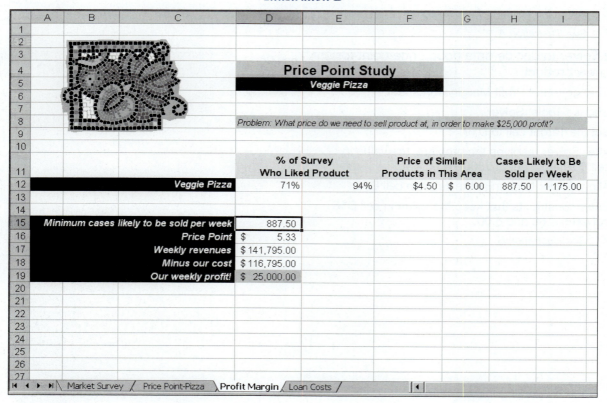

Price Point Study
Veggie Pizza

Problem: What price do we need to sell product at, in order to make $25,000 profit?

	% of Survey Who Liked Product		Price of Similar Products in This Area		Cases Likely to Be Sold per Week	
Veggie Pizza	71%	94%	$4.50	$ 6.00	887.50	1,175.00

Minimum cases likely to be sold per week	887.50
Price Point	$ 5.33
Weekly revenues	$ 141,795.00
Minus our cost	$ 116,795.00
Our weekly profit!	$ 25,000.00

Sheet tabs: Market Survey | Price Point-Pizza | **Profit Margin** | Loan Costs

428

Illustration C

	A	B	C	D	E	F	G	H
7								
8				Problem: How much will our start up loan cost us?				
9								
10								
11		Maximum cases likely to be sold per week		1,175.00		Best Case Scenario		
12		Likely Price Point	$	5.33		Loan rate	7%	
13		Maximum weekly revenues	$	187,728.59		Term (in years)	15	
14		Maximum weekly cost	$	154,630.00		Monthly payment	$ 8,804.43	
15		Maximum weekly profit	$	33,098.59				
16		Maximum monthly profit	$	132,394.37		Worst Case Scenario		
17		Maximum costs for first month	$	618,520.00		Loan rate	9.5%	
18		Manufacturing gear-up costs	$	250,775.00		Term (in years)	15	
19		Start-up advertising costs	$	110,250.00		Monthly payment	$ 10,228.65	
20		Total loan needed	$	979,545.00				
21								
22				$8,804.43				
23			7.00%	$ 8,804.43				
24			7.25%	$ 8,941.90				
25			7.50%	$ 9,080.50				
26			7.75%	$ 9,220.22				
27			8.00%	$ 9,361.04				
28			8.25%	$ 9,502.96				
29			8.50%	$ 9,645.97				
30			8.75%	$ 9,790.05				
31			9.00%	$ 9,935.20				
32			9.25%	$ 10,081.40				
33			9.50%	$ 10,228.65				
34								

Market Survey / Price Point-Pizza / Profit Margin \ Loan Costs /

On Your Own

1. Start Excel and create a new workbook.

2. Save the workbook as **OXL32**.

3. Set up a two-input data table to help you determine the monthly payments for buying a car. Assume the interest rates range from 6% to 7% in quarter percent increments and that used cars you've been looking at range from $7,000 to $12,000 in $500 increments. Also assume that the loan term is three years.

4. Set up another scenario in the same workbook, in which you use Goal Seek to determine exactly how much money you can borrow in order to maintain a monthly loan payment of $250. Assume the interest rate is 6.2%, and the loan term is three years.

5. Format the worksheets as you wish.

6. Spell check the worksheet.

7. Print the worksheet.

8. Close the workbook, saving all changes.

Exercise 33

On the Job

With the lookup functions, you can look up information in a table based on a known value. For example, you can look up the salesperson assigned to a particular client. At the same time, you can look up that client's address and phone number. You can also look up the sales discount for a particular customer or calculate the bonuses for a group of salespeople based on a bonus structure. If needed, you can nest a function such as SUM within a lookup function, in order to lookup a sum total within a table. For example, you might want to lookup the total cost of the items in an invoice in order to calculate the cost of delivering them.

As the owner of Coastline Gourmet Importers, it's important that you keep close track of your growing business. In an effort to save time and keep the money flowing more smoothly, you've decided to automate the process of invoicing your customers. In this exercise, you'll use Excel to create an invoice, and with the help of the lookup functions you'll build in, you'll be able to compute the pricing and delivery costs easily.

Terms

Table A series of columns and rows used to organize data. Each column typically represents a different field, and each row represents an entire record.

Range name The name given to a set of adjacent cells. You might name a range in order to make it more convenient to reference that range in a formula or a function, such as VLOOKUP.

Notes

Create Lookup Functions

- The lookup functions, VLOOKUP and HLOOKUP, locate a value in a **table**.

- There are two ways to look up data, depending on the way the data is arranged: vertically or horizontally.
  - VLOOKUP (vertical lookup) looks up data in a particular column in the table.
  - HLOOKUP (horizontal lookup) looks up data in a particular row in the table.

- The VLOOKUP function uses this format: =VLOOKUP(*item,table-range,column-position*)
  - Item is the text or value for which you are looking.

- The item to look up must be located in the first column of the VLOOKUP table.
- Upper- and lowercase are treated the same.
- If an exact match is not found, the next smallest value is used.
- ✓ *You can use a function here to calculate the item's value. For example, suppose you were trying to look up the delivery cost for several items in an invoice. The delivery cost is based on the total sale, so you could use SUM to calculate the total sale, then look up that total in your delivery cost table.*

- Table-range is the range reference or **range name** of the lookup table.
  - Do not include the row containing the column labels.

- ◆ If you are going to copy the lookup function, you should express the range as an absolute reference or as a range name.
- ● Column-position is the column number in the table from which the matching value should be returned.
  - ✓ *The far-left column of the table is one; the second column is two, etc.*
- ■ For example, to look up the mortgage payment for a $110,000 loan for 20 years at 9% in the following table, use this formula:
  =VLOOKUP(110000,D12:I38,4)

        Item   Table range   Column position

VLOOKUP table

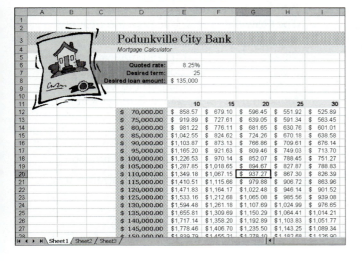

- ■ You may use a similar formula in a horizontal lookup table:
  =HLOOKUP(*item,table-range,row-position*).
  - ● Item is the text or value for which you are looking.
  - ● Table-range is the range reference or **range name** of the lookup table.
    - ✓ *Do not include the column that contains the row labels in this range.*
  - ● Row-position is the row number in the **table** from which the matching value should be returned.
- ■ For example, to look up the mortgage payment for a $110,000 loan for 20 years at 9% in the same table shown here, use this formula:
  =HLOOKUP(20,E11:I38,10)

       Item   Table range   Row position

Procedures

Insert VLOOKUP or HLOOKUP Function Using Function Wizard

1. Click desired cell .... ⬚
2. Press = (equal sign) .... ⬚
3. Type function name:
   - **VLOOKUP (**
   - **HLOOKUP(**
4. Type item in **Lookup_value** positionbox.

- ✓ *This function's syntax appears in a ScreenTip underneath the Formula bar. With complex functions such as this, it's helpful to click the function's name in the ScreenTip in order to display the related Help screen. Also remember that at any time, you can click the Insert Function button to display a dialog box into which you can enter the function's arguments.*

- ✓ *Item can be an actual item or a reference to cell containing item.*

- ✓ *You can click a cell in worksheet to insert cell reference.*

5. Type range in **Table_array** box.
   - ✓ *You can select a range in worksheet to insert cell references.*
6. Type row or column number in **Row** or **Col_index_num** box.
7. Click **OK** .... Enter

Exercise Directions

1. Start Excel, if necessary.

2. Open ⊘ **33CGIINVOICE**.

3. Save the file as **CGIINVOICE**.

4. If needed, switch to the Invoice Template worksheet.

5. In cell D13, enter a formula to look up the price per case of the item entered in cell B13.

   - Use the VLOOKUP function.

   - The Lookup Value is the item name, which will be typed into cell B13.

   - The table that contains the information you need is located on the Item List worksheet. Make sure you do not include row 1, which contains the column labels, in the range you select.

     ✓ *Since you'll be copying this formula, make sure the range address is absolute.*

   - The Column Index is 2, because the cost per case of each item is located in column 2 of the table.

6. Copy this formula to other cells in the Cost per Case column.

   ✓ *You've probably noticed that your formula causes an error, "N/A." That's because there's currently nothing entered into cell B13. Since we will be entering some items, you can ignore the error if you like, or, if you want the challenge, before copying the formula, you can modify it by nesting the VLOOKUP function within an IF function, which tests if B13="", and, if so, displays 0 (zero). If cell B13 is not blank, then have the IF function perform the VLOOKUP function.*

7. In cell E29, enter a formula to look up the delivery cost, which is based on the number of cases ordered.

   - Use the HLOOKUP function.

   - The Lookup Value is the SUM of the numbers entered into the range C13:C26.

     ✓ *Remember, you can use a function or a formula to calculate the value you want to look up in a table.*

   - The delivery costs table is located in rows 10 and 11 on the Delivery Costs worksheet. When you select your range, be sure not to include the row labels which appear in columns B and C.

   - The Row Index is 2, because the delivery costs are located in row 2 of the table.

   - To avoid the N/A error, you may want to nest the HLOOKUP function in an IF function as well, in a manner similar to the VLOOKUP function described earlier. Simply nest the HLOOKUP function within an IF function which tests if the SUM of C13:C26 is equal to 0, and, if so, displays 0 (zero). If not, then have the IF function perform the HLOOKUP function.

8. Test your new invoice by entering in a few items:

   a. In cell B9, type **China Garden**.

   b. In cell B10, type **2135 Restaurant Row**.

   c. Beginning in cell B13, type the item names and number of cases ordered as shown in Illustration A.

9. Spell check the worksheet.

10. Print the worksheet.

11. Close the workbook, saving all changes.

Illustration A

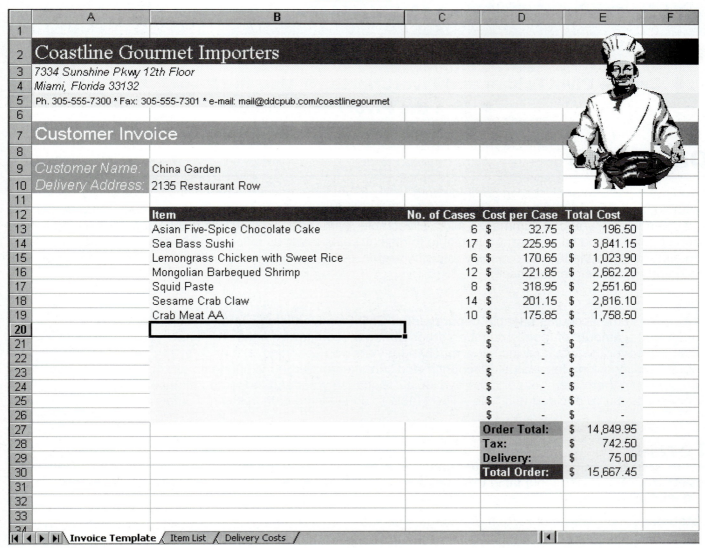

On Your Own

1. Start Excel and open **OXL32**, the workbook you used in the On Your Own section of Exercise 32, or open ⊙ **33CARLOAN**.

2. Save the file as **OXL33**.

3. Use the VLOOKUP function to locate the monthly loan payment for a $11,000 loan at 6.5% interest.

   ✓ *As a challenge, you can nest the MATCH function within the VLOOKUP function, and use MATCH to lookup the Column Index for you. Simply tell MATCH to look for the value 11000 in the row of column labels, B6:M6.*

4. Make sure the cell where the result is displayed is labeled.

5. Use the HLOOKUP function to locate the monthly loan payment for a $10,500 loan at 6.25% interest.

   ✓ *As an additional challenge, use a nested MATCH function here as well to look up the value .0625 in the column of row labels, B6:B11.*

6. Make sure the cell where the result is displayed is labeled.

7. Save the worksheet, close it, and exit Excel.

Exercise 34

Skills Covered:

◆ **Create PivotTables and PivotCharts** ◆ **Use the PivotTable Field List**
◆ **Use the PivotTable Toolbar**

On the Job

If you must perform analyses on complex data, a PivotTable can make the process a lot easier. For example, if you had a database containing lots of information, such as sales data by product, store, region, and salesperson, you can summarize it in a PivotTable. With the table, you can display totals by region for each product or you can rearrange the table to display sales totals by office and individual salesperson. You can also combine the tables to display totals by region, office, salesperson, and product. The flexibility of the PivotTable is its greatest asset.

You work in the accounts payable department at California Cardiology, and you've been asked to analyze the amount of money spent on drugs during the last few months. You know you'll need to look at the data several ways, such as "How much money are you spending with each of your suppliers, and does it justify asking for a larger discount?" and "Are certain surgeons spending too much on particular drugs, when there are cheaper ones available?" Because you need these and many other questions answered, you've decided to create a PivotTable to analyze the data in several different ways.

Terms

PivotTable A rearrangeable table that allows you to analyze complex data in a variety of ways.

Database An organized collection of records. For example, in an employee database, one record might include the following:

> Employee name
> Date of hire
> Address
> Phone number
> Salary rate

PivotChart A chart based on PivotTable data.

Page field A field from the database that you can use to create different "pages" or views within the PivotTable.

Field A single part of a record, such as "Phone number." Multiple related fields, such as one employee's name, address, phone number, etc., make up one record.

Notes

Create PivotTables

- A **PivotTable** allows you to summarize complex data, such as a company's sales or accounting records.

- The advantage of the PivotTable over a regular table of information is that it lets you quickly change how data is summarized. For example, you can change from a report that summarizes sales data by region and office to one that summarizes the same data by salesperson and product.

Sample PivotTable

	A	B	C	D	E	F
1	Region	Southern ▼				
2						
3	Sum of Total Sale		Month ▼			
4	Office ▼	Drug ▼	April	May	June	Grand Total
5	Atlanta	Bludadoze	$ 38,310.00	$ 51,053.00	$ 20,966.00	$110,329.00
6		Havcore	$ 53,665.00	$ 25,519.00	$ 15,648.00	$ 94,832.00
7		Pardox	$ 20,315.00	$ 31,779.00	$ 11,958.00	$ 64,052.00
8	Atlanta Total		$112,290.00	$108,351.00	$ 48,572.00	$269,213.00
9	Dallas	Bludadoze	$ 18,974.00	$ 32,102.00	$ 34,308.00	$ 85,384.00
10		Havcore	$ 20,355.00	$ 29,796.00	$ 16,541.00	$ 66,692.00
11		Pardox	$ 40,459.00	$ 59,197.00	$ 49,083.00	$148,739.00
12	Dallas Total		$ 79,788.00	$121,095.00	$ 99,932.00	$300,815.00
13	Grand Total		$192,078.00	$229,446.00	$148,504.00	$570,028.00

- The source data for your PivotTable may be a **database**, text file, a query file, or even a list within an Excel workbook.

- After creating a PivotTable report, you can create a matching **PivotChart**.

  ✓ *You can create a PivotChart without creating a PivotTable first, although most users create the table prior to creating the chart.*

- You can publish your PivotTable/PivotChart to the Internet or your company's intranet.

Use the PivotTable Field List

- To help you create a pivot table, use the PivotTable Wizard.

  ✓ *The PivotTable Wizard creates the framework for your PivotTable. You then use the items on the PivotTable Field List to arrange (and rearrange) the data to create the table you want.*

- The PivotTable Field List contains a list of every field (column) in your database/list.

PivotTable Field List

- By dragging these items onto various parts of the PivotTable, you can instantly change how your data is summarized.

  ✓ *You can also select items from the list and use the Add To button to add the item to the PivotTable without dragging.*

- The PivotTable has three basic areas into which you can drag the items on the PivotTable Field List: the row area, the column area, and the body area.

- Drag numerical items into the body of the table to summarize them.

  ✓ *In the sample on the left, the Total Sale item was placed in the body area of the PivotTable.*

- Drag items into the row area to have them appear in the rows of the table. Items that you drag into the column area appear in the columns of the table.

  ✓ *In the sample, the Office and Drug items were added to the row area, and the Month item was added to the column area of the table.*

- In addition to dragging items into the body, row, and column areas of the table, you can drag them into the **page fields** area as well.

- The page fields area allows you to create "pages" of the report in which only the items relating to a particular category are displayed.

  ✓ *In the sample, the Region item was added to the Page Fields area. This allows the user to quickly view data for each region separately, or for all regions.*

- When you add an item to a PivotTable, that item becomes a button with a down arrow.

- You can limit what's displayed in the PivotTable by clicking the down arrow on the appropriate item button and selecting the item(s) you want to display.

  ✓ *In the sample, the down arrow on the Region button was clicked, and "Southern" was selected. This caused the PivotTable to display only the data for the Southern Region. A user could further limit the report to display only the Atlanta office or only the drug sales for Bludadoze and Pardox or only the sales for June.*

Use the PivotTable Toolbar

- When you create a PivotTable, the PivotTable toolbar automatically appears.

- Use the toolbar to format your PivotTable, hide or display data, create a PivotChart, and so on.

Format Report   Show Detail   Include Hidden Items in Totals   Field Settings

PivotTable

PivotTable ▾

Chart Wizard   Refresh Data

Hide Detail   Always Display Items   Hide Fields

Procedures

Create PivotTable with Excel List

1. Click within Excel list.
2. Click **Data** .... `Alt`+`D`
3. Click **PivotTable and PivotChart Report** .... `P`
4. Click **Microsoft Excel list or database** .... `Alt`+`M`
5. Click **Next** .... `Enter`
6. Make sure that the range you want to create the table from is selected, then click **Next** .... `Enter`

   ✓ *The Wizard should automatically select a range for your list. If selection is wrong, you can select range yourself.*

7. Select
   New worksheet .... `Alt`+`N`
   OR
   Select
   Existing worksheet ... `Alt`+`E`
8. Click **Finish** .... `Alt`+`F`

   ✓ *PivotTable Field List appears, displaying a list of the columns (fields) in your list.*

9. Drag the name of item(s) you wish to appear in separate columns in the table from the PivotTable Field List box into area on the worksheet marked **Drop Column Fields Here**.

   ✓ *As an alternative to dragging, you can also select the item you want, choose Column Area from the drop-down list on the PivotTable Field List box, and click **Add To**.*

10. Drag the name of the item(s) you wish to appear in separate rows in table from the PivotTable Field List into area on the worksheet marked **Drop Row Fields Here**.

    ✓ *You can also select the item you want, choose Row Area from the drop-down list, and click **Add To**.*

11. Drag the name of item that you wish to appear in the body of the table from the PivotTable Field List into area on the worksheet marked **Drop Data Items Here**.

    ✓ *This item is typically a numerical item, such as total sales.*

    ✓ *As mentioned earlier, you can also select the item you want, choose Data Area from the drop-down list, and click **Add To**.*

12. If you wish to display only items related to a particular category, you can add a page field as well by dragging that item from the PivotTable Field List into area marked **Drop Page Fields Here**.

    ✓ *You can also select the item you want, choose Page Area from the drop-down list, and click **Add To**.*

    ✓ *To remove an item from the table, drag it outside table area.*

    ✓ *To format PivotTable, click **Format Report** button on PivotTable toolbar and select format you like. You can also quickly apply color fills, fonts, font colors and attributes, and number formats manually using the Formatting toolbar.*

Create PivotChart from PivotTable

1. Click inside PivotTable.
2. Click **Chart Wizard** button on PivotTable toolbar.
3. Make any adjustments you like:

   • To remove a field from a chart, drag it off chart area.

   • To add a field to a chart, drag it from PivotTable Field List onto chart area.

   • To change chart type, click **Chart Type** button on Chart toolbar and select chart type you want to use.

Exercise Directions

1. Start Excel, if necessary.
2. Open ⊙ **34PHARMACY**.
3. Save the file as **PHARMACY**.
4. Create a PivotTable.
   a. Use the range C9:G88 of the Drug Purchases worksheet.
   b. Place the PivotTable on the Analysis worksheet, beginning in cell C6.
5. Drag the Supplier item into the area marked *Drop Row Fields Here*.
6. Drag the Drug item to the right of the Supplier item.
7. Drag the Month item into the area marked *Drop Column Fields Here*.
8. Drag the Total Sale item into the area marked *Drop Data Items Here*.
9. Drag the Surgeon item into the area marked *Drop Page Fields Here*.
10. Select *Dr. Mei Rong Lu* from the Surgeon list.
11. Format the table:
    a. Click the Format Report button on the PivotTable toolbar.
    b. Select Table 2 and click OK.
    c. Click in cell E8.
    d. Click the Field Settings button on the PivotTable toolbar.

e. Click Number.
f. Select *Currency* and click OK.
g. Click OK again.
h. Adjust the column widths on the table if needed, to fully display the data.
12. Spell check the workbook. See Illustration A.
13. Print the PivotTable.
14. Create a PivotChart from your table.
15. Print the chart.
16. Rearrange the PivotTable:
    a. Move the Drug button in front of the Month button.
    b. Move the Month button above the Surgeon button.
    c. Move the Surgeon button in front of the Supplier button.
    d. Drag the Supplier button off the table to remove it.
    e. Select *June* from the Month list. See Illustration B.
17. Print the table.
18. Print the chart.
    ✓ *Notice that the chart has changed to reflect the reorganization of the table.*
19. Close the workbook, saving all changes.

Illustration A

Surgeon	Dr. Mei Rong Lu				
Total Sale		**Month**			
Supplier	**Drug**	April	May	June	**Grand Total**
Caldecott Drug Sup	Ciberan		$8,965.00	$15,648.00	$24,613.00
	Tyledan	$20,355.00			$20,355.00
	Xydocan		$16,554.00		$16,554.00
Caldecott Drug Supply Total		**$20,355.00**	**$25,519.00**	**$15,648.00**	**$61,522.00**
Harcourt Drugs	Ciberan			$20,966.00	$20,966.00
	Hearteze		$32,102.00		$32,102.00
	Tyledan	$19,665.00	$12,654.00		$32,319.00
	Xydocan		$19,452.00		$19,452.00
Harcourt Drugs Total		**$19,665.00**	**$64,208.00**	**$20,966.00**	**$104,839.00**
Nuvo Pharmaceutic	Hearteze	$17,954.00	$9,874.00		$27,828.00
	Nockout		$21,645.00		$21,645.00
	Tyledan		$10,215.00		$10,215.00
	Xydocan			$11,958.00	$11,958.00
Nuvo Pharmaceuticals Total		**$17,954.00**	**$41,734.00**	**$11,958.00**	**$71,646.00**
Grand Total		**$57,974.00**	**$131,461.00**	**$48,572.00**	**$238,007.00**

Illustration B

Month	June						
Total Sale	**Drug**						
Surgeon	Ciberan	Hearteze	Mycodal	Nockout	Tyledan	Xydocan	**Grand Total**
Dr. Che Ramirez	$19,875.00		$16,554.00			$10,654.00	$47,083.00
Dr. Mei Rong Lu	$36,614.00					$11,958.00	$48,572.00
Dr. Raj Shad			$32,886.00				$32,886.00
Dr. Tejan Williams	$16,451.00		$42,136.00	$36,993.00	$6,584.00		$102,164.00
Dr. Yong Kwan Choi		$99,932.00					$99,932.00
Grand Total	**$72,940.00**	**$99,932.00**	**$91,576.00**	**$36,993.00**	**$6,584.00**	**$22,612.00**	**$330,637.00**

On Your Own

1. Start Excel and open ⊙ **34CDLIST**.

2. Save the workbook as **OXL34**.

3. Create a PivotTable on the Sheet 2 worksheet to show:

   a. CDs listed by artist

   b. The total cost of CDs per artist

   c. The total cost of CDs

   d. Format the PivotChart using your choice of format.

4. Create a PivotChart from the same data.

5. Spell check the workbook.

6. Print the PivotTable and PivotChart.

7. Display only CDs by Sarah McLachlan, Barenaked Ladies, and Sheryl Crow.

8. Print this new table.

9. Close the workbook, saving all changes.

Exercise 35

◆ **Critical Thinking**

You're the owner of Northwest Gear, a clothing store for teenagers. You're assembling this month's sales data for items that were placed on special sales during the month, and you want answers to questions such as "What items sold only if they were heavily discounted?" and "Which day of the week is the best one on which to hold a sale?" You want to use your analysis to help you determine the best price for a new item, given a goal of $150,000 for its first three months of sales. Finally, you're also interested in learning which item sold the most on any given sales day.

Exercise Directions

1. Start Excel, if necessary.

2. Open 🌀 **35NWGEAR**.

3. Save the file as **NWGEAR**.

4. Create a PivotTable using the database on the August Sales Items worksheet (see Illustration A):

   a. Place the table on the Sales Analysis worksheet, beginning in cell B12.

   b. Show the days of the week in separate rows.

   c. Show the discount in separate columns.

   d. Use the "No. Sold That Day" in the body of the report.

5. Create a second PivotTable:

   a. Click cell B14 on the August Sales Items worksheet.

   b. Use the data in "another PivotTable report" to create your second report.

   c. Place the second report on the Sales Analysis worksheet, beginning in cell B25.

   d. Show the discount amounts in separate columns.

   e. Show the item names in separate rows.

   f. Again, use the "No. Sold That Day" in the body of the report.

   g. Create different "pages" for each store, and show the data for the Mission Street store only.

6. Spell check the worksheet, and print the two PivotTables.

7. Change to the New Product worksheet. In cell B15, enter a formula that computes the average sales per day at 20% discount, using the data shown in the first column of the first PivotTable. Multiply this daily average times 24 (the number of workdays in a month).

   ✓ Use the AVERAGE function, and select as your range the data in the 20% column in the first PivotTable. Do not include the Grand Total cell in your range.

8. In cell B16, create a similar formula using the data in the second column of the first PivotTable, calculate the average sales per day at the 25% discount rate, then multiply this average times 24.

9. In cell B17, calculate the average sales per day at 40% discount, and multiply that average times 24.

10. Use Goal Seek to change the proposed price of hip hugger shorts (cell B11) so that the projected sales (cell C19) equals $150,000. See Illustration B.

11. Spell check and print the worksheet.

12. Change to the August Sales Items worksheet. In cell H9, enter a formula to display the name of the best-selling single day item (see Illustration C):

    a. Use the HLOOKUP function.

    b. Use "Item" as the lookup value, or just click cell C13.

    c. Use the range B13:H92 as the table array range.

    d. To calculate the number of the row in which the best selling item appears, use the MATCH function: MATCH(MAX(F14:F92),F14:F92,0)+1.

✓ The MAX function finds the highest value in the Number Sold That Day column. MATCH then looks for this value in the No. Sold That Day column, and calculates the row number. However, this row number is one off, because HLOOKUP counts the column label row as row 1. So add 1 to the value that MATCH comes up with, and you'll have the right number to give to HLOOKUP.

✓ If you want to step through this formula to see how it works, click cell H9, then choose Tools, Formula Auditing, Evaluate Formula.

13. Close the workbook, saving all changes.

Illustration A: PivotTables

Sum of No.Sold☐That Day	Discount ▾			
Day of the Week ▾	20%	25%	40%	Grand Total
Monday	24	41	113	178
Tuesday	48	85	109	242
Wednesday	57	65	108	230
Thursday	35	86	78	199
Friday	70	38	47	155
Saturday	134	47	50	231
Grand Total	368	362	505	1235

Store	Mission Street ▾			

Sum of No.Sold☐That Day	Discount ▾			
Item ▾	20%	25%	40%	Grand Total
Cropped Tank Top	57	91	136	284
Skinny Mini	54	64	98	216
Surfer Shorts	46	112	51	209
Grand Total	157	267	285	709

Illustration B: Goal Seek Solution

	A	B	C
2	**Northwest Gear, Inc.**		
3	2749 Mission St., Seattle, WA 98122		
4	Ph. 206-555-3922		
5	Fax: 206-555-3923		
6			
7			
8			
9			
10	Item	Hip Hugger Shorts	
11	Proposed Price	$ 19.89	
12			
13		Quantity	Total
14	Est. Sales at Full Price	2,600	$ 51,724.14
15	Est. Sales at .20%	1,472	$ 29,283.82
16	Est. Sales at .25%	1,448	$ 28,806.37
17	Est. Sales at .40%	2,020	$ 40,185.68
18			
19		Total Estimated Sales	$ 150,000.00
20			

Illustration C: HLOOKUP Function

H9   *fx* =HLOOKUP("Item",B13:H92,MATCH(MAX(F14:F92),F14:F92,0)+1)

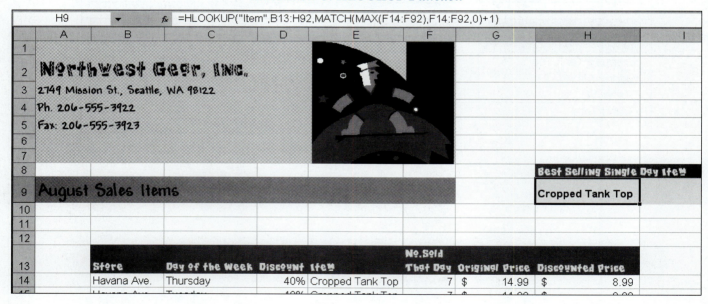

	A	B	C	D	E	F	G	H	I
1									
2	**Northwest Gear, Inc.**								
3	2749 Mission St., Seattle, WA 98122								
4	Ph. 206-555-3922								
5	Fax: 206-555-3923								
6									
7									
8								Best Selling Single Day Item	
9	August Sales Items							Cropped Tank Top	
10									
11									
12									
13	Store	Day of the Week	Discount	Item	No. Sold That Day	Original Price	Discounted Price		
14	Havana Ave.	Thursday	40%	Cropped Tank Top	7	$ 14.99	$ 8.99		
15	Havana Ave.	Tuesday	40%	Cropped Tank Top	7	$ 14.99	$ 8.99		

Exercise 36

Skills Covered:

◆ **Save a Worksheet as a Web Page** ◆ **View and Change Web Data**

On the Job

Save a worksheet in HTML format to publish it on the World Wide Web or company intranet, or to add the data to an existing Web page.

As the owner of Northwest Gear, you've put a lot of hard work analyzing last month's revenues for sale items, and now you want to share its data on the company's new intranet. You also want to get your manager's feedback on the pricing for a new item, hip hugger shorts, so you'll publish that data on the intranet as well, and let them adjust the price as they see fit.

Terms

HTML Hypertext Markup Language, used to publish information on the World Wide Web.

World Wide Web A network of computers located in businesses, research foundations, schools, and homes that allows users to share and search for information.

Web browser Software that enables you to view Web sites on the Internet.

Publishing The process of saving data to an intranet or Internet.

Intranet A private network of computers within a business or organization.

Web page Information published on the World Wide Web, which can include text, graphics, and links to other pages.

Notes

Save a Worksheet as a Web Page

■ Excel worksheet data can be saved in **HTML** format for publication on the **World Wide Web**.

✓ *HTML (Hypertext Markup Language) is a series of codes that help a **Web browser** properly display text, graphics, and animations on a Web page.*

■ The process of saving data in HTML format is called **publishing**.

■ You can publish worksheet data to the Internet or to a company **intranet**.

■ The Save as Web Page command from the File menu helps you convert a worksheet to a **Web page**.

■ Before Excel publishes the page, it displays a dialog box to confirm the item(s) to publish, viewing options, and publish options.

■ Using the options in the Publish as Web Page dialog box, you can publish your worksheet data as static data (unchangeable, except through the process of publishing) or interactive data (changeable by any user, through a Web browser).

✓ *Changes made by a user to an interactive Web page are not saved permanently to that Web page—they are intended for that user's purposes only.*

■ Once your worksheet is published, you can republish it (resave it to the Internet) at any time.

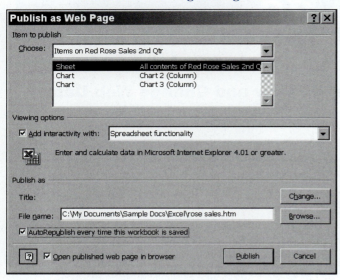

View and Change Web Data

- When you want to view your Web page file, you must use a Web browser, such as Internet Explorer.

- If a worksheet was published with static data, you will only be able to view that data.

- If a worksheet was published with interactive data, you will be able to view it and make changes.

✓ To make changes, a user must have Excel 2002 installed, or at least Web Components (an Office XP feature).

■ To make changes to an interactive worksheet, you follow the same procedures as in Excel—click a cell and type new data, or double-click to edit data.

■ A Commands and Options dialog box provides extra tools for changing formats, adjusting formulas, and so on.

A published worksheet

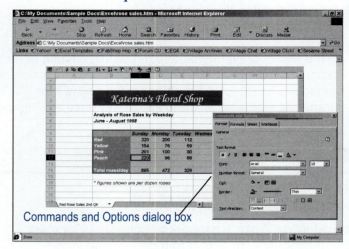

Commands and Options dialog box

Procedures

Save a Worksheet as a Web Page

1. If you want to publish a selected range, then select those cell(s).

2. Click **File** .... Alt+F

3. Click **Save as Web Page**.... G

   ✓ You may save either the range you selected on the worksheet, or the entire book.

4. Click **Selection:** .... Alt+E
   OR
   Click **Entire Workbook** .... Alt+W

5. Click **File name** text box....................... Alt+N

6. Type file name.

7. Click **Publish** .... P

To change the title for the Web page:

a. Click **Change** .... H

b. Type new title.

c. Click **OK** .... Enter

To add interactivity

• Click **Add interactivity with** .... A

8. Click **AutoRepublish every time workbook is saved** .... U

9. Click **Open published web page in browser** .... Alt+O

10. Click **Publish** .... P

   ✓ The Web page is complete and automatically displays in the browser. It will be published as a static page unless you chose to add interactive functionality.

Open a Web Page File in Browser

   ✓ Use this procedure to open a published Web page that was not opened automatically by the Publish as Web Page dialog box.

1. Click **Start** .... Ctrl+Esc

2. Select **Programs** .... P

3. Click **Internet Explorer** .... ↓, Enter

4. Click **File** .... Alt+F

5. Click **Open** .... O

6. Click **Browse** .... Alt+R

To select a different drive:

a. Click **Look in** .... Alt + I

b. Select
   desired drive ..... ↑↓ , Enter

To select a folder in the specified drive:

• Double-click
  folder name .... ↑↓←→ , Enter

7. Double-click file to open in **File name** list box.

8. Click **Open** .... Enter

   ✓ You can also view the Web page by typing its address (file path) into the Address box of your Web browser.

Exercise Directions

1. Start Excel, if necessary.

2. Open 💾**NWGEAR** or 💿**36NWGEAR**.

3. Save the file as **NWGEAR**.

4. Publish the August Sales figures:

   a. Publish only the August Sales Items worksheet.

   b. Use the file name **NWGEAR.htm**.

   c. Publish the worksheet as static data (no interactivity).

   d. Change the title of the Web page to **Sales Items – August**.

   e. Select the AutoRepublish option.

   f. Display the Web page in your browser. (See Illustration A.)

      ✓ Notice that you can not change any of the data. You can print it, however, using the File, Print command in the browser.

5. Publish another part of the workbook:

   a. Publish only the New Product worksheet.

   b. Use the file name **NEWPROD.htm**.

   c. Publish the worksheet as interactive data.

   d. Change the title of the Web page to **Hip Hugger Shorts**.

   e. Select the AutoRepublish option.

   f. Open the Web page in your browser. (See Illustration B.)

      ✓ You'll see a warning telling you that the formulas on the New Product worksheet that refer to cells on other worksheets will be converted to their values. That's fine for our purposes, so just click OK to continue.

6. Make changes to the Web page:

   a. Let's see what the revenues would be if the shorts sell for $19.50. Change cell B11 to 19.50.

   b. Let's change cell B11 to $17.75 and see what the total estimated revenues look like.

   c. Now try a compromise: change cell B11 to $18.25.

7. Close the Web browser and return to Excel.

   ✓ You'll notice that the changes you made to the Web page have not affected the workbook at all.

8. Close the workbook, saving all changes.

Illustration A

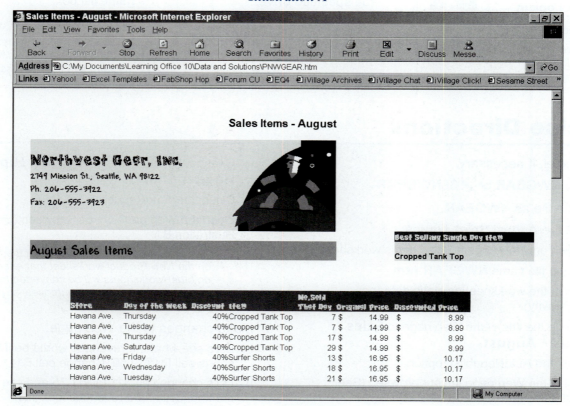

Illustration B

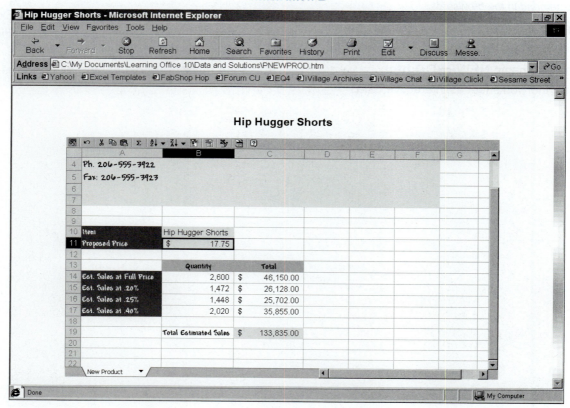

On Your Own

1. Open the **OXL26** file created in the On Your Own section of Exercise 26, or open the file ⊛**36GRADES**.

2. Save the file as **OXL36**.

3. Create a grade conversion chart on the Grades worksheet, similar to the one shown in Illustration C:

   a. Enter the minimum score needed to achieve each letter grade—you can copy the ones shown, or use your own.

   b. Note that the scores are listed from F to A—you must use this reverse ordering system so that the VLOOKUP formulas you'll enter in step 5 will work correctly.

   c. Format the grade conversion chart however you like.

4. Add a column next to Final Grade called **Grade**.

5. Using VLOOKUP, create formulas for the Grade column that look up a student's letter grade, based on their Final Grade score.

6. Publish the entire workbook:

   a. Use the file name **GRADES.htm**.

   b. Publish the worksheet with interactivity.

   c. Change the title of the Web page to **Final Grades – English 101**.

   d. Select the AutoRepublish option.

   e. Display the Web page in your browser.

7. Through the browser, change some of the second semester scores for a few of the students, so that you create changes to their final scores.

8. Make these same changes to the workbook.

9. Close the browser.

10. Close the workbook, saving all changes.

   ✓ When you save the workbook, the changes you made will automatically be republished. If you want to verify this, open the Web page in your browser.

Illustration C

Exercise 37

◆ **Copy Data from a Web Page** ◆ **Create a Web Query**

On the Job

The Internet contains a vast amount of data, some of it useful, some of it not. When you find some useful data, such as table that lists the pricing structure for a supplier's services, you can copy this data easily into an Excel worksheet, where you can calculate, sort, format, and analyze it at your leisure. You can also create a refreshable Web query to copy current data from the Web at the click of a button.

You're a legal assistant at Perry, Hawkins, Martinez and Klein, and you've been assigned the task of creating a worksheet that lists the firm's cases appearing in court this week. You've also been asked to create a listing of news sites with coverage of important cases. You've decided to combine the two into one updateable worksheet using Excel's Web query feature.

Terms

Web Query The process of pulling data from a Web page into an Excel worksheet.

Refresh The process of updating the data copied to a worksheet through a query.

Notes

Copy Data from a Web Page

- If you find data on the Internet or your company's intranet that you wish to use in Excel, you can import it.

- The process of importing the data into a worksheet is as simple as copying and pasting.

- After pasting the data into a worksheet, you can use the Paste Options button to change its formatting.

- You can also use the Paste Options button to convert the pasted data into a **Web query**.

Create a Web Query

- There are many ways in which you can create a Web query:

  - By copying and pasting the data from a Web page into Excel.

  - By initiating a query in Excel with the Create New Query command.

  - By initiating a query in Internet Explorer with the Export to Excel command.

    ✓ *These methods are all similar, and very easy to do. So you're free to create the query using the process you find most convenient at the time.*

- After a query is created, data from the associated Web page is copied to the worksheet.

- If the data on the Web page changes, you can **refresh** your query.

- When a query is refreshed, current data from the associated Web page is copied to the worksheet, replacing the existing data.

Procedures

Copy Data from a Web Page

1. In your Web browser, navigate to the Web page of your choice and select the data you wish to copy.
2. Click **Edit** .... Alt + E
3. Click **Copy** C
4. Change to Excel, and click the cell located in the upper-left corner of the range in which you want the data to appear.
5. Click **Edit** .... Alt + E
6. Click **Paste** .... P

   ✓ The data appears in the worksheet.

   ### To change the format of the pasted data:

   a. Click the arrow on the

   Paste Options button 📋▾.

   b. Click **Keep Source**
   Formatting .... K
   OR

   Click **Match Destination**
   Formatting .... M

   ✓ You can change the pasted data to a Web query by choosing the option, **Create Refreshable Web Query** from the Paste Options menu—then follow the steps in the next procedure to create the query.

Create Web Query in Excel

1. Click **Data** .... Alt + D
2. Click **Import**
   External Data .... D
3. Click **New Web Query** .... W
4. Click **Address** .... D
5. Type address of Web page containing data to import and click **Go** .... G
6. Click the yellow arrow next to table(s) whose data you wish to import.

   ✓ The arrows change to green check marks to indicate that they are selected.

   ✓ If you click Import without selecting any tables, the entire page will be imported.

7. Click **Import** I
8. Select where you want the data to appear:

   a. Click **Existing**
   worksheet .... Alt + E

   b. Click in worksheet where you want the data to appear.
   OR

   • Click **New**
   worksheet .... Alt + N

9. Click **OK** .... Enter

Create a Web Query from Internet Explorer

✓ You must use Internet Explorer version 5.0 or later.

1. Navigate to the Web page whose data you wish to import to Excel.
2. Right-click the table you want to import and choose **Export to Microsoft Excel** X

   ✓ The data should appear in a new Excel workbook. If Excel is unsure which table to import, you'll need to select it from the New Web Query dialog box that appears.

Refresh a Web Query

1. Click within the query area.
2. Click the **Refresh** button ⬍ on the External Data toolbar.
OR
1. Click **Data** .... Alt + D
2. Click **Refresh Data** .... R

   ✓ You can set the query to update periodically by clicking the **Data Range Properties** button on the External Data toolbar.

Exercise Directions

1. Start Excel, if necessary.

2. Open ⊘ **37TRIALS**.

3. Save the file as **TRIALS**.

4. Copy data from the Web:

   a. Start Internet Explorer and open the Web page ⊘ **COURTTV.htm** on the CD.

   b. Select the **In the News**, **Upcoming Trials**, and **Recent Trials** sections.

   c. Click Copy.

   d. Switch back to Excel, and click cell C20 on Sheet1.

   e. Click Paste.

      ✓ *The data is pasted to the worksheet, but it is not refreshable.*

   f. Click the arrow on the Paste Options button and select Create Refreshable Web Query.

   g. Click the arrows next to the **In the News**, **Upcoming Trials**, and **Recent Trials** sections to select them.

   h. Click Import.

5. Set up a Web Query:

   a. Select Data, Import External Data, New Web Query.

   b. In the Address box, type D:\Datafiles\Excel\FINDLAW.htm and click Go.

      ✓ *If your CD-ROM drive is not the letter D or you've copied the files to your hard drive, substitute the correct letter for the letter D.*

   c. Click the arrows next to the "Top Legal Headlines" and "US Law" sections.

      ✓ *You'll need to select the headline, US Law, and each section under it.*

   d. Click Import.

   e. Select cell E20 in Sheet1 and click OK.

6. Adjust the formatting of the imported data (see Illustration A):

   a. Select the range E20:E72 and use the Format Cells dialog box to apply Wrap Text alignment.

   b. Change the width of column E to 33.50.

7. Spell check the worksheet.

8. Print the worksheet.

9. Close the workbook, saving all changes.

Illustration A

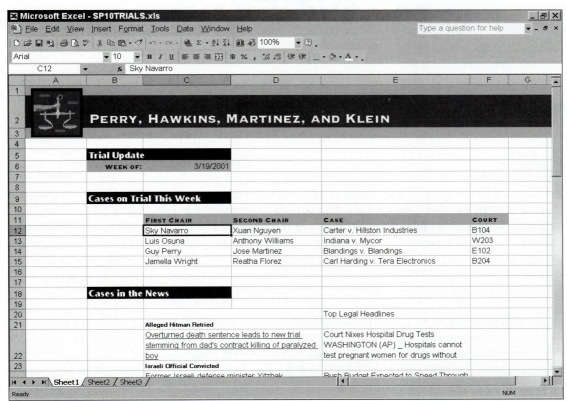

On Your Own

1. Create a new workbook.

   ✓ *You're looking for a job, so you want to create a workbook of up-to-date job postings.*

2. Save the file as **OXL37**.

3. Visit at least two job search Web sites (such as Monster.com), and use your preferred method to create a Web query to import their data.

4. Add additional columns to the imported data to help you in your job search, such as "Resume Sent?" and "Follow-up Call," so you can track your activities related to each potential job.

5. Format the worksheet as you like.

6. Close the workbook, saving all changes.

Exercise 38

Skills Covered:

◆ **Link and Embed Excel Data** ◆ **Pasting a Picture** ◆ **Link Data**
◆ **Edit Linked Data** ◆ **Embed a File** ◆ **Edit Embedded Data**

On the Job

When you need to use Excel data within another document, such as a Word document or PowerPoint presentation, you can link the document to the Excel data, and keep the document automatically updated whenever the Excel data is changed. If you'd like to make changes in the other document without affecting the original Excel data (or vice-versa), you can embed that data instead of linking it. In Exercise 29, you learned how to link and embed Excel charts in other documents; in this exercise you'll learn how to link and embed Excel data.

Although you've just spent a lot of time creating a Web site to provide instant access to current cases and law news for all of the lawyers in your firm, you've been informed that one of the senior partners does not use a computer, and doesn't want to learn. This means that you must now create a Word memo listing roughly the same data—this week's trials and their locations, and next week's as well. Luckily, since the data is still in Excel, you can quickly draft a memo and then link and embed the Excel data in it.

Terms

Link A reference to data stored in another file. When that data is changed, the data is updated in the destination file automatically.

Embed A special process of copying data from one document to another, so that the tools from the original application are made available in the destination application for editing. No link to the original data is created, so such editing does not affect the original data.

OLE Object Linking and Embedding enables Windows applications to share data.

Picture A graphic image of your data, which is neither linked or embedded into another document. Since it's a picture, the only way to change the data would be to change it in Excel, take another picture, and insert that new picture into the destination document, replacing the original document.

Notes

Link and Embed Excel Data

- If you copy data from Excel and simply paste it into a document, that data does not maintain any connection to its source. For some applications, this process may be all you need.

- However, if you want to maintain a connection to the original Excel data, you can opt to **link** or **embed** it.

- Linked data is changed when the original data is changed; embedded data is not. However, embedded data retains a connection to the program that originated it, providing you with tools you might need to make changes.

- **OLE**, which is short for Object Linking and Embedding, is the mechanism that allows data to be linked or embedded between Windows documents.

- Typically, all Windows programs support OLE, so you can apply the process you learn in this lesson to link or embed Excel data wherever you want.

Pasting a Picture

- You can paste a **picture** of your Excel data into another document instead of linking or embedding it, but that means you won't be able to change the data at all without completely starting over.

Link Data

- Use linking to create a special communication between two files. For example, you can insert an Excel worksheet (source file) into a Word document (destination file).

- As covered in Exercise 29, when you create a link between files, the data in the destination file changes if you update the source file.

  - ✓ Thus, if you link Excel data to a Word document and then change that data, the changes are automatically updated within the Word document.

  - Although linked data is updated automatically, you can change the link so that it updates manually—when you tell it to.

  - You can perform other maintenance tasks with the links in your destination file, such as updating the location of the source file, breaking a link, and retaining any local formatting changes whenever a link is updated.

- Linked data is not stored in the destination file, so the resulting destination file is smaller than if you embed data.

- You can display linked data as an icon within the source document; this does not affect the link's ability to keep that data current.

Edit Linked Data

- When you double-click data linked to an Excel workbook, Excel automatically starts and opens the workbook so you can make changes.

  - ✓ So for example, if you link Excel data in a Word document, you can open that Word document and double-click the data to start Excel so that you can make changes whenever you need to.

- After you make your changes and save them, the changes are automatically updated through the link to the destination file.

  - ✓ If the destination file is not currently open, then the changes will be updated when it is opened later.

Embed a File

- With embedding, there is no direct link to the source data. Thus, you can make changes to the source data that do not affect the destination file, and vice-versa.

  - ✓ For example, if you change embedded Excel data within a Word document, the changes won't affect the original data in its Excel workbook.

- When you embed Excel data into another document, that data is copied to the destination file, making it larger than if you used linking.

- To link or embed files, use the Edit, Paste Special command. Shown here is the Paste Special dialog box from Word.

Paste Special dialog box

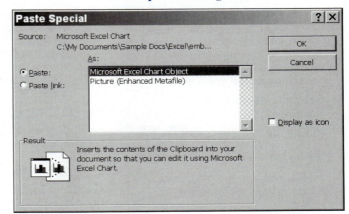

Edit Embedded Data

- When you double-click data embedded from an Excel workbook, the toolbars and menus from Excel appear within the destination application, making it possible to make whatever changes are necessary to the embedded data.

  - ✓ For example, if you double-click embedded Excel data while viewing a Word document, Excel's menus and tools appear within the Word window.

- Remember, the changes you make to embedded data do not affect the original data in the Excel workbook—the two sets of data are separate.

Procedures

Paste a Picture of Data

1. Select data.
2. Press and hold **Shift** as you click **E**dit. .... `Shift`+`Alt`+`E`
3. Click **C**opy Picture .... `C`
4. Select appearance:
   - **As shown on screen** .... `S`
   - **As shown when printed** .... `P`
5. Select format:
   - **Pic**ture .... `T`
   - **B**itmap .... `B`
     - ✓ *Select Picture (Windows metafile) in most instances —the Bitmap option results in a smaller file size, but lower quality, and may not appear correctly if the destination file is viewed with a different resolution than yours.*
6. Switch to destination document.
7. Click **E**dit .... `Alt`+`E`
8. Click **P**aste .... `P`
   - ✓ *You can also insert a picture of Excel data in PowerPoint by simply copying and pasting it using the Standard toolbar buttons, then selecting the option Picture of Table from the Paste Options menu. This method does not work in the other Office XP programs.*

Link Data

- ✓ *For automatic links to update data properly, make sure that the Update remote references option is turned on in Excel's Tools, Options, Calculation tab.*

1. Select data.
2. Click **Copy** button 📋 .
3. Switch to destination file, and position cursor where you want data inserted.
4. Click **E**dit .... `Alt`+`E`
5. Click **Paste S**pecial .... `S`
6. Click **Paste l**ink .... `L`

7. Select **Microsoft Excel Worksheet Object.**
8. If you want to display data as an icon, select **D**isplay **as icon** option .... `D`
   - ✓ *To change the icon that's displayed, click Change Icon and select one from those listed.*
9. Click **OK** .... `Enter`
   - ✓ *When you create a link, it is updated automatically. However, you can change updating to manual if you like.*
   - ✓ *You can also link Excel data to Word by simply copying and pasting it using the Standard toolbar buttons, then selecting the option Keep Source Formatting and Link to Excel or Match Destination Table Style and Link to Excel from the Paste Options menu. This method does not work in the other Office XP programs.*

Change Link Information

1. In the destination file, click **E**dit .... `Alt`+`E`
2. Click **Lin**ks .... `K`
3. Select link you want to update.
4. To change location of linked file, click **Chan**ge Source .... `N`
   a. From **Look in** list, type (or select) folder in which file is currently located ..... `Alt`+`I`
   b. Type name of file you want to link to in **File n**ame text box .... `Alt`+`N`
   c. Click **Open** button 📂 .
5. To remove link, click **B**reak Link .... `B`
6. To change way in which link is updated, select option:
   - **A**utomatic update .... `A`
   - **M**anual update .... `M`
   - **Locked** .... `K`
     - ✓ *Locked option, if present, prevents linked object from being updated.*

7. To retain local formatting changes you make to the linked data in Word, click **Preserve f**ormatting **after update** .... `Alt`+`F`
8. Click **OK** .... `Enter`

Update Manual Link

1. Open destination file.
2. Click **E**dit .... `Alt`+`E`
3. Click **Lin**ks .... `K`
4. Select link you want to update.
5. Click **U**pdate Now .... `U`
   - ✓ *You can also press F9 after selecting object to update it.*

Embed Data

1. Select data.
2. Click **Copy** button 📋 .
3. Switch to destination document, and position cursor where you want data inserted.
4. Click **E**dit .... `Alt`+`E`
5. Click **Paste S**pecial .... `S`
6. Click **P**aste .... `P`
7. Select **Microsoft Excel Worksheet Object**.
8. If you want to display data as an icon, select **D**isplay **as icon** option .... `D`
9. Click **OK**.
   - ✓ *You can also embed Excel data in PowerPoint by simply copying and pasting it using the Standard toolbar buttons, then selecting the option Excel Table from the Paste Options menu. This method does not work in the other Office XP programs.*

Edit Linked Data

1. Double-click linked data or icon.
   - ✓ *Excel starts and displays data.*
2. Make desired changes.
3. Click **F**ile .... `Alt`+`F`
4. Click **E**xit .... `X`

5. When prompted, select **Yes** to save your changes .... [Y]

Edit Embedded Data

1. Double-click embedded data or icon.
   - ✓ *A border appears around data, and Excel's menus and toolbars appear.*
2. Make changes as needed.
3. Click outside data border.

Exercise Directions

1. Start Excel, if necessary.

2. Open 💾**TRIALS** or 💿 **38TRIALS**.

3. Save the file as **TRIALS**.

4. Start Word and open 💿 **38WKTRIALS.doc**. Save the Word file as **WKTRIALS.doc**.

5. In the **TRIALS** workbook, select the range C11:F15 and click Copy.

6. In **WKTRIALS.doc**, select the text **[embed data here]** then press Delete to remove it.

7. Open the Edit menu and select Paste Special.

8. Select Paste, Microsoft Excel Worksheet Object, and click OK to embed the data.

9. Switch back to Excel, and open 💿 **38NXTTRIALS**.

10. Save the file as **NXTTRIALS**.

11. Select the range C11:F16 and click Copy.

12. Switch back to Word, and select the text **[link data here]**. Press Delete to remove the text.

13. Open the Edit menu and select Paste Special.

14. Select Paste link, Microsoft Excel Worksheet Object, and click OK to link the data.

15. First, make a change to the embedded data:
    a. Double-click the listing of this week's trials.
    b. Change the court location for the Indiana v. Mycor trial to **W205**.
    c. Click outside the embedded data area to save your change.
    d. View the **TRIALS** workbook and notice that your changes have not affected the original data.
    e. Close the **TRIALS** workbook, saving all changes. See Illustration A.

16. Now, make changes to the linked data:
    a. Double-click the listing of next week's trials.
    b. Change the case name for the fourth trial to **Anderson Roofing v. Williams**.
    c. Change back to Word, and notice that the link has updated the data there.
    d. Click outside the linked area.

17. Spell check the Word document.

18. Print the Word document.

19. Close **WKTRIALS.doc**, saving all changes.

20. Close **NXTRIAL**, saving all changes.

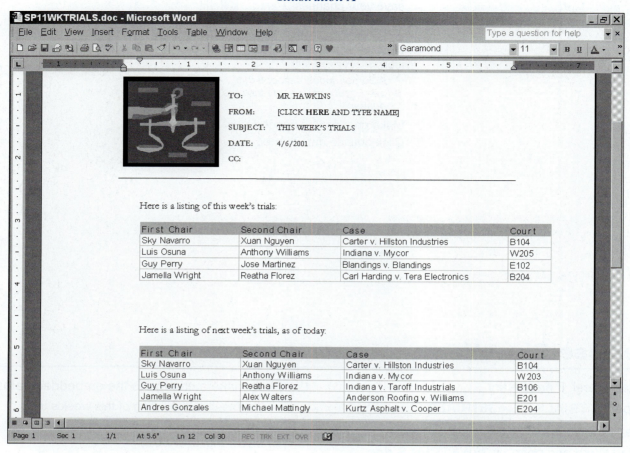

On Your Own

1. Open the file **OXL36**, created in the On Your Own of Exercise 36, or open ☉**38GRADES**.

2. Save the file as **OXL38**.
   ✓ *When asked, disable the AutoRepublish feature.*

3. Start Word and create a memo.
   ✓ *You need to report to the principal the scores for first and second semester and the final grades for each member of your class. Write a memo to this effect.*

4. Save the file as **38GRADES.doc**.

5. In the memo, tell the principal that you've included below the first and second semester test and quiz scores, then insert the appropriate ranges from **OXL38** as pictures into the memo.

6. At the end of the memo, tell the principal that you've included a listing of final scores for all the students, then link the appropriate range from **OXL38** to the memo.

7. Use the link to change the lowest score for a C from 73 to 71.
   ✓ *Even though you didn't copy the range that listed the grades and the minimum score associated with them, you can still change that information through the link.*

8. Spell check the Word document.

9. If you want, you can resize the linked data by dragging its edges. This small size change will enable you to reduce the document to two pages instead of three.

10. Print the Word document.

11. Close the Word document, saving all changes.

12. Close the workbook, saving all changes.

Exercise 39

◆ **Critical Thinking**

You're a medical assistant at California Cardiology, Inc, and you've been asked to create several new pages for the company's Web site. First you'll import some data from the Web into an existing workbook, and then you'll publish various worksheets on the company intranet. Finally, you'll create a memo to your boss detailing your progress and showing off some of your work.

Exercise Directions

1. Start Excel, if necessary.

2. Open ⌨**PHARMACY** or open 💿**39PHARMACY**.

3. Save the file as **PHARMACY**.

4. Insert a new worksheet after the Analysis worksheet, and name it **Heart Surgery Forum**.

5. Start Internet Explorer, and open the Web page 💿**HEARTFORUM.htm** from the CD.

6. Select the *Current Issue* section, and click Copy.

7. Switch back to Excel and click cell C4 on the Heart Surgery Forum worksheet.

8. Click Paste.

9. Click the arrow on the Paste Options button, and select Create Refreshable Web Query.

10. Click the arrow next to the Current Issue section, then click Import.

11. Close Internet Explorer.

12. Publish a worksheet:

    a. Publish the Drug Purchases worksheet, with interactivity.

    b. Use the file name **DRUGPUR.htm**.

    c. Use the title **Drug Purchases – April to June**.

    d. Turn on AutoRepublish.

    e. Display the page in your Web browser. See Illustration A.

13. Using the Web browser, add a total to the Web page:

    a. Scroll down to cell F90, and type **Totals**.

    b. Use the AutoSum button on the toolbar to enter a formula in cell G90 that computes the total drug purchases.

    c. Display the Commands and Options dialog box, and add bold formatting to cell F90.

    d. Close the Web browser.

14. Publish the data you copied from the Internet:

    a. Publish the Heart Surgery Forum worksheet, *without* interactivity.

    b. Use the file name **HRTSURGY.htm**.

    c. Use the title **Heart Surgery Forum – April 9, 2001**.

    d. Do not turn on AutoRepublish.

    e. Display the page in your Web browser. See Illustration B.

    f. After viewing the Web page, close the Web browser.

15. Create a memo to your boss:

    a. Start Word, and create a new document using the Elegant Memo template.

    b. Save the file as **39DRUGMEMO.doc**.

    c. Enter the text shown in Illustration C

    d. Select the range C9:G40 on the Drug Purchases worksheet, and click Copy.

    e. Link the data into the memo at the location shown in the illustration.

    f. Select the range, C41:G88, click Copy, and paste link the data to the next page in the memo.

    ✓ *You pasted the drug purchase data in two sections because if you had pasted it in one large section, it would not fit on a page. Since Word is not able to break the linked data into sections that fit your pages comfortably, you have to do that manually.*

    g. Using the link, change the value of the first sale from $5,698 to $6103.

16. On the third page of the memo, enter the text shown in Illustration D.

17. Embed some data:

    a. Select the range, C4:D19 on the Heart Surgery Forum worksheet, and click Copy.

    b. Embed the data into the memo at the location shown in the illustration.

18. Spell check the memo.

19. Print the memo.

20. Close the memo, saving all changes.

21. Close the workbook, saving all changes. When prompted, enable the AutoRepublish feature.

Illustration A: Drug Purchases Web Page

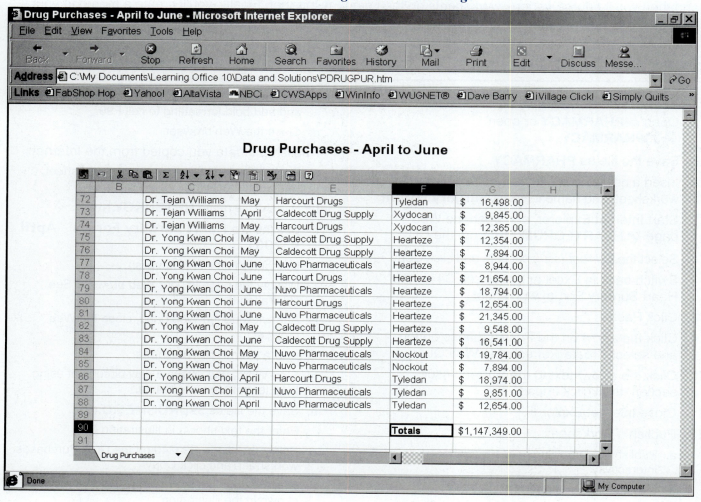

Illustration B: Heart Surgery Forum Web Page

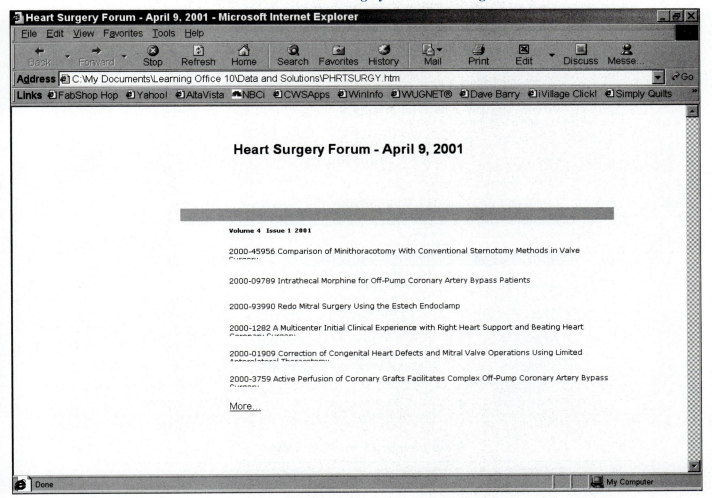

Illustration C: Memo, Page One

INTEROFFICE MEMORANDUM

TO:	MR. HIGGINS
FROM:	JENNIFER FULTON
SUBJECT:	APRIL TO JUNE DRUG PURCHASES
DATE:	4/10/2001
CC:	

Per your request, I have recently updated our intranet with a listing of drugs purchased over the last three months. This data is now available to all the doctors for their review. For your convenience, I've included the purchase data here as well:

Link data

Surgeon	Month	Supplier	Drug	Total Sale
Dr. Ashesh Shah	April	Nuvo Pharmaceuticals	Mycodal	$ 6,103.00
Dr. Ashesh Shah	April	Caldecott Drug Supply	Mycodal	$ 16,654.00
Dr. Ashesh Shah	May	Nuvo Pharmaceuticals	Mycodal	$ 9,486.00
Dr. Ashesh Shah	April	Nuvo Pharmaceuticals	Nockout	$ 7,612.00
Dr. Ashesh Shah	May	Nuvo Pharmaceuticals	Nockout	$ 16,452.00
Dr. Ashesh Shah	April	Nuvo Pharmaceuticals	Tyledan	$ 4,691.00
Dr. Ashesh Shah	April	Harcourt Drugs	Tyledan	$ 21,546.00
Dr. Ashesh Shah	April	Caldecott Drug Supply	Tyledan	$ 18,654.00
Dr. Ashesh Shah	May	Nuvo Pharmaceuticals	Tyledan	$ 12,345.00
Dr. Che Ramirez	June	Harcourt Drugs	Ciberan	$ 19,875.00
Dr. Che Ramirez	April	Nuvo Pharmaceuticals	Ciberan	$ 7,998.00
Dr. Che Ramirez	April	Harcourt Drugs	Ciberan	$ 18,645.00

Illustration D: Memo, Page Three

In addition to the drug purchase data, I added a page to our Web that lists the latest articles at the Heart Surgery Forum Web site. Here's a sample of the articles available this week for review:

Volume 4 Issue 1 2001

Embed data

2000-45956 Comparison of Minithoracotomy With Conventional Sternotomy Methods in Valve Surgery

2000-09789 Intrathecal Morphine for Off-Pump Coronary Artery Bypass Patients

2000-93990 Redo Mitral Surgery Using the Estech Endoclamp

Surgery

Thoracotomy

2000-3759 Active Perfusion of Coronary Grafts Facilitates Complex Off-Pump Coronary Artery Bypass Surgery

More...

Access 2002

Directory of Data Files on CD

Exercise #	File Name	Page #
1	AC01	472
2	AC02	477
3	AC03	482
4	AC04	486
5	AC05	492
6	AC06	493
7	AC07	498
8	AC08	504
9	AC09	508
10	AC10	509
11	AC11	513
12	AC12	519
13	AC13	524
14	AC14	528
15	AC15	533
16	AC16	535
17	AC17	539
18	AC18	541
19	AC19	546
20	AC20	549
21	AC21	555
22	AC22	560
23	AC23	563
24	AC24	566
25	AC25	571
26	AC26	576
27	AC27	579
28	AC28	580

Database Basics

Skills Covered:

◆ **What is Access?** ◆ **What is a Database?**

◆ **What is a Database Management System?**

◆ **How is an Access Database Organized?**

◆ **How are Access Tables Related?**

Notes

What is Access?

- Microsoft Access is the best-selling personal computer database management system. The notes below describe what a database management system is in more detail.

- You can share data created in Access with other Microsoft Office applications, especially Word and Excel.

What is a Database?

- A **database** is an organized collection of information about a subject.

- Examples of databases include an address book, the telephone book, a CD tower full of music CDs, or a filing cabinet full of documents relating to clients.

- A name, address, and phone listing in an address book is an example of a common manual database. To update an address of a friend in Denver, you would search for the name, erase or cross out the existing address, and write in the new address.

Examples of manual database records

Name: Jim Ferrara Address: 84 Winthrop Rd. City: Denver State: CO Zip: 80209 Telephone: 303-555-5576 Notes: Note new address and phone number.	Part Number: 001759 Part Description: Socket wrench Cost: $3.50 List Price: $14.99 Date Received: 2/23/99
Address Book Entry	Inventory Card

- While updating one or two address in a manual database may not take a lot of effort, searching for all friends in one city or sorting all clients who have done business with you in the last month would take considerable effort.

- An **Access database** is a computer-based equivalent of a manual database. Access makes it easy to organize and update information electronically.

What is a Database Management System?

- A **database management system** such as Access includes both the database information and the tools to use the database. These tools allow you to input, edit, and verify your data.

- With Access, you can sort, find, analyze, and report on information in your database. For example, in a sales management database you could find all clients who bought a mountain bike in the last year and create mailing labels in order to send them an announcement of a new bike trails book.

How is an Access Database Organized?

- Unlike other database software programs, Access maintains all its objects in one database file. This file uses the MDB extension.

The Database Window Organizes Objects

- When you open a database file, you see the **database window**, which displays seven buttons under the Objects button.

- Each button changes the database window to display a list of the database **objects** for each object type. (See next page for a description of each object type.) For example, click on the Forms button to see a list of all forms.

Access database window

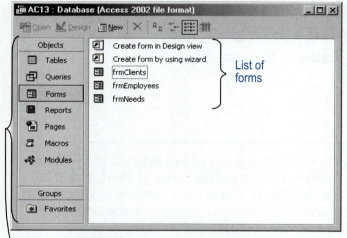

Types of database objects

Tables Store Information

- All Access database information is stored in tables. Each table contains information about a particular topic. For example, a sales inventory database may have separate tables for clients, products, and sales.

- Each row of an Access table is a **record**. A record is a set of details about a specific item. For example, a record for a client may contain the client's name, address, and phone number. A record about a product could include the part number, serial number, and price.

- Each column of an Access table is a **field**. Fields provide the categories for the details describing each record. In the client example above, there would be separate fields for name, address, and phone number.

- Each column is headed by a **field name**.

- The specific field data within a record is the **field contents**.

Tables store information in rows and columns

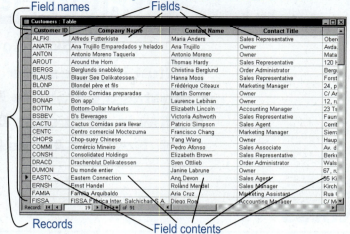

- Good database design may require you to break what you originally thought may be one field into multiple fields. For example, you would use separate fields for a client's first name, last name, address, city, state, and ZIP code.

- You can decide what to make into fields by thinking about how you will sort or look up the information. Many client lists, for example, sort by last name and then by first name.

Database Objects Help You Search, Analyze, and Present Data

- Database objects are the elements that make up a database. Although each Access database has numerous objects, there are seven major object types that are visible as soon as you open a database.

  - **Table**
    You store database information in one or more tables. You view, edit, and input information in tables in Datasheet view, which has rows and columns, just like an Excel spreadsheet.

  - **Form**
    A form is a window for viewing the data in one or more tables. Forms make it easy to view, input, and edit data because forms typically show all the information for one record on a single page.

Forms help you view, input, and edit data

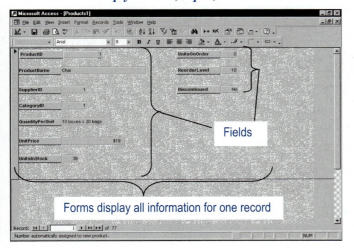

Fields

Forms display all information for one record

- **Query**

  A query allows you to see or work with a portion of a table by limiting the number of fields and by selecting specific records. For example, a bank may choose to see just the name, phone, and amount for all clients in Texas whose accounts are over $10,000.

Design queries to sort and analyze data

Table selected for query

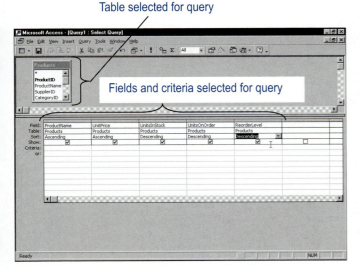

Fields and criteria selected for query

Query results show a portion of table data

Only selected fields appear in query result

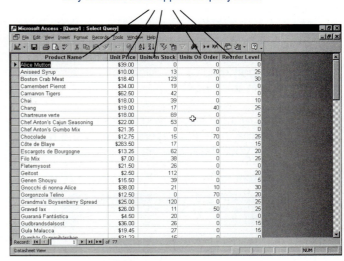

- **Report**

  A report is formatted information from a table or query that you can send to a printer. Reports can include a detailed list of records, calculated values and totals from the records, mailing labels, or a chart summarizing the data.

Use reports to create printed summaries of data

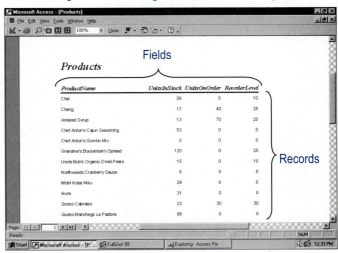

Fields

Records

- **Macro**

  Macros allow you to automate some processes within Access. Macros are beyond the scope of this book.

- **Module**

  Modules help automate Access tasks. Modules give you more flexibility for each automated process than macros do. Modules are also not included in this book.

- **Page**

  This new feature allows you to create Web-based forms that allow users to input and read data from your database via the Internet.

Pages let users input and read data on the Web

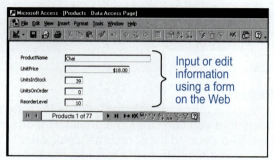

How are Access Tables Related?

- Database tables that share common fields are **related**. Most Access databases have multiple tables that are related to each other, which means you can use Access to create a **relational database**.

- A relational database breaks the "big picture" into smaller, more manageable pieces. For example, if you were gathering information about a new product line, each type of information—product, suppliers, customers—would be stored in its own, related table rather than in one large, all-inclusive table.

- You relate one table to another through a common field. For example, the Products table will have a ProductID field that also appears in the Customers table.

- This capability to store data in smaller, related tables gives a relational database great efficiency, speed, and flexibility in locating and reporting information.

Exercise 1

Skills Covered:

◆ **Copy Data Files and Deselect the Read-only Attribute**
◆ **Start Access and Open a Database** ◆ **Navigate in a Database**
◆ **Sort Records**

On the Job

Your first goal in working with a database is to start Access and open a database. You must then be able to identify and move around each of the various objects in the database. A quick sort of the data lets you find data quickly and perform a simple analysis of the information.

You've just been hired as the manager of Steel Dreams Motorcycle Emporium. One of your responsibilities is going to be maintaining and updating the store's databases. The owner of the shop wants you to explore the information stored in two of the database's tables and forms. You'll also perform a few simple sorts of the information to see how databases are used to analyze information.

Terms

Database file The file that contains all objects of your database.

Database window The on-screen container that has a separate button for each object type (tables, queries, forms, reports, pages, and others).

Switchboard An Access form with command buttons or other controls that lead to other switchboard forms, input forms, and reports.

Datasheet view The view of a table that shows you the data in each record. Like a spreadsheet, the datasheet shows rows (records) and columns (fields).

Sort To organize data alphabetically or in numerical order.

Ascending To sort from the smallest to the largest (from A to Z and from 1 to 9).

Descending To sort from the largest to the smallest (from Z to A and from 9 to 1).

Notes

Copy Data Files and Deselect the Read-only Attribute

- Access does not let you use the Save As command on a database as a whole.

- To use the data files for the Access exercises in this book, you must first copy the files from the CD to your hard drive. You can copy them all at once, or you can copy individual files as you need them.

- Files stored on a CD-ROM drive, when copied to another disk, have the read-only attribute turned on. You must turn it off in order to save your changes to the files.

- To turn off the read-only attribute for a file, you right-click it and choose Properties, and then deselect the Read-only check box in the Properties box that appears.

- You can remove the read-only attribute from many files at once by selecting multiple files before you right-click.

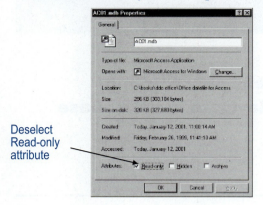

Deselect
Read-only
attribute

Start Access and Open a Database

- As with other Office programs, you can start Access using the Start button, an icon on the desktop, or a button on the Office Shortcut bar.

- When you start the program, Access displays the New File Task Pane at the right, from which you can open an existing database or start a new one.

Access's Task Pane provides shortcuts for opening and creating database files

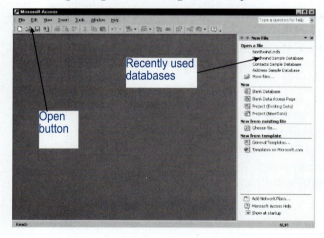

Recently used
databases

Open
button

- The last four databases you have opened appear in the *Open a file* section at the top of the Task Pane. You can quickly reopen one of them by clicking its name.

- If the database you want to open does not appear on that list, click More Files to use the Open dialog box to locate the file you want.

- You can also display the Open dialog box by clicking the Open button on the toolbar.

- If you need help with the Open dialog box, see Exercise 9 in Lesson 2 of the Word section in this book.

- After the **database file** opens, you see the **database window.**

The database window is a central point from which you can open tables, queries, forms, and so on

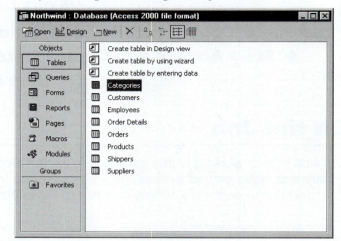

✓ *Notice that the title bar of the database window shown above reports that the database is in Access 2000 format. By default, all files created in Access 2002 are in Access 2000 format, for compatibility with the earlier Access version. You will learn more about file formats in upcoming exercises*

- Some databases, such as those created with the Database Wizard, display a **Switchboard** window when you open them. You can close the Switchboard window by clicking its Close button [X].

- After closing the Switchboard, you might need to maximize the minimized Database window. Double-click it to do so.

Close the Switchboard window if it appears when you open a database, and restore the Database window

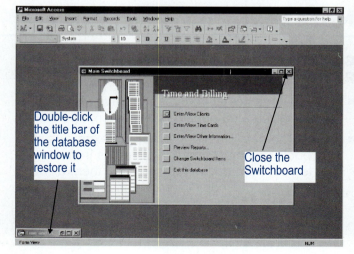

Double-click
the title bar of
the database
window to
restore it

Close the
Switchboard

■ You can start Access and open a database file at the same time by double-clicking the database file you want to open from Windows Explorer or My Computer.

■ You can also use the Open Office Document command on the Start menu in Windows to select a database to open and start Access at the same time.

Navigate in a Database

Open Objects with the Database Window

■ Use the database window to select the type of object you want to work with in Access. Click one of the Objects buttons in the Objects bar to view the available objects of that type, which are displayed in the right portion of the window.

To open an object from the database window, double-click it

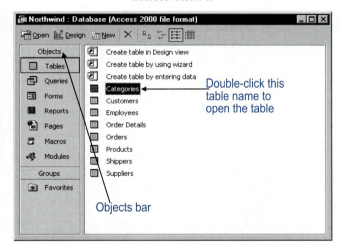

■ Double-click an object to open it and begin work. For example, if you want to open a table called *Customers*, click the Tables button, and then double-click the icon for Customers. You can also click on the object icon and click the Open button.

Move through a Datasheet

■ When you open a table, data displays in a row and column format similar to a spreadsheet. Each column heading displays the caption or field name for the field, and each row contains all the information for a single record.

■ This row and column display is called **Datasheet view**. This view enables you to see more than one record at a time on the screen.

Datasheet view displays data in rows and columns

■ To move through the datasheet, you can use the navigation buttons at the bottom of the window.

■ The navigation buttons also show the current record and the total number of records. You can type a record number in the specific record box and press Enter to move to that record.

Datasheet navigation buttons

■ When you move into a field, you are in one of two modes: *field edit mode* or *navigation mode*. The insertion point displays in the field in edit mode; the entire field entry is highlighted when you are in navigation mode. To switch back and forth between the two modes, press F2.

■ Press Tab to go from one column to the next column. In the last column, press Tab to go to the first column in the next record.

■ You can use the arrow keys to move around the datasheet, and you can also use a number of shortcut keys to move to specific points in the datasheet.

Move through a Form

■ You can navigate through records on a form using the same navigation buttons that appear in Datasheet view of a table or form.

■ If you are in navigation mode, you can also use the shortcut keys such as Ctrl+Home and Ctrl+End, to move to the first or last record on a form.

Sort Records

- Sorting rearranges records in order by one or more fields. Most types of fields can be sorted.

- You can **sort** in **ascending** order (A to Z or 1 to 9) or **descending** order (Z to A or 9 to 1).

- Before sorting, you must first move the insertion point to the field you want to sort. For example, if you want to sort a table of clients by last name in ascending order, move to the Last Name field, then click the ![A-Z] button.

- Some reasons to sort might be to:
  - See groups of data (for example, all clients who live in New York or all of yesterday's sales).
  - See information organized from smallest or largest values.
  - Group all records that have blanks in a field.
  - Look for duplicate records.

- You can sort in Datasheet or Form view. It is easier to see the sort results in Datasheet view.

You can sort a table by any field

Sort buttons

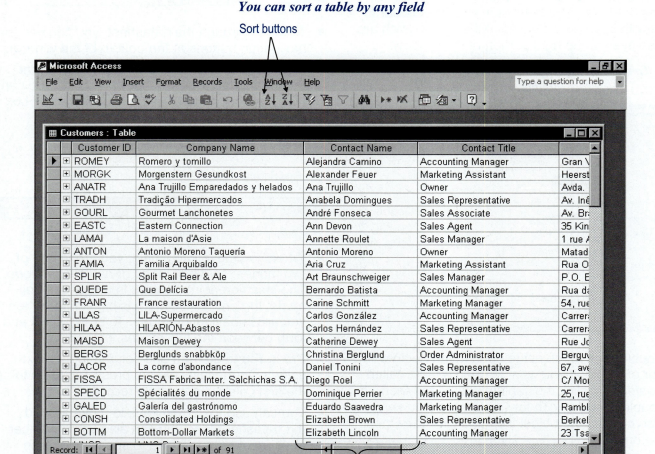

Ascending sort has been done by this column

Procedures

Copy Data Files and Deselect the Read-only Attribute

1. Copy the Access data file(s) from your CD to a hard drive.
2. Open Windows Explorer, and locate the drive and folder where you stored the copies.
3. Click to select the file(s) you want to open.

   ✓ To select all the files in a folder at once, right-click and choose Select All.

4. Click **F**ile .... `Alt`+`F`
5. Click **P**roperties .... `R`
6. Deselect **R**ead-only in the Attributes section ...`Alt`+`R`
7. Click **OK** .... `Enter`

Start Access

1. Click **Start** button `Start`.
2. Click **P**rograms.
3. Click **Microsoft Access**.

Open an Existing Database File when You Start Access

1. Click **Start** button `Start`.
2. Click **Open Office Document**.
3. Click the desired file.

   ✓ You can change to another folder, if needed, to locate file you wish to open.

   ✓ To change folders, select a new folder from Look in drop-down list.

4. Click **O**pen.

Open a Recently Used Database File

- Click the **file name** in the Open a file section of the New File Task Pane.

  OR

1. Click **F**ile .... `F`
2. Click the **file name** at the bottom of the File menu.

Open a Database File

1. Click **More files** on the Task Pane.

   OR

   Click the **Open** button `💾` on the toolbar.
2. Click the file you want to open.
3. Click **O**pen .... `O`

Navigate in a Database

Open objects with the database window:

1. Click an **Objects** button.
2. Double-click the object you want to open.

   OR

1. Click on object icon to select it.
2. Click **O**pen in datasheet window .... `Alt`+`O`

Move through a datasheet:

- **Tab** into a field .... `Tab`
- Press **Ctrl+End** to move to last field and last row .... `Ctrl`+`End`
- Press **Ctrl+Home** to move to first field and first row .... `Ctrl`+`Home`
- Press **End** to move to last field in row .... `End`
- Press **Home** to move to first field in row .... `Home`

In Navigation mode, to move to:

- **Last field, last record of table** .... `Ctrl`+`End`
- **First field, first record of table** ...... `Ctrl`+`Home`
- **Last field, current record** .... `End`

- **First field, current record** .... `Home`
- **Last record, current field** .... `Ctrl`+`↓`
- **First record, current field** .... `Ctrl`+`↑`
- **Next field (or if in last field to first field of next record)** .... `Tab`
- **Previous field** .... `Shift`+`Tab`

Sort Records

1. Open datasheet or form.
2. Click in column to be sorted in Datasheet view or one field in Form view.
3. Click **R**ecords .... `Alt`+`R`

   a. Click **S**ort .... `S`

   b. Select **A**scending or **D**escending ...... `A` or `C`

   OR

   Click **Ascending** button `A↓` or

   Descending button `Z↓`.

Close a Table

1. Click **F**ile .... `F`
2. Click **C**lose .... `C`

   ✓ Text changes are saved automatically.

3. If you are prompted to save design changes, click **Y**es to save changes or **N**o to cancel changes.

Close Access

1. Click **F**ile .... `F`
2. Click E**x**it .... `X`

   OR

   Click the **Close** button `X` for the Access window.

Exercise Directions

1. Start Access, if necessary.
2. Open ☉**AC01**.
   - ✓ *You may have to copy the data files from your CD to the hard drive and deselect the read-only attribute.*
3. In the database window, click **Tables** on the Objects list.
4. Open the **tblClients** table.
5. Scroll vertically to review some of the client names.
6. Scroll horizontally to review the number of fields in the table.
7. Use the navigation buttons to find the record for **Anar Mitra**.
8. Move to the Last Name field and sort the client names in ascending order. After the sort, your table should look like the one shown in Illustration A.
   - ✓ *Choose Records, Sort, Sort Ascending or click the Sort Ascending button.*
   - ✓ *Now sort the table in ascending order by Client ID.*
9. Close the table without saving any changes.
10. Click the Forms button on the Database window.
11. Open the form **frmClients**.
12. Go to the record for **Jamal Joyner**.
13. Now go back to the first record. Scroll through the records and count how many of the clients have been to the store (have a check mark in the field). How many of the client prospects are classified as "Hot One"?
14. Sort the records in ascending order by City.
    - ✓ *Move to the City field, then choose Records, Sort, Sort Ascending.*
15. Scroll through the records. Note that this sort groups the clients by city, starting with **Avon** and ending with **Westminster**.
16. Close the form.
17. Exit the database.
    - ✓ *Close button ☒ or File, Exit.*

Illustration A

On Your Own

1. Start Access and open the ☉**AC01** database.
2. Open the **tblClients** table.
3. Use keystroke shortcuts to go to the following locations in the table:
   - The current field of the last record.
   - The last field of the current record.
   - The previous field.
   - The first field of the first record.
4. Find the record for **Ellen Mills**. What is her address?
5. Sort the table in ascending order by ZIP. How many clients live in the **80444** ZIP Code?
6. Close the table without saving any changes.

Exercise 2

Skills Covered:

◆ **Enter Records** ◆ **Edit Records** ◆ **Delete Records**
◆ **Print Datasheets and Forms** ◆ **Print Preview**

On the Job

Your main task as a user of a database is to enter and edit data stored in the database. You must be able to enter new records, typically in a form or a datasheet. You will also edit records already stored in the database and correct entries as you enter them. Printing a table or form provides you with a hard copy of the database, which can be used, for example, by a manager for reviewing and on-paper editing.

As the manager of the Steel Dreams Motorcycle Emporium, you must keep the customer database up-to-date by entering records using both a form and a datasheet. You will make changes to existing records and correct information as you enter it. You will then print the updated database to create a hard copy of the information.

Terms

Enter To type in data and press Tab to move to the next field.

Preview To produce a screen view of what a printed page will look like.

Notes

Enter Records

- To **enter** records in a datasheet or in a form, type the information you want in a field, and press Tab or Enter to go to the next field.

Enter Records in a Datasheet

- To enter records in a datasheet, type the data below each field name as you would in an Excel worksheet.

- Type the information you want for the record, and press Tab or Enter to go to the next field.

- When you enter data in the last field for a record, press Tab or Enter to go to the first field of the next record. If you are at the last record of the table, this will automatically create a new record.

- Unlike other Office applications where you have to choose the Save command, Access automatically saves a record when you go to another record.

✓ *Each field has a drop-down list containing previous entries for that field; you can select from it instead of retyping an entry. You'll learn more about this feature in later exercises.*

Enter Data Quickly Using Shortcut Keys

- Use shortcut key combinations shown in the Procedures on page 476 to enter data quickly.

Copy Data

- Use the Copy and Paste commands to enter repetitive data. Select the data you want to copy, and then use the Copy command. Then move the insertion point to the location you want the data to appear. Use the Paste command to insert the copied data.

- There are three ways to issue the Copy and Paste commands. To copy, you can choose the Copy command from the Edit menu, press Ctrl+C, or click the Copy button .

- To paste, you can choose the Paste command from the Edit menu, press Ctrl+V, or click the Paste button 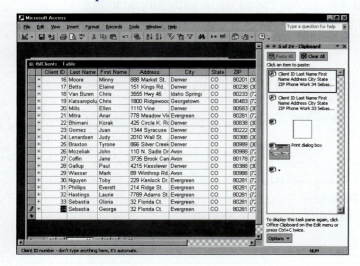.

- When you copy (or cut) twice in a row before you paste, the Clipboard appears in the Task Pane. This is a new feature in Access 2002.

- The Clipboard Task Pane enables you to store and paste multiple selections.

- If you want to paste a copied selection other than your most recently copied one, you can click it on the Task Pane before pasting.

The Clipboard is available on the Task Pane

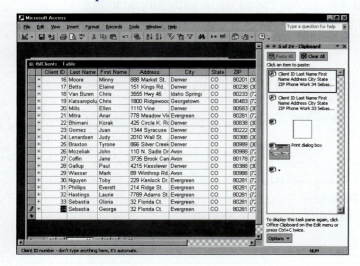

Move Data

- Moving data works the same way as copying it (see above, except you use the Cut command instead of the Copy command).

- To issue the Cut command, choose it from the Edit menu, press Ctrl+X, or click the Cut button.

Copy an Entire Record

- To copy an entire record in Datasheet view, select the record by clicking its record selector button to the left of the record in the gray record selector bar. Copy it with the Copy command. Then select the destination location and use the Paste Append command (on the Edit menu). Existing information will be overwritten with the new information.

- The Paste Append command does not have a keyboard shortcut or toolbar button equivalent.

Select a record, then copy it; then use
Paste Append to paste a copy of it elsewhere

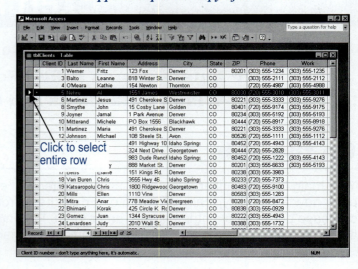

Enter Records in a Form

- You enter records in Form view the same way you do in Datasheet view. Type in a field and press Tab or Enter to go to the next field.

- When you are on the last field of the form and you press Tab or Enter, Access automatically saves the current record and the insertion point moves to the first field of the next record.

- If you are displaying a current record and want to add a new record, choose the New Record command from the Insert menu or click the New Record button on the toolbar or navigation bar.

Edit Records

- You may want to correct field information after you enter it. You can delete and add text in the same way you would in Word or Excel.

- Click to position the insertion point. Press Backspace to remove text before the insertion point or press Delete to remove text after the insertion point.

- You can also drag the mouse pointer to select text and then press Delete to remove the text.

- Select text and type new text to replace the selected text. You can double-click on a word to select a word, then type to replace it.

- If you move the mouse pointer to the beginning of a field, the pointer changes to a white plus sign. Click to select the entire content of that field.

- While you are making changes to a record, a pencil icon appears on the record selector button (to the left of the record). The pencil indicates that any changes are not currently saved.

- If you want to undo your changes, press Esc once to undo the change to the current field and press Esc again to undo all changes to the current record.

- Changes are automatically saved to the record when you go to another record or close the table or form.

Delete Records

- You can delete the current record or one or more contiguous records.

- When you delete one or more records, Access will ask you to confirm the deletion. After you select *Yes*, you cannot reverse the deletion.

- Access shows the total number of records at the bottom of the window.

- If you have an AutoNumber field in the table, when you delete a record, Access will not reuse the numbers of the deleted records. AutoNumber fields are discussed in Exercise 5.

Print Datasheets and Forms

- Print all the records of the current screen in Datasheet or Form view by clicking the Print button.

- If you want to set print options, open the Print dialog box by choosing Print from the File menu.

Print dialog box

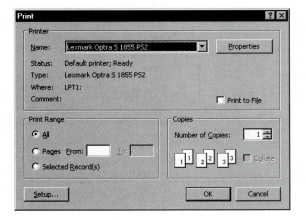

- The Name drop-down arrow in the Print dialog box allows you to choose a different printer.

- To print selected records, click the record selector to the left of one or more records in Datasheet or Form view. Then click File, Print and choose to print Selected Record(s) in the Print dialog box.

- If desired, type more than 1 in the Number of Copies box and then check Collate if you want to print the document in a complete set, or leave Collate unchecked if you want to print multiple copies of page 1, then page 2, and so on.

Print Preview

- Click the Print Preview button on the toolbar to see a screen **preview** of what your printing will look like.

- While in Print Preview, click the magnifying glass to see more details or to return to full-page view.

- The Navigation buttons at the bottom of the screen in Print Preview allow you to see the first, previous, specific, next, or last page.

Print Preview shows what the data will look like when printed

Zoom

Leave Print Preview

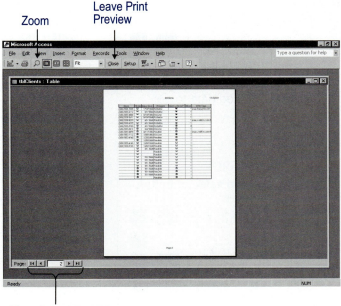

Move between pages

Procedures

Enter Records

To enter records in a datasheet:

1. Click in the first blank cell in the first field (the first column and first row).
2. Type data for field.
3. To correct an error, press **Backspace** .... `Backspace` and type again.
4. Press **Tab** to go to next field .... `Tab`
5. Repeat steps 2–4 for each field in record.
6. Click in first cell in the next row to begin new record.

To enter data quickly using shortcut keys:

- Copy value from current field in previous record .... `Ctrl`+`'`
- Enter current date .... `Ctrl`+`;`
- Enter current time .... `Ctrl`+`:`

To copy data:

1. Select data to copy.
2. Click **Edit** .... `Alt`+`E`
3. Click **Copy** .... `C`
4. Move insertion point to where you want copied data to go.
5. Click **Edit** .... `Alt`+`E`
6. Click **Paste** .... `P`

To copy entire record:

1. Click on record selector button to left of record.
2. Click **Edit** .... `Alt`+`E`
3. Click **Copy** .... `C`
4. Click **Edit** .... `Alt`+`E`
5. Click **Paste Append** .... `N`

To enter records in a form:

1. Type data in first field.
2. Press **Tab** .... `Tab`
3. Repeat steps 1 and 2 until complete.

Edit a Field Entry

1. Click in the field you want to edit.
2. Position the insertion point:
   - Click where you want it.

   OR

   - Use arrow keys .... `↕↔`
3. Remove unwanted text using these keys:
   - **Backspace** .... `Backspace` to delete to left.
   - **Delete** .... `Del` to delete to right.
4. Type replacement text.

Replace a Field Entry

1. Select entire field.
2. Click at beginning of field, when mouse pointer shows black arrow.
3. Retype field content.

Delete a Record

1. Select the record you want to delete.
2. Click **Delete Record** button .

   OR

   a. Click **Edit** .... `Alt`+`E`
   b. **Click Delete Record** ..... `R`

   OR

   - Press **Ctrl** + minus sign .... `Ctrl`+`-`

   OR

   - Press **Delete** .... `Del`
3. Click **Yes** .... `Enter`

Print Datasheets and Forms

1. Open datasheet or form to print.
2. If desired, click on record selector button on left of datasheet or form to select record(s) to print.
3. Click **File** .... `Alt`+`F`
4. Click **Print** .... `P`
5. Click **Print Range** option to select:
   - **All** .... `Alt`+`A`
   - **Pages** .... `Alt`+`G`
   - **Selected Record(s)** .. `Alt`+`R`
6. Select **Properties** .... `Alt`+`P` to make any changes to printer setup.
7. Choose desired option tab and select options:
   - **Paper**
   - **Graphics**
   - **Fonts**
   - **Device Options**
   - ✓ *The tabs may be different depending on your printer.*
8. Click **OK** .... `Enter`
9. Type number in **Number of Copies** text box .... `Alt`+`C` if you want multiple copies.
10. Click **OK** .... `Enter`

Print Preview

- Click **Print Preview** button .

OR

1. Click **File** .... `Alt`+`F`
2. Click **Print Preview** .... `V`
3. Click magnifying glass to see more or less detail.
4. Click navigation buttons to see the first, previous, specific, next, or last page.

Exercise Directions

1. Start Access, if necessary.

2. Open ⊙ **AC02**.
   - ✓ *You may have to copy the data files from your CD to the hard drive and deselect the read-only attribute.*

3. Open the **tblClients** table.

4. Move to the blank record after client 27, **Jane Coffin**.

5. Make sure the insertion point is in the Last Name field, then enter the three new records shown in Illustration A.
   - ✓ *Press Tab or Enter to move from one field to the next.*

6. Change **Mark Wasser's** address to **89 Winthrop Rd**.

7. Add three more records shown in Illustration B. Use shortcut keys to enter the repeated information in the City, State, and ZIP fields.

8. Copy the entire record for **Gloria Sebastia** and paste it in the row for the next new record at the bottom of the table.

9. Change the First Name of the new record to **George**.
   - ✓ *This new record is for Gloria's husband. All other record information is the same.*

10. Preview the datasheet and print one copy.

11. Close the table.
    - ✓ *Close button ☒ or File, Close.*

12. Open the **frmClients** form.

13. Insert a new record (Insert, New Record) and enter a new record with the following information:
    Tracy Richards, 532 W. Albion Dr., Blackhawk, CO, 80356, (303) 555-7275

14. Change the ZIP for **Tracy Richards** to **80444** and change the phone number to **(720) 555-2237**.

15. Delete the record for **Jane Coffin**.

16. Select the records for **George** and **Gloria Sebastia** as well as **Tracy Richards**.

17. Preview and print the selected records.

18. Close the table.

19. Exit the database.

Illustration A

		Client ID	Last Name	First Name	Address	City	State	ZIP	Phone	Work
	+	23	Gomez	Juan	1344 Syracuse	Denver	CO	80222	(303) 555-4943	
	+	24	Lenardsen	Judy	2010 Wall St.	Denver	CO	80388	(303) 555-1732	
	+	25	Braxton	Tyrone	866 Silver Creek	Denver	CO	80989	(303) 555-8928	
	+	26	Mozeliak	John	110 N. Sadle Dr	Avon	CO	80988	(720) 555-1788	
	+	27	Coffin	Jane	3735 Brook Can	Avon	CO	80178	(720) 555-8917	
▶	+	28	Gallup	Paul	4215 Kessler Av	Denver	CO	80388	(303) 555-9256	(303) 555-3920
	+	29	Wasser	Mark	89 Guilford Ln.	Avon	CO	80988	(720) 555-3840	
	+	30	Nguyen	Toby	229 Kenlock Dr.	Evergreen	CO	80281	(720) 555-0035	(303) 555-1182
✱		oNumber)								

		Client ID	Last Name	First Name	Address	City	State	ZIP	Phone	Work
	+	23	Gomez	Juan	1344 Syracuse	Denver	CO	80222	(303) 555-4943	
	+	24	Lenardsen	Judy	2010 Wall St.	Denver	CO	80388	(303) 555-1732	
	+	25	Braxton	Tyrone	866 Silver Creek	Denver	CO	80989	(303) 555-8928	
	+	26	Mozeliak	John	110 N. Sadle Dr	Avon	CO	80988	(720) 555-1788	
	+	27	Coffin	Jane	3735 Brook Can	Avon	CO	80178	(720) 555-8917	
	+	28	Gallup	Paul	4215 Kessler A\	Denver	CO	80388	(303) 555-9256	(303) 555-3920
	+	29	Wasser	Mark	89 Winthrop Rd.	Avon	CO	80988	(720) 555-3840	
	+	30	Nguyen	Toby	229 Kenlock Dr.	Evergreen	CO	80281	(720) 555-0035	(303) 555-1182
▶	+	31	Phillips	Everett	214 Ridge St.	Evergreen	CO	80281	(720) 555-9387	
	+	32	Hastings	Laurie	7789 Adams St.	Evergreen	CO	80281	(720) 555-8886	(720) 555-3381
	+	33	Sebastia	Gloria	32 Florida Ct.	Evergreen	CO	80281	(720) 555-9402	
*		oNumber)								

On Your Own

1. Start Access and open the ☉ **OAC02** database.

2. Open the **tblClients** table.

3. Enter records for 5 of your friends and family members into the table. Use their real addresses and phone numbers—or make up the address and phone information as you go.

4. Change the address information of the records you entered to fit with the Colorado city, state, ZIP, and phone number information already in the table. For example, use the cities of Denver, Thornton, Westminster, Golden, Blackhawk, etc., use CO for the state abbreviation, use phone numbers with either the 303 or 720 area code, and use some of the ZIP Codes already in the table.

5. Preview and print the table, then close it.

6. Open the **frmClients** form.

7. Scroll through the new records you added, then add 5 more records for your friends and family members. Make up Colorado city, state, ZIP, and phone number information similar to what you used in the **tblClients** table.

   ✓ You can press Tab to move from field to field.

8. Close the form, and open the **tblClients** table.

9. Select the new records you added.

10. Preview and print the selected records.

11. Close the form.

12. Close the database and exit Access.

Skills Covered:
◆ **Plan a Database** ◆ **Create a New Database File**
◆ **Create a Table in Datasheet View**
◆ **Change Field Names in Datasheet View** ◆ **Save a Table Design**

On the Job

As well as learning to work with existing databases, you must also learn to plan and create a new database of your own. In planning the database, you need to consider how the database will be used by asking: What information will it store? How will you use the database to analyze the information? After planning the database, you can easily create the new database file and the tables that store the data.

Now that you have become familiar with the Steel Dreams Motorcycle Emporium's current database, you've decided to create a new database and add a table to store information about the shop's client names, addresses, and phone numbers.

Terms

Primary key The field that uniquely identifies each record in a table.

Blank database A database file that does not yet contain any objects (that is, tables, queries, reports, and so on).

Template A predefined group of settings for creating a new database, including what tables will be included, what fields will be used, and so on.

Notes

Plan a Database

- Before you create a database, you must decide which fields you want to include—and if you need a single table or more than one. Consider what information the database will store and how the information will be used.

- To begin, make a list of the fields you want to store in your database, such as last name, first name, address, phone, and so on.

- If you have a lot of categories in mind, break down the field list into specific categories such as Customers, Vendors, Inventory, and so on. Each category will form a separate table in your database.

- If you envision repeated information in a table, plan to split it into separate tables. For example, you might want to store employee contact information in a separate table and employee vacation usage data in another table so that you don't repeat information you already have in the contact table (address, phone, e-mail account, and so on).

- Think about the ways you will want to search or sort the data, and plan the fields to support them.

- For example, if you want to sort by last name, make sure you have separate fields for First Name and Last Name. The same goes for City, State, and ZIP Code. It would be hard, for example, to create mailing labels if client addresses are in one field.

- Each table should have a field in which each record will be unique, such as an ID Number field. This field will be the table's **primary key**.

- Plan the relationships between your tables. Make sure that tables to be related have a common field. For example, the Employee ID field in the Employee Contacts table might link to the Employee ID field in the Vacations table.

  ✓ *Relationships between tables are covered more thoroughly in Lesson 2, Exercise 9.*

- When you've finished identifying fields and tables, you are ready to create your new database file and create the tables within it.

Create a New Database File

- The database file contains all Access objects, including tables, forms, queries, pages, and reports. Each database file is stored with an .mdb extension.

- You must create a database file, or open an existing one, before you can enter any data or create any objects (such as tables or queries).

- When you start Access, the New File Task Pane provides shortcuts for starting a new database or opening an existing one.

- You can reopen the task pane at any time by clicking the New button on the toolbar.

Start a new database from the Task Pane

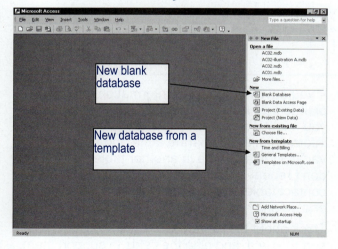

- To start a new database, you can choose to create a **blank database** or create a database based on a **template**.

  ✓ *You can also choose to start a new data access page for a Web page or a new project, but these are not covered in this course.*

✓ *A new feature in Access 2002 is the ability to create a new database by copying an existing one. Use the New from Existing File link in the Task Pane.*

Create a New Blank Database

- To create a blank database, use the Blank Database link in the New File Task Pane.

- The File New Database dialog box appears, and you enter a file name and click Create.

Enter a name for the database file you are creating

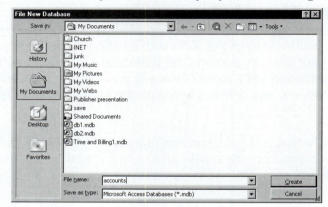

Create a Table in Datasheet View

- There are three ways to create a table: using Table Design view, using a wizard, and by entering data in a new datasheet.

- In this exercise, you will learn about the latter method. Other methods are covered in upcoming exercises.

- To create a new table with a datasheet, click the *Create table by entering data* shortcut from the database window. A new, blank datasheet appears with placeholder field names (Field1, Field2, etc.) in the column heads.

A new table from Datasheet view

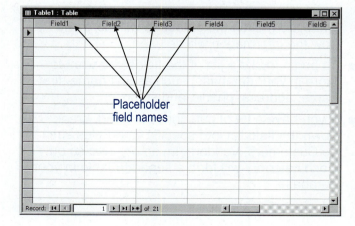

Change Field Names in Datasheet View

- A new table in Datasheet view provides placeholder names for each field at the top of each column.

- To change a field name, double-click the existing name and then type a new one.

Save a Table Design

- When you close a table after making design changes to it, Access asks whether you want to save your changes.

- This refers to the structural changes to the table, such as the field names, not to any data you have entered. Data is saved automatically.

- The first time you save changes to a table, Access prompts for a table name.

Name the new table

- If there is no primary key field defined for the table, Access asks whether you want to create one.

Define the primary key

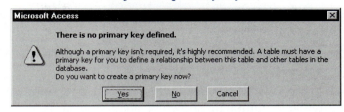

- If you choose *Yes*, it creates a new field called *ID* in the table and sets it as the primary key.

- If you choose *No,* it saves your table without a primary key.

  ✓ *You cannot choose an existing field to be the primary key field from Datasheet view. In Exercise 5 you will learn about Table Design view.*

Procedures

Display the Task Pane
1. Click **File**...................Alt + F
2. Click **New**.............................N

Create a New Blank Database
From Task Pane:
1. Choose **Blank Database**.
2. Type file name.
3. Choose folder in **Save in** drop-down list.
   OR
   Click folder on the Places bar.
4. Click **Create**....................Enter

Create Table in Datasheet View
From database window:
- Double-click **Create table by entering data**.
  OR
  a. Click **Insert**............Alt + I
  b. Click **Table**....................T

c. Choose **Datasheet View**.
d. Click **OK**......................Enter

Change Field Names in Datasheet View
1. Double-click field name in column header.
2. Type new field name in column header.
3. Press **Enter**....................Enter
   OR
   Click in column to change.
4. Click **Format**...............Alt + O
5. Click **Rename Column**.......N
6. Type new field name in column header.
7. Press **Enter**....................Enter

Save a Table Design
1. Close the table....................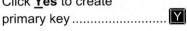
   ✓ *If this is the first time you've saved the table, continue with the following.*
2. Click **Yes** ....Y
3. Type table name.
4. Click **OK** ....Enter
5. Click **No**.............................N
   ✓ *To bypass creation of primary key.*
   OR
   Click **Yes** to create primary key ....Y

Exercise Directions

1. Start Access and select Blank Database from the Task Pane.

2. Replace the default file name, *db1*, with **AC03** and press **Enter**.

3. Double-click on **Create table by entering data** in the database window.

4. In the Datasheet view for the new table, change the field names as shown in Illustration A.

   ✓ *As you can see, the field names for this table do not use spaces. Although you can use spaces in file names, spaces can sometimes result in database errors for certain advanced operations.*

   ✓ *Double-click on Field1 and type the new name.*

5. Add the records shown in Illustration A.

   ✓ *Press Tab after each entry to move to the next column.*

6. Save the table as **tblClients** and have Access create a primary key.

7. Close the table.

8. Exit the database.

Illustration A

FirstName	LastName	Address	City	State	ZIP	Phone
Fritz	Werner	123 Fox	Denver	CO	80201	(303) 555-1234
Jenny	Zimdahl	234 Ivy	Aurora	CO	80014	(303) 555-2345
Leanne	Balto	83 Winter St.	Denver	CO	80224	(303) 555-2111
Kathie	O'Meara	154 Newton	Thornton	CO	80221	(303) 555-4987
Al	Nehru	1551 James	Westminster	CO	80030	(303) 555-3010
Jesus	Martinez	17 Tar Drive	Arvada	CO	80030	(303) 555-9275
Pam	Wong	3954 Maple	Evergreen	CO	80219	(303) 555-7283
John	Smith	15 Cosby Lane	Golden	CO	80456	(303) 555-9174
Jamal	Joyner	1 Park Avenue	Denver	CO	80234	(303) 555-5192
Michele	Mitterand	PO Box 1556	Blackhawk	CO	80444	(303) 555-8917

Table1 : Table

Record: 11 of 11

On Your Own

1. Start Access and create a new database.

2. Save the database file as **OAC03**.

3. Create a table for storing a telephone list or roster. You can use friends, relatives, associates, club or organization members, or the members of a sports team.

4. Include fields for first name, last name, and telephone number.

5. Save the table with the name **Roster**.

6. Let Access create the Primary Key field.

7. Enter at least five records in the table.

8. Close your database and exit Access.

Exercise 4

Skills Covered:

◆ **Create a Database with Database Wizards**
◆ **Start Database Wizards** ◆ **Use Database Wizards**
◆ **Use Switchboards**

On the Job

Microsoft Access comes with several databases designed for typical purposes. You simply choose the desired wizard—which you can customize to more closely match your needs—and enter data. If you create a database using one of the database wizards, you can save a significant amount of time compared to designing a database from scratch. Access switchboards provide a convenient way to automate your database and make its features and data more *access*ible.

Before you spend a lot of time creating the database objects for Steel Dreams Cycle Emporium, you want to check out the templates that come with Access to see whether one of them might provide a suitable head start for your work. You will create a new database using the Database Wizard, to see whether it meets your needs.

Terms

Template A predefined group of settings for creating a new database, including what tables will be included, what fields will be used, and so on.

Database Wizard A step-by-step process for creating a new database using a template.

Switchboard An Access form with command buttons or other controls that lead to other switchboard forms, input forms, and reports.

Notes

Create a Database with Database Wizards

- Access offers ten different **templates** that help you create a database that may match what you need in a database.

    ✓ *You can also download additional templates from the Microsoft Web site if you have Internet access. Just click the* Templates on Microsoft.com *hyperlink on the New File Task Pane.*

- In Access, **templates** are accessed through **Database Wizards**, so the terms *template* and *database wizard* are roughly synonymous in Access. This is not always the case in other Office programs, however.

- These templates provide a basic set of tables, queries, forms, and reports, plus a Switchboard to help beginners navigate among them.

- You cannot pick and choose among the tables and other objects that Access creates when you use a database wizard. However, you can delete any unwanted objects, or make changes to them, after the database wizard is finished creating the objects.

- Using a template is helpful primarily if you want to create a database similar to one of the templates. If your database is fairly specific in purpose, whether simple or complex, it is probably easier to build from scratch.

Start Database Wizards

- You can start a database wizard from within Access by clicking General Templates in the task pane to display the Templates dialog box.

- The Templates dialog box has two tabs: General and Databases. The General tab contains a template for a blank database, a data access page for the Web, and blank databases that are not designed around a specific purpose.

- Click the Databases tab to see icons for the database templates that Access offers. Then double-click the one you want, or click it and then click OK.

  - ✓ *A preview pane exists in the Templates dialog box, but it only shows a simple graphic representation of the database. If you need more help choosing the right database template, open it up and examine its features.*

Choose the template you want

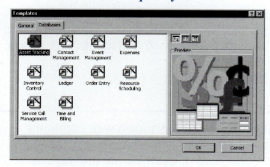

- After you choose a template, a File New Database dialog box appears, just like when you create a new blank database. Enter a name for the new database file in it and click Create. The database wizard then starts.

Use Database Wizards

- The database wizard leads you through a series of dialog boxes that:
  - Show you the tables that appear in the new database and allow you to select optional fields for each table.

    - ✓ *The basic list of fields for a particular table is fixed. The field names that appear in italics and that do not have a check mark next to them by default are optional. You can select any or all of these optional fields to include in the table.*

Select optional table fields

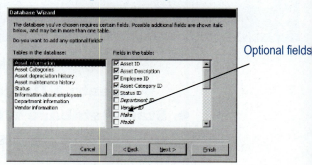

Optional fields

- Provide choices for form and report formatting.
- Enable you to enter a title for the database (different from the file name).
- Enable you to specify a graphic to use as a logo on reports.

- The database wizard does not create any data; you will enter the data yourself, as you learned to do in Exercise 2.

- You can customize the tables and other database objects (queries, forms, and reports) after Access creates them for you.

Use Switchboards

- Databases created with a database wizard automatically include a **switchboard** that allows you to navigate to forms and reports created for the database.

- The switchboard is actually a group of linked forms with buttons for opening certain forms, reports, or queries.

- The main switchboard form opens automatically each time you open that database.

- The database window starts minimized when the main switchboard appears; double-click it (in the bottom-left corner of the Access window) to restore it. You can minimize or close the main switchboard if desired to get it out of your way.

A main switchboard

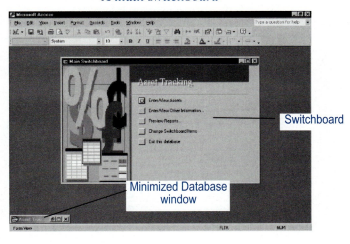

Switchboard

Minimized Database window

- You can change the content of a switchboard form, or choose a different form as the default, by clicking Change Switchboard Items on the main switchboard. Such editing is beyond the scope of this book, but you can try it on your own or with the assistance of an instructor.

Modifying the Switchboard

- You can prevent the main switchboard from opening at startup by choosing Tools, Startup, and choosing None as the Display Form/Page entry.

Procedures

Create a Database with a Template

From Task Pane:

1. Choose **General Templates**.
2. Click the **Databases** tab.
3. Click the template.
4. Click **OK**...........................Enter
5. Type file name.
6. Choose folder in **Save in** drop-down list.
   OR
   Click folder on left side of dialog box.
7. Click **Create**.....................Enter
8. Click **Next**. ....Enter
9. If desired, click on each table in database and click on check box in front of italicized entries to add optional fields.
10. Click **Next** ....Enter
11. Click style for screen displays.
12. Click **Next** ....Enter

13. Click style for printed reports.
14. Click **Next**........................Enter
15. Type a title for database.
    ✓ *This name appears on the title bar. It need not be the same as the file name.*
16. If you want a picture on every report, click **Yes, I'd like to include a picture** and click **Picture** button to choose picture.
17. Click **Next**........................Enter
18. Click **Finish**.....................Enter
    ✓ *Some templates prompt you to enter your company's contact information after the database wizard runs; do so if prompted.*

Use Switchboard

1. Click on button to open form, report, or another switchboard.
2. If another switchboard appears, click on **Return to Main Switchboard** to return.

Close Switchboard

- Click **Close** ✖ on the Switchboard window.

Restore Database Window

- Double-click the database window's **title bar**.
  ✓ *The database window's title bar is in the bottom-left corner of the Access window.*

Prevent Switchboard from Opening Automatically

1. Click **Tools** ....Alt+T
2. Click **Startup** ....U
3. Click down arrow next to **Display Form/Page** .
4. Choose **(none)**.
   ✓ *(none) is at the top of the list; scroll up to find it.*
5. Click **OK** ....Enter

Exercise Directions

1. Start a new database using the Order Entry template.
   - ✓ *Click the General Templates link in the New File Task Pane, and choose Order Entry from the Databases tab.*

2. Name the database **AC04**. The database wizard starts.

3. In the Customer information table, add the E-mail Address and Notes fields (at the bottom of the Fields in customer information table list).

4. Pick your own styles for screen displays (forms) and reports.

5. Title the database **Orders** and choose Finish.

6. Access prompts you for company information. Click OK and enter the following information for the company:

   Company: **Steel Dreams Cycle Emporium**
   Address.: **P.O. Box 765**
   City: **Oyster Bay**
   State: **NY**
   ZIP: **11771**
   Sales Tax Rate: **8%**
   Default Terms: **Net 30**
   Phone Number: **(516) 555-2200**

7. Click the Close button ❌ to exit the form.

8. On the switchboard, click Enter/View Other Information.

9. Click Enter/View Products, add the Products as follows.

Product Name	Unit Price
Leather saddlebag	109.95
Vinyl seat cover	24.95
Chrome polish	9.50
Steel Dreams T-shirt	10.95

   - ✓ *You do not enter the Product ID; Access enters this automatically.*

10. Click the Close button ❌ to exit the form.

11. Close the switchboard and restore the database window.

12. Turn off the automatic display of the switchboard at startup.
    - ✓ *To do so, choose Tools, Startup and set Display Form/Page to None.*

13. Exit Access.

On Your Own

1. Start Access and create a database using the Inventory Control Wizard.

2. Save the database as **OAC04**. You can use this database to store information about items sold as part of a fundraiser for a club or organization, for items sold in a retail store, or for items that you own, such as books or CDs.

3. Close the main switchboard and open the **Categories** table in Datasheet view.

4. Enter at least five product categories.

5. Open the **Products** table in Datasheet view.

6. Enter at least three products. Notice that the categories you created appear on a drop-down list in the Category ID field.

   - ✓ *You do not have to fill in all the fields in the Products table. Try to fill in the Product Name, Production Description, Category ID, and Unit Price, though.*

7. View the existing forms and tables and make modifications if you want.

8. Open the switchboard form. (Click on Forms in the Objects bar; click on switchboard to open it.)

9. Make some changes to the switchboard using the Switchboard Manager. To access it, click Change Switchboard Items on the Main Switchboard.

10. Close the database and exit Access.

Exercise 5

Skills Covered:

◆ **Open a Database File** ◆ **Create a Table with the Table Wizard**
◆ **Start a New Table in Table Design View**
◆ **Work with Table Design View** ◆ **Select a Field for the Primary Key**
◆ **Open a Database Exclusively** ◆ **Set a Database Password**

On the Job

You will probably want more than one table in your database. Good database design means having tables for different types of information as you learned in Exercise 3. Client information should be in one table (or tables) and employee information should be in another (or others) as you specialize tables for the different types of information. In this exercise, you will open the database file you created in Exercise 3 and add a few new tables to it. You will also learn how to set a password to protect your database from being modified by others.

You have decided to stick with creating your database from scratch rather than using the database wizard version from Exercise 4. You now need to create a new table to keep track of your employees, as well as a table to log customer inquiries and requests. You will also experiment with password-protecting the database.

Terms

Table Design view A view in which you can add, edit, and delete fields from the table, change field types and descriptions, set a primary key, and more.

Data type The type of data that a particular field is designed to hold. Common types include *Text*, *Number, Date,* and *Memo*.

Field description An optional brief comment or explanation of a field. The field description appears in the status bar at the bottom of the window when its field is selected.

Field properties Characteristics of a field that determine how long an entry can be, how the entry will be formatted, whether there should be a default entry, and what can be entered (for example, numbers only or valid dates only).

Notes

Open a Database File

■ To get to any tables or other objects within a database, you need to open the database first.

■ Depending on when you last opened the database, you can choose from a list of recently used files on the New File Task Pane or at the bottom of the File menu.

■ If you have not used the database recently, you may need to use the Open dialog box (File, Open) or the More Files link in the Task Pane.

Create a Table with the Table Wizard

- The Table Wizard is a handy utility for creating new tables. You can choose fields from many different sample tables that Access provides.

- To create a table using the Table Wizard, you can double-click *Create table by using wizard* in the list of tables of the database window.

- Another way to start the Table Wizard is to display the list of tables in the Database window, click New , and then click Table Wizard in the New table dialog box that appears.

- The Table Wizard walks you step-by-step through all the decisions you must make.

Two ways to start the Table Wizard

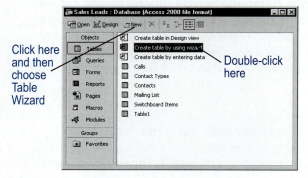

Choosing Table Fields

- The first decision to make is what fields to include. The Table Wizard lets you choose any field from any table in any of the database templates. There are over a hundred tables to choose from.

- The sample tables are broken into two categories: *Business* and *Personal*. Choose one of the two options to switch the sample table listing.

- When you select a sample table, a list of all its fields appears. You can select a field by clicking the > button, or select all the fields in that table at once by clicking the >> button.

- You can choose fields from as many of the sample tables as you like before moving on.

The Table Wizard helps you choose fields

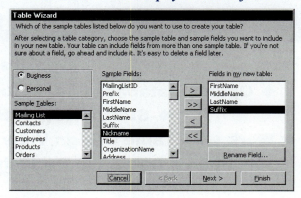

- You can rename a chosen field by clicking the Rename Field button. This keeps the field's properties but enables you to call it something else.

Completing the Table Wizard

- The Table Wizard also prompts you for a table name, and lets you specify whether Access should create a primary key field.

- If you choose to create your own primary key field, the Table Wizard displays a list of the fields you have chosen, so you can specify which one should be the primary key.

  ✓ You won't see this screen (below) if you let Access create a primary key field.

Select the primary key field

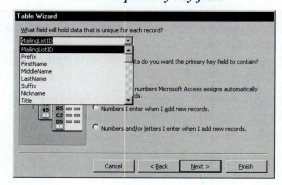

- The Wizard also prompts you for a data type for your primary key field. You can make it an AutoNumber field, a Numeric field, or a Text field.

  ✓ Data types are explained in the table on the next page.

- The Table Wizard also asks about relationships to other tables in your database. The default is for the table to have no relationships.

  ✓ You will learn about relationships in Exercise 9.

Start a New Table in Table Design View

- You can also create a new table in **Table Design view**. The Table Design view method is more complex, but also more powerful and flexible.

- To start a new table using Design view, you can double-click *Create Table in Design View* in the tables list of the Database window.

- Another way is to click the New button 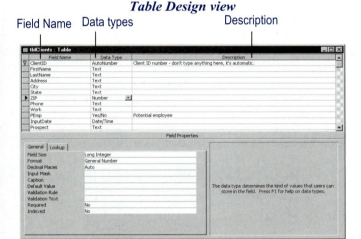 in the Database window, choose Design View from the New Table dialog box, and click OK.

Work in Table Design View

- Table Design view contains a list of the fields in the table, including name, **data type**, and **field description**.

- When a field is selected, its **field properties** appear in the lower half of the Table Design view window. Field properties specify advanced options for the field, such as maximum entry length and default value.

  ✓ *Field properties will be covered in Exercise 7.*

Table Design view

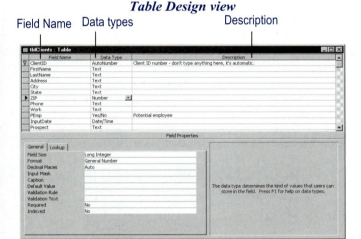

Field Names

- Type or edit a name in the Field Name column. Although you may use up to 64 characters, you should keep the name short.

  ✓ *As previously discussed, even though you can include underscores or spaces in the field name, you should avoid doing so. This will help avoid problems with formulas, programming, or converting your database to a different format.*

Field Descriptions

- The field description is optional. You can enter anything you want here, but most people use it to provide comments or hints about the intended use and/or limitations of the field.

- The text you type in the description will appear on the status bar (bottom of the screen) when the user is in this field in Datasheet view or on a form.

Data Types

- The Data type column tells you what kind of information your field can store. Click the drop-down arrow in this cell to choose from the list of data types. You can also type the first letter of the data type to make this choice, if you prefer to use the keyboard:

Data Type	Description
Text	Includes any characters up to a maximum of 255 characters (determined by field size). If the data includes a mix of numbers and any amount of letters, choose Text. Examples include name and address fields. ✓ *The default data type is Text.*
Memo	Use this data type when Text is not large enough. Like Text, this data type can also have letters and numbers but can be much larger—up to 65,536 characters. Don't use Memo unless you need that extra length, however, because you can't perform certain actions (indexing, for example) on a memo field.
Number	Includes various forms of numerical data that can be used in calculations.
Date/Time	Date and time entries in formats showing date, time, or both.
Currency	Use for currency values with up to four digits after the decimal place. This data type is more accurate for large numbers than the Number data type, but generally takes up more space.
AutoNumber	Usually this is used to create an identification number for each record. The value for each record increases by one.

Data Type	Description
Yes/No	Only two possible values can be in this field. Options include Yes/No, True/False, or On/Off. The default style shows a check box with a 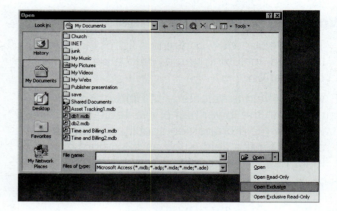 for *Yes* or blank ☐ for *No*.
OLE Object	This data type allows you to place another file type into your record. Within the field, you can insert a picture (a company logo, for example), a Word document (employee resume), or an Excel spreadsheet (client summary chart).
Hyperlink	This allows you to insert a Web address such as *www.ddcpub.com*, which will launch when you click it in Datasheet view or on a form. You could also type a path and file name to a file on your hard drive (C:\docs\myres.doc) or a network drive.
Lookup Wizard	Creates a lookup column, which creates a list of values from which to choose when entering data.

Select a Field for the Primary Key

- As explained in Exercise 3, a table can have a primary key field that contains unique data for each record. The primary key field helps avoid duplicate records in a table.

- Each table can have only one primary key field.

- For the primary key field, choose a field that will be unique for each record. FirstName and LastName would not be good choices for the primary key because different records could have the same value.

- For an employee database, the primary key could be the Social Security Number, for example. You could also create an Employee ID field specifically to be the primary key field.

- When you create a table without choosing a primary key field, Access asks whether you want a primary key field to be created automatically. If you do so, the new field receives the name "ID."

- From Table Design view, you can choose an existing field to be your primary key by selecting it and then clicking the Primary Key button 🔑 on the toolbar.

Open a Database Exclusively

- To set a database password, you have to open the database in exclusive mode (no one else can be in the database).

- Open Exclusive is most often used to ensure that only one user at a time is trying to change the design of database objects.

- In the Open dialog box, choose the down arrow on the Open button and select Open Exclusive.

Use Open Exclusive rather than the normal Open operation when you want to set a password

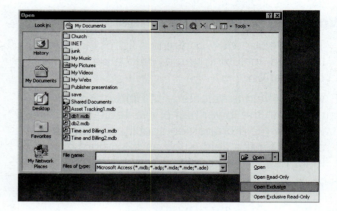

Set Database Password

- When you set a password, you must type the password again to verify accuracy. The password does not show when you type; asterisks display instead. Note that passwords are case-sensitive.

Enter the password to use, then reenter it to confirm

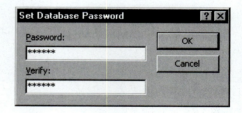

Remove Database Password

- You have to type the password again when you want to remove the password.

- If you forget your password, you will not be able to open the database.

Procedures

Open a Recently Used Database File

From the New File Task Pane:

- Click the file name.

From the menu bar:

1. Click **File**....................`Alt`+`F`
2. Click the file name.

Open a Database File

1. Click **Open** button 📂.

   OR

   a. Click **File**.................`Alt`+`F`

   b. Click **Open**......................`O`

   OR

   - Click **More Files** on the Task Pane.

2. Select file to open.
3. Click **Open**...................`Alt`+`O`

Create a Table with Table Wizard

From the Database window:

1. Click **Tables**.
2. Double-click **Create table by using wizard**.
3. Click **Bu**s**iness**....................`S`

   OR

   Click **Personal**.................`P`

4. Click a sample table.
5. Click a field you want.
6. Click > to add the field.........`>`

   ✓ Click >> to choose all fields from the sample table at once. Click < or << to remove fields from your list.

7. Repeat steps 5–6 as needed.
8. Repeat steps 4–6 to choose more fields from another table.
9. (Optional) Rename a field:

   a. Click a **field** on the Fields in my new table list.

   b. Click **Rename Field**........`R`

   c. Type the new name.

   d. Click **OK**...................`Enter`

10. Click **Next**.............................`N`
11. Type the table name.
12. Choose one:

    - Click **Yes**, **set a primary key for me**.............`Alt`+`Y`

    - Click **No**, **I'll set the primary key**...........`Alt`+`N`

13. Click **Next**.............................`N`

    ✓ If you chose Yes in step 12, skip to step 18 now.

14. Click the down arrow next to **What field will hold data that is unique for each record?**..............`Alt`+`W`

15. Click the primary key field you want.

16. Choose the data type for the primary key field:

    - **Consecutive numbers Microsoft Access assigns automatically to new records**...............`Alt`+`C`

    - **Numbers I enter when I add new records**..`Alt`+`A`

    - **Numbers and/or letters I enter when I add new records**.................`Alt`+`L`

17. Click **Next**.............................`N`

18. (Optional) Set relationships to other existing tables.

    ✓ Relationships are covered in Exercise 9. You can skip them for now.

19. Click **Next**.............................`N`

20. Click **Finish**.........................`F`

Create Table in Table Design View

From the Database window:

1. Click **Tables**.
2. Double-click **Create table in Design view**.

Create a Field in Table Design View

1. Click in the **Field Name column** of an empty row.

2. Type field name.
3. Press **Tab**...........................`Tab`
4. Click the **down arrow** in the Data Type column......🔽
5. Click the field type.
6. Press **Tab**...........................`Tab`
7. (Optional) Type field description.

Select a Field for the Primary Key

1. Click in the field to use.
2. Click **Primary Key** button 🔑 on toolbar.

   ✓ Click Primary Key button again to remove primary key.

   ✓ Click in another field and click Primary Key button to change primary key.

Open a Database Exclusively

1. Click **File**....................`Alt`+`F`
2. Click **Open**......................`O`
3. Move to database file.
4. Click on **Open** drop-down arrow.
5. Click **Open Exclusive**.........`V`

Set Database Password

1. Open database exclusively.
2. Click **Tools**.................`Alt`+`T`
3. Click **Security**....................`T`
4. Click **Set Database Password**..........................`D`
5. Type password.
6. Press **Tab**...........................`Tab`
7. Type password again.
8. Click **OK**.........................`Enter`

Remove Database Password

1. Click **Tools**.................`Alt`+`T`
2. Click **Security**....................`T`
3. Click **Unset Database Password**..........................`D`
4. Type password.
5. Click **OK**.........................`Enter`

Exercise Directions

1. Start Access, if necessary.

2. Open 💿 **AC05**.

3. Start a new table using the Table Wizard.

4. Choose the **Employees** sample table, and transfer all of its fields to the Fields in My New Table list.

5. Remove the BillingRate, EmployeeID, and NationalEmplNumber fields from your Fields in My New Table list.

6. Rename the SocialSecurityNumber field to **SSN**.

7. Name the table **tblEmployees**.

8. Choose to set your own primary key field, and set it to the SSN field.

9. Specify that the primary key field should contain numbers that you will enter yourself.

   ✓ *Do not create any relationships at this point for the new table.*

10. Create a new table using Table Design view with the following information:

Field Name	Data Type
NeedID	AutoNumber
ClientID	Number
Needs	Memo

11. Make the NeedID field the primary key.

12. Save the table as **tblNeeds**.

13. Close the **tblNeeds** table.

14. Close the database and reopen it with Open Exclusive.

15. Create a password for the database.

    ✓ *Start with Tools, Security.*

16. Close and reopen the file by typing the password.

17. Remove the password.

18. Close the database.

On Your Own

1. Open 💿 **OAC05**, which contains a simple database with the beginnings of a sports team roster.

2. Create a new table with the Table Wizard that will hold data about the equipment that the organization owns.

   ✓ *You might want to pull fields from several different sample tables.*

3. Create another new table, this time using Table Design view, to hold data about various categories of membership in the organization.

4. Password-protect the database, and then close it and reopen it.

5. Remove the password.

6. Close the database and exit Access.

Exercise 6

You are in charge of tracking customer feedback for Wee-Soft, a company that produces educational software for children. The company includes a Feedback card with each product, which customers fill out and mail in. You need to create a database that records the feedback from those cards.

Exercise Directions

1. Create a blank new Access database named **AC06**.

2. Create a new table using the fields in Part I of Illustration A.
   - ✓ Do not use spaces in the field names.
   - ✓ Separate the parent's first name and last name into separate fields: FirstName and LastName.
   - ✓ Abbreviate long names; for example, abbreviate the How many children live in your home? field to NumChildren.
   - ✓ Choose appropriate field types (Text or Number). The ZIP field should be set to Text rather than Number.

3. Insert a field at the top of the field list called **CustomerID**, set its type to Number, and make it the primary key.

4. Save the table design; name it **tblCustomers**.

5. Create another table using the fields shown in Part II of Illustration A.
   - ✓ Use the Yes/No field type for the yes/no questions on the form.
   - ✓ Abbreviate the question names; for example, you could use the following abbreviations:

Field Name on Form	Field Name in Table
How old is the child who will use the product the most	ChildAge
Was the program easy to install?	InstallEasy
Did you encounter any installation errors or problems?	InstallProblems
Does your child enjoy using the program?	ChildEnjoy

Field Name on Form	Field Name in Table
Do you think that the program is helping your child learn?	ChildLearn
If you had it to do over, would you buy this program?	BuyAgain
Would you recommend this program to others?	Recommend

   - ✓ Use the Memo type for the Comments field.

6. Add a CustomerID field with the Number type at the top of the field list.
   - ✓ You will use this field to join the two tables in a later exercise.

7. Add a FeedbackID field above the CustomerID field with the AutoNumber type, and make it the primary key.
   - ✓ Since one customer might send in more than one feedback card on different products, the CustomerID field cannot be the primary key field in this table. The FeedbackID field serves that function instead.

8. Save the table design; name it **tblFeedback**.

9. Enter the data from the completed customer form shown in Illustration A into the tables.

10. Close the Access database.

Wee-Soft
Customer Feedback

Part I: About You

Parent Name: _Janice Rand_

Address: _108 Ponting Street_

City: _Macon_ State: _IL_ ZIP: _62544_

Telephone: (_217_) _555-2340_

How many children live in your home? _1_

Part II: About the Product

Product Purchased: _Learning Adventure_

Product Version: _2.0_

Date of Purchase: _3/15/01_

Place of Purchase: _Best Shopper_

How old is the child who will use the product the most? _8_

Was the program easy to install? .... Yes ☒ No ☐

Did you encounter any installation errors or problems? .... Yes ☐ No ☒

Does your child enjoy using the program? .... Yes ☒ No ☐

Do you think that the program is helping your child learn? .... Yes ☒ No ☐

If you had it to do over, would you buy this program? .... Yes ☒ No ☐

Would you recommend this program to others? .... Yes ☒ No ☐

Comments:

I would like to see a version for younger children (ages 3-5).

Exercise 7

Skills Covered:

◆ **Open a Table for Editing in Table Design View**
◆ **Rename a Field** ◆ **Add a Field** ◆ **Delete a Field**
◆ **Reorder Fields** ◆ **Change Field Properties**

On the Job

After you design a table and begin to add data, you may discover that you don't have a place to put some of the information or that the data you have for a field doesn't fit. In this case, you will have to edit the design of the table. You may also want to set some field properties that help speed up data entry or help ensure that you enter the data correctly.

Now that you have begun working with the tables you created in Lesson 1, you realize that they could stand some improvement. You need to add more fields, rename some existing fields, and make changes to field type and field properties,

Terms

Field properties Characteristics of a field that determine how long an entry can be, how the entry will be formatted, whether there should be a default entry, and what can be entered (for example, numbers only or valid dates only).

Notes

Open a Table for Editing in Table Design View

- To edit an existing table's design, select it from the list of tables in the Database window and then click Design Design .

- You can also right-click an existing table and choose Design View.

- While viewing an existing table in Datasheet view, you can also click the Design button ▾ on the toolbar to switch to Design view.

  ✓ *The Design button on the toolbar is also a drop-down list. You can switch among Design view, Datasheet view, PivotTable view, and PivotChart view.*

Table Design view

Field Name   Data types   Description

Field properties for current field

- You can edit the name, data type, and field description just as you did when you created the table initially (see Exercise 5). Even if you created the table some other way, such as with the Table Wizard, you can still edit it in Table Design view.

- When a field is selected, its **field properties** appear in the Field Properties half of the Table Design window. Field properties specify advanced options for the field, such as maximum entry length and default value.

Rename a Field

- To rename a field, move to the Field Name box and edit or replace the name there.

- Any forms, reports, or queries based on this table will need to be changed or recreated; the name change does not automatically transfer to related objects.

Add a Field

- You can add new fields to your table in Design view. Move to a blank row and type the field name you want. Select a data type and enter a description for the field if you like.

- To insert a new field between two existing ones, or at the top of the list, select the field above which the new one should appear and click the Insert Rows button ⇥ on the toolbar (or choose Insert, Rows).

Delete a Field

- If you make a mistake creating new fields, you can remove a field from Table Design view.

- Removing a field deletes all data that was entered in that field from the table.

- To delete a field, select it and press the Delete key, or click the Delete Rows button ⇥ on the toolbar.

- You can also delete a row (that is, a field) by choosing Edit, Delete Rows from the menu bar.

Reorder Fields

- The order in which fields appear in Table Design view does not directly affect objects based on the table, like queries and reports.

- However, when you build reports, queries, forms, and so on with a table, you work with a *field list,* and the order shown on that list is the order shown in Table Design view.

- To move a field on the list, select it by clicking the field selector (the gray square to the left of the field name) to select the entire row. Then drag it up or down on the list.

Select a field and then drag it up or down

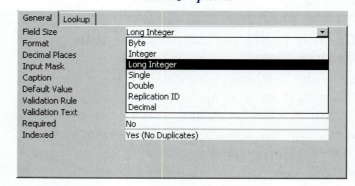

Change Field Properties

- In most cases you do not have to change the field properties at the bottom of the Table Design view window; you can accept the defaults.

- To see an explanation of each field property, click in the property and see the description on the right side of the screen or press F1 to see more detailed help.

Set Field Size

- The field size for Text data types determines the maximum number of characters you can type.

- Choose a Field Size option on the drop-down list for Number data types to determine how large the number can be and if you can have decimal places. For numbers 0 to 255 with no decimal places, choose Byte. For the largest numbers without decimal places, choose Long Integer, and for the largest numbers with decimal places, choose Double.

Field size options

Choose a Format

- Especially for number and date/time data types, choose an option on the Format drop-down list to choose how you want the values displayed. Each drop-down choice shows an example of what the value will look like.

Format options for date/time data types

General Date	6/19/94 5:34:23 PM
Long Date	Sunday, June 19, 1994
Medium Date	19-Jun-94
Short Date	6/19/94
Long Time	5:34:23 PM
Medium Time	5:34 PM
Short Time	17:34

- You can also type codes in the Format box. (See Help for an explanation for codes). For example, type m/d/yyyy for a date type to display 1/1/2002.

Enter a Caption

- A caption is an alternative name for the field. For example, if you have a field called FNAME, you might assign a caption of First Name.
- Captions appear on forms and reports instead of the field name, helping make those objects more understandable.

Enter a Default Value

- You can type a Default Value you want to appear in new records.
- The Default Value is used for the most common value for records but the user can always type over any value in the field.
- An example would be 0 for a sales field or CO for the state field in a table where addresses, for example, are typically located in Colorado.

Use an Input Mask

- The Input Mask is a field template to validate how each character is entered into the field.
- For example, you can show parentheses for a telephone field or dashes for a social security number field. Some of the fields you worked with in the first few exercises used input masks for data like phone numbers and ZIP Codes.

Use Data Validation

- The Validation Rule property allows you to verify data as the user enters it into the table.

- Examples include <Date() (less than today's date), Between 0 and 100, "CO", "TX", or Is Null (blank).
- You can use the Expression Builder by clicking the Build button [...] to the right of the field property box.
  - ✓ *The Expression Builder is a dialog box from which you can choose various fields or objects and math operators. It is a very powerful tool, but not covered in any detail in this book; you might want to experiment with it on your own.*
- The Validation Text appears in a dialog box when a Validation Rule is broken.

Require an Entry

- Required means that a user has to fill in this field before going to another record.
- You might want to set a field to Required if that field is an essential part of the record, such as Invoice # or Customer ID.

Index a Field

- Indexed makes searches and sorts on this field go quicker.
- Do not set all fields to Indexed; instead, set this value only for the field (or two) on which you think you will search or sort most often.

Switch between Views

- To switch to Datasheet view from Table Design view, click the View button on the Standard toolbar. It is the left-most button on the toolbar.
- When in Datasheet view, the button's face changes, and clicking it switches you to Table Design view.
- This button also has a drop-down list, so you can choose other views from it.
- You can also choose a view from the View menu if you prefer.

Procedures

Open a Table for Editing

In Database view:

1. Click **Tables**.
2. Click the table to edit.
3. Click **D**esign .... `Alt`+`D`

Rename a Field

1. Double-click the field's name.
2. Type a new name.

Insert a Field

1. Select the field above which the new field should appear.
2. Click **Insert Rows** button 🔲.
   OR
   a. Click **I**nsert .... `Alt`+`I`
   b. Click **R**ows..................... `R`
3. Click in the **Name column** of the new row.
4. Type field name.
5. Press **Tab** .... `Tab`

6. Click the down arrow 🔲 in the Data Type field.
7. Click the field type.
8. Press **Tab** .... `Tab`
9. (Optional) Type field description.

Delete a Field

1. Select the field.
2. Click **Delete Rows** button 🔲.
   OR
   a. Click **E**dit................ `Alt`+`E`
   b. Click **Delete R**ows .... `R`

Move a Field

1. Select the field.
2. Drag it up or down on the list.

Change Field Data Type

1. Click in the field's Data Type column.
2. Click the down arrow 🔲.
3. Click the new field type.

Set Field Properties

1. Select a field.
2. Click the property you want to change.
3. Type a value, or select from the drop-down list.
   ✓ *For example, to enter a caption, click in the caption field and enter the caption you wish to display.*
4. Repeat steps 2–3 as needed to set properties in other fields.

Switch Between Views

1. Click **V**iew.................... `Alt`+`V`
2. Click **Data**sheet View.......... `S`
   OR
   Click **D**esign View.............. `D`
   ✓ *You can also use the View button, the left-most button on the Standard toolbar, to switch views.*

Exercise Directions

1. Start Access, if necessary.
2. Open ⊘**AC07**.
3. Open the **tblClients** table in Design view.
4. Change the ID field name to **ClientID** and include the description **Client ID number -- don't type anything here; it's automatic**.
5. Change the caption to **Client ID**.
6. Add an InputDate field with a Date/Time data type, Input Date caption, and Short Date format.
   ✓ *In Design view, move to a blank row and type the field name and then change the properties in the bottom of the window. For example, move to the Caption property and type **Input Date** and move to the Format property and choose Short Date on the drop-down list.*
7. Add a BeenToStore field with a Yes/No data type and **Been To Store?** as the caption.
8. Add a Cycles field with a Number data type, **Number of Cycles in Household** in the description, and Byte for the Field Size.
9. Add a WebPage field with a Hyperlink data type.
10. Add a Notes field with a Memo data type.
11. Create captions for all field names that contain more than one word. For example, type **First Name** as the caption for the FirstName field.
12. Save the table's design.
    ✓ *Click the Save button.*
13. Look at the table in Datasheet view.
    ✓ *Click first toolbar button.*
14. Return to Design view.
    ✓ *Click again on the first toolbar button.*
15. Insert a Suffix field (Text type) before the FirstName field.
16. Set the Suffix field's size to 5 characters.
17. Move the Suffix field below the LastName field.
18. Close the **tblClients** table, saving any changes, and open the **tblEmployees** table.
19. Delete the MiddleName field.
20. Close the **tblEmployees** table, saving your changes to it.
21. Close the database.

On Your Own

1. Open the database **OAC05** that you worked with in the On Your Own section of Exercise 5, or open ⊕ **OAC07**.

2. In Design view, edit the **Roster** table to add two new fields. Make one of the fields a different data type. For example, you can add a Position field or a birthday field. If you add a birthday field, you can also add a Yes/No field to indicate whether or not you should send a card.

3. Enter captions for the FirstName, LastName, and SendACard fields that include spaces between the words.

4. Save the changes to the table.

5. Switch to Datasheet view. Scroll the window so you can see the new fields added to the table.

6. Close the table.

7. Close the database and exit Access.

Exercise·8

Skills Covered:

◆ **Switch among Open Objects** ◆ **Insert a Column** ◆ **Delete a Column**
◆ **Move a Column** ◆ **Hide and Unhide Columns** ◆ **Change Datasheet**
Column Width ◆ **Freeze Columns** ◆ **Remove Gridlines**

On the Job

If you plan to work with your data in Datasheet view a lot, you might want to adjust the layout so you can see your data more clearly as you work. You can make changes that affect the underlying table, such as inserting and deleting columns (fields). You can also make cosmetic changes that affect only Datasheet view, such as hiding certain columns, freezing certain columns so they remain visible when you scroll, and adjusting the width of a column.

At the Steel Dreams Cycle Shop, customers can sign up for the shop's quarterly newsletter. You would like to add a field to your tblClients table to indicate whether each customer has signed up. You would also like to make some on-screen formatting changes to the tblClients table so you can enter and view records in it more easily.

Terms

Column header The gray box containing the column (field) name.

Hide To remove an object, such as a column, from view on the screen without deleting it.

Freeze To fix the position of certain columns so that when you scroll to the right, those columns remain on-screen while other columns move.

Gridlines Lines that outline each row and column on-screen.

Notes

Switch among Open Objects

- The bottom of the Window menu shows you a list of all objects that are currently open. Click or type the number on the menu to move to the object.

- You can also see each object or document that is open on the Windows taskbar. Click on the document button on the taskbar to go to the object.

  ✓ You can press F11 to go to the database window, no matter which window is currently displayed.

Switch between open windows within Access with the taskbar or Window menu

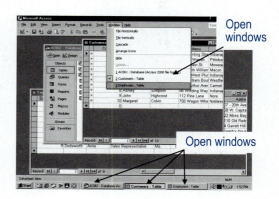

500

Insert a Column

- When you add a column in Datasheet view you are adding a field to the underlying table.

- To insert a column, open the Insert menu and choose Column. The field name will be a placeholder name (Field#); you can change the name as you learned in Exercise 3.

- When you insert a column, it appears to the left of the column that was selected before you issued the insertion command.

A new field inserted between two existing fields

- If you want to add a description, change the data type, or change any properties, you must go to Design view.

- If you have already entered data into the table, you will need to go back and fill in the value for the new field for each record.

- Adding, deleting, and moving a column from a table does not change any forms, reports, or queries that you've created based on that table. You must modify these objects separately. For this reason, it is advantageous to finalize the lists of fields you plan to use in a table before you create forms, reports, or queries based upon it.

Delete a Column

- Deleting a column on the datasheet removes the field from the underlying table, including any data that was stored in it.

  ✓ *To hide a field temporarily without deleting it, see Hide and Unhide Columns later in this exercise.*

- After deleting a field, you cannot get the data back that the field contained, so be careful when deleting fields.

Move a Column

- After you select the column header, you can use the drag-and-drop method to move a column in Datasheet view.

- Click the **column header** to select it. The entire column becomes highlighted. Then drag the column name left or right to move the column.

- A black vertical line shows where the column is going. When you release the mouse button, the column drops into the new location.

Move a column by dragging its header

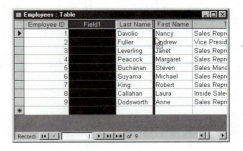

Hide and Unhide Columns

- If you don't want to view or print certain columns in Datasheet view, you can **hide** them. Simply select the column(s) and choose the Hide Columns command from the Format menu. To redisplay the columns, choose the Unhide Columns command from the Format menu and check all the columns you want displayed.

Change Datasheet Column Width

- If the field entry is too wide to see in Datasheet view, you can change the width to display more of the column.

- The column width does not affect the field size in table design; it is only for your convenience when viewing the datasheet.

- You can change column width for automatic fit to the widest entry by double-clicking the double-headed arrow mouse pointer between two column headers.

- Or, change the column width manually by dragging the right border of the column header to the desired width.

Address	City
123 Fox	Denver
818 Winter St.	Denver
154 Newton	Thornton
1551 James	Westminster

Mouse pointer

- You can also change column width by choosing the Column width command from the Format menu and typing the width or clicking the Best Fit button.

Freeze Columns

- If there are too many columns, you may not be able to see all fields at once in Datasheet view.

- If certain columns are important to view at all times, you can **freeze** them so that they remain on the screen as you scroll to the left or right.

- Before you can freeze a column, select it. To do so, move the mouse pointer over a column until the pointer becomes a down arrow. Then click and drag to the left or right to select multiple columns. Then open the Format menu and choose Freeze Columns.

- A divider line appears between the frozen columns and the unfrozen ones.

Three columns have been frozen at the left

Columns to the left of this line are frozen

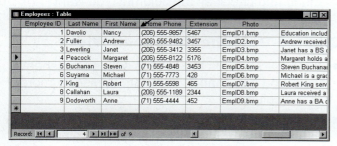

- You can unfreeze columns by choosing the Unfreeze All Columns command from the Format menu.

Remove Gridlines

- If you don't want the **gridlines** between rows and columns to appear on-screen and when you print the datasheet, you can choose to remove the gridlines.

- In the Datasheet Formatting dialog box, you can also change the color of the gridlines and background as well as the effect of shown gridlines.

Datasheet Formatting dialog box

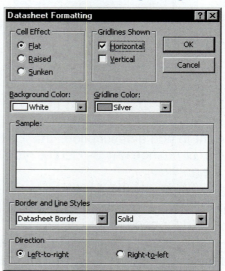

Procedures

Switch among Open Objects

1. Click **Window** .... Alt + W
2. Click number of desired object.
   OR
   Click desired object in
   Windows taskbar.
   OR
   Press **F11** to go to the
   database window. F11
   OR
   - Press **Alt+Tab** .... Alt + Tab

Insert a Column

1. Display Datasheet view.
2. Click in column to right of
   location for new column.
3. Click **Insert** .... Alt + I
4. Click **Column** C
   OR
1. Right-click column header.
2. Click **Insert Column** C

Delete a Column

1. Click on column header you
   want to delete.
2. Click **Edit** .... Alt + E
3. Click **Delete Column** .... M
4. Click **Yes** .... Y
   OR
1. Right-click column header.
2. Click **Delete Column** .... M
3. Click **Yes** .... Y

Move a Column

1. Click on column header you
   want to move.
2. Click and drag the selected
   column to new position.

Hide and Unhide Columns

Hide Columns:

1. Click in column you would like
   to hide.
2. Click **Format** .... Alt + O
3. Click **Hide Columns** .... H

Unhide Columns:

1. Click **Format** .... Alt + O
2. Click **Unhide Columns** ...... U
3. Check column(s) to unhide.
4. Click **Close** .... Enter

Change Datasheet Column Width

Menu:

1. Click in field for column.
2. Click **Format** .... Alt + O
3. Click **Column Width** C
4. Click **Best Fit** .... Alt + B
   OR
   Type column width.
5. Click **OK** .... Enter

Mouse:

- Double-click on right edge of
  field name cell.
OR
- Drag double-headed mouse
  pointer on right edge of field
  name cell.

Freeze/Unfreeze Columns

1. Select one or more columns.
2. Click **Format** .... Alt + O
3. Click **Freeze Columns** .... Z
   OR
   - Click **Unfreeze**
     All Columns .... A

Remove Gridlines

In Datasheet view:

1. Click **Format** .... Alt + O
2. Click **Datasheet** .... E
3. Deselect Gridlines Shown for:
   - **Horizontal** .... H
   - **Vertical** V
4. Click **OK** .... Enter

Exercise Directions

1. Start Access, if necessary.

2. Open ⊙ **AC08**.

3. Open the **tblClients** table.

4. Switch back to the database window without closing the datasheet.

5. Switch back to the datasheet again.

6. Delete the Suffix column.

7. Hide the ClientID column.

8. Increase or decrease the width of each column so that it is large enough to see all data within it but small enough that it does not waste space on-screen.

   ✓ *Double-click the column heading borders.*

9. Freeze the first two columns.

10. Scroll all the way to the right, so the last field is visible on-screen (Notes).

11. Insert a new field to the left of the Notes field, and name it Newsletter.

    ✓ *Select the Notes field, then choose Insert, Column. Then double-click the column header and type the new field name.*

12. Change the field type to Yes/No for the Newsletter field.

    ✓ *Hint: you will need to go into Table Design view.*

13. Return to Datasheet view, and place a check mark in the Newsletter column for Leanne Balto.

14. Unfreeze all columns.

    ✓ *Format, Unfreeze All Columns.*

15. Move the Newsletter field to the right of the Notes field.

16. Turn off the vertical gridline display. (Leave the horizontal gridlines showing.)

17. Unhide the ClientID column.

18. Close the datasheet, saving your changes to it.

On Your Own

1. Open the database ⊙ **OAC08**.

2. Open the **Roster** table in Datasheet view, resize the columns as needed to create a pleasing display that shows all data in each column.

3. Place a checkmark in the Send a Card column for Leo, Shenille, Justin, and John.

   ✓ *The best way to accomplish this is to freeze the first three columns. Then you can scroll to the right and see the Send a Card field on-screen at the same time as the First Name field. Unfreeze when you are finished.*

4. Make a printout that contains just the First Name, Last Name, and Position fields, and that does not contain any gridlines.

   ✓ *To do so, hide all the fields except the ones you want, hide the gridlines for the table, and then print the datasheet. Don't forget to unhide the fields when you're finished.*

5. Insert a new field called OtherTeams, to the left of the Birthday field.

6. Use Design view to create a caption for the new field that includes a space between **Other** and **Teams**. Then go back to Datasheet view to see the change in the column header.

7. Close the table, saving your changes.

8. Close the database and exit Access.

Exercise 9

Skills Covered:

◆ **Relate Tables** ◆ **Enforce Referential Integrity**
◆ **Print Relationships** ◆ **Close Relationships Window**
◆ **Show Related Records**

On the Job

When you create relationships between tables, you associate a field in one table with an equivalent field in another. Then the two tables can be used in queries, forms, and reports together, even if there is not a one-to-one relationship between entries. For example, a Customers table can be linked to an Orders table by the customer ID number, so that you can pull up a customer's contact information on a form when entering a new order.

Since each entry in the tblNeeds table corresponds to a request made by one of the clients in your tblClients table, you have decided to create a relationship between those two tables so they can be used together in queries, forms, and reports.

Terms

Foreign key A field in the child table that is related to the primary key in the parent table.

Parent table The main table of a relationship. When creating a relationship, this is the "one" side of the relationship and contains the primary key.

Child table The second table of a relationship. When creating a relationship, this is generally the "many" side of the relationship. One record from the parent table (such as clients) can be related to one or more records of the child table (such as sales).

Referential Integrity A property of a relationship between two tables. When Referential Integrity is on, the child table cannot contain a foreign key value that does not have a corresponding value in the primary key of the parent table.

Orphan A value in the foreign key that does not have a corresponding primary key in the parent table.

Cascade Update When the primary key field is updated in a relationship, the corresponding foreign key value(s) in the child table's related records automatically updates.

Cascade Delete When a record in a parent table is deleted, Access deletes all the related records from the child table where the value from the primary key matches the value in the foreign key.

Subdatasheet A child table related to the main (parent) table.

Master field The related field from the main (parent) table of the relationship.

Child field Related field from the child table of the relationship.

Notes

Relate Tables

- To create a relationship between two tables, the same field (or equivalents) must appear in both tables. It is desirable, but not required, to use the same field name in both tables.

- In most cases the field is unique in one table (usually the primary key) but not unique in the other. This results in a one-to-many relationship.

- The related field in the second table is called the **foreign key**. The foreign key field must have the same data type as the related primary key, unless the primary key is an AutoNumber type. In that case, the foreign key field must be a Number type.

- The table containing the primary key field being linked is in the **parent table**, and that field is the "one" side of the relationship, indicated by a "1" in the Relationships window.

- The table containing the foreign key field is the **child table**, and that field is the "many" side of the relationship, indicated by an infinity sign (∞) in the Relationships window.

- You set relationships in the Relationships window. In the Relationships window, primary key fields are indicated in bold.

- In the Relationships window, drag a primary key to the related foreign key to open the Edit Relationships dialog box. You can also double-click on the space between two tables in the Relationships window to open the Edit Relationships dialog box.

Relationships window and Edit Relationships dialog box

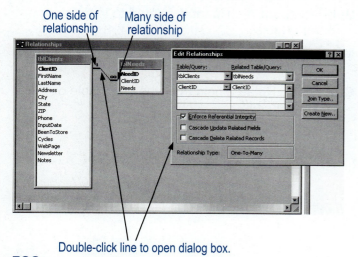

One side of relationship   Many side of relationship

Double-click line to open dialog box.

Enforce Referential Integrity

- On the Edit Relationships dialog box, you can choose to Enforce **Referential Integrity** so that you won't have an **orphan** in the child table. For example, you won't be able to enter an order for a customer that does not exist.

- If you select Enforce Referential Integrity, you can choose two additional options: Cascade Update Related Fields and Cascade Delete Related Records.

- **Cascade Update** Related Fields means that when you change the value in the primary key of the parent table, the related foreign key field in all related records of the child table will automatically change as well. If you don't check this box, Access will give an error message when you try to change the primary key.

- **Cascade Delete** Related Records means that when you delete the record in the parent table, all related records in the child table will delete as well. If you don't check this box, Access will give an error message when you try to delete the record in the parent table.

- When referential integrity is enabled, the parent table shows a "1" next to the primary key and the child table most often shows an infinity symbol next to the foreign key.

- If the two related fields are primary keys, you'll see an "I" on both fields.

Print Relationships

- To print the Relationships window contents, open the File menu and choose Print Relationships. Access creates a report that contains a replica of the window contents. Print it using the Print button on the toolbar or the File, Print command.

Close Relationships Window

- After setting table relationships, click File, Close or click the window's Close button to close the Relationships window.

Show Related Records

- You can view the parent table and the child table in Datasheet view. After you create a relationship between tables, return to the Datasheet view of the parent table and click on the plus sign (+) on the left edge of a record to see the related rows from the child table.

✓ If you have more than one child table, you can change the **subdatasheet** attached to the datasheet. Choose Insert, Subdatasheet and in the dialog box choose the child table and if necessary, identify the **master fields** and **child fields**.

Subdatasheet for current record

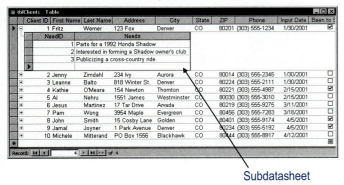

Subdatasheet

Insert Subdatasheet dialog box

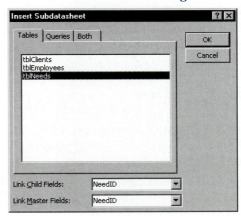

Procedures

Relate Tables

1. Click the **Relationships** button ![icon] on the Standard toolbar.

   OR

   a. Click **Tools** .... Alt + T

   b. Click **Relationships** .... R

   ✓ *Relationships Window opens. The Show Table dialog box may open automatically. Use step 2 if it does not.*

2. Click the **Show Table** button ![icon].

   OR

   a. Click **Relationships** .... Alt + R

   b. Click **Show Table** .... T

3. Click table you want to include.

4. Click **Add** .... Alt + A

5. Repeat steps 5–6 for all tables that are part of relationships.

6. Click **Close** .... Alt + C

7. Drag from primary key of one table to foreign key of another table.

✓ *Edit Relationships dialog box opens. See next procedure to enforce referential integrity.*

8. Click **Create** .... Enter

Enforce Referential Integrity

1. If necessary, open Edit Relationships dialog box again and do steps a–c:

   a. Click **Enforce Referential Integrity** .... Alt + E

   b. Click **Cascade Update Related Fields** .... Alt + U

   c. Click **Cascade Delete Related Records** ... Alt + D

2. Click **OK** .... Enter

Print Relationships

1. Click **File** .... Alt + F

2. Click **Print Relationships**... R

3. Click **Print** button ![icon].

   OR

   a. Click **File** .... Alt + F

   b. Click **Print** .... P

   c. Click **OK** .... Enter

✓ *After printing the relationships, a report remains on-screen.*

4. Click the **Close** button ![X] to close the report.

5. Click **No** to not save changes .... N

Close Relationships Window

- Click the **Close** button ![X].

   OR

1. Click **File** .... Alt + F

2. Click **Close** C

Show Related Records

1. Click **Tables** object button on database window.

2. Click name of table.

3. Click **Open** .... Alt + O

4. Click **+** before record to show subdatasheet for selected record.

5. Click **−** before record to hide subdatasheet.

1. Open main table in Datasheet view.
2. Click **I**nsert .... `Alt`+`I`
3. Click **S**ubdatasheet .... `S`

4. Choose child table.
5. If necessary, choose an option from **Link C**hild **Fields** drop-down list .... `Alt`+`C`
6. Click **OK** .... `Enter`

Exercise Directions

1. Start Access, if necessary.
2. Open 💿 **AC09**.
   - ✓ *Do not open any tables, queries, or forms. You cannot create a relationship to a table already in use.*
3. Relate the ClientID primary key from the **tblClients** table to the ClientID field of the **tblNeeds** table.
   - ✓ *Choose Tools, Relationships. Click Show Table button and add tables. Then drag between the fields.*
4. In the Edit Relationships dialog box, Enforce Referential Integrity between these two tables.
5. Set Cascade Update and Cascade Delete.
6. Print the Relationships window content, and then close the Relationships window. Close the report without saving it.

7. Open the **tblClients** table in Datasheet view.
8. Click on the + before Client ID to see the subdatasheet **tblNeeds** for Fritz Werner.
9. Click on the - before Client ID to close the **tblNeeds** subdatasheet for Fritz Werner.
10. Open the subdatasheet for Jenny Zimdahl.
11. Enter the following need for Jenny: **Wheel covers for 1968 Harley-Davidson**.
    - ✓ *Do not enter the NeedID; it is an AutoNumber field. Simply tab past it.*
12. Close the **tblClients** table, and open the **tblNeeds** table in Datasheet view. Verify that the new record you entered appears there.
13. Close the database and exit Access.

On Your Own

1. Open 💿 **OAC09**.
2. Create a new field in the **Roster** table called CategoryID and set its type to Number.
3. Create a relationship between the **Roster** table and the **Categories** table based on the CategoryID field in each. Enforce Referential Integrity, and turn on Cascade Update Related Fields.
4. Set the category of each player in the Roster table to 1 (Active) except John Smith; set his to 5 (Inactive).
5. In the **Categories** table, try to delete record 5 (Inactive).
6. Go back to the Relationships window and turn off Enforce Referential Integrity for the relationship.

7. Go back to the **Categories** table and try again to delete record 5.
8. Return to the Relationships window and try to turn on Enforce Referential Integrity again.
9. Return to the **Roster** table and change John Smith's status to 4 (Retired).
10. Return to the Relationships window and turn on Enforce Referential Integrity.
11. Close the Access database, saving all changes, and exit Access.

Exercise 10

◆ Critical Thinking

Because of your experience with databases at Steel Dreams, you have volunteered to be the database coordinator for the Central Indiana Shetland Sheepdog Club. The club's secretary has started a database file, but now that you have taken over the project, you want to improve the database using the skills you have learned in the preceding exercises.

Exercise Directions

1. Open the ⊙ **AC10** database.

2. Open the **tblMembers** table.

3. Widen the Address column so that the complete addresses display.

4. Narrow the State and ZIP columns so that they are not wider than required to hold the data they contain.

5. In Datasheet view, move the JoinDate field between MemberID and FirstName.

6. In Table Design view, create captions for the fields in which the field names consist of two or more words, so that there are spaces in the captions between the words. For example, the caption for FirstName would be First Name.

7. Close the **tblMembers** table, saving your changes.

8. Open the **tblDogs** table.

   ✓ Notice that owner names in tblDogs have been entered with both the first and last names in a single field. You know from your work in this lesson that in order to create a relationship between the two tables, you must join the MemberID field from tblMembers to a field in tblDogs, but since MemberID is an AutoNumber field and Owner is a Text field, some work will be required.

9. Edit the entries in the Owner field so they show the owners' MemberID number rather than their names.

   ✓ You will need to open the tblMembers table for reference, and switch back and forth between the two tables using the Window menu or the taskbar.

10. Switch the **tblDogs** table to Table Design view and change the field type of the Owner field to Number.

11. Close all tables, saving your changes.

12. Open the Relationships window and create a relationship between the MemberID field in **tblMembers** and the Owners field in **tblDogs**. Choose all three Referential Integrity checkboxes.

    ✓ When you finish, the Relationships window should resemble Illustration A.

13. Close the Relationships window.

14. Open **tblMembers** in Datasheet view and hide the MemberID field.

15. View the list of Kenneth Kwan's dogs on the subdatasheet.

16. Using a subdatasheet, add the following information for Ralph Orton's dog:

    • Registered Name: **Orton's Spice of Life**
    • Call Name: **Skip**
    • Birthdate: **9/12/00**
    • Coloring: **Sable**

17. Close **tblMembers**, saving your changes.

18. Close the Access database.

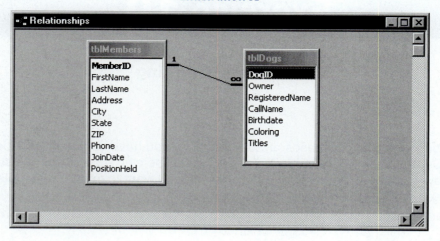

Exercise 11

◆ **Create a Lookup for a Field** ◆ **Create a Value List with the Lookup Wizard** ◆ **Lookup Field Values from another Table**

On the Job

Some fields store data that can contains only a limited range of valid values, such as Marital Status or Gender. To simplify data entry and prevent entry errors, you can create a lookup for a field that presents the user entering records with a list of options from which to choose.

As you have started to fill in data in the Employees table in your Steel Dreams Cycle Shop database, you have noticed that some fields can contain only a few different entries. You would like to create lookups so that there are no typing mistakes in those fields that would prevent you from querying or generating reports based on those fields later.

Terms

Lookup Field A list of values from which to choose when entering information into a field.

Notes

Create a Lookup for a Field

- If you have several values that can appear in a field, consider using a **lookup field**.

- A lookup field appears as a drop-down list during data entry, and you can choose from the list rather than typing an entry. This minimizes data entry errors and ensures consistent formatting (such as capitalization).

- When you enter data for a record, an arrow appears within the lookup field indicating that you can choose from a list of options.

A lookup field during data entry

- You can use the Lookup Wizard to create a lookup field with values you enter.

- You can also use the Lookup Wizard to create a lookup field that looks up values from another table.

- To create a lookup for a field, go to Table Design view and change the field's type to Lookup Wizard. The Lookup Wizard will automatically run.

Create a Value List with the Lookup Wizard

- The Lookup Wizard provides a list in which you can type the values you want to appear on the list.

- This method works well when the values on the list will seldom or never change. If the values change frequently, use the table lookup method instead.

  ✓ *When creating your list, try to enter the values in a useful order. An alphabetical list of states, for example, is easier to use than one that doesn't have a recognizable order. A list of prospect levels might be ordered by the frequency with which they are used.*

Lookup Field Values from Another Table

- If your list often varies, you can create a separate table for the list instead and then create a lookup field that looks into that table.

- Before creating the lookup, you must first create the additional table. Then run the Lookup Wizard and select the table to be used.

- The Lookup Wizard first helps you choose the lookup table or query.

Select the table from which to look up values

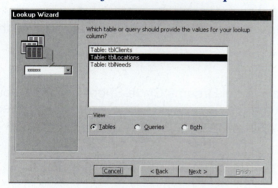

- It then prompts you to choose which fields from the table or query to include.

  ✓ If the table you choose for the lookup has a primary key field, it's a good idea to choose it along with the field that you actually want to appear in the lookup list. You can then hide the primary key field. The users will choose from the "friendly" field, such as the text names, but the entry in the table will be the unique primary key value for that choice.

Select the fields to include

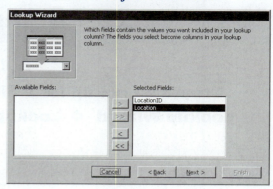

- You next choose how wide to make each chosen field. By default the primary key field is hidden.

Select the column widths for the lookup field(s)

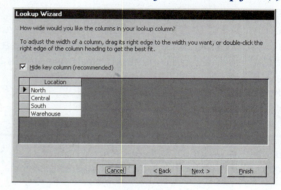

- On the last step of the wizard, you can change the field name. Keep the field name the same if you are changing an existing field and if you've already created a query, form, or report based on this table.

  ✓ If you have text values in a field that you are converting to a lookup field, and the new lookup will contain the numeric ID numbers from the corresponding table rather than the values, creating the lookup will delete all the nonnumeric previous entries in that field, and you will need to reenter them. For this reason, it's best to set up any lookups you want to use before you do much data entry.

Procedures

Create a Lookup List for a Field

1. Open the table in Table Design view.
2. Click in the **Data Type** column for the field.
3. Click the **down arrow** ▾.
4. Click **Lookup Wizard**.
5. Click **I will type in the values that I want** .... Alt + T
6. Click **Next** .... Alt + N
7. Press **Tab** .... Tab
8. Type a value for the list.
9. Press **Tab** .... Tab
10. Repeat steps 8–9 as needed.
11. Click **Next** .... Alt + N
12. Click **Finish** .... Enter

Use a Table as a Lookup

1. Create a **table** to be used as a lookup.
   OR
   Decide on an **existing table** to use as a lookup.
2. Open the **table** containing the field in which you want to use the lookup in Table Design view.
3. Click in the **Data Type** column for the field to receive the lookup.
4. Click the **down arrow** ▾.
5. Click **Lookup Wizard**.
6. Click **I want the look up column to lookup the values in a table or query** ..... Alt + L
7. Click **Next** .... Alt + N

8. Click the table to use.
9. Click **Next** .... Alt + N
10. Click a **field** to include.
11. Click > button .... >
12. Repeat **steps 10–11** as needed.
13. Click **Next** .... Alt + N
14. Adjust column width if desired.
15. Click **Next** .... Alt + N
16. Click **Finish** .... Enter

Use a Lookup Field in Data Entry

1. Click the **down arrow** ▾.
2. Click the **value** you want.

Exercise Directions

1. Open ⊙ **AC11**.
2. Create a new table called **tblLocations** using Design view. Include these fields:

LocationID	AutoNumber
Location	Text

3. Make LocationID the primary key field. Then save the new table.
4. Switch to Datasheet view and enter the following locations:

North
Central
South
Warehouse

5. Close **tblLocations**.
6. Open **tblEmployees** in Design view.
7. Change the data type for the OfficeLocation field to Lookup Wizard.
8. Create a lookup using the Lookup Wizard:
   - Choose to look up the values in the tblLocations table.

- Choose to include both fields from that table.
- Leave the column width and field name at the defaults.

9. Save **tblEmployees**, and switch it to Datasheet view.
10. Enter the following locations using the new drop-down list in the Office Location field:
    - Central: **Taiko, Raoul, and Shanda**
    - North: **Stanley and Peter**
    - Warehouse: **Richard**
11. Switch back to Design view and create a lookup for the DepartmentName field that uses the following internal list:

Administration
Distribution
Sales
Maintenance

12. Save the table, and then go to Datasheet view and change Taiko's department to **Administration** using the new drop-down list.
13. Save and close the table and the **AC11** database.

On Your Own

1. Start Access and open ⊙ **OAC11**.

2. Remove the relationship between the Roster and **Categories** table.

3. In the **Roster** table, set up the CategoryID field to use the **Categories** table to look up values.

4. Save and close all tables, then go back to the Relationships window. Notice that the lookup recreated the relationship between the tables.

5. Edit the relationship to Enforce Referential Integrity.

6. Open the **Roster** table in Datasheet view, and notice that the CategoryID field now shows the text names of the categories rather than the numbers.

7. Enter the caption for the CategoryID field to **Category**.

8. Create a lookup for the Position field with these values:

Catcher	Center field	First base
Second base	Third base	Right field
Left field	Center field	Left-center field
Shortstop	Any	

9. Close the database and exit Access.

Skills Covered:

◆ **Compare Datasheet and Form View** ◆ **Create an AutoForm**
◆ **Create a Form with the Form Wizard**
◆ **Create a Form from Scratch** ◆ **Enter Form Design View**
◆ **Work with Form Design View** ◆ **AutoFormat a Form**

On the Job

If your table contains many fields, entering records in Datasheet view can become cumbersome. Many people find it easier to create a data entry form that displays all the fields on-screen at once, one record at a time.

As you add more information to the Steel Dreams Cycle Emporium database, you're finding that you're spending too much time scrolling through the records in Datasheet view. You've decided to create a form to help you navigate the information.

Terms

Form view The view that generally shows many fields for one record on one screen.

Form Design view The view in which you can edit the controls on a form.

Form selector A box at the upper left of Form Design view, where the two rulers intersect. Clicking this box selects the form as a whole.

Control An item such as a text box, label, or line on a form or report.

AutoFormat A feature that applies a formatting template to a form, including background and fonts.

Notes

Compare Datasheet and Form View

- In Datasheet view, each row is a record and each column is a field.

- If there are many fields, you must scroll to the left/right to move among them.

Datasheet view

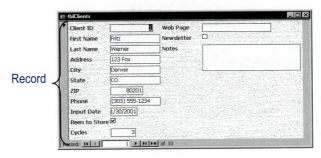

- **Form view**, on the other hand, displays one record at a time, and shows all the fields at once (in most cases).

Form view

- Think of a form as a window to the table. When you add data to a form, it automatically fills in the underlying table(s).

Create an AutoForm

- There are several ways to create a new form. The easiest is to use AutoForm, which creates a simple form containing all the fields in a particular table or query.

- An AutoForm is very basic and might not be formatted exactly the way you want. However, you can edit it in **Form Design view** after you create it.

- You have a choice of several types of AutoForms. The most common type is Columnar, which arranges the field names in columns. The form shown on the preceding page is a columnar AutoForm.

- Other types resemble datasheets, or enable you to drag-and-drop fields into a PivotTable or PivotChart.

- To create an AutoForm, display the Forms tab on the database window, click the New button, and choose the type of AutoForm you want and the table or query on which the form should be based.

Create a Form with the Form Wizard

- The Form Wizard offers a good compromise between the simplicity of an AutoForm and the time needed to create a form from scratch.

- It asks questions in a series of dialog boxes, walking you step-by-step through the process of selecting tables/queries, fields, and formatting.

- To start a form with the Form Wizard, display the Forms tab in the database window and double-click *Create form by using wizard.*

The Form Wizard

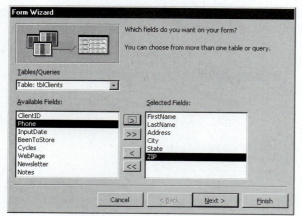

Create a Form from Scratch

- You can also create a new form from scratch in Form Design view. This creates a blank form, onto which you can place fields and other controls.

- To start a form in Design view, double-click Create form in design view from the Forms tab of the database window.

Form selector   *A blank form*

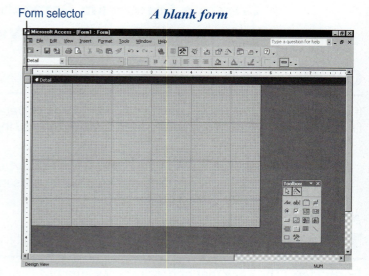

- If you start a new form using the above method, no table or query is associated with it. You can edit the form properties to attach one by right-clicking the **form selector** (the box in the top left corner, where the rulers intersect) and choosing Properties, and then choosing a table or query from the Record Source list on the Data tab.

Edit a form's properties to change the table or query on which it is based

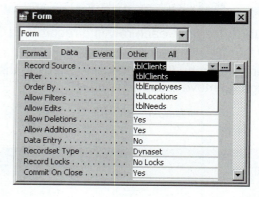

- The attached table/query will become important in Exercise 13, when you learn how to add fields to a form from the Field List.

■ If you would prefer to specify a table or query when creating a new form, use the New button in the database window. The New Form dialog box enables you to choose a table or query before creating the form.

Using the New Form dialog box enables you to select a table or query for your new blank form

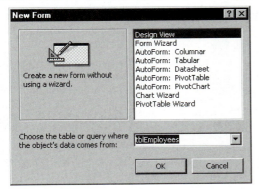

Enter Form Design View

■ If you start a form using AutoForm or the Form Wizard, you might want to edit the form in Design view.

■ You can switch between Form view and Form Design view by making a choice on the View menu or by clicking the View button ![View button] ▾ on the toolbar.

■ You can open a saved form in Design view by selecting it in the database window and clicking the Design button.

Work with Form Design View

■ Each item on a form (or report) is called a **control**. Controls include text boxes where you type in the information for a field, labels to describe the field and the form, lines, and many other items.

■ While you are in Form Design view, click on a control to select it. Selection boxes surround the control.

Form Design view   Selected Control

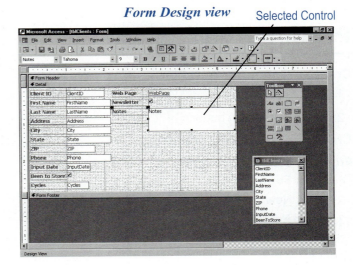

■ You will learn more about controls and Form Design view in upcoming exercises.

AutoFormat a Form

■ When you create a form with the Form Wizard, it asks you to choose a design to apply. The design includes a background, font choices, and color choices.

■ You can choose a different design at any time, or apply a design to a form that was not created with the Form Wizard at all.

■ To choose a different format, choose Format, **AutoFormat** or click the AutoFormat button ![AutoFormat button] on the toolbar.

■ Then select a format from the AutoFormat dialog box that appears.

Select an AutoFormat

Procedures

Create a Columnar AutoForm

1. Open table in Datasheet view.
2. Click **AutoForm** button ▣ ▾ .

Create Any Type of AutoForm

From the database window:

1. Click **Forms**.
2. Click **New** .... `Alt`+`N`
3. Click **AutoForm: Columnar**.
   OR
   Click **AutoForm: Tabular**
   OR
   Click **AutoForm: Datasheet**
   OR
   Click **AutoForm: PivotTable**
   OR
   Click **AutoForm: PivotChart**
4. Click **down arrow** next to Choose the table or query where the object's data comes from.
5. Click the **table** or **query** to use.
6. Click **OK** .... `Enter`

Create a Form with the Form Wizard

From the database window:

1. Click **Forms**.
2. Double-click **Create form by using wizard**.
3. Click **down arrow** next to Tables/Queries.
4. Click **table** or **query**.
5. Click **Available Fields** to include.
6. Click **right arrow button** `>` .
7. Repeat steps 5–6 as needed.
8. Return to step 4 to select fields from other tables/queries if needed.
9. Click **Next** .... `Alt`+`N`
10. Click a layout:
   - **Columnar** .... `Alt`+`C`
   - **Tabular** .... `Alt`+`T`
   - **Datasheet** .... `Alt`+`D`
   - **Justified** .... `Alt`+`J`

   - **PivotTable** .... `Alt`+`I`
   - **PivotChart** .... `Alt`+`V`
     ✓ *Columnar is the most common type, and the one that produces a traditional type of form.*
11. Click **Next** .... `Alt`+`N`
12. Click a format style.
13. Click **Next** .... `Alt`+`N`
14. Type a title.
15. Click **Finish** .... `Enter`

Create a New Form from Scratch

From the database window:

1. Click **Forms**.
2. Double-click **Create form in Design view.**
   ✓ *The above steps do not attach a table or query to the form.*
   OR

From the database window:

1. Click **Forms**.
2. Click **New** .... `Alt`+`N`
3. Click **Design View**.
4. Click **down arrow** ▾ .
5. Click the **table** or **query** name.
6. Click **OK**.

Attach a Table or Query to a Form

✓ *You can also use the following procedure to change which table or query is attached.*

1. In Design view, right-click **form selector**.
   ✓ *The form selector is the box at the top left, at the intersection of the vertical and horizontal rulers.*
2. Click **Properties** .... `Alt`+`P`
3. Click the **Data** tab.
4. Click **down arrow** ▾ next to Record Source.
5. Click **table** or **query** to use.

Switch from Form View to Form Design View

1. Click **View** .... `Alt`+`V`
2. Click **Design View** .... `D`
   OR
   Click **Design View** button ▨ ▾ .

Switch from Form Design View to Form View

1. Click **View** .... `Alt`+`V`
2. Click **Form View** .... `F`
   OR
   Click **Form View** button ▦ ▾ .

AutoFormat a Form

From Form Design view:

1. Click **Format** .... `Alt`+`O`
2. Click **AutoFormat** .... `F`
3. Click the desired format.
4. Click **OK** .... `Enter`

Exercise Directions

1. Start Access, if necessary.

2. Open 💿 **AC12**.

3. Create a columnar AutoForm based on the **tblNeeds** table.

4. Save the new form as **frmNeeds** and close it.

5. Create a form based on the **tblClients** table using the Form Wizard. Use the following settings:
   - Use all the fields.
   - Use a Columnar layout.
   - Choose the Industrial design.
   - Name the form **frmClients**.

6. Change the form's AutoFormat to the Expedition style.

7. Close the form, saving your changes.

8. Start a new, blank form without specifying a table.

9. Attach the **tblEmployees** table to the form using the form's Properties box.

10. Save the form as **frmEmployees** and close it.

11. Close the form and database.

On Your Own

1. In Access open the 💿 **OAC12** database.

2. Create a form for the **Roster** table using the Form Wizard. Include all fields.

3. Save the form with the name **Roster**.

4. Display the form in Design view.

5. Apply an AutoFormat to it.

6. Switch to Form view, and enter a new record into the table using the form.

7. Close the form, saving your changes.

   ✓ *When you enter Form view through Form Design view, the design changes you have made to the form are not immediately saved. They are not saved until you close the form, whether from Form view or Form Design. That's why you're prompted to save your changes when you close the Form view in step 7.*

8. Create a new form for the Equipment table using AutoForm:Tabular. Name it **Equipment**.

9. Close the database and exit Access.

   ✓ *In these On Your Own exercises, you are creating some forms and tables with the same names. Although this is not such a great idea from a database design perspective because of the potential for confusion, many people do create databases that way in real life. These exercises give you the opportunity to try it out and see whether you find it confusing or convenient.*

Skills Covered:

◆ **Add a New Field to a Form** ◆ **Select Controls on a Form**
◆ **Delete a Control from a Form** ◆ **Move Controls** ◆ **Reset Tab Order**
◆ **Change Control Formatting** ◆ **Resize Fields and Other Controls**
◆ **Align Controls** ◆ **Form Backgrounds**

On the Job

Regardless of how you created your form, you might like to make some changes to it. The AutoForm and Form Wizard methods create nice basic forms, but sometimes field labels are truncated or there is not enough space between fields. In addition, you might want to add more fields to the form that you originally omitted, or change the text formatting.

> You have decided to add another field to your tblClients table, and you want it to appear on the frmClients form as well. You would also like to apply some additional formatting on the form to make it more attractive.

Terms

Field List A floating box in Form Design view containing the names of all the fields in the associated table or query.

Control A field, label, option group, box, or other object on a form.

Selection handles Black squares around the border of a control that indicate it is selected.

Tab order The order in which the insertion point moves from field to field on a form.

Notes

Add a New Field to a Form

- To add a new field, drag it from the **Field List**. If the Field List does not appear, click the Field List button on the toolbar.

Adding fields to the form

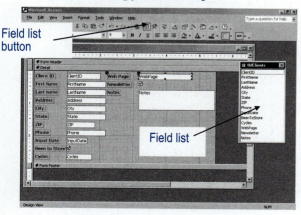

Field list button

Field list

✓ Don't worry if you don't get the positioning exactly right; you can move the field and/or its associated label at any time.

Select Controls on a Form

- To select a field or other **control**, click on it. **Selection handles** appear around it.

- When you select a field, its associated text label is also selected, so that moving the field also moves the label. It works in reverse, too: clicking a text label also selects the associated field.

A selected field and label

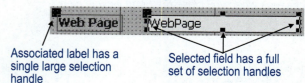

Associated label has a single large selection handle

Selected field has a full set of selection handles

■ To select multiple controls, click on the first control, hold the Shift key down, and click on additional controls. You can also "lasso" controls by dragging a box around them.

Delete a Control from a Form

■ To delete a field or other control, select it and press the Delete key.

■ When selecting a field for deletion, click on the field itself, not its associated text label. If you select the label before pressing Delete, only the label will be deleted, and the field itself will remain.

Move Controls

■ To move a field, select it, and then position the mouse pointer anywhere over it *except* over a selection handle, so the pointer becomes an open hand. Then drag to a new location.

Drag a field and its label as a pair with the open-handed mouse pointer

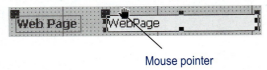

Mouse pointer

■ The field and its associated label move as a pair when you drag with the open-hand mouse pointer.

■ If you want to move the field or the label separately from one another, click on the one you want to move and then drag it by the large selection handle in the top-left corner. The mouse pointer appears as a pointing finger in this case.

Drag a field or label separately by dragging by the selection handle in the upper-left corner

Mouse pointer

Reset Tab Order

■ If you add or move controls, you may want to reset the order in which each field appears when you or another database form user presses Tab to navigate in the form.

■ You might also want to set an alternate **tab order** so that users don't have to tab past a seldom-used field such as Suffix or Middle Initial during data entry.

■ Choose the Tab Order command from the View menu.

■ In the Tab Order dialog box, drag the fields into the order you want them.

■ Click the Auto Order button to set the order from left to right and top to bottom based on the fields' current positions on the form.

Set tab order

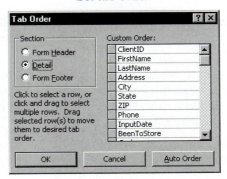

Change Control Formatting

■ While a control on a form is selected, you can click on the Formatting toolbar to do any of the following:

- Change the item's font type or font size.
- Change whether the text is bold, italic, or underlined.
- Choose left-aligned, centered, or right-aligned.
- Choose the color of the background, text, and border.
- Choose the style and width of the line or of the border surrounding the box.

■ All of the above formatting features work just as they do in other Office programs that you might already be familiar with.

■ When you select multiple objects, you can use the Formatting toolbar to change more than one at a time.

■ If you make an error while formatting, choose the Undo command immediately after a change.

■ To copy all enhancements, select a control with the enhancements you want to copy, click the Format Painter button and then click the object to change.

- If you want to change multiple objects with Format Painter, double-click the Format Painter button and click on each control you want to change. Click the Format Painter button again to turn it off.

Resize Fields and Other Controls

- To resize a control, drag any selection handle except the one in the upper-left corner.

- To resize several controls at once, select them all and then resize one; the others will resize, too.

- If you need to resize a text box so that text is not truncated, double-click a selection handle to automatically expand or contract the size so that the text exactly fits.

- To make a group of controls the same size, select them all, choose Format, Size, and then select To Widest, To Narrowest, To Tallest, or To Shortest.

Align Controls

- One of the challenges in creating a form from scratch is to get all the fields precisely aligned with one another.

- To align several fields, place the first one where you want it, and then choose Format, Align. You can choose alignment options such as Left, Center, Top, or To Grid.

  ✓ *The dots on the background in Form Design view form the grid referred to in the To Grid option.*

Form Backgrounds

- You can change the color of any part of a form by clicking on the background in Design view, and then clicking the drop-down arrow of the Fill/Back Color button on the Formatting toolbar and choosing a color from the palette.

Make a choice from the Fill/Back Color palette

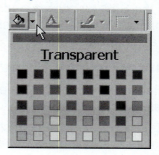

- You can add a logo or other graphic as a background for the form. You do this through the Property sheet of the form.

- Double-click on any object to open its Property sheet. For the form, use the Form selector above the vertical ruler and to the left of the horizontal ruler.

Property sheet

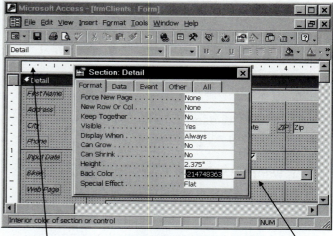

Double-click on the Form Selector to Open the Property Sheet for the Form

Build button

- The Build button appears on the toolbar and as an ellipses (…) button at the end of some properties when you select them, such as the Picture property. This button opens a dialog box that allows you to make a choice from a list.

- If you want the picture repeated throughout the form, change Picture Tiling to Yes.

Procedures

✓ *All the following procedures take place in Form Design view.*

Display the Field List

1. Click **V**iew .... [Alt]+[V]
2. Click **Field L**ist .... [L]
   OR
   Click the **Field List**
   button [▤].

Add a Field

- Drag field from field list to form.

Select a Field or Other Control

- Click on a **control** to select it.
OR
1. Click on first control.
2. Hold down **Shift** and click on additional controls to select them.
OR
1. Position **mouse pointer** outside first control.
2. Drag a box around all controls to select.

Delete a Field or Other Control

1. Select **control** to delete.
   ✓ *If deleting both a field and its label, click on the field itself, rather than the label.*
   ✓ *If deleting only a field label, select the label.*
2. Press **Delete key** .... [Del]

Move a Field or Other Control

Move a field and label as a pair, or move other type of control:

1. Click on **field** you want to move.
2. When the mouse pointer is a hand ✋, drag control and attached label and drop in new location.

Move a field or label separately:

1. Click on **field** or **label** you want to move.
2. Point **mouse pointer** to upper-left selection handle.
3. When mouse pointer is a pointing hand 👆, drag and drop to new location.

Reset Tab Order

1. Click **V**iew .... [Alt]+[V]
2. Click **Tab** Order .... [B]
3. Click **A**uto Order .... [A]
   OR
   Drag fields into order you want.
4. Click **OK** .... [Enter]

Change Control Formatting

1. Select **control** you want to format.
2. Click desired button from Formatting toolbar.
OR
1. Click **F**ormat .... [Alt]+[O]
2. Click desired change from Format menu.

Resize Controls

1. Click on **control** you want to size.
2. Point to **selection handle** so mouse pointer becomes an arrow  .
3. Drag to resize.
OR
1. Change first item to proper size.
2. Select first item and other items to size.
3. Click **F**ormat .... [Alt]+[O]
4. Click **S**ize .... [S]
5. Click **To W**idest .... [W]

Align Controls

1. Move first item to proper location.
2. Select first item and other items to align.
3. Click **F**ormat .... [Alt]+[O]
4. Click **A**lign .... [A]
5. Click desired alignment option.

Change Form Background Color

1. Click the **form background**.
2. Click down arrow on **Fill/Back Color** button [▨▾].
3. Click the desired **color**.

Use a Background Image

1. Click the **Form Selector**.
2. Click **V**iew .... [Alt]+[V]
3. Click **P**roperties .... [P]
4. Click **Format** tab.
5. Scroll down to **Picture** field and select it.
6. Click **Build** button [⋯] next to Picture field.
7. Choose a file that contains the picture you want.
8. Click **O**pen .... [Enter]
9. Click the **Close** button [✖].

Remove a Background Image

1. Click the **Form Selector**.
2. Click **V**iew .... [Alt]+[V]
3. Click **P**roperties .... [P]
4. Click **Format** tab.
5. Delete the entry in the **Picture** field.
6. Click the **Close** button [✖].

Exercise Directions

1. Start Access, if necessary.

2. Open ⊘**AC13**.

3. Open the **tblClients** table in Table Design view, and add a new field directly above the Notes field called **WhenBuy**.

4. Set the field type to Text and set its caption to **Anticipated Purchase**.

5. Close the table, saving changes.

6. Open the **frmClients** form in Form Design view, and add the new field to a blank spot on the form.

7. Move the field to the right (separately from its label) so that the label and field do not overlap.

8. Remove the colon from the end of the Anticipated Purchase label.

9. Rearrange the form fields so that the new field is directly above the Notes field.

10. Resize the Web page, Anticipated Purchase, and Notes fields, and right align the text boxes, as in Illustration A.

11. Use the Align feature to make sure that those three fields are precisely aligned at their right edges.

12. Reset the tab order so that the WhenBuy field falls between Newsletter and Notes.

13. Select all the field labels and italicize them (as a group).

14. Change the font color of the field labels to dark green.

15. Set the background color for the Detail area of the form to pale yellow.

16. Remove the background image from the form so that the yellow background shows.

17. Preview the form in Form view; then return to Form Design view and save your changes.

18. Close the form and database.

Illustration A

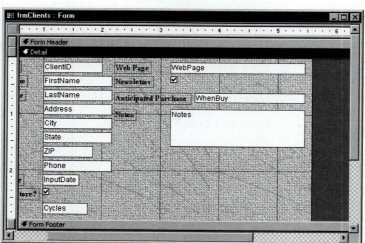

On Your Own

1. Open ⊘ **OAC13**.

2. Create a new blank form with the **Equipment** table associated with it.

3. Manually add and arrange the fields from the Field List.

   ✓ *You can enlarge the form size by dragging its bottom-right corner of the grid area outward.*

4. Format the fields in whatever way you think is attractive. This can include:

- Aligning fields with one another
- Changing font, text size, and color
- Rearranging fields
- Increasing or decreasing field or label size
- Changing the background color or adding a background picture

5. Check the tab order, and reset it if needed.

6. Save the new form as **Equipment2**.

7. Close the database and exit Access.

Exercise 14

Skills Covered:

◆ **Use Form View Toolbox** ◆ **Add Labels** ◆ **Add Lookups to Forms**
◆ **Add an Option Group** ◆ **Add a List Box or Combo Box**

On the Job

You might want to dress up your basic form with some extra text labels, or place special controls on the form that make data entry easier for the user. Some of these extras include option groups, list boxes, and combo boxes. They're similar in function to the lookups you created in Exercise 11, but work only within the form on which they are created.

As store employees use the frmClients form you have created, you notice that they are making some data entry errors. You think that perhaps creating option groups or combo boxes for some fields will help improve data entry accuracy. You would also like to add a note to clarify the purpose of the Notes field.

Terms

Toolbox A floating toolbar in Form Design view that provides buttons for adding various types of controls to the form.

Option group A set of buttons or check boxes on a form that present a finite set of acceptable values from a lookup.

List box A box on a form that lists a finite set of acceptable values for a field from a lookup.

Combo box Like a list box, except the user can also enter new values of none if the existing values in the lookup are appropriate.

Label A frame containing descriptive text on a form. A label is different from a text box in that a text box can be bound to a field in a table, while a label exists only on the form.

Text box A box on a form that contains text and that can be bound to a field in a table. Fields on a form appear as text boxes, for example.

Notes

Use Form View Toolbox

- The **Toolbox** appears in Form Design view. It can be used to add items (controls) to a form.

- If the toolbox does not appear, click the Toolbox button on the toolbar.

Display the Toolbox if it does not already appear

Toolbox button

- The toolbox contains a Wizard button near the top. It is an on/off switch; by default it is on.

The Toolbox

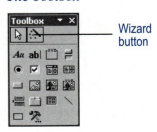

Wizard button

- When the Wizard feature is on, a wizard walks you through the process of creating certain types of controls (such as **option groups** and **list/combo boxes**).

- When the Wizard button feature is off, all types of controls can be manually placed on the form without using a wizard.

- Using the wizards makes learning about the different kinds of controls easier.

Add Labels

- A **label** is a descriptive bit of text that you add to a form that is not associated with a field in a table. The label exists only on the form.

- To add a label, click the Label button **Aa** on the Toolbox and then drag on the form to create the label's frame. Then type your text.

Create a new label from the Toolbox

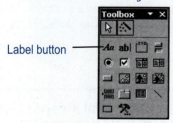

Label button

- The button to the right of the Label button is the **Text Box** button **Aa**. You can use it to create unbound text boxes that will later be associated (manually) with fields. Beginners will not do this very often.

Add Lookups to Forms

- Access offers various types of lookups you can add on a form. These are like the lookups you can set for fields in Table Design view (see Exercise 11), except you create them from the form.

- You do not need to create lookups on the form for fields that have already been set up with the Lookup Wizard in Table Design view; these appear with lookups by default when placed on a form.

- The default setting for a field with a lookup is Combo Box when placed on a form, but you can change that setting. To do so, go to the Lookup tab for that field's properties in Table Design view and set the Display Control setting to Text, List Box, or Combo Box.

Add an Option Group

- An option group is a group of mutually exclusive buttons representing various lookup choices. You can make them appear as square buttons, as round dots, or as check boxes.

An option group

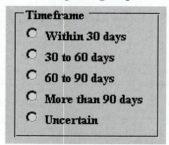

- The Option Group Wizard makes it easy to create an option group on a form. Click the Option Group button in the Toolbox and then click or drag on the form where you want it to appear.

Create an option group from the Toolbox

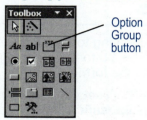

Option Group button

- Then step through the wizard to complete the option group.

The Option Group Wizard at work

- A limitation of an option group is that you cannot specify that it take its values from a table or query; you must manually type in the values to appear in the group.

- If you need the values to come from a table or query, use a list box or combo box instead.

Add a List Box or Combo Box

■ List boxes and combo boxes work the same way, except a combo box enables users to enter additional values, while a list box restricts them to the choices you provide.

■ Both a list box and a combo box can either take their values from a list you provide or from a table or query, just like a lookup (from Exercise 11).

✓ *Make sure you have completed Exercise 11 before working on this exercise, so you will understand the concepts behind lookups.*

■ A combo box, by default, appears as a single-line text box with an associated drop-down list. Users can type in the text box normally, or select from the list.

■ If there are more entries for a list box than will fit in the allotted space on the form, Access automatically adds a scroll bar to the list box.

A combo box (left) and a list box (right)

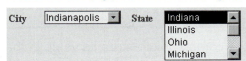

■ To create a list box or combo box, click the corresponding button on the Toolbox and then follow the Wizard's prompts. Just like with the Lookup Wizard, you can specify a table or query, or you can type the values you want.

Create a list box or combo box

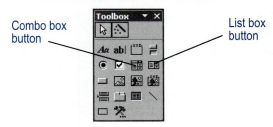

Adding Other Types of Controls

■ The Toolbox has other buttons as well, for other kinds of controls you can place on a form.

■ To find out what type of control a button inserts, point to it and review the ScreenTip that appears.

■ Some of the more common additional controls include Image, Page Break, Tab Control, Line, and Rectangle. These can be used to dress up the form or to organize a complex form into manageable sections.

Procedures

Display the Toolbox
From Form Design view:

• Click on **Toolbox** button ⚒.
OR
1. Click **View** .... Alt + V
2. Click **Toolbox** X

Add a Label
1. Click **Label** button *Aa*.
2. Drag diagonally on form.
3. Enter text.
4. Resize box as necessary.

Create an Option Group
1. With the Control Wizard on, click **Option Group** button.
2. Click on form.
3. Type **label names**, pressing Tab after each.
4. Click **Next** .... Alt + N

5. Do one of the following:
   a. Click **down arrow** ▼.
   b. Click choice of **default label**.
   OR
   • Click **No, I don't want a default**.
6. Click **Next** .... Alt + N
7. Accept the default values.
   OR
   Enter values to correspond to each label.
8. Click **Next** .... Alt + N
9. Click **down arrow** ▼.
10. Click the **field** to store the value in.
11. Click **Next** .... Alt + N
12. Click the **button type** to use.
13. Click the **button style** to use.
14. Click **Next** .... Alt + N
15. Type a caption.
16. Click **Finish** .... Enter

Create a List Box or Combo Box using Values from a Table or Query
1. Click **List Box** button.
   OR
   Click **Combo Box** button.
2. Click **Next** .... Alt + N
3. Click the table to use.
   OR
   a. Click **Queries** .... Alt + Q
   b. Click the query to use.
4. Click **Next** .... Alt + N
5. Click the field from which to take data.
6. Click **>** [>].
   ✓ *Usually you will want only one field. However, in some cases you might want two or more, such as First Name and Last Name.*
7. Click **Next** .... Alt + N

8. Drag edge of sample list to adjust width.

9. Click **Next**.................... `Alt`+`N`

10. Click **down arrow** `▼`.

11. Click field to store value in.

12. Click **Next**.................... `Alt`+`N`

13. Type a label for the list or combo box.

14. Click **Finish**...................... `Enter`

Create a List Box or Combo Box by Typing Values

1. Click **List Box** button `⊞`.

   OR

   Click **Combo Box** button `⊞`.

2. Click **I will type in the values that I want**.................. `Alt`+`T`

3. Click **Next**.................... `Alt`+`N`

4. Type the number of columns you want.

   ✓ *One column is sufficient in most cases.*

5. Press **Tab**. .... `Tab`

6. Type a list entry.

7. Repeat steps 5-6 as needed.

8. Drag edge of list to adjust width.

9. Click **Next** .... `Alt`+`N`

10. Click **down arrow** `▼`.

11. Click field to store value in.

12. Click **Next** .... `Alt`+`N`

13. Type a label for the list or combo box.

14. Click **Finish** .... `Enter`

Exercise Directions

1. Start Access, if necessary.

2. Open ⊘ **AC14**.

3. Open **frmClients** in Form Design view.

4. Move the Notes field down, and add a label above it with the following text:

   Enter any information gathered during conversation with customer, such as spouse name, hobbies, or favorite brands.

5. Format the text in the new label as 8-point italic.

6. Switch to Form view to check your work. It should resemble Illustration A. Then switch back to Form Design view.

7. Delete the City field from the form, and create a combo box in its place called **City** that takes its values from the following list:

   **Denver
   Indianapolis
   Noblesville
   Beech Grove
   Lafayette**

8. Set the combo box to store its value in the City field, and name the combo box **City**.

9. Delete the State field from the form, and create a list box called **State** in its place that takes its values from the **tblStates** table and stores its value in the State field.

10. Use Format Painter to copy the label formatting from existing fields and field labels to the new ones.

11. Resize/reposition fields as needed. You might want to move some fields into the second column to make room for the new State list box, as in Illustration B.

12. Close the database.

Illustration A

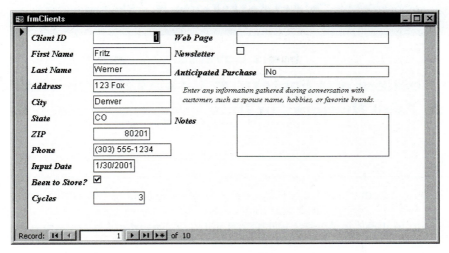

Illustration B

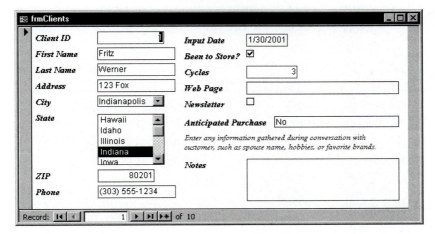

On Your Own

1. In Access, open the database ⊘**OAC14**.

2. Display the **Equipment** table in a datasheet. Which fields do you think would benefit from a combo box, list box, or option group?

3. Create a new table based on one of the fields you identified in step 2, and include values in that table for all the current field entries.

   ✓ *For example, if you decided to create a combo box for Item Type, your new table would include Ball, Bat, Miscellaneous, and Safety.*

4. Open the **Equipment2** form in Form Design and create a combo box based on the table you just created that replaces the existing field on the form.

5. Create other combo boxes, list boxes, or option groups for any other fields that you identified in step 2.

   ✓ *For example, you might change the Insured field to Yes and No option buttons in an option group.*

6. Close the database and exit Access.

Exercise 15

Skills Covered:

◆ **Work with Headers and Footers** ◆ **Display Header and Footer Areas**
◆ **Add Page Numbers or Date and Time** ◆ **Page Setup**

On the Job

Form headers and footers help users to identify a form's purpose and to give the form a professional, attractive appearance both on-screen and in printouts. If you think you might want to print your records in Form format at some point, the Page Setup features in Access will be helpful in setting margins and page orientation.

You would like to add a title to the form you have been working on, and you think the form header might be a good place to add it. You would also like to print a copy of your client list using the form and would like to adjust the margins and page layout before you print.

Terms

Page header Same as form header except it applies to individual printed pages instead of to the form as a whole.

Form header An area at the top of the form, above the Detail area, in which you can enter titles, explanatory text, graphics, or anything else that applies to the form as a whole.

Page footer Same as form footer except it applies to individual printed pages.

Form footer Same as form header, except it appears below the Detail area.

Margin The space on all sides of a page where no printing appears.

Orientation The direction the printing appears on the page, either across the width of the page (portrait) or the length of the page (landscape).

Notes

Work with Headers and Footers

- Headers and footers on a form provide a place to enter objects that relate to the entire form or entire page, rather than to an individual record.

- On-screen, headers and footers appear at the top and bottom of a form (or page, on a multipage form), providing information. For example, you might enter a form title in the Form Header area.

- When you print in Form view, the headers and footers appear on the printout.

- There are two kinds of headers: page header and form header.

- Whatever you enter in the **page header** appears in each page of a multipage form or printout. You might place a page numbering code here, for example, to print a page number at the top of each page.

- Whatever you enter on the **form header** appears only once, at the top of the on-screen form or at the beginning of the printout.

- The **form footer** displays in Form view and on the last page of a printout. The form's footer is a good place for controls that you always want to see if the detail section requires scrolling.

- Footers work the same way; you can have a **page footer** and a **form footer** that appear on the bottom of each page and at the bottom of the last page, respectively.

Display Header and Footer Areas

- By default, only the Detail area appears in Form Design view. To display form headers/footers or page headers/footers, choose them from the View menu.

- You can drag the bars for each section up or down to increase or decrease the section's size.

- Refer to the vertical and horizontal rulers on-screen to help gauge the size of the header or footer when printed. However, the actual size that appears on-screen will depend on the monitor size and resolution.

Form with all headers and footers displayed

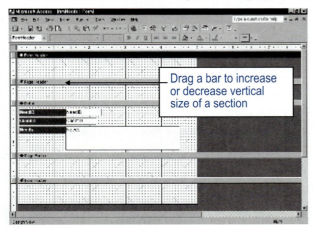

Drag a bar to increase or decrease vertical size of a section

- The page header and footer prints at the top and bottom of the page but does not display in Form view.

- After displaying the header or footer area, use the Toolbox tools to place objects into it, such as text labels.

Add Page Numbers or Date and Time

- You can also add controls that will show page numbers and the date in the header or footer section of a form.

- To do so, click on the section in which you want the item, and then use the Page Numbers or Date and Time command on the Insert menu.

- These commands place codes in text frames on the form.

- Page Numbers codes can be inserted only in a page header or footer, and do not display anything on-screen.

- Date and Time codes can be inserted only in a form header or footer, and *do* display in the on-screen form.

Page Setup

- Page Setup enables you to change the way your datasheet or form appears on the page. You can set Page Setup settings from either Form Design or Datasheet views.

  ✓ *Page Setup settings are saved with a form, but not with a datasheet. The settings go back to the defaults when you close a table after changing page setup. If you want to save settings with a datasheet, create a datasheet-style form.*

- The Page Setup dialog box contains tabs for Margins and Page for both Datasheet and Form view, and an additional tab, Columns, in Form view.

- To open the Page Setup dialog box, choose File, Page Setup.

Margins Tab

- Use the **Margins** tab of the Page Setup dialog box to change the margins.

  ✓ *Before you print, use File, Print Preview to check what the page settings will look like.*

- The Print Data Only option specifies that the field names not be printed, only the data within the fields will be printed.

Set print margins

Page Tab

- Use the Page tab of the Page Setup dialog box to change the print **orientation** to landscape or portrait.

Set page orientation and size

Set number and width of columns

- You can also specify a paper size and source, and choose to use a specific printer for the print job. This can be useful if you have multiple printers with different capabilities.

Columns Tab

- Here you can set the spacing between rows and the number and width of columns in which to print.

✓ *The width of the detail section plus the left and right margins must be equal to or less than the width of the page for the form to print correctly. If you get two pages for each form when you expect one, try reducing the margins or decreasing the form width in Form Design view.*

Procedures

Display or Hide Headers or Footers

From Form Design view:

1. Click **View** .... Alt+V
2. Click desired option to select or delete:
   - **Page Header/Footer** ..... A
   - **Form Header/Footer** ..... H

Insert Page Numbering

From Form Design view:

1. Click **Insert** .... Alt+I
2. Click **Page Numbers** .... U
3. Select page number format:
   - **Page N** .... Alt+N
   - **Page N of M** .... Alt+M
4. Select location:
   - **Top of Page** .... Alt+T
   - **Bottom of Page** .... Alt+B

5. Select **Alignment**:
   - **Left**
   - **Center**
   - **Right**
   - **Inside**
   - **Outside**
6. Click **OK** .... Enter
   ✓ *Control is inserted on document.*
7. If desired, drag control to different location.

Insert Date and Time

From Form Design view:

1. Click **Insert** .... Alt+I
2. Click **Date and Time** .... T
3. Select options.
4. Click **OK** .... Enter
5. If desired, drag control to different location.

Page Setup

Change page orientation:

1. Click **File** .... Alt+F
2. Click **Page Setup** .... U
3. On **Page** tab, select orientation:
   - **Portrait** .... Alt+R
   - **Landscape** .... Alt+L
4. Click **OK** .... Enter

Change margins:

1. Click **File** .... Alt+F
2. Click **Page Setup** .... U
3. On **Margins** tab, enter margins:
   - **Top** .... Alt+T
   - **Bottom** .... Alt+B
   - **Left** .... Alt+F
   - **Right** .... Alt+G
4. Type margin in inches.
5. Click **OK** .... Enter

Change columns settings:

1. Click **File** .... Alt + F
2. Click **Page Setup** .... U
3. On **Columns** tab, enter settings for:
   Grid Settings:
   - **Number of Columns** .... Alt + C
   - **Row Spacing** .... Alt + W

Column Size:
- **Width** .... Alt + I
- **Height** .... Alt + E

Column Layout:
- **Down, then Across** .... Alt + O
- **Across, then Down** .... Alt + N
4. Click **OK** .... Enter

Exercise Directions

1. Start Access, if necessary.
2. Open ⊚ **AC15**.
3. Open **frmClients** in Design view.
4. Enlarge the Form Header area to about 3/4" in height.
5. Change the form header's background color to match that of the Detail area.
6. Create a **Clients** label in the center of the form header area (using the Label tool in the Toolbox), and format it as Arial 28-point bold. See Illustration A.
7. Display the page header/footer, and place a page number code in the footer. Make the page number right-aligned.
8. Save your work.
9. Use Print Preview to see how the printout will look; then return to Form Design view for the form.
   ✓ *Click the Print Preview button on the toolbar. When you are finished, click the Design View button to return.*

10. Insert a date code only (no time) in this format: dd/mm/yy in the form header.
11. Move the date code to the form footer.
    ✓ *By default the form footer has no area; drag the Form Footer bar downward to create some space for it.*
12. Change the form footer's background color to match that of the Detail area.
13. Change the page margins to .5" on all sides.
14. Change the page layout to Landscape.
15. Change the number of columns to 2.
16. Preview your printout in Print Preview.
    ✓ *Access reports a problem. Why?*
17. Change the paper size to Legal.
18. Preview the printout again.
19. Close the database, saving all changes.

Illustration A

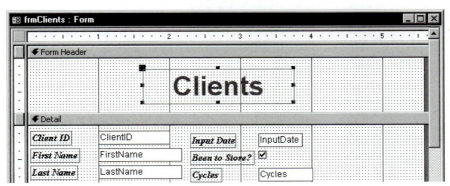

On Your Own

1. In Access, open ⊙ **OAC15**.

2. Add a title to the **Equipment2** table in the Form Header area. Use any font, size, and color you like.

3. Place page numbering in the page footer area. Then turn off the page footer with the View menu. What happens?

4. Experiment with various settings to find settings that allow you to print on the fewest number of pages possible. Use different sizes of paper, different orientations, and different numbers of columns. You can adjust the form size too if that will help.

5. When you find the right combination of settings, print your work.

6. Close the database and exit Access.

Exercise 16

◆ **Critical Thinking**

As you learn more about Access, you have new ideas for improving the database for the Central Indiana Shetland Sheepdog Club that you worked on in Exercise 10. Now that you know about lookups and forms, you would like to use some of those elements to enhance the club's database.

Exercise Directions

1. Open the ⊚AC16 database.
2. Create a new form using AutoForm:Columnar based on the **tblDogs** table.
3. Save the form as **frmDogs** and close it.
4. Create a new form using the Form Wizard based on the **tblMembers** table.
   - Use all the fields.
   - Use a columnar layout.
   - Choose the Expedition style.
   - Name the new form **frmMembers**.
5. In Form Design view, add the title **Membership List** to the form header area. Center the label and format it as 18-point.
6. Switch to Form view to review the changes. Use Window, Size to Fit Form if necessary to view the entire form.
7. Close the form, saving your changes.
8. Create a new table called **tblPositions** with a single field called **Positions**. Make that field the primary key.
9. Create these entries in the new table:
   - **President**
   - **Vice-President**
   - **Secretary**
   - **Treasurer**
10. Use the newly created table as a lookup for the PositionHeld field in the **tblMembers** table (in Table Design view). Then close **tblMembers**, saving changes.
11. Return to **frmMembers** in Design view, and delete the PositionHeld field.

12. Re-add it to the form from the Field List, so that the new lookup takes effect there.
13. Format and reposition the added field and its label to match the other fields on the form.
14. Save and close the **frmMembers** form, and open the **frmDogs** form in Form Design view.
15. Add the title **Dogs** to the form header and format it attractively.
16. Add a page number code to the page footer.
17. Replace the Owner field with a list box that takes its values from the FirstName and LastName fields from the **tblMembers** table.
18. Rearrange the other fields on the form, and make the form larger overall, if necessary, to accommodate the larger size of the new list box. Illustration A shows an example, previewed in Form view.
19. Replace the Coloring field with a Coloring list box that uses the following values, and stores its value in the Coloring field in **tblDogs**:
   - **Bi-black**
   - **Bi-blue**
   - **Blue merle**
   - **Sable**
   - **Sable merle**
   - **Tri-color**
20. Resize the new list box so that it takes up only a single line.
21. Switch to Form view to inspect your work; then save the form and close it.
22. Save your work and exit Access.

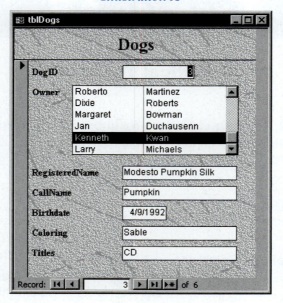

Exercise 17

Skills Covered:

◆ **Find and Replace Data** ◆ **Find Data**
◆ **Replace Data** ◆ **Search Using Wildcards**

On the Job

One of the primary purposes of a database is to store data so you can look it up later. You use the Find procedures to locate data and Find and Replace to locate data and change it to something else. You can search on an exact match or use wildcards that help you find information if you don't know the exact spelling.

You have received some updated information for some of your customers and need to enter the changes into your tblClients table. Since you find it easier to work with a form than with raw data in a datasheet, you will make these changes to tblClients from the frmClients form.

Terms

Find To locate text within a record that matches characters you type.

Replace To substitute new text after finding a string of text.

Wildcard A character (? or *) that signifies one or more unspecified characters when finding text.

Notes

Find and Replace Data

- You can **find** and **replace** data in Datasheet view and in Form view.

- Move to the field where you want to search for data (unless you want to search all fields). Then open the Find and Replace dialog box to begin your search.

Find Data

- The Find and Replace dialog box contains options for how you want to search for data. The options include:

  - *Find What*
    Type the word or phrase you want to look for. You can include **wildcards**. You can also pick from your last six searches.

  - *Look In*
    This defaults to the current field. You can choose this field for the entire table or form from the drop-down list.

Find and Replace dialog box, Find tab

  - *Match*
    Using the text in the Find What text box, find an exact match using the entire field, any part of the field, or the start of the field.

  - *Search*
    You can choose to search the entire list or in a particular direction through the records.

- *Match Case*
  Check this box if you want the capitalization of the Find What entry to match the case of the value in the field exactly. For example, "Broadway" will not match with "broadway."

- *Search Fields as Formatted*
  Find exact matches for date and number formats. When checked, 2/21/99 will not match February 21, 1999. When unchecked, these two dates will match.

■ Click Find Next to find the next record that matches (in the direction indicated by the Search box).

Replace Data

■ When you have some text that needs to be replaced with other text, use the Replace tab of the Find and Replace dialog box. For example, if area code 303 changes to 720, you can replace each occurrence of 303 with 720.

Find and Replace dialog box, Replace tab

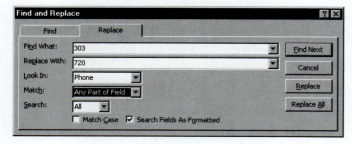

- In the Replace With text box, you type the text that will replace Find What text.

■ Click the Find Next button to find a match.

■ If the text is found, choose Replace to replace the text in the current record or Replace All to replace all occurrences in all records.

■ Unless you are sure you won't create errors in your database, you should choose Replace rather than Replace All. You can undo only the last replace.

Search Using Wildcards

■ You can use wildcards in the Find What text box if you don't know the exact spelling, but do know some of the characters.

■ The most common wildcard is the asterisk (*). The asterisk can replace any number of characters. For example, Sm*th will find Smyth, Smith, and Smooth.

■ You can use more than one asterisk. Sm*th* will find Smith, Smooth, Smothers, and Smythe.

■ To speed up filling in the Find or Replace dialog boxes, you don't need to change the Match choice from the default Whole Field option. Type *Broadway* to find a record when Broadway is anywhere within the field.

■ The question mark (?) wildcard is a substitute for an unknown single character. ?oss will find Boss and Hoss, but not Floss.

Procedures

Find and Replace Data

Find data:

1. Click field to match.
   OR
   In Datasheet view, click field selector or any field in column.

2. Press **Ctrl + H** .... Ctrl+H
   OR

   Click the **Find** button .
   OR

   a. Click **Edit** .... Alt+E

   b. Click **Find** .... F

3. Type data to find in **Find What** text box.

4. Click **Look In** list box to select current field, form, or table.

5. Click **Match** list box to select desired option:
   - **Start of Field**
   - **Any Part of Field**
   - **Whole Field**

6. Click **Match Case** .... Alt+C
   to restrict search to the case that you typed in Find What box.

7. Click **Search Fields As Formatted** .... Alt+O
   to match dates and numbers as they are displayed in the field.

8. Click **Search** list box to select desired option:
   - **All**
   - **Up**
   - **Down**

9. Click **Find Next** .... Alt+F

10. Click **Close** button
    when finished.

Replace data:

1. Click field to match.
   OR
   In Datasheet view, click field selector or any field in column.

2. Press **Ctrl+H** .... Ctrl+H
   OR

   a. Click the **Find** button 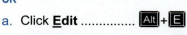.

   b. Click the **Replace** tab.
   OR

   a. Click **Edit** .... Alt+E

   b. Click **Replace** .... E

3. Type data to replace in **Fi̲nd What** text box.

4. Type replacement data in **Repl̲ace With** text box.

5. Click **Loo̲k In** list box to select current field, form, or table.

6. Click **Matc̲h** list box to select desired option:
   - **Start of Field**
   - **Any Part of Field**
   - **Whole Field**

7. Click **Match C̲ase** .... Alt + C to restrict search.

8. Click **Search Fields As F̲ormatted** .... Alt + O to match dates and numbers as they are displayed in the field.

9. Click **S̲earch** list box to select desired option:
   - **All**
   - **Up**
   - **Down**

10. To replace text in current field:
    - Click **R̲eplace** .... Alt + R

11. To replace text in all matching fields at once:
    - Click **Replace A̲ll** ... Alt + A

12. To view next matching field:
    - Click **F̲ind Next** ...... Alt + F

13. Click **Close** button ☒ when finished.

Search Using Wildcards

In **Fi̲nd What** text box on Find or Replace tab:
- Type text and * to replace multiple characters.
- Type text and ? to replace one character.

Exercise Directions

1. Start Access, if necessary.

2. Open 💿 **AC17**.
   - ✓ *You might want to turn on gridlines again (if you turned them off in an earlier exercise.) It will make it easier to work with the data in datasheets. To do so, choose Tools, Options and mark the appropriate check boxes on the Datasheet tab.*

3. Open **frmClients** in Form view.

4. Jesus Martinez was recently in the store and bought another cycle. Find his record, and mark the Been to Store check box. Also change his Cycles entry to 1.
   - ✓ *Locate his record with the Find command.*

5. Leanne Balto sent you an announcement that she got married and changed her last name to Harvey. Find her record and change her name. Her address is now **9820 Berry Road**, **Beverly, CO 88988**, and phone **303-555-1223**.
   - ✓ *Search the LastName field for Balto and use the Replace feature to replace it with Harvey for Leanne's record.*

6. Jamal Joiner (or Joyner?) calls for information. While he's on the phone, you look up his record and update his information. Find his record using a ? wildcard.
   - ✓ *Use Jo?ner to find his record, since you are not sure about the spelling of his last name.*

7. Close the database.

On Your Own

1. In Access, open 💿 **OAC17**.

2. Open **frmRoster**.

3. There is a spelling error in the Roster table. The city "Noblesville" has been spelled "Nobelsville" in some records. Make the correction using Replace All.

4. Search for all instances of the word "base" in the position field. Make sure that you have at least one person in the roster who can cover each base (First, Second, and Third).

5. Find Bianca Sellerton's entry and change her phone number to **555-7899**.

6. Use wildcards to look up the street address of the person whose house number is 8173.

7. Close the database and exit Access.

Exercise 18

On the Job

When you have unorganized lists, the data is sometimes difficult to digest or use. If you sort records by the field(s) such as last name, you can look up the information quickly. If you are interested in the most or least active customers or largest orders you can quickly view this information through sorting. You learned about basic sorts back in Exercise 1; in this lesson you will learn about more complex sorting options.

Not everyone at Steel Dreams has a computer at his or her workstation. However, it is very important for employees to be able to look up information quickly about a client, so you will print the tblClients table for employees to refer to. Some employees need a printout sorted by Last Name and First Name; others need one sorted by State and City.

Terms

Multiple sort To use more than one field to sort. If there are duplicates for the first field, the second field is used to organize the records for each set of duplicated values in the first field.

Sort To arrange records alphabetically or numerically according to a specific field.

Ascending From A to Z or 1 to 9.

Descending From Z to A or 9 to 1.

Notes

Multiple Sorts

- With a **multiple sort** you can **sort** by more than one column. For example, you could sort by State and then by City. All the records containing CA as the State, for example, would be grouped together, and then all the records with San Diego as the City would be grouped within the CA grouping.

- You can sort on multiple columns through Datasheet view but not Form view.

- You can sort fields with Text, Number, Currency, Date/Time, and Yes/No data types.

- You cannot sort fields that have Memo, Hyperlink, or OLE Object data types.

- You can sort in **ascending** order (A to Z or 1 to 9) or **descending** order (Z to A or 9 to 1).

  ✓ You can also use filters and queries to sort records (see later exercises in this lesson).

Change Column Order

- When you sort by multiple columns, columns are sorted from left to right. You cannot specify a different sort priority.

- However, you can temporarily rearrange the columns before you sort so that the column by which you want to sort first appears to the left of the other columns that should be subordinate in the sort.

- If the fields you want to use for the sort are not adjacent, you can rearrange them before sorting, just as you did in Exercise 8.

- If you do not want the rearrangement to be permanent, do not save your changes when you close the datasheet.

Remove a Sort

- If you save a table or form after sorting, the sort order becomes a property of the table or form. You can change this property by sorting on a different field.

- To undo any sort, choose Records, Remove Filter/Sort.

- If there is no primary key, records within a table (and its corresponding forms) are placed in input order when you remove the sort.

- If there is a primary key, records are ordered by the primary key when you remove the sort.

Procedures

Change Column Order

1. Click on column header.
2. Drag column to desired position in table.

Multiple Column Sort

1. Drag across field names to select columns.
2. Click **Ascending** button 🔼 or

   Descending button 🔽.

   OR

   a. Click **Records** .... Alt + R
   b. Click **Sort** .... S
   c. Select **Ascending** or **Descending** ...... A or C

Remove Sort

1. Click **Records** .... Alt + R
2. Click **Remove Filter/Sort** .... R

Exercise Directions

1. Start Access, if necessary.
2. Open ⊙ **AC18**.
3. Open **tblClients** in Datasheet view.
4. Hide the following columns: ClientID, Input Date, Been to Store, Cycles, WebPage, Newsletter, Anticipated Purchase, and Notes.
   - ✓ Format, Hide Columns.
5. Change Fritz Werner's state from Indiana to **IN**, for consistency with the other entries.
6. Widen the Address column enough that no addresses are truncated.
   - ✓ Double-click between columns to autosize them.
7. Narrow the State and ZIP columns so there is no wasted space.
8. Sort the list by Last Name, then First Name. To do this:
   - Move the Last Name column to the left of the First Name column.
   - Select the Last Name and First Name columns.

- Click the Sort Ascending button.
   - ✓ In this data, there don't happen to be any people with the same last name as another, so sorting only by last name would have given the same effect. However, as your database grows, you will probably have duplicate last names and need this multi-field sort capability.

9. Print the datasheet.
10. Close the datasheet, saving your changes to it; then reopen it. Notice that your sort, field arrangements, and hidden fields are all just as you left them.
11. Remove the sort, and move the Last Name column back to its previous position.
12. Sort the list by State, then by City.
13. Print the datasheet.
14. Remove the sort.
15. Unhide all the hidden fields.
16. Close the datasheet, saving your changes.
17. Close the database.

On Your Own

1. Open ⊚ **OAC18**.

2. Open the **Roster** table in Datasheet view.

3. Create a printout of the roster sorted by ZIP code and then by last name. The printout must contain at least the names, addresses, phone numbers, and positions, and must fit on a single sheet of paper.

   ✓ *Need some help? Here's how to do it:*

   - Hide all the fields except those containing names, addresses, phone numbers, and positions.

   - Sort the list in Ascending order by ZIP code and then by Last Name. (You'll need to move the ZIP column.)

   - After sorting, move the ZIP column back to its normal position.

   - Preview the printout, and then close Print Preview.

   - Return to the datasheet and make any adjustments needed for a better printout. You might change the page layout to Landscape, for example, and/or adjust column widths.

   - Print the datasheet.

4. Close the datasheet, saving your changes to it.

5. Reopen the datasheet and remove the sort.

6. Unhide all the hidden columns.

7. Close the database, saving changes, and exit Access.

Exercise 19

Skills Covered:

◆ **Filter a Record Subset** ◆ **Filter By Selection**
◆ **Filter Excluding Selection** ◆ **Filter For Entry** ◆ **Filter By Form**

On the Job

Sometimes you will want to look at all records that match certain criteria. Although you could sort a list, it may be easier to isolate (filter) only the records you want to see. Then when you use the navigation buttons or keys to move through records, you see only relevant records.

Business at the cycle shop is slow. You've decided to call all customers who have visited the store to invite them to a reception with free food and snacks. You need to print a list of those customers so your assistant can call them. You also want to create a list of your most loyal customers—those who subscribe to your newsletter and who have visited the shop—and send a mailing to them that includes a 25% off coupon for purchases made on the day of the reception. Finally, you want a list of customers who do not live in Denver so you can send them a mail-order form.

Terms

Filter To display only certain records.

Filter By Selection To filter based on the data in current field.

Filter By Form To show a form that allows you to enter criteria for the filter.

Notes

Table Datasheet toolbar   Filter By Form

Filter By Selection   Apply (or Remove) Filter/Sort

Filter a Record Subset

- When you **filter** records, you see a subset of the records in the datasheet or form.

- The number of records that match the filter displays to the right of the navigation buttons at the bottom of the datasheet or form.

- You can filter using toolbar buttons (see above), by right-clicking a field and choosing a filter from the shortcut menu that appears, or by choosing a filter from Records, Filter. Not all filter types are available using all filtering methods.

- Here are types of filters available:
  - Filter By Selection: choose only records that match the current field. Available from the toolbar, shortcut menu, and Records menu.
  - Filter Excluding Selection: choose all records that don't match the current field. Available only from the shortcut menu and the Records menu.
  - Filter For: choose records containing a field that matches what you type. Available only from the shortcut menu. This is a short version of Filter By Form that works with only a single field at a time.

- Filter By Form: choose records where one or more field entries match what you type. Available only from the toolbar and Records menu.

- Advanced Filter/Sort: create more complicated filters in conjunction with sorting. Available only from the Records menu and covered in Exercise 20.

Filter By Selection

- The Filter By Selection option is the easiest way to filter your records.

- When you click in a field and then choose Filter By Selection, Access shows all records that match the value that is in the field.

- You can also select a portion of a field and then choose Filter By Selection. If the selection is at the beginning (or end) of the field, Access will show all records that have the same text at the beginning (or end) of the field.

- If you select text in the middle of the selection before Filter By Selection, Access shows all records that have the selected text anywhere in the field.

- You can do Filter By Selection more than once to limit your records further. For example, in the tblClients table, you could filter for CO and then filter for Cycles=3. After you apply the second filter, you will find all client records where the State is Colorado and Cycles is 3. Such a multi-level filter might be more easily accomplished with Filter By Form, however.

Filter Excluding Selection

- When you want to find all records that do not match the current field, choose Filter Excluding Selection.

Filter For Entry

- If you want to type in the text that will become the filter, choose Filter For, then enter the text. You can use wildcards in specifying the criteria. (See Exercise 17 for information on using wildcards.)

Filter By Form

- Filter By Form gives you options to filter on multiple fields and to use wildcards in the filter criteria.

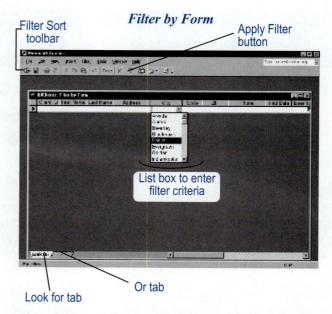

Filter by Form

Filter Sort toolbar

Apply Filter button

List box to enter filter criteria

Look for tab

Or tab

- The Filter By Form opens a form that allows you to do the following in each field in either Datasheet or Form view:
  - Click the drop-down arrow to the right of the field and choose from the entries in the field.
  - Type the value you want.
  - Type the value with a wildcard asterisk (*) for any number of characters or question mark (?) for one character.
  - Type > (greater than), < (less than), >= (greater than or equal to), or <= (less than or equal to) and then a number.
  - Type Between *firstvalue* and *secondvalue*. For example, Between 1/1/99 and 3/31/99.

- If you have entries in multiple fields on the Look for tab, Access finds all records that match for all entries. For example, if Smith is in Last Name and Denver is in City, records that have both Smith and Denver show.

- If you have an entry on the Look for tab and then an entry on the Or tab(s), Access finds all records that match any of the entries. For example, if Smith is on the Look for tab and Denver is the Or tab, Access will find all the Smiths whether or not they live in Denver and all people who live in Denver whether or not their name is Smith.

- After you enter in your criteria in the Filter By Form window, you can:

- Choose the Save to Query button 💾 to create a query from these criteria. The Load from Query button 📇 brings in criteria from a query. (Queries are covered in later exercises.)

  ✓ *Filters are saved automatically with the table or form if you close the object with the filter applied; the Save to Query feature merely saves them as separate entities. To get rid of a filter so that it is not saved with the table or form, clear the filter grid and then choose Apply Filter.*

- Click Close `Close` to return to the form or datasheet without filtering data.

- Click Clear Grid ✕ to remove all entries and start over.

- Click Apply Filter ▽ to filter the data.

Procedures

Apply or Remove a Filter

Apply filter:

1. Create a filter (see following procedures).

2. Click **Apply Filter** button ▽ .

   OR

   a. Click **Records**.........`Alt`+`R`

   b. Click **Apply Filter/Sort**...`Y`

Remove filter:

- Click **Remove Filter** button `▽` .

   OR

1. Click **Records**.............`Alt`+`R`

2. Click **Remove Filter/Sort**....`R`

Filter By Selection

   ✓ *Filters and displays records that match selected item.*

1. View desired form or datasheet.

2. Select desired item in field location.

3. Click **Filter By Selection** button `▽✓` .

   OR

   a. Click **Records**.........`Alt`+`R`

   b. Click **Filter** ....`F`

   c. Click **Filter by Selection**.................`S`

   OR

   a. Right-click field.

   b. Click **Filter by Selection**.................`S`

   ✓ *Records that match selected item will appear.*

Filter Excluding Selection

1. Select field data you want to exclude.

2. Right-click field.

   OR

   Click **Records**............`Alt`+`R`

3. Select **Filter Excluding Selection** ....`X`

   ✓ *Records that do not contain selected data will appear.*

Filter For Entry

1. Right-click field in datasheet or form.

2. Select **Filter for:** ....`F`

3. Type filter value, using wildcards if desired.

4. Press **Enter** ....`Enter`

   ✓ *Records that match will appear.*

Filter By Form

   ✓ *Filters and displays records that meet specified criteria.*

1. View desired form or datasheet.

2. Click **Filter By Form** button `▣` .

   OR

   a. Click **Records** ....`Alt`+`R`

   b. Click **Filter**.....................`F`

   c. Click **Filter By Form** ......`F`

3. Type entries in the appropriate fields, using wildcards if desired.

   OR

   a. Click on desired field list box arrow.

   b. Select desired entry.

4. Click **Apply Filter** button ▽ .

   OR

   a. Click **Filter**.............`Alt`+`R`

   b. Click **Apply Filter/Sort**...`Y`

   ✓ *Result of filter will appear.*

Exercise Directions

1. Start Access, if necessary.
2. Open 💿 **AC19**.
3. Open **tblClients**.
4. Use Filter By Selection to display only the customers who have visited the store.

   ✓ *When you click the check box to select a field, be careful you do not change the check box state for that record. You might need to click it a second time to restore its original state.*

5. Hide all fields except First Name, Last Name, and Phone.
6. Print the datasheet.
7. Without removing the first filter, use Filter By Form to further filter the list to show only customers who have visited the store *and* who subscribe to your newsletter.

   ✓ *Unhide the Newsletter column and Filter By Selection.*

8. Hide the Phone field, and unhide the Address, City, State, and ZIP fields.
9. Print the datasheet.
10. Remove the filter to show all clients.
11. Using Filter Excluding Selection, exclude all records for customers who do not live in Denver.
12. Print the datasheet.
13. Remove the current filter, and then using Filter By Form, create a filter that finds people who *either* have been to the store or receive the newsletter.
14. Print the datasheet
15. Unhide all fields and remove all filters.
16. Close the database.

On Your Own

1. Open 💿 **OAC19**.
2. Open the **Roster** table in Datasheet view.
3. Use any filtering method to create separate roster datasheet printouts for players in each city.
4. Remove all filters.
5. Display the **Roster** form, and filter out players from Noblesville.
6. Without removing the existing filter, add another criterion: show only players with Active in the Category field.
7. Print the filtered roster from form view.
8. Close the database, saving all changes, and exit Access.

Skills Covered:

◆ **Advanced Filter/Sort** ◆ **Set Up Sorting** ◆ **Criteria Row**

On the Job

If you have multiple sorts and criteria you want to use to filter a table or form, use Advanced Filter/Sort. For example, you may want to sort a datasheet by Last Name and then by First Name and also display only the records for newsletter subscribers.

> The mailing service that you use for your newsletters has requested that you provide the list of newsletter recipients sorted by ZIP Code. You need to pull out the addresses of the people who have signed up for the newsletter and sort the list by ZIP Code, then print the list.

Terms

Recordset A subset of a table created by a filter or a query.

Criteria Specifications that a record must meet in order to be included in the recordset.

Relational operators Characters you use to define criteria, such as > (greater than sign).

Dynaset A recordset in which records can be updated to change the underlying table(s).

Notes

Advanced Filter/Sort

- If you want to combine filtering and sorting, choose Advanced Filter/Sort. It is very similar to a query, which you'll learn about in Exercise 21.

  ✓ *Any filters/sorts saved with the table appear in the grid. Clear the grid before starting your new filter/sort if needed.*

Advanced Filter window

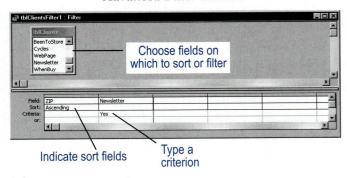

Choose fields on which to sort or filter

Indicate sort fields

Type a criterion

- The top part of the Advanced Filter window shows a Field List. You need not select all fields that you want to appear—only the ones by which you want to filter or sort.

  ✓ *This is one way in which an advanced sort/filter differs from a query. With a query, any fields that you do not select are not included in the result. With an advanced filter/sort, all fields are included in the result.*

- To choose a field for sorting or filtering, double-click on a field in the Field List, drag the field list to the grid, or click the drop-down arrow on the right of the field box and choose the field.

- When you apply the filter, a portion of the table (**recordset**) displays in Datasheet view.

Set Up Sorting

- To sort by a field, double-click the Sort box under the field name in the Advanced Filter window, or click the drop-down arrow and choose Ascending or Descending.

- Ascending will sort fields in alphabetical order from A-Z or numbers from lowest to highest.
- Descending will sort fields in reverse alphabetical order from Z-A or numbers from highest to lowest.

Criteria Row

- The **criteria** row of the Advanced Filter window allows you to enter characters to filter data.
- You can type the complete value in the criteria row or use wildcards. For example, you can type Denver or Den* to choose Denver.
- For a Yes/No field, you can type Yes or No. For a date/time field, you can type a specific date or time.
- You can also type the following **relational operators** or text in the criteria row:

Use:	For and example:
<	Less than. <30
<=	Less than or equal to. <=#1/1/99#
>	Greater than. >100
>=	Greater than or equal to. >=Date()
<>	Not equal to. <>"Denver"
Like	Match a pattern of characters. Like "Den*"
And	Match 2 or more conditions. >5 And <10
Or	Match any of the conditions. "CO" or "CA"
Between … And	Match values in a range. Between #1/1/98# And #1/15/98#
In	Select from a list of values. In("NM","NY","NJ")
Is Null	If there are no values in the field.
Is Not Null	If the field has any values.

- After you type characters in the criteria cell under a field, press Tab to see if Access accepts your entry.
- Access may change the entry to include characters that it needs to apply the filter. Text is surrounded by quotation marks, a date is surrounded by pound signs (#), and Access adds the keyword *Like* when you use wildcards.
- An exception is with a Yes/No field; since Yes and No are exact values and not text strings, Access does not use quotation marks.
- If you type multiple entries on one criteria row, Access finds only records that meet all the criteria.
- If you type separate criteria in the Criteria and Or row(s), Access finds records that meet *any* of the criteria.

Procedures

Start an Advanced Filter/Sort

1. View desired form or datasheet.
2. Click **Records** .... [Alt]+[R]
3. Click **Filter** .... [F]
4. Click **Advanced Filter/Sort**... [A]

Select a Sort/Filter Field

- Drag desired field from field list to field cell in lower part of window.

Sort by a Field

1. Click in **Sort** box.
2. Click **down arrow** [▼].
3. Click **Ascending** or **Descending**.

Filter by a Field

1. Place insertion point in Criteria cell.
2. Enter a criterion.
   - ✓ Use wildcards or relational operators as needed.

Apply an Advanced Filter/Sort

- Click **Apply Filter** button .

OR

1. Click **Filter** .... [Alt]+[R]
2. Click **Apply Filter/Sort**........ [Y]

Remove an Advanced Filter/Sort

- Click **Remove Filter** button .

OR

1. Click **Records** .... [Alt]+[R]
2. Click **Remove Filter/Sort**.... [R]
   - ✓ Removing an advanced filter/sort is the same as removing any other filter or sort.

Delete a Filter/Sort

From the Advanced Filter/Sort grid:

1. Click **Edit** .... [Alt]+[E]
2. Click **Clear Grid**.................[G]

Exercise Directions

1. Start Access, if necessary.

2. Open ⊘ **AC20**.

3. Open **tblClients**.

4. Use an advanced filter to show records without ZIP Codes.

   ✓ *Records, Filter, Advanced Filter/Sort. Use Is Null in the criteria cell.*

5. After you look up the records, enter the ZIP Code **80211** for each of them.

6. Remove the filter.

7. Use a filter to find clients with no date in the InputDate field.

   ✓ *Advanced Filter Input Date Is Null.*

8. Enter today's date as the input date for the found records.

9. Remove the filter.

10. Use an advanced filter to find records of people who have Yes (a check mark) in the Newsletter field, and sort the list in Ascending order by ZIP Code.

11. Print the list.

    ✓ *Adjust print settings as desired, as you learned in earlier lessons. You might want to use Landscape page orientation, for example.*

12. Use an advanced filter to find records of people who have an InputDate between January 1, 2001 and March 1, 2001, and sort the list by Last Name.

13. Print the list.

14. Remove the filter.

15. Close the database.

On Your Own

1. Open ⊘ **OAC20**.

2. Open the **Roster** table.

3. Use the Advanced Filter/Sort feature to sort the table both in ascending order by last name and first name and to display only those records of people in the city of Noblesville.

4. Print the resulting **dynaset**.

5. Remove the filter.

6. Use the Advanced Filter/Sort feature to sort the table in descending order by last name, and display only players whose ZIP Code begins with 462 and whose Category is Active.

7. Print the resulting dynaset.

8. Remove the filter.

9. Use Advanced Filter/Sort to find records with no birthdates, and make up birthdates for those people.

10. Remove the filter.

11. Close your database, saving all changes, and exit Access.

Exercise 21

Skills Covered:

◆ **Compare Query to Sorts/Filters** ◆ **Ways to Start a New Query**
◆ **Create a Query with a Wizard** ◆ **Create a Query in Query Design View** ◆ **Choosing Fields for a Query** ◆ **Sorting Records in a Query**
◆ **Criteria in Query** ◆ **Display the Query Datasheet** ◆ **Save a query**

On the Job

When advanced sorting/filtering isn't enough, you're ready to move up to queries. With a query, you can create a very powerful sort/filter specification and save it to be reused over and over again.

As manager of Steel Dreams, you need to create some permanent lists for customer mailings, prospects, and phone numbers. The owner also asked questions about some characteristics of the customers, which you can answer with queries.

Terms

Query A defined set of operations to be performed on a table (or on the results from another query).

Select query A query that sorts and filters a table or other query to extract certain fields and records based on criteria you specify. This is by far the most common type of query.

Query Design view A window that allows you to choose the fields in a query, to sort, and to set criteria.

Query design grid The lower half of the Query Design view that shows the field name, table name, sort order, show box, and criteria rows for selecting records. In earlier versions of Access, this was called the QBE grid.

Show box The check box on the query design grid that allows you to display or hide a column that may be used in criteria or sorting.

Notes

Compare Queries to Sorts/Filters

- **Queries** are like advanced sort/filters except you can save a query and store it in the database window.

- Queries also make possible some specialized operations like performing calculations on field values and placing the result in a new column in a datasheet.

- Like sorting/filtering, queries let you sort and define criteria to select the records you want to see.

- Unlike sorting/filtering, a query enables you to choose a subset of fields to display. You need not hide the columns you don't want; they simply don't appear in the query results.

- You can also use certain fields in the query as filters without including those fields in the query output.

- Queries, like tables, can be used as a starting point for reports or forms.

- There are several kinds of queries, but the most common type is a **select query**. The main purpose of a select query is to extract fields and records from a larger table and present the results in a specific sort order.

Ways to Start a New Query

- As with most other database objects in Access, you can start a new query using a wizard or using **Query Design view**.

- To create a new query in Query Design view, the fastest method is to double-click *Create query in Design view* from the database window.

- If you want to create a new select query using a wizard, the fastest way is to double-click *Create query by using Wizard* from the database window.

- If you want some other type of specialized query, you must use the New button in the database window (with Queries selected at the left). This displays the full list of the various query wizards.

New Query dialog box

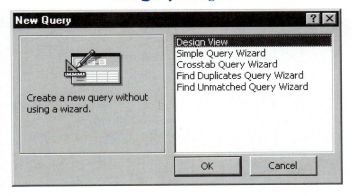

- Choosing the Simple Query Wizard from the New Query dialog box is the same as double-clicking the Create query using Wizard shortcut in the Database window.

- Another way to open the New Query dialog box is to display the table on which you want to base the query and then open the drop-down list for the New Object button and choose Query.

Select Query from the New Object button

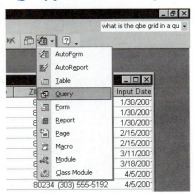

Create a Query with a Wizard

- The Simple Query Wizard walks you step-by-step through the process of selecting fields to include in a query. It lets you create a version of a table (or other query) that contains a subset of fields.

- For example, you might want to see only the name and address fields for a contact list rather than all data about each person.

Simple Query Wizard

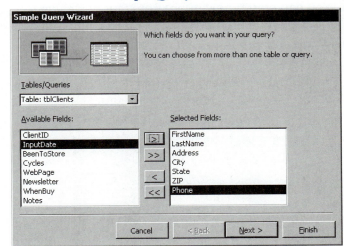

- If your selections include numeric fields, the Simple Query Wizard also allows you to specify whether you want a summary or detail query. A detail query displays all records individually; a summary query summarizes based on a particular field value.

- If you choose a summary query, you can choose to present the sum, average, minimum value, or maximum value of any numeric fields.

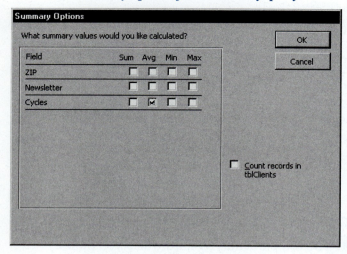

■ Query results appear in a Datasheet view, similar to a table.

  ✓ *The Simple Query Wizard cannot filter records and cannot sort them in a particular order, so you will probably need to use Query Design view to get the exact query results you need.*

Create a Query in Query Design View

■ You can start a new query from Query Design view, or you can modify any existing query there.

■ When you start a new query in Query Design view, the Show Table dialog box automatically appears. Choose the tables you want for the query.

Choose the tables/queries

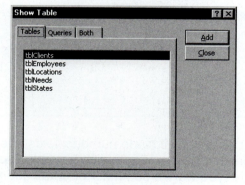

■ If you choose more than one table, the tables must have a relationship between them.

  ✓ *A query is a great way to create a single object containing fields from multiple related tables. For example, suppose you want to create a form that includes fields from both a Customers and an Orders table. You could create a relationship between the tables, then create a query that includes the fields from both, and then create a form based on that query (see Exercise 9).*

■ Query Design view consists of two sections. At the top are field lists for the tables/queries to work with. At the bottom is the **query design grid**, where you place the individual fields (one per column) and define how they should be acted upon.

Query Design view

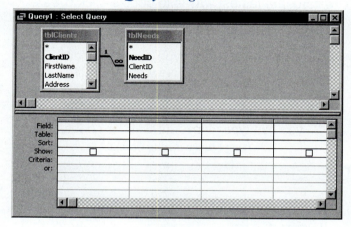

Choosing Fields for a Query

■ The order you choose fields in the Query design determines the column order for the resulting datasheet.

■ You can choose a field in any of the following ways:

  • Double-click on the field in the Field List to place the field to the right of the previous field.

  • Drag the field from the Field List to a field in the query design grid to insert this field where you want it in the grid.

  • Click on the drop-down arrow or type in the Field cell to choose a field from the list of fields.

■ You may need to use fields for sorting or criteria but not want to see the fields in Datasheet view. If you don't want to see the fields in Datasheet view, uncheck the **show box**.

Sorting Records in a Query

■ Underneath the fields you want to sort, do one of the following in the Sort box to choose a sort order:

- Double-click in the Sort box to cycle through Ascending, Descending, or no sort (blank).
- Click on the drop-down arrow and choose Ascending or Descending.
- Type **a** for Ascending or **d** for Descending.

■ The position of the sort fields from left to right determines the sort order. The left-most field with a sort specified is the primary sort; the remaining fields with sorts specified are subsorts and are sorted in order from left to right.

Criteria in a Query

■ The same rules for filters apply to queries for criteria as well as sorting. Here is a review:

- You can type the complete value in the criteria row or use wildcards. For example, you can type Denver or Den* to choose Denver.
- You can also type the following symbols or text in the criteria row:

Use:	For and example:
<	Less than. <30
<=	Less than or equal to. <=#1/1/99#
>	Greater than. >100
>=	Greater than or equal to. >=Date()
<>	Not equal to. <>"Denver"
Like	Match a pattern of characters. Like "Den*"
And	Match 2 or more conditions. >5 And <10
Or	Match any of the conditions. "CO" Or "CA"
Between … And	Match values in a range. Between #1/1/98# and #1/15/98#
In	Select from a list of values. In ("NM","NY","NJ")
Is Null	If there are no values in the field.
Is Not Null	If the field has any values.

- All entries in one criteria row mean that every condition must match to find the record.
- Entries in the Criteria and Or rows mean that a record must match one of the conditions to be included in the result to find a record.

Display the Query Datasheet

■ There are two ways to see the results of a query. One is to preview the results in Datasheet view, by switching to Datasheet view. The other is to run the query with the Run button ![Run button].

■ For a select query, there is no real difference between these two methods. However, when you get into action queries that actually perform operations on the data rather than just displaying it, the difference becomes important.

■ Query results appear in Datasheet view and resemble a table.

Save a Query

■ When you close a query window, if you have made design changes to it, you are prompted to save your work.

■ You can also save a query from Design view before you are ready to close it.

■ The first time you save a query, you will be prompted for a name. Although the name can be a maximum of 64 characters including spaces, you should keep the name short and use no spaces.

■ Many people use the convention of preceding the query name with qry to identify the object type.

Procedures

Start the Simple Query Wizard

From the database window:

1. Click **Queries**.
2. Double-click **Create query by using wizard**.

From a datasheet:

1. Open table or query that will be the source for new query.
2. Click down arrow on **New Object** button.

   ✓ *The image on the New Object button changes depending on your last selection.*

3. Click **Query** .... `Q`
4. Click **Simple Query Wizard**.
5. Click **OK** .... `Enter`

Complete the Simple Query Wizard

1. Start the Simple Query Wizard using one of the methods just described.
2. Click **Tables/Queries** down arrow `▼`.
3. Click table or query to use.
4. Click a field to include in the query.
5. Click **Add Field** button `>`.
6. Repeat steps 4-5 to add more fields from same table or query.
7. Return to step 2 to select fields from other tables/queries if desired.
8. Click `Next >` .... `Alt`+`N`

   ✓ *If you included any Numeric fields, you are prompted to choose between Detail and Summary.*

9. If prompted, do one of the following:

   To create a detail query (i.e. a normal query):

   - Click `Next >` ... `Alt`+`N`

   Or, to create a summary query:

   a. Click **Summary** ...... `Alt`+`S`
   b. Click **Summary Options** .... `Alt`+`O`

   c. Click check box(es) for fields to summarize.
   d. (Optional) Click **Count records in *tablename*** check box.
   e. Click **OK** .... `Enter`

10. Click `Next >` .... `Alt`+`N`
11. Type query name.
12. Click `Finish` .... `Alt`+`F`

Start a Query in Design View

From the database window:

1. Click **Queries**.
2. Double-click **Create query in Design view**.

From a datasheet:

1. Open table or query that will be the source for new query.
2. Click down arrow on **New Object** button.

   ✓ *The image on the New Object button changes depending on your last selection.*

3. Click **Query** .... `Q`
4. Click **Design View**.
5. Click **OK** .... `Enter`

Select Tables/Queries to Use

1. With Select Query Window displayed, click **Show Table** button (if the Show Table dialog box does not automatically appear).
2. Click table to use.
3. Click `Add` .... `Alt`+`A`

   ✓ *To select a query instead, click the Queries tab. The Both tab shows both tables and queries at once.*

4. Repeat steps 2-3 to add more tables or queries.
5. Click `Close` .... `Alt`+`C`

Add Fields to a Query

- Double-click a field in the field list.

OR

- Drag a field into the query design grid.

Sort by a Field

1. Click in the **Sort** row for a field in the query design grid.
2. Click the **down arrow** `▼`.
3. Choose **Ascending** or **Descending**.

   ✓ *To remove a sort, choose (not sorted).*

Enter Filter Criteria

1. Click in the **Criteria** row for a field in the query design grid.
2. Enter criteria.
3. Repeat steps 1 and 2 for additional fields.

   ✓ *To enter either-or criteria, enter each criterion on a separate Or row in the grid.*

Preview Query Results

1. Click **View** .... `Alt`+`V`
2. Click **Datasheet View** .... `S`

   OR

   Click the **View** button .

Return to Query Design View

1. Click **View** .... `Alt`+`V`
2. Click **Design View** .... `D`

   OR

   Click the **View** button `▼`.

Save a Query

1. Click **Save** button `💾`.

   OR

   a. Click **File** .... `Alt`+`F`
   b. Click **Save** .... `S`

2. Type query name if saving query for first time.
3. Click **OK** .... `Enter`

Save and Close a Query

1. Click **Close** button ⊠ on query window.
2. Click **Yes**........ Alt + Y or Enter
3. Type query name.
4. Click **OK**.......................... Enter

Run a Query

From Query Design view:

- Click the **Run** button ❗.

From the database window:

1. Click **Queries**.
2. Double-click the query name.

Exercise Directions

1. Start Access, if necessary.

2. Open ⊙ **AC21**.

3. Open **tblClients**.

4. Using the New Object button, create a new query with the Simple Query Wizard that:

   a. Includes FirstName, LastName, Phone, and Cycles fields only.

   b. Is a Detail query.

   c. Is named **qryClientPhone**.

5. Close all open datasheets.

6. Start a new query in Query Design view.

7. Add the **tblClients** table.

8. Add the FirstName and LastName fields to the query design grid.

9. Sort in Ascending order by LastName.

10. Add the **tblNeeds** table to the query.

    ✓ *Click the Show Table button to open the Show Table dialog box.*

11. Add the Needs field to the query design grid.

12. Save the query as **qryNeeds** and switch to Datasheet view to check it out; then close it.

13. Start a new query in Query Design view.

14. Add the **tblClients** table.

15. Add all fields necessary for mailing (FirstName, LastName, Address, City, State, and ZIP) to the query design grid.

16. Sort in Descending order by ZIP.

17. Add a criterion so that only records in which the State is CO are included.

18. Add a second criterion on the OR line so that records without CO in the State field can be included if the Newsletter field value is Yes.

    ✓ *You will need to add the Newsletter field to the grid, and add criteria for it on the OR line, but then you must clear the Show check box for it so that the Newsletter field does not display in the query results.*

19. Preview the query results in datasheet view.

20. Save the query as **qryMailing1** and close it.

21. View **qryMailing1** from the database window.

22. Close the database and exit Access.

On Your Own

1. In Access, open ⊙ **OAC21**.

2. Using the Simple Query Wizard, create a query that would be useful for creating mailing address labels for a team mailing. Include only the fields you need for mailing labels. Name it **qryLabels.**

3. Edit the query in Design view so that the records are sorted by ZIP Code and so that only Active players are included.

   ✓ *One way to do this would be to add the Categories table, add the Category field to the query, filter by it, and turn off its display in the query results.*

4. Save the query and close it.

5. Create a new query that displays the first and last names and birthdates for people with birthdays in March.

   ✓ *One way to do this would be to enter the following criteria for the Birthday field: Like "3*". This finds all records in which the Birthday field begins with 3. This would not work, however, if you wanted all birthdays in January because "1*" would find January, October (10), November (11), and December (12) since they all begin with a 1.*

6. Save the new query as **qryMarchBday.**

7. Create a new query that displays FirstName, LastName, and Birthday for all players who were born between 1975 and 1980.

   ✓ *One way to do this would be to enter Between #01/01/75# and #01/01/80# for the Birthday field's criteria. Notice that you use # signs rather than quotation marks in this case because you want the value rather than a character in a text string. If you don't type the # signs, Access will insert them automatically for you.*

8. Save the new query as **qry1975-1980**.

9. Close the database and exit Access.

Exercise 22

Skills Covered:

◆ **Open a Query for Editing** ◆ **Delete a Field** ◆ **Move a Field**
◆ **Use All Fields of a Table for a Query**
◆ **Rename a Query** ◆ **Save a Query with a Different name**

On the Job

After you have built simple queries, you may need to change your initial query design. You can change query design by adding, deleting, or moving fields. You can also quickly add all fields from a table to your query. After changing the design, you may want to rename the query and print a query datasheet.

The staff member for whom you created the qryMailing1 query in Exercise 21 has requested that the last names come first, to make it easier to look up names. Also, the employee using the qryNeeds query wants the customer phone numbers to appear on that list, so she doesn't have to look them up. You will make these changes. You will also create a new query that generates listing of employees sorted by last name.

Terms

Field selector The gray bar above a field in the query grid; click it to select that field, in preparation for moving or deleting it.

Property sheet A dialog box that shows properties for all aspects of an object. Each query has a property sheet, as does each individual object (such as a field or label).

Notes

Open a Query for Editing

- If you want to edit a query after you've saved it, choose the query name on the Queries window of the database window and click the Design button.

- You can add more fields to the query by dragging them into the grid, as you learned in Exercise 21.

Select a Field

- To delete or move a field, you must first select it in the grid.

- To select a field in the grid, click the **field selector**. When the mouse pointer is over the field selector, the pointer appears as a down-pointing black arrow.

Mouse pointer over field selector

Delete a Field

- To delete a field, select it and press the Delete key.

Move a Field

- To move a field, select it and then point to the field selector. The mouse pointer changes to a white arrow. Drag to the new position. (A vertical line will indicate the new position.)

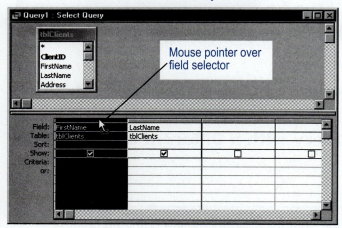

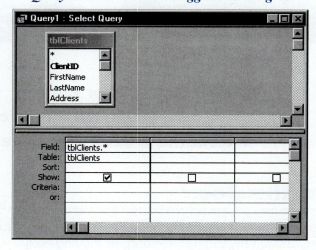

- You can also move a field in the query results datasheet. Then when you close the datasheet and save your changes, the column order will be saved, too, and will override the order specified in Query Design view.

- Making design changes to a query in Datasheet view is useful when you have added the fields to the query using one of the methods that inserts a single entry that represents all fields (as in the following section).

Use All Fields of a Table for a Query

- You saw in Exercise 21 how to place individual fields in a query. You can include all fields from a particular table by placing each one individually in the query grid.

- There are also three shortcut methods for including all fields in a query.

- One method is to double-click the title bar of the field list, so that all fields are selected, and then drag them as a group to the grid.

- Another method is to select and drag the asterisk from the top of the field list into the grid. It represents all fields as a group.

✓ *If you want to sort or enter criteria, you will need individual fields to appear in the grid. If you have included all fields using the asterisk method, add the needed fields to the grid individually, too, and enter your sorting or filtering criteria. Then deselect the Show box for the individual field, so it won't appear in the query twice.*

- The third method is to set the query properties to include all fields.

- After you create the query, double-click in the gray area behind Field List. The **property sheet** appears for the query. Change the Output All Fields property to Yes.

Property sheet for the query

Query Properties	
General	
Description	
Default View	Datasheet
Output All Fields	Yes
Top Values	All
Unique Values	No
Unique Records	No
Run Permissions	User's
Source Database	(current)
Source Connect Str	
Record Locks	No Locks
Recordset Type	Dynaset
ODBC Timeout	60
Filter	

Rename a Query

- You may want to change the name of a query because of a typo or you may want to include the *qry* naming convention.

- To rename a query, right-click it in the database window and choose Rename.

✓ *If you change the name of a query, any reports or forms you already created based on this query will not run. To avoid recreating all your forms and reports, you can modify the properties of the existing ones to point to the new query. To do so, display the property sheet for the report or form and change the Record Source property to the new query name.*

Save a Query with a Different Name

■ After making changes to a query, you might want to save it with a different name to preserve the original version.

■ To do so, with the query displayed in Datasheet or Design view, use the File, Save As command.

Procedures

Open a Query for Editing
From the database window:
1. Click **Queries**.
2. Click the query.
3. Click **Design** button
    ....

Select a Field in the Grid
● Click the field selector.
   ✓ *The entire column is highlighted.*

Delete a Field from the Grid
1. Select the field.
2. Press **Delete**......................Del

Move a Field in the Grid
1. Select the field.
2. Position mouse pointer over field selector.
3. Drag to new location.

Place All Fields in Query Grid
1. Double-click title bar of field list.
2. Drag selection to query grid (lower pane).

Place a Single Field Representing All Fields in Query Grid
● Double-click asterisk at top of table field list.
   OR
● Drag asterisk to query grid.
   ✓ *Any fields that appear individually in the query will now appear twice unless you turn off their Show check boxes.*

Edit Query Properties to Include All Fields
1. Right-click gray area behind field lists.
2. Click **Properties**.................P
3. Click in the **Output All Fields** box.
4. Click **down arrow** .
5. Click **Yes**.
6. Click **Close** button .
   ✓ *Any fields that appear individually in the query will now appear twice unless you turn off their Show check boxes.*

Rename a Query
1. View database window.
2. Click **Queries** button.
3. Right-click query to rename.
4. Click **Rename**.....................M
5. Type new name.
6. Press **Enter**.....................Enter

Save a Query with a Different Name
From Query Design view:
1. Click **File**.....................Alt+F
2. Click **Save As**.....................A
3. Type new name.
4. Click **OK** ....Enter

Exercise Directions

1. Start Access, if necessary.

2. Open ⊛ **AC22**.

3. Open **qryMailing1** in Design view.

4. Transpose the order of the FirstName and LastName columns.

5. Save the query as **qryMailing2** and switch to Datasheet view to see its result. Then close it.

6. Create a new query in Design view that includes all the fields from the **tblEmployees** table (using the asterisk).

7. Sort the list alphabetically by last name.

   ✓ To do this, you will need to add the LastName field individually to the query, set up the filter, and deselect the Show check box for the field.

8. Save the query as **qryEmployeeList** and close it.

9. View the **qryEmployeeList** query results in a datasheet.

10. Hide the first two columns; then close the datasheet saving changes.

11. Reopen the query results to confirm that your design changes were saved.

12. Still in Datasheet view, move the DateHired field to the left-most column position.

13. Preview the query results.

14. Close the datasheet, saving your changes.

15. Open the **qryNeeds** query in Design view.

16. Add the Phone field to the grid, in the first empty column.

17. Move the Phone field to the left of Needs.

18. Preview the query results in Datasheet view.

19. Close the datasheet and save the changes.

20. Exit the database.

On Your Own

1. In Access, open ⊛ **OAC22**.

2. Open the **qry1975-1980** query, and add all fields to it by setting the query properties.

3. Preview the query results. If any fields appear in duplicate, return to Query Design view and fix this.

4. Hide the ID column in the query.

5. Close the query, saving the changes.

6. Open the **qryMarchBday** query, and arrange the fields so Birthday comes first.

7. Save the changes to the query.

8. Save the query again, this time as **qryAprilBday**, and modify the filter criteria so it finds April rather than March birthdays.

9. Close the query, saving your changes.

10. Create a new query that shows all fields for the Roster table and is sorted in descending order by city.

11. Name the new query **qryCities**.

12. Create a query that shows all fields from the Roster table but only includes records from Indianapolis or Noblesville. Sort by ZIP Code in ascending order.

13. Name the new query **qryZIP**.

14. Print the query.

15. Close the database, saving all changes, and exit Access.

Exercise 23

◆ Critical Thinking

The Central Indiana Shetland Sheepdog Club has been using the database you created for them, but several users expressed wishes for sorted and filtered data. Some of these are one-time requests; others are requests for data that will be needed repeatedly. You know that queries can answer these needs, so you will create several queries that will take care of them.

Exercise Directions

Kenneth Kwan has reported that the coloring for his dogs is not Sable, but rather Shaded Sable.

1. Open ⊙ **AC23**.

2. Make the change in the Dogs table for Kenneth's dogs only (dog id's 3 and 5). You can either use Find and Replace or a filter.

The membership chairman wants a list of members sorted by last name.

3. Sort the **tblMembers** table and print it.

The recording secretary would like a list of dogs who have a CD or CDX title.

4. Using an advanced filter, create and print the data from the **tblDogs** table for dogs that have CD or CDX in the Titles field.

    ✓ *Use wildcards. Remember that the Titles field might include more than one title. You want to include records that have "CD" anywhere within that field.*

5. Save the filter as a query called **qryCD/CDX**.

The recording secretary says this is a helpful list, but she only needs the Owner, Registered Name, and Title fields.

6. Open the query in Query Design view, and then switch to Datasheet view to see the result. Then switch back to Query Design view.

    ✓ *Even though only one field appears in the grid, all fields appear in the query. Why is this?*

7. Modify the query properties so that Output All Fields is set to No.

8. Add the Owner and RegisteredName fields to the query, and position them to the left of the Titles field.

    ✓ *You can move fields to the left or right in the grid by clicking at the top of the column to select it and then dragging with the mouse.*

9. Preview the query results.

    ✓ *The Titles field does not appear. Why?*

10. Return to Query Design view and make the Titles field appear in the query.

11. Preview the query results; then close the query and save changes to it.

The club president would like a list of the club officers and their phone numbers.

12. Create a new query that uses the following fields from the **tblMembers** table: FirstName, LastName, Phone, and PositionHeld.

13. Add a criterion so that only records where the PositionHeld field is not blank are included.

    ✓ *Use Is Not Null as the criterion for that field.*

14. Sort the query results by LastName in ascending order.

15. Save the new query as **qryOfficers**.

16. Display the query in Datasheet view and print it. Then close it.

    ✓ *Before you print, check column widths. Widen any where entries appear truncated.*

Exercise 24

Skills Covered:

◆ **Report Layouts** ◆ **Ways to Create a Report** ◆ **Create an AutoReport**
◆ **Create a Report with the Report Wizard** ◆ **Work with Report Preview**
◆ **Print a Report** ◆ **Save a Report**

On the Job

Reports give you much more flexibility in producing output than simply printing tables and queries. You can print records in a tabular format that looks like a datasheet but with more attractive fonts, and you can print records one below the other in a columnar format.

After seeing your printouts of queries and tables, the owner and other employees of the cycle shop have been asking if you could make the print-outs more readable, and in some cases if you could add totals to the details. You realize it is time to learn about reports.

Terms

Report A way to structure your data for printing with format enhancements.

AutoReport A report that is automatically generated at the click of a button.

Report Design view A view of the report that lets you change its appearance and contents.

Preview A view of the report as it will appear when printed.

Notes

Report Layouts

- While you can print tables, queries, and forms, **reports** are designed specifically for printed output.

- Reports give you more options for formatting, calculating, and totaling your data.

- There are three main types of report layout:
  - In a tabular report, each row is a record and each column is a field. It's similar to the printout you get when printing a datasheet.
  - In a columnar report, all the fields for each record appear together, followed by those for the next record, and so on.

- In a mailing label report, records are arranged in blocks across and down the page, ready to print on a sheet of self-stick labels.

- Reports can also contain sorting, grouping, and summary statistics.

Ways to Create a Report

- There are several methods of creating a new report:
  - There are two **AutoReports** available: Tabular and Columnar. These create a basic no-frills report from a single table or query.
  - The Report Wizard takes you step by step through the process.

- You can create a report from scratch through **Report Design view**, which is similar to Form Design view. Report Design view is covered in Exercise 25.

- You can use the Label Wizard for mailing labels and the Chart Wizard for creating charts. These specialized Report Wizards are covered in Exercise 26.

- You can also copy an existing report and then make changes to it.

- Regardless of the method you use to create the report, you can modify its appearance and content in Design view.

Create an AutoReport

- To create an AutoReport, open the New Report dialog box (with the New button in the Database window) and choose one of the two types of AutoReports. Then select the table or query on which to base it and click OK. Access generates the report.

New Report dialog box

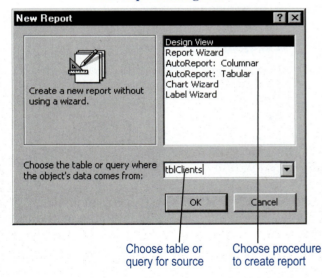

Choose table or query for source

Choose procedure to create report

- You can also use the New Object button when viewing a datasheet. Open its drop-down list and choose Report, and a new columnar AutoReport will be generated.

- AutoReport assumes that you want all fields in the report in the order in which they appear in the table or query. There are no options you can specify for an AutoReport.

Create a Report with the Report Wizard

- The Report Wizard works like other wizards you have already seen in Access.

- You choose the table/query and fields, the layout, and other options for the report, and then Access creates it according to your specifications.

- As with other wizards, you can start the Report Wizard by double-clicking its shortcut in the database window or by choosing it from the New Report dialog box.

- The wizard asks whether you want grouping. You can group the records by one or more fields, and then sum, count, or perform some other calculation for each group. For example, you could count the number of clients from each ZIP Code.

Specifying grouping with the Report Wizard

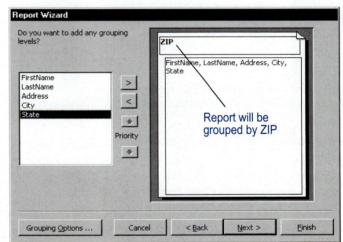

Report will be grouped by ZIP

- You can also specify a sort order. Grouping takes precedence over sorting, so, for example, if you group by ZIP and then sort by LastName, the records within each ZIP Code will be sorted by LastName.

- You can choose a layout for the report from among several choices: Stepped, Block, Outline 1, Outline 2, Align Left 1, and Align Left 2. You can also choose between Portrait and Landscape page orientation.

- Also, as with forms, you can choose a style, which includes background color, font choices, and so on.

Work with Report Preview

- The report appears in **Preview** view, which is like Print Preview in other Office programs. Since reports are designed primarily to be printed, a report's native view is Preview (rather than Datasheet, as is the case with a table or query).

- You can also get to Preview mode by double-clicking the report in the database window, or by clicking it once and then clicking the Preview button.

Report Preview view

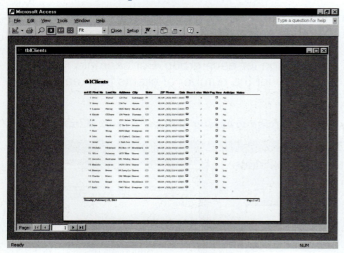

- In Preview mode, the mouse pointer displays as a magnifying glass . Click anywhere in the report display to toggle between a view of the whole page (choose Fit in the Zoom drop-down list on the Preview toolbar) and the most recent zoom value.

  ✓ *When you zoom in, you might notice that some of your column headings are truncated. You can fix this in Exercise 25, when you learn about modifying a report layout in Design view.*

- The Preview toolbar has buttons similar to those in other Office XP applications.

- The navigation buttons on the bottom of the Preview window are similar to those for tables, queries, and forms except they are for moving from page to page within a report.

Report Preview toolbar

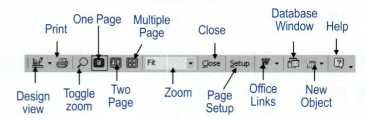

Print a Report

- To print the report, click the Print button in Preview view. This prints one copy of the entire report.

- You can also use the File, Print command if you prefer. As with other views (and other Office programs), this opens the Print dialog box, from which you can choose certain pages, a specific printer, or additional copies.

Save a Report

- When you create a report with AutoReport, it is not saved or named automatically. You are prompted to supply a name when you close the Preview window.

- When you create a report with the Report Wizard, you specify a name as the last step of the Wizard, and it is automatically saved.

- Just like with queries and other objects, you can use File, Save As to save it under a different name (for example, if you want to make changes to a copy while preserving the original version).

- To rename a saved report (or any object in the database window), right-click on the name, choose Rename from the shortcut menu, type the new name, and press Enter.

Procedures

Create an AutoReport

From the database window:

1. Click **Reports**.
2. Click **New**......................Alt+N
3. Click **AutoReport: Tabular**.
   OR
   Click **AutoReport: Columnar**.
4. Click **down arrow** ▼.
5. Choose table or query to use.
6. Click **OK**..........................Enter
   ✓ *The report displays in Preview.*

Create New Report Using Report Wizard

From the database window:

1. Click **Reports**.
2. Double-click **Create report by using wizard**.
3. Select fields..... Alt+A, ↓↑ to be included in report.
4. Click > to choose field.
   OR
   Click >> to choose all fields.
5. Click Next > ....Alt+N
   ✓ *If your data source is a query that contains fields from more than one table, you're asked by which table you want to view data.*
6. If prompted:
   a. Click the table by which to view data.
   b. Click Next > ....Alt+N
7. To choose a grouping field (optional):
   a. Select field to group by ....↓↑
   b. Click > to choose field.
      ✓ *If you do not choose a grouping field, records will appear in normal order.*
8. To set grouping options:
   a. Click Grouping Options ... ...Alt+O

b. Click **down arrow** ▼.
c. Click interval for grouping.
d. Click **OK**.....................Enter
   ✓ *You can choose intervals of 10s, 100s, and so on. If you do not specify an interval, each different entry will constitute a new group.*
9. Click Next > ....Alt+N
10. To choose a sort order (optional):
    a. Click drop-down arrow to choose a field.
    b. Click sort button for
       Ascending [Ascending] or
       Descending [Descending]
       sort.
    ✓ *If you do not specify a sort order, records appear in the order in which they appear in the table or query on which the report is based.*
    ✓ *Repeat step 10 for additional sort criteria.*
11. Click Next > ....Alt+N
12. Choose a report layout:
    • **Stepped**.................Alt+S
    • **Block** ....Alt+K
    • **Outline 1**...............Alt+O
    • **Outline 2**...............Alt+U
    • **Align Left 1** ....Alt+A
    • **Align Left 2** ....Alt+I
13. Choose a page orientation
    • **Portrait** ....Alt+P
    • **Landscape** ....Alt+L
14. Click Next > ....Alt+N
15. Choose a report style.
16. Click Next > ....N
17. Type a report name.
18. Choose to preview the report or modify its design:
    • **Preview the report**.....................Alt+P

OR
    • **Modify the report's design**....................Alt+M
19. Select **Display Help on working with the report?** ....Alt+H
    if you wish to use Access's report editing help feature.
20. Click Finish ....Alt+F
    ✓ *The report appears in Preview unless you select to Modify the report's design after typing the report name in step 17.*

Print the Report

From Preview:

• Click the **Print** button .
OR
1. Click **File**....................Alt+F
2. Click **Print**...........................P
3. Set any print options.
4. Click **OK** ....Enter

From the database window:

1. Click the report to print.
2. Click the **Print** button .
   OR
   a. Click **File** ....Alt+F
   b. Click **Print** ....P
   c. Set any print options.
   d. Click **OK** ....Enter

Save the Report

From Preview view:

1. Click **File**....................Alt+F
2. Click **Save** ....S
3. If the report has not been saved before:
   a. Type a name for the report.
   b. Press **Enter**...............Enter

Exercise Directions

1. Start Access, if necessary.

2. Open ☉ **AC24**.

3. Create a tabular AutoReport based on **qryClientPhone**.

4. Save it as **rptClientPhone**.

5. Print two copies of the report, and then close it.

6. Create a columnar AutoReport based on **qryMailing1**.

7. Save it as **rptMailing1** and close it.

8. Create a report with the Report Wizard based on **qryEmployeeList**. Use the following specifications:

   - Use only these fields: FirstName, LastName, DepartmentName, and OfficeLocation.
   - Group by OfficeLocation.
   - Sort by DepartmentName, then LastName in ascending order for both.
   - Use Align Left 1 as the layout.
   - Use Portrait as the page orientation.
   - Use Corporate as the style.
   - Name it **rptEmployeesByLocation**.

9. Examine the report in Preview. Notice that the locations appear as numbers, rather than as descriptive locations.

10. Close the report, and delete it from the database window.

11. Modify the **qryEmployeeList** query to add the Location field from the **Locations** table to it.

    ✓ *You will need to add the **Locations** table to the query.*

12. Recreate the query from step 8, this time with the Location field instead of the OfficeLocation field.

    ✓ *Notice that the Report Wizard now asks by which table you want to display data, because you now have data from two tables in the report.*

13. Print the report.

14. Close the database.

On Your Own

1. Start Access and open ☉ **OAC24**.

2. Create a Columnar AutoReport from the **qry1975-1980** query, and save it as **rpt1975-1980**.

3. Preview and print the report, then close it.

4. Create a Tabular AutoReport from the **qryAprilBday** query, and save it as **rptAprilBday**.

5. Preview and print each report.

6. Create a report using the Report Wizard from the **qryCities** query with the following:

   - Use all the fields.
   - Group first by State, then by City.
   - Sort by LastName in ascending order.
   - Choose any layout and style you like.
   - Save the report as **rptCities**.

7. Preview and print each report.

8. Close the database and exit Access.

Exercise 25

Skills Covered:

◆ **About Design View** ◆ **About Controls** ◆ **About Report Sections**
◆ **Change Section Size** ◆ **Edit a Report Layout** ◆ **Move a Control**

On the Job

While AutoReports and the Report Wizard option may produce acceptable reports, you will often find that you need to edit a report to change its title, enhance its appearance, and reposition fields to make it more readable and pleasing to the eye. Access provides a number of ways to enhance a report's appearance and change its content.

You are not satisfied with the basic reports you created in Exercise 24, and want to make some formatting changes to them.

Terms

Report Design view The editing screen in which you can change the way a report looks.

Control Any selectable item on a report or form layout.

Label A control that displays text. Labels include column or row headings and titles.

Report Section An area of a report that specifies where on the page information is displayed. The sections include report header, report footer, page header, page footer, group headers and footers (if any), and the detail section.

Header Items that appear at the top of a section. The items can be text, calculations, or graphics.

Footer Items that appear at the bottom of a section.

Report header/footer Sections on a report that display only at the beginning and end of the report.

Page header/footer Sections on a report that display at the beginning and end of each page.

Detail Section of a report that displays the data from the source table or query.

Value Control that displays data from a source table or query or the results of a formula or expression.

Notes

About Design View

■ If you need to make changes to a report after you've created it with AutoReport (or a wizard), you need to work in **Report Design view**.

■ While in Preview, click on the View button to get to Design view or click on the Design button in the database window when the report is selected.

■ As with Form Design view, Report Design view consists of a grid on which you can add, remove, resize, and reposition **controls**.

■ Unlike with forms, however, Report Design view does not precisely reflect the finished look of the report. That's because the report design contains single placeholders that represent multiple records.

- When you preview and print the report, those single placeholders will be filled in with many records.
- Each field placeholder appears in the Detail section, while the field labels form column headings in the Page Header section.

Report Design view

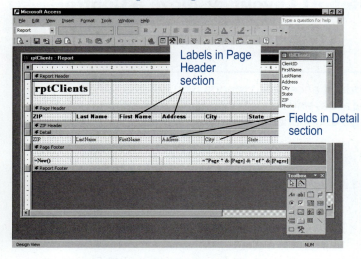

- To return to Preview from Design view, click the Preview button .

About Controls

- Each element of a report is called a control, just as it is on a form. Controls include:
  - **Labels** that identify fields
  - Fields that derive their contents from the source table or query. Different fields may have different control types, including:
    - ◆ Text boxes (the most common)
    - ◆ List or combo boxes
    - ◆ Check boxes, toggle buttons, or option buttons, usually used for Yes/No fields
  - Command buttons
  - Images
  - Formulas or expressions in text boxes
  - Borders and lines

About Report Sections

- Reports are divided into **Report sections**. As in a form, each section determines where the controls it contains will appear.

- At a minimum, a report contains the following sections:
  - **Report header**, which contains the report's title. Sometimes, you may wish to enhance the report header with a company logo or other graphic. Information in the report header appears only on the first page of the report.

  - **Page header**, which contains information repeated at the top of each report page. In a tabular report, like the one shown below, the page header usually contains labels that identify the fields. In a columnar report, this section may be empty.

  - **Detail**, which contains the **values** for the fields. In a columnar AutoReport, the field names usually appear in this section.

  - **Page footer**, which contains information that appears at the bottom of each report page. In AutoReports, Access includes the date and the page number in this section. Most reports generated by wizards include the date and page number here.

  - **Report footer**, which contains information that appears only on the last page of the report. In AutoReports, the report footer is usually empty.

- You can hide any section by changing its Visible property (on the section's property sheet Format tab) to No.

Sections of a tabular report in Design view

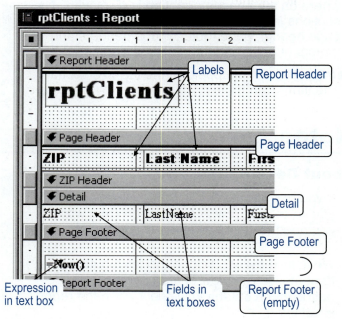

- To delete page headers and footers in Design view, choose View, Page Header/Footer. This toggles them off and removes their content.

- You can re-add the page header and footer sections by choosing View, Page Header/Footer again, but they'll be blank, and you will have to insert new controls into them.

- If you want a page footer and not a header (or vice versa), delete any controls and drag the border so there is no height to the section, or set the section's Visible property to No.

Change Section Size

- First move, delete, or resize any controls if you want to make the section smaller. (To edit controls, see below.)

- Move to the edge of the section. The mouse pointer becomes a double-arrow ✛.

- Drag the mouse pointer up or down to resize the section. This works just like on a form in Form Design view.

Edit a Report Layout

- Report Design view is similar to Form Design view.

- You already have most of the knowledge you need to work in Report Design view, because you already know how to move, resize, and delete controls. The following sections provide a brief review.

Delete a Control

- To delete a control, select it and press the Delete key.

Resize a Control

- To resize a control, point to any selection handle on the control except the upper-left one, so the pointer becomes a two-headed arrow. Then drag.

- If the control is a label, you can double-click the double-headed arrow to size the control to fit text automatically.

- If multiple controls are selected, choose Format, Size and then select one of the options, such as To Fit, To Tallest, To Shortest, To Widest, or To Narrowest.

Move a Control

- To move a control, position the mouse pointer over a control so the mouse pointer becomes an open hand ✋, and drag.

- When the label and the field are in the same section, as in most columnar reports, they are usually attached so that selecting one selects the other. The hand then moves both label and field at the same time.

- To move only one control of a pair (a field and its label), move the mouse pointer to the upper-left sizing handle box until it becomes a pointing finger ☝. Then you can move that control separately.

- However, when the label and field are in separate sections, they are separate units, and you must select them both together before dragging if you want them to move as a pair.

- To align a group of controls, select the controls, then choose Format, Align and choose one of the options, such as Left, Right, Top, or Bottom. This action aligns the controls themselves, not the text within a label or the value in a field.

Edit a Label

- You may wish to change a label to make it easier to understand. If the report is based on a query or table and its name appears at the top of the report (like qryClients), you might want to change it to something friendlier like Clients.

- To change a label, select the control and click inside it. Then use cursor movements, Delete, Backspace, and character keys to change the label to read as you wish.

Add a Field

- To add a field to the report, drag it from the field list. If the field list does not appear, click the Field List button 🗒 on the toolbar to display it.

  ✓ *Many people find it easier to recreate a report using the Report Wizard than to add fields because of the extensive moving and repositioning of fields and labels usually required to make the report look good after a field has been added or removed.*

Format a Control

- Select a control or controls and then click the appropriate button on the Formatting toolbar. The formatting is exactly the same as that for forms.

- To copy the formatting from one control to another, click the control whose format you want to copy, click the Format Painter button 🖌, then click the control to change. As in other Office applications, you can double-click the Format Painter to format multiple controls without having to re-click Format Painter.

Procedures

Go to Design View

From Preview:

1. Click **View** .... `Alt`+`V`
2. Click **Design View** .... `D`

   OR

   Click the **View** button 📐 ▾.

From database window:

1. Click **Reports**.
2. Select report name.
3. Click **Design** .... `Alt`+`D`

   All the following steps are done in Design view.

Change Section Size

1. If necessary, remove or resize controls within section.
2. Move mouse pointer to edge of section.
3. Drag double-headed mouse pointer up or down.

Add a Field

1. If Field List does not appear, click **Field List** button .
2. Drag a field into Detail section (or whatever section you wish to place it in).
3. Edit the section as necessary to accommodate the field.
4. If necessary, move the label to a different section such as a header that contains field labels.

Select Controls

1. Click control.
2. Hold down **Shift** and click additional controls. .... `Shift`

   All the following steps are done with control(s) selected.

   To deselect a selected control without deselecting others, hold down **Ctrl** and click the control .... `Ctrl`

Change Control Size

- Drag double-headed mouse pointer on sizing handle.

  OR

1. Select one or more controls.
2. Click **Format** .... `Alt`+`O`
3. Click **Size** .... `S`
4. Choose one:
   - To **Fit**. .... `F`
   - To **Tallest** .... `T`
   - To **Shortest** .... `S`
   - To **Widest** .... `W`
   - To **Narrowest** .... `N`

Move Controls

- Drag selected control with hand mouse pointer.

Align Controls

1. Select one or more controls.
2. Click **Format** .... `Alt`+`O`
3. Click **Align** .... `A`
4. Choose one:
   - **Left** .... `L`
   - **Right** .... `R`
   - **Top** .... `T`
   - **Bottom** .... `B`

Delete Controls

- Press **Delete** to remove selected control(s).

Edit a Label

1. Click in selected label to position insertion point.
2. Press **Delete**.

   OR

   Press **Backspace**.

   OR

   Type new text.

Format a Control

- Click one of the Formatting toolbar buttons.

  OR

1. Select control with format to copy.
2. Click **Format Painter** button 🖌️.
3. Click control to be formatted.

   OR

1. Double-click **Format Painter** button 🖌️.
2. Click each control to be formatted.
   - ✓ *While Format Painter is active, you can change the formatting of the original control and apply the change to other controls without having to reactivate Format Painter.*
3. Click **Format Painter** button 🖌️ or press **Esc** when you've formatted all desired controls .... `Esc`

Exercise Directions

1. Start Access, if necessary.
2. Open 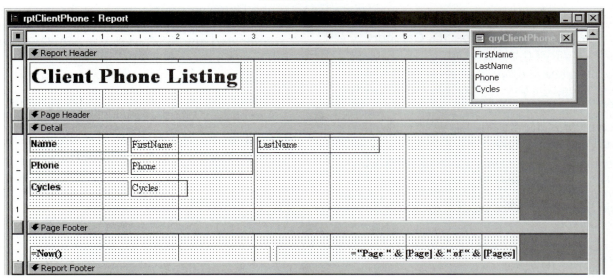**AC25**.
3. Open **rptClientPhone** in Design view.
4. Change the report title to **Client Phone Listing**.
5. Delete the label for the Last Name field, and move the field itself up next to the First Name field.

   ✓ *To delete the label but leave the field itself, make sure the label is selected, rather than the field, before you delete.*

6. Change the label for the First Name field to **Name**.
7. Move the Phone and Cycles fields up to close the space. At this point it should resemble Illustration A.
8. Preview the report, then close it, saving your changes.
9. Open **rptEmployeesByLocation** in Design view.
10. Change the report title to **Employees by Location**.
11. Change the font for all controls to Arial.
12. Add the SSN field to the report. To do this:

    a. Drag the SSN field into the Detail area.

    b. Position the field to the right of the First Name field.

    c. Select the SSN label and cut it to the Clipboard.

    d. Select the Location Header area, and then paste the SSN label.

    e. Position the SSN label above the SSN field, so it serves as a column heading.

    f. Set the alignment for the SSN content (the field, not the label) to Left.

    g. Use Format Painter to copy the formatting from the Last Name label to the SSN label. Illustration B shows the result at this point.

13. Delete the horizontal lines above and below the labels in the Location Header area.

    ✓ *You might want to temporarily enlarge the Location Header section so you have more room to work, and/or drag one of the labels to the side temporarily so you can more easily select the lines.*

14. Draw a new, single horizontal line below the labels.

    ✓ *You will need to display the Toolbox to access the Line tool. The toolbox works just as it did in Form Design view.*

15. Preview the report, and then print it.
16. Save your work and close the database.

Illustration A

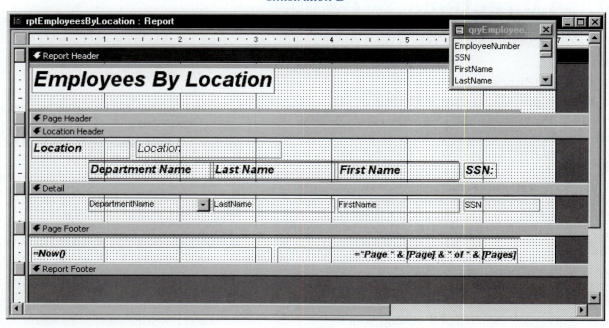

On Your Own

1. Start Access and open ☉ **OAC25**.

2. Open the **rptCities** in Design view.

3. Remove the following fields: ID, Category, Phone Tree, and Send a Card.

   ✓ *You will need to delete the field in the Detail section and the label in the Page Header section separately.*

4. Shorten or eliminate any labels to make the report more readable.

   ✓ *For example, you might remove the First Name and Last Name labels and replace them with a single Name label, or you might remove the City and State labels since those fields are self-explanatory.*

5. Spread out and enlarge the remaining fields in the Detail section so they use the empty space from the deleted fields as needed to prevent truncated entries. Switch between Preview and Design view to check your work.

6. Make any font size changes desired.

7. Switch the order of two fields (First Name and Last Name, for example).

8. Change the report title to something more understandable (for example, Roster by City).

9. Save the report.

10. Print the report.

11. Close the database and exit Access.

Exercise 26

Skills Covered:

◆ Create a Chart Report

On the Job

A chart presents data graphically, making it easier to see relationships among categories of data. The Chart Wizard creates a report that contains a chart; you can create a chart and then modify its layout in Report Design view.

You have received two requests for specific data from the database. The personnel manager would like a chart that shows how many employees work at each location, and the marketing manager would like to see how many cycles customers have. You will satisfy these requests with charts.

Terms

Chart A graphical representation of data.

Notes

Create a Chart Report

- Access provides a Chart Wizard that creates a **chart** from the data in a table or query.

- You can start the Chart Wizard from the New Report dialog box.

- On the first step of the Chart Wizard, choose which fields you want as part of the chart.

- Generally, you will have at least two fields: a data field (values associated with pie slices, lines, or bars) and a label field (x-axis labels or numbers).

- However, you might use the same field for both. The Wizard enables you to reuse one of your chosen fields as a "count" field. For example, suppose you want to count the number of employees at each location. The data field would contain the count of each location, and the label field would contain the various locations.

Chart Wizard – Choose Fields

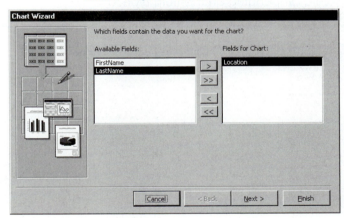

- On the next step of the wizard, choose the type of chart you want.

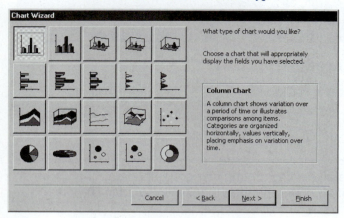

- The next step of the wizard shows you a sample chart and allows you to drag the fields to the places you want them on the chart.

- For example, drag a field on the horizontal axis to have this field become the labels for each bar or line point.

- Drag a different field to the vertical axis for the values of the bars or lines.

- There are three positions for fields for a bar chart: Axis, Data, and Series. You can leave one of these empty, and fill in whichever of the other two you want.

- The Data position does a sum or count of the field, depending on the field type.

Chart Wizard – Drag Fields for Chart Items

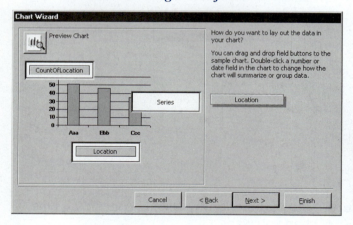

- To see what your chart will look like, click the Preview Chart button. If the results are not what you expected, rearrange the fields in the sample and try again.

- On the final step of the wizard, give the chart a title. This will appear at the top of the chart.

- You can also choose to display a legend (box that shows what each color of bar or line means). If you used a series in the step before, you'll probably want a legend. If you left the Series box unfilled, a legend will not be useful.

- You can also choose to view the report or go to the design of the report.

- When the report is done, you can resize the chart, click on the title and edit it, and add labels or fields to the report.

Modify a Chart Report

- You can format a chart report's layout in much the same way as any other report.

- You can edit label text and change fonts and control sizes.

- One of the most common changes to make to a chart is to enlarge the size of the chart object. To do this, you might need to enlarge the Detail section of the chart.

Modify the Chart Itself

- The chart exists as a control on the report. You cannot modify the chart directly using Access.

- However, you can enter Microsoft Graph, the mini-application that created the chart, and gain access to a wide variety of chart-modification commands and tools. Microsoft Graph is very similar to the charting tools in Excel.

- To modify the chart, double-click it. This opens the chart in Microsoft Graph within Access. The toolbar and menus change.

Using Microsoft Graph to edit a chart

Microsoft Graph toolbar and menus

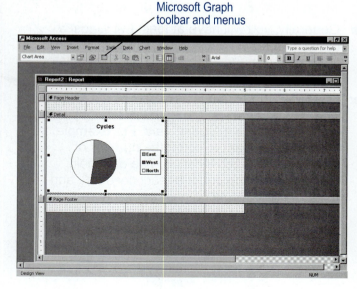

■ To modify something about the chart, use the menus or right-click on the part to change and choose from the shortcut menu. For example, to format a pie slice, right-click it and choose Format Data Series. Or to format the chart title, right-click it and choose Format Chart Title.

Choosing Format from the
shortcut menu opens a dialog box

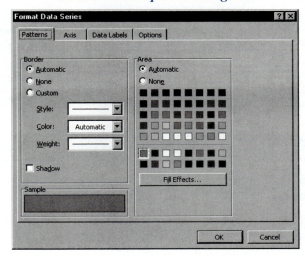

Editing part of a chart in Microsoft Graph

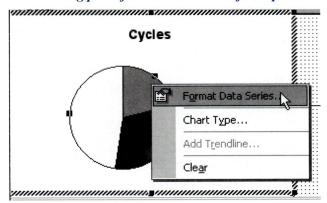

■ Choosing Format *object* (the exact name varies depending on what you clicked on) opens a dialog box from which you can make changes to that aspect of the chart.

■ A placeholder chart appears rather than your actual chart when working in Microsoft Graph. You can see the result of your changes on your actual chart by exiting Microsoft Graph and switching to Preview view.

■ To exit Microsoft Graph, click anywhere outside the chart. This returns you to Access and to Report Design view.

✓ *Don't worry if the legend in Design view shows the default "East, West, North" from Microsoft Graph. When you preview the chart in Preview view, your own chart's legend will appear.*

Procedures

Create a Chart Report

From the database window:

1. Click **Reports**.
2. Click **New**.................... Alt + N
3. Click **Chart Wizard**...........
4. Click **down arrow** ▾.
5. Click table or query on which to base the chart.
6. Click **OK**........................... Enter
7. Select a field .... to be included in chart.
8. Click > to add field.
   OR
   Click >> to add all fields.
9. Repeat steps 7 and 8 to select other fields if needed.
10. Click Next > .... Alt + N

11. Click the button on the type of chart you want.
12. Click Next > .... Alt + N
13. If necessary, drag the fields from the right side of screen to the different parts of the chart.
14. Click Next > .... Alt + N
15. Type a title for the chart.
16. Click **Yes, display a legend**.
    OR
    No, don't display a legend.
17. Click to open the report with the chart displayed on it.
    OR
    Modify the design of the report or chart.
18. Click Finish .... Alt + F

Edit a Chart Report

Open in Design view from the database window:

1. Click **Reports**.
2. Click the report to edit.
3. Click **Design**............... Alt + D

Open in Design view from Preview:

● Click the **View** button ⬚ ▾.

Open Microsoft Graph

● Double-click the chart in Design view.

Exercise Directions

Create a Bar Chart Showing Employees Per Location

1. Start Access and open ✆ **AC26**.

2. In Query Design view, create a new query based on the **tblEmployees** and **tblLocations** tables that contains the following fields: First Name, Last Name, and Locations. Save it as **qryEmpLocations**.

3. Use the Chart Wizard to create a chart based on the Locations field of your new query. Use the following settings:

   • Choose only the Location field.
   • Choose Bar Chart as the chart type.
   • Use the Location field for both Data and Axis. Leave Series blank.
   • Choose not to display a legend.

4. In Design view, make the chart larger so that the vertical axis labels all have room to display.

5. Enter Microsoft Graph, and remove the chart title from the chart.

6. Create a new label in the Page Header section for the title, and call it **Employees Per Location**.

7. Format the new title as 16-point bold dark green.

   ✓ *You may have to enlarge the object.*

8. Double-click the chart, and then right-click a blue bar and choose Format, Data Series.

9. Change the blue bar to orange. Then return to Report Design view.

10. Preview your report in Preview, and print it.

11. Save the report as **rptEmpLocations** and close it.

Create a Pie Chart Showing Cycles Per Customer

1. Create a new chart report based on **tblClients**.

   • Include only the Cycles field.
   • Choose Pie as the chart type.
   • Use Cycles for the Series and leave Data blank.
   • Name the chart **rptCycles**.

2. In Design view, change the title on the chart to **How Many Cycles Do Customers Own?**.

3. Preview and print the chart.

4. Close the database.

On Your Own

1. Start Access and open ✆ **OAC26**.

2. Create a bar chart report that shows the amount spent for each ItemType in the **Equipment** table.

3. Format the report and its chart so it looks attractive and readable.

4. Give it a title such as **Expense by Item Type**, and don't display a legend.

5. Use the Chart Options in Microsoft Graph to enter a Y-axis label of Dollars.

6. Format the Category Axis (the vertical one) so that the equipment types appear in 8-point lettering.

7. Make any other modifications to the report that you think will improve its appearance.

8. Save the chart report as **rptExpenseByType**.

9. Print the report.

10. Save the database, close it, and exit Access.

Exercise 27

On the Job

There are many ways to create mailing labels using Microsoft Office products. Word has the strongest mailing label creation features, but you can also create them directly from Access, using a table or query as the data source.

Steel Dreams is preparing a new catalog, and you need to print mailing labels to affix to them.

Terms

Label Wizard A series of dialog boxes that guides you through the creation of labels.

Notes

About Labels

■ In label format, records are arranged in blocks across and down the page. This format is used to make mailing labels and includes field values, not field names.

■ Labels usually are printed on special self-adhesive labels. A variety of manufacturers make such labels, and Access provides automatic formatting for many of the self-adhesive label styles available.

■ Although mailing labels are the most common type of label, you can also find labels for diskettes, manila folders, and video tapes. If you create a database that contains information on your video collection, you can create labels from the database to identify the videos.

Use the Label Wizard

■ The **Label Wizard**, like the Chart Wizard, is accessed from the New Report dialog box.

■ In the first Label Wizard dialog box, you choose the label manufacturer and type or specify the dimensions of the label type you are using.

Label Wizard: Choose label type

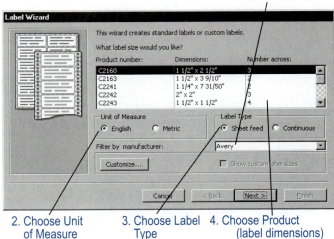

1. Choose Manufacturer
2. Choose Unit of Measure
3. Choose Label Type
4. Choose Product (label dimensions)

■ In the preceding illustration, the manufacturer (Avery) is selected from the drop-down list. The Unit of Measure is specified as English (inches), and the label type is Sheet feed.

■ When the manufacturer is selected, a list of the standard labels by that manufacturer appears. Choose the label by product number, as shown.

577

- If the label type you are using is not shown, you can specify the dimensions of your label stock by clicking the Customize button.

- In the second Label Wizard dialog box, you select the font and font size for the label. Access offers a default font and font size suitable to the label type. You may wish to accept the default and make any changes to it later in Design view.

Label Wizard: Choose label font

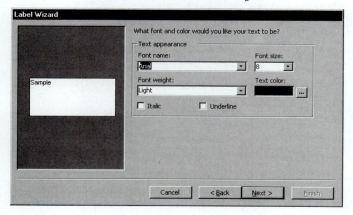

- In the third dialog box, you select the fields to be included on the label.

- Use the select field button ⟩ to include a field on the label. Press the spacebar and type punctuation as necessary to separate the fields. Press Enter to start a new line.

Label Wizard: Select fields

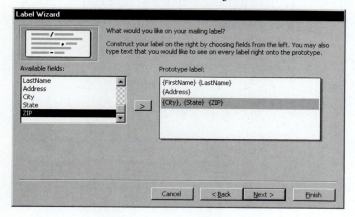

- To remove a field, press the Delete key when the insertion point is to the left of the field or press the Backspace key when the insertion point is to the right of the field. (The field name is treated as a single character.)

- Don't forget to type any spaces or punctuation you need between fields, such as a space between FirstName and LastName or a comma and space between City and State.

Spacing and punctuating labels

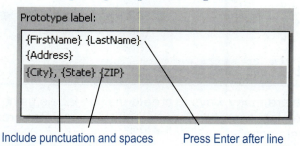

Include punctuation and spaces   Press Enter after line

- The fourth Label Wizard dialog box lets you choose the fields by which you want the labels sorted. Given the choices in the illustration below, the records will be sorted by ZIP Code.

Label Wizard: Select sort fields

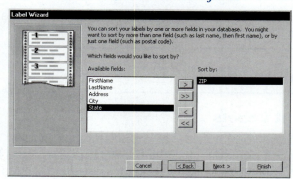

- The final dialog box asks you to name the report.

- When you click Finish, Access creates the label report and displays it in Preview.

- You can switch to Design view to make any changes. In Design view, only one label is shown and the codes for the fields are presented as shown below.

Label Design view

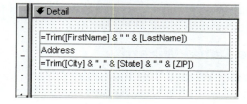

- If you wish to change the font, font size, or text style, select the field and use the Formatting toolbar buttons to apply the desired format.

Procedures

Create Mailing Labels

1. Click **Reports**.
2. Click **New**.....................Alt+N
3. Click **Label Wizard**............⊠
4. Click on the down arrow and select a **table** or **query** to base the labels on.
5. Click **OK**...........................Enter
6. Choose the label manufacturer, unit of measure, label type, product number, and so on; or click the **Customize** button Customize... and specify the label dimensions.
7. Click Next > ....Alt+N

8. If necessary, change the font.
9. Click **Next**...................Alt+N
10. Click > to move field to prototype label.
11. Press Enter to move down a line.
    OR
    Press the Spacebar.
    OR
    Type a comma or any other character.
12. Repeat steps 9–10 for all parts of the label.
13. Click Next > ....Alt+N

14. To choose a sort order:
    a. Click field by which you want to sort.
    b. Click > to move field.
    c. Repeat steps a and b for each sort field.
15. Click Next > ....Alt+N
16. Give the report a title in the provided text box, and choose to **See the labels as they will look printed** or **Modify the label design**.
17. Click Finish ....Alt+F

Exercise Directions

1. Start Access, if necessary.
2. Open ⊙ **AC27**.
3. Start the Label Wizard based on **qryMailing1**.
4. On the first dialog box of the wizard, choose:
   - Filter by Manufacturer: Avery
   - Unit of Measure: English
   - Label Type: Sheet feed
   - Product Number: 5160
5. Accept the defaults for fonts.
6. Insert the name (first and last) and address (Address, City, State, ZIP) information for the label.

7. Sort the labels by ZIP Code, then by last name.
8. Save the labels as **rptLabels**.
   ✓ *If you see a warning about there not being enough horizontal space, click OK. This appears to be a bug in the program.*
9. Display the labels in Design view.
10. Change the font size for all fields to 9 points.
11. Print one copy of the labels. Print them on regular paper if you do not have the Avery 5160 product stock.
12. Close the database.

On Your Own

✓ *You need to print mailing labels from **qryLabels**. You have some generic labels that are on a standard 8.5" x 11" sheet. Each label is $1^1/_3$" x 4" and there are two labels per row.*

1. Start Access and open ⊙ **OAC27**.
2. Use the Label Wizard to create the labels. You will need to find a label type that matches the labels you have, or create your own Custom label settings. Use whatever font size and sorting you like.

3. Save the label report as **Mailing Labels**.
4. Print the labels. (Use regular paper.)
5. Edit the label layout to use a different font or font size.
6. Edit the label layout to include some regular (non-field) text, such as **To:** above the first line.
7. Print the labels.
8. Close the database and exit Access.

Exercise 28

Everyone in the Central Indiana Shetland Sheepdog Club appreciates the great job you've done on the database, but the printouts of the tables and queries don't seem as professional looking as they should. You will create some reports that can substitute for printouts of these items.

Exercise Directions

1. Start Access, if necessary.

2. Open ☉ **AC28**.

3. Create a report that contains all the information except DogID from the **Dogs** table and shows the Owner's first and last name instead of the owner number.
   - ✓ To do this, you must create a query that includes the **Dogs** and **Members** tables, and then base the report on that query.

4. Format the report so that it looks attractive in Preview view, and then print it.

5. Create a report that shows member names and phone numbers only, sorted by first name.

6. Change the headings for the report to a different font, size, and color.

7. Create a report that will print member mailing labels on Avery 5160 labels.

8. Create a report containing a pie chart that shows the breakdown of dog colorings among dogs owned by club members.

9. Format the chart in MS Graph to make it more attractive, and then print it.

10. Close the database.

PowerPoint 2002

Lesson 1

Getting Started with PowerPoint 2002
Exercises 1-7

Lesson 2

Editing and Formatting a Presentation
Exercises 8-16

Lesson 3

Setting up a Slide Show
Exercises 17-24

Directory of Data Files on CD

Exercise #	File Name	Page #
1	N/A	N/A
2	02Gourmet	594
3	03Gourmet	598
4	04Gourmet	602
5	05Gourmet	606
6	06IMPORTOUTLINE 06WORKSH.xls	610
7	N/A	N/A
8	08West	619
9	09West	623
10	10WestPrinting	629
11	11WestPrinting	636
12	N/A	N/A
13	13Marvel	643
14	14Marvel	649
15	15Marvel	654
16	N/A	N/A
17	17Marvel	664
18	18Marvel 18Marvel2	668
19	19Marvel	672
20	20Marvel2	676
21	21Marvel2 21Marvel	679
22	22Marvel2	682
23	23Marvel2, Internet Simulation	686
24	24DitexInc	687

Exercise 1

Skills Covered:

◆ **About PowerPoint** ◆ **Start PowerPoint**
◆ **The Blank Presentation Option** ◆ **Apply a Slide Layout**
◆ **The PowerPoint Screen** ◆ **Use Shortcut Menus**
◆ **Use Slide Design Templates** ◆ **Use Placeholders**
◆ **Add Slides to a Presentation** ◆ **Save a Presentation**
◆ **Save File as a Web Page** ◆ **Close a Presentation/Exit PowerPoint**

On the Job

Use a presentation to supplement a speech or lecture. You can show an audience the main topics you will discuss as you illustrate items with charts or tables. For example, you might present a talk to prospective customers about services your company performs or products you sell.

You are in charge of creating a slide presentation for Coastline Gourmet Importers. Coastline Gourmet Importers is importing a new line of Indian spices and wants you to create a presentation advertising some of their newest products. As a bonus, you will save the presentation for the Web because you know the company uses the Internet to sell many products.

Terms

Presentation A set of slides or handouts that contain information you want to convey to an audience.

Clip art Predrawn artwork that you can insert into your files.

Design template A preformatted slide design that contains colors and graphics to make your presentation consistent and attractive.

Slide layout Pre-determined sets of placeholders for various types of slide content.

Placeholder Designated areas in PowerPoint layouts that can be used to easily insert text, graphics, or multimedia objects.

HTML Hypertext Markup Language is the file format used for files accessed on the World Wide Web.

Notes

About PowerPoint

- PowerPoint is a presentation graphics program that lets you create slide shows that can be shown with a projector, a computer screen, or as a Web page.

- A **presentation** can include handouts, outlines, and speaker notes.

- PowerPoint slides may contain text and various objects, such as charts and **clip art**.

- You can import data from other Office programs to a PowerPoint slide.

Start PowerPoint

- When you start PowerPoint, the screen appears with a slide, ready for you to work.

The PowerPoint Screen

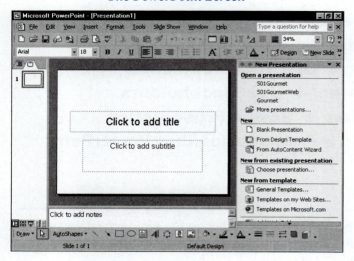

- PowerPoint offers a variety of designs and **design templates** on which to base a new presentation. There is also a blank template so you can create your own design.

The Blank Presentation Option

- A blank presentation doesn't have any graphics or backgrounds applied to it, but it does contain a single slide with the Title Slide layout applied. You can change the layout, create additional slides, apply colors, background patterns, and other formatting. You can then insert text, charts, drawings, clip art, and various multimedia effects to build your presentation content.

- The different kinds of slide layouts offer placeholders for entering content and text formats.

- After you create the presentation, you can add design elements, such as backgrounds, font styles, and color, if you want.

- If you do not have time to create your own design—or if you're new to creating presentations—you can use one of PowerPoint's predesigned design templates to enhance the appearance of your slides quickly and consistently.

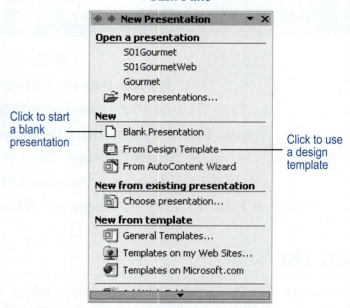

Click to start a blank presentation

Click to use a design template

Apply a Slide Layout

- When you start a new presentation or add a slide to a presentation, it will appear with a default **slide layout**. You can use that layout, or select a new layout from the Slide Layout Task Pane.

- The Slide Layout Task Pane supplies 27 different slide layouts you can use to build your own unique presentation.

- Slide layout arranges the standard objects of a presentation—titles, charts, and clip art, for example—on the slide to make it attractive.

- The placeholders and options for slide layouts help you create the text and content for each slide of a presentation.

Slide Layout Task Pane

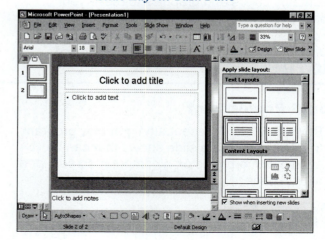

The PowerPoint Screen

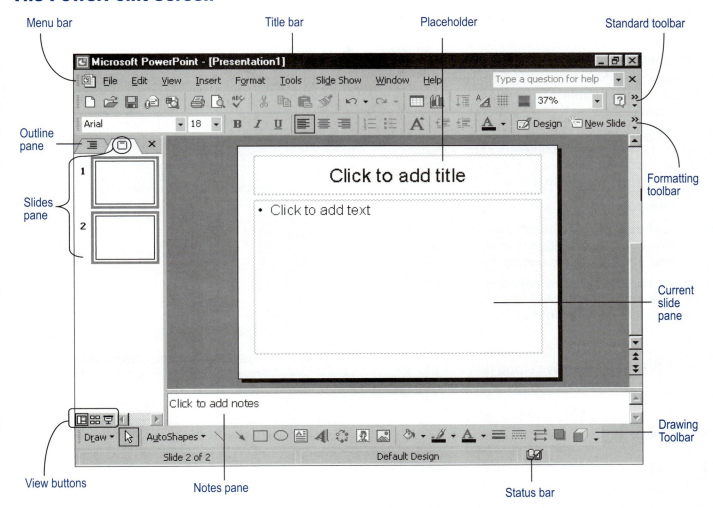

Menu bar   Title bar   Placeholder   Standard toolbar

Outline pane

Slides pane

Formatting toolbar

Current slide pane

Drawing Toolbar

View buttons   Notes pane   Status bar

- PowerPoint supplies the default title "Presentation" and a number in the title bar of each presentation you create. This title can be changed when you save the presentation with a new and descriptive name.

- A menu bar displays below the title bar.

- The Standard toolbar contains some buttons you'll see in other applications, such as Open, Save, and Print, as well as buttons unique to PowerPoint.

- The Formatting toolbar, which also contains some familiar buttons, lets you change font styles and sizes, among other things.

- The Formatting toolbar also includes buttons for common tasks, such as adding a design or a new slide by activating the Task Pane.

- The Drawing toolbar contains line, color, shape, and other drawing tools to use in your presentation.

- View buttons can be used to quickly switch among the three views: Normal (where you enter content on slides or in an outline format), Slide Sorter (the view used to rearrange and organize slides), and Slide Show (the presentation mode).

- The status bar displays information about the presentation, such as the slide number and template name.

- Normal view contains four panes: Slides, Current slide, Notes panes, and Outline, which you can access by clicking its tab. You can use these panes to enter information, arrange objects on the slide, and navigate between different slides.

Use Shortcut Menus

- Right-clicking elements in PowerPoint—such as **placeholders**, slides, text, and graphics— displays a shortcut menu that lets you quickly perform tasks and procedures.

Use Slide Design Templates

- The Template option lets you create slides with a planned layout. There are two types of templates—design templates and content templates.

- Design templates contain various colorful backgrounds, graphics, and text colors to apply to a presentation.

- Content templates contain sets of slides with design elements and content suggestions for specific presentations, such as a company handbook or financial overview.

Use Placeholders

- PowerPoint displays placeholders to define the arrangement and location of text and other objects you can add to a slide.

- There are three types of text placeholders: title, subtitle, and text (bulleted lists of content). Each of these contains preset formatting for text font and size.

- When you type into a placeholder, PowerPoint selects the box, displays sizing handles for sizing, and a cursor for typing.

Placeholders

Placeholders   Handles

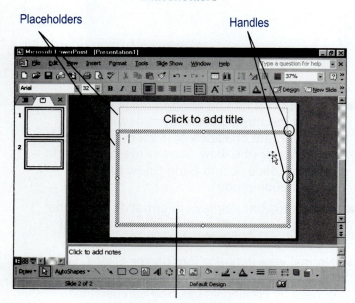

Selected placeholder

- Graphic placeholders provide a place for charts, clip art, tables, and other objects you can add to the presentation.

- If you are new to creating presentations, placeholders can help you create a professional-looking slide set.

Add Slides to a Presentation

- PowerPoint inserts a new slide immediately after the slide currently displayed or selected.

- When you add a second slide to your presentation, the Title and Text slide layout is automatically applied. You can replace it with another layout from the Slide Layout Task Pane.

Title and Text Slide Layout

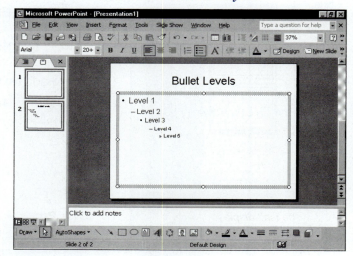

- The bulleted list layout supplies a title placeholder plus a text placeholder with five bullet levels, each with a different bullet shape to identify it.

Save a Presentation

- If you want to have a file available for future use, you must save it on a removable disk or on an internal fixed drive.

- Save a PowerPoint presentation using the same procedures you use to save a Word document or Excel spreadsheet.

- PowerPoint automatically adds a .ppt extension to a saved presentation and changes the presentation's name in the title bar when you give the slide a new name.

- As in Word, you can also add summary information—title, author, keywords, and so on—about the presentation and view statistics.

Save File as a Web Page

- You can save a presentation in **HTML** (Hypertext Markup Language) format for publishing on the World Wide Web.

- When you save a presentation in HTML, you can open it in a browser, such as Internet Explorer.

Close a Presentation/Exit PowerPoint

- PowerPoint prompts you to save a presentation that has not been saved or has been modified before letting you close the presentation or exit the program.

- Follow the same procedures for closing a presentation file and exiting PowerPoint as in Word and Excel applications.
- Close a document when you are finished working on it.

Procedures

Start PowerPoint

1. Click **Start** `Start` .... `Ctrl`+`Esc`
2. Click **Programs**.
3. Click **Microsoft PowerPoint 2002**.

Open a New Presentation

1. Start PowerPoint.
2. In the Task Pane, click **Blank Presentation**

   `Blank Presentation`

   ✓ *If the New Presentation Task Pane isn't displayed, click View, Task Pane.*
3. In the Task Pane, click the Slide Layout you want to use.

Use Template Option

1. Start PowerPoint.
2. In the New Presentation Task Pane, click **From Design Template**

   `From Design Template`
3. Click the design template you want to use.

Use Right-clicks

1. Point to a PowerPoint item.
2. Right-click the mouse.
3. Click a command.

Use Placeholders

1. Click once in text placeholder.
2. Enter text.

OR

1. Click on content placeholder.
2. Insert specific type of content, such as clip art.

Insert New Slide (*Ctrl+M*)

1. Click **Insert** .... `Alt`+`I`
2. Click **New Slide** .... `N`

   OR

   Click **New Slide** button .
3. From Slide Layout Task Pane, select layout.

Add Summary Information about Presentation

1. Click **File** .... `Alt`+`F`
2. Click **Properties** .... `I`
3. Add desired information.
4. Click **OK** .... `Enter`

Save Presentation (*Ctrl+S*)

1. Click **File** .... `Alt`+`F`
2. Click **Save** .... `S`

   OR

   Click **Save** button `🖫`.
3. Click **Save in** drop-down arrow .... `Alt`+`I`
4. Select **drive** and **folder**.
5. Double-click **File name** text box .... `Alt`+`N`
6. Type **file name**.
7. Click **Save** .... `Alt`+`S`

Save as Web Page

1. Click **File** .... `Alt`+`F`
2. Click **Save as Web Page** .... `G`
3. In **File name** text box, type file name .... `Alt`+`N`
4. Click **Save** .... `S`

Close Presentation

1. Click **File** .... `Alt`+`F`
2. Click **Close** .... `C`

Exit PowerPoint

1. Click **File** .... `Alt`+`F`
2. Click **Exit** .... `X`

Exercise Directions

1. Start PowerPoint, if necessary.
2. Create a new blank presentation.
3. Save the file as **01Gourmet**.
4. Accept the default Title Slide layout for the first slide.
5. Type the title and subtitle as shown in Illustration A.
6. Insert a new slide and accept the Title and Text layout for the second slide.
7. Type the title and bulleted list as shown in Illustration B.
8. Fill in the summary information for the file as follows:

Title:	**Coastline Gourmet Importers**
Subject:	**Indian Spices**
Author:	**Your name**
Manager:	**Your supervisor or teacher's name**
Company:	**Communications Solutions, Inc.**
Category:	**Promotion**
Keywords:	**Spices, Indian**

9. Save the file, but don't close it.
10. Save the presentation as a Web page using the same name.
11. Close the file and exit PowerPoint, saving all changes.

Illustration A

Coastline Gourmet Importers

Indian Spices

Illustration B

New Indian Spices

- Arrowroot-a starch used for sweetmeats
- Asafoetida-a sour spice with a strong aroma
- Carom seeds-a digestive seasoning spice
- Mace-a sedative and carminative spice
- Nigella-a seed used in pickles
- Fenugreek-a strong flavor, rich in iron

On Your Own

1. Start PowerPoint and use a design template to create a presentation about yourself.

2. Select the default title slide layout and type a title for the presentation. For example, you might type My Life, or All About Me. Enter your name as the subtitle.

3. Insert a second slide using the Bulleted list layout.

4. Type a title on the second slide, and then type at least three items describing what the presentation will be about. For example, the first item might be "The Early Years," the second item might be "A Budding Athlete," and so on.

5. Insert a third slide using the Title, Text, and Clip Art layout.

6. Type a title on the third slide based on the first bulleted item that you entered on the second slide.

7. Type at least three bulleted items related to the topic.

8. Insert a fourth slide using the Title, Clip Art, and Text layout.

9. Type a title on the fourth slide based on the second bulleted item that you entered on the second slide.

10. Type at least three bulleted items related to the topic.

11. Save the presentation with the name **OPP01**.

12. Close the presentation and exit PowerPoint.

Exercise 2

Skills Covered:

◆ **Open an Existing Presentation** ◆ **Slide Views**
◆ **Move from Slide to Slide** ◆ **Spell Check** ◆ **Print a Presentation**
◆ **Change a Slide's Layout or Design Template**

On the Job

Check the spelling and otherwise refine the design of your presentation to make the best impression possible. For example, you may show a presentation to a prospective client who might purchase your product. A well-designed presentation can be the turning point in a sale.

You want to make some changes to the slide presentation for Coastline Gourmet Importers to make sure that your client will like it. Any presentation you plan to show a client should be spell checked. Also, you should review the design and organization of the presentation to make sure it is suitable for the client's tastes and requirements. Often, printing the presentation to hard copy gives you a better idea of how it will look to the customer.

Terms

Views PowerPoint offers several different ways you can view the presentation as you work on it: Normal view, which includes the Slide, Note, and Outline panes, Slide Sorter, and Slide Show views. Each view has its own advantages and features.

Automatic spell checking A feature that checks spelling as you enter text. A wavy red line in the text indicates a possible spelling error.

Notes

Standard toolbar

Open an Existing Presentation

■ PowerPoint opens with a blank presentation, consisting of a title slide, ready to work on.

■ Open an existing presentation to modify, add or delete material, print, or run the presentation as a slide show.

Slide Views

■ In PowerPoint, you can create and view a presentation in three different **views** plus two tabs that display panes within Normal view.

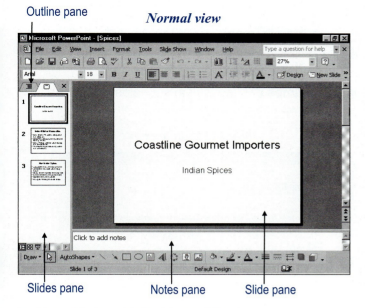

Outline pane

Normal view

Slides pane   Notes pane   Slide pane

- Normal view (default) provides two panes, or views, of the slide and its contents—Slide pane and Notes. It also includes two tabs—Slides and Outline.
  - The Slide pane displays the contents as it will look on the slide.
  - The Notes pane lets you add text for personal reference.
  - The Slides tab lets you organize slides and easily see a thumbnail of each slide.
  - The Outline tab lets you view the slides content in outline format.
- Slides pane in Normal view displays the slides in the presentation so that you can quickly switch to the slide you want to view.
- The Outline pane in Normal view displays the outline of the presentation (slightly reducing the size of the Slide pane as it does so).

Outline pane

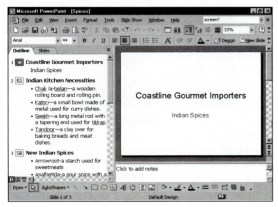

- Slide Sorter view displays the entire presentation in large thumbnails so you can easily identify slides as well as add, delete, and rearrange slides. This view is also suitable for easily adding and previewing animations, transitions, and sound effects to an entire presentation.
- Slide Show view displays one slide at a time, displaying a slide as it would be displayed in a slide show. This view is used to run an on-screen slide show.

Move from Slide to Slide

- Most presentations include multiple slides.
- You will need to move from slide to slide to enter text and modify the presentation.
- PowerPoint offers a variety of ways to select and display slides.

Move from slide to slide on scroll bar

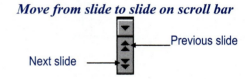

Previous slide

Next slide

Spell Check

- PowerPoint provides two methods of spell checking in your presentations: automatic and manual.
- **Automatic spell checking** works while you're typing.
- Automatic spell checking displays a wavy red line under words PowerPoint doesn't recognize.
- PowerPoint activates the automatic spell checker by default.
  - ✓ *You can use manual spell checking at any time.*
- The use of the spell checker is similar to that in other Microsoft Office applications.
- A professional presentation must have no spelling errors.

Print a Presentation

- Printing PowerPoint slides is similar to printing pages in other Office programs, with a few exceptions.
- A presentation can be printed as speaker's notes, handouts, slides, or as an outline. You choose the settings in the Print dialog box.

Print dialog box

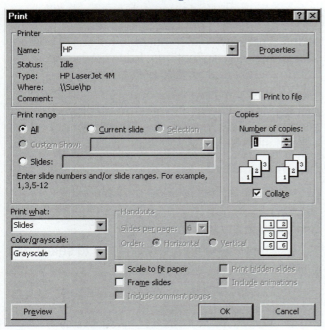

- You specify page setup before you print the contents of the presentation. Select Page Setup from the File menu.
- Page setup lets you define the page size and orientation.
- Sometimes printing a slide set helps you to see any flaws to the design and to proofread content.

Page Setup dialog box

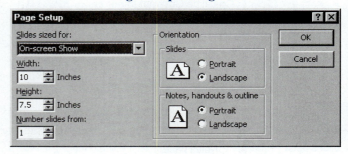

Print Options

Option	Description
Properties	Click to change printer conditions, such as paper size, orientation, and graphics.
Print to file	Creates a printer file (.PRN) that can be printed on another computer that doesn't have the PowerPoint program.
Print range	Defines whether to print all slides, the current slide only, or a range of slides in the presentation.
Copies	Defines the number of copies to print.
Collate	Prints the slides in their order in the presentation.
Print what	Select to print slides, handouts, notes, or an outline.
Handouts	Select the number of slides to print per page.
Order	Select horizontal or vertical order of the slides on the handout page.
Grayscale	Select to print colors in shades of gray.
Pure black and white	Select this option to print slides in only black and white.
Scale to fit paper	Changes the size of the slide to fit the selected paper size.
Frame slides	Adds a frame border around the slides when printed.
Include animations	Check the option to include animations in the printed slides.
Print hidden slides	Prints any hidden slides in the presentation.

Change a Slide's Layout or Design Template

- You may need to change a slide's layout or a presentation's template as you work.
- Change a slide's layout to add additional text or elements, like a graph or chart.
- Change the template to modify background, text color, or design elements.

Slide Design Task Pane

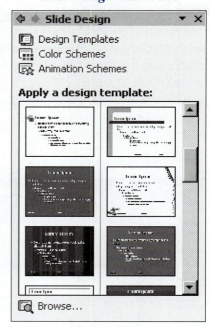

- Try to choose a template design that suits the subject matter.

- You can view a color presentation in black and white or grayscale while you are working on it.

- When viewing a presentation in grayscale or black and white, PowerPoint automatically displays a Grayscale View toolbar.

Black and White view

Procedures

Open Existing Presentation

1. Start PowerPoint.
2. Click **File** .... Alt + F
3. Click **Open** .... O
4. Click on file to open.
5. Click **Open** button .... O

OR

1. Click the **Open** button 📂 on the Standard toolbar.
2. Browse to locate and open the file.

OR

- Click to open a file on the New Presentation Task Pane.

Slide Views

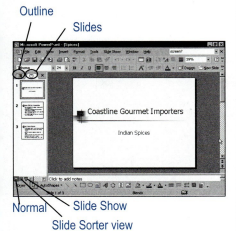

Outline

Slides

Normal

Slide Show

Slide Sorter view

- To change views, click appropriate button on View bar or click appropriate tab.

OR

1. Click **View** .... Alt + V
2. Click one of the following:
   Normal .... N
   Slide Sorter .... D
   Slide Show .... W or F5

Move from Slide to Slide

1. Press **Page Down** to display next slide.
2. Press **Page Up** to display previous slide.

OR

1. Click **Next Slide** button ⬇ on vertical slide scroll bar.
2. Click **Previous Slide** button ⬆ on vertical slide scroll bar.

OR

- Click on a slide on the Slides or Outline pane.

OR

- Double-click on a slide in Slide Sorter view.

Disable or Activate Automatic Spell Checker

1. Click **Tools** .... Alt + T
2. Click **Options** .... O
3. Click **Spelling and Style** tab .... Ctrl + Tab
4. To disable, select **Hide all spelling errors** check box .. S
   OR
   To activate, check **Check spelling as you type** .... P
5. Click **OK** .... Enter

Manually Spell Check Presentation (*F7*)

1. Click **Tools** .... Alt + T
2. Click **Spelling and Grammar** .... S
   OR
   Click **Spelling and Grammar** button ✓.

Change Page Setup

1. Click **File** .... Alt + F
2. Click **Page Setup** .... U
3. Indicate page specifications.
4. Click **OK** .... Enter

Change Slide Layouts

1. Click **Format** .... Alt + O
2. Click **Slide Layout** L
3. Click layout you want to apply.
4. Click the **Close** button ✕.

Change Design Templates

1. Click **Format** .... Alt + O
2. Click **Slide Design** .... D
3. Select template design from Slide Design pane.
   ✓ *Clicking the arrow on the design preview gives the option of applying the design to all slides or selected slides.*
4. Click the **Close** button ✕.

View Slide in Black and White

1. Click **View** .... Alt + V
2. Click **Color/Grayscale** C
3. Click **Pure Black and White**... U
4. To change view back to color, repeat steps 1 and 2 and then click **Color**.

Print Presentation (*Ctrl+P*)

1. Click **File** .... Alt + F
2. Click **Print** .... P
3. Choose desired print options.
4. Click **OK** .... Enter

OR

- Click **Print** button 🖨.
  ✓ *Your presentation will print based on the default or last options you selected in the Print dialog box.*

Exercise Directions

1. Start PowerPoint, if necessary.
2. Open ⌨01Gourmet or 💿02Gourmet.
3. Save the file as **02Gourmet**.
4. Move to slide 1 and insert a new slide using the Title Slide layout.
5. Enter the text as shown in Illustration A.
6. Switch to Outline pane. In the Notes pane, enter the following text:
   Add recipes for some spices in sidebars.
7. Switch to Slide pane.
8. Move to slide 3 and insert another slide using the Title and 2-Column Text layout.
9. Enter the text shown in Illustration B.
10. Change to Slide Sorter view.
11. Check the presentation for spelling errors.
    - ✓ *Note the spelling checker will find errors in some of the Indian words. Check the spelling yourself for these and then simply ignore the words in question.*
12. Apply the design template Edge.
13. Print a handout with three slides per page.
14. Close the file and exit PowerPoint, saving all changes.

Illustration A

Indian Cookery

Exotic Spices, Ingredients, and Kitchen Accessories

Illustration B

Indian Essentials

- Beans
  - Lentils
  - Chick Peas
  - Black Beans
- Baked flat breads
  - Naan
  - Chapati
  - Wafers
  - Roti

- Preserves
  - Apple
  - Carrot
- Pickles
  - Chili Pickles
  - Lemon Pickles
- Desserts
  - Sweetmeats
  - Puddings
  - Toffee

On Your Own

1. Open the **OPP01** presentation you created in the On Your Own section of Exercise 1, or open ⊙ **02MYLIFE**.
2. Save the file as **OPP02**.
3. Check the spelling in the presentation.
4. Scroll through the second, third, and fourth slides.
5. Change to Slide Sorter view.
6. Display the Outline pane.
7. Change to Normal view.
8. Display the slide in black in white.
9. Display the title slide.
10. Change back to color.
11. Change the design template.
12. Display slide four.
13. Change the slide layout to Title, Text, and Clip Art.
14. Print the entire presentation.
15. Save the presentation, close it, and exit PowerPoint.

Exercise 3

Skills Covered:

◆ **Work with Content Layouts** ◆ **Use Undo**

On the Job

Add objects to your slides to make them more interesting to the audience. You might, for example, add clip art to a slide presentation to break up the text or emphasize certain points.

The client has supplied your company with information for use in a chart and other slides. They also asked that you add clip art to the presentation to make it more interesting for their prospective clients. In this exercise, you will enhance your presentation with clip art and **WordArt**.

Terms

WordArt A feature used to transform text into a picture object.

Object An item other than text, such as a table, chart, clip art, WordArt, or worksheet.

Embed Inserting an object created in another application into your PowerPoint presentation. Embedded objects are easy to edit and update.

Notes

Work with Content Layouts

- The Slide Layout Task Pane supplies placeholders for **objects**, such as clip art and charts, in addition to placeholders for text.

- In PowerPoint, the Slide Layout Task Pane provides previews of various layouts that use text placeholders, or a combination of text and content placeholders.

- A content placeholder helps you add objects by displaying an icon box in the placeholder.

- You can also insert objects manually into new and preexisting slides using menus and toolbar buttons.

- **Embed** a content object, such as an Excel worksheet, so you can edit it easily within PowerPoint.

- Objects add interest to a presentation.

Icon box for adding an object

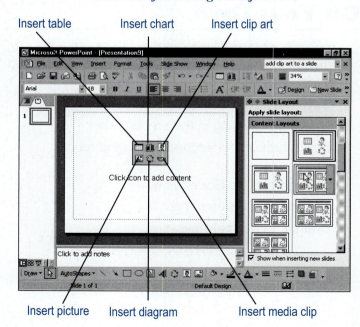

596

Add clip art to a presentation

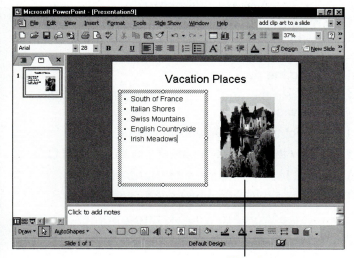

Clip art

Use Undo

- PowerPoint contains an Undo feature, as in other Microsoft applications, that reverses the most recent action.

- With Undo, you can often reverse one or multiple actions you have performed in PowerPoint.

- You can redo actions after you undo, if you change your mind.

Procedures

Insert Object into Placeholder

1. Add new slide layout that contains a content placeholder.
2. Click the appropriate object icon.
3. In the resulting dialog box, choose the appropriate options.
4. Click **OK**..........................Enter

Insert Clip Art

1. Add new slide layout that contains a content placeholder.
2. Click **Insert Clip** Art icon 🖼️.
3. In Select Picture dialog box, click desired art.
   OR
   a. Type a keyword in the Search text box.
   b. Click Search.
4. Select desired clip art.
5. Click **OK**.

Insert WordArt

1. Click **Insert** .... Alt + I
2. Click **Picture** .... P
3. Click **WordArt** .... W
   ✓ *You can add WordArt to a new or existing slide.*
4. Click the WordArt style you'd like to apply.
5. Click **OK**.
6. Type text.
7. Click **OK** ....Enter
8. Select options from WordArt toolbar.

Insert Object using No Placeholder

1. Open a new or existing slide.
2. Click **Insert**................. Alt + I
3. Click one of the following:
   - **Picture**........................... P
   - **Diagram**....................... G
   - **Te_x_t box**....................... X
   - **Mo_v_ies and Sounds** V

- **C_h_art**............................. H
- **Table** .... B
- **Object** .... O

4. Choose from the submenu or dialog box that appears depending on the object you selected.

Insert a Text Box

✓ *Drawing toolbar must be displayed.*

1. Click **Text Box** button 📇 on the Drawing toolbar.
2. Click and drag the text tool on the slide.
3. Type the text.

Undo (*Ctrl+Z*)

1. Click **Edit** .... Alt + E
2. Click **Undo** .... U

Undo Multiple Actions

1. Click **Undo** button's down arrow ▾.
2. Click the recent actions you want to undo.

Insert WordArt Object toolbar

Insert WordArt

Edit Text   Format Placeholder   WordArt Same Letter...   WordArt Alignment

WordArt gallery   WordArt Shape   WordArt Vertical text   WordArt Character Spacing

Exercise Directions

1. Start PowerPoint, if necessary.
2. Open ⌨02Gourmet or 💿03Gourmet.
3. Save the file as **03Gourmet**.
4. Move to slide 4 and insert a new slide.
5. Select Title, Content, and Text slide layout.
6. Enter the text as shown in Illustration A.
7. Insert a relevant clip art in the content placeholder. Select a clip and then double-click it to insert into the document.
8. Insert a new slide at the end of the presentation.
9. Double-click the Title Only slide layout.
10. Type the title shown in Illustration B.
11. Insert a text box and type the text as shown in Illustration B.
    - ✓ *See procedures for inserting text boxes.*
12. Insert a relevant clip art. Resize or move the art as necessary.
    - ✓ *To resize the clip art click on the clip to select it and then drag one of the sizing handles. To move a clip, click on the clip to select it. Holding down the mouse button, drag the clip to a new location.*
13. Insert a new slide after slide 5 using any Slide Layout.
14. Undo the new slide insert.
15. Move to the end of the presentation and insert a new slide.
16. Select the Title Only slide layout.
17. Enter the title text as shown in Illustration C.
18. Click Insert, Picture, and WordArt.
19. Choose a WordArt style and click OK.
20. For the WordArt, type **Sizzling Spices**.
21. From WordArt's toolbar, choose any design or text formatting you want and close the WordArt by clicking OK. You can resize or reformat the WordArt.
22. Spell check the presentation.
23. Print the slides as handouts, with four slides to the page.
24. Close the file and exit PowerPoint, saving all changes.

Illustration A

Make Your Own or Buy Our GHEE

- Melt 5 pounds of butter in a saucepan. Bring to boil, stirring constantly.
- Simmer butter for 30 minutes then remove from heat.
- Skim the top layer. Let cool 2 hours.
- Transfer to jar.

Illustration B

Presentation

Unless a dish looks nice, it doesn't matter how many exotic spices and wonderful flavors you add. Make sure the presentation of the dinner is attractive. Use fresh flowers, play some soft music, and arrange the napkins and dishes in an attractive manner.

Illustration C

Just what you need:

On Your Own

1. Open the **OPP02** presentation you created in Exercise 2, or open 💿 **03MYLIFE**.

2. Save the file as **OPP03**.

3. Insert a clip art picture on to slide 3. Try to select a picture that is somehow related to the text on the slide.

4. Insert a clip art object on slide 4.

5. Undo the insertion.

6. Insert a different clip art object on slide 4.

7. Print the presentation as handouts with two slides on a page.

8. Save the presentation, close it, and exit PowerPoint.

Exercise 4

On the Job

As you work on a presentation, you can move slides around, copy slides, and even delete slides you don't want in the presentation to make it more compact or descriptive. You might also, for example, create a presentation for one group of people in your company and then customize the presentation for another group by copying and changing some slides.

After reviewing your presentation, you decided to change the presentation's organization and make some additional changes before showing it to the client. In this exercise, you will duplicate slides and add new slides to your presentation.

Terms

Duplicate To create a copy of a slide that includes all text, content objects, and formatting of the original. A duplicate slide is inserted after the original slide in the presentation.

Slide Sorter view A method of viewing multiple slides in the presentation at one time so you can easily move them.

Notes

Move, Copy, Duplicate, and Delete Slides

- A presentation contains multiple slides, any of which you can move, copy, **duplicate**, or delete.

- To move a slide, click the slide in the Slides tab or Outline tab in Normal view or in Slide Sorter view and drag it to the new position.

- You can also move and copy slides from one presentation to another.

- Duplicating creates a copy of a slide so you can make use of custom formatting and other features of the original slide to create a new slide.

- If you move, copy, duplicate, or delete a slide, you can use the Undo command to reverse the action.

- Save a presentation before you edit a slide so you can revert to the previous version if you make a mistake or lose data.

Move slides

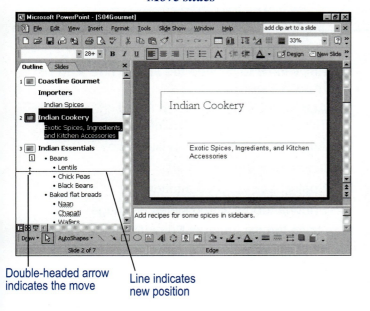

Double-headed arrow
indicates the move

Line indicates
new position

Slide Sorter View

- **Slide Sorter view** enables you to organize your presentation as a whole.

- Slide Sorter view displays slides as miniatures so you can arrange them as you work or as the final step to completing the presentation.

- You cannot edit slide content in Slide Sorter view.

- To edit slide content, double-click a slide to display it in Normal view.

Slide Sorter view

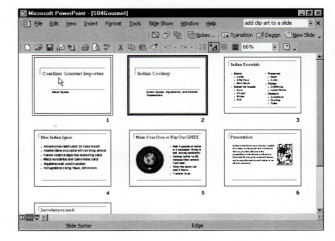

Procedures

Copy Slide (*Ctrl+C*) and Paste Slide *(Ctrl+V)*

1. In the Slides or Outline pane of Normal view or in Slide Sorter view, select slide to copy.

2. Click **Copy** button 🗈.

   OR

   a. Click **Edit** .... Alt + E

   b. Click **Copy** C

   ✓ *If you want to copy slide from one presentation to another, display the other presentation.*

3. In the Slides or Outline pane of Normal view or in Slide Sorter view, select slide after which the copied slide will be pasted.

4. Click **Paste** button 🗈.

   OR

   a. Click **Edit** .... Alt + E

   b. Click **Paste** .... P

Duplicate Slide

1. In the Slides or Outline pane of Normal view or in Slide Sorter view, select slide.

2. Click **Insert** .... Alt + I

3. Click **Duplicate Slide** .... D

Delete Slide

1. In the Slides or Outline pane of Normal view or in Slide Sorter view, select slide.

2. Press **Delete** key .... Del

   OR

   a. Click **Edit** .... Alt + E

   b. Click **Delete Slide** .... D

   OR

1. Right-click slide in the Slides or Outline pane of Normal view or in Slide Sorter view.

2. Click **Delete Slide** .... D

Move Slide

1. In the Slides or Outline pane of Normal view or in Slide Sorter view, select the slide thumbnail.

2. Drag the slide thumbnail button to new position.

3. Release mouse button.

Change to Slide Sorter View

- Click **Slide Sorter View** button 🔳.

   OR

1. Click **View** .... Alt + V

2. Click **Slide Sorter** .... D

Exercise Directions

1. Open ⌨03Gourmet or ⊙04Gourmet.

2. Save the file as **04Gourmet**.

3. Select slide 2 and copy it.

4. Paste the slide so it becomes slide 3.

5. Change the contents of slide 3 as shown in Illustration A.

6. If necessary, switch to the Slides pane in Normal view.

7. Duplicate slide 5.

8. Switch to Slide Sorter view.

9. Delete slide 5.

10. Move slide 4 to the second slide position.

11. Edit slide 8 to change the title to **The Key to Indian Cooking**.

12. Add a new slide after slide 8 and choose the Title, Text, and Content slide layout.

13. Add the text as shown in Illustration B.

14. Insert appropriate clip art.

15. Spell check the presentation.

16. Print handouts with 6 slides per page.

17. Close the file and exit PowerPoint, saving all changes.

Illustration A

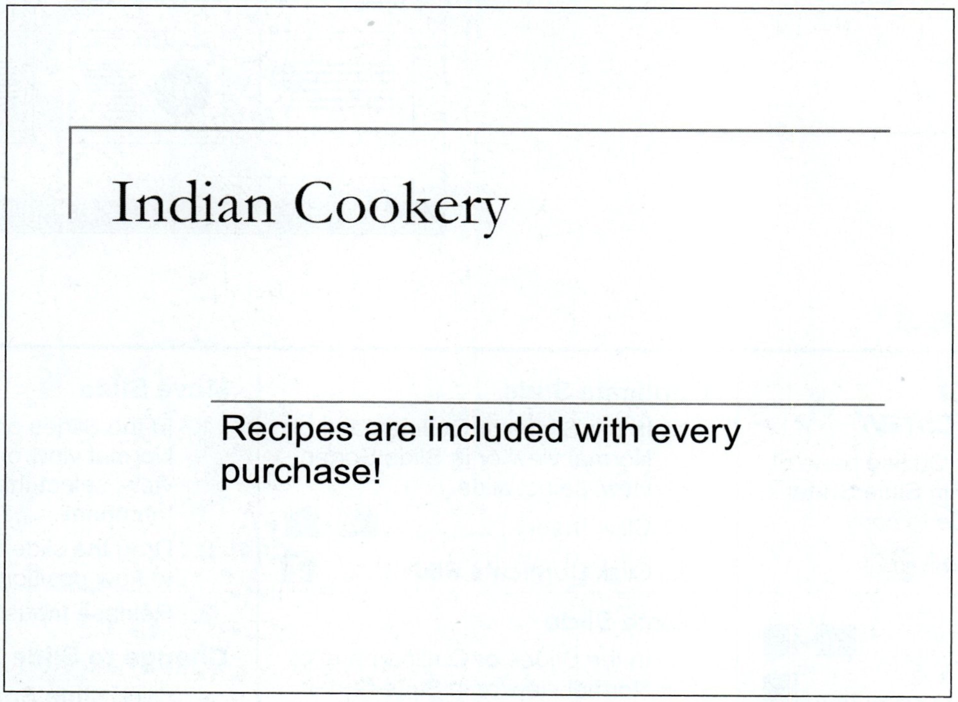

Indian Cookery

Recipes are included with every purchase!

Illustration B

Indian Ingredients

- Almonds
- Aniseed
- Artichokes
- Bay leaves
- Lamb
- Buttermilk
- Cabbage
- Lemons
- Mangos

On Your Own

1. Open the **OPP03** presentation you created in Exercise 3, or open ⊙ **04MYLIFE**.

2. Save the file as **OPP04**.

3. Insert a new slide after slide 2 using the Title and 2-Column Text layout.

4. Give the slide a title related to the third topic on slide 2.

5. Type at least two items in each column.

6. Change to Slide Sorter view.

7. Move the new two-column slide to the end of the presentation.

8. Make of copy of the fourth slide and paste it at the end of the presentation.

9. Undo the paste.

10. Save the presentation.

11. Close the presentation and exit PowerPoint.

Exercise 5

Skills Covered:
◆ Outline Pane ◆ Summary Slide

On the Job

Use the Outline pane in Normal view to help you organize a presentation. For example, you can add new slides and move slides around in the Outline pane so you can better organize the slides you already have.

You will continue working on the sample slide presentations for your client, Coastline Gourmet Importers. In this exercise, you will check each slide for organization, spelling, and other details in the Outline pane, so that you can easily rearrange text and make modifications to the presentation.

Terms

Outline pane Selecting the Outline pane in Normal view lets you see the outline of a slide presentation in text form on the Outline pane, as well as with slide thumbnails on the Slide pane.

Collapse Hiding all except main, or selected, headings in an outline.

Expand Showing all levels of an outline.

Outline A technique of arranging topics and their subordinates to organize a presentation.

Notes

Outline Pane

- The **Outline pane** displays a presentation so that you can see an overview and organize content more easily.

- You can create a presentation in Normal view with the Outline pane displayed.

- Use the Outline pane to check the text content of a presentation for consistency and an overall flow of information.

- You can print a customized Outline view by **collapsing** or **expanding** certain headings or showing all formatting, for example.

- The Outlining toolbar makes it easy to rearrange content throughout the entire presentation.

- The Outlining toolbar also helps you view the **outline** in different ways, for easier organization.

Outline pane

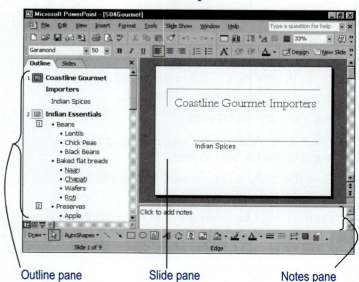

Outline pane   Slide pane   Notes pane

Outlining toolbar

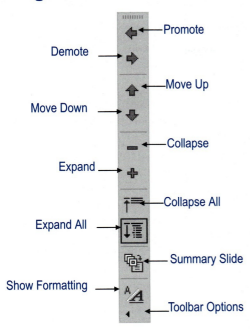

- Promote/Demote buttons change the heading levels and apply styles, such as bulleted text to selected text.

- Move Up/Move Down buttons let you move text up or down on the outline.
- Expand button displays the title, subtitle, and all bullet levels of the text in the selected slides.
- Collapse button hides the text levels in the selected slides and displays only the title text.
- Expand All button displays all levels of text for all slides in the presentation.
- Collapse All button displays only the title text for all slides in the presentation.
- Summary Slide button creates a new slide consisting of the titles of selected slides in Outline view.
- Show Formatting button displays text formatted as it will look on the slide.

Summary Slide

■ Create a Summary Slide made up of the titles of each slide in your presentation.
■ A Summary Slide can be used as an agenda or overview.

Procedures

Display Outlining Toolbar
1. Click **View** .... Alt + V
2. Click **Toolbars** .... T
3. Click **Outlining**.

Move Text in Outline View
1. Select the text to move.
2. Click **Move Up** 🔼 or **Move Down** 🔽 buttons.
3. Click **Demote** ➡️ or **Promote** ⬅️ buttons to change the outline level of the text.

OR
1. Select the text to move.
2. Drag the text to new location.
3. Release mouse button.

Select Slides in Outline View
1. Click the slide's number or Slide icon 5 🔲 .
2. To select additional slides, press Shift and then click Slide button for each slide.

Display Titles in Outline View
- Click the **Collapse All** button 📑 .

Insert Summary Slide
1. Select all slides in presentation .... Ctrl + A
2. Click **Summary Slide** button 📑 on the Slide Sorter toolbar.

Print an Outline (*Ctrl+P*)
✓ *Collapse or expand slide titles and text as you want them to appear on printout.*
1. Click **File** .... Alt + F
2. Click **Print** .... P
3. Click Outline View in **Print what** drop-down list .... Alt + W
4. Click **Outline View**.
5. Click **OK** .... Enter

Exercise Directions

1. Open 04Gourmet or 05Gourmet.

2. Save the file as **05Gourmet**.

3. If necessary, click the Outline pane.

4. Move slide 4 to the third slide position.

5. Move slide 2 so it appears after slide 4.

   ✓ *Hint: Collapse the slides before you move slide 2.*

6. Move the following bullets on slide 9:
   - Lamb to the first bullet position on the slide.
   - Cabbage to the second bullet position.
   - Buttermilk to the third bullet position on the slide. See Illustration A.

7. Collapse all.

8. Select all slides and add a summary slide at the beginning of the presentation.

9. On the summary slide, as shown in Illustration B:
   - Delete one of the Indian Cookery bullets.
   - Move the Presentation bullet to the second position on the Summary Slide.

10. Expand the outline.

11. Spell check the presentation.

12. Print the outline.

13. Close the file and exit PowerPoint, saving all changes.

Illustration A

Indian Ingredients

- Lamb
- Cabbage
- Buttermilk
- Almonds
- Aniseed
- Artichokes
- Bay leaves
- Lemons
- Mangos

Summary Slide

- Coastline Gourmet Importers
- Presentation
- Indian Cookery
- Indian Essentials
- New Indian Spices
- Make Your Own or Buy Our GHEE
- The Key to Indian Cooking
- Indian Ingredients

On Your Own

1. Create a new, blank presentation.

2. Save the new presentation as **OPP05**.

3. In the Outline pane, enter text for at least four slides. Make the presentation about an organization or club to which you belong, about the place where you work, about a class you are taking, or about school in general.

4. Change to Slide Sorter view.

5. Create a Summary slide from the headings on the slides in the presentation.

6. Move the Summary slide to the end of the presentation.

7. Change back to Normal view and the Outline pane.

8. Use the Outlining toolbar to rearrange slides and promote/demote text.

9. Print the collapsed outline and then print the expanded outline.

10. Apply a design template to the presentation

11. Check the spelling.

12. Save the presentation.

13. Close the presentation and exit PowerPoint.

Exercise 6

- ◆ **Import/Export an Outline**
- ◆ **Link an Excel Worksheet**

On the Job

Use data created in other programs for slide material to save time. You might have written a paper that when collapsed in Word creates the perfect outline for a presentation. Or, you created an Excel worksheet that you can link to a presentation that gives your audience the most up-to-date material.

Your client, Regency General, Inc., has supplied you with files that they want you to use in the presentation you're creating for them. Using the client's files from Word and Excel means the data is accurate and up-to-date and the organization is already arranged as the client wants. You'll also add some design elements to spice up the presentation.

Terms

Import To bring a copy of text or data created in another program into PowerPoint.

File formats Each program saves a file as a specific type, or format. Many programs can convert file types so they can be used by several different programs.

Export To send a copy of text or data from one program, such as PowerPoint, to another program.

Link To connect two files so that when an original file is updated, the linked file reflects the changes.

Source The file from which you are copying or moving information.

Destination The file to which you are copying or moving information.

Notes

Import/Export an Outline

- You can use text created in other programs, such as Word, in your PowerPoint presentation.

- You might want to **import** text so that you don't have to retype the text or because you prefer organizing the presentation in Word.

- Import a DOC, RTF, TXT, or HTM format, as well as other formats from Excel, WordPerfect, and other programs.

  - ✓ *You may need to install a file converter to load certain types of files.*

- PowerPoint recognizes many **file formats**. When you open a file created in another format, PowerPoint automatically converts it to a PowerPoint outline.

  - ✓ *Some files you open may not be suitable for a PowerPoint outline. When you choose the Outline Files type when importing an outline, PowerPoint lists only those formats that do work as outlines.*

- Word formats an outline exported from PowerPoint with headings and bullets that are indented.

- You might **export** an outline to Word so that you can use the text in another document, such as a report or letter.

Import an Excel worksheet

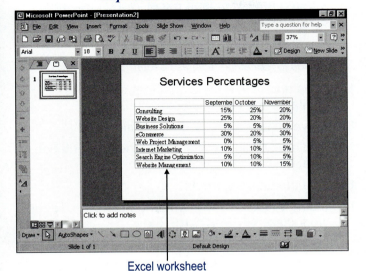

Excel worksheet

Link an Excel Worksheet

- You can **link** an Excel worksheet to a PowerPoint presentation to keep your information up-to-date and accurate.

- A linked object is one that's created in a **source** file and inserted into a **destination** file.

- A linked object does not become a part of the destination file.

- The link connects the files so that when the source is modified, the destination automatically updates the information.

- You can link to any program that supports linked and embedded objects.

- PowerPoint lets you create a new object to link or select an existing file to link to your PowerPoint presentation.

- An inserted worksheet may display empty cells, but you can crop unnecessary cells and resize the worksheet to better fit the slide.

- When you click in an inserted Excel worksheet, the Excel toolbar appears for you to use.

Procedures

Import Outline from Word
(Ctrl+O)

1. Click **File** .... Alt + F
2. Click **Open** .... O
3. In **Files of type**, click **All Outlines**.
4. In **Look in** list, select the folder where the Word file is stored.
5. Select file to import.
6. Click **Open** .... O

Export Outline to Word

1. Click **File** .... Alt + F
2. Click **Send To** .... D
3. Click **Microsoft Word** .... W
4. Click **Outline only** .... O
5. Click **OK** .... Enter

Insert New Excel Worksheet
(Ctrl+M)

1. Click **Insert** .... Alt + I
2. Click **Object** .... O
3. Click **OK** .... Enter
4. In Insert Object dialog box, select **Create new** .... Alt + N
5. In **Object type** list box, select **Microsoft Excel Worksheet**.
6. Click **OK** .... Enter
7. Enter data in worksheet.
8. Click outside of worksheet to return to presentation and display data.

Insert Existing Object File

1. Click **Insert** .... Alt + I
2. Click **Object** .... O
3. Click **OK** .... Enter
4. In Insert Object dialog box, click **Create from file** .... Alt + F

5. Click **Browse** .... B
6. Select file.
7. Click **OK** .... Enter
8. Select **Link** check box L
9. Click **OK** .... Enter

Crop Excel Worksheet

1. Double-click worksheet.
2. Click any of the eight handles on border of object.
3. Drag double-headed arrow to resize object box.

Size Worksheet

1. Select worksheet by clicking it once.
2. Drag corner handle to resize.

Move Worksheet

1. Click worksheet to display four-headed arrow.
2. Drag object box to new position.

Exercise Directions

1. Start PowerPoint, if necessary.

2. Open **06IMPORTOUTLINE.doc** as an outline in PowerPoint.

   ✓ *You will need to select All Outlines from the Files of type drop-down list in the Open dialog box.*

3. Save the file as **06InternetServices**.

4. Apply an appropriate design template to the presentation.

5. Go to slide 1 and add the bulleted text shown in Illustration A.

6. Go to slide 2 and insert a clip art. Resize and move the clip art to fit the slide content.

7. Insert a new slide after slide 3. Choose the Title Only text layout slide.

8. Add the title: **Communications**.

9. Insert a new Microsoft Excel Worksheet and add the data as shown in Illustration B.

   ✓ *Set the view to 100% to make working in the worksheet easier. The toolbar changes, which allows you to format the table as needed.*

10. Crop and resize the worksheet so it looks similar to the one in Illustration B.

11. Move slide 4 to the slide 3 position.

12. Add a new slide to the end of the presentation. Use the Title Only text layout.

13. Add the title: **Services**.

14. Insert an existing worksheet and link it. Use the worksheet **06WORKSH.xls**.

15. Crop, size, and move the worksheet if necessary, as shown in Illustration C.

16. Modify the chart in Excel and then go to PowerPoint to view the modified chart.

17. Spell check the presentation.

18. Print the presentation as slides.

19. Close the file and exit PowerPoint, saving all changes.

Illustration A

Regency General, Inc.

- Single Web pages to custom integration
- Business-2-Business Internet Services
- Small businesses to large enterprises
- Government and educational institutions
- Leased-line access

Illustration B

Communications

	Consulting	Sales	Return Business
Intranet	25%	20%	20%
Extranet	15%	15%	15%
Telecommunications	35%	30%	35%
Internet	25%	35%	30%

Illustration C

Services

	September	October	November
Consulting	15%	25%	20%
Website Design	25%	20%	20%
Business Solutions	5%	5%	0%
eCommerce	30%	20%	30%
Web Project Management	0%	5%	5%
Internet Marketing	10%	10%	5%
Search Engine Optimization	5%	10%	5%
Website Management	10%	10%	15%

On Your Own

1. Start PowerPoint and create a presentation outline from the ⊙ **OPP06OUT.doc** Word document file.

2. Save the presentation as **OPP06**.

3. Use the outline to create a presentation telling people why they should donate money to a particular charity. You can select any charity you want. Personalize the outline text by replacing the sample text in the outline.

4. Apply a design template to the presentation.

5. Change slide layouts as necessary to set up the slides for titles and bulleted lists. Include space for clip art and an Excel worksheet.

6. Insert clip art where necessary.

7. Save the presentation.

8. Start Excel and create a new workbook, or open ⊙ **OPP06XL.xls**.

9. Save the worksheet as **OPP06-2**.

10. Enter or edit the data to set up a worksheet to insert in your presentation. For example, list the income and expenses for the charity, or how much money comes from fundraising.

11. Save the worksheet, close it, and close Excel.

12. Insert the **OPP06-2.xls** worksheet on a slide in the **OPP06** presentation.

13. If necessary, move, crop, or resize the worksheet on the slide so it looks good.

14. Print the slides.

15. Save the presentation and exit PowerPoint.

Exercise 7

When presenting an advertising campaign to a client, you want to offer two or three different designs so that the client can compare layouts and then make a choice. In this exercise, you will create another sample presentation for your client Coastline Gourmet Importers.

Exercise Directions

1. Start PowerPoint, if necessary.
2. Create a new presentation using the Watermark design template.
3. Save the file as **07Gourmet**.
4. Use the Title Slide design as your first slide.
5. In the Outline pane of Normal view, enter the text as shown in Illustration A.
6. Move to slide 1. Add a clip art or WordArt to one corner of the slide that serves as a logo for Coastline Gourmet Importers. You might use a food or herb clip art.
7. Resize and move as necessary. The logo should be small.
8. Create three more slides adding text to each slide and clip art, if you want.
9. Switch to Slide Sorter view.
10. Move slide 2 after slide 4.
11. Switch back to Normal view.
12. Edit slide 6 by inserting an Excel spreadsheet using the following data:

	1st Qtr	2nd Qtr	3rd Qtr	4th Qtr
Spices	125	175	200	250
Ingredients	75	125	150	125
Accessories	75	100	125	75

13. Resize the worksheet so it fits on the slide and is easy to read.
14. If necessary, switch to the Outline pane in Normal view.
15. Collapse all and print the outline.
16. Select all slides and create a summary slide.
17. Move the summary slide to the end of the presentation and insert a logo on to that slide.
18. Spell check the presentation.
19. Expand all and print the outline.
20. Switch to Normal view and print handouts with 3 slides per page in pure black and white.
21. Save the file.
22. Close the file and exit PowerPoint, saving all changes.

¹■ **Coastline Gourmet Importers**

Indian Spices and Cookery

²■ **Indian Spice Line**

- Cookery
- Tools and Equipment
- Ingredients
- Spices
- Recipes

³■ **Indian Spices**

- Arrowroot
- Asafoetida
- Carom seeds
- Mace
- Nigela
- Fenugreek

⁴■ **Indian Ingredients**

- Beans
- Flat breads
- Preserves
- Pickles
- Desserts
- Rice
- Ghee

⁵■ **Indian Recipes**

- Check out our cookbooks and printed recipes for Indian foods.

⁶■ **Sales Statistics**

- Spices
- Ingredients
- Accessories

⁷■ **Contact Information**

- Coastline Gourmet Importers
- 7334 Sunshine Pkwy.
- 12th Floor
- Miami, FL 33132
- Voice: 305-555-7300
- Fax: 304-555-7301
- E-mail: mail@ddcpub.com/coastlinegourmet

1

Skills Covered:

◆ **Select Text** ◆ **Align Text** ◆ **Change the Appearance of Text**
◆ **Change Case** ◆ **Change Slide Color Scheme**
◆ **Change Slide Background**

On the Job

You can change the appearance of text to make it fit the space on the slide better or to add emphasis and interest. Change color schemes or text styles to give a presentation more interest or excitement. For example, a presentation about a sale would use bright colors and informal font styles, whereas a presentation about a financial institution would use more simple colors and formal fonts.

You work for Regency General, Inc. as a Web site designer. West Printing Company, a company that prints books and other publications, wants you to help them with a Web site to which they can refer prospective customers. One of West Printing Company's employees created a PowerPoint presentation. West's owner wants you to improve upon the design of the presentation.

Terms

Justified Text is spaced so that both left and right edges of text are even.

Format To change the text appearance by applying a new font face, size, alignment, color, or style.

Color scheme A set of compatible colors in a slide used for background, type, lines, and objects.

Notes

Select Text

■ You select text so that you can modify it in some way, like making it larger or bold.

■ You can use the mouse pointer either as an I-beam or arrow to select text in PowerPoint. Drag the I-beam across the text you want to select. Point the arrow at a line of text to select one or more lines.

■ You can select and edit text in Normal view.

Align Text

■ Align text to the left, center, or right in a placeholder to add interest and to enhance the design.

■ You can also use **justified** text alignment, although too much justified text can be difficult to read.

■ You can align any one paragraph of text in a text placeholder without changing the other paragraphs of text. In a title placeholder, however, aligning one paragraph realigns all of the paragraphs.

■ Align text in the slide pane in Normal view to see the effects on the slide.

Change the Appearance of Text

■ You can **format** the appearance of text to emphasize it or to make your presentation more interesting and unique.

Formatting toolbar

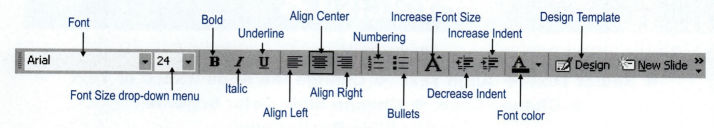

- Text appearance attributes include font face, size, color, style, and special effects.

- You can change text attributes using techniques similar to those that you used in Word and Excel.

- As in Word, when changing the appearance of a single word, you do not need to select the word first. You can simply click in the word and apply a new text attribute.

- Use the Formatting toolbar to change one text attribute at a time.

  ✓ *If you cannot see all of the above buttons, drag the Formatting toolbar below the Standard toolbar to display all of its tools.*

- Use the Font dialog box to change multiple attributes at one time.

Font dialog box

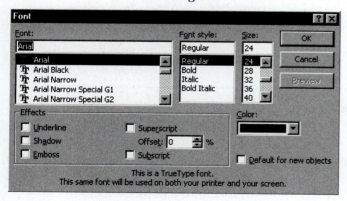

- You can modify text appearance in Normal view.

  ✓ *Formatting doesn't change the appearance of the outline in the Outline pane even though you can format the text of the slide by selecting and formatting outline text.*

- When changing a font face, you can change a selection on one slide or you can replace one font with another throughout the entire presentation.

- Be aware that too many text attributes can make a presentation appear "busy" instead of adding to its power to communicate.

Change Case

- You can change the case of existing text to make it consistent or to correct a typing error.

- As in Word, you can change the case of text to one of the following:

  - Sentence case: Initial capital letter and lowercase for the rest of the text in the sentence.

  - lowercase: All selected text is lowercase.

  - UPPERCASE: All selected text is uppercase.

  - Title Case: Each word is capitalized.

  - tOGGLE cASE: Reverses the case of the selected text.

Change Slide Color Scheme

- PowerPoint's design templates each come with a set of predesigned **color schemes** from which you can choose.

- Each color scheme consists of eight colors that are applied to the slide background, text, lines, shadows, title text, fills, and accents.

- Click Design on the Formatting toolbar to access the Slide Design Task Pane. Click Color Schemes to view the different color schemes.

Color Schemes in Task Pane

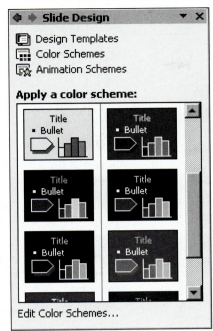

- You can apply a different color scheme to an entire presentation or to just one slide. You might, for example, change the colors on one slide to emphasize that portion of the presentation.

- You can customize a color scheme by changing the colors of individual items, such as the background, title text, or shadows.

Edit Color Scheme Custom tab

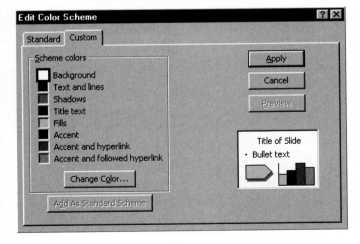

- Avoid using too many different colors, which can make a presentation hard to read.

Change Slide Background

- You can change the color of a slide background, enhance it with a color gradient or pattern, or replace it with a texture effect or picture.

- Change background colors in the Background Color dialog box.

Background Color dialog box

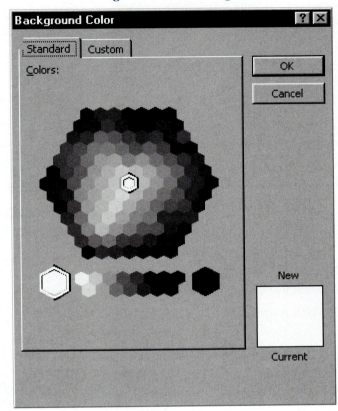

- Although you can combine a background color with a pattern or color gradient, you cannot combine a picture or texture with any other effect.

- You can change the background for a single slide, selected slides, or all slides in a presentation.

Procedures

Select Text

- Double-click to select word.
- Triple-click to select paragraph.
- Point mouse arrow at text in Outline pane and click to select it.
  - ✓ *When you select an upper-level title all sub-titles and bullets beneath it are selected as well.*
- Click the I-beam at the beginning of the text and drag the mouse to the end of the text to select it.
- Click the text placeholder border to select the text box.

Align Text *(Ctrl+L, Ctrl+E, Ctrl+R)*

1. Select text or click mouse anywhere in paragraph you want to align.
2. Click **Left Align** 📄, **Center** 📄, or **Right Align** 📄 button.

OR

1. Click **Format** .... `Alt`+`O`
2. Click **Alignment** .... `A`
3. Click appropriate alignment:
   - **Align Left** .... `L`
   - **Center** .... `C`
   - **Align Right** .... `R`
   - **Justify** .... `J`

Change Appearance of Text

1. Select text or click mouse within text to be changed.
2. Click appropriate button on Formatting toolbar.

OR

1. Click **Format** .... `Alt`+`O`
2. Click one of the following:
   - **Font** .... `F`
   - **Bullets and Numbering** .... `B`
   - **Line Spacing** .... `S`
   - **Replace Fonts** .... `R`
3. Make desired changes.
4. Click **OK** .... `Enter`

Change Case

1. Select text.
2. Click **Format** .... `Alt`+`O`
3. Click **Change Case** .... `E`
4. Click one of the following:
   - **Sentence case.** .... `S`
   - **lowercase** .... `L`
   - **UPPERCASE** .... `U`
   - **Title Case** .... `T`
   - **tOGGLE cASE** .... `G`
5. Click **OK** .... `Enter`

Change Slide's Color Scheme

1. Click **Format** .... `Alt`+`O`
2. Click **Slide Design** .... `D`
3. Click **Color Schemes** in the Task Pane.
4. Click one of the color scheme drop-down arrows to display the pop-up menu.
5. Click one of the following:
   - **Apply to All Slides** to apply the scheme to all slides.
   - **Apply to Selected Slides** to apply scheme to selected slides.
   - **Show Large Previews** to view the color schemes in a larger preview.

Change Color within Color Scheme

1. Click **Format** .... `Alt`+`O`
2. Click **Slide Design** .... `D`
3. Click **Edit Color Schemes** in the Task Pane.
4. Click the **Custom** tab .... `Ctrl`+`Tab`
5. In the **Scheme colors** list, select an element .... `Alt`+`S`
6. Click **Change Color** button `Change Color...` .... `O`

7. Click **Standard** tab ..... `Ctrl`+`Tab` for standard colors.

   OR

   Click **Custom** tab .... `Ctrl`+`Tab` to add custom color.
8. Click **OK** .... `Enter`
9. Click one of the following:
   - **Preview** `Preview` .... `Alt`+`P` to view scheme on slide.
   - **Apply** `Apply` .... `Alt`+`A` to apply scheme to selected slides.

Change Slide Background

1. Click **Format** .... `Alt`+`O`
2. Click **Background** .... `K`
3. Click color drop-down box and choose one of the following:
   - **Automatic** to choose assigned scheme color.
   - **Color box** to choose color within scheme.
   - **More colors** to choose custom color .... `M`
   - **Fill effects** to choose gradient, texture, or pattern .... `F`
4. Select **Omit background graphics from master** check box to remove any lines, boxes, or other graphics but retain color on all slides.......................... `Alt`+`G`
5. Click one of the following:
   - **Preview** `Preview` .... `Alt`+`P` to view scheme on slide.
   - **Apply** `Apply` .... `Alt`+`A` to apply scheme to selected slides.
   - **Apply to All** `Apply to All` .... `Alt`+`T` to apply scheme to all slides.

Exercise Directions

1. Start PowerPoint, if necessary.

2. Open ◎ **08West**.

3. Save the file as **08West**.

4. In slide 1, select the title **West Printing Company** and enlarge its font size to 72 points.

5. Select the subtitle text that begins **Printing Services**… and change it to Times New Roman, italic, 42 points.

6. In slide 2, change the title to **Full-Service Printing** and left align it. Change the title to uppercase.

7. In slide 3, left align the title. Change the title to uppercase.

8. Change the remaining slide titles in the presentation to uppercase and left aligned.

9. In slide 4, select the title **Typesetting**… and change that text to Algerian, centered, and enlarge the text size to 66 points.

10. In slide 5, change the bulleted list to a numbered list.

11. Replace all occurrences of the Arial font with Times New Roman.

12. In slide 7, select row 1 of the table and change the font to Arial, 18-point bold.

13. Select column 1 of the table and change the text to Arial, 18-point bold. Select the rest of the table and right-align the text.

14. Select the text **Prices are per page** and change it to Arial, 14 point. See the example in Illustration A.

15. Change the design template to the Network template.

16. Change the slide color scheme to the first color scheme. Change the background color in the scheme to a dark blue and look at each slide.

17. Change the color scheme to another scheme and change the background color in that scheme to a lighter color. Apply the change to all of the slides in the presentation.

18. Spell check the presentation.

19. Print the slides.

20. Close the file and exit PowerPoint, saving all changes.

Illustration A

Sample Prices

	One-Color	Two-Color	Three-Color	Four-Color
2-page	$1.09	$1.60	$2.05	$2.55
4-page	$2.09	$2.60	$3.05	$4.55
8-page	$3.09	$3.60	$4.05	$6.55
16-page	$4.09	$4.60	$5.05	$7.55
24-page	$5.09	$5.60	$6.05	$8.55

Prices are per page

On Your Own

1. Open **OPP06**, the presentation you used in the On Your Own section of Exercise 6, or open ⊚ **08DONATE**.

2. Save the file as **OPP08**.

3. Change the case of the titles on all of the slides.

4. Change the font of the subtitle on the Title slide.

5. Change the color scheme for all slides.

6. Change the background for the first slide and the last slide.

7. Save the changes, close the presentation, and exit PowerPoint.

Exercise 9

◆ **Copy Text Formatting** ◆ **Move and Copy Text**
◆ **Increase/Decrease Paragraph Spacing**
◆ **Move, Size, Copy, and Delete Placeholders and Other Objects**

On the Job

Modify text formatting and size placeholders to make more room on a slide for text or objects. For instance, you might need to add an extra bullet to the list, add a chart to a slide, or move text from one slide to another.

Your client asked that you revise the presentation to make it a bit less crowded and change some of the formatting. In this exercise, you'll enhance and edit the presentation for West Printing Company.

Terms

Format Painter A tool that lets you copy text formatting from one selection and apply it to any other text in the presentation.

Paragraph spacing The amount of space between two blocks of text, such as two bullets.

Placeholder border A screened area around the edge of a placeholder, used to move a placeholder. You can also click on a placeholder to select the text or apply font changes.

Sizing handles Any of eight small black boxes located on a placeholder's border, used to resize the placeholder.

Notes

Copy Text Formatting

- Just as in Word, you can quickly copy and apply text formatting in PowerPoint by using the **Format Painter**.
- You can copy text and object formatting and apply it to one or multiple text blocks or objects.

Move and Copy Text

- As you review a slide or presentation, you may rearrange the text to make it easier to follow.
- Just as in Word, you can move text in PowerPoint using drag-and-drop or cut-and-paste methods.

- Use the drag-and-drop method to move text to a nearby location. When you move text, a vertical line moves with the mouse to help you position the text.
- Use the cut-and-paste method to move text between two locations that are set far apart.
- You can use the drag-and-drop feature to move text on a slide or between slides in a presentation from the Outline pane. You can move text within a slide in the Slide pane.
- You can cut and paste text to a new location on the same slide, a different slide, or a different presentation using either the Slides or the Outline pane.
- You can also copy and paste text between slides and between presentations.

Increase/Decrease Paragraph Spacing

- Adjust **paragraph spacing** between bullets or other paragraphs to make it easier to read or to fill the space better.

- You can adjust the space between paragraphs gradually by using the Increase  and Decrease Paragraph Spacing buttons.

- To set paragraph spacing to a specific amount, use the Line Spacing dialog box.

Line Spacing dialog box

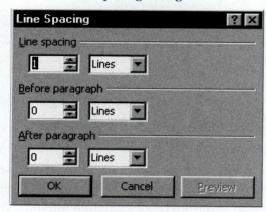

Move, Size, Copy, and Delete Placeholders and Other Objects

- You can move or size any text or object placeholder or any other object, such as a clip art image.

- You can also delete or copy any placeholder or other object.

- To move, size, copy, or delete an object, you need to select it first so that its **placeholder border** and **sizing handles** appear.

Placeholder border and handles

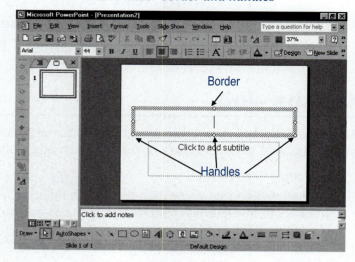

- Then drag the border or sizing handles to complete the task.

- When you click on a placeholder and drag it, the border changes from cross-hatching to dots.

Procedures

Copy Text Formatting to One Item

1. Select text containing format you want to copy.
2. Click **Format Painter** button on the Standard toolbar.
3. Select text that you want to change.

Copy Text Formatting to Multiple Items

1. Select text containing format you want to copy.
2. Double-click **Format Painter** button on the Standard toolbar·
3. Select text that you want to change.
4. When you're done formatting, press **Esc** or click the **Format Painter** button to deactivate Format Painter.

Drag-and-Drop Text

1. Position mouse to left of text so pointer changes to four-headed arrow .
2. Click once to highlight a bullet item and its subitems.
3. Drag mouse pointer to its new position.
4. Release mouse button.

   ✓ *When moving text, make sure horizontal line representing text is in appropriate position before you release mouse button.*

Cut or Copy and Paste Text

1. Select text to be moved or copied.

2. Click **Cut** button ✂ to move text.

   OR

   Click **Copy** button 📋 to copy text.

3. Position mouse where you want to insert text.

4. Click **Paste** button 📋.

Add Increase/Decrease Paragraph Spacing Buttons to Toolbar

1. Display Formatting toolbar.

2. Click **More Buttons** button ▾.

3. Click **Add or Remove Buttons** .... 🄰

4. Click the **Increase Paragraph Spacing** ⭾≡ and **Decrease Paragraph Spacing** ⭰≡ buttons.

5. Click outside of menu to close it.

Increase/Decrease Paragraph Spacing

1. Select paragraphs you want to adjust.

2. Click **Increase** ⭾≡ or **Decrease** ⭰≡ **Paragraph Spacing** button until space is as you want it.

Move Placeholder or Other Object

1. Click in placeholder or graphic to select it.

2. Position mouse on border so pointer changes to four-headed arrow ✛.

3. Drag object to new position.

Size Placeholder or Other Object

1. Click in placeholder or graphic to select it.

2. Position mouse on sizing handle so pointer changes to two-headed arrow ↘.

3. Drag handle until placeholder is desired size.

Copy Placeholder (Ctrl+C, Ctrl+V)

1. Click in object placeholder to select it.

   OR

   Select text placeholder and click placeholder border.

2. Click **Edit** .... Alt+E

3. Click **Copy** C

4. Move to slide, presentation, or position in which you want the copied material to appear.

5. Click **Edit** .... Alt+E

6. Click **Paste** .... P

Delete Placeholder

1. Click in object placeholder to select it.

   OR

   Select text placeholder and click placeholder border.

2. Press **Delete** key. .... Del

   ✓ *The placeholder "Click to add" returns when you delete the placeholder's contents.*

Exercise Directions

1. Start PowerPoint, if necessary.

2. Open 📼**08West** or 💿**09West**.

3. Save the file as **09West**.

4. In Normal view, go to slide 2. Change the text in the title **FULL-SERVICE PRINTING** to Times New Roman, 44 point.

5. Copy that formatting to all titles in the remaining slides of the presentation, except for the title on slide 4, **TYPESETTING**.

6. In slide 3, delete the third and fourth bullets: **Work with your word processing document** and **Multiple layouts for every document**.

7. Resize the placeholder to close up empty space left by the deleted bullets and add an appropriate clip art image.

8. Move and size the clip art to fit in the lower-right corner, as shown in Illustration A.

9. In slide 4, change the first bullet to read: **We provide over 200 typefaces for your printing needs**. Move the first bullet to the end of the bulleted list.

10. Change the text format of all of the bullets on slide 4 to Times New Roman, 28 point. Resize the placeholder so the text appears more to the left side of the slide. Add a clip art to the right corner of the slide, as shown in Illustration B.

    ✓ *Resizing a placeholder can result in changing the font size.*

11. Change the slide layout in slide 6 to Title and 2-Column Text and move the **Four-color work** bullet to the second bulleted list. Move the headings, resize the placeholders and adjust positions, as shown in Illustration C.

12. In slide 7, move the text box (**Prices are per page**) down about ½". Move the table down about ½" as well.

    ✓ *Moving text boxes and tables is the same as moving a placeholder.*

13. Change the title **Sample Prices** to uppercase to match the other titles in the presentation, as shown in Illustration D.

14. Spell check the presentation.

15. Print the slides in Slide view.

16. Close the file and exit PowerPoint, saving all changes.

Illustration A

LAYOUT AND DESIGN

- Graphic artists available
- Free consultation
- Logo design

Illustration B

TYPESETTING

- We use multiple desktop publishing programs to suit your needs
- We can scan your documents or work from scratch
- Bring in a disk with the material typed for a typesetting discount
- We provide over 200 typefaces for your printing needs

Illustration C

ONE-, TWO-, AND FOUR-COLOR

- We can print your documents in one-color if you prefer black, red, or blue ink
- Two-color jobs include red and blue, green and yellow, or any other combinations

- Four-color work with Pantone colors gives your publications that professional look

Illustration D

SAMPLE PRICES

	One-Color	Two-Color	Three-Color	Four-Color
2-page	$1.09	$1.60	$2.05	$2.55
4-page	$2.09	$2.60	$3.05	$4.55
8-page	$3.09	$3.60	$4.05	$6.55
16-page	$4.09	$4.60	$5.05	$7.55
24-page	$5.09	$5.60	$6.05	$8.55

Prices are per page

On Your Own

1. Open **OPP08**, the presentation you used in Exercise 8, or open **09DONATE**.

2. Save the file as **OPP09**.

3. Copy the formatting from the subtitle on the Title slide to the bulleted text on all other slides.

4. Move the bulleted items on slide 5 to rearrange them.

5. Increase the paragraph spacing on all slides to improve the appearance of bulleted items.

6. Decrease the size of a clip art object on a slide and position it so it looks good.

7. Save the presentation, close it, and exit PowerPoint.

Exercise 10

◆ **Use Slide and Title Masters** ◆ **Slide Master View**
◆ **Insert Slide Numbers, Date and Time, and Footer Text**
◆ **Format Bullets**

On the Job

Use a slide or title master to make each slide in the presentation consistent with the others. You might, for example, want to add the same art or logo to each slide and to change the format of the bullets so they all match throughout the presentation.

You have created a second presentation to show your client West Printing Company because you know it is always best to give a client at least two ideas from which to choose. You still need to go over the second presentation to make it more interesting and professional.

Terms

Slide master A template slide that contains colors, text, placeholders, and other items that appear on all slides in a certain design. If you make a change to the slide master, all slides in the set change, too.

Title master A template slide that contains text or design elements for the title slide only.

Footer An area at the bottom of a slide in which you can enter a date, slide number, or other information. A footer appears on all slides in the presentation.

Notes

Use Slide and Title Master

- Each design template has its own **slide master**.

- A slide master contains text characteristics, background and other colors, and placeholders.

- If you want to make a change to all the slides in a presentation (except for the title slide), change the slide master. You might, for example, want to add a logo or slogan to each slide.

- Changes that affect all slides might include adding a picture, adjusting a placeholder, or changing fonts.

- To add text or objects to a slide master, insert a text box or an object box.

- If you want to use different default elements for the title slides in a presentation, use the **title master**.

- A title master contains characteristics and elements for only the title slide.

Slide Master View

- You edit the slide master in Slide Master view.

Slide Master view

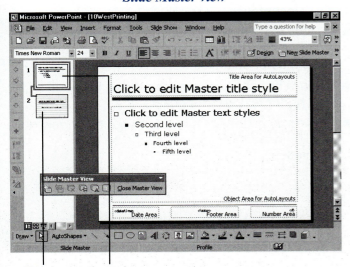

Title master   Slide master

- Changes you make in Slide Master view apply to all slides within the presentation, except title slides.

- You can make changes to the title or master slide at any time during the creation of a presentation.

- Formatting changes that you make to individual slides after you finalize the slide master will override slide master settings.

- You can also customize individual slides to omit slide master background graphics.

Insert Slide Numbers, Date and Time, and Footer Text

- Include a slide number in the **footer** of a slide to identify the slide's position in the presentation.

- Add the date and time to a slide footer so you can tell when it was created or updated.

Slide footer with date and time

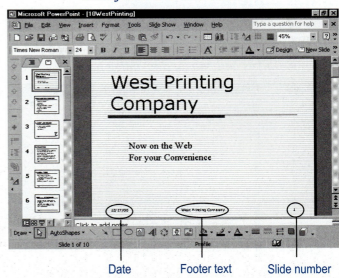

Date   Footer text   Slide number

- You can use a slide footer to identify a presentation's topic, author, client, or other information.

Header and Footer dialog box

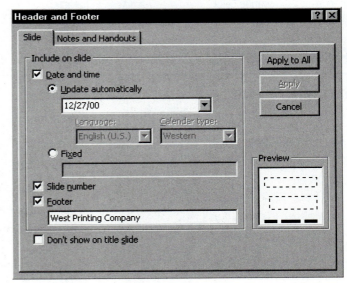

- You can include numbers, dates, times, and other footer text on one slide or every slide in a presentation.

- Placeholders for slide numbers, the date and time, and footer text appear on the slide and title masters.

- If you want to change the location of an element in the footer, you must do so on the slide master.

Format Bullets

- You can change the color, size, and/or character of any bullet.

Bullets and Numbering dialog box

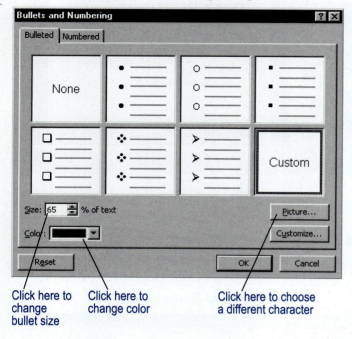

Click here to change bullet size

Click here to change color

Click here to choose a different character

- Change the characteristics of a bullet on one slide to make the item stand out.
- Change the characteristics of bullets in a slide master so the bullets change throughout the presentation.
- Bullets that you format on individual slides after you finalize the slide master will override the slide master settings.
- As in Word or Excel, you can turn a bullet off if you prefer text without bullets.
- Too many bullet types in a slide put emphasis on design instead of on the content, so use discretion.

Procedures

View Slide Master

1. Click **View** .... `Alt`+`V`
2. Click **Master** .... `M`
3. Click **Slide Master** .... `S`

   OR

   Press Shift and click the **Slide Master View** button `⊞`.

   ✓ *The Normal View button changes to the Slide Master View button when Shift is pressed.*

4. In the Slide pane, click on either the slide master or title master to make changes.

Create Text Boxes

✓ *The Drawing toolbar must be displayed.*

1. Click **Text Box** button `📄`.
2. Click or drag text box mouse

   pointer `↓` on slide.

3. Enter text.

View Footers

1. Click **View** .... `Alt`+`V`
2. Click **Header and Footer** .... `H`

Enter Date and Time

1. Click **View** .... `Alt`+`V`
2. Click **Header and Footer** .... `H`
3. Select **Date and time** check box .... `D`
4. Click one of the following:
   - **Update automatically** .... `Alt`+`U`
     Select date/time format.
   - **Fixed** .... `Alt`+`X`
     Enter date and/or time.
5. Click one of the following:
   - **Apply** button `Apply` to apply change to one slide .... `Alt`+`A`

- **Apply to All** button
  `Apply to All` to apply change to all slides ... `Alt`+`Y`

Enter Slide Number

1. Click **View** .... `Alt`+`V`
2. Click **Header and Footer** .... `H`
3. Select **Slide number** check box .... `Alt`+`N`
4. Click one of the following:
   - **Apply** button `Apply` to apply change to one slide .... `Alt`+`A`
   - **Apply to All** button
     `Apply to All` to apply change to all slides ... `Alt`+`Y`

Enter Footer Text

1. Click **View** .... Alt + V
2. Click **Header and Footer** .... H
3. Click **Footer** check box .... F
4. Enter text in **Footer** text box.
5. Click one of the following:

   - **Apply** button Apply to apply change to one slide .... Alt + A

   - **Apply to All** button Apply to All to apply change to all slides... Alt + Y

Format Bullets

1. Select bulleted text.
2. Click **Format** .... Alt + O
3. Click **Bullets and Numbering** .... B
4. Click **Bulleted** tab ...... Ctrl + Tab
5. Click bullet example or choose your own **Picture** to use art or **Customize** to change the bullet character.
6. Click **Color** .... Alt + C to change bullet color. (You may need to repeat steps 1-4 if the dialog box closed.)
7. Click **OK** .... Enter

Exercise Directions

1. Start PowerPoint, if necessary.
2. Open the file ⊙ **10WestPrinting**.
3. Save the file as **10WestPrinting**.
4. Go to title Slide Master view and display the title master. Reduce the width of the title placeholder by about 1" on the right so you can fit a logo in the upper-right corner of the slide.
5. Follow the steps to create a logo for West Printing Company using an appropriate clip art image with a text box over it, as shown in Illustration A.

   a. Insert appropriate clip art.

   b. Resize and move the clip art to the upper-right corner as shown in the illustration.

   c. Insert a text box and enter the text **WPC**.

   d. You may want to change the color or typeface of the text so it stands out (Format, Font, Color or Font).

6. Follow these directions to copy the logo (hold the Shift key as you select the clip art and the logo text) and paste it to the bulleted list slide master.

   a. Copy the logo in Slide Master view.

   b. Click the slide master in the Slides pane.

   c. Paste the logo in the upper-right corner.

7. Resize the title text placeholder so that the text does not interfere with the logo.

   ✓ If text interferes with the logo, you can resize the placeholder of the bulleted text to make room for the logo.

8. Display the title master. Change the color scheme on the title master. Add a striped background (Format, Background).
9. Switch back to Normal view.
10. Go to the end of the slide presentation and add a slide. Choose the Title Slide layout. Enter the text as shown in Illustration B.
11. Add a new slide using the Title and 2-Column Text slide layout. Add text as shown in Illustration C.
12. Move to slide 1. Insert an automatically updating date and a descriptive footer, as shown in Illustration D.
13. Move to slide 3 and change the color of the bullets.
14. Resize the placeholder to close up the empty space on the bottom.
15. Add a clip art to the bottom of the slide, as shown in Illustration E.
16. Increase the paragraph spacing between the bullets in slide 5.
17. On slide 5, change the bullets into a different character, size, and color to make them stand out more than the others in the presentation. Illustration F offers one example.
18. Spell check the presentation.
19. Save the file.
20. Print handouts of the slide presentation with 4 slides per page.
21. Close the file and exit PowerPoint, saving all changes.

West Printing Company

WPC

Now on the Web
For your Convenience

Customer Service

WPC

Personal service on the Web
New Teleconferencing!

Illustration C

Teleconferencing

WPC

- Talker display
- Participant list
- Online orders
- Online call control
- Shared presentations
- Conference calling
- Low costs
- Flat rates

West Printing Company

WPC

Now on the Web
For your Convenience

4/10/01   West Printing Company

LAYOUT AND DESIGN

WPC

- Graphic artists available
- Free consultation
- Logo design

4/10/01   West Printing Company

CAMERA WORK

WPC

- ❖ Expert camera operators
- ❖ Professional paste-up artists
- ❖ Metal plates are checked thoroughly for accuracy
- ❖ Bluelines provided for every job

4/10/01   West Printing Company

On Your Own

1. Open **OPP09**, the presentation you used in Exercise 9, or open 🔗**10DONATE**.

2. Save the file as **OPP10**.

3. Add the date, time, and slide number in the footer of all slides except the title slide.

4. Change the slide master to include the name of the organization in the upper-right corner of all slides.

5. Select a different marker for the bullets on the slide master.

6. On one slide in the presentation, use a different bullet marker in a different color.

7. Save the presentation, close it, and exit PowerPoint.

Exercise 11

Skills Covered:

◆ **Use Rulers and Guides** ◆ **Floating Toolbars**
◆ **Draw Graphic Objects** ◆ **AutoShapes**
◆ **Group and Ungroup Objects** ◆ **Layer Objects**

On the Job

Use PowerPoint's many drawing tools to help enhance a presentation. You might use rulers and guides to line up text or drawing objects, for example. You might draw logos, illustrations, or other objects to add to your slides.

The owner of West Printing Company is thinking about putting the presentation that you are designing on the Web. In this exercise, you will add design elements to the second presentation you created for West. You'll also add some buttons that make the presentation more suitable to the Web.

Terms

Guides Nonprinting vertical and horizontal lines you can use to align objects on a slide.

Floating toolbar Any toolbar that you can move with the mouse around on the screen for easier access and viewing.

Dock To affix a floating toolbar to the edge of the PowerPoint screen.

AutoShapes A set of tools that makes drawing common geometric shapes fast and easy.

Group To join multiple objects into a single object so that they are easier to move and manipulate.

Notes

Use Rulers and Guides

Rulers in Normal view

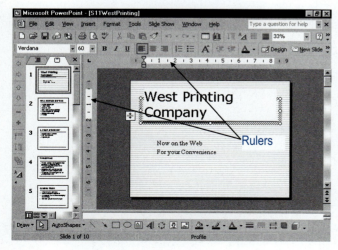

- PowerPoint provides a vertical and horizontal ruler that you can show or hide at any time.
- Use the rulers to adjust indents or add tabs to text.
- You can also use rulers to align objects on the slide.
- The ruler's origins (0 measurement on the ruler) change depending on whether you're using text or an object.
- The origin appears on the edge of the ruler when you're working with text and in the center point of the ruler when you're working with an object.
- As you move the mouse pointer, an indicator moves on each ruler showing your horizontal and vertical locations.

■ **Guides** are alignment tools that help you line up objects and text.

Guides in Normal view

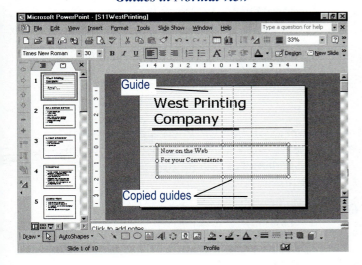

■ PowerPoint supplies one vertical and one horizontal guide that you can move and copy.

■ Use rulers and guides to make your work look more exact and professional.

Floating Toolbars

■ A **floating toolbar** is one that is not attached to the edge of the program window. Certain toolbars float by default, such as the WordArt and Tables and Borders toolbars. The Standard and Formatting toolbars do not float by default, but they can be dragged from their position and float anywhere in the program window.

■ A move handle on a floating menu's submenu enables you to create a floating toolbar from the submenu.

■ You can resize a floating toolbar and move it anywhere on the screen.

Floating toolbars

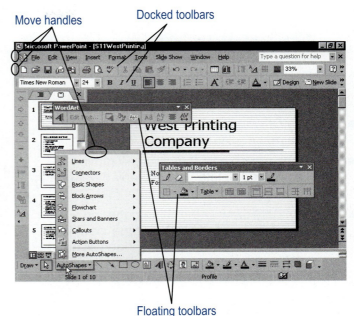

■ Use a floating toolbar to see all available buttons on it or to move it closer to a section on which you're working.

■ You can **dock** a floating toolbar on the left, top, or bottom of the program window. The Standard and Formatting toolbars are typically docked by default.

Draw Graphic Objects

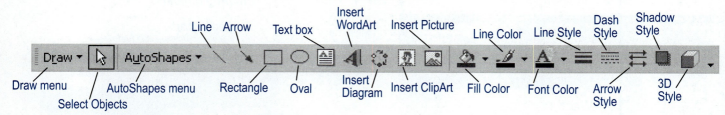

Drawing toolbar

Draw menu — Select Objects — AutoShapes menu — Line — Arrow — Text box — Insert WordArt — Insert Diagram — Insert Picture — Insert ClipArt — Line Color — Line Style — Dash Style — Shadow Style — Rectangle — Oval — Fill Color — Font Color — Arrow Style — 3D Style

- Use the Drawing toolbar to create objects such as lines, rectangles, and ovals.

- Drawings are objects that you can move, size, copy, and delete, just like any other object in PowerPoint.

- You can only draw in the Slide pane, on a slide master, or on a slide in Notes Page view, but whatever you draw on a notes page will not be reflected on slides in any other view.

- Using the Drawing toolbar, you can also fill the shapes and draw lines with colors. You can change line styles and colors, arrow styles, and fill colors.

- The Drawing toolbar displays with all views except Slide Sorter.

AutoShapes

- Use AutoShapes to draw arrows, stars, circles, and other shapes into a slide quickly and easily.

- AutoShapes are objects, so they can be copied, resized, and moved just like placeholders and other objects.

- You can use the tools on the Drawing toolbar to enhance and modify AutoShapes.

  - Use Lines to create curves, arrows, and freeform lines.

  - Use Connectors to connect objects on a slide.

  - Basic Shapes include circles, rectangles, triangles, parentheses, brackets, and so on.

  - Block Arrows are decorative arrows of all kinds.

  - Use Flowchart to create organizational chart shapes.

  - Stars and Banners include ribbon and star shapes.

  - Use Callouts to create special text boxes that can be used to create labels in slides. There are several styles, including cartoon bubbles.

- Use Action buttons to create navigation buttons such as Next, Back, and Help. You use Action Buttons to give users control over the presentation.

Group and Ungroup Objects

- You can **group** the objects within a drawing to make them into one composition that will keep the position of each object. Grouped objects are also easier to copy or move.

- When you group objects, you only need to click once to select the entire group of objects.

- You can ungroup objects when you want to edit or delete an individual object in the group.

Ungrouped and grouped objects

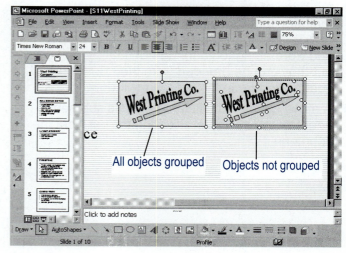

Layer Objects

- You can layer objects one on top of another to create depth or add perspective in a drawing.

- After drawing an object, you can move it to the front or to the back of a layered stack.

- You can also move objects forward or backward in a layer one object at a time.

Procedures

Display Rulers and Guides

1. Click **V**iew .... Alt + V
2. Click **R**uler .... R
3. Click **V**iew .... Alt + V
4. Click **Gri**d and Guides I
5. Click **Di**splay drawing guides on screen I
6. Click **OK**.

Copy Guide

- Hold **Ctrl** key and drag existing guide.

Delete Guide

- Drag guide off screen.

Floating Toolbars

To create floating toolbar:

1. Drag toolbar's handle away from program window's edge.
   - ✓ *Some toolbars float by default but can be docked.*

   OR

   Drag move handle away from submenu to create floating toolbar.
2. Move floating toolbar by dragging its title bar.
3. Size floating toolbar by dragging its border.

To dock floating toolbar:

- Move toolbar to edge of program window.

Draw Graphic Objects

1. Click **Line** 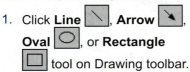, **Arrow**, **Oval**, or **Rectangle** tool on Drawing toolbar.
2. Position crosshair + on slide and drag to create object.
3. Click **Select** tool.
4. Select object by clicking it.
5. Click one of the following buttons on Drawing toolbar to apply to selected object:

   - **Fill Color** to display colors and fill effects
   - **Line Color** to display colors and fill effects
   - **Line Style** to display various line widths
   - **Dash Style** to display available dash types
   - **Arrow Style** to display various arrow shapes
     - ✓ *Press Shift key as you draw rectangle or oval to create a straight line, a perfect square, or circle.*

Draw AutoShapes

1. Click **A**utoShapes menu ..... Alt + U on Drawing toolbar.
2. Click one of the following:

   - **L**ines L
   - **Co**nnectors .... N
   - **B**asic Shapes .... B
   - Block **A**rrows .... A
   - **F**lowchart .... F
   - **S**tars and Banners .... S
   - **C**allouts C
   - Action Buttons I
   - More AutoShapes .... M

3. Select shape you want from submenu.
4. Click or drag mouse on slide to create shape.

Group Objects

1. Click first object.
2. Hold down **Shift** key while clicking other objects to be grouped.
3. Click **D**raw .... Alt + R
4. Click **Group** .... G

Ungroup Objects

1. Select object.
2. Click **D**raw .... Alt + R
3. Click **U**ngroup .... U

Layer Objects

1. Select object.
2. Click **D**raw .... Alt + R
3. Click **Order** .... R
4. Click one of the following:

   - **Bring to Front** .... T
   - **Send to Back** .... K
   - **Bring Forward** .... F
   - **Send Backward** .... B

Exercise Directions

1. Start PowerPoint, if necessary.

2. Open 📇**10WestPrinting** or 💿**11WestPrinting**.

3. Save the file as **11WestPrinting**.

4. Display the Slide Master view and click on the title master. Add two horizontal lines near the bottom of the slide, above the footer area, similar to those in Illustration A.

   ✓ *Press and hold the Shift key while drawing the line to make it absolutely straight. Release the mouse button before you release the Shift key.*

5. Apply colors to the lines that match the slide color scheme by selecting the line and clicking the Line Color button.

6. Create a West Printing Company logo in the title master. You can use AutoShapes, lines, WordArt, and other drawing tools. Apply a color fill to part of the logo, such as gray or yellow. An example appears in Illustration B.

7. Change to Normal view.

8. Switch to slide 7. Draw three AutoShape stars as in Illustration C, and apply a different fill color to each. Make sure the colors match the slide's color scheme.

9. Overlap the stars as shown in Illustration C. Move the last star you drew to the back and the first star to the front. Group the stars and position them as shown in Illustration C.

10. Add a text box below the stars with the text shown in Illustration C. Format the text to Times New Roman, 24 points, bold, and italic.

11. Display the rulers.

12. Move to slide 3. Remove the bullets from the bulleted text.

13. Widen the placeholder so it reaches the right side of the slide and, using the ruler, set tabs so that the second line of text is 1" and the third line another 1".

   ✓ *Note: You may have to adjust the indent markers.*

   ✓ *Refer to the Word section for information about setting tabs.*

   ✓ *You can set tabs easily using the horizontal ruler.*

14. Resize the placeholder.

15. Add a clip art to the bottom of the slide. Resize the clip art if necessary.

16. Go to slide 10. Insert any Action button from AutoShapes. In the Action Settings dialog box, select the First Slide hyperlink. Select any sound option you want. Position the button as shown in Illustration D.

17. Run the presentation to make sure the effects work.

   ✓ *To run the presentation, Click View, Slide Show.*

18. Spell check the presentation.

19. Print the presentation.

20. Save the file, but don't close it.

21. Save the file as a Web page using **11WestPrinting-2.htm** as the file name.

22. Close the file and exit PowerPoint, saving all changes.

Illustration A

West Printing Company

Now on the Web
For your Convenience

Illustration B

West Printing Company

Now on the Web
For your Convenience

Illustration C

FOUR-COLOR PRINTING

☐ Four-color work with Pantone colors gives your publications that professional look

All-Star Printing!

Illustration D

MAILINGS

☐ We can include mailing information on the printed piece
☐ Mailing labels printed
☐ We can sort your mailings
☐ We can even take them to the post office for you

On Your Own

1. Open **OPP10**, the presentation you used in Exercise 10, or open ⊙ **11DONATE**.

2. Save the file as **OPP11**.

3. Display the slide rulers.

4. Insert an AutoShape on the title slide. For example, insert a lightning bolt, a star, or any other object.

5. Use the drawing tools to draw a simple picture on a different slide. For example, draw a bunch of balloons, or a flower.

6. Group the drawn objects and move them to a different location on the slide.

7. Save the presentation, close it, and exit PowerPoint.

Exercise 12

On the Job

Customize a template to create your own unique presentations. Your custom template, for example, might contain the same color scheme and graphic images that you use in your other company materials, such as a newsletter, letterhead, and brochure.

You work for Murray Hill Marketing, LLC. Marvel Enterprises is a client of your company. Marvel Enterprises produces cleaning products for home and businesses. The owner of Marvel Enterprises wants you to create a custom template in PowerPoint that you can use for several presentations as part of a special public relations campaign for the company.

Terms

Template A foundation on which to build a presentation; a template may contain colors, graphics, fonts, and type styles.

Notes

Customize a Template

- You can customize a **template** to suit your presentation topic better. Or, you can create a template from a presentation you have already created. Any text, graphics, or other contents of the existing presentation will be saved with the template.

- Customize a template to change color schemes, background graphics, font formatting, and so on.

- Use the slide master to add modifications to all slides in a template.

- After you create the look you want, save the template so you can base other presentations on it.

Save and Apply a Custom Template

- You can save any presentation as a custom template.

- After you save a custom template, you can use it as a basis for other presentations.

- Modifying a content template can make creating custom presentations quick and easy.

Procedures

Create Custom Template

1. Open existing presentation.
   OR
   Open new blank design template or content template presentation.
2. Modify slide master, fonts, contents, color schemes, and other design elements.
3. Click **File** .... `Alt`+`F`
4. Click **Save As** .... `A`
5. Click **Save as type** ...... `Alt`+`T`
6. Select **Design Template**.
7. Save template in default folder: Windows/Application Data/Microsoft/Templates.
8. Name the template.
9. Click **Save** .... `Alt`+`S`

Add Custom Template to AutoContent Wizard *(Ctrl+N)*

1. Click **File** .... `Alt`+`F`
2. Click **New** .... `N`
3. In the Task Pane, click **From AutoContent Wizard**.
4. Click **Next** .... `Alt`+`N`
5. Click **General** button ... `Alt`+`G`
   ✓ You cannot add content template to All category.
6. Click **Add** .... `Alt`+`D`
7. Select your custom template.
8. Click **OK** .... `Enter`
9. Click **Finish** .... `Alt`+`F`

Apply Custom Template

1. Click **File** .... `Alt`+`F`
2. Click **New** .... `N`
3. In the Task Pane, click **General Templates**.
4. Click the **General** tab.
5. Select the custom template on which to base new presentation.
6. Click **OK** .... `Enter`

Exercise Directions

1. Start PowerPoint, if necessary.
2. Add a slide color scheme. You can customize the colors, if you want. Apply the color scheme to all slides.
3. Go to the Slide Master view. Replace all Arial or Times New Roman fonts with Goudy Old Style or any other serif font.
4. On the slide master, add some graphic lines, shapes, clip art, and/or other design effects to make the slide interesting. See Illustration A for an example.
5. Create a logo for Marvel Enterprises. You can use clip art images or create a drawing. Place the logo on the slide master.
6. Save the file as a template: **Marvel.pot**.
7. Close the file.
8. Start a new presentation using the custom template.
9. Save the file as **12Marvel.ppt**.
10. Enter text in the title slide as shown in Illustration B.
11. Add a bulleted list slide and enter the text as shown in Illustration C.
    ✓ You may have to resize the placeholder.
12. Spell check the presentation.
13. Print the presentation.
14. Close the file and exit PowerPoint, saving all changes.

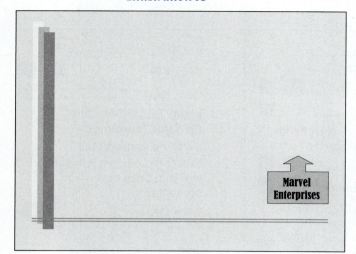

Illustration C

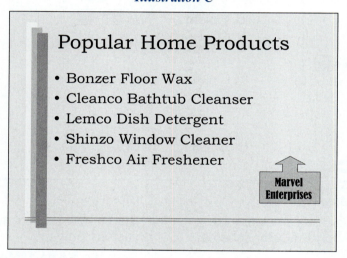

On Your Own

1. Create a new presentation based on a blank template.

2. On the master slide apply colors, select fonts, select bullets, and insert graphics as desired to customize the template.

3. Save the presentation as a template with the name **OPP12.pot**.

4. Create a new presentation based on the **OPP12.pot** template.

5. Save the presentation as **OPP12-2.ppt**.

6. Create a presentation about a friend, family member, or pet. Include at least three slides.

7. Save the presentation, close it, and exit PowerPoint.

Exercise 13

◆ Insert Organization Chart Slide

On the Job

Add an organization chart to your presentation to illustrate the structure of your organization. For example, show the relationship between store managers and their staff or between the vice presidents of the company and their assistants and managers.

Recently there have been changes in employee status at Marvel Enterprises—several people were promoted and others left the company. The owners of Marvel have asked you to create an organization chart showing the current company structure.

Terms

Organization chart An illustration of the top-down structure (the *hierarchy*) of positions within an organization, usually starting with the chief executive.

Notes

Insert Organization Chart Slide

- An **organization chart** can illustrate a company's or organization's structure.

Organization chart

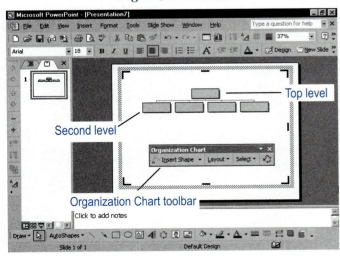

Organization Chart toolbar

- It can also show the structure of a department, project, exercise, process, procedure, or family tree.

- You can create an organization chart using any layout that includes a content placeholder and clicking the Insert Diagram or Organization Chart icon or insert one without a placeholder using the Insert menu.

- You can choose to insert any diagram type, including the Organization Chart, a Pyramid Diagram, Target Diagram, or others.

- When you insert an organization chart, five boxes appear. You can add, delete, and type in the boxes as desired.

- PowerPoint includes an Organization Chart toolbar that has menus for adding boxes, changing the layout of the chart, and selecting parts of the chart.

- An organization chart can be moved, copied, and deleted like any other object.

Procedures

Create Organization Chart

1. Apply a layout that contains a content placeholder.
2. Click the Insert Diagram or Organization Chart icon.
3. Click the Organization Chart diagram style.
4. Click **OK**.
5. Click in any box and begin typing to enter text.
6. Press **Enter** to add another line of text in box.
7. Click mouse on box to which you want to attach new box.
8. To add box, click **Insert Shape** .... `Alt`+`N` and then press up or down.
   - **Subordinate** .... `S`
   - **Coworker** .... `C`
   - **Assistant** .... `A`
9. Repeat steps 8 and 9 until chart is complete.

Select Box

- Click the border of a box.

Type in a Box

- Click within the box and enter text.

Select Multiple Boxes

1. From Organization Chart toolbar, click **Select** ..... `Alt`+`C`
2. Choose one of the following:
   - **All Assistants** .... `A`
   - **Branch** .... `B`
   - **Level** .... `L`
   - **All Connecting Lines** ... `C`
   OR
- Hold down **Shift** key and click on multiple boxes.

Delete Box

1. Select box.
2. Press **Delete** key .... `Del`

Format Fonts

1. From Organization chart, select text.
2. Click **Format** .... `Alt`+`O`
3. Click **Font** .... `F`
   ✓ *Format fonts the same as you would any font in PowerPoint.*
4. Click **OK** .... `Enter`

Change Chart Layout

1. From Organization Chart toolbar, click **Layout** .... `Alt`+`L`
2. Click one of the following:
   - **Standard** .... `S`
   - **Both Hanging** .... `B`
   - **Left Hanging** .... `L`
   - **Right Hanging** .... `R`
   - **Fit Organization Chart to Contents** .... `F`
   - **Expand Organization Chart** ...... `E`
   - **Scale Organization Chart** ...... `C`
   - **AutoLayout** .... `A`

Change Alignment

1. From Organization chart, select text.
2. Click **Format** .... `Alt`+`O`
3. Click **Alignment** .... `A`
4. Click one of the following:
   - **Align Left** .... `L`
   - **Align Right** .... `R`
   - **Center** .... `C`
   - **Justify** .... `J`

Change Box Color

1. From Organization chart, double-click box.
2. Click **Colors and Lines** tab.
3. Click **Color** .... `C`
4. Select color.
5. Click **OK** .... `Enter`
   OR

1. Select the box to be formatted.
2. Click the drop-down arrow of the **Fill** button on the Tables and Borders or the Draw toolbar.
3. Select a color from the display.

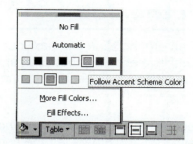

- **More Fill Colors** .... `M`
  ✓ *This option displays a color palette from which you can select a suitable color.*
- **Fill Effects** .... `F`
  ✓ *This option displays a dialog box from which you can choose:*
  - **Gradient**
  - **Texture**
  - **Pattern**
  - **Picture**
  ✓ *The row of colors under Automatic lets you apply a color that is consistent with the color scheme of the design template you are using for the presentation.*
  ✓ *Other colors may appear if you have selected fill colors on other slides.*

Change Box Border

1. From Organization chart, double-click box.
2. Click **Colors and Lines** tab.
3. Click one of the following:
   - **Line Color** .... `O`
   - **Style** .... `S`
   - **Weight** .... `W`
   - **Dashed** .... `D`
4. Click **OK** .... `Enter`

Edit Organization Chart

- Click chart.

Exercise Directions

1. Start PowerPoint, if necessary.

2. Open 📠**12Marvel** or 💿 **13Marvel**.

3. Save the file as **13Marvel**.

4. Add a slide after slide 2 and choose a Content slide layout that includes a title.

5. Add the title **Sales Staff**.

6. Add an organization chart.

7. Use the toolbar buttons to add a co-worker, subordinates, and assistants as shown in Illustration A and enter the text in each box as shown.

   ✓ Hint: Colin Smith is a subordinate of Mary Frank.

8. Scale the chart to better fit the slide. Move the chart as necessary to fit the chart on the slide.

9. Select the boxes and change the color to any color that matches the color scheme.

   ✓ Hint: You should make all assistants one color, all associates another color, and so on, to differentiate between levels.

10. Click outside of the chart to deselect the organization chart.

11. Add another slide, using a Content slide layout that includes a title.

12. Enter the title on the slide **Human Resources**.

13. Add an organization chart. Enter text and boxes as shown in Illustration B.

    ✓ Hint: Use the both hanging layout.

14. Change the color of the boxes to similar colors you used on the previous chart.

15. Scale and move the chart to center it on the slide.

16. Spell check the presentation.

17. Print the presentation.

18. Close the file and exit PowerPoint, saving all changes.

Illustration A

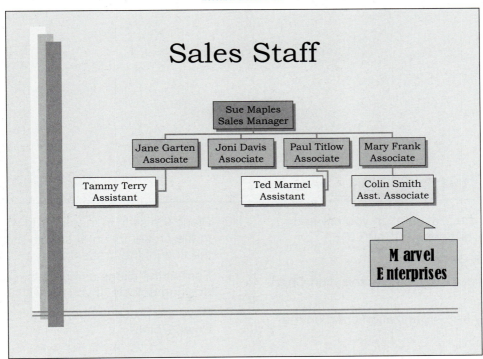

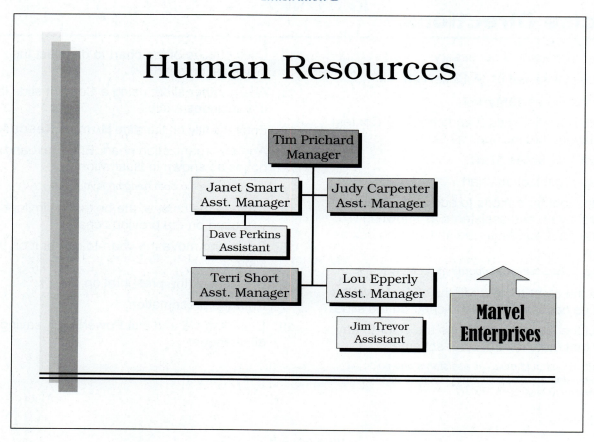

On Your Own

1. Open **OPP04**, the presentation you created about yourself, or open 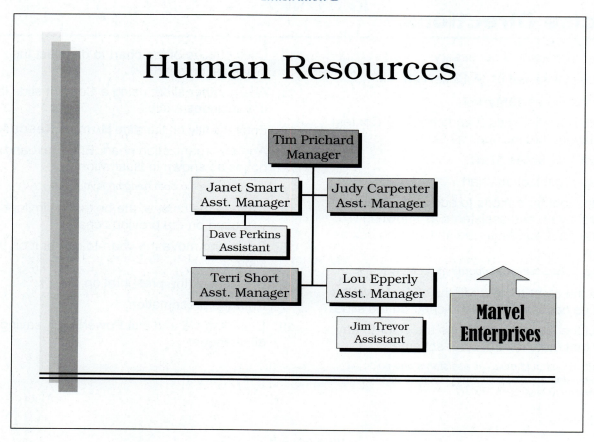**13MYLIFE**.

2. Save the file as **OPP13**.

3. Insert a new slide using the Organization Chart slide layout.

4. Create a family tree organization chart on the new slide.

5. Format the chart any way you want.

6. Place the slide in the order in which it belongs in the presentation. It should make sense in the flow of the presentation.

7. Format the slides using fonts, colors, and drawing objects, if you want.

8. Save the presentation, close it, and exit PowerPoint.

Exercise 14

On the Job

Add charts or tables to a presentation to illustrate data in an easy-to-read format. Sales figures represented in a chart, for example, are easier to understand than if they're simply listed or just read aloud to the audience.

The owner of Marvel Enterprises has given you some data that you can add to the presentation in the form of charts, tables, and worksheets. In this exercise, you will continue work on the Marvel Enterprises project using the custom template you created.

Terms

Chart A graphic illustration of numbers, percentages, or other data.

Datasheet A worksheet for the graph and charting program. A datasheet contains columns and rows in which you can enter text.

Data label Text that identifies your data.

Table A structure for organizing data in rows and columns.

Notes

Create a Chart

- You can add a **chart** to your presentation to illustrate data in an easy-to-understand format or to compare and contrast sets of data.

- You can create a new chart and data in PowerPoint using Microsoft Graph, a charting program that comes with PowerPoint.

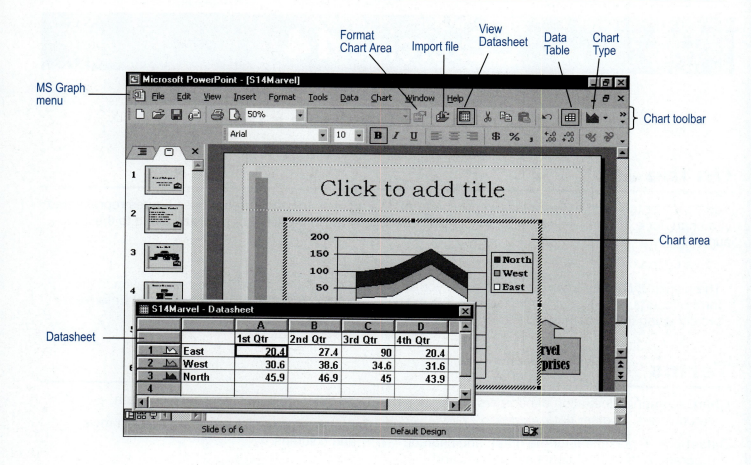

- As you learned in Exercise 6, you can also insert an existing chart as an object from Excel to use in a slide.

Import Data Options dialog box

- You can insert a chart into a content slide layout or add it without a placeholder using the Insert Chart button on the Standard toolbar.

- When you insert a new chart, a Chart toolbar is added to the Standard toolbar and several charting tools appear on the Formatting toolbar.

- A sample chart and a **datasheet** window containing sample data also appear. You can type in replacement data or import data from an existing Excel file.

Datasheet window

		A	B	C	D
		1st Qtr	2nd Qtr	3rd Qtr	4th Qtr
1	East	20.4	27.4	90	20.4
2	West	30.6	38.6	34.6	31.6
3	North	45.9	46.9	45	43.9
4					

- The default chart type is 3-D Column. You can, however, choose from several chart formats, including bar, line, pie, area, scatter, doughnut, radar, surface, bubble, and stock.

- You can move, copy, size, and delete a chart just like any other slide object.

- You can show or hide gridlines, or measurement guides, within a chart to help you read the chart information.

- You can include a title, **data labels**, and a legend with your chart. A legend identifies the data in a chart by listing each type of data with a color key to its corresponding chart element.

Create a Table

- Use a **table** to organize information into rows and columns.

- You can create a new table using the placeholder in a Title and Table layout, or insert a table without a placeholder by using the Insert Table button on the Standard toolbar.

- When you insert a table, you may need to adjust row or column width or resize and move the table.

- When you insert a new table or click an existing table, the Tables and Borders toolbar appears with tools you can use to edit the table.

- The Tables and Borders toolbar appears on the right side of the screen. You can move the toolbar to show more buttons.

- After creating a table, you can format the text, resize the cells, insert and delete columns and rows, and change borders on the table.

- You can format the font, color, and size of table text just as you would regular slide text.

Insert Table dialog box

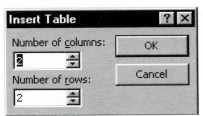

Tables and Borders toolbar

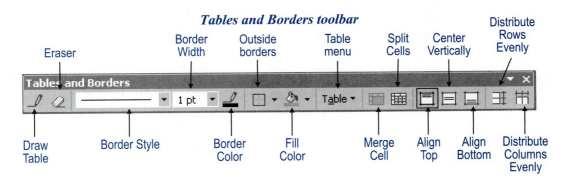

Procedures

Create New Chart

1. Click **Insert Chart** button .
   OR
   a. Click **I**nsert .... `Alt`+`I`
   b. Click **N**ew Slide .... `N`
   c. Select any layout with a chart object included.
   d. Double-click chart placeholder.
2. Enter data for chart in datasheet.
3. Click outside chart and datasheet to close datasheet and update chart on slide.
4. Return to chart for edits by double-clicking chart.

Import Chart from Excel

1. Click **Insert Chart** button.
   OR
   a. Click **I**nsert .... `Alt`+`I`
   b. Click **C**hart..................... `H`
   c. Double-click chart placeholder on Chart slide.
2. Click **Import File** button.
3. In the **Look in** drop-down list, locate the folder where the Excel chart is stored.
4. Select Excel file to insert.
5. Click **O**pen .... `Alt`+`O`
6. Select sheet you want to use from list.
7. Click **OK**............................ `Enter`
8. Click outside chart and datasheet to close datasheet and update chart.
9. Return to datasheet for edits by double-clicking chart.

View Datasheet

- Double-click chart.

Close Datasheet

1. Click datasheet.
2. Click the **Close** button.

Change Chart Type

1. Double-click chart to display the datasheet.
2. Click down arrow on **Chart Type** button.
3. Select chart type from drop-down palette.

OR

1. Click **C**hart .... `Alt`+`C`
2. Click **Chart Ty**pe .... `Y`
3. Select chart type.
4. Click **OK** .... `Enter`

Show/Hide Gridlines and Show/Hide Legend

1. Double-click chart.
2. Click **Category Axis Gridlines** button.
   OR
   Click **Value Axis Gridlines** button.
   OR
   Click **Legend** button.

Insert Table

1. Click **Insert Table** button and drag down and to the right to select number of cells to include in table.
   OR
   a. Click **I**nsert............ `Alt`+`I`
   b. Click **N**ew Slide .... `N`
   c. Select any layout with a table object included.
   d. Double-click table placeholder in the slide.
   e. Enter **Number of columns**.. `Alt`+`C`, *number*
   f. Enter **Number of r**ows.... `Alt`+`R`, *number*
   g. Click **OK** .... `Enter`
2. Click in a cell to enter text.
3. Press **Tab** key to move insertion point from cell to cell.
4. Click outside of table to return to slide.
5. Return to table for edits by clicking table.

Format Table

1. Click **Table and Borders** button if necessary to display Tables and Borders toolbar.
   OR
   Right-click the Standard toolbar and click Table and Borders.
2. Use Table and Borders toolbar to format table.
3. To format a border:
   a. Click from following buttons and make selection:
      - **Border Style**: choose solid, dashed, or dotted lines for table border.
      - **Border Width**: choose thickness of border line.
      - **Border Color**: choose color for borders.
      - **Outside Borders**: use Borders button to apply formatting to selected borders: outside, inside, all, or individual.

b. Click the border to apply formatting, or draw lines to add new cells in the selected border settings.

4. Select cell(s) and then click from the following buttons.

- **Fill Color** [icon]: fill table with color. Select a color or fill effect.
- **Merge Cells** [icon]: joins two or more cells.

- **Split Cell** [icon]: divides cell in half.
- **Align Top** [icon]: aligns table text to top of cell.
- **Center Vertically** [icon]: aligns table text to vertical center of cell.
- **Align Bottom** [icon]: aligns table text to bottom of cell.

Change Column Width/Row Height of Table

1. Position mouse over border line.
2. Mouse pointer changes to double-headed arrow [icon].
3. Click and drag border to move it.

Exercise Directions

1. Start PowerPoint, if necessary.

2. Open 📖**13Marvel** or 💿**14Marvel**.

3. Save the file as **14Marvel**.

4. Add a new slide at the end of the presentation using the Title and Chart layout. Enter the slide title **Cleaning Agents**.

5. Insert a chart and delete the data from the datasheet. Enter the data as shown in Illustration A.

6. Close the datasheet and adjust the chart position or resize the chart so you can view all of the data.

7. Change the chart type to a 3-D Bar Chart.

8. Add value axis gridlines if they are not showing.

9. Add a new slide at the end of the presentation using the Title only slide layout. Enter the slide title **Best Sales**.

10. Insert a chart using the Chart button and import Sheet 1 of the file 💿**14Marvel.xls** to the datasheet.

11. Close the datasheet and adjust the chart on the slide as shown in Illustration B.

✓ *Hint: You can resize the chart separately from the chart area placeholder. You can also move the legend.*

12. Add a new slide at the end of the presentation using the Title and Table slide layout. Add the slide title **Sales Analysis**.

13. Insert a 5 x 5 table and enter the text as shown in Illustration C. Do not press Enter after typing the chart information.

14. Format the text in the first row and the first column of the table as Arial Narrow, 18 points, and centered. Format the rest of the table text to 18 points and centered.

15. Resize the table to fit on the slide without overlapping other elements and adjust the row and column widths to fit the text.

✓ *To resize the table, click on the table to select it and drag the sizing handles.*

16. Spell check the presentation.

17. Print the slides as handouts with four per page.

18. Close the file and exit PowerPoint, saving all changes.

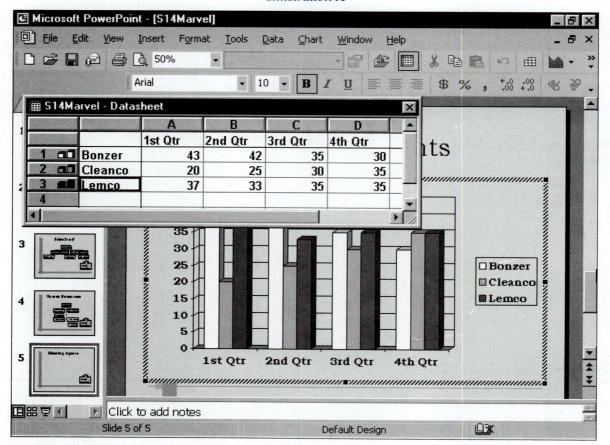

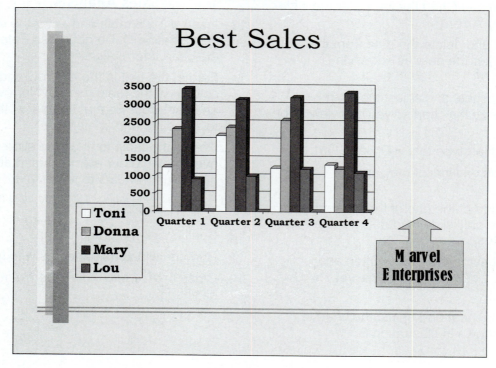

Illustration C

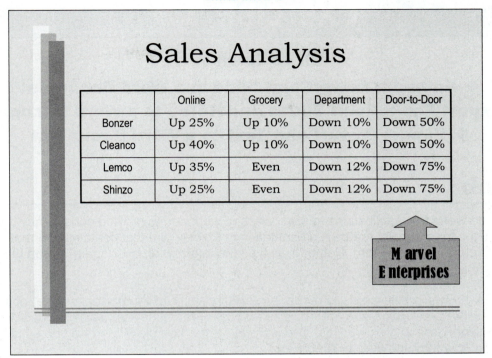

On Your Own

1. Open **OPP11**, the charity presentation you last worked with in Exercise 11, or open ⊙**14DONATE**.

2. Save the file as **OPP14**.

3. Insert a chart slide illustrating where income for the organization came from last year. For example, it might come from donations, fundraising, grants, membership dues, and so on.

4. Insert another chart slide and import the Breakdown of Expenses pie chart from the ⊙**14CHART.xls** Excel workbook file.

5. Format the chart so it is easy to read and looks good on the slide.

6. Insert another slide showing a table listing the officers of the organization.

7. Save the presentation, close the presentation, and exit PowerPoint.

Exercise 15

Skills Covered:

◆ **Embed a PowerPoint Slide in a Word Document**
◆ **Export PowerPoint Slides and Notes to a Word Document**
◆ **Export PowerPoint Text to a Word Document**

On the Job

Share information between two applications to save yourself work and to provide consistency between documents. You might, for example, create a presentation in PowerPoint that contains information you can use in a report you're preparing in Word. Rather than type the information over again, export the text to Word.

The owner of Marvel Enterprises wants to create a report in Word for the partners of her company. Since she's not familiar with PowerPoint, you are going to help by creating several sample documents using various data and slides from the PowerPoint presentation. After she picks the one she wants, you can then explain to her how to complete her report.

Terms

Embed To insert a copy of an object from one application into another so that object in the second program is not affected by changes to the original object. Compare *Link*.

Object Any text, table, picture, slide, spreadsheet, or data treated as a unit for formatting, copying, or moving.

Link To insert a copy of an object from one application to another so that the copied object is automatically updated when it is changed in the original file.

Export To send a copy of an object from one application to another application. The object may be embedded in the other application or it may be linked to the original.

Notes

Embed a PowerPoint Slide in a Word Document

■ You can use simple copy and paste to **embed** a slide in a Word document to illustrate a report or enhance the document.

■ The slide appears in Word in full color, with graphics and text.

■ You can size and move the slide after it's copied to the Word document.

■ Embedded **objects** are similar to **linked** objects except that the embedded object does not change when the original file changes.

Export PowerPoint Slides and Notes to a Word Document

■ You can send PowerPoint slides and notes to a Word document to enhance a report or other document.

■ When you use the Send To command to export slides, miniatures of your slides appear in the Word document. You also can print blank lines with the slides for notes or comments.

■ You can choose to link to the PowerPoint source document. Then, when you make a change to the presentation, the linked document in Word updates automatically.

Export PowerPoint Text to a Word Document

■ You can **export** PowerPoint text to a Word document to save yourself from retyping the text.

■ You can choose to export only the text to the document, not graphics.

Procedures

Embed PowerPoint Slide in Word

1. Open presentation in PowerPoint.
2. Go to Slide Sorter view.
3. Select slide to copy.
4. Click **Copy** button 📋 ... `Ctrl`+`C`
5. Switch to Word document and position cursor.
6. Click **Paste** button 📋 ... `Ctrl`+`V`

   OR

   a. Click Paste **S**pecial .... `S`
   b. Click **Paste l**ink .... `L`
   c. Click **OK** .... `Enter`

Export PowerPoint Slides and Notes to Word

1. Open presentation in PowerPoint.
2. Click **File** .... `Alt`+`F`
3. Click **Send To** .... `D`
4. Click **Microsoft W**ord .... `W`
5. Select one of the following options for Page layout in Microsoft Word.

   ✓ *The images beside each option indicate the Page layout.*

- **Notes n**ext to slides ..... `N`

  ✓ *The presentation is inserted into a new Word document in a three-column table. The slide number appears in the left column, the slide in the center column, and any notes in the right column.*

- **Bl**ank lines next to slides .... `A`

  ✓ *The presentation is inserted into a new Word document in a three-column table. The right column contains blank lines for notes or comments.*

- **Notes b**elow slides ...... `B`

  ✓ *The presentation is inserted into a new Word document with one slide per Word page. The slide is preceded by its number in the upper left and any notes are displayed below the slide image.*

- **Bl**ank lines below slides .... `K`

  ✓ *The presentation is inserted into a new Word document with one slide per Word page with blank lines under each slide for notes or comments.*

- **O**utline only .... `O`

  ✓ *Only the text of the presentation is inserted into a new Word document.*

6. For all options except Outline only, select either:

   - **P**aste .... `Alt`+`P`
   - **Paste l**ink .... `Alt`+`I`

7. Click **OK** .... `Enter`
8. Save the Word document.

Export PowerPoint Outline to Word

1. Open presentation in PowerPoint.
2. Click **File** .... `Alt`+`F`
3. Click **Save A**s .... `A`
4. Click **Save as type** ...... `Alt`+`T`
5. Select **Outline/RTF (*.rtf)**.
6. Click **S**ave .... `Alt`+`S`
7. Switch to Word.
8. Click **File** .... `Alt`+`F`
9. Click **O**pen .... `O`
10. Click **Files of type** .... `Alt`+`T`
11. Select **Rich Text Format (*.rtf)**.
12. Select the file.
13. Click **Open** .... `Alt`+`O`

    OR

1. Open presentation in PowerPoint.
2. Click **File** .... `Alt`+`F`
3. Click **Send To** .... `D`
4. Click **Microsoft W**ord .... `W`
5. Select **O**utline only .... `O`

Exercise Directions

1. Start PowerPoint, if necessary.

2. Open ⌨️**14Marvel** or 💿**15Marvel**.

3. Save it as **15Marvel**.

4. In Slide Sorter view, copy slide 5 and paste it into a new Word document. Press Enter in the Word document to leave space at the top of the page. Enter the text you see in Illustration A to show how the slide and text look together in a document.

5. Select the slide and center it.

   ✓ *Hint: you can use View, Print Layout in Word or check the results in Print Preview if you're not sure of the position of the slide.*

6. Save the document in Word as **15Marvel.doc**. Print the document and close it.

7. In PowerPoint, using the same presentation, export the file to a new Word document using the Send To command. Show the slides next to notes, as shown in Illustrations B, C, and D.

8. Save the document as **15Marvel2.doc**. Print the document and close it.

9. In PowerPoint, using the same presentation, save the file as an Outline/RTF file named **15Marvel3.rtf**. Switch to Word and open that file into a new Word document.

   ✓ *Note: Only the text saves in Outline/RTF format. The tables, charts, and organization charts do not save to the Word document.*

10. Save the file as **15Marvel3.doc**. Print the document and close it. Exit Word.

11. Close the file and exit PowerPoint, saving all changes.

Illustration A

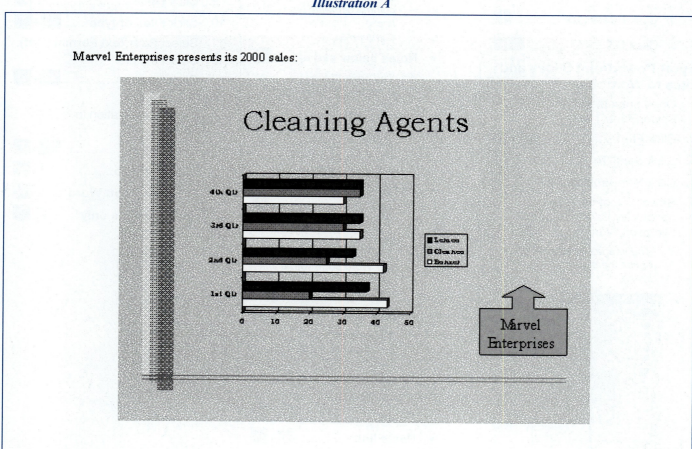

Illustration B

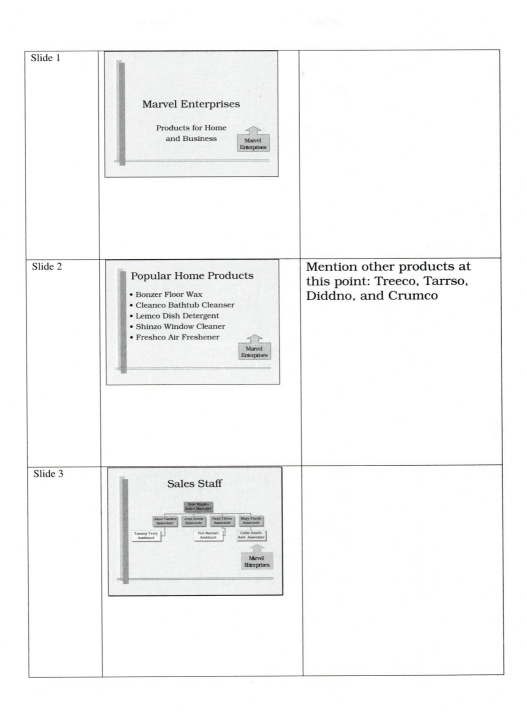

Illustration C

Slide 4	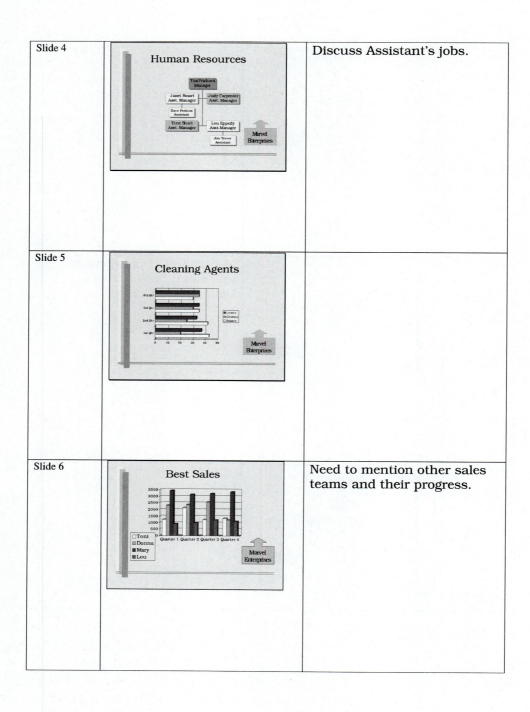 Human Resources	Discuss Assistant's jobs.
Slide 5	Cleaning Agents	
Slide 6	Best Sales	Need to mention other sales teams and their progress.

Illustration D

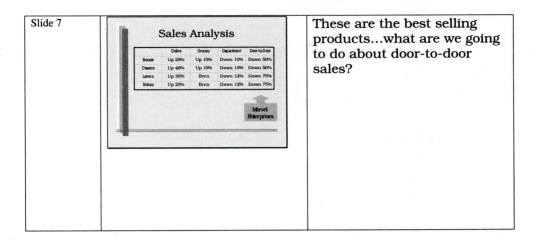

On Your Own

1. Open **OPP14**, the presentation you were working with in Exercise 14, or open ⊙ **15DONATE**.

2. Save the file as **OPP15**.

3. Start Word, create a new document, and type a letter to the president of your organization explaining the presentation you have created, or open the document ⊙ **15LETTER**.

4. Save the Word document as **OPP15-2.doc**.

5. Select the Income chart in the **OPP15** presentation, and paste it at the end of the **OPP15-2.doc** document.

6. Export the entire presentation to a new Word document, including blank lines for notes.

7. Save the document as **OPP15-3.doc**.

8. Save all open Word documents, close them, and exit Word.

9. Save the PowerPoint presentation, close it, and exit PowerPoint.

◆ **Critical Thinking**

Although the owner of Marvel Enterprises is pleased with your work so far, she would like another presentation design to choose from. She's also given you some additional information to use for this presentation. In this exercise, you will create one more presentation for Marvel Enterprises.

Exercise Directions

1. Start PowerPoint, if necessary.
2. Create a new blank presentation.
3. Save the file as **16Marvel**.
4. Using the slide master, create a new presentation background for Marvel Enterprises. Apply a color scheme, clip art, AutoShapes, or other design elements to make it attractive. Make sure that you insert at least one clip art graphic and that you apply a custom color scheme or background colors.

   ✓ *Hint: The background for the illustration is changed in the Background dialog box accessed by choosing Format, Background; instead of picking a color, try Fill Effects in the Background fill drop-down list.*

5. Create a logo for Marvel Enterprises and place it on the slide master. Combine a clip art image or an AutoShape with a text box to create the logo to fit in the corner of the slide as shown in Illustration A.
6. Change all Arial fonts on the slide master to Times New Roman or any other serif font. Return to Normal view.
7. On the title slide, enter the text as shown in Illustration A. Select the title text and enlarge it to 48 points and left align the title text.
8. Show the rulers and use tabs to indent the subtitle text as shown.
9. Add a slide based on the Title and Table slide layout. Enter the text as shown in Illustration B.
10. Resize the cells to fit the text as shown in Illustration B. Center the text in the heading row both horizontally and vertically. Resize the table on the slide if necessary.
11. Add a Bulleted List slide and enter the text as shown in Illustration C.
12. Change the bullet characters to any desired shape. Increase the paragraph spacing in the bullet text.

    ✓ *Hint: Use Wingdings characters for the larger bullets.*

13. Add a fourth slide and use the Title Only slide layout. Add the title **Product Sales**.
14. Insert a bar chart using the following data:

	Qtr 1	Qtr 2	Qtr 3	Qtr 4
Bonzer	2349	2400	2300	2250
Cleanco	3030	3230	3123	3144
Lemco	1800	1989	1956	2000

15. Adjust the position of the chart on the slide to fit the space without overlapping other slide items.
16. Change the chart type, as shown in Illustration D.
17. Send the PowerPoint presentation to Word with blank lines below the slides for notes to be added.
18. Spell check the presentation.
19. Save the file as **16Marvel.doc** and print it.
20. Close the file and exit PowerPoint.

Illustration A

Marvel Enterprises

Products for your future…

Products for your life…

Products for you…

Illustration B

Alternate Product Uses

	Original	**New**	**Improved**	**Best Yet**
Bonzer	Floor wax	Car wax	Window polisher	Siding cleaner
Cleanco	Tub cleanser	Tile cleanser	Floor cleanser	Window cleaner
Lemco	Dish detergent	Car cleaner	Dog wash	Bath soap
Shinzo	Window cleaner	Tile cleaner	Floor cleaner	Car cleaner

Illustration C

Product Benefits

➤ All of our products are environmentally safe.

➤ Our products are concentrated, so you can add water to extend their usefulness.

➤ All of our products have multiple uses.

➤ You can order our products from a catalog, from our Web page, or from your local grocery store.

Illustration D

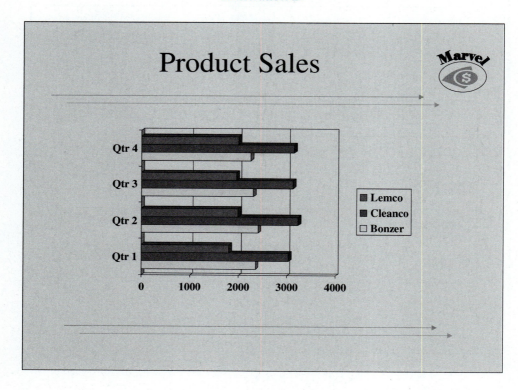

Exercise 17

Skills Covered:

◆ **Check Slides for Style and Consistency** ◆ **Show a Presentation**
◆ **Add Transitions** ◆ **Add Sound** ◆ **Advance Slide** ◆ **Hide Slides**

On the Job

When you show your presentation, you can add certain elements to make it more interesting. You might want to show a presentation automatically, in which case you can use timings to give the audience the right amount of time to read each slide. Transitions and sound can be set to play as each slide changes into the next.

The owner of Marvel Enterprises informed you that she will present the slide show to a large audience. She wants automatic timings, although she also wants the capability to advance the slides manually. Additionally, she wants transitions and sounds. In this exercise, you will prepare the custom presentation you created for viewing.

Terms

Kiosk A computerized machine that displays continuously running presentations, usually found in visitors' centers, trade shows, or conventions.

Transitions The visual effect used when one slide moves off of the screen and another moves onto the screen.

Sound clip Recorded audio clips that you can play automatically as a slide changes from one to the next or by clicking a sound button on the slide.

Advance Slide timing A setting that controls the amount of time a slide displays on the screen.

Notes

Check Slides for Style and Consistency

- You can set PowerPoint to check your slides as you create them for style and consistency, such as the number of font types and the minimum font sizes.
- PowerPoint displays a light bulb to warn you of errors. Click the light bulb to read suggestions.
- You can change the style items that PowerPoint checks or turn the Check style feature off.

Show a Presentation

- You can show a presentation on your computer screen, project it on a larger screen, or show it using a **kiosk**.
- You can present a slide show automatically or manually when you click the mouse.

- You can also run a show continuously.
- Each slide displayed in the slide show fills the entire computer screen.
- PowerPoint displays a black screen with the words *End of slide show* at the end of the presentation.

Add Transitions

- PowerPoint provides **transitions** that you can use to make the slide show more interesting.
- You can apply transitions in any view. However, Slide Sorter view is the easiest because it provides several transition tools on its toolbar and you can apply transitions to several slides at once.
- Apply an animation effect to one slide by selecting the effect. Apply to all slides by clicking the Apply to All Slides button on the Slide Transition Task Pane.

661

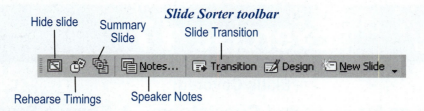

Slide Sorter toolbar

- To access all of the transition options at once, open the Slide Transition Task Pane.

Slide Transition Task Pane

- You can preview transitions before you apply them and you can control the speed of each transition from the Slide Transition Task Pane.

- Slides with transitions are marked by a Slide Transition icon in Slide Sorter view. You can click the icon to preview the transition.

Slide with transition

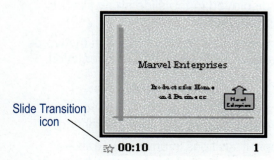

Slide Transition icon

- If you use too many different transitions, the viewer may find it distracting.

Add Sound

- Use a **sound clip** in your presentations to add interest and emphasis.

- You can add any sound file to a slide. Sound files often have a .wav or .mid extension. You can insert a sound from Microsoft's Clip Gallery or from any file on your computer. You can even record your own sounds.

- Sound files play when you move from one slide to another, or when you click the sound button on the slide.

- You can also play CD tracks or recorded narration in a slide show. See Exercise 19 for information.

Advance Slide

- If you do not want to advance slides manually, by mouse clicks in a presentation, you can have PowerPoint advance each slide automatically.

- **Advance Slide timing** defines the amount of time a slide is on the screen before PowerPoint automatically advances to the next slide.

- You can set Advance Slide timing in the Slide Transition Task Pane for individual slides or for all slides in a presentation. Set advance slide timing in seconds or minutes and seconds.

- Even if you set advance timings for your slides, you can also choose to advance the slide manually.

- PowerPoint provides a play feature you can use to set and check advance slide timings.

- The advance slide timing for each slide is indicated in Slide Sorter view by a number below each slide.

Slide with advance slide timing

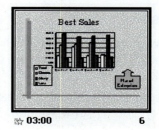

Hide Slides

- You can hide slides in your presentation so they do not show when you run the slide show. For example, you might hide some slides to shorten the presentation, or hide slides that don't apply to a specific audience.

- Hidden slides remain in the file and can be displayed again at any time.

- PowerPoint places an indicator under a hidden slide in Slide Sorter view.

Hidden slide

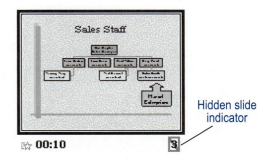

Hidden slide
indicator

Procedures

Set Options for Style and Consistency

1. Click **Tools**....................Alt+T
2. Click **Options**.......................O
3. Click **Spelling and Style** tab ....Ctrl+Tab
4. Click **Check style** C
5. Click **Style Options** button Style Options... ......Alt+T
6. Make necessary changes in Style Options dialog box.
7. Click **OK**...........................Enter
8. Click **OK** again ....Enter

Start Slide Show *(F5)*

1. Click **Slide Show** button 🖳.
   OR
   a. Click **Slide Show**............D
   b. Click **View Show** V
2. Press Page Down to advance to next slide. Press Page Up to go to previous slide.
   OR
   Click mouse to advance slide show.
3. Click the page to end the show.
   OR
   Click **Esc** to end slide show ....Esc
   OR
   Right-click and select **End Show**...........................S

Add Transitions

1. Display slide to add transition effect in Normal view.
   OR
   Select one or multiple slides to affect in Slide Sorter.
2. Click **Slide Show** ....Alt+D
3. Click **Slide Transition** ....T
4. Select a transition in the **Apply to selected slides** list.
5. Click modify transition speed:
   - **Slow**
   - **Medium**
   - **Fast**
6. Click Apply to All Slides if you want the transition to apply to more than the selected slide.

Add Transition Effect from Slide Sorter Toolbar

1. Switch to Slide Sorter view.
2. Select slide or slides to affect.
3. Select options from Slide Transition Task Pane.

Add Sound

1. Select slide or slides to affect.
2. Click **Slide Show** ....Alt+D
3. Click **Slide Transition** ....T
4. Select a sound in the **Modify Transition** Sound drop-down list.
5. Click **Loop until next sound** for continuous sound.
6. Click Apply to All Slides if you want the sound to apply to more than the selected slide.

Insert Sound Objects

1. Display slide in Normal view.
2. Click **Insert** ....Alt+I
3. Click **Movies and Sound** V
4. Click one of the following:
   - **Sound from Media Gallery**...............S
   - **Sound from file**............N
5. Select sound.
6. Click **OK** .... Enter
7. Choose **Yes** to play sound automatically or **No** to play sound when you click **Sound** button 🔊.

Add Advance Slide Timings

1. Switch to Slide Sorter view.
2. Select a slide to apply timing to or select multiple slides by pressing the **Shift** key as you click the slides.
3. Click **Slide Show** ....Alt+D
4. Click **Slide Transition**.........T
5. In **Advance slide**, click **Automatically after.**
6. Enter time in spin box.
7. Click **On mouse click** to add manual advance as option.
8. Click Apply to All Slides if you want the timing to apply to all slides.

Check Timings

1. In Slide Sorter view, click **Rehearse Timings** button 🖅.
2. Walk through the presentation, reading slide contents and any comments you intend to make in the presentation.
3. Advance from slide to slide as you intend to during an actual presentation.
4. When you're done, press **Esc** .... ⌫Esc
5. PowerPoint asks if you wish to save these timings. Select **Yes** to save them.

Hide Slide

1. Switch to Slide Sorter view.
2. Select slide to hide.
3. Click **Hide Slide** button 🖾.
4. Click **Hide Slide** button 🖾 a second time to redisplay hidden slide.

Remove Slide Transition.

1. Click the slide.
2. Display the Slide Transition Task Pane.
3. Click **No Transition** in the **Apply to selected slides** list.

Exercise Directions

1. Start PowerPoint, if necessary.
2. Open ⌨️**15Marvel** or 💿**17Marvel**.
3. Save the file as **17Marvel**.
4. Check the presentation for any spelling errors or style inconsistencies.
5. Show the presentation as a slide show.
6. Switch to Slide Sorter view.
7. Apply the Random Transition effect to all slides using a slow speed. Show the presentation.
8. Apply one or two transitions to the entire slide show.
9. Rehearse the show to set transition timings. As you rehearse, read each slide. Allow enough time for the speaker to discuss the topics.

10. After rehearsal, in slide 2, set the timing to 2 minutes. On slides 5, 6, and 7, set the timing to 3 minutes.
11. Hide slides 3 and 4.
12. Run the presentation.
13. Add transition sounds to the slides. You can add one sound to all slides or use different sounds for multiple slides.
    ✓ *Your computer may not be equipped to play sound.*
14. Spell check the slide presentation.
15. Print the presentation.
16. Show the slide presentation.
17. Close the file and exit PowerPoint, saving all changes.

On Your Own

1. Open **OPP15**, the presentation for the charity that you last used in Exercise 15, or open 💿**17DONATE**.
2. Save the file as **OPP17**.
3. Run the slide show.
4. Set the slide show to run automatically with an interval of 5 seconds.
5. Add a dissolve transition effect to all slides at a medium speed.
6. Add the sound of applause to the title slide and the final slide.
7. Run the slide show again.
8. Save the presentation, close it, and close PowerPoint.

Exercise 18

Skills Covered:

◆ **Animate Text and Objects** ◆ **Preset Animation**
◆ **Custom Animation**

On the Job

Animate text and objects to add interest and emphasis to certain slides and items in the presentation. Animate a bulleted list of topics that build in importance, for example, with timed pauses to catch the audience's attention.

The owner of Marvel Enterprises liked your presentation but she wants more movement and some sound added for emphasis. The owner also asks that you prepare a second presentation with sound and movement, so she has a choice. In this exercise, you will add animation to the custom presentation you created.

Terms

Animate To apply movement to text or an object. For example, text might fly onto the screen from the left or drop in from above.

Preset animation Several types of movements included in PowerPoint that you can apply quickly and easily.

Notes

Animate Text and Objects

- You can **animate** text on slides to add interest to your presentation or to emphasize special points.

- You can make animated text appear one letter or one paragraph at a time, for example. Or, you can animate text to fly in or bounce in, for example.

- You can use PowerPoint's **preset animations** or design your own custom animations.

- You can preview animations and adjust timing before you show the presentation.

- Apply an animation effect to one slide by selecting the effect. Apply to all slides by clicking the Apply to All Slides button in the Animation Schemes Task Pane.

Slide Design - Animation Schemes Task Pane

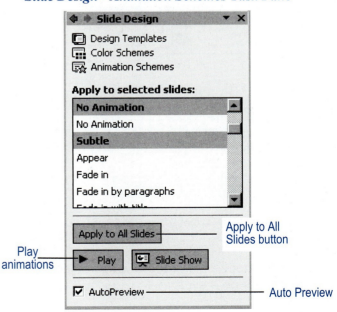

- Use the Animation Schemes Task Pane to apply preset animation effects quickly and preview those effects.

Preset Animation

- PowerPoint supplies Subtle, Moderate, and Exciting animation schemes you can apply to your slides.

- Use preset animations on bulleted lists, titles, subtitles, and other text.

- You can apply preset animations from Normal or Slide Sorter view using the Animation Schemes Task Pane.

- You can click AutoPreview to preview an animation when you select it from the Animation Scheme list box.

Custom Animation

- Use the Custom Animation Task Pane to set animation effects, direction, property and speed for text in a slide.

- You can apply custom animations to tables, charts, and organization charts. You can also apply custom animations to lines, shapes, clip art, and AutoShapes.

Custom animation order

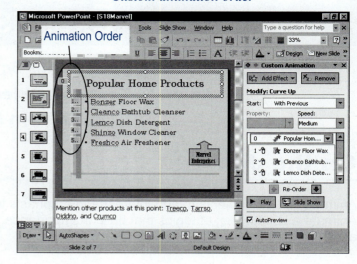

Custom Animation Task Pane

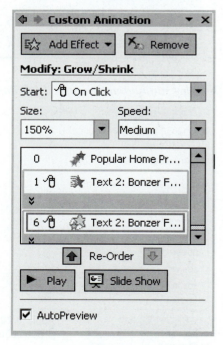

- You can choose the order in which objects and text appear on a slide.

- You can also apply various properties to the animations. For example, you can choose the amount of spin or the direction of a checkerboard effect.

- You can set the speed of the animation.

- You can set details for each effect applied to bullet text, for example.

Set details for single animations

- You can set effect details, such as direction or size. Most effects also include sound enhancements.

Set effect details

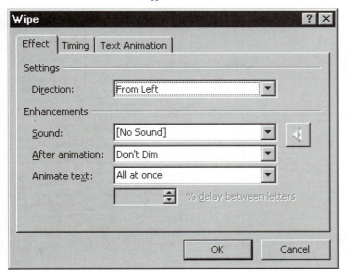

■ You can set timing details, such as speed, delay, or repeat, for each effect.

Set timing details

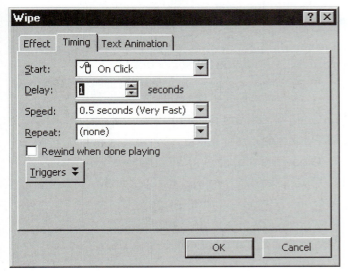

■ You can set details for text animation, such as text grouping and order of the effect.

Set text animation details

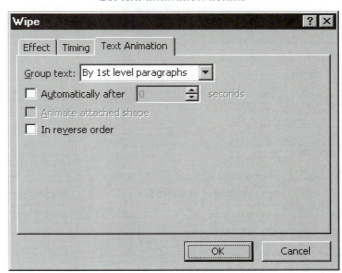

Procedures

Display Animations Effects Task Pane

1. Click **Slide Show** .... D
2. Click **Animation Schemes**.. C

Preset Animation

1. In Normal or Slide Sorter view, display slide.
2. Click in text or object to be animated.

3. Click desired animation effect in Animation Schemes Task Pane.

OR

Click **Apply to All Slides**.

Preview Animations

- Click **Animation Preview** button ⭐.

OR

1. Open Animation Schemes Task Pane.

2. Click **Play**.

Custom Animation

1. In Normal view, display slide.
2. Click the item to be animated.
3. Click **Slide Show** .... Alt + D
4. Click **Custom Animation**.... M
5. Click **Add Effect** button

   ⭐ Add Effect ▾ .

6. Choose appropriate command:
   - **Entrance**......................... E
   - **Emphasis**..................... M
   - **Exit** X
   - **Motion Paths** .... P

7. Choose effect you want to apply.

8. Click **Start** drop-down arrow. Choose appropriate option:
   - **On Click**
   - **With Previous**
   - **After Previous**

9. Click the property drop-down arrow and choose appropriate option.

10. Click **Speed**. Choose appropriate option:
    - **Very Slow**
    - **Slow**
    - **Medium**
    - **Fast**
    - **Very Fast**

11. Click **Close** button X to close the Task Pane.

Set Effect Details

1. Open the Custom Animation Task Pane.
2. Click the effect in the Effects list.
3. Click the drop-down arrow.
4. Click **Effect Options**........... E

5. Click the appropriate tab:
   - **Effect**
   - **Timing**
   - **Text Animation**
6. Set the details.
7. Click **OK** .... Enter

Turn Animation Off

1. Select text or object from which to remove animation.
2. Open Animation Schemes Task Pane.
3. Click No Animation in the Apply to selected slides list box.

Exercise Directions

1. Start PowerPoint, if necessary.
2. Open ▦**17Marvel** or ☉**18Marvel**.
3. Save the file as **18Marvel**.
4. Switch to Slide Sorter view.
5. Remove all transition effects from all slides; keep the timings.
6. Switch to Normal view.
7. In the first slide, select the title text and apply the preset animation Big Title (an Exciting animation).
8. Remove Hide Slide from slides 3 and 4.
9. Select slide 3 and apply the Faded zoom animation.
10. Select slide 4 and apply Faded Zoom.
11. Switch to slide 2.
12. Apply the following custom animation:
    - Display the title first, using any entrance effect.
    - Display the bulleted text with applause and by word.
13. Switch to slide 6 and apply any custom Emphasis effect to the chart. Repeat the effect 3 times.
    - ✓ Hint: Use the Timing tab to set the details of the effect.

14. Switch to slide 7 and apply any custom exit effect to the table.
15. Switch to Slide Sorter view.
16. Play the effects on each slide and make any adjustments you think necessary.
    - ✓ Illustration A shows that you do not see transitions and animations in this view.
17. Spell check the presentation.
18. Print the presentation.
19. Close the file, saving all changes.
20. Open ▦**16Marvel** or ☉**18Marvel2**.
21. Save the file as **18Marvel2**.
22. Apply transitions, preset animations, timings, and custom animations to the show any way you'd like.
23. Preview the slide show and make any adjustments.
24. Close the file and exit PowerPoint, saving all changes.

Illustration A

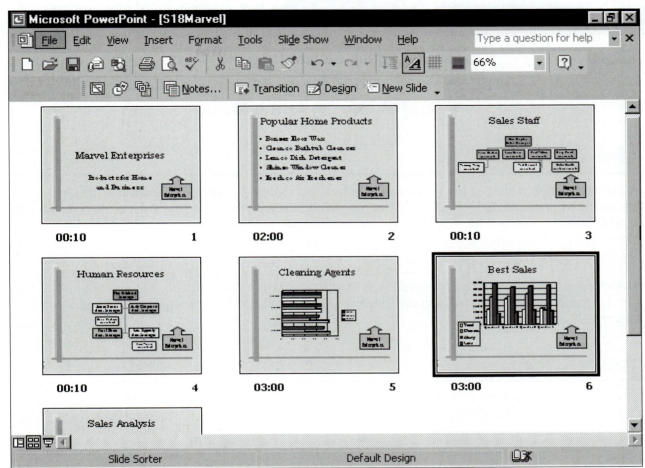

On Your Own

1. Open **OPP17**, the presentation you used in the On Your Own section of Exercise 17, or open 🖱 **18DONATE**.

2. Save the file as **OPP18**.

3. Display the Animation Schemes Task Pane.

4. Apply an animation scheme to the AutoShape on the title slide. (If you do not have an AutoShape on the title slide, use one on a different slide or create one.)

5. Animate the slide text for all slides with bullet lists.

6. Use Custom Animation to animate one of the charts in the presentation.

7. Run the presentation.

8. Save the presentation, close it, and exit PowerPoint.

Exercise 19

Skills Covered:
◆ **Annotations** ◆ **Pause and Resume Show**
◆ **Add Music** ◆ **Add a Movie**

On the Job

Use annotations during a slide show to highlight certain information or items. For example, you can underline points to emphasize or check off topics as you discuss them. For a really dynamic presentation, you can add music or movie clips. Adding a limited amount of multimedia to a presentation can make it more interesting and entertaining.

The owner of Marvel Enterprises is pleased with the content of the presentation, but she wants you to add some pizzazz to it. She is planning on showing the presentation to a new group of investors and wants to really impress them.

Terms

Annotation feature A method of writing or marking on the slide during a presentation.

Notes

Annotations

- You can add annotations such as writing or drawing to a slide during a slide show.
- When you use the **annotation feature**, the mouse becomes a pen.
- You may want to annotate a chart or data in a table, for instance, as you present a slide show.
- Annotations do not change the slide; they only appear during the presentation.
- PowerPoint suspends automatic timings while you use the annotations feature.
- You can choose different colors to use for the pen.

Pause and Resume Show

- You can pause a slide show when you want to discuss elements in the show. When you are ready, you can resume the show.

Add Music

- You can add music clips to your presentation to make it more interesting or to emphasize a slide.
- Your computer must have speakers and a sound card to play music during the presentation.
- You might want music to play in the background as the viewer reads the slide or as you talk.
- Insert a music clip as a slide object in Normal view.
- A music clip is indicated by a sound button .
- You can choose to have the music play when you advance to the slide containing the clip or when you click its icon.
- You can insert a music file, CD track, or music from Microsoft's Clip Gallery.
- Microsoft's Windows\Media folder often includes sounds, music, and other clips for you to use with a presentation. You can also find additional sound files on the Internet.

Add a Movie

- You can insert movie clips or videos into a presentation.
- Insert a movie clip in Normal view.

- You can choose to have the video begin when you advance to the slide containing the object or to play when you click the movie icon.
- Movies are often files ending with an .avi, .mpe, or .mpg extension.

Procedures

Add Annotations

1. Show the presentation.
2. Click the shortcut menu 🖼 ╱ that appears in the lower-left corner of the screen.
3. Click **P**ointer Options ....O
4. Click **P**en..............................P

   OR

   Press **Ctrl+P** ....Ctrl+P

Erase Annotations

- Press **E** on keyboard............E

OR

1. Right-click the slide or click the Annotation icon.
2. Click **S**creen ....S
3. Click **E**rase Pen ....E

Change Pen Color

1. Click the shortcut menu 🖼 ╱ that appears in the lower-left corner of the screen.
2. Click **P**ointer Options ....O
3. Click Pen **C**olor..................C
4. Click one of the following:
   - **B**lack ....B
   - **W**hite..............................W
   - **R**ed ....R
   - **G**reen ....G
   - B**l**ue L
   - **C**yan C
   - **M**agenta ....M
   - **Y**ellow ....Y
   - Gr**e**y................................E
   - Re**s**et ....S

Pause Show

1. Right-click the screen.
2. Click **S**creen C
3. Click **P**ause.......................S

Resume Show

1. Right-click the screen.
2. Click **S**creen C
3. Click Re**s**ume ....S

Turn Off Annotation Feature

1. During slide show, right-click any slide.
2. Click **P**ointer Options ....O
3. Click A**u**tomatic..................U

OR

- Press **Esc**...........................Esc

Add Sound

Insert sounds and movies in Normal view.

1. Select slide with which to associate music.
2. Click **I**nsert ....Alt+I
3. Click Mo**v**ies and Sounds...V
4. Click one of the following:
   - **S**ound from Gallery......S
   - Sou**n**d from File............N
   - Play **C**D Audio Track....C
5. Select a sound and click **OK**...........................Enter
6. Click **Y**es to play music automatically when slide advances.

   OR

   Click **N**o to have music play when you click Sound button.

Add Movie

1. Open slide presentation.
2. Select slide with which to associate video clip.
3. Click **I**nsert................Alt+I
4. Click Mo**v**ies and Sounds...V
5. Click one of the following:
   - **M**ovie from Media Gallery ....M
   - Movie from **F**ile ....F
6. Choose file to add.
7. Click **OK** ....Enter
8. Click **Y**es to have movie play automatically in the slide show or **N**o to have it played when you click it.

Exercise Directions

1. Start PowerPoint, if necessary.
2. Open ⌨ **18Marvel** or 💿 **19Marvel**.
3. Save the file as **19Marvel**.
4. Run the slide show. On the second slide, activate the annotation feature and circle **Bonzer Floor Wax** with the pen. Change the color of the pen and draw an arrow to point to **Shinzo Window Cleaner**. Erase the annotations.
5. On slide 5, draw a star beside the first quarter in the chart.
6. On slide 6, circle **Mary's** name in the legend. Erase the annotations.
7. Move to slide 7 and pause the show.
8. Resume the show and end it.
9. In Slide view, insert a Title Only slide at the end of the presentation.
10. Insert the title **Marvel Enterprises Rocks**.
11. Insert a sound or movie clip. Have the sound or movie play automatically in the slide show.
12. Size the sound or movie clip as you would size any type of object.
13. Show the presentation.
14. Close the file and exit PowerPoint, saving all changes.

On Your Own

1. Open **OPP18**, the presentation you used in the On Your Own section of Exercise 18, or open 💿 **19DONATE**.
2. Save the file as **OPP19**.
3. Add a music clip or a video clip to one or more of the slides.
4. Run the slide show. Stop the show to annotate one of the slides. For example, circle important text.
5. Run the presentation.
6. Save the presentation, close it, and exit PowerPoint.

Exercise 20

Skills Covered:

◆ **Create Notes Pages and Handouts**

◆ **Notes Master and Handout Master** ◆ **Pack and Go**

◆ **Meeting Minder** ◆ **Incorporate Meeting Feedback**

On the Job

PowerPoint provides ways for you to maximize your presentations. You can distribute handouts with a presentation, for example. Or, you can also pack up your presentation to display it on another computer. You can even show a presentation to different people on different computers during an online meeting.

The owner of Marvel Enterprises wants you to create notes pages and handouts of a presentation for her audience. She also needs the presentation saved to a disk so she can show it on a computer that doesn't have PowerPoint. Finally, the owner has asked you to show her how to take notes during an online presentation so she can create a report of the notes after the presentation.

Terms

Notes Comments added to the presentation that can be for the speaker's eyes only.

Handouts Printed copies of the presentation for the audience to refer to during and after the slide show.

Pack and Go A feature that lets you save the presentation to a floppy disk and then show it on a computer that doesn't have PowerPoint loaded.

Notes

Create Notes Pages and Handouts

- **Notes** help you remember key points about each slide in the presentation.

- You can enter speaker's notes for a slide in the Notes pane in Normal view, or in a placeholder below the slide in Notes Page view.

- You can then print your presentation in Notes Page format for reference while giving a presentation or to hand out to the audience.

- You can also print and hand out notes pages with a blank notes' area, so that audience members can take their own notes in the empty placeholders.

- You can give the audience **handouts** of the presentation for future reference.

- Printed handouts do not show notes.

Notes Master and Handout Master

- You can add text, pictures, and other information to a notes or handout master.

Notes Master view

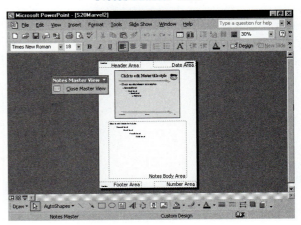

Handout Master view

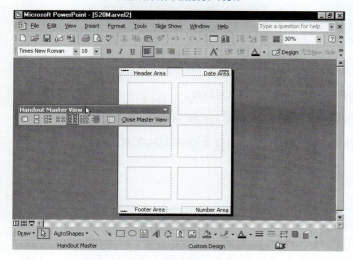

- Anything added to a master appears in all notes or handouts you print.

- Either master can list your company logo, the date, and your phone number, for instance.

- You can enter a header or footer, page numbers, and dates in a master as well.

Pack and Go

- Use the **Pack and Go** Wizard when you want to run a slide show on another computer.

- If the computer you plan to run the packed show on doesn't have PowerPoint, you can include the Viewer in the Pack and Go file.

- The Viewer is a program that lets you run a PowerPoint slide show without the use of PowerPoint.

- The Pack and Go Wizard guides you through saving the presentation and Viewer.

- You can unpack the slide show on any PC.

Pack and Go Wizard

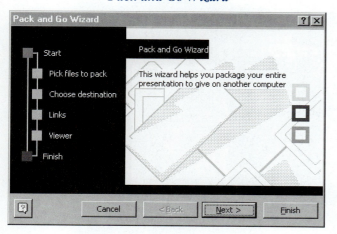

Meeting Minder

- You can use the Meeting Minder to take notes during a slide show.

Meeting Minder dialog box

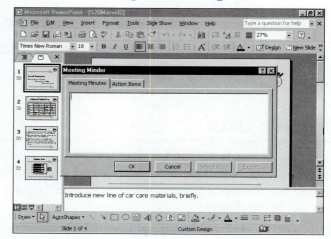

- During an online meeting, anyone can take notes in the Meeting Minder and everyone can view those notes while online.

- After the slide show, you can view the notes and comments in the Meeting Minder.

Incorporate Meeting Feedback

- During a slide show, you can enter action items in the Meeting Minder as a way of involving online participants. Action items direct the participants to complete tasks related to the meeting.

- An action item may be a task you want someone to complete, such as performing research on a meeting topic and reporting back to the group.

Meeting Minder dialog box: Action Items tab

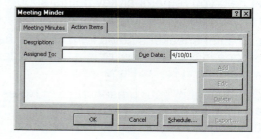

- After the show, you can e-mail the interested parties by exporting the action item.

- PowerPoint also creates a slide at the end of the presentation on which you can store the action items so you can discuss them with your audience.

- You can also send meeting minutes and action items to Word to use in a report or other document.

Procedures

Create Notes Pages

- Enter notes in Notes pane in Normal view.

OR

1. Click **V**iew .... `Alt`+`V`
2. Click **Notes P**age................. `P`
3. Click in notes placeholder and enter notes.

Print Notes Pages *(Ctrl+P)*

1. Click **F**ile..................... `Alt`+`F`
2. Click **P**rint........................... `P`
3. Click **Notes Pages** in **Print what** drop-down list.
4. Click **OK** .... `Enter`

Create Handouts *(Ctrl+P)*

1. Click **F**ile..................... `Alt`+`F`
2. Click **P**rint........................... `P`
3. In the **Print what** drop-down list, click **Handouts**.
4. In **Slides per page** drop-down list, choose 2, 3, 4, 6, or 9............... `Alt`+`R`
5. Choose slide order:
   - **Hori**z**ontal** .... `Alt`+`Z`
   - **V**ertical.................. `Alt`+`V`
6. Click **OK** .... `Enter`

Edit Notes or Handout Master

1. Click **V**iew..................... `Alt`+`V`
2. Click **M**aster .... `M`
3. Click **N**otes master............. `N`

   OR

   Click **Hand**o**ut master** .... `D`
4. Enter any text or graphic you want to display on all notes or handouts.
5. Click **Close Master View** button `Close Master View`

Pack and Go

1. Open presentation.
2. Click **F**ile .... `Alt`+`F`
3. Click **Pac**k **and Go**............. `K`
4. Follow directions in Pack and Go Wizard.
5. Unpack show and run it to check for errors.

   OR

   Click the **Close** button `X` in the Master toolbar.

Unpack Presentation

1. Insert floppy disk in computer.
2. Open Windows Explorer and locate the pack and go file.
3. Double-click **Pngsetup** on floppy disk.
4. Enter hard drive destination in which to unpack presentation.

   ✓ *Note: Use an empty folder on the hard drive. Pack and Go overwrites everything in the folder.*
5. Click **Y**es to run unpacked show.

   OR

   Click **N**o to wait to run show.

Show Presentation

1. Open destination folder in Explorer.
2. Right-click presentation.
3. Click **Show**.

Take Notes during Slide Show

1. Right-click slide in Slide Show view.
2. Click **Mee**t**ing Minder** .... `T`
3. Enter notes or comments.
4. Click **OK** .... `Enter`

Read or Enter Notes after Presentation

1. Click **T**ools.................. `Alt`+`T`
2. Click **Meeting Minder** .... `T`

Create Action Items in Meeting Minder

1. During slide show, right-click slide.

   OR

   After show,
   click **T**ools................... `Alt`+`T`
2. Click **Meeting Minder** .... `T`
3. Click **Action Items** tab.
4. Enter appropriate text.
5. Click **A**dd .... `Alt`+`A`
6. Click **E**xport................ `Alt`+`E`
7. Click **Post action items to Microsoft Outlook** .... `P`

   OR

   Click **Send meeting minutes and action items to Microsoft Word** .... `S`
8. Click **E**xport **Now** .... `E`

Exercise Directions

1. Start PowerPoint, if necessary.
2. Open ⌨ **18Marvel2** or 💿 **20Marvel2**.
3. Save the file as **20Marvel2**.
4. Switch to Normal view and select the first slide. Add the following notes in the Notes pane:

   Mention research and development of future products.

5. View notes pages. Print the notes page for slide one.
6. Print as handouts with 4 per page.
7. Go to the Notes Master view and add a header and date. Use your name as the header and the month and year as the date as shown in Illustration A. Print all slides as notes pages.
8. Go to the slides master and copy the logo plus logo text.
9. Switch to the handout master and copy the logo and text to the top middle of the page. Add the following footer **Marvel Enterprises**, as shown in Illustration B.
10. Print the handout for the slide show.
11. Run the presentation. During the presentation, open the Meeting Minder and enter the following notes in the meeting minutes:

   Suggestions:

   Personal care products such as foot pumice, foot powders, foot creams and lotions.

   Dog care products? Shampoo and dips?

12. In Normal view, open the Meeting Minder and add the following to the Action Items tab:

   Research Dog Products

   Timothy

   6-01

   and

   Research Foot Care Products

   Debbie

   6-01

   ✓ *Hint: Type the first action item, click the Add button. Type the second action item, click the Add button.*

13. Export the action items and meeting minutes to Word and print the Word document.
14. Save the document as **20Marvel2.rtf**.
15. Close the Word document and the file. Return to PowerPoint.
16. Save the file.
17. Pack the presentation to a floppy disk.

   ✓ *Hint: Embed the fonts. Include the Viewer only if you plan to show the presentation on a computer that does not have PowerPoint installed.*

18. Close PowerPoint.
19. Unpack the presentation and run it to make sure it works.

Illustration A

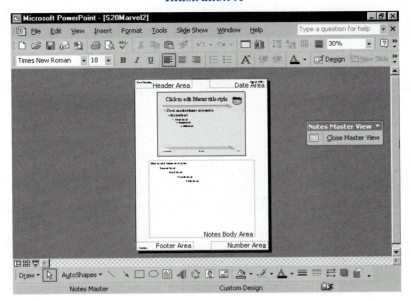

Illustration B

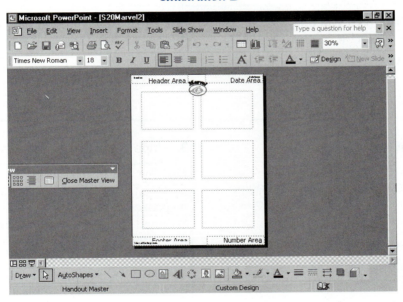

On Your Own

1. Open **OPP19**, the presentation you used in Exercise 19, or open 🖴 **20DONATE**.

2. Save the file as **OPP20**.

3. Type notes for at least three slides.

4. Open the handouts master.

5. Add your name, the date, and the page number to the notes master and the handouts master.

6. Insert a clip art image on the handouts master.

7. Set formatting options as desired.

8. Insert a different clip art image on the notes master.

9. Set formatting options as desired.

10. Create notes and handouts for the presentation and print them.

11. Save the presentation, close it, and exit PowerPoint.

Exercise 21

Skills Covered:

◆ **Set Up a Presentation** ◆ **Set Up Show Dialog Box Options**

On the Job

Set up a slide show so you can use it in different situations. For example, if you run a slide show on a kiosk, you will want the show to run continuously so no one has to monitor it. At the same time, you don't want anyone to alter the show or add to it while it's running. You can control this by setting up the show.

The owner of Marvel Enterprises wants you to set up two presentations—one she can use on a kiosk and a second she can use at a computer at a trade show.

Terms

Custom Show A show in which you specify the slides and the order in which the slides appear during presentation.

Narration A voice recording that describes or enhances the message in each slide.

Notes

Set Up a Presentation

- You can set up PowerPoint to show a presentation on a computer, either accompanied by a speaker, or running on its own continuously in a kiosk or trade show booth.

Set Up Show dialog box

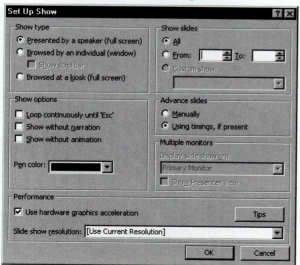

Set Up Show Dialog Box Options

Option	Description
Presented by a speaker	Shows the presentation full screen.
Browsed by an individual	Shows the presentation in a window on the screen with menus and commands an individual can use to control and change slide show.
Browsed at a kiosk	Shows the presentation full screen; automatically sets the show to loop continuously; viewer can advance slides and use action buttons/hyperlinks but cannot change slide show.
Loop continuously until 'Esc'	Runs a presentation over and over continuously.
Show without narration	Displays the slide show with no voice.
Show without animation	Displays the show with no animation.
Pen Color	Enables you to choose a pen color for annotation.

Option	Description
Show scrollbar	Shows scrollbar on-screen with presentation; available only when Browsed by an individual is selected.
Slides	Choose All or enter numbers of specific slides to show.
Custom show	Choose specific slides or presentations.
Advance slides	Choose Manually or Using timings if present.
Multiple monitors	Default is primary monitor; choose if second monitor is attached.

- You may want to show the presentation at a trade show or convention or at your place of business.

- You can choose to set up a presentation so that the viewer can manipulate the screen or set it up so the viewer cannot manipulate or change the slide show.

- You can run a presentation in a continuous loop.

- PowerPoint lets you run a presentation with or without **narration** and animation.

- If you run a slide show that is unattended you should include timings and voice narration.

Procedures

Set Up and Run Presentation

1. Open presentation.
2. Click **Slide Show** .... Alt + D
3. Click **Set Up Show** .... S
4. Choose one of the following show types:
   - **Presented by a speaker** .... P
   - **Browsed by an individual** .... B
   - **Browsed at a kiosk** ...... K
5. Choose other options.
6. Click **OK** .... Enter

Set Up Custom Slide Show

1. Click **Slide Show** .... D
2. Click **Custom Shows** .... W
3. Click **New** .... N
4. Click slide to add to presentation.
5. Click **Add** .... A
6. Click **OK** .... Enter
7. Name the show.
8. Click **Close** C

Exercise Directions

1. Start PowerPoint, if necessary.
2. Open ⌨️ **20Marvel2** or 💿 **21Marvel2**.
3. Save the file as **21Marvel2**.
4. Set the slide show up to be browsed by an individual, with all slides and using timings.
5. Loop the show continuously.
6. View the show.
7. Change the setup so it doesn't show the animation.
8. View the show.
9. Close the file, saving all changes.
10. Open ⌨️ **19Marvel** or 💿 **21Marvel**.
11. Save the file as **21Marvel**.
12. Set the show up to run on a kiosk. Change timings in the show so it runs more quickly on the kiosk.
13. View the show.
14. Close the file and exit PowerPoint, saving all changes.

On Your Own

1. Open **OPP20**, the presentation you used in Exercise 20, or open 💿 **21DONATE**.
2. Save the file as **OPP21**.
3. Set up the slide show to be presented by a speaker and to loop continuously.
4. Run the slide show. (Press Esc to stop it.)
5. Save the file as **OPP21-2**.
6. Set up the slide show to be browsed at a kiosk without animation.
7. Run the slide show.
8. Save the presentation, close it, and exit PowerPoint.

Exercise 22

Skills Covered:

◆ **Save a Presentation as a Web Site** ◆ **Publish a Presentation**
◆ **Make Your Web Presentation More Efficient**

On the Job

Publish a presentation to the Web so that a larger audience can view it. You might, for example, already have a Web site established for customers to view your products or services. Add a presentation to the site to interest more customers and provide an additional resource.

The owner of Marvel Enterprises wants to use one of the presentations you created as a Web site. You will need to check the presentation for consistency and add a few things to it before you save it as a Web page and publish it.

Terms

Web site A collection of Web pages; a site usually contains information with a common focus.

HTML (Hypertext Markup Language) A formatting language used on the Internet.

Browser A program, such as Internet Explorer, used to view Web pages and sites.

Web page One document on the Web, usually containing information related to one topic.

Publish To set options to make the presentation more suitable for viewing on the Web.

Notes

Save a Presentation as a Web Site

- Save a presentation as a **Web site** so you can publish it to the World Wide Web.

- PowerPoint lets you save a presentation in **HTML** format so you can open it in a Web **browser**, such as Internet Explorer.

- When you save as a **Web page**, PowerPoint stores all HTML files in a folder named for the saved file. PowerPoint also saves the original file so you can open the presentation any time you want.

- You can save a PowerPoint slide as a Web page or save multiple PowerPoint slides as a Web site.

Publish a Presentation

- You **publish** a presentation to prepare it for the Web.

Publish as Web Page dialog box

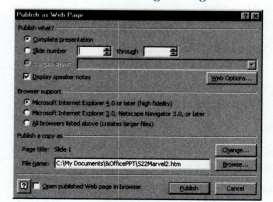

■ Publishing lets you choose options for how people will view the pages.

Web Options dialog box

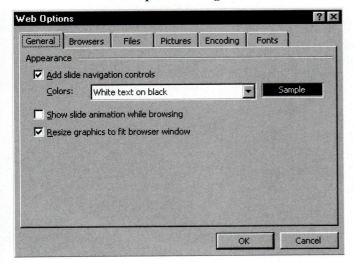

■ Choose browser support when you publish a presentation. Browser support determines which browsers can view the Web page.

Browsers tab of the Web Options dialog box

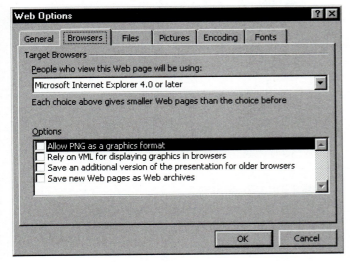

■ Change colors and resize graphics when you publish to the Web so the text and objects look their best on the page.

■ Organize files and locations in the Web site for efficiency.

Files tab of the Web Options dialog box

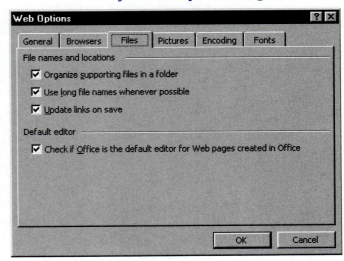

Make Your Web Presentation More Efficient

■ An efficient Web site makes it easy for people to display topics quickly. If your site is easy to navigate, people will spend more time looking at your site.

■ Add Action buttons for easier navigation.

■ Use small graphics and pictures to cut downloading time.

■ Use one major heading on each page to let viewers know where they are.

■ Don't squeeze too much text on one slide or one page.

■ Use lists or tables when possible, because they are easier and faster to read than paragraphs of text.

■ Use the GIF image format for cartoons, line drawings, or pictures with few colors.

■ Use JPEG format for scanned photographs or images with several colors.

■ Use PNG format for buttons, bullets, and small images.

Procedures

Preview Presentation in Web Page View

1. Open a presentation.
2. Click **File** .... `Alt`+`F`
3. Click **Web Page Preview**.... `B`
4. Close browser to return to PowerPoint.

Save Presentation as Web Page

1. Open or create presentation.
2. Click **File** .... `Alt`+`F`
3. Click **Save as Web Page**.... `G`
4. Click **Save in** and select a folder in which to save the Web page .... `Alt`+`I`
5. Accept or change suggested **File name** .... `Alt`+`N`

   ✓ *See your system's administrator for information on saving your Web page to a Web server.*

---

6. Click **Change Title** button
   `Change Title...` .... `Alt`+`C`
   to display the Set Page Title dialog box and change the page title:
   a. Type the **Page title** .... `Alt`+`P`
   b. Click **OK** .... `Enter`
7. Click **Save** button 🖫 .... `Alt`+`S`

Publish Web Page

1. Open or create presentation.
2. Click **File** .... `Alt`+`F`
3. Click **Save as Web Page**.... `G`
4. Click **Save in** and select a folder in which to publish the Web page .... `Alt`+`I`
5. Accept or change suggested **File name** .... `Alt`+`N`

---

6. Click **Publish** button
   `Publish` .... `Alt`+`P`
7. Click desired options.
8. Click **Web Options** button `Web Options...` .. `Alt`+`W`
9. Click desired options.
10. Click **Browsers** tab .... `Ctrl`+`Tab`
11. Click desired options.
12. Click **Files** tab............ `Ctrl`+`Tab`
13. Click desired options.
14. Click **Pictures** tab....... `Ctrl`+`Tab`
15. Click desired options.
16. Click **OK** .... `Enter`
17. Click **Publish** button
    `Publish` .... `Alt`+`P`

Exercise Directions

1. Start PowerPoint, if necessary.
2. Open 🖴**21Marvel2** or 💿 **22Marvel2**.
3. Save the file as **22Marvel2**.
4. Switch to Normal view and add the following Action buttons to the presentation (AutoShapes, Action Buttons). You can place the buttons anywhere on the slide, as shown in Illustration A.

   Slide 1: add the End button
   Slide 5: add the Home button
   ✓ *See Exercise 11 for review of Action Buttons.*

   ✓ *Hint: Leave the hyperlinks as they are by clicking OK in the Action Settings dialog box.*

5. Save the presentation.
6. Save the presentation as a Web page and publish the complete presentation. Do not display speaker notes. Set browser support for Microsoft Internet Explorer 4 or later.
7. Change the following Web option when you publish the presentation:

   Show slide animation while browsing.

8. View the Web pages using your browser.
9. Close Internet Explorer.
10. Close the file and exit PowerPoint, saving all changes.

    ✓ *Some formatting may change when you save in HTML.*

Illustration A

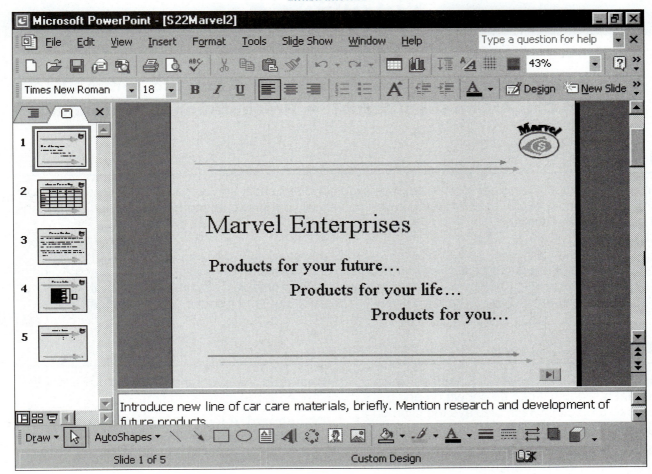

On Your Own

1. Open **OPP21**, the presentation you used in Exercise 21, or open ⊙ **22DONATE**.

2. Save the file as **OPP22**.

3. Save the presentation as a Web page, changing the name to **OPP22-2**.

4. View the presentation in your Web browser.

5. Close the browser.

6. Save the presentation, close it, and exit PowerPoint.

Exercise 23

Skills Covered:

◆ **Export to Overhead Transparencies** ◆ **Export to 35mm Slides**
◆ **Find Clip Art on the Internet** ◆ **Presentation Conferencing**

On the Job

Export a presentation to another format, such as slides or overheads, so you can show it on a projection system. For instance, export to overheads so you can show your presentation to a larger audience than you could on a computer screen.

Marvel Enterprises has asked you to prepare a presentation to send to an imaging company for slides and transparencies. Also, they've asked you to assist them in holding an online meeting with the owner of Marvel Enterprises and co-workers to review the presentation and discuss possible modifications.

Terms

Transparencies Clear sheets of plastic on which you print a slide so it can be shown on an overhead projector, which displays the slide on a large screen.

Imaging company A company that specializes in printing 35mm slides, transparencies, and other computerized images to various media.

Real time An event that is taking place live, as opposed to in delayed time.

Whiteboard A tool, similar to a blackboard, on which you can enter text.

Notes

Export to Overhead Transparencies

■ PowerPoint lets you save a presentation so you can create **transparencies** to show on an overhead projector.

Export to Overhead in Page Setup dialog box

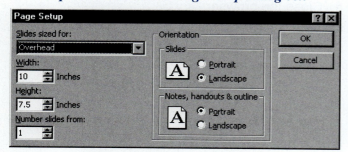

■ For best results, let a professional **imaging company** print the transparencies for you.

■ Check with the imaging company for the correct file format, although the PPT file format generally works well.

Export to 35mm Slides

■ You can save a presentation in a format appropriate for creating 35mm slides.

■ You should send your presentation to a professional imaging company to have the slides made.

■ Avoid a blue and red color scheme because it can be hard to read or visually distracting.

Find Clip Art on the Internet

■ In addition to the clip art that is included with Office XP, you can also buy clip art collections from other resources or download clip art from the Internet.

Presentation Conferencing

■ You can share your presentation with others online via NetMeeting, Microsoft's **real** (actual) **time** conferencing program.

■ Your computer must be networked or attached to the Internet to use NetMeeting.

■ You can start a spontaneous meeting as long as co-workers are running NetMeeting and are online. You can schedule the meeting beforehand using e-mail or the telephone.

■ During a meeting, you can show and edit a presentation.

■ The person who initiates and controls an online meeting is called the host. The host can show the presentation to others without allowing them to edit the presentation.

■ The host controls the online meeting by clicking the appropriate button on the Online Meeting toolbar, which appears when you connect with NetMeeting.

■ The host can also allow co-workers to edit the presentation, if desired, by turning on the collaboration feature.

■ Only one person can control/edit the presentation at a time. The initials of that person are displayed next to the mouse pointer.

■ While others edit the presentation, the host cannot use the cursor.

■ Only the host of an online meeting needs to have the file and application installed.

■ The host can start the Chat feature to allow participants to discuss the presentation with co-workers.

■ The host can start the **whiteboard** feature to allow participants to make notes and record comments.

■ Several people can simultaneously send messages or files in Chat or add notes to the whiteboard if the collaboration feature is turned off.

■ The first time you use the online conferencing feature, you must enter some basic information.

Procedures

Export to Overhead

1. Open presentation.
2. Click **File** .... Alt + F
3. Click **Page Setup** .... U
4. Click **Slides sized for** .... Alt + S
5. Click **Overhead**.
6. Click **OK** .... Enter
7. Save presentation.

Export to 35mm Slides

1. Open presentation.
2. Click **File** .... Alt + F
3. Click **Page Setup** .... U
4. Click **Slides sized for** .... Alt + S

5. Click **35mm slides**.
   ✓ Image size changes to 11.25 x 7.5. Leave it at this size.
6. Click **OK** .... Enter
7. Save presentation.

Start Online Meeting

1. Click **Tools** .... Alt + T
2. Click **Online Collaboration** .... N
3. Click **Meet now** .... M
   ✓ If you've never used NetMeeting, the NetMeeting dialog box appears.
   a. Enter your personal and server information for NetMeeting.
   ✓ For help with this information, see documentation on NetMeeting.

   b. Click **OK** .... Enter
   OR
   ✓ If you have used NetMeeting or after you enter your information in NetMeeting dialog box, continue with:
4. Click **Type name or select from list** .... Alt + T
5. Enter names of desired participants or select them from list.
6. Click **Call**.
7. Computer dials number.
8. When the receiving computer answers and displays NetMeeting, you can begin the meeting.

Exercise Directions

✓ *Use the Internet simulation provided on the CD that accompanies this book to complete this exercise.*

1. Start PowerPoint, if necessary.

2. Open 📖 **22Marvel2** or 💿 **23Marvel2**.

3. Save the file as **23Marvel2**.

4. Display the Web toolbar.

5. On the Address line, type the following and press Enter:

   D:/Internet/Ppt/Ex23/barrysclipart.htm

   ✓ *If you've copied the Internet simulation on to your hard drive or your CD-ROM drive is not D:, substitute the correct letter for D.*

6. To find appropriate clip art for your online presentation follow these steps:

   a. Type **business** in the Find box and click **Go**.

   b. Scroll the page to locate a clip art.

   c. Right-click the second clip art in the second row and click Save Picture As.

   d. In the Save As dialog box, choose the folder in which to save the clip art and click Save.

7. Close the Internet simulation by clicking the Close button ☒.

8. View slide 1 of the presentation.

9. Insert the picture from a file (Insert, Picture, From File).

10. Size and position the clip art above the slide's title.

11. Change the page setup of the presentation to overhead transparencies.

12. Print the presentation as slides.

13. Change the page setup to 35mm slides.

14. Print the presentation as slides and compare the size and shape of the slides to the first set you printed.

15. Schedule an online meeting with others in your network.

    ✓ *If your computer is not networked or NetMeeting is not installed to your computer, you may skip this part of the exercise.*

16. Start the online meeting and run your presentation.

    ✓ *You run a presentation the same way, whether you're online or not.*

17. End the meeting by clicking the End Meeting button on the Online Meeting toolbar.

18. Close the file and exit PowerPoint, saving all changes.

On Your Own

1. Open **OPPT 22**, the presentation you used in Exercise 22, or open 💿 **23DONATE**.

2. Save the file as **OPPT23**.

3. Change the page setup of the presentation to overhead transparencies.

4. Print the presentation as slides.

5. Change the page setup to 35mm slides.

6. Print the presentation as slides and compare the size and shape of the slides to the first set you printed.

7. If you're attached to a network, hold an online meeting and run the presentation during the meeting.

8. Save the presentation, close it, and exit PowerPoint.

Exercise 24

◆ Critical Thinking

When you show a presentation, you want to make sure the audience gets the most out of the information you present. By setting transitions, adding sound, and otherwise setting up a presentation, you can present the slide show in the best possible way for your audience to understand and enjoy.

Exercise Directions

1. Start PowerPoint, if necessary.

2. Open 💿 **24DitexInc**.

3. Save the file as **24DitexInc**.

4. Apply transitions, sounds, and timing to all slides. View the presentation.

5. Hide slide 3.

6. Animate the bullets on slide 2 with preset animations.

7. Animate the text and objects on slides 3 and 4 with custom animations. You can choose to use sounds, if desired. View the presentation.

8. Save the timings.

9. Add a slide at the end of the presentation using the Title Only layout. Add the title **Thank You!**

10. Add a music or video clip to the last slide. The clip should play automatically when the slide is displayed.

11. On the notes master, add the following header:
    DitexInc
    Sue Bender, owner

12. In Notes Page view, add notes to slide 3 as shown in Illustration A.

13. Add notes to slide 5 as shown in Illustration B.

14. Print the notes pages as handouts, 4 per page.

15. Pack the presentation onto a disk and view it on another computer.

16. Show the presentation from your own computer. During the presentation, open the Meeting Minder and enter these notes:
    Get price quote for 3 types of Input data: Catalog, Brochures, Annual Reports.

17. In the Action Items, add the following:
    Annual report Dave   3/01
    Catalog design Tom   4/01
    Catalog final   Willa   4/01

18. Export the information from Meeting Minder to Word.

19. Save the Word file as **24DitexInc.rtf** and print it.

20. Close the file and exit Word. Click OK to close the Meeting Minder.

21. Finish showing the presentation and then set up the slide show to run on a kiosk. View the slide show.

22. Save the presentation as a Web page (**24DitexInc.htm**). Publish the presentation using all slides, no speaker notes, and open it to a Web browser.

23. Run the presentation and then close the browser.

24. Close the file and exit PowerPoint, saving all changes.

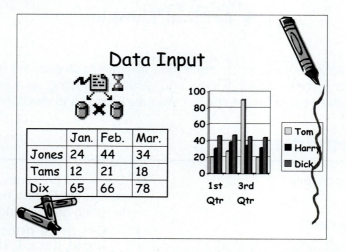

DitexInc
Sue Bender, owner

Our prices include data input, plus double-proofing. Every fact, word, and figure is double-checked by special proof-readers so you are guaranteed correct data. We guarantee our services with your money back if you find one single mistake.

Backups are also stored on tape for up to 6 months, longer if you want to pay for that option.

DitexInc
Sue Bender, owner

Please contact us if you have any questions or comments. For a free estimate of your input data, call us today. You can also email us or stop by the office.

Challenge Lesson

Lesson 1

Exercises 1-9

Directory of Data Files on CD

Exercise #	File Name	Page #
1	01HANDHELD.doc, Internet Simulation	691
2	02COSTS.xls, 02RATES.doc, Internet Simulation	694
3	03OUT.doc, 03OFFRATES.xls, Internet Simulation	697
4	04CCIHOME.doc, 04CCIPRES.ppt, Internet Simulation	700
5	05INVENT.mdb	702
6	06SALES.mdb, 06MEETING.doc, 06RESULTS	704
7	07PRICES.xls, 07NEWPRICE.doc	707
8	08LINAMES.xls, 08INTRO.doc, 08CONTACTS.mdb	710
9	09EARNINGS.xls, 09REGENCY.ppt, 09TOALL.doc, Internet Simulation	712

Exercise 1

Skills Covered:

◆ **Locate Data on the Internet**

◆ **Make Web Data Available for use Offline**

◆ **Edit and Format a Table in a Word Document**

◆ **Send a Word Document via E-mail**

You are the assistant to the president of Northwest Gear, Inc. The president wants a new handheld computer to use when he is away from the office. He has asked you to research the current features and prices and then forward the information to him so he can make a decision. You will use the CNET Web site to locate information about handheld devices. You will save the information in a Word document, edit the document, and then e-mail the document to Northwest Gear's president.

If you are connected to the Internet, use the suggested site to gather the required information, or select other appropriate Web sites. If you are not connected to the Internet, use the Internet simulation on the CD-ROM that accompanies this book. All the steps involving the Internet described in the exercise are simulated on the CD.

Exercise Directions

✓ *Use the Internet simulation provided on the CD that accompanies this book to complete this exercise.*

Locate Data on the Internet

1. Start Word if necessary.

2. Open ☉ **01HANDHELD.doc**.

3. Save the file as **HANDHELD**.

4. Enter the current date and your name in the appropriate locations.

5. Display the Web toolbar.

6. On the Address line, type the following and press Enter:
   D:/Internet/Challenge/Ex01/cnet.htm

   ✓ *If you've copied the Internet simulation files to your hard drive or your CD-ROM drive is not D:, substitute the correct drive letter for D.*

8. On the CNET home page, click the Hardware Reviews link.

9. Click the Handhelds link.

10. Under the heading Buying Advice, click the Top picks by OS link.

11. Click the Pocket PC link.

12. Click the See all handhelds with Pocket PC link.

13. Scroll down to the Products & Reviews: section, and click the check box for each of the following three devices:

    • Compaq iPaq H3650 Pocket PC

    • Casio Cassiopeia E-125

    • HP Jornada 720

14. Click the **Compare** button at the top of the product list.

15. Click the Printer-friendly format link in the upper-right corner.

Make Web Data Available for Use Offline

1. Save the page in Web Archive format with the file name **COMPARE**.

2. Disconnect from the Internet, or close the Internet simulation by clicking the Close button ⊠.

3. Open the **COMPARE** file in Word.

   ✓ *If necessary, select All Files from the Files of type drop-down list.*

4. Scroll down in the file and select the 13 table rows beginning with the row labeled **Processor**.

5. Copy the table to the Windows Clipboard.

6. Paste the table from the Clipboard onto the last line of the **HANDHELD** document.

Edit and Format a Table in a Word Document

1. Use the following steps to modify and format the table as shown in Illustration A.

2. Select the entire table.

3. On the Table page of the Table Properties dialog box, set the Preferred Width of the table to 6".

4. In the Format Paragraph dialog box, set left and right indents and before and after spacing to 0, set line spacing to single, and set special indents to None.

5. Delete the blank row between OS and Product Name.

6. Delete the row labeled **Full Specifications**.

7. Remove all hyperlinks from the **Product Name** row.

8. Delete the hypertext **Check Latest Prices**, the soft line break, and the text **Price Range**: from all cells in the **Where to Buy** row, so that only the price range remains.

9. Increase the font size of the pricing values to 10 points.

10. Delete the graphics image following the product name **Compaq iPaq H3650 Pocket PC**.

11. Move the **Product Name** and **Where to Buy** rows to the top of the table.

12. Replace the label **Where to Buy** with the label **Price Range**.

13. Use the Table 3D effects 2 AutoFormat to format the table.

14. Right-align the table on the page.

15. Preview the **HANDHELD** document. It should look similar to the one in the illustration.

Send a Word Document via E-Mail

1. Send the document via e-mail to: northwestgear@ddcpub.com.

   ✓ *You will be prompted to connect to the Internet. If you do not have an Internet connection, your e-mail will not go through.*

2. Disconnect from the Internet.

3. Close all open documents, saving all changes.

Illustration A

Northwest Gear, Inc.

Memo

To: Company President

From: Your name

Date: Today's date

Re: Handheld devices

I used the CNET web site to research the available handheld devices, and I recommend you purchase one of these three. Let me know which one you prefer and I'll go ahead and order it.

Product Name	HP Jornada 720	Casio Cassiopeia E-125	Compaq iPaq H3650 Pocket PC
Price Range	$798-999	$486-699	$485-849
Processor	Intel SA-1110 206 MHz	MIPS VR4122 150 MHz	Intel 206 MHz
Memory / ROM installed (max)	ROM	16 MB (16 MB) - ROM	16 MB ROM
Memory / RAM installed (max)	32 MB (32 MB) - SDRAM	32 MB (32 MB) - integrated	32 MB (32 MB) - SDRAM
Memory / Flash installed (max)	Flash CompactFlash Card	Flash CompactFlash Card	None
Display type	6.5" integrated	TFT active matrix integrated	4" TFT active matrix integrated
Audio output	Speaker(s)	Speaker(s)	Speaker(s)
Audio input	Microphone	Microphone	Microphone
Input device(s)	Keyboard, touch-screen, keypad	Wheel, stylus	Touch-screen, stylus
OS provided	Microsoft Windows for Pocket PC	Microsoft Windows for Pocket PC	Microsoft Windows CE

1

Exercise 2

Skills Covered:

◆ **Locate Data on the Internet** ◆ **Enter Data into an Excel Worksheet**
◆ **Insert Worksheet Data into a Word Document**

You are organizing a corporate retreat in Vancouver, British Columbia, for Murray Hill Marketing executives. You have received information about lodging, but the costs are in Canadian dollars. You will search the Web for the current exchange rate, and then you will enter the data into an Excel worksheet to convert the costs to U.S. dollars. Finally, you will insert the Excel worksheet into a Word document for distribution.

Exercise Directions

✓ *Use the Internet simulation provided on the CD that accompanies this book to complete this exercise.*

Locate Data on the Internet

1. Start Excel if necessary.
2. Open ⊙ **02COSTS.xls** and save it as **COSTS**.
3. Display the Web toolbar.
4. On the Address line, type the following and press Enter:
   D:/Internet/Challenge/Ex02/xrates.htm
   ✓ *If you've copied the Internet simulation files to your hard drive or your CD-ROM drive is not D:, substitute the correct drive letter for D.*
5. From the Exchange rates drop-down list, select **Canadian Dollars**.
6. Click **Submit**.
7. Locate the United States Dollar exchange rates. Write down the rates.
   ✓ *The first column provides the number of U.S. dollars per each Canadian dollar; the second column provides the number of Canadian dollars per one US dollar.*
8. Disconnect from the Internet, or close the Internet simulation by clicking the Close button ⊠.

Enter Data into an Excel Worksheet

1. In the **COSTS** worksheet, enter the number of Canadian dollars per one U.S. dollar in cell C5, then copy it to cells C6, C7, and C8.

2. Create a formula in cell D5 to calculate the current cost in U.S. dollars of lodging in a four star hotel.
   ✓ *Divide the cost in Canadian dollars by the exchange rate.*
3. Copy the formula to cells D6:D8.
4. Preview the worksheet. It should look similar to the one in Illustration A.
   ✓ *Keep in mind that the current exchange rates may not be the same as those in the illustrations.*
5. Save the worksheet and leave it open.

Insert Worksheet Data into a Word document

1. Start Word if necessary.
2. Open ⊙ **02RATES** and save it as **RATES**.
3. Insert your name and today's date.
4. Copy the range A1:D10 from the **COSTS** worksheet and paste it at the end of the **RATES** document.
5. Apply the Table 3D effects 3 AutoFormat.
6. Increase the width of columns 2 and 4 if necessary so the data fits on one line.
7. Center the table.
8. Check the spelling and grammar in **RATES**.
9. Display the document in Print Preview. It should look similar to the one in Illustration B.
10. Print the document.
11. Close all open documents, saving all changes.

Lodging Packages; Four Nights, Five Days*
Vancouver

Accommodation	Cost (CAD)	Exchange Rate	Cost (USD)
Four Star	$ 575.00	1.5388	$ 373.67
Three Star	$ 515.00	1.5388	$ 334.68
Economy	$ 465.00	1.5388	$ 302.18
Budget	$ 350.00	1.5388	$ 227.45

*Rates Based on Double Occupancy

Illustration B

MEMORANDUM

To: Jenni Waldron
From: Your Name
Date: Today's Date
Re   Current Lodging Costs

Jen –

I received the lodging costs from the travel agency in Vancouver, but they were in Canadian dollars. I converted them to U.S. dollars based on today's rates -- which happen to be fantastic! Of course there's no guarantee they'll be this low in April when we go, but there's no guarantee they'll be higher, either!

Lodging Packages; Four Nights, Five Days*			
Vancouver			
Accommodation	**Cost (CAD)**	**Exchange Rate**	**Cost (USD)**
Four Star	$ 575.00	1.5238	$ 377.35
Three Star	$ 515.00	1.5238	$ 337.97
Economy	$ 465.00	1.5238	$ 305.16
Budget	$ 350.00	1.5238	$ 229.69
*Rates Based on Double Occupancy			

Exercise 3

Skills Covered:

◆ **Create a PowerPoint Presentation from a Word Outline**
◆ **Download Clip Art from the Web**
◆ **Link Excel Data to a Table on a PowerPoint Slide**

The president of Murray Hill Marketing has decided he would prefer to hold the corporate retreat in the United States. He has asked you to prepare a presentation about a few different locations for him. In this exercise, you will create a presentation about Martha's Vineyard Island for his consideration. To create the presentation, you will export a Word document to PowerPoint and then apply formatting to improve it. You will link a slide to an Excel worksheet object listing costs, and you will locate clip art on the Internet that you can use to illustration the slides.

Exercise Directions

✓ *Use the Internet simulation provided on the CD that accompanies this book to complete this exercise.*

Create a Presentation from a Word Outline

1. Start Word.
2. Open ✆ **03OUT.doc**.
3. Export the Word outline to create a PowerPoint presentation.
4. Save the presentation as **VINEYARD**.
5. Apply the Layers design template.
6. Apply the Title Slide layout to the first slide and replace the text **Your Name** with your own name. The slide should look similar to Illustration A.

Download Clip Art from the Web and Insert it in a PowerPoint Presentation

1. Apply the Title, Text, and Content layout to Slide 3.
2. Display the Web toolbar.
3. On the Address line, type the following and press Enter: **D:/Internet/Challenge/Ex03/designgallery.htm**

   ✓ *If you've copied the Internet simulation files to your hard drive or your CD-ROM drive is not D:, substitute the correct drive letter for D.*

4. In the Search for: text box, type **island**. Choose **Clip Art** from the Results should be: drop-down list. Click the **Go** button.
5. Check the check box for the sunny 3KB island scene clip art located top right.
6. Click Download 1 Clip.
7. Click Download Now!.

   ✓ *The clip art will be added to your Microsoft Clip Gallery.*

   ✓ *If you have an Internet connection and wish to locate the clip art picture online, choose Insert, Picture, Clip Art in the Word document, then click the Clips Online button in the Microsoft Clip Gallery dialog box. Follow steps 4-7 above to download the image from the Web. The clip art picture should look similar to Illustration B.*

8. Disconnect from the Internet, or close the Internet simulation by clicking the Close button ☒.
9. Insert the clip.
10. Save the presentation.

Link Excel Data to a Table on a PowerPoint Slide

1. Apply the Title and Table layout to Slide 4.
2. Open the file ✆ **03OFFRATES.xls** and save it as **OFFRATES**.

3. Create a table on the fourth slide of the **VINEYARD** presentation by linking the data in cells A3:D8 of the **OFFRATES** worksheet to the slide as an Excel Worksheet Object.

    a. Copy cells A3:D8 in **OFFRATES.xls**.

    b. In **VINEYARD.ppt**, click the object placeholder on the slide.

    c. Choose the Edit, Paste Special command, and select to link the data as an Excel worksheet object.

4. Resize the table to fill the slide.

5. Save the presentation. Slide four should look similar to Illustration C.

6. Change the cost of meals per day in cell B5 of the **OFFRATES** workbook to $42.

7. See if the change is reflected in the table on slide 4 of the presentation.

    ✓ If necessary, update the link.

Complete the Presentation

1. Insert a clip art picture of a seashell on slide 5.

    ✓ If you cannot locate an appropriate picture in the Clip Organizer, insert the file ✪ **SHELL1.wmf** supplied with this book.

2. Apply the Checkerboard across slide transition to all slides in the presentation, set to advance automatically after 4 seconds at a medium speed.

3. Check the spelling and grammar in the presentation.

4. Use Slide Show view to view the presentation.

5. Close all documents, saving all changes.

Illustration A

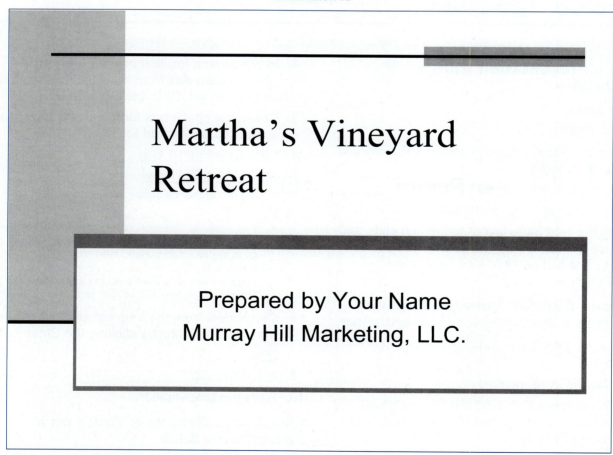

Illustration B

Highlights

- Enjoy relaxed island atmosphere.
- Explore beautiful nature preserves.
- Visit quaint seaside villages.
- Appreciate fine dining, shopping, nightlife.

Illustration C

Per Person Cost – Off Season

	Per day/night	# days/nights	Total
Lodging (per night)	$ 185.00	4	$ 740.00
Meals (daily)	42.00	5	210.00
Miscellaneous	30.00	5	150.00
Round Trip Transportation			52.00
Total			$ 1,152.00

Exercise 4

Skills Covered:

◆ **Save a Word File as a Web Page**

◆ **Publish a Presentation to a Web Site**

◆ **Link a Web Page and a Presentation Web Site**

◆ **Link a Web Page to an Internet Site**

You are a Web site designer hired to design a Web site for California Cardiology, Inc. They are particularly interested in providing their patients with useful information about their practice and about heart health. In this exercise, you start by creating a Web site from a PowerPoint presentation provided by California Cardiology. You then create a home page with Word, which you link to the presentation site. You also provide links from the presentation site to a site on the Internet about heart disease and prevention.

Exercise Directions

Save a Word File as a Web Page

1. Start Word if necessary.

2. Open 🔘 **04CCIHOME.doc**.

3. Save the document as a Web Page with the name **CCIHOME** and the title **California Cardiology Home Page**.

4. Apply the Profile theme to the page.

5. Save the document and keep it open.

Publish a Presentation to a Web Site

1. In PowerPoint, open the file 🔘 **04CCIPRES.ppt** and save it as **CCIPRES**.

2. Create a hyperlink to the CCI Home Page (file **CCIHOME**) from the text **CCI Home Page** on both Slide 1 and Slide 5.

3. Publish the presentation to the Web with the name **ABOUTCCI**. Publish all slides, include navigation controls, and change the title to **About California Cardiology**.

4. Close the **CCIPRES** presentation and open the **ABOUTCCI** presentation.

5. Preview the presentation as a Web site.

6. Close the preview, then close the presentation, saving all changes.

7. Exit PowerPoint.

Create Hyperlinks in a Word Document

1. In Word, switch to the CCI home page, **CCIHOME**.

2. Use the text **online presentation** to create a hyperlink to the About CCI presentation Web site (file **ABOUTCCI.htm**).

3. Use the text **American Heart Association** to create a hyperlink to the American Heart Association's homepage, at URL address:
   http://www.americanheart.org/
   OR

   If you are not connected to the Internet, create the hyperlink to point to the following file:
   D:/Internet/Challenge/Ex04/ americanheart.htm

   ✓ *If necessary, substitute the correct drive letter for D:.*

Preview and Test the Web Site

1. Use Web Page Preview to check the CCI Home Page (**CCIHOME.htm**). It should look similar to the one in Illustration A.

2. Test the link to the **ABOUTCCI** presentation.

3. View the slides in the presentation.

4. Test one of the links back to the CCI Home Page (**CCIHOME.htm**).

5. Test the link to the American Heart Association's Web site.

   ✓ *If you are working online, you will be prompted to sign in.*

6. Use the Back button on your Web browser toolbar to return to the CCI Home Page.

7. Close Web Page Preview and disconnect from the Internet.

   OR

   Exit the simulation by clicking the Close button ☒.

8. Close all open documents, saving all changes.

9. Exit all open applications.

Illustration A

California Cardiology, Inc.

Maintaining Healthy Hearts for Life

Welcome to **CCI on the Web**, your link to California Cardiology! We have designed this site to provide you, our patients, with useful information about our practice and about cardiology care in general. Explore the links below to learn more about **CCI** and how you can maintain a healthy heart for life!

About CCI

California Cardiology is a medical practice servicing the greater Los Angeles area. Our physicians and support staff specialize in cardiology and diseases of the heart.

◻ Learn more about CCI by viewing our online presentation.
◻ Learn more about heart disease and caring for your heart by accessing the Web site for the American Heart Association.

Publications and Periodicals

CCI publishes a newsletter at regular intervals throughout the year. In addition, we offer special reports, reprinted articles, and other printed information about cardiology and maintaining a healthy heart.

◻ Newsletter
◻ Caring for your Heart

Physician Directory

A listing of our associates, including direct phone numbers and e-mail addresses.

Exercise 5

Skills Covered:

◆ **Export an Access Table to Excel** ◆ **E-mail an Excel Worksheet**
◆ **Receive an Excel Worksheet via E-mail and Save it in HTML Format**
◆ **Edit an HTML Worksheet in Excel**

You are the assistant manager of one of Coastline Gourmet's retail stores. The company has recently started selling promotional items featuring the store logo. The manager has asked you to do an inventory analysis of promotional items that have been ordered. To accomplish this, you will export the data from an Access table into an Excel worksheet and then modify the worksheet. You will then send the worksheet via e-mail to the manager for approval.

Exercise Directions

Export an Access Table to Excel

1. Copy the database ⊙ **05INVENT.mdb** and name the copy **INVENT.mdb**.

   ✓ *To copy an Access database, right-click the file and select Copy. Then go to where you wish to copy the file. Right-click on the destination folder, and select Paste. Right-click on the copied file and select Rename to rename the file.*

2. Open the **INVENT** database and open the table **STOCK**.

3. After viewing the table, close it, but keep it selected in the Database window.

4. Using the Office Links command, export the table into an Excel workbook.

   ✓ *The file is named **STOCK** by default.*

Analyze Access Data in Excel

1. Make the following changes to the Excel worksheet. When you are finished, the worksheet should look similar to the one in Illustration A.

   a. Insert three rows at the top of the worksheet so you have room to enter a title.

   b. In cell A1 type **Coastline Gourmet Importers**, in 12-point Arial bold.

   c. In cell A2 type **Promotional Item Inventory**, also in 12-point Arial bold.

   d. Delete the ORDERED column.

   e. In cell J4 enter the column label **TOTAL**.

   f. In cell J5, enter the formula for calculating the total number of each item ordered, and then copy the formula to cells J6:J21.

      ✓ *Use the AutoSum function.*

   g. Format columns K and L as currency with no decimal places, then in cell K4, enter the column label **PRICE**, and in cell L4 enter the column label **VALUE**.

   h. In column K, fill in the pricing information shown in the illustration.

   i. In cell L5 enter a formula for calculating the value of each item, and then copy the formula to cells L6:L21.

      ✓ *Total number of items ordered multiplied by the item price.*

   j. In cell B23, type the row label **TOTAL**.

   k. In cell L23, calculate the total value of the entire inventory.

   l. Select cells A4:L23 and apply the Classic 3 AutoFormat.

2. Display the worksheet in Print Preview. It should look similar to the one in the illustration.

   ✓ *If necessary, adjust column widths so the worksheet fits on a single page.*

3. Save the worksheet, then print it.

Send a Worksheet as E-Mail

1. In Excel, send the worksheet as an e-mail message.

   ✓ *The steps for this are the same as sending a document as an e-mail message in Word, as covered in Exercise 22 of the Word section. Either click the E-Mail button on the Standard toolbar, or click File, Send To, E-Mail Recipient.*

2. If you have an e-mail account, address the message to yourself. If you have access to the Internet but do not have an e-mail account, address the message to **coastlinegourmet@ddcpub.com**.

3. Skip the cc: field and enter in the Introduction field: **Here's the information you requested re: promotional item inventory analysis**. (The file name Stock is entered in the Subject field by default).

4. Send the worksheet, and then close it.

Receive, Save, and Edit an E-Mailed Worksheet

1. If you have an e-mail account, use Outlook or Outlook Express to check for messages.

2. If you sent the message to yourself, save the file in HTML format as **MESSAGE**.

   ✓ *Disconnect from the Internet.*

3. Open the **MESSAGE.htm** document in Excel.

4. Change the number of Black Oven Mitts from 25 to **30**.

5. Print the **MESSAGE.htm** worksheet.

6. Close all open documents, saving all changes, and exit all open applications.

Illustration A

	A	B	C	D	E	F	G	H	I	J	K	L
1	Coastline Gourmet Importers											
2	Promotional Item Inventory											
3												
4	ITEM #	DESCRIPTION	COLOR	XS	S	M	L	XL	One Size	TOTAL	PRICE	VALUE
5	M8510	Shirt - Long	Multi	4	4	8	10	10		36	$ 25	$ 900
6	M5540	Shirt - Short	Multi	5	6	6	8	10		35	$ 23	$ 805
7	M4309	Apron	White	2	8	8	10	10		38	$ 25	$ 950
8	M3254	Apron	Teal	4	8	8	10	10		40	$ 25	$ 1,000
9	M7654	Apron	Multi	5	8	8	10	10		41	$ 25	$ 1,025
10	M7455	Oven Mitt	Black						25	25	$ 18	$ 450
11	M3280	Oven Mitt	Navy						25	25	$ 18	$ 450
12	M5532	Oven Mitt	Red						25	25	$ 18	$ 450
13	M4230	Cap	Teal						35	35	$ 15	$ 525
14	M5550	Dish Towels	White						50	50	$ 8	$ 400
15	M7676	Dish Towels	Navy						45	45	$ 10	$ 450
16	M7405	Dish Towels	Multi						50	50	$ 8	$ 400
17	M5555	Sweatshirt	Multi	5	6	8	8	10		37	$ 30	$ 1,110
18	M3290	Sweatshirt	Black	4	5	6	6	8		29	$ 30	$ 870
19	M3317	Sweatshirt	Navy	5	5	6	8	8		32	$ 30	$ 960
20	M2222	Sweatshirt	White	10	10	12	14	16		62	$ 25	$ 1,550
21	M3290	Sweatpants	Multi	10	10	12	14	16		62	$ 20	$ 1,240
22												
23		TOTAL										$ 13,535

Exercise 6

Skills Covered:

◆ **Create Queries in an Access Database**

◆ **Merge a Word Document with Access Queries**

◆ **Embed Excel Data in a Word Document**

◆ **Create Merge Envelopes using an Access Table**

As the sales assistant for Electron Consumer Industries, a large manufacturer of computer electronics based in Chicago, IL, you are planning the annual sales meetings—one for salespeople in the North territories and one for salespeople in the South territories. You have the name and address information for all of the salespeople in one Access table; however, you want to send one letter to the North territory and one to the South territory. First, you will create queries in the Access database to separate the North territory salespeople from the South territory salespeople. Then, you will create one merge document in Word that includes the information that will go in both letters. You will copy the document so you have two letters, and then you will customize one letter for the North and one for the South, including embedded Excel data. After merging the documents, you will use the complete Access table to generate envelopes for all of the letters.

Exercise Directions

Create Queries in an Access Database

1. Copy the database ☉ **06SALES.mdb** and name the copy **SALES.mdb**.

   ✓ To copy an Access database, right-click the file and select Copy. Then go to where you wish to copy the file. Right-click on the destination folder, and select Paste. Right-click on the copied file and select Rename to rename the file.

   ✓ You must deselect the Read-only attribute on the database. To do so, right-click on the file, select Properties, and deselect Read-only.

2. Open the **SALES** database.

3. Using the **Salespeople** table, create a query that shows the complete records for all salespeople in the North territory.

4. Save the query as **North**.

5. Using the **Salespeople** table again, create a query that shows the complete records for all salespeople in the South Territory.

6. Save the query as **South**.

7. Close the Access database.

Use an Access Query as a Data Source for a Form Letter Mail Merge

1. In Word, create the document shown in Illustration A, or open the document ☉ **06MEETING.doc**

   ✓ If you are creating the document, leave out the merge fields; you will insert them in step 5. If you want, simply type the field names as placeholders for the actual fields.

2. Check the spelling and grammar in the document.

3. Save the document as **NMEETING**.

4. Set up a form letter mail merge, using the **NMEETING** file as the main document and the **North** query of the **SALES.mdb** database as the data source.

5. Insert merge fields into **NMEETING** as shown in the illustration.

   ✓ You may use the Address Block or individual merge fields. Also, don't forget the Territory merge field in the second sentence of the first paragraph.

6. Save the document.

7. Make a copy of the document by saving it with the name **SMEETING**.

8. Change the data source for the **SMEETING** document to the **South** query of the **SALES.mdb** database.

Embed Excel Data in a Word Document

1. In Excel, open the workbook ⊙ **06RESULTS** and save it as **RESULTS**.

2. Embed the North Territory data from the **RESULTS** workbook (A5:G16) in the **NMEETING** letter document, on the line above the closing as marked on Illustration A.

   ✓ *Use the Paste Special command to embed the data.*

3. Embed the South Territory data from the **RESULTS** workbook (A19:G29) in the **SMEETING** letter document, on the line above the closing as marked on Illustration A.

Complete the Merge

1. Merge the **NMEETING** letter to a new document and save the new document with the name **NLETTERS**.

2. Print the document **NLETTERS**, then close it.

3. Merge the **SMEETING** letter to a new document and save the new document with the name **SLETTERS**.

4. Print the document **SLETTERS**, then close it.

Use an Access Table as a Data Source for an Envelopes Mail Merge

1. Use the mail merge wizard to create envelopes using the **Salespeople** table of the **SALES.mdb** database as the data source.

2. Insert the merge fields or merge blocks as necessary to set up the envelope correctly for mailing.

3. Merge the envelopes to a new document and save the new document with the name **ENVELOPE**.

4. Print the envelopes.

5. Save the main document as **EMEETING**.

6. Close all open documents, saving all changes.

7. Exit all open applications.

Electron Consumer Industries, Inc.
8740 South Crawford Road◆Chicago, IL 60619◆(312) 555-7700

Today's Date

«FirstName» «LastName»
«Company»
«Address1»
«Address2»
«City», «State» «PostalCode»

Dear «FirstName»:

This year we have decided to hold two sales meetings – one for the North territories and one for the South territories. You will attend the meeting for the «Territory» territory.

In preparation for the meeting please check the sales totals below. If you notice any discrepancies, use Excel to edit the worksheet, then send it back to me via e-mail.

Sincerely,

Embed data here

Your Name
Sales Assistant

Exercise 7

Skills Covered:

◆ **Save an Excel Worksheet as a Web Page**
◆ **Link a Word Document to an Excel Web Page**
◆ **Send a Word Document via E-mail**

You are a project manager at Regency General, Inc. You want to let your customers know that Regency General has recently increased pricing for products and services. First, you will update a pricing table in Excel. Then, you will save the worksheet as a Web page so it can be made available on the Internet. Next, you will create a Word document announcing that the pricing table is available on the Internet and provide a hyperlink to the Web page. Finally, you will e-mail the Word document to your clients.

Exercise Directions

Save an Excel Worksheet as a Web Page

1. Start Excel.
2. Create the worksheet shown in Illustration A, or open ☉ **07PRICES.xls**.
3. Save the file as **PRICES**.
4. In cell E6, create a formula to calculate the new price of an initial consultation.
   - ✓ *Multiply the old cost by the percent of the increase, and then add the result to the old cost.*
   - ✓ *You may have to adjust column widths.*
5. Copy the formula as necessary to calculate the new pricing of all other services.
6. Select the worksheet (A1:E13) and apply the Colorful 2 AutoFormat.
7. Print the **PRICES.xls** worksheet.
8. Publish the worksheet only as a Web Page with the file name **WEBPRICE.htm**.
9. Save and close the **PRICES.xls** worksheet.
10. Open the **WEBPRICE.htm** worksheet and preview it as a Web page.
11. Close Web Page Preview, then save and close the **WEBPRICE.htm** worksheet, and exit Excel.

Link a Word Document to an Excel Web Page

1. In Word, create the document shown in Illustration B, or open ☉ **07NEWPRICE.doc**.
2. Save the document as **NEWPRICE.doc**.
3. Select the text **PRICING TABLE** in the second paragraph and create a hyperlink to the **WEBPRICE.htm** Web page.
4. Save the document, and then test the link.
5. Close your Internet browser.
6. Print the **NEWPRICE** document.

Send a Word Document via E-Mail

1. Send a copy of the Word document via e-mail.
   a. If you have an e-mail account, send it to yourself. If you do not have an e-mail account send it to regencygeneral@ddcpub.com.
   b. Skip the cc: line
   c. Enter **Regency General Pricing Increase** on the Subject line.
   d. Enter **Information about our new pricing structure** on the Introduction line.
2. Disconnect from the Internet.
3. Close all open documents, saving all changes.

	A	B	C	D	E
1	Regency General				
2	Pricing Table				
3					
4			Old	% Increase	New
5	Consultation				
6	(per hour)	Initial	$ 100.00	5%	
7		Development	$ 75.00	3%	
8		Maintenance	$ 85.00	3%	
9					
10	Database Management				
11		Up to 100 records	$ 350.00	3%	
12		100 - 500 records	$ 450.00	5%	
13		More than 500 records	$ 550.00	5%	

Regency General, Inc.

1500 W. High Tech Blvd. ❖ Suite 700 ❖ Austin, TX 73301
(512) 555-3900 ❖ regencygeneral.com

Today's Date

Dear Valued Client:

Due to an increase in the cost of doing business, and in order to guarantee the same high quality work and service you have come to expect from Regency General, Inc., we have been forced to increase our pricing structure. The cost of most services has increased by 3%, while the cost of a few services has increased by 5%.

We have made the new pricing information available on the World Wide Web at our own Web site. You may access the PRICING TABLE directly from this letter to see how the increases will affect you.

I would like to take this opportunity to thank you for your loyalty to Regency General. We value and appreciate your business, and we hope you continue to come to us for all of your Business-to-Business Internet service needs.

Sincerely,

Your Name
Project Manager

Exercise 8

Skills Covered:

◆ **Link an E-mail Message to an Excel Worksheet**
◆ **Link an Excel Worksheet to an Access Database**
◆ **Use an Excel Worksheet as a Data Source for a Mail Merge**

In this exercise, you will wear "two hats." First, you will be a regional sales manager for Electron Consumer Industries, Inc. You will create and send an e-mail message to the new Long Island sales representative providing a hyperlink to a list of contact names and addresses stored in Excel. You will then become the Long Island sales rep, receive the message, and open the Excel worksheet. Since you already have an Access database of customers, you will link the Excel worksheet as a table to your database. Finally, you will send a letter introducing yourself to the contacts in the Excel list.

Exercise Directions

Link an E-Mail Message to an Excel Worksheet

1. Start Excel.

2. Open ◉ **08LINAMES.xls**.

3. Save the file as **LINAMES**, and then close the workbook and exit Excel.

4. Start Word and create a new e-mail message.

5. If you have an e-mail account, address the message to yourself. If you do not have an e-mail account, address the message to electron@ddcpub.com.

6. Enter **Welcome Aboard!** in the Subject line.

7. Type the following message in a 12-point sans serif font:

   Welcome to Electron Consumer Industries. As promised, I have stored a list of CUSTOMER CONTACTS for the Long Island area in an Excel worksheet on the company intranet. I suggest you get in touch with them to introduce yourself as soon as possible. Let me know if you have any questions.

8. Create a hyperlink from the text **CUSTOMER CONTACTS** to the **LINAMES.xls** workbook.

9. Before sending the message, save it as a Word document file with the name **WELCOME**.

10. Send the message.

11. If you sent the message to yourself, use Outlook or Outlook Express to retrieve it and save it as an HTML file with the name **GETNAMES**.

   ✓ *If your e-mail program displays a warning about viruses because the file has a link, go ahead and open the file. However, be aware that if you do not know the source of the file, you should not open it. Viruses are real and dangerous, and they are easily transmitted via e-mail.*

12. Disconnect from the Internet.

13. Open the **GETNAMES.htm** document or the **WELCOME.doc** document and use the hyperlink to open the Excel worksheet.

14. Close the Excel worksheet and exit Excel.

Prepare a Word Document for Use as a Form Letter

1. In Word, create the document shown in Illustration A, or open ◉ **08INTRO.doc**.

2. Save the file as **INTRO.doc**.

3. Check the spelling and grammar in the document.

4. Close all open Word documents, and exit Word.

Link an Excel Worksheet to an Access Database

1. Copy the ⊙ **08CONTACTS.mdb** database and name the copy **CONTACTS.mdb**.

   ✓ *To copy an Access database, right-click the file and select Copy. Then go to where you wish to copy the file. Right-click on the destination folder, and select Paste. Right-click on the copied file and select Rename to rename the file.*

   ✓ *You must deselect the Read-only attribute on the database. To do so, right-click on the file, select Properties, and deselect Read-only.*

2. Open the **CONTACTS.mdb** database.

3. Link the **LINAMES** worksheet from Excel to the **CONTACTS** database. Name the linked table **LINAMES**.

4. Using the Office Links command, create a form letter mail merge using **INTRO.doc** as the main document and the linked **LINAMES** table as the data source.

5. Merge the letters to a new document and save the document with the name **LILETTER**.

6. Print the merge letter document.

7. Save and close all open documents.

8. Exit all open applications.

Illustration A

Electron Consumer Industries, Inc.
8740 South Crawford Road◆Chicago, IL 60619◆(312) 555-7700

Today's Date

«Title» «FirstName» «LastName»
«JobTitle»
«Company»
«Address1»
«Address2»
«City», «State» «PostalCode»

Dear «Title» «LastName»:

This is just a quick note to introduce myself. I have recently joined Electron Consumer Industries as the Long Island Sales Representative. Rest assured that I will uphold the high standards set by my predecessor. Feel free to contact me with any questions about your current account, or if you want to explore new options.

«Title» «LastName», I look forward to meeting you in the not too distant future.

Sincerely,

Your Name
Sales Representative

Exercise 9

Skills Covered:

◆ **Download Clip Art from the Web**

◆ **Insert Clip Art in an Excel Worksheet**

◆ **Copy Charts from a Worksheet onto PowerPoint Slides**

◆ **Save a Presentation as a Web Site**

◆ **Link a Word Document to a Presentation Web Site**

You are the assistant to the president of Regency General, Inc. The president has asked you to modify a PowerPoint presentation by adding information from an Excel worksheet and then make the presentation available on the company's intranet. In addition, you will create a memo for electronic distribution to all employees, providing a link to the presentation on the intranet.

Exercise Directions

✓ *Use the Internet simulation provided on the CD that accompanies this book to complete this exercise.*

Insert Downloaded Clip Art in an Excel Worksheet

1. Start Excel.

2. Open ⊙ **09EARNINGS.xls**.

3. Save the file as **EARNINGS.xls**.

   ✓ *Note that this workbook contains multiple worksheets.*

4. Display the Web toolbar.

5. On the Address line, type the following and press Enter: **D:/Internet/Challenge/Ex09/msngallerylive.htm**

   ✓ *If you've copied the Internet simulation files to your hard drive or your CD-ROM drive is not D:, substitute the correct drive letter for D.*

6. Click the **Accept** button.

7. In the Search for: text box, type **eagles**. Choose **Clip Art** from the Results should be: drop-down list. Click the **Go** button.

8. Click the **>>** link on the top right three times, to go to page 4 of 10 of the eagle clip art pictures.

9. Check the check box for the 15KB eagle clip art located second from left on the second line of clip art pictures.

10. Click Download 1 Clip.

11. Click Download Now!.

✓ *The clip art will be added to your Microsoft Clip Gallery.*

✓ *If you have an Internet connection and wish to locate the clip art picture online, choose Insert, Picture, Clip Art in the Excel document, then click the Clips Online button in the Microsoft Clip Gallery dialog box. Follow steps 7-11 above to download the image from the Web. The clip art picture should look similar to Illustration A.*

12. Disconnect from the Internet, or close the Internet simulation by clicking the Close button ⊠.

13. Insert the image into the worksheet.

14. Close the Clip Gallery

15. Close your browser and disconnect from your service provider (if you are connected).

16. Size and position the clip art image on the worksheet as shown in Illustration A.

17. Display the worksheet in Print Preview. It should look similar to Illustration A.

18. Save and print the workbook.

Paste Excel Charts in a PowerPoint Presentation

1. Open the presentation ⊙ **09REGENCY.ppt** in PowerPoint, and save it as **REGENCY.ppt**.

2. On the title slide, insert the downloaded clip art of the eagle you used in the worksheet.

3. Size and position the clip art as shown in Illustration B.

   ✓ *If necessary, click the Draw button on the Drawing toolbar and use the Order, Send to Back command to position the picture behind the text on the slide.*

4. On slide 4, enter the title **Three-Year Column Graph**.

5. Copy and paste the column chart from the 3-year Sales worksheet in **EARNINGS.xls** to slide 4 of **REGENCY.ppt**.

6. Increase the size of the chart object to fill the slide.

7. On slide 5, enter the title **Year 1999**.

8. Copy and paste the pie chart showing year 1999 categories from the Pie Comparisons worksheet in **EARNINGS.xls** to slide 5 of **REGENCY.ppt**.

9. Increase the size of the chart object to fill the slide.

10. On slide 6, enter the title **Year 2001**.

11. Copy and paste the pie chart showing year 2001 categories from the Pie Comparisons worksheet in **EARNINGS.xls** to slide 6 of **REGENCY.ppt**.

12. Increase the size of the chart object to fill the slide.

13. Check the spelling and grammar in the presentation.

14. Apply the Strips Right-Down transition to all slides, at medium speed, set to advance on a mouse click or automatically after 5 seconds.

15. Preview the presentation, then save it.

Save Office Files in HTML format

1. Publish the entire presentation to the Web with the file name **SOARPRES.htm** and the Web page title **Regency General Soars**.

2. Save and close the **REGENCY.ppt** presentation and exit PowerPoint.

3. In Word, open ☉ **09TOALL.doc**.

4. Save the file as **TOALL.doc**.

5. Insert your name and today's date.

6. Insert the clip art image of the eagle into the **TOALL** document. See Illustration C.

Insert and Test Hyperlinks

1. Create a hyperlink from the clip art image to the **SOARPRES.htm** Web presentation.

   ✓ *Simply select the graphics image, then click Insert, Hyperlink, and continue as when creating a hyperlink from text.*

2. Save the **TOALL.doc** document in HTML format with the name **REGMEMO.htm**.

   ✓ *If Word warns you that some features are not supported, select Continue.*

3. Use Web Page Preview to view the **REGMEMO.htm** document.

4. Test the link to the **SOARPRES.htm** Web presentation.

5. Run the presentation slide show in Internet Explorer.

6. Close Internet Explorer.

7. Close all open documents, saving all changes.

8. Exit all open applications.

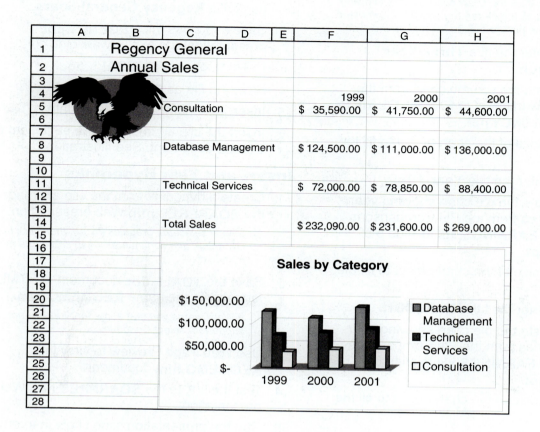

	A	B	C	D	E	F	G	H
1		Regency General						
2		Annual Sales						
3								
4						1999	2000	2001
5			Consultation			$ 35,590.00	$ 41,750.00	$ 44,600.00
6								
7								
8			Database Management			$ 124,500.00	$ 111,000.00	$ 136,000.00
9								
10								
11			Technical Services			$ 72,000.00	$ 78,850.00	$ 88,400.00
12								
13								
14			Total Sales			$ 232,090.00	$ 231,600.00	$ 269,000.00
15								

Sales by Category

$150,000.00
$100,000.00
$50,000.00
$-

1999 2000 2001

- Database Management
- Technical Services
- Consultation

Illustration B

Illustration C

Memorandum

To: All Employees

From: Your Name

Date: Today's date

Re: Presentation on the Web

I recently posted a presentation detailing some of the more exciting aspects of Regency General's financial growth on our company intranet. To access the presentation quickly, just click the image below!

Have fun!

Index